Historical Dictionary
of Law Enforcement

HISTORICAL DICTIONARY OF LAW ENFORCEMENT

Mitchel P. Roth

James S. Olson, Advisory Editor

GREENWOOD PRESS
Westport, Connecticut • London

Library of Congress Cataloging-in-Publication Data

Roth, Mitchel P., 1953–
    Historical dictionary of law enforcement / Mitchel Roth.
       p.   cm.
    Includes bibliographical references and index.
    ISBN 0–313–30560–9 (alk. paper)
    1. Police—History—Dictionaries.   2. Police—Biography—Dictionaries.   3. Law
enforcement—History—Dictionaries.   I. Title.
    HV7903.R67   2001
    363.2'03—dc21   00–024646

British Library Cataloguing in Publication Data is available.

Library of Congress Catalog Card Number: 00–024646
ISBN: 0–313–30560–9

First published in 2001

Greenwood Press, 88 Post Road West, Westport, CT 06881
An imprint of Greenwood Publishing Group, Inc.
www.greenwood.com

Printed in the United States of America

The paper used in this book complies with the
Permanent Paper Standard issued by the National
Information Standards Organization (Z39.48–1984).

10 9 8 7 6 5 4 3 2 1

This book is dedicated to Bernard L. Roth (1929–1972) and Melville C. Roth
and
to all peace officers killed in the line of duty

Contents

Preface

Historians generally acknowledge that modern professional policing began with the creation of the London Metropolitan Police model in 1829. Indeed, much of this book is devoted to British policing and its antecedents in the British Isles, dating back to the sheriffs and constables of the eleventh century. However, police organizations and law enforcement entities have been in existence since classical antiquity. The earliest accounts of organized policing can be traced as far back as Caesar Augustus's Vigiles, Praetorian Guards, and Urban Cohorts. Until the eighteenth century, such military and paramilitary police forces were the general rule rather than the exception. Since that time, however, European Continental police innovations stemming from Napoleonic France have had a dramatic impact on the development of centralized state policing throughout the world. These developments and hundreds of others are chronicled in this historical dictionary on law enforcement around the world.

While there are a handful of reference books covering the history of policing, they are usually parochial in approach, dealing with specific countries or continental traditions. This book is designed to fill this void by providing a reference work that views policing from an international vantage point. One of the weaknesses of existing reference works on criminal justice is that many authors attempt to tell both sides of the story in one volume, as in the "encyclopedia of lawmen and outlaws" genre or those devoted to "cops and robbers." On the other hand, this book is devoted solely to the discipline of policing.

Several guidelines have been followed in preparing the more than nine hundred entries contained in this volume. Biographical entries were selected with police experience in mind. This could include a supervisory capacity without actual field work, as in the cases of FBI directors and police officials such as Theodore Roosevelt. While policy mavens, criminologists confined to laboratories, and academics do not fit this criterion, several are included because of their impact on police issues or crime-fighting strategies and technology. Biographical entries cover significant personages who had short careers in law enforcement, such as New York City Police Commissioner Theodore Roosevelt, as well as those who spent entire careers in the profession, such as J. Edgar Hoover. Birth and death dates have been provided when available.

Many topics are tangential yet significant to the history of policing, including individuals like "Boss" William Marcy Tweed of Tammany Hall, who dispensed police appointments to supporters, and Jacob Riis, the chronicler of New York City immigrant life who accompanied Theodore Roosevelt as he covered the police beat and crime-ridden areas of the city. White men have dominated American policing since the colonial era. However, this volume also includes important policewomen and matrons such as Lola Baldwin and Mina van Winkle; forgotten, but exceptional, African-American peace officers such as Bass Reeves and Samuel Battle; and the Indian police forces that ranged the Oklahoma Territory on horseback prior to statehood.

While American policing dominates the entries in this work, this is in part due to its decentralized nature, which has led to the development of more than twenty thousand police forces at the local, state, and federal levels. In a book of this size it would be impossible to chronicle all the American police forces; therefore, it was necessary to select those that have been in the forefront of police professionalism as well as those that have been marked by scandal or media scrutiny. Much emphasis is given to the histories of the New York City, Los Angeles, Berkeley (California), and Chicago police departments, which are probably the most storied departments in American criminal justice history. While other city police departments merit attention for their contributions to American criminal justice, such an endeavor would be beyond the scope of the present volume. A similar argument can be made for state policing. Within these pages, the Texas, Pennsylvania, New York, and New Jersey state police forces are examined. A survey of the Massachusetts, California, and Louisiana State police forces could also be instructive, but again, this too would be beyond the scope of a one-volume work.

The same care was taken in selecting entries for the history of law enforcement in other countries. Although much attention is devoted to Scotland Yard, the French Sûreté, and the Royal Canadian Mounted Police, this volume also reveals the unfamiliar histories of the Iranian SAVAK, the Haitian Tonton Macoutes, and the Saudi Arabian religious police. The South African Police, the Gestapo, and the Soviet KGB also make their appearance, along with the Mexican Rurales.

Unlike traditional reference books on criminal justice history, this work also includes nontraditional examples of law enforcement such as private detectives; vigilante groups; little-known Western lawmen; detective organizations such as Wells Fargo, Pinkerton's National Detective Agency, and the agency of William Burns; and forgotten members of Scotland Yard, the Sûreté, and the FBI. The

Texas Rangers are well represented in this volume, as are derivative police forces such as the short-lived Arizona Rangers. Asterisks indicate a cross-reference to major entries in this volume. It is hoped that the reader will enjoy and find instructive this blending of history, criminology, and police science.

I would like to acknowledge the aid and assistance of the Newton Gresham Library Staff at Sam Houston State University, who were especially gracious in extending renewal times for reference books and other sources. I am also grateful for the friendship and support of Jim Olson, the best history chair in America, who proposed the project to me three years ago. A special thanks goes to my editor at Greenwood Press, Cynthia Harris, and to Jurg Gerber and Richard Ward for their support of my project. A special thanks goes as well to my canine-buddy Dillon for his advice and constant companionship as I whiled away hundreds of hours in my study working on this manuscript. Finally, this book is dedicated to my wife, Rosanne Barker, who has never wavered in her support of my various writing projects.

Abbreviations

A

ABBERLINE, FREDERICK GEORGE. (1843–1929) Born in Blandford, England, to a saddler and sometime local peace officer, Abberline worked as a clocksmith prior to joining the London Metropolitan Police* in 1863. Three years later he was promoted to sergeant and soon after became a plainclothes (see PLAINCLOTHES OFFICERS) detective. By 1873 he had risen to the rank of inspector, and he eventually attained the rank of chief inspector in 1890, before retiring two years later. Following retirement he worked in Monte Carlo as a private enquiry agent, and in 1898 he joined the European branch of Pinkerton's National Detective Agency.*

Abberline is best-known as the lead inspector for Scotland Yard* during the Jack the Ripper murder case in 1888. He was criticized for his inability to solve the case and remains a controversial and elusive figure. Little is known about Abberline and no photographs of him have been identified. However, some clues have been provided by a friend, for whom Abberline provided a collection of press clippings in the last years of his life.

The press cutting collection was extensively annotated, filling in some of the blanks in Abberline's life. He apparently was the recipient of eighty-four commendations and awards, and he explained that he did not immediately write his memoirs because it violated the protocol of his era (in part because authorities feared it would reveal police crime-fighting methods). Abberline did embark on a work titled *Reminiscences*, but only forty pages exist, which chronicle insubstantial cases. No mention is made of the Ripper case or any other significant cases.

The inspector by all accounts was a capable officer and reportedly knew more about the East End and Whitechapel underworld than any of his contemporaries. Legions of "Ripperologists," enthusiasts of the Jack the Ripper case, believe that

Abberline actually knew the identity of the real killer. They point to the fact that in 1889 Abberline took part in concealing a raid on a homosexual brothel catering to an exclusive clientele, including Queen Victoria's son, the Duke of Clarence. The allegation that Clarence was the Ripper was given wide currency beginning in the 1960s, but no historical evidence has surfaced to support this claim. Once Abberline resigned from the force in 1892 he never again mentioned the case.

SOURCES: Paul Begg, Martin Fido, and Keith Skinner, *The Jack the Ripper A to Z,* 1991; Paul Begg and Keith Skinner, *The Scotland Yard Files,* 1992.

ABERNATHY, JOHN R. (1876–1941) Born in Bosque County, Texas, the musically precocious Abernathy was playing the piano in saloons by the age of six. By the age of eleven he had participated in his first cattle drive, and four years later he was working as a wrangler on the legendary Goodnight Ranch.

After stints capturing wolves and selling musical instruments, Abernathy gravitated to law enforcement, becoming a deputy U.S. marshal and then a deputy sheriff* in southwestern Oklahoma in the late 1890s. His friendship with President Theodore Roosevelt* led to his appointment to marshal of Oklahoma in 1905. During his tenure he commanded such noted Oklahoma lawmen as Chris Madsen* and Henry Andrew "Heck" Thomas.* Abernathy has been credited with sending 782 men to prison without ever killing any of his adversaries, earning him the moniker "Catch-'em-alive Jack."

Following his resignation as Oklahoma marshal he served as a U.S. Secret Service* agent in New York and as a Mexican secret service agent under President Francisco Madero. Subsequently he made, and lost, fortunes as a wildcat oil driller in Texas; survived a serious drilling rig accident; and moved to Long Beach, California, where he died in 1944. His body was returned to Texas and buried in Wichita Falls.

SOURCES: John R. Abernathy, *"Catch 'Em Alive Jack": The Life and Adventures of an American Pioneer,* 1936; Dan L. Thrapp, ed., *EFB,* Vol. 1, 1988.

ABSCAM. In 1980 the Federal Bureau of Investigation (FBI)* conducted an undercover investigation into political corruption involving several members of the U.S. Congress as well as a number of high-profile local and state politicians. The term *ABSCAM* is short for "Arab scam" and refers to a sting operation in which FBI agents posed as wealthy Arab businessmen and offered bribes to influential politicians in exchange for favors. This investigation led to the conviction of one senator and six members of the House of Representatives. Despite claims of entrapment, the videotape evidence showing the politicians greedily accepting envelopes of money was incontrovertible.

SOURCE: George C. Kohn, *Encyclopedia of American Scandal,* 1989.

ACCOUNT OF THE ORIGINS AND EFFECTS OF A POLICE, AN. This 1758 pamphlet by Sir John Fielding* emphasized the preventative nature of policing and offered sketchy descriptions of a "Flying Squad" of horse police and details of police organization.

SOURCE: Patrick Pringle, *Hue and Cry*, 1955.

ACTON, THOMAS C. (1823–1898) Born in New York City, Acton overcame many obstacles in his youth and gained admission to the New York State Bar without ever attending college. He never went into practice himself, instead opting for a career in public service. In 1860 he began a nine-year stint on the Board of Police Commissioners in New York City.

During the New York City Draft Riots* of 1863 Acton assumed personal command of the Metropolitan Police after Superintendent John Alexander Kennedy* was severely beaten by a mob. Acton is credited with marshaling whatever resources were available to quell the rioting. He ordered all available officers from unaffected parts of the city to report to duty and appropriated every mode of transportation to rush officers to the riot scene. The rioting was beyond Acton's control and would only end after Union troops were rushed from Gettysburg to bring the end to three days of carnage.

Ultimately Acton's actions limited the destruction to the city and were responsible for saving the financial center of Wall Street from ruin. Under Acton's orders, police were instructed to take no prisoners and to "kill every man who has a club." Acton's methods of riot control were widely studied in the years following the rioting. Because of poor health, he resigned from the post of police commissioner in April 1869.

SOURCES: James F. Richardson, *The New York Police*, 1970; Augustine E. Costello, *Our Police Protectors*, 1885; reprint, 1972.

ADAMS, FRANCIS W. H. (1904–1990) After earning his law degree from Fordham Law School in 1923, Adams embarked on a law career that would take him from assistant U.S. attorney for the southern district of New York to special assistant to the attorney general in charge of investigating the burning of the *Morro Castle* off the New Jersey coast in 1934.

He returned to private practice in 1937 and, after several stints on various New York City civil commissions in the 1940s, was persuaded by the mayor to accept the position of New York City Police Department (NYPD)* commissioner. Assured of a free rein in rooting out corruption in the department, in 1954 he embarked on a campaign to take officers from the glee club and the departmental band and place them on the streets.

Adams is credited with increasing the number of officers on the street and adding close to two thousand officers to the force over the nineteen months he served prior to retirement. He implemented Operation Efficiency, which served as a watchdog unit to scrutinize officers on patrol. By the time his tour of duty ended, serious crime in the city had dropped 13 percent.

SOURCE: Charles Phillips and Alan Axelrod, *CCC*, 1996.

ADAMS, JAMES B. (b. 1926) Born in Corsicana, Texas, during World War II, Adams served in the army, where he gained a proficiency in Japanese while attending specialized training programs at Louisiana State University, the University of Minnesota, and Yale University. Following the war he returned to college; he received his law degree from Baylor University in 1949. After a short stint as assistant county attorney, he won election to the Texas State House of Representatives. However, he resigned in 1951 to join the Federal Bureau of Investigation (FBI)* as a special agent. Over the next two decades he served in a variety of capacities in field offices in Seattle, Washington; San Francisco, California; Minneapolis, Minnesota; and San Antonio, Texas. Adams became prominent in 1975 when he testified before the U.S. Senate and House committees investigating alleged civil rights violations committed by the FBI.

By 1978 Adams had risen to the second highest position in the FBI, as associate director under FBI Director William H. Webster.* The next year he retired from the FBI and was selected as the executive director of the Texas Criminal Justice Division. In 1980 Adams was appointed director of the Texas Department of Public Safety* and chief of the Texas Rangers.* Seven years later he retired from public service. Adams was the recipient of numerous awards, including the National Intelligence Distinguished Service Medal (1979) from the Central Intelligence Agency and the Attorney General's Distinguished Service Award (1978).

SOURCES: Mitchel Roth (historical text by), *Courtesy, Service, and Protection: The Texas Department of Public Safety's Sixtieth Anniversary*, 1995; Athan G. Theoharis, ed., *The FBI*, 1999.

AHRENS, ROBIN. (1952–1985) Born in St. Paul, Minnesota, and educated at Utah State and James Madison Universities, Ahrens joined the Federal Bureau of Investigation (FBI)* in 1984. The following year she was posted to the Phoenix, Arizona, field office. While arresting a suspected armed robber on October 4, 1985, Ahrens became the first female special agent to be killed in the line of duty. She was apparently killed by friendly fire, when agents mistook her for an armed affiliate of the suspect and shot her. Subsequently, the new Phoenix field office was named in her honor.

SOURCE: Athan G. Theoharis, ed., *The FBI*, 1999.

ALCOCK, JOHN. In 1917 Alcock became first deputy superintendent of the Chicago Police Department (CPD),* and for several months in 1918 he was acting chief while Chief Herman Schuettler* was on furlough. Appointed acting chief in 1930 by Mayor William H. Thompson for the seventh time during his eleven years as mayor, Alcock began an immediate shake-up of the corrupt police department. Known to the underworld as "Saltwater Jack" and "Eyes and Ears," Alcock initiated a plethora of disciplinary measures to assure the public that the alliance between the police department and gangsters had ended. He created a Bureau of Criminal Information and Statistics to put an end to the tradition of suppressing criminal reporting, which was clearly an attempt to mislead the public. This new records division would then furnish the Chicago Crime Commission with information on crime in the city. The crime commission compiled a list of twenty-eight Chicago criminals designated as public enemies.* Topping the list was Al Capone, who was warned to leave town when he returned to the city from Philadelphia in March 1930.

SOURCE: Raphael W. Marrow and Harriet I. Carter, *In Pursuit of Crime*, 1996.

ALCOHOL, TOBACCO AND FIREARMS. The Bureau of Alcohol, Tobacco, and Firearms (BATF) can be traced back to its inception as the Alcohol, Tobacco, Tax Unit in 1862. The following year, this unit within the Internal Revenue Service engaged three detectives to help prevent, detect, and punish tax evaders. A division of the U.S. Treasury Department,* since 1972, it was renamed the Bureau of Alcohol, Tobacco and Firearms.

During the Prohibition era this agency targeted bootleggers and speakeasies. By the late 1980s, however, the BATF had become responsible for regulating the production of the nation's alcoholic beverages, firearms traffic, high explosives, and automatic weapons. The ATF was especially prominent during the initial shootout at the Branch Davidian compound near Waco, Texas, in 1992. In 1990, of its 3,731 employees, 1,400 were special agents and 450 were inspectors and specialists.

SOURCE: Kenneth J. Peak, *Policing America*, 1993.

ALDERMEN. Contrary to the model of policing of Sir Robert Peel,* which championed professional independence from local politicians, the New York City model that developed in the 1840s and 1850s was characterized by partisan control of the police. Aldermen were powerful local politicians who had the power to appoint, upon nomination by the mayor, a police chief and as many police officers as the ordinances of the city council required. Conversely, police officers could be removed for misconduct at the request of the Board of Aldermen. Until the New York City charter was revamped in 1853, aldermen had the power to discharge prisoners arrested by the police, which resulted in tension between the policemen and the aldermen. Although their powers were restricted by the 1853 act, aldermen still retained the right to free prisoners between the time they were arrested and when they appeared before a magistrate.

SOURCES: Wilbur R. Miller, *Cops and Bobbies*, 1973; James F. Richardson, *The New York Police*, 1970.

ALDRICH, ROY W. (1869–1955) Born in Quincy, Illinois, Aldrich relocated to Missouri with his family in his youth. In the late 1880s he worked in the timber industry in the Pacific Northwest and held a series of jobs, including horsetrader, coffee plantation manager, miner, and stagecoach driver. He enlisted in the U.S. Army in 1898 and served in the Philippines theater of the Spanish American War. Aldrich moved to Texas in 1907 and, after a stint in real estate, joined the Texas Rangers* in 1915. During his tenure he patrolled the Rio Grande border and then was transferred to the Austin headquarters for the remainder of his career. Aldrich saw action trying to suppress the 1919 Longview race riot and restoring law and order to the East Texas oil boomtown of Mexia in 1922. During the 1920s he successfully investigated sensational murders, chased bootleggers, and handled labor strife in Borger. Aldrich continued to work for the Rangers into the 1930s.

SOURCE: Mike Cox, *Texas Ranger Tales: Stories That Need Telling*, 1997.

ALEXANDER, RICHARD C. (1841–1907) Raised on a Suffolk, England, farm, Alexander joined the military in 1857. Reportedly the best shot in the army, he saw action in India during the Sepoy uprising and mutiny. In 1876 he moved to Durban, South Africa, where he was appointed superintendent and chief constable (see CONSTABLES), a position he would hold for forty years. Having spent twelve years as a senior noncommissioned officer, he had the perfect background for the position according to the standards set by Colonel Sir Charles Rowan.* Alexander, who was better known by now as "The Old Super," retired in 1906 and died the following year.

SOURCE: Alan, F. Hattersley, *The First South African Detectives*, 1960.

ALLEE, ALFRED Y. (1855–1896) Born in DeWitt County, Texas, Allee entered law enforcement as deputy sheriff of Karnes County, Texas, in 1882. It was not long before he was embroiled in controversy, as he was accused of murdering a robbery suspect. Following his acquittal, he won the same policing position in Frio County. Soon after, he killed a deputy in a gunfight, and he was again tried and exonerated. Although he was often criticized for shooting unprepared victims, he was applauded in 1888 for his heroism in tracking down and killing the brutal robber Brack Cornett in a pitched gunfight. Noted for his animosity towards blacks, he once reportedly killed a black porter who got in his way. On August 19, 1896, Allee was stabbed to death in a barroom fight in Laredo, Texas.

SOURCE: Jay Robert Nash, *EWLD*, 1994.

ALLEN, JOHN OLIVER. (1850–1928) Born in Kaufman County, Texas, Allen joined Company D of the Texas Rangers* in 1874. In his less than one-year stint with the Rangers, he was wounded four times in Indian battles.

SOURCE: "John O. Allen," *Frontier Times*, August 1927, p. 8.

ALLISON, WILLIAM DAVID. (c. 1861–1923) Born in Ohio, Allison moved to Texas, where he gained a reputation as the most proficient sheriff* in the history of the state. He joined the Arizona Rangers* in 1903 and served until it was disbanded in 1905. During his tenure with the short-lived rangers, he rose to the rank of lieutenant and was credited with killing the train robber Three Finger Jack and capturing the Owens Brothers and other bandits of note. Following his Arizona service he returned to Texas, where he killed a former general under Mexican President Francisco Madero, Pascal Morosco, when he reportedly caught him rustling cattle. Allison was shot and killed in Seminole, Texas, in 1923.

SOURCES: Joseph Miller, *The Arizona Rangers*, 1972; Dan L. Thrapp, ed., *EFB*, Vol. 1, 1988.

ALLMAN, JAMES. (1876–1956) Born in Ireland, Allman joined the Chicago Police Department (CPD)* at the age of twenty-four. Allman had been nicknamed the "Iron Man" for his strict discipline and no-nonsense manner, and during a thirteen-year stint as captain, he was moved to fourteen different stations to reorganize and improve their police units. During his forty-five years on the force, he was untainted by scandal, a rare accomplishment in that day and age. In October 1931, Chicago Mayor Anton Cermak appointed him police chief, a position he held for the next fourteen years. Allman served in this role longer than any other chief of the department.

Succeeding acting chief John Alcock,* who returned to the department as first deputy, Allman led the cleanup of the city in the waning days of Prohibition. In particular, he led the reorganization of the CPD following the release of the Bruce Smith* report. According to the new organizational plan, the force was structured into major units, consisting of the uniform force, Detective Bureau, Traffic Bureau, Bureau of Department Records and Property, Bureau of Criminal Information and Statistics, Personnel Bureau, Crime Prevention Division, and Morals Division.

SOURCE: Raphael W. Marrow and Harriet I. Carter, *In Pursuit of Crime*, 1996.

ALVORD, BURT. (1866–c. 1910) The career of Burt Alvord illustrates the thin line that often distinguished peace officers from outlaws in the nineteenth-century American West. Alvord arrived in Tombstone, Arizona, with his justice of the peace* father in the early 1880s. Soon after his arrival he witnessed the gunfight at the O.K. Corral while employed there as a stable boy.

In 1886 Alvord was appointed deputy by Sheriff John Horton Slaughter* of Cochise County. Slaughter was made aware of Alvord's dexterity with a sixgun after he killed a Tombstone desperado in a gunfight the previous year. In 1890 Alvord worked as a peace officer in the mining camp of Pearce, Arizona, and then Willcox, where he performed the duties of constable (see CONSTABLES) and killed "Cowboy Bill" King under mysterious circumstances. During the 1890s Alvord participated in numerous gun battles with outlaws and rustlers and achieved a reputation as a dependable peace officer, but in 1899 his choice of running pals led to his involvement in a drunken gunfight in which one of his friends was killed. Chastised publicly by his mentor Slaughter, Alvord left Tombstone for Fairbank, Arizona, where he became the town constable.

Alvord's drinking and carousing spiraled out of control, and he was forced to resign as town constable. Despite his penchant for law enforcement earlier in his career, by 1899 Alvord had stepped over the line and would never hold another peace-keeping position. While leading a gang of train robbers, he was arrested for the first time in 1900. Freed from jail by a gang member, Alvord spent the next few years on the lam before being arrested again in 1903. Released after a two-year stint in the Yuma penitentiary, Alvord sought new fortunes south of the border and was last seen in either Panama or Venezuela in 1910. According to one source he was seen working on the Panama Canal project, while another reported he was happily married and living in Honduras.

SOURCES: C. L. Sonnichsen, *Billy King's Tombstone*, 1972; Joseph Miller, *The Arizona Rangers*, 1972; Bill O'Neal, *The Arizona Rangers*, 1987.

AMBLER, HORACE. (c. 1849–after 1880) Ambler was born in Pennsylvania. Following service in the U.S. Army, he was appointed chief of the Indian police* on the San Carlos Apache Reservation in Arizona. He stepped down after less than one month, being succeeded by Albert D. Sterling in August 1880.

SOURCE: Dan L. Thrapp, ed., *EFB*, Vol. 1, 1988.

AMOS, JAMES EDWARD. (1879–1953) Born in Washington, D.C., Amos worked as a telephone repairman and steam engineer before getting the law enforcement bug while serving as a bodyguard for President Theodore Roosevelt* and then working for the William John Burns* International Detective Agency. As director of the Federal Bureau of Investigation* in 1921 Burns appointed Amos as a special agent, making him one of the first African-American agents in the history of the Bureau. The most prominent cases investigated by Amos included the Lepke Buchalter syndicate, black nationalist Marcus Garvey, and German spy Frederick Joubert Duquesne. Amos also participated in the capture of mobster Dutch Schultz. He retired in October 1953, two months before he died.

SOURCE: Athan G. Theoharis, ed., *The FBI*, 1999.

ANDERSON, SIR ROBERT. (1841–1918) Born in Dublin, Ireland, Anderson was educated at Trinity College before being called to the bar in 1870. Prior to joining the London Metropolitan Police,* he worked for an intelligence unit investigating Fenian activites and as secretary to the prison commissioners. In 1888 he was appointed assistant commissioner of the Criminal Investigation Department (CID)* a position he held until he retired thirteen years later. He was the officer in charge of the Whitechapel murder investigation, popularly known as the Jack the Ripper case, from October 1888 until the file was closed in 1892. He is remembered as having admitted on several occasions that the identity of the Ripper had been discovered, making him the only member of the police to state conclusively that the case had been solved.

Anderson's recommendation that all prostitutes working the streets after midnight be arrested was rejected by the authorities, leading to Anderson's proclamation that prostitutes should not expect police protection. Although he provided any names, he claimed that the Ripper was a "poor Polish Jew" from the Whitechapel area and that he had been sent to an asylum, where a witness later identified him. However, of the two possible names associated with this suspect, both have been discredited.

Upon his retirement in 1901 Anderson was knighted. During the last seventeen years of his life he wrote numerous articles and over twenty books, including *Criminals and Crime* (1907) and his autobiography, *The Lighter Side of My Official Life* (1910). Being plagued by deafness, his last years were spent somewhat isolated. Anderson eldest son wrote a biography of his parents in 1947.

SOURCES: Paul Begg, Martin Fidc, and Keith Skinner, *The Jack the Ripper A to Z*, 1991; H. L. Adam, *Police Encyclopedia*, 1920; Martin Fido and Keith Skinner, *The Official Encyclopedia of Scotland Yard*, 1999.

ANDREWS COMMITTEE. In 1895 this committee to investigate corruption on the Philadelphia police force was convened at the urging of a bipartisan reform group called the Citizens' Municipal Association of Philadelphia. Two years later the committee issued a report that characterized the police force as nothing more than political agents of the Republican machine. In the findings the committee cited numerous instances of police corruption, including the discarding of hundreds of votes for opposition candidates and even police presence in the voting booths to make sure that the "correct" ballots were cast.

In a reciprocal relationship with the political leaders, the police received carte blanche to engage in police brutality and to offer protection to local vice lords. However, despite the seriousness of the committee findings, the police force remained unchanged. For example, when General Smedley Darlington Butler* was appointed public safety director in 1923 he found that many Philadelphia policemen collected payoffs of up to $200 per month.

SOURCE: Carl Sifakis, *The Encyclopedia of American Crime*, 1982.

ANGUS, WILLIAM GALISPIE. (1849–1921) Born in Janesville, Ohio, Angus served in the army before moving to Wyoming in 1880. Although he reportedly worked as a pimp, gambler, and bartender, in 1889 he was elected sheriff* of Johnson County. His four-year tenure coincided with the Johnson County War, in which he allied himself with the small ranchers, or nesters, against the cattlemen. He was criticized for not pursuing a murder case against Frank M. Canton (Joe Horner)* and in 1892 he led the siege against the Texas mercenaries at the TA Ranch. Considered an adequate peace officer, Angus turned to ranching in 1893.

SOURCE: Helena Huntington Smith, *War on the Powder River*, 1966.

ANSLINGER, HARRY J. (1892–1975) Born in Altoona, Pennsylvania, and educated at Pennsylvania State University and the Washington College law school, Anslinger rose to national prominence as the first commissioner of the Bureau of Narcotics of the U.S. Treasury Department in the 1930s.

Anslinger initially entered public service with the War Department before moving to the Treasury Department in 1926. During the early Prohibition years he attended seminars on international drug and alcohol smuggling, which eventually led to his appointment, in 1929, to commissioner of Prohibition. The following year he was appointed to head the new Bureau of Narcotics.

As commissioner of the Bureau of Narcotics, Anslinger embarked on a get-tough policy against drug users. During the 1930s he led the crusade against marijuana, which culminated in the passage of the Marijuana Tax Act of 1937. During World War II Anslinger claimed that the Japanese were using an "Opium Offensive" as part of a strategy to enslave conquered countries through drug trafficking. In response to examples of this policy in Korea and China, the U.S. government was sufficiently alarmed to grant Anslinger access to the Coast Guard, the U.S. Customs Service,* and the Internal Revenue Service in his battle against the narcotics trade. With William F. Tompkins, Anslinger coauthored *The Traffic in Narcotics* (1953). He remained an outspoken adversary of illegal drug use until his death in 1975.

SOURCES: Carl Sifakis, *The Mafia Encyclopedia*, 1999; Charles Phillips and Alan Axelrod, *CCC*, 1996.

ANTHROPOMETRY. Anthropometry, or the science of human measurement, was based on an identification system created by Alphonse Bertillon.* This French system (see BERTILLON SYSTEM) predated fingerprinting* as a method for criminal classification and was influenced by the findings of the French statistician Lambert Adolphe Jacques Quetelet, who calculated the odds of any two individuals with comparable physical features being exactly the same height at four to one. Bertillon figured that by including other physical measurements, identification could be made even more dependable.

SOURCES: Eugene B. Block, *Science vs. Crime*, 1979; William G. Bailey, ed., *The Encyclopedia of Police Science*, 1995.

ANTI–HORSE THIEF ASSOCIATION. In 1859 the Anti–Horse Thief Association was established at Fort Scott to confront the horse theft problem in Kansas and its bordering states. Following the Civil War, criminal bands flourished in this sparsely policed area, using the Indian Territory as their base of operations. Made up more of vigilantes than peace officers, association justice was typically dispensed at the end of a hanging rope. After the horse theft problem diminished the organization continued to meet as a social group into the twentieth century.

SOURCE: Frank Richard Prassel, *The Western Peace Officer*, 1981.

ARGENSON, MARC RENÉ DE VOYER. (1652–1721) Born in Venice, Argenson succeeded Gabriel La Reynie* as the lieutenant-general of police* of Paris and is credited with building on the improvements of his predecessor. One of his accomplishments involved changing police patrol patterns. Originally, all police patrolled from a fixed location, but in 1698 Argenson established a post at the Pont-Neuf so that in the event of an emergency, any citizen could be secure with the knowledge that soldiers would be posted there rather than having to wait for them to make their designated rounds. Historians consider this the progenitor of the police station.

Argenson was also instrumental in creating the office of inspector of police in 1708, whereby forty inspectors were assigned different sections of the city, where they served under the direction of local commissioners. Argenson's tenure saw more improvements in street lighting and cleaning and the suppression of the vagabond problem. Following his resignation in 1718 he was appointed minister of justice.

SOURCES: Philip John Stead, *The Police of Paris*, 1957; Alan Williams, *The Police of Paris: 1718–1789*, 1979.

ARIZONA RANGERS. Created in 1901, the Arizona Rangers, like the Texas Rangers,* existed before actual statehood. A consortium of cattlemen, mine owners, railroad officials, and newspaper officials, Republicans all, convinced the Territorial Governor that a force modeled on the Texas Rangers was required to dispatch the growing lawlessness in Arizona. Resistance came from the usual suspects: local peace officers, who felt their autonomy and power might be threatened. However, support was strong in the legislature, and a ranger force was inaugurated over objections like that of one newspaperman who claimed that the only activity he associated with the rangers was for them "to go camping around the country making coffee" (O'Neal).

Funded similarly to their Texas counterparts, the Arizona force was required to supply its own weapons, equipment, and mounts, although the state would reimburse for horses killed in action. Like the Texas Rangers, who wore suitable range clothes, they were issued no uniform, which further protected their identities. However, in a harbinger of what was to come in the development of state police professionalization, it was noted that the "force was to be governed by the rules and regulations of the Army of the USA." Rangers were hired for twelve-month enlistments and given the power to arrest anywhere in the territory and deliver the prisoner to the county where the crime had been committed.

Throughout its short history it remained a custom to not publicly identify Ranger members, although some were well known in their home communities. Since there was a high turnover rate, many concealed their identities. Some had previous experience as peace officers, others as cowboys and cattlemen.

Shortly after its creation, Democrats complained to the governor that the Rangers were all Republicans. The patronage issue would continue to creep into any discussion of the Rangers. Republican virtues included a zealous stand on temperance. In 1907, under General order number 1, it was mandated that "Rangers will not congregate in saloons; nor in any bawdy house, for the purpose of amusement, or out of idleness" (O'Neal).

By 1908, the Rangers' strength was approved at twenty-three officers and men as outlawry began a decline in Arizona. The group's strength was concentrated in the southwestern part of the territory, where the Rangers found themselves undermanned and outgunned. In 1907 the force requested a machine gun for the company plus the replacement of the Ranger-issue 1895 Winchester rifle with the 1903 Springfield. Other requests included better tracking dogs and expenditures for inspection trips by train. However, the demise of this short-lived force was on the horizon as opposition to its expenditures increased and payroll was cut by reducing its strength. As a result, the machine gun and the Winchesters would not be forthcoming. The mission of the Rangers was to reduce outlaw depredations, which they did within eight years. Then, after reporting less than two dozen arrests in a month, it became apparent that the Rangers had worked themselves out of a job.

In 1909 an anti-Ranger effort was in progress, supported by county sheriffs (see SHERIFF) and district attorneys. That same year they were used to suppress labor unrest in the mining town of Globe. However, political issues refused to go away, as the Ranger company, which was widely viewed as the creation of the Republican governor, became a political football and Democratic target. Democrats campaigned on an anti-Ranger platform, addressing the complaints and jealousy of local law officers. One of the main laments was that Ranger arrests took fees and rewards from local peace officers. Another reason for resentment stemmed from the fact that the Rangers served as monitors of sheriffs and reported the activities of local lawmen to the governor. Considerable opposition came from the north, where few were stationed. Crackdowns in crime-infested regions were resented locally. Thus, despite the wide support of Arizonians at large, the Arizona Rangers were disbanded on February 15, 1909.

The Rangers' legacy suggests that they had much better relations with the

Mexican government than their Texan counterparts. Unlike the relationship between the Texas Rangers* and the Mexican Rurales,* Arizona Rangers cooperated with the Mexican government, which permitted them to launch manhunts and extradite criminals to the United States, albeit in an informal manner.

Ultimately, in 1912 Arizona achieved statehood, and a highway patrol* was created in 1931. As with past mounted police forces,* the introduction of the automobile, rapid population growth, and political infighting signaled the end of the Arizona Rangers. The exploits of the Arizona Rangers inspired the short-lived 1958 television series *26 Men*, with actor Tris Coffin portraying Captain Thomas H. Rynning.* Hollywood was not immune to the charm of the former police force, and in 1948 RKO released the low-budget film *Arizona Ranger*.

SOURCES: Bill O'Neal, *The Arizona Rangers*, 1987; Joseph Miller, *The Arizona Rangers*, 1972; Mitchel Roth, "Mounted Police Forces: A Comparative History," *Policing* 21(4), 1998.

ARMSTRONG, JOHN BARCLAY. (1850–1913) Born in McMennville, Tennessee, Armstrong is best remembered for his capture of noted gunman John Wesley Hardin. Leaving home in his youth, Armstrong drifted through the southwest before landing in Austin, Texas, in 1870. Marriage, children, and a brief ranching career followed before he joined the Texas Rangers* in 1875. During the next decade he became one of the most prominent members of the Rangers and a favorite of Ranger commander Leander H. McNelly.* As McNelly's protégé Armstrong earned the nickname "McNelly's Bulldog" as well as a promotion to sergeant.

Armstrong began his pursuit of the noted Texas badman John Wesley Hardin in early 1877. With a $4,000 reward offered for Hardin's arrest, it was not long before the intrepid ranger tracked the outlaw down to the Gulf states and then to Florida. Although, Armstrong had no legal authority in the state, he commissioned several men as deputies and, on a tip, found Hardin and several gang members on a train in the Pensacola area. Hardin was captured before he could fire a shot when he uncharacteristically caught one of his pistols in his suspenders. However, one of his accomplices was able to get off a round, narrowly missing Armstrong's scalp but close enough to knock off his stetson hat. The ranger returned fire, mortally wounding Hardin's associate in the chest. Hardin put up a fight and was only subdued when hit over the head with a gun butt. The remaining members of the gang were taken into custody without further violence.

After collecting his $4,000 reward, Armstrong purchased more than 50,000 acres of cattle land, forming the nucleus of one of the largest cattle ranches of that time, the XIT. He continued his ranger career and rose to the vaunted position of captain before retiring in 1882 to supervise operations on his ranch. He returned to law enforcement for a brief spell as U.S. marshal (see U.S.

MARSHALS SERVICE) in his locale. The remaining years of his life were not without incident. In 1908 one of his cowboys took umbrage with a particular directive and shot Armstrong off his horse. However, the hardy veteran of numerous shooting scrapes survived and died with his boots off at home on his ranch five years later.

SOURCES: Jay Robert Nash, *EWLO*, 1994; Richard C. Marohn, *The Last Gunfighter: John Wesley Hardin*, 1995.

ARRINGTON, GEORGE W. (1844–1923) Born in Greensboro, Alabama, Arrington served with Mosby's Raiders during the Civil War. With the subsequent defeat of the Confederacy, he headed to Mexico with many of his compatriots to offer assistance to Maximilian's faltering government. Following a series of adventures in Central America, Arrington returned to the United States in 1867.

Moving to Texas, Arrington joined the Texas Rangers* in 1875, where his cavalry experience under John S. Mosby led to his rapid promotion through the ranks to captain of Company C in 1878. Arrington's unit patrolled the Texas Panhandle, one of the most dangerous territories during the post–Civil War years. His company made quick work of the outlaw scourge, and in 1879 he established Camp Roberts, the first ranger camp in the Panhandle region.

Remembered as an uncompromising disciplinarian, Arrington left the Texas Rangers in 1882 to become a ranch manager and continue his law enforcement career as sheriff* of Wheeler County and its fourteen adjacent counties. He retired from law enforcement in 1891, and except for another brief stint as sheriff in 1894, spent his remaining years on his Rocking Chair Ranch near the Washita River.

SOURCES: Walter Prescott Webb, *The Texas Rangers*, 1935; Robert W. Stephens, *Texas Ranger Indian War Pensions*, 1975.

ASKARS. The sultanate of Muscat and Oman employed a traditional tribal police known as the Askars as late as the 1960s. Each of the country's thirty-five districts was controlled by a Wali, who was responsible for maintaining law and order. The Wali commanded the Askars who were garbed in robes and equipped with rifles. Today, Askars have been replaced by the Royal Omani Police.

SOURCES: James Cramer, *The World's Police*, 1964; George Thomas Kurian, *World Encyclopedia of Police Forces & Penal Systems*, 1989.

ASTOR PLACE RIOT. In 1849 a New York City riot developed out of a rivalry between two thespians at the Astor Place Theater. When a mob tried to prevent one of the actors from taking the stage, a wild melee ensued, with the mob throwing rocks at a small, outmatched police detachment. A local militia force was called to the scene and fired into the horde, killing twenty-two people and wounding forty. This was a turning point in New York City crowd control;

in response, the police force instituted riot control training and military drills for police officers and began equipping them with their first police weapon, a 22-inch club, to be used only in self-defense.

SOURCE: Richard Moody, *The Astor Place Riot*, 1958.

ATEN, IRA. (1863–1953) Born in Illinois, Aten's family moved to Texas during his childhood. In 1883 he joined the vaunted Texas Rangers.* As a member of Company D of the Frontier Battalion, Aten found himself guarding the Rio Grande border region, a hotspot for criminal activity. In 1887 Aten's accomplishments in the field led to his promotion to sergeant. Aten is credited with persuading John Reynolds Hughes* to enlist in the Rangers. In 1889 Aten was so upset after killing two horse thieves in a gunfight that he retired.

Soon after leaving the Rangers, Aten was appointed sheriff* of Fort Bend County, which was at that time embroiled in a violent political feud known as the Jaybird-Woodpecker War. Aten has been recognized for ending this conflict in 1890. Three years later he was elected sheriff of Castro County, where he was credited with treating prisoners humanely. A superb marksman, Aten usually brought fugitives back alive rather than dead. In 1895 he left law enforcement for ranching. Two of his brothers also served as Texas Rangers.

SOURCE: Jay Robert Nash, *EWLO*, 1994.

AUBLE, WALTER H. (1862–1908) Auble joined the Los Angeles Police Department (LAPD)* in 1887 and the following year was promoted to detective. He left the department to become a deputy U.S. marshal (See U.S. MARSHAL SERVICE) in 1893 but returned to the LAPD in 1898. In 1905 he began a one-year stint as police chief. Preferring to work as a detective, he stepped down in 1906 and returned to the field. In September 1908 he became the third LAPD officer to be killed in the line of duty. Auble was killed while attempting to thwart a burglary. When the perpetrator was surrounded following a manhunt, he swallowed a capsule of cyanide and died an hour later. As of 1984, Auble, having served as police commissioner, is the highest-ranked LAPD officer to be killed on duty.

SOURCE: Arthur W. Sjoquist (historical text by), *Los Angeles Police Department Commemorative Book, 1869–1984*, 1984.

AUGUSTUS CAESAR. (63 B.C.–A.D. 14) The grand-nephew and heir of Julius Caesar, Augustus was born Gaius Octavius. He carved out a brilliant military career, and following the suicides of Marc Antony and Cleopatra in 31 B.C., consolidated his power with the support of the Roman army. He subsequently garnered the support of the Roman populace as well, and in 27 B.C. was given the title Augustus. Among the most enduring achievements of his administration was the law enforcement network he created.

Augustus introduced a law enforcement apparatus composed of several separate organizations. The elite Praetorian Guard, more like a military police, consisted of nine cohorts of a thousand men each. Three cohorts were stationed in Rome, while others were posted in provincial towns. They functioned more as military support for police rather than actual peace officers. The three Urban Cohorts, troops of soldiers with police powers that patrolled Rome, were commanded by a leader in civilian garb, whom one historian has referred to as the "chief constable of Rome" (see CONSTABLES).

Besides the Praetorian Guard and the Urban Cohorts, Augustus created the Vigiles, which were more akin to policemen-firemen and composed of nonmilitary personnel. To ensure the force remained so, he only recruited freedmen from the civilian population. The Vigiles were armed with short swords and either a baton or club. The firefighting Vigiles saw their police powers increase over time as they were imbued with police duties such as inflicting corporal punishment on serious lawbreakers and individuals who violated fire regulations. They were also notably responsible for nighttime policing in Rome and shared day duties with the Urban Cohorts. During the Augustan era, Rome, then a city of 750,000, was protected by a force of 10,000 police. With a police-to-civilian ratio of 1 to 75, London's 1989 ratio of 1 to 278 paled in comparison.

SOURCES: Charles Reith, *The Blind Eye of History*, 1952; Gaius Suetonius Tranquillus, trans. by Robert Graves, *The Twelve Caesars*, 1957; George Thomas Kurian, *World Encyclopedia of Police Forces & Penal Systems*, 1989.

AULL, CHARLES. (1849–1899) Aull was born near Liberty, Missouri, and at the age of three traveled with his physician father to California during the waning months of the gold rush. After a short stint in the mercantile business, Aull was appointed undersheriff of Modesto, California, in 1870. Five years later he was designated turnkey of the state prison at San Quentin. He resigned in 1880 and joined the Wells Fargo Detective Bureau,* under the command of the legendary James Bunyan Hume.*

During his tenure with Wells Fargo, Aull was credited with capturing the stagecoach bandit Dick Fellows, in 1881. Later that year he was instrumental in tracking down the stage robbers Bill Miller and Bill Miner. In 1883 Aull returned to the field of corrections as deputy warden of San Quentin. Four years later he left law enforcement when he was promoted to warden of Folsom Prison, where he earned a reputation as a judicious and professional penologist.

SOURCES: Richard Dillon, *Wells Fargo Detective*, 1969; Kenneth Lamott, *Chronicles of San Quentin*, 1961.

B

BACA, ELFEGO. (1865–1945) Born in Socorro, New Mexico, and educated in Topeka, Kansas, Baca returned with his family to Socorro in 1880 when his father became the marshal of a nearby town. In 1884 Elfego followed his father into law enforcement, albeit as a self-appointed peace officer, at Frisco, New Mexico, after the mail order purchase of a badge and a brace of six shooters. Never one to shy away from gunplay, in October 1884 Baca participated in one of the most heralded gunfights of Western lore. In an altercation with cowboys from a local ranch, their foreman was killed in a fall from his horse. The following day Baca found himself besieged by eighty employees from the ranch, culminating in a thirty-six-hour gunfight. Baca withstood a withering fusillade of bullets, and then dynamite, before surrendering to a friend, but still in possession of his six guns. At least fourteen cowboys were wounded in the siege, four fatally.

After serving four months in jail and beating a murder charge, Baca set his sights on entering the law profession and pursuing a career as a peace officer. Baca's future in law enforcement was assured following this episode. Over the ensuing years he became a lawyer and was elected to a variety of offices including deputy sheriff, county sheriff, mayor of Socorro, and district attorney, and he barely lost in the governor's race.

Despite his reputation, Baca rarely drew his weapons. However, in 1915 at the age of fifty Baca was ambushed by an old adversary and his gunmen. Baca returned fire, killing the ringleader with shots from both pistols. Following his acquittal on murder charges, he was elected sheriff* of Socorro County. After his term as sheriff he returned to legal practice in New Mexico for his remaining years.

SOURCES: Larry D. Ball, *Elfego Baca*, 1992; Leon Claire Metz, *The Shooters*, 1976; Dan L. Thrapp, ed., *EFB*, Vol. 1, 1988.

BADGE, THE. *Dragnet** creator Jack Webb paid homage to Los Angeles Police Department (LAPD)* chief William H. Parker* in this reverent biography.

SOURCE: Joe Domanick, *To Protect and Serve*, 1994.

BAKER, LAFAYETTE "LAFE." (1826–1868) Born in Stafford, New York, and raised in Lansing, Michigan, Baker was a member of the San Francisco Vigilance Committee* in the 1850s and was reportedly one of the finest marksmen in the country. In 1861 William Seward, who was suspicious of President Abraham Lincoln's close relationship with Allan J. Pinkerton,* appointed Baker to head up the new U.S. Secret Service, commanded by Lafayette Baker. In 1866 Baker was succeeded as head of the U.S. Secret Service by Colonel William P. Wood.*

   Subsequently, Baker, whom some scholars suspect of complicity along with Edwin Stanton in the assassination plot against Lincoln, was appointed to command the First District of Columbia Cavalry, a unit characterized as an unsavory paramilitary force composed of former criminals and ne'er-do-wells. The unscrupulous Baker earned a reputation for brutality and became known in some quarters as "Czar of the Underworld." Under his direction the cavalry unit arrested suspects without warrants and held them for weeks in a dungeon-like setting in the basement of the Treasury Building. After Baker was forced into retirement in 1867 he began writing a history of the U.S. Secret Service. Its publication earned Stanton's wrath for the unpleasant portrait it painted of him. In the months following the book's publication, Baker was harassed and narrowly escaped several murder attempts. When he died at the age of forty-two, his obituary listed typhoid as the cause of death, while his death certificate cited meningitis. Although his physician suspected arsenic poisoning, this was never followed up. Conspiracy theorists point to Stanton's embarrassment as the likely impetus for his death.

SOURCE: James Mackay, *Allan Pinkerton: The First Private Eye*, 1996.

BALDWIN, LOLA. One of the early pioneers in female law enforcement, Baldwin was working for the Portland, Oregon, National Traveler's Aid Association when she was asked to perform protective work on behalf of women who would be attending the Lewis and Clark Exposition in 1905. She performed her duties with such distinction that when the fair ended, she continued to provide the same services for women visitors to Portland and was eventually imbued with police powers by the Portland police. She focused much of her energies on closing down saloons and brothels. By 1913 she held the rank of captain, and she directed her officers to prohibit young women from working in sordid environments such as pool halls and bowling alleys.

She weathered several death threats and one poisoning attempt and later became the director of the Department of Public Safety for the Protection of Young Girls and Women. During her long career with the organization, she outlasted six police chiefs and five mayors. Women were not referred to as policewomen until 1927, preferring the title "worker" or "operative."

SOURCES: Dorothy Moses Schulz, *From Social Worker to Crimefighter*, 1995; Kerry Segrave, *Policewomen: A History*, 1995.

BALTIMORE POLICE DEPARTMENT. Baltimore was established as Baltimore Towne in 1729, but it was not until 1784 that any attempts were made to create an organized law enforcement apparatus, when constables* were appointed and imbued with police powers. In 1853 the Maryland State Legislature authorized the creation of a police force to enforce the laws and protect public and private property. According to the new statute, officers were required to be armed and to carry a badge. During the Civil War the department was controlled by the state, beginning in 1862.

The 1880s saw numerous innovations and attempts at modernization. In 1885 the call box system and a Harbor Patrol were adopted and the first patrol wagon saw service. In the 1890s a Bertillon Bureau (see BERTILLON, ALPHONSE; BERTILLON SYSTEM) was created for identification purposes, followed by a Traffic Division (1908) and a Police Academy (1913).

The Board of Police Commissioners was created in 1920, and General Charles D. Gaither was selected as the first Baltimore police commissioner. The first radio communications were installed in patrol cars in 1933. Numerous other developments followed, including the establishment of the Accident Investigation Unit (1938), the Laboratory Division (1950), and the Central Records Division (1951). In 1961 the Park Police and the Baltimore Police Department (BPD) were consolidated. Today the BPD is responsible for a jurisdiction covering eighty-six square miles.

SOURCE: "The Baltimore City Police Department," November 1999, available at: cw. cibaltimore.md.us/government/police/history, Internet.

BANGS, GEORGE HENRY. (d. 1883) Born and raised in New England, Bangs claimed he could trace his lineage back to the *Mayflower*. He worked as a reporter for his father's newspaper prior to entering law enforcement. When Allan J. Pinkerton* inaugurated his detective agency in the 1850s he selected Bangs as his first employee. Over the next three decades Bangs served as general superintendent and Pinkerton's most trusted employee. Bangs came close to losing his job on several occasions when he was reported drunk in public. As superintendent he was often in the field, rarely spending time in the Chicago office. Bangs retired as general superintendent in 1881, and in 1887 his son, George D. Bangs, joined the agency. George D. would assume his father's old position in 1892 and hold it for the next thirty years.

SOURCES: James Mackay, *Allan Pinkerton: The First Private Eye*, 1996; Frank Morn, *"The Eye That Never Sleeps,"* 1982.

BANKS, E. J. "JAY." (1913–1987) As captain of the Texas Rangers,* Banks helped quell the Lone Star Steel Strike and the integration of Mansfield, Texas, schools in the 1950s. While commanding Company C in Dallas, his photograph was featured in *Time* magazine in 1956 in connection with the integration problems in Mansfield. He was selected as the model for the Texas Ranger statue that was dedicated at Love Field in Dallas in 1960. Banks participated in the Fort Worth chase and gunfight that culminated in the killings of multiple murderers Gene Paul Norris and William Carl Humphrey. He retired in 1960, but continued his law enforcement career as police chief with the Big Spring, Palestine, and Gladewater police departments. He also served as consultant to the Southern Methodist University Department of Public Safety and helped establish training academies across the state of Texas.

SOURCE: Susie Mills, *Legend in Bronze*, 1982.

BARRY, JAMES BUCKNER "BUCK." (1821–1906) Born in North Carolina, Barry became one of the early Texas Rangers* legends. He joined the force in 1845 and, over the next twenty years, fought outlaws and Indians and saw action in the Mexican and Civil Wars. During his career in law enforcement, Barry also served as sheriff* of Navarro County in East Texas. The town of Rangerville was reportedly named for a Texas Ranger camp in the vicinity that was commanded by Barry in 1859 or 1860. Barry's memoirs were edited by James K. Greer and published in 1932.

SOURCES: James Greer, ed., *Buck Barry: Texas Ranger and Frontiersman*, 1932; reprint, 1978; Mike Cox, *Texas Ranger Tales*, 1997.

BARTELS, JOHN R. (b. 1936) Following graduation from Harvard Law School in 1960, Bartels began his career with the federal government. As an assistant U.S. attorney general in New York, he investigated organized crime families and in 1969 was tabbed to head the Justice Department's New Jersey Organized Crime Strike Force. Credited with making inroads on the growing organized crime problem, he was appointed by President Richard Nixon as the first director of the Drug Enforcement Agency (DEA) in 1973. However, his honeymoon with the former Bureau of Narcotics and Dangerous Drugs was short-lived, and two years later he was forced to resign under a cloud of controversy. Critics accused him of violating constitutional protections and failing to halt the flow of illegal drugs into the United States.

SOURCE: Charles Phillips and Alan Axelrod, *CCC*, 1996.

BASSETT, CHARLES E. (1847–1896) Bassett was born in New Bedford, Massachusetts, and, following service in the Union Army during the Civil War,

he was elected as the first sheriff* of Ford County, Kansas, in 1873. He was reelected two more times, but because of term limits he was prohibited from running a third time in 1878. In 1877 he had collaborated with undersheriff William Bartholomew "Bat" Masterson* in the pursuit of bank robber Sam Bass. Masterson replaced Bassett as sheriff of Ford County and appointed him as undersheriff.

When Bat's brother, Edward J. Masterson,* was killed, in April 1878, Bassett replaced him as marshal of Dodge City and hired Wyatt Berry Stapp Earp* as deputy marshal. He resigned the following year and moved to Colorado and then Texas for short stints before returning to Dodge City in 1881. Although he was present at several notable gunfights, Bassett rarely participated in the actual violence, opting instead to back up fellow peace officers like Earp and Masterson, who were more inclined toward gunplay. In his last years Bassett ran several saloons in between stints in law enforcement.

SOURCES: Nyle L. Miller and Joseph W. Snell, *Great Gunfighters of the Kansas Cowtowns, 1867–1886*, 1967; Dan L. Thrapp, ed., *EFP*, Vol. 1, 1988.

BASSETT, FRANCIS. (1593–1645) In 1625 Bassett was appointed vice admiral of Cornwall, England, thanks in part to his marriage into a prominent Cornish family in 1620. This position would lead to a seat in Parliament in 1639 and then his appointment to sheriff* in 1642. As sheriff he was mainly concerned with collecting money and munitions as he supported Parliament during the English Civil War. He took part in several battles and left the sheriffship to concentrate on military affairs. Appointed governor of St. Michael's Mount, he succumbed to exhaustion while preparing to defend the Mount during the Civil War.

SOURCE: Irene Gladwin, *The Sheriff*, 1984.

BATON CHARGE, ORIGINS OF. In 1830 the London Metropolitan Police* participated in its first organized baton charge, which was occasioned by an impending mob attack on the Lord Mayor's Show. Responding to rumors of the brewing trouble, sixty policemen, who were armed with batons, assembled and charged into the approaching mob. This incident was hailed as one of the first successful examples of police crowd control that did not require the participation of the military.

SOURCE: James Cramer, *The World's Police*, 1964.

BATTLE, SAMUEL J. (1883–1966) The son of former slaves, Battle was born in New Bern, North Carolina. He moved north, seeking to escape segregation. Prior to relocating to New York City he briefly attended a manual training school in New Haven, Connecticut. Early on he set his sights on becoming a police officer, a rare accomplishment for an African-American in turn-of-the-century America. While working grueling twelve-hour days as a porter at New York

City's Grand Central Terminal, Battle prepared for the civil service exams that were required to join the police force. He passed the exam in 1910; nonetheless, administrators vacillated on whether to hire him.

Battle was finally hired but was given the silent treatment by fellow officers at the West 68th Street Station. Battle accepted his rejection while maintaining a cordial presence, and in 1913 he was transferred to Harlem's West 135th Street Station. In this growing African-American community, Battle flourished, and by 1919 he was being encouraged to prepare for the sergeant's exam with the caveat that he would only be allowed into the police preparatory school if the class approved. After he saved the life of a white police officer during a race riot in Harlem, Battle's entry into the preparatory program was secured.

Despite passing the exam, Battle was forced to wait seven years before becoming the first black police sergeant in the New York City Police Department (NYPD).* Battle continued his march through the ranks, becoming the first black lieutenant on the force in 1935 and then, six years later, parole commissioner, charged with rehabilitating black delinquent youths in Harlem.

Battle made headlines in 1943 when Mayor Fiorello LaGuardia authorized him to quell race riots in Harlem following a police shooting of a black youth. In order to restore order, Battle ordered whites to keep a low profile in Harlem while he directed horse mounted police* on the streets and police sharpshooters on roofs. Battle's high profile in the black community enabled him to end the disturbance in short order. He returned to his position as parole commissioner following the riot and retired in 1951. In 1964 he was honored in a special ceremony as "the father of all Negroes in the Police Department."

SOURCE: W. Marvin Dulaney, *Black Police in America*, 1996.

BAUM, W. CARTER. (1904–1934) Born in Washington, D.C., Baum joined the Federal Bureau of Investigation (FBI)* in 1930 and served in the New York and Chicago field offices. Baum was part of the team pursuing Depression-era bandits John Dillinger and Lester "Baby Face Nelson" Gillis. On April 22, 1934, Baum was killed by Gillis during the attempted capture of the gang at the Little Bohemia resort in Wisconsin. Baum's wife later served in the FBI (1935–1944), as did his daughter (1949–1957).

SOURCE: Athan G. Theoharis, ed., *The FBI*, 1999.

BEADLES. Beadles were parish officers used for law enforcement in England in the early eighteenth century. One of the earliest paid positions in parish law enforcement, beadles were responsible for a multitude of duties ranging from town crier and vestry clerk to church warden and rate collector. Beadles assisted parish constables* by suppressing the vagrancy problem and acting as supervisor of the night watch.* By the early nineteenth century the beadle had become a minor salaried official responsible for night watch several nights a week and enforcing the Poor Law during the day. Each parish had four or five beadles to supplement the constables and watchmen (see NIGHT WATCH, WATCH AND WARD SYSTEM) prior to 1829.

SOURCES: Elaine A. Reynolds, *Before the Bobbies*, 1998; J. J. Tobias, *Nineteenth-Century Crime in England*, 1972.

BEALL, WILLIAM. Beall became the fifth chief of the Berkeley, California Police Department* in 1966, succeeding Addison Fording.* Beall grew up in Berkeley and attended high school and college in the vicinity before joining the force as a patrolman in 1941. The next year he joined the Federal Bureau of Investigation (FBI)* and worked out of the Washington, D.C., Chicago, and Detroit offices before returning to the Berkeley police in 1944. Five years later he was promoted to sergeant, then lieutenant in 1952, inspector in 1952, and captain in 1961.

As police chief Beall initially focused his attentions on the rising crime problem along Telegraph Avenue, an area frequented by drug dealers, runaways, bikers, and students. According to the 1967 crime reports, Berkeley had one of the highest major crime rates in the country. In July 1968 violent demonstrations once again threatened the peaceful enclave of Nobel prize winners and professors. Several highway patrolmen were injured by fire bombs, and in the ensuing five days of rioting, fifty-eight people were injured. In January and February of 1969, the police force was once again backing up the University Police during violent protests of the Third World Liberation Front. Events had gotten so far out of control that Governor Ronald Reagan declared a state of emergency on the University of California campus. Police and protestors skirmished in tear gas and rock-throwing confrontations. In May 1969 Beall stepped down from the force after twenty-seven years and accepted the position of chief of police of the University of California, Berkeley, campus. Not long afterward he was named chief of police of all nine University of California campuses.

SOURCE: Alfred E. Parker, *The Berkeley Police Story*, 1972.

BEATY, CLARENCE L. Clarence L. "Chapo" Beaty served in the Arizona Rangers* from 1903 to 1907. Formerly a cowboy, Beaty rose to prominence in 1904 when he assisted in the capture of noted bandit Antonio Nunez and then, the following year, apprehended horse thief Simon Juarez. Beaty was known to complement his weaponry with a sawed-off shotgun, about which he noted "You could shoot it from the hip like an automatic."

SOURCE: Bill O'Neal, *The Arizona Rangers*, 1987.

BECKER, CHARLES. (1870–1915) Becker was one of the most corrupt police officers of his era; in fact, the novelist Stephen Crane reputedly based the brutal policeman who beats the title character in *Maggie: A Girl of the Streets* on this notorious member of the New York City Police Department (NYPD).*

Becker served two masters during his nefarious career. While working as police lieutenant under Police Commissioner Rhinelander Waldo,* he handled payoffs for Tammany Hall boss Tim Sullivan, whom, by most accounts, Becker hoped to succeed. As head of the department's special criminal squad, he provided protection for gangsters and proved capable of physically disciplining those who did not pay their share of the protection racket.

On July 15, 1912, a tenderloin* gambler named Herman Rosenthal who was tired of paying for police protection dared stand up against the system by reporting on police corruption to New York district attorney and future governor Charles Seymour Whitman. The following day Becker ordered the murder of Rosenthal, who perished in a hail of gunfire from four killers just outside the Hotel Metropole on West 43rd Street.

Becker was put in charge of the investigation and in quick order made sure the police lost the license number of the getaway car and hid a witness to the murder in a police jail cell. However, District Attorney Whitman soon rescued the witness from the police station. Subsequently, the killers were captured and the chain of command for the murder was traced to Becker. Becker and the four hit men were all sentenced to death. Although Becker received another trial after irregularities were discovered in his original trial, he received the same penalty and, despite pleas from his family, was executed at Sing Sing Prison on July 7, 1915. (In a postscript to the story, Becker's electrocution was one of the more indelicate executions in the prison's storied history.) Becker's wife placed a plate with the inscription "Charles Becker, Murdered July 7, 1915, by Governor Whitman" on his gravestone. However, police warned her she could be prosecuted for libel so she removed the offending plate.

SOURCES: Andy Logan, *Against the Evidence: The Becker-Rosenthal Affair*, 1970; Jonathan Root, *One Night in July*, 1961.

BEHAN, JOHN HARRIS. (1845–1912) Born in Westport, Missouri, after a colorful career as a soldier, freighter, and miner, Behan reached Prescott, Arizona, in the 1860s. In the 1870s he served as sheriff of Yavapai County and also served several terms in the territorial legislature. He moved to Tombstone, Arizona, in 1880 and was appointed deputy and then sheriff* following the organization of Cochise County.

Behan is best remembered for his role in the conflict between the Wyatt Berry Stapp Earp* and Doc Holliday–led contingent and the local cowboy faction that culminated in the gunfight at the O.K. Corral in 1881. Although Behan's reputation was untarnished by the subsequent events, his competition with Wyatt Earp over the actress Josie Marcus, who later became Earp's wife, probably contributed to the bloody turn of events. In addition, rancor existed between Earp and Behan stemming from political considerations. Earp and his brothers were Republicans while Behan was a Democrat, being more in tune with the cowboy element than the Republican merchants and gambling house and saloon owners.

One of the more controversial, and probably overresearched, events in American Western history, the gunfight at the O.K. Corral in 1881 was over in little more than thirty seconds. Behan unsuccessfully attempted to prevent the confrontation between the Earps and Holliday, on the one hand, and the Clanton and McLaury factions, on the other. He arrested Wyatt Earp and Doc Holliday after the gunfight, but they were eventually acquitted and left the county before they could be tried again.

Following the Tombstone years Behan served as a state clerk and as superintendent of the Yuma Territorial Prison from 1880 to 1890. In 1895 he worked as U.S. treasury agent in El Paso, Texas, before enlisting in the Rough Riders of Theodore Roosevelt* during the Spanish-American War. He would eventually serve in most theaters of the war, including Cuba and the Philippines, and later in China during the Boxer Rebellion.

SOURCES: Casey Tefertiller, *Wyatt Earp*, 1998; Dan L. Thrapp, ed., *EFB*, Vol. 1, 1988.

BEIDLER, JOHN X. (1831–1890) Born in Mount Joy, Pennsylvania, Beidler pursued the shoemaking, brickmaking, and broom manufacturing trades before moving to the Illinois frontier prior to the Civil War. The diminutive, but foul-tempered, Beidler favored the name "X" as a first name. He reportedly served with John Brown's abolitionist force on the Kansas frontier shortly before Brown left for Harper's Ferry and immortality.

In 1863 Beidler arrived in Virginia City, Montana, where he became a vigilante leader. A controversial figure in Western lore, he reportedly orchestrated the hanging of five highwaymen on January 14, 1864, and rose to prominence during the reign of the Montana Vigilance Committee. Following the dispersal of the vigilance group, Beidler served as a stagecoach guard and was appointed deputy U.S. marshal, reportedly putting his vigilante tendencies to great use. His last years were anticlimactic. Destitute in the end, he relied on handouts from former colleagues and admirers, and when a bill was tendered in the Montana territorial legislature to afford him some type of financial support, it was soundly defeated.

SOURCES: Helen Fitzgerald Sanders, ed., *X. Beidler, Vigilante*, 1957; Dan L. Thrapp, ed., *EFB*, Vol. 1, 1988.

BELL, HAMILTON BUTLER. (1853–1947) Born in Hagerstown, Maryland, after a peripatetic childhood as an orphan Bell arrived in Kansas and then in Colorado, where he opened a dance hall in the 1870s. By 1874 he had become adept at virtually all Western trades, working in Dodge City as a saloon manager, undertaker, and peace officer. He served more than thirty years as a Kansas peace officer, including two terms as Ford County sheriff.* During his last years, Bell reportedly ran a Dodge City junk shop, where no doubt he regaled visitors with stories of the old Kansas cowtowns.

SOURCE: Ed Bartholomew, *Wyatt Earp: The Untold Story*, 1963.

BELL, JAMES W. (c. 1842–1881) Born in Maryland, Bell entered law enforcement as a member of the Texas Rangers* in 1875. After service in Company D of the Frontier Battalion, he drifted into New Mexico in time for the Lincoln County War. Appointed deputy by Sheriff* Patrick Floyd Jarvis "Pat" Garrett,* Bell and deputy Robert Ameridth Olinger* were killed by Billy the Kid during his escape from the Lincoln jail, where he was being confined in preparation for execution following his conviction for murder. Bell was reportedly soft-spoken and of average height, his appearance only accented by a knife scar that ran from his left ear to his mouth. He apparently treated Billy the Kid kindly prior to the escape since the outlaw reportedly told confidants he hated to kill Bell and did so only in order to make good his escape.

SOURCES: William A. Keleher, *Violence in Lincoln County, 1869–1881*, 1957; Don Bullis, *New Mexico's Finest: Peace Officers Killed in the Line of Duty, 1847–1996*, 1996.

BERIA, LAVRENTI PAVLOVICH. (1899–1953) Like Joseph Stalin, Beria was descended from humble peasant origins. Beria would become head of the Soviet secret police* and one of the most feared men in the Soviet Union during the reign of Stalin, who referred to Beria as "Our Himmler."

Beria joined the Communist party in 1917 and by the early 1920s was well versed in the skills of intelligence and counterintelligence. Upon his appointment to the leadership of the NKVD, an offshoot of the Cheka* and precursor to the KGB,* Beria had the former secret police chief, N. I. Ezhov, executed. With the full support of Stalin, the Soviet secret police under Beria would infiltrate every facet of Soviet society.

During World War II Beria was given unprecedented domestic power as Stalin directed the war effort. Following the war, Stalin, with the assistance of his chief of secret police, purged tens of thousands of imagined political adversaries from the Soviet ranks. Subsequently, Stalin diverted blame for this bloody and controversial episode to his protégé Beria. However, Stalin died in 1953 before he could bring his scapegoat to justice. Beria tried to fill his former mentor's shoes as dictator but was arrested in 1953. The following year he was found guilty of treason and executed.

SOURCES: Amy W. Knight, *The KGB: Police and Politics in the Soviet Union*, 1988; Amy Knight, *Beria: Stalin's First Lieutenant*, 1993.

BERKELEY, CALIFORNIA, POLICE DEPARTMENT. Following its incorporation in 1878, Berkeley, California, was policed by an elected city marshal and constables.* Crime increased into the twentieth century, and in 1905 August Vollmer* was elected town marshal. Four years later he was appointed Berkeley's first chief of police. Vollmer quickly made his mark as a perspicacious police reformer. Among his earliest achievements was to establish a department code of ethics that barred the acceptance of gratuities and favors under penalty of dismissal.

Credited as the father of modern law enforcement, Police Chief Vollmer was instrumental in inaugurating a series of innovations during his tenure as police chief, including the first Modus Operandi System (1906), the first use of scientific investigation (in the 1907 Kelinschmidt case), the first police motorcycle patrol (1911), one of the earliest fingerprinting * systems (1924), and many others. From 1905 to 1932 Vollmer molded the Berkeley police force while leading a national police professionalism movement.

SOURCES: Alfred E. Parker, *The Berkeley Police Story*, 1972; Gene E. Carte and Elaine H. Carte, *Police Reform in the United States: The Era of August Vollmer*, 1975.

BERRYER, NICOLAS-RENÉ. (1703–1762) Born in Paris, Berryer was the eighth lieutenant-general of police,* of Paris beginning his ten-year tenure in 1747. Berryer is credited with the creation of the Bureau de Sûreté, or Security Office, where citizens could report thefts and police officials recorded information without charging fees from the complainants. Antagonism developed toward Berryer among the vagabonds and transients for what seemed to be a his indiscriminate policy of arresting those who matched a certain profile, not unlike the racial profiling that has come under fire today.

Berryer was also responsible for setting up a domestic espionage system. During his tenure he weathered numerous death threats from the street people, harassed the freemasons, and tolerated local brothels as long as they agreed to file weekly reports on their customers. With this information Berryer had the opportunity to gather incriminating information on a clientele that ranged from wanted thieves and deserters to the new papal nuncio. Following retirement in 1757 he served as secretary of the navy from 1758 to 1761 and keeper of the Seals from 1761 to 1762.

SOURCES: Alan Williams, *The Police of Paris, 1718–1789*, 1979; Philip John Stead, *The Police of France*, 1983; Philip John Stead, *The Police of Paris*, 1957.

BERTILLON, ALPHONSE. (1835–1914) Born in Paris into a middle-class family, the son of a physician with a keen interest in anthropology and statistics, Bertillon was drawn to the sciences at an early age. In 1878 Bertillon found employment as a records clerk for the Paris Prefecture of Police, leading to a lifelong interest in identifications systems that would give him his moniker, the "Father of Scientific Detection." Over the next seven years Bertillon developed a methodology to identify recidivist offenders. Through the use of anthropometry* he created the system that became known as *bertillonage* based on human body measurements prior to the introduction of a fingerprinting* system.

In recognition of his feat of rationalizing the police department's record-keeping system, Bertillon was appointed chief of the Service of Judicial Identity on February 1, 1888. Subsequently he would add photographic methods to other identification techniques and would become an expert in using photography to identify forged documents. Bertillon's reputation was tarnished after he identified a forged signature of the French army captain Alfred Dreyfus as legitimate, leading to the captain's imprisonment for treason on Devil's Island. The Bertillon system* was brought into question in 1904 when American officials at Leavenworth Prison came across two inmates with exactly the same measurements. With the increased emphasis on fingerprint identification, *bertillonage* fell into disfavor.

SOURCES: Henry T. F. Rhodes, *Alphonse Bertillon: Father of Scientific Detection*, 1956; David R. Johnson, *American Law Enforcement: A History*, 1981.

BERTILLON SYSTEM. The Bertillon system, or *bertillonage*, was named after its creator, Alphonse Bertillon.* By applying anthropometry,* the study of human body measurements, law enforcement had a more efficient, although not exact, method of identifying criminals. According to Bertillon's system, identifying measurements included length and width of the head; length of the left, middle, and little fingers; length of the left foot, left forearm, and right ear; height of the individual; measurement of outstretched arms, the trunk, and measurement of the person while seated from the bench to the top of the head. Other identifying characteristics included scars, birthmarks, hair and eye color, and a description of the nose.

Bertillon insisted that an examiner and an assistant perform the measurements independently of each other for more accurate results. The system was first used by the Police of Paris in 1882, and by the following year, forty-nine men had been identified; in 1885, over five hundred criminals had been positively identified.

Another important component of the system was the use of photography to create frontal and profile photos of convicts, replete with a register number. An antecedent to fingerprinting,* *bertillonage* was well regarded until the 1890s, when fingerprinting replaced it to the relief of peace officers burdened by the laborious identification procedures required by the Bertillon system.

SOURCES: Henry T. Rhodes, *Alphonse Bertillon: Father of Scientific Detection*, 1956; Alphonse Bertillon, *Alphonse Bertillon's Instruction for Taking Descriptions for the Identification of Criminals and Others by the Means of Anthropometric Indication*, reprint, 1977.

BERTIN DE BELLISLE, HENRI BAPTISTE. (1720–1792) Born in Perigreux, France, Bertin served as Paris lieutenant-general of police* from 1757 to 1759, he is generally credited with extending street lighting to most streets in Paris and relocating the putrid city dumps to outside the city limits. Like his predecessor Nicholas-René Berryer,* he owed his position to the support of Madame de Pompadour. Following his retirement in 1757 he served as secretary of state for a specially created department from 1763 to 1780 and as controller general from 1759 to 1763.

SOURCES: Alan Williams, *The Police of Paris, 1718–1789*, 1979; Philip John Stead, *The Police of Paris*, 1957.

BIAGGI, MARIO. (b. 1917) The son of Italian immigrants, Biaggi was born in Manhattan's Little Italy. Following a childhood of grinding poverty, he graduated high school in 1934 and worked as a letter carrier before joining the New York City Police Department (NYPD)* in 1942. Over the next twenty-three years he would carve out an exemplary career, earning twenty-eight citations for bravery and meritorious service and, in 1960, the Police Medal of Honor for Valor, the department's highest honor.

However, Biaggi's career was often surrounded in controversy. In 1955 he was accused of being absent without leave during an inspection. Four years later, while off duty, he shot and killed a man who, he claimed, abducted and forced him to drive to a secluded spot. Despite unanswered questions surrounding this incident, the following year he received the department's medal of honor.

Biaggi took a leave of absence to pursue a law degree at the New York Law School, and in 1965 he retired from the force on a disability pension based on an injury received on duty in 1946. He passed the New York bar on his third attempt, and in 1968 ran successfully for Congress. His political career was as dogged by scandal as his law enforcement years. In 1987 he was found guilty of obstruction of justice and of taking illegal gratuities. The following year Biaggi was snared in the Wedtech scandal. Upon conviction for bribery, racketeering, and influence pedaling, he resigned from Congress in disgrace; however, this did not dissuade him from running unsuccessfully for Congress in 1992.

SOURCES: Charles Phillips and Alan Axelrod, *CCC*, 1996; George C. Cohn, *Encyclopedia of American Scandal*, 1989.

BICYCLE POLICE. By the late 1890s traditional methods of police patrolling had become inadequate for the changing nature of urban America. While patrolling on horseback or by foot had certain advantages, the introduction of the "steam carriage," a precursor to the automobile, demanded better and faster traffic control because the increasingly crowded streets were filled with horse-drawn trucks, steam carriages, and other forms of transportation. This made big city streets unsafe for pedestrians. In 1895 New York City Police Commissioner Theodore Roosevelt* inaugurated a "scorcher squad" composed of four bicycle officers to regulate traffic in the most dangerous areas. Roosevelt also implemented an eight-mile-an-hour speed limit. Violators would be stopped by bicycle cops who then inspected their driver's license. Within seven years the squad had been increased to one hundred members, and it was credited with making 1,366 arrests in 1902 alone. By the end of the decade horseless carriages had become affordable to the masses and the Bicycle Squad was overwhelmed in its attempt to control New York City's traffic maelstrom. By 1912 it was decided that using automobiles instead of bicycles would be a better way of controlling traffic and New York City established a Traffic Division. The Bicycle Squad was not disbanded until 1934. Instead of consigning the bicycles to auction or the dumpster, the police department commendably sold them to local children for as little as 25 cents each.

SOURCE: H. Paul Jeffers, *Commissioner Roosevelt*, 1994.

BIKO, STEVE. (1946–1977) The death of South African activist Steve Biko at the hands of the South African Police (SAP)* while in custody in the late 1970s was one of the most controversial incidents of police brutality in the era of apartheid. Biko was just one of forty-four students and activists to die under police detention in South Africa between March 1976 and July 1978. The SAP alleged that some of those whose bodies were missing simply left the country. Following a five-minute inquest into Biko's death from head injuries, the minister of police submitted that Biko, who was an advocate of violence, was injured while resisting arrest. However, word soon leaked out that Biko had been detained naked in a cell chained to a heating vent on the wall and that the police prevented physicians from treating him even though he was obviously suffering from brain damage. By the early 1980s, criticism by the liberal South African newspapers following the deaths of more detainees led to a new code of conduct designed to offer more humane treatment to political prisoners.

SOURCES: John D. Brewer, *Black and Blue: Policing in South Africa*, 1994; John D. Brewer, *After Soweto: An Unfinished Journey*, 1986; Thomas Plate and Andrea Darvi, *Secret Police*, 1981.

BILL. This British police slang has a variety of possible origins. Originally it may have referred to a tipstaff carried by police, which announced their office. The inside of the staff was hollow in order to carry arrest warrants. The staff was often called "Bill," and if an officer touched a person with it, he or she was under arrest. The term is also used by cabdrivers in reference to the licenses issued by the London Metropolitan Police* that allow them to apply for hire. Following World War I, Old Bill was a cartoon character used to recruit new police candidates. The term has enjoyed renewed popularity as the title of a recent television series.

SOURCE: Bill Waddell, *The Black Museum*, 1993.

BIRNIE, RICHARD. (1760–1832) As assistant Bow Street magistrate, Birnie commanded the Bow Street Runners,* who helped foil the 1820 Cato Street conspiracy. The following year he was appointed chief magistrate of Bow Street, the last nonbarrister to hold the position and the final magistrate to act as unofficial chief of police. With the creation of the New Police in 1829, Birnie joined the opposition, knowing full well that the days of the Bow Street Runners were numbered. With his death in 1832 it was announced that the chief magistrate position would be abolished.

SOURCE: Anthony Babington, *A House in Bow Street*, 1969.

BISHOP, LEO. (b. 1903) Born at Junction, Texas, Bishop quit ranching in 1932 and joined the Texas Rangers.* During the 1930s he was generally regarded as the best rifle shot on the force. Bishop patrolled the Mexican border near Eagle Pass and reportedly engaged in weekly gunfights with smugglers, cattle rustlers, and the like. In 1933 Bishop and most of the other Rangers were dismissed by Governor Miriam Amanda Wallace "Ma" Ferguson. Not long afterward he was hired by another former Ranger, Manuel Trazazas "Lone Wolf" Gonzaullas,* to work as a night guard for an oil company. The following year, with a change in governors, Bishop was once more a Ranger. Bishop would rise to prominence suppressing an outbreak of crime in San Augustine, Texas, in the mid-1930s. Departing San Augustine in 1935, he spent a three-year stint in South Texas. He quit the Rangers after observing one of his superiors accepting payoffs from gamblers.

SOURCE: Ben Proctor, *Just One Riot*, 1991.

BLACK HUSSARS. Supporters of the Pennsylvania State Police,* formed in 1905, conferred the moniker "Black Hussars" on this military-inspired police force, which was active in suppressing immigrant strikers and other unpopular foreigners during the first decade of the twentieth century. The opposition referred to the force as the "Cossacks."*

SOURCE: Thomas A. Reppetto, *The Blue Parade*, 1978.

BLACKJACK. The origins of the blackjack can be traced back to the medieval star, a weapon that was essentially a studded metal ball attached to a chain. Over the years this instrument was modified into the slung shot, a piece of lead attached or welded to a metal rod. By the 1700s this more compact weapon was favored by street thugs in an era where handguns were not reliable or readily available. Today's blackjack is a flat or round piece of lead covered in leather. The flat incarnation is called the slapjack and is reportedly preferred by patrolmen who work out of squad cars because it fits comfortably into a back pocket. The round blackjack is the lighter of the two and is known as a convoy. Not all police officers carry this weapon, preferring the more threatening dimensions of a nightstick. Many police forces, such as the Philadelphia force, require officers to purchase their own blackjack.

SOURCES: Jonathan Rubinstein. *City Police*, 1973; Rex Applegate, *Crowd and Riot Control*, 1964.

BLACK MARIA. This early prototype of the police van was introduced in Boston, Massachusetts. Newspapers in 1847 heralded its arrival, although there is no substantiated proof that it was required to be painted black. According to one version, the "Black Maria" was named after a huge black woman named Maria Lee, who ran an unruly boardinghouse for sailors. Apparently, one of the early deliveries of prisoners included a group from Black Maria's establishment. However, J. E. Lightner cites another source suggesting that the term originated in Philadelphia in 1843.

SOURCES: J. E. Lighter, *Historical Dictionary of American Slang*, Vol. 1, 1994; Carl Sifakis, *The Encyclopedia of American Crime*, 1982.

BLACK MUSEUM, THE. New Scotland Yard,* the current, more modern headquarters of the London Metropolitan Police* houses, in its own Black Museum, a unique collection of exhibits, photographs, and memorabilia related to Great Britain's most celebrated crimes. Closed to the public, this crime museum was originally established in 1874. The current museum was opened in 1981.

SOURCES: Gordon Honeycombe, *The Murders of the Black Museum*, 1982; Bill Waddell, *The Black Museum*, 1993.

BLOODY CHRISTMAS. This early 1950s scandal was the inspiration for James Ellroy's novel *L.A. Confidential* and the hit 1997 movie of the same name. One of the worst scandals of the Chief William Henry Parker* era, it began after two Los Angeles Police Department (LAPD)* officers were badly beaten after responding to a "trouble call" at a local bar. Backup units arrived and transported seven of the troublemakers back to the Central Station. Meanwhile, over one hundred officers were celebrating the holiday season at the station. When the officers were alerted to what had happened, they descended on the suspects and severely beat the prisoners. When they had finished, the walls and floors were covered in blood and Parker's force was tainted by brutality complaints. Parker faced the issue head-on and initiated an investigation that led to the suspension of almost three dozen officers. However, allegations of police brutality have dogged the force into the twenty-first century.

SOURCES: Arthur W. Sjoquist, *Los Angeles Police Department Commemorative Book, 1869–1984*, 1984; Brian Helgeland and Curtis Hanson, *L.A. Confidential* (screenplay), with introduction by James Ellroy, 1997.

BLUEBOTTLES. This colloquial reference to constables* can be traced back to sixteenth-century Shakespearean drama and enjoyed more prominent usage from the 1800s into the twentieth century.

SOURCE: Bill Waddell, *The Black Museum*, 1993.

BLUE COCOON. This slang term refers to the insular world of policing, where police associate with police, talk shop, and rarely allow outsiders in. Over the years police culture has taken on a siege mentality in which it is felt that outsiders could not possibly conceive of their job pressures or understand their language—a culture in which the cops are pitted against the rest of the world. Police officers only drink in cop bars and socialize with other cops.

SOURCE: William Bratton, with Peter Knobler, *Turnaround*, 1998.

BOCEKCI BASI. In the fourteenth century the Ottoman Empire established a detective division, known as the Bocekci basi, to complement its military police force. Like the thief-takers (see THIEF-TAKER GENERAL), this unit employed many ex-criminals who were familiar with the milieu of the underworld. The typical operative worked the city streets and markets in disguise and acted as an informant or spy.

SOURCE: James Cramer, *The World's Police*, 1964.

BOGGS, JOHN C. (1825–1909) Born in Greencastle, Pennsylvania, Boggs moved to California in 1849 following the discovery of gold. After three peripatetic years of prospecting he entered law enforcement informally as a watchman (see NIGHT WATCH; WATCH AND WARD SYSTEM) at the Dry Diggings mining camp. In the 1850s he helped capture several well-known desperadoes, including Tom Bell and Rattlesnake Dick. Despite three unsuccessful campaigns for the office of Placer County sheriff,* he continued to lead crime-fighting efforts through various citizens' organizations. After a stint as undersheriff in 1877 he was elected to the long-sought-after position of sheriff in 1879. While sheriff, Boggs brought Placer County's first train robbers to justice. However, in 1880, when a jury refused to convict one of the robbers, Boggs retired and left law enforcement.

SOURCE: Charles Phillips and Alan Axelrod, *CCC*, 1996.

BOGIES. This is a British slang term for police officers, which was used prior to 1914.

SOURCE: Bill Waddell, *The Black Museum*, 1993.

BONAPARTE, CHARLES JOSEPH. (1851–1921) Born in Baltimore, Maryland, and educated at Harvard the nephew of French emperor Louis Napoleon Bonaparte III served as attorney general under President Theodore Roosevelt* and earned a reputation as an advocate for civil service reform. Bonaparte is credited with proposing the creation of a Bureau of Investigation in 1907. Congress initially demurred, citing such a force as a threat to civil liberties and chiding Bonaparte for introducing a secret service modeled after the notorious French secret police. However, in 1908 Roosevelt directed the creation of such an agency by executive order, laying the groundwork for the eventual creation of the Federal Bureau of Investigation (FBI)* in 1935.

SOURCES: J. B. Bishop, *Charles Joseph Bonaparte: His Life and Public Services,* 1922; Athan G. Theoharis, ed., *The FBI,* 1999.

BONNEY, EDWARD. (1807–1864) Born in Essex County, New York, Bonney moved to Indiana in 1843 and eventually settled in the Mormon community of Nauvoo along the Mississippi River. Incensed by the murders of Joseph and Hyrum Smith at Carthage, Illinois, in 1845 and such acts as the destruction of the Mormon newspaper, he developed a fixation on a criminal element plying the rivers of the Midwest. In 1845 he became a bounty hunter, and, over time he developed into a skilled detective. During a four-month pursuit through Illinois, Missouri, Indiana, and Ohio, Bonney tracked down the four men responsible for the 1845 torture-murder of Colonel George Davenport, for whom Davenport, Iowa, was named.

In 1852 Bonney decamped for Aurora, Illinois, and then Chicago as he continued his detective work to the end. Bonney rose to prominence with the 1850 publication of *The Banditti of the Prairies, or, The Murderer's Doom! A Tale of the Mississippi Valley.* A huge success, it ran through six editions over the next eight years and is considered an accurate chronicle of his life as a detective in the Mississippi Valley.

SOURCE: Edward Bonney, with introduction by Philip D. Jordan, *The Banditti of the Prairies,* 1963.

BOSTON POLICE DEPARTMENT. Six years after the settlement of Boston in 1630, a night watch* was created. Shaped by English antecedents, the night watch was soon supplemented by a daytime ward force. In 1712 the constable watch made the transition to a paid and better qualified law enforcement apparatus. For the next 110 years Boston was policed by constables* and night-watchmen (see WATCH AND WARD SYSTEM) under the supervision of the town selectmen. When Boston became a city in 1822, the charter required a new system of policing. Control of the force was passed from the selectmen to the mayor and aldermen, and in 1853 the day and night forces were consolidated into a modern, twenty-four-hour police organization, based in part on the London model of Sir Robert Peel.* The early history of the Boston police was best chronicled by former police officer Edward Hartwell Savage in *Police Records and Recollections; or Boston by Daylight and Gaslight* (1873).

During the 1850s and 1860s the Boston police contended with a devastating cholera epidemic and anti–Civil War draft riots. During its first decade the new force established a rank structure, erected its first station house and police telegraph, and embraced blue uniforms and brass badges. During the 1860s the Boston force inaugurated a rogues' gallery and introduced a traffic squad, civil service code, and policeman's ball. It was not long before firearms were added to the accoutrements of the beat cop.

Except for the Boston Police Strike of 1919,* the force has been relatively untainted by controversy and corruption, especially in light of the checkered history of the nearby New York City Police Department (NYPD).* Leading police chiefs during its first seventy-five years included Commissioners Stephen O'Meara (1906–1918), Edwin Upton Curtis* (1919–1922), Herbert A. Wilson (1922–1930), and Eugene C. Hultman.

SOURCES: Leonard V. Harrisor, *Police Administration in Boston*, 1934; Roger Lane, *Policing the City: Boston 1822–1885*, 1967.

BOSTON POLICE STRIKE OF 1919. When Edwin Upton Curtis* became Boston police commissioner in 1918, he inherited a disgruntled, poorly paid police force. Together with the reluctance of the mayor to consider pay raises, the rank and file had no choice, if they wanted to raise their standard of living, but to organize a local union. Following the Bolshevik Revolution in 1917, labor unions had yet to win wide approval in America, so when Curtis heard about this affiliation with the upstart American Federation of Labor, he suspended all the union members from duty. In response, three-quarters of the force went on strike on September 9, 1919. Curtis then compounded his actions by proclaiming that none of the strikers would be reinstated.

With the police on strike, the Boston criminal element seized the moment, assaulting passersby, setting off fire alarms, and looting businesses. The anarchy lasted for several days until volunteer police officers, loyal policemen, and the Massachusetts National Guard quelled the disorder. The rioting led to eight deaths (including one police officer), seventy-one injuries, and hundreds of thousands of dollars in property damage. Curtis never reinstated the strikers, and he remained popular with the public for his resolve. He endeavored to rebuild the force during the remaining three years of his life. However, he was vilified by union sympathizers and is credited with setting back the police union movement by forty years.

SOURCE: Francis Russell, *A City in Terror: 1919, the Boston Police Strike*, 1975.

BOWMAN, ALONZO. (b. 1835) Born in Vermont, the longtime resident of Brookline, Massachusetts, joined the Brookline police force in 1871, after fighting for the Union in the Civil War between 1861 and 1864. In 1876 Bowman was promoted to police chief, and by 1893 he had served seventeen of his twenty-three years on the force in that capacity.

SOURCE: George W. Hale, *Police and Prison Cyclopaedia*, 1893.

BOW STREET RUNNERS. Novelist and police reformer Sir Henry Fielding* forecast methods for crime prevention in his *Enquiry into the Causes of the Late*

Increase in Robbery, published in 1751. As a senior magistrate at the Bow Street
Magistrates' Office, he concluded that the only way to suppress London's rising
crime problem was to recruit a special police force that would be headquartered
at Bow Street and would be paid 100-pound rewards for each criminal apprehended. Following Henry's death in 1754, his half-brother, Sir John Fielding,*
continued his work and introduced this precursor to Peel's police force following
the recruitment of six or seven thief-catchers (see THIEF-TAKER GENERAL).
Over time the force became better known as the Bow Street Runners, as they
were expected to run to the scene of a crime.

By 1763 Sir John Fielding had introduced a mounted night patrol as well.
With the support of government financing, the force flourished. Following Fielding's death in 1780, six more police forces, based along the lines of the Bow
Street Runners, had been introduced in London by 1792. It was easy to spot the
Runners, who, while on duty, wore red waistcoats, as well as a badge, and
carried a short mace replete with a metal receptacle for holding rolled-up arrest
warrants. In addition, each carried a thirteen-inch-long truncheon* bearing the
name Bow Street.

SOURCES: Anthony Babington, *A House in Bow Street*, 1969; Patrick Pringle, *Hue
and Cry*, 1955.

BRADLEY, CYRUS P. (1819–1865) Born in Concord, New Hampshire, Bradley moved to Chicago in 1837. He was appointed tax collector for South Chicago in 1849 and distinguished himself as a member of a local fire company.
In 1860 he began the first of two terms as fire marshal. He also served two
terms as sheriff* before becoming the city's first police chief, on May 26, 1855.
During his tenure as chief he also led a private detective agency.

The Chicago Police Department (CPD)* was credited with solving every
crime reported during its first three months in operation. Chief Bradley played
an active role in crime control, personally capturing a handful of felons, including a murderer, a rapist, and a forger. The next year the new mayor dismissed
Bradley and his police force as was the custom in the days of political patronage,
when each politician appointed his own supporters. The mayor also abolished
the position of police chief. This action set a precedent for Chicago, where, over
the next eighty-five years, forty-three different police chiefs would be appointed.

In 1861 the police chief position was restored and Bradley was selected to
the post once more. That same year Bradley was appointed provost marshal* of
the army following the outbreak of the Civil War. Among his first acts was the
posting of policemen on Chicago's wharves and docks in order to check for
draft dodgers. As police chief Bradley recommended doubling the size of the
force. He also introduced a new uniform for officers, consisting of a dark blue
frock coat with buttons sporting the words "Chicago Police." Each officer also
wore a blue cap, which was heavily ribbed in case he was assaulted with bricks
or bludgeons. Each hat was marked by the officer's number. While mustaches

were banned, military whiskers were allowed. In 1861 Bradley also organized the department's first detective division. He resigned in 1863 to concentrate on his role as provost marshal for the army. During his last years he worked for the U.S. Secret Service* and was credited with nabbing several counterfeiters.

SOURCES: John J. Flinn, *History of the Chicago Police*, 1887; revised, 1973; Raphael W. Marrow and Harriet I. Carter, *In Pursuit of Crime*, 1996.

BRADLEY, THOMAS "TOM." (b. 1917) Born in Calvert, Texas, in 1923 Bradley moved to Los Angeles with his family. He attended the University of California at Los Angeles, where he excelled both athletically and academically. He left the university in his junior year to join the Los Angeles Police Department (LAPD).* During the next fifteen years he rose from beat cop to become the first African-American lieutenant on the force.

While on the force Bradley earned a law degree, in 1956. Five years later he retired from the force, convinced that racism in the LAPD would prevent him from ever rising higher than lieutenant. He entered private practice after two decades as a policeman; leaders of the African-American community soon approached him to run for political office, and in 1963 he began a three-decade career in politics, eventually serving five terms as mayor.

Bradley presided over Los Angeles during one of the most controversial episodes in the history of the LAPD. In 1991 four white police officers were videotaped brutally beating black motorist Rodney King.* The subsequent acquittal of the officers, followed by four days of rioting, led to the forced resignation of police chief Daryl F. Gates.* Bradley was also criticized for his failure to provide adequate leadership over the LAPD, and in 1992 he retired.

SOURCE: Joe Domanick, *To Protect and Serve*, 1994.

BRADY, WILLIAM. (1825–1878) The Irish-born Brady immigrated to the United States in time to join the Second New Mexico Volunteers in 1851. In 1865 he was promoted to brevet major for his performance in the campaign against the Navajo Indians. Brady remained in New Mexico following the cession of hostilities and in 1869 became sheriff* of the newly organized Lincoln County.

In 1875 he was reelected to a second, nonconsecutive term as sheriff. During the infamous Lincoln County War, he sided with the Murphy-Dolan faction against the Tunstall group, which included Billy the Kid. Following the murder of John Tunstall in 1878, Sheriff Brady was blamed for the murder by the Tunstall contingent, and on April 1, 1878, he was ambushed and killed by three members of the anti-Dolan faction, which on that day included Billy the Kid.

SOURCES: Donald R. Lavash, *Sheriff William Brady: Tragic Hero of the Lincoln County War*, 1986; Don Bullis, *New Mexico's Finest: Peace Officers Killed in the Line of Duty, 1847–1996*, 1996.

BRAIN. This term is British police slang typically used by other officers when referring to detectives.

SOURCE: Bill Waddell, *The Black Museum*, 1993.

BRANNAN, SAM. (1819–1889) An elder in the Mormon Church, Brannan led a party of several hundred Mormons from New York to San Francisco in 1846. However, he was soon expelled from the church for diverting tithe money to his own investments. Brannan became California's first millionaire in the late 1840s by wisely cornering mining equipment to sell to the gold miners. Brannan was heralded for his role in cofounding the 1851 San Francisco Vigilance Committee* in an attempt to stifle the city's growing lawlessness and was a zealous proponent of hanging, but he was soon replaced as leader by William Tell Coleman.*

SOURCES: Robert M. Senkewicz, *Vigilantes in Gold Rush San Francisco*, 1985; Louis J. Stellman, *Sam Brannan, Builder of San Francisco*, 1953.

BRASCO, DONNIE. *See* PISTONE, JOSEPH D.

BRATTON, WILLIAM J. (b. 1947) Born and raised in New York City, Bratton was educated at Boston State College and enlisted in the army in 1966. Following service in Vietnam he returned to Boston and joined the Boston police force in 1970. During the early 1970s he studied law enforcement at Boston State College, was promoted to sergeant in 1975, and three years later made lieutenant. Frustrated by the bureaucracy of the Boston Police Department, in 1983 Bratton won appointment as chief of the Massachusetts Bay Transportation Authority (MBTA). Three years later he was appointed superintendent of the Metropolitan Police (Mets), the third largest police department in Massachusetts. Between 1986 and 1989 Bratton was credited with resurrecting the Mets and adding luster to its once tarnished image. In 1990 Governor Michael Dukakis merged the Mets and three other state law enforcement agencies into one force.

In 1990 Bratton began a two-year stint as chief of the New York City Transit Police and was credited with its turnaround when he left office in 1992. A keen observer of criminal justice trends and research, Bratton applied James Q. Wilson and George Kelling's "Broken Windows"* theory to crime in the New York City subway system.

Following the high-profile killing of Utah tourist Brian Watkins in the New York City subway, the Transit Police was given forty million dollars to improve its performance. Bratton credited this killing with providing the catalyst for causing a turnaround in the crime rate in New York City, causing it to begin dropping. Bratton redesigned transit uniforms, renovated and upgraded the Transit Police Academy, introduced better weapons and communications equipment, and improved morale on the force by arming transit cops with nine-millimeter weapons even before the New York City Police Department had them.

In 1992 Bratton was appointed Boston superintendent-in-chief, and named Boston Police commissioner in 1993, whereupon he incorporated community policing and brought in Jack Maple* as executive assistant to make changes in the detective bureau. To aid in the transformation of the department, Bratton introduced new technology, a neighborhood-policing program, and the training of neighborhood beat officers.

In 1994 Mayor Rudolph Guliani appointed Bratton New York City Police Commissioner. Although he was credited with improving the quality of life, this fact is often overstated (although he did get rid of many of the street vendors). Jack Maple served as Bratton's deputy commissioner for crime control strategies during his tenure in New York. One of their first initiatives was a gun strategy to determine the origin of every gun used in a crime, whereby every gun suspect was interviewed by a detective. Bratton's crime-fighting agenda was influenced Maple's strategies. Maple insisted that in order to bring down crime, the NYPD would need to have more accurate and timely intelligence, rapid deployment, effective tactics, and a relentless follow-up and assessment. Other crime strategies would follow. Among the most important was a youth violence strategy designed to stem the juvenile crime wave. He also incorporated drug, domestic violence, quality of life, auto crime, and integrity strategies. He essentially took the handcuffs off police officers and used civil law and the "Broken Windows" strategy to enforce regulations against harassment, assault, disorderly conduct, and vandalism. Enforcement was stepped up to uphold laws against public intoxication and public urination. Within twenty-seven months of Bratton taking over as police commissioner, the murder rate was cut in half and serious crime was down 33 percent. In the forefront of the community-policing movement, he was often in conflict with Mayor Giuliani over credit for the turnaround. Bratton, Maple, and his dream team created the Compstat system, a combination of computer statistics analysis and an unrelenting demand for accountability.

SOURCE: William Bratton, with Peter Knobler, *Turnaround: How America's Top Cop Reversed the Crime Epidemic*, 1998.

BREAKINRIDGE, WILLIAM MILTON "BILLY." (1846–1931) Born in Watertown, Wisconsin, Breakinridge left home at an early age and, after a series of jobs, landed in Denver, Colorado. He served in the Third Colorado Cavalry and was with Colonel John M. Chivington's forces during the notorious Sand Creek Massacre. In 1878 he was appointed deputy sheriff* in Phoenix, and the following year he took a similar position in Tombstone, Arizona, under Sheriff John Harris Behan.* He left law enforcement for ranching and surveying in 1883, but he returned to peacekeeping as deputy U.S. marshal and then as a special investigator for the Southern Pacific Railroad. In 1918 he retired and ten years later, at the age of eighty-two, published his reminiscences of the frontier Southwest, *Helldorado*.

SOURCES: William M. Breakinridge, *Helldorado*, 1928; Carl W. Breihan, *Great Lawmen of the West*, 1963.

BREAUTÉ, FAUKES DE. (d. 1226) One of the most prominent of King John's sheriffs, de Breauté immigrated from France, where he had started life a poor serf. His meteoric rise to power began in 1207 when he was appointed bailiff in Wales. King John continued his policy of hiring foreign mercenaries as sheriffs, eventually appointing de Breaute sheriff* of seven shires. He in turn supported John during the period following the signing of the Magna Carta of 1215. De Breauté would marry into wealth, power and royal patronage, but he soon earned notoriety for torturing and imprisoning innocent people in order to extort their property. His predilection for destroying churches and ignoring the law led to his excommunication and finally to his imprisonment in the Tower of London for several weeks. Stripped of his wealth and landholdings, he was banished to France and died a pauper in 1226.

SOURCE: Irene Gladwin, *The Sheriff*, 1984.

BREWER, WILLIAM. (d. 1227) Beginning in 1157, during a fifty-year career as sheriff,* Brewer served English kings from Henry II to Henry III. A favorite of King John (signer of Magna Carta in 1215), Brewer served as sheriff in eleven different shires during his rule. Demonstrating the lucrative potential of the sheriff's position, King John presented William with land grants, fisheries, manors, and timber, enough for William to build a new chamber for one of his manor houses. As sheriff, Brewer would serve as intermediary between the king and the Pope under John, and his name appears on the list of witnesses to the signing of the Magna Carta. He was a loyal subject to the end; most historians suggest that he only signed the document under duress.

A brutal dispenser of the king's justice, he was such an unpopular man among his constituents in Dorset and Somerset that they collected a large sum of money, which they offered to the king if he would get rid of Brewer. Never one to reject a gift, John accepted the donation but merely moved Brewer to a different vicinity. John named him the executor of his will and Brewer served John's son, Henry III, with the same allegiance as his father.

SOURCE: Irene Gladwin, *The Sheriff: The Man and His Office*, 1984.

BRIANT, ELIJAH S. (1861–1933) Born in Simpson County, Kentucky, Briant moved to Texas in the 1880s and worked as a school teacher and then as a surveyor. From 1893 to 1897 he was the postmaster for Sonora, Texas, and also worked as a sheepherder. He entered law enforcement in 1893 when he was elected Sutton County sheriff.* Over the next several years he suppressed the local bandit element, culminating in a 1901 gunfight in which he participated in the killing of fugitive Will Carver. After collecting a thousand-dollar award, Briant admitted that he wished the shooting had never occurred. He later served as a county judge and became involved in several business ventures in San Angelo, Texas.

SOURCES: John Eaton, *Will Carver, Outlaw*, 1972; "E. S. Briant a Texas Sheriff," *Frontier Times*, February 1933.

BRIDGES, JACK L. (1838–c. 1883) Reportedly born "at sea." Bridges moved from Maine to Kansas where he worked as a deputy U.S. marshal (see U.S. MARSHALS SERVICE) by the late 1860s. In 1871 he was seriously injured in a gunfight with horse thief John E. Ledford in Wichita, Kansas. He returned home to Maine to recuperate and then headed west to Colorado and Kansas, serving as marshal in Dodge City beginning in 1882. However, little is known of his career after 1883 except that William Matthew "Bill" Tilghman Jr.* replaced him as Dodge City marshal.

SOURCE: Nyle H. Miller and Joseph W. Snell, *Great Gunfighters of the Kansas Cowtowns 1867–1886*, 1967.

BRIL, JACQUES L. (1906–1981) Born in New York City and educated at the University of Michigan, Bril made numerous contributions to the field of lie detection. In 1931 he founded the firm Jacques L. Bril, Criminology Consultants and Investigators, which specialized in deception detection. Five years later he codeveloped a lie detector* apparatus called the Pathometer. He later played a role in the development of the Biograph and the Bril deception test.

SOURCE: Charles Phillips and Alan Axelrod, *CCC*, 1996.

BRODERICK, JOHN "JOHNNY." (1894–1966) Born in the Gashouse District of New York City, Broderick rose to prominence as a member of the New York City Police Department (NYPD)* during the Prohibition years. Known as "The Boff" for his predilection for violence, Broderick served stints as a fireman, labor tough, and bodyguard to Samuel Gompers before joining the force.

After joining the NYPD in 1923 Broderick quickly developed a reputation as one of the toughest cops on the beat and reputedly knocked out known criminals on sight. With a lead pipe hidden in the folds of a newspaper, Broderick roughed up countless gangsters. Edward G. Robinson's character in the 1936 film *Bullets or Ballots* was supposedly based on Broderick.

"The Boff" was a controversial police officer during his quarter-century career, manhandling the notorious Jack "Legs" Diamond by carrying him out of a movie theater and sticking him head first into a garbage can, and in 1926 shooting three escaped prisoners after they killed the warden and a guard at Tombs Prison. In 1931, along with John H. F. Cordes,* he helped capture "Two Gun" Crowley. His reputation as a tough guy led heavyweight champ Jack Dempsey to declare that "The Boff" was the only man he feared outside the ring. Despite his preference for violence, many of his peers felt Broderick had more bark than bite, saving some of his most ferocious beatings for the unsuspecting and sometimes innocent. On several occasions Broderick himself was severely beaten by his adversaries.

A favorite of newspaper reporters, who embellished his image, "The Boff" was also popular with Broadway luminaries such as Ed Sullivan, Gene Fowler, and Toots Shor, whom he regaled with stories from the mean streets. Broderick retired in 1947.

SOURCES: Thomas A. Reppetto, *The Blue Parade*, 1978; *New York Times*, January 18, 1966; *New Yorker*, December 26, 1931.

"BROKEN WINDOWS." In the March 1982 issue of *Atlantic Monthly*, authors James Q. Wilson and George Kelling argued, in the article "Broken Windows," that the police role should be expanded to include less traditional law enforcement goals such as improving the quality of community life by concentrating on maintaining order. Their findings were in part inspired by study findings about the foot patrol in Newark, New Jersey, which indicated that increased foot patrols did not necessarily lead to crime reduction but did lead to increased public order. By maintaining a vigilant presence, foot patrol officers could suppress community threats posed by drug addicts, prostitutes, and rowdy gang members and lead to the perception that public safety had increased.

The Wilson and Kelling article used the "broken windows" concept to link the deterioration of the community environment, characterized by graffiti, broken windows, and litter, with an increased potential for "criminal invasion." As the neighborhoods continued to decline, there seemed to be a natural progression toward more crime and a sense that public safety was decreasing. Therefore, according to this controversial theory, a greater police presence should be mandated for neighborhoods in decline.

SOURCE: James Q. Wilson and George L. Kelling, "Broken Windows," *Atlantic Monthly*, March 1982.

BROOKS, JOHN A. (1855–1944) Born in Bourbon, Kentucky, Brooks moved to Texas in 1876, working as a cowboy and miner before joining the Frontier Battalion of the Texas Rangers* in 1883. Six years later he was promoted to captain. During his twenty-three-year tenure with the Rangers he survived gunshot wounds and skirmishes with a variety of intrepid foes. In 1906 he resigned from the force and actively pursued political office, winning terms in the Texas State Legislature and appointment as judge in 1911, a position he held until 1939.

SOURCE: Mike Cox, *Texas Ranger Tales II*, 1999.

BROOKS, PIERCE. (1923–1998) Known as "the father of officer survival training," Brooks rose to prominence in 1963 when he figured in the apprehension of *Onion Field** killers Gregory Ulas Powell and Jimmy Lee Smith while serving on the Los Angeles Police Department (LAPD).* Brooks also served as police chief for Lakewood, Colorado, and the Springfield and Eugene, Oregon, police departments.

SOURCE: Michael Stone, "Remembering Pierce Brooks, a Law Enforcement Legend," *American Police Beat*, May 1998.

BROOKS, WILLIAM L. (1849–1874) In 1872 Brooks was elected as the first city marshal of Newton, Kansas. In June of the same year he survived three gunshot wounds following an altercation with Texas cowboys. Two months later he was working as a peace officer in Ellsworth, Kansas. In December he was wounded in a Dodge City gunfight but managed to shoot two of his assailants, one fatally. "Billy" Brooks survived several other scrapes before falling in with a bad crowd, and in 1874 he was hanged with several other horse thieves when a mob seized them from the Caldwell, Kansas, jail.

SOURCE: Nyle H. Miller and Joseph W. Snell, *Great Gunfighters of the Kansas Cowtowns*, 1967.

BROWN, HENRY NEWTON. (1857–1884) Born in Rolla, Missouri, Brown worked on cattle ranches in Colorado in his teens and drifted through the Texas panhandle before arriving in Lincoln County, New Mexico, in the late 1870s. During the Lincoln County War in 1878 he sided with Billy the Kid and the McSween-Tunstall bloc. He was with the Kid when he gunned down Sheriff William Brady* in Lincoln. Brown participated in several gunfights and took part in the killing of Andrew "Buckshot" Roberts. He was also present during the siege of the McSween house and managed to escape with Billy the Kid and several others.

Subsequently, the remnants of the Kid faction journeyed to the Texas panhandle and began a horse-stealing enterprise. However, Billy returned to New Mexico and death at the hands of Patrick Floyd Jarvis "Pat" Garrett,* while Brown stayed in Texas. Appointed deputy sheriff in Oldham County, Texas, he was fired for drinking and carousing. After some time ranching in Oklahoma, he next donned a star as deputy marshal and then city marshal of Caldwell, Kansas. Brown survived several gunfights with desperadoes in 1883 before teaming up with several outlaws and a deputy to rob a bank in Medicine Lodge, Kansas. During the robbery the erstwhile marshal shot the bank president as he reached for a gun. A cashier was also killed in the melee. Pursued by a posse of citizens, the four bank robbers were cornered and arrested in a box canyon. Figuring it was only a matter of time before a lynch mob seized them from their temporary shelter, Brown made a break but was by mowed down at point-blank range by a man with a shotgun. His prescience was confirmed: a lynch mob dragged the remaining prisoners to the nearest tree and hanged them.

SOURCES: Nyle H. Miller and Joseph W. Snell, *Great Gunfighters of the Kansas Cowtowns*, 1967; Bill O'Neal, *Encyclopedia of Western Gunfighters*, 1979.

BROWN, LEE PATRICK. (b. 1937) Born in the small town of Wewoka, Oklahoma, Brown's family moved to central California in 1942, where his father picked grapes as a seasonal laborer. Brown joined the San Jose police force in 1960 after receiving a bachelor's degree in criminology from Fresno State University. During his early career in policing he was engaged in undercover work in vice and narcotics.

Brown went on to earn a master's degree in criminology at the University of California at Berkeley in 1966 before joining the faculty at Portland State University in Oregon, where he established the school's first criminal justice program. In 1970 he was awarded a doctorate degree in criminology from Berkeley. After academic stints at several other schools, he returned to law enforcement as the sheriff* of Multnomah County, Oregon, in 1975.

Brown held a variety of administrative posts in the 1970s, including, in 1977, public safety commissioner of Atlanta, Georgia, where he came under heavy criticism for his handling of the 1981 Atlanta child murders. The following year, Brown was appointed police chief of Houston, Texas. During the next nine years he inaugurated a community policing program and helped heal racial divisions through extensive minority recruitment. However, his tenure in Houston as police chief was fraught with controversy. His attempts at implementing Neighborhood Oriented Policing (NOP)—the program was derided by his officers as standing for "Nobody on Patrol" because of its strategy of having police work indoors with community groups rather than on the streets apprehending offenders. When Brown resigned in 1989, crime was on the rise in Houston.

In 1990 Brown continued his meteoric rise through the ranks when appointed police commissioner of the New York City Police Department (NYPD) with a force seven times larger than Houston's. With the support of Mayor David Dinkins, Brown initiated the "Safe Streets, Safe City" campaign, which increased police manpower by 25 percent. As part of his plan, headquarters personnel, who were typically relegated to desk jobs, were ordered to participate in street duty at least once a week. During his two years as police chief Brown increased minority representation in the force and professionalized the NYPD. Shortly after his arrival he could point to the first major decline in city crime statistics in thirty-six years. His record as New York police commissioner was marred by several episodes, however, including an investigation into the police handling of racial violence between blacks and Orthodox Jews in the Crown Heights section of Brooklyn, which concluded that "a leadership vacuum existed at the highest levels of the department" (Bernstein).

In 1992 Brown returned to Houston and joined the faculty at Texas Southern University. The following year he served as President Bill Clinton's drug czar in Washington, D.C., and in 1997 Brown became the first black mayor of Houston, America's largest city to have never before had one.

SOURCES: W. Marvin Dulaney, *Black Police in America*, 1996; Lee P. Brown, *Community Policing: A Practical Guide for Police Officials*, 1989; Alan Bernstein, "Brown Embraces Latest Challenge," *Houston Chronicle*, August 17, 1997.

BRUSSEL, JAMES ARNOLD. (1905–1982) Born in New York City, Brussel attended the University of Pennsylvania before beginning his psychiatry career with the New York State Department of Mental Hygiene in the 1930s. Brussel was an early pioneer in criminal profiling and one of the first to use it in criminal investigations, notably in the New York "Mad Bomber" case of the 1950s and later the "Boston Strangler" case.

SOURCE: Charles Phillips and Alan Axelrod, *CCC*, 1996.

BRYCE, JACOB ADOLPHUS "JELLY." (1906–1974) Born in Mountain View, Oklahoma, Bryce joined the Oklahoma City Police Department (OCPD) in 1928, where he became better known by his nickname, "Jelly," and lightning-quick dexterity with a handgun. Many of his contemporaries compared him favorably with the legendary Oklahoma lawman William Matthew "Bill" Tilghman,* and in his first year on the force he killed three men in the line of duty. In 1933 Bryce rose to prominence following his role in the killing of the "Tri-State Terror," noted badman Wilbur Underhill.

Bryce reportedly practiced his quick-draw technique for hours at a time in front of a mirror. The practice paid off in 1934 when Federal Bureau of Investigation (FBI)* chief John Edgar Hoover* selected him to teach firearms tactics to his agents. During his tenure with the FBI Bryce created the bureau's concealed fast-draw holster and introduced the crouched firing stance later adopted by most police organizations. By the mid-1940s Bryce had killed ten men while with the FBI and OCPD. One colleague noted that Bryce had shot and wounded nine others as well. Bryce served in a variety of FBI offices and in 1941 was promoted to special agent in charge of the El Paso, Texas; San Antonio, Texas; Oklahoma City, Oklahoma, and Albuquerque, New Mexico, offices before he retired in 1958.

SOURCE: Ron Owens, "Jelly Bryce," in Craig W. Floyd and Kelley Lang Helms, eds., *To Serve and Protect*, 1995.

BUFFALOING. Buffaloing was a form of police brutality utilized by such Western peace officers as James Butler "Wild Bill" Hickok* and Wyatt Berry Stapp Earp.* The term referred to the predisposition these men had for subduing lawbreakers by hitting them over the head with the butt end of their revolvers. Buffaloing reportedly originated as a condescending reference toward cowboys, whom lawmen viewed as no more intelligent than the notoriously vapid buffalo, which stood still while hunters wiped them out.

SOURCE: Carl Sifakis, *The Encyclopedia of American Crime*, 1982.

BULLOCK, SETH G. (1847–1919) Born near Windsor, Ontario, Canada, Bullock moved to Montana when he was twenty and four years later was elected to the Territorial Senate. Following his stint as a politician he won election as sheriff* of Clark County, Montana in 1873. Three years later he traveled to Deadwood, South Dakota and was nearby when James Butler "Wild Bill" Hickok* was killed. Bullock was informally appointed sheriff soon after, and the following year, when a formal government was established, he was officially appointed sheriff by the governor. He is credited with bringing a period of calm to Deadwood before he stepped down in 1878. He served as deputy marshal in the area for several years while pursuing various sideline businesses.

In 1879 Bullock turned to ranching and five years later began a long friendship with Theodore Roosevelt.* Roosevelt later appointed him to a conservation post in 1900 and then in 1905 to U.S. Marshal (see U.S. MARSHALS SERVICE) of South Dakota. Bullock is credited with having a mountain in the Black Hills named after his friend Roosevelt, who died not long before Bullock himself.

SOURCES: Kenneth C. Kellar, *Seth Bullock—Frontier Marshal*, 1972; Dan L. Thrapp, ed., *EFB*, Vol. 1, 1988.

BURNS, WILLIAM JOHN. (1861–1932) Born in Baltimore, this son of Irish immigrants rose to become one of America's greatest detectives. The greatest influence on his chosen profession probably came from his childhood, when his father was appointed police commissioner of Columbus, Ohio. The future U.S. Secret Service agent soon began helping his father solve the more difficult cases. Burns rose to prominence in his early twenties when he helped determine how an Ohio state election was fraudulently rigged.

Bombarded with job offers, Burns joined the U.S. Secret Service* in 1889. During his stint with the Secret Service he helped crack several notorious counterfeiting cases, and in 1897 he worked undercover in Indiana in order to ascertain who was responsible for the vigilante lynching of five suspected criminals.

Burns joined the Department of the Interior as an investigator in 1903. One of his greatest cases was the investigation of San Francisco political boss Abe Ruef, who was sent to prison after a three-year inquest. The ever-restless Burns soon left government employ to form the Burns and Sheridan Detective Agency with partner William P. Sheridan, which, like its main competitor, the Pinkerton's National Detective Agency,* operated as a quasi-private police force. The following year Sheridan sold out his share to Burns and the William J. Burns National Detective Agency was born, with regional offices soon opening throughout the country.

The Burns agency came under heavy criticism for its unpopular support of big business interests against labor unions. Despite such controversy and Burns's heavy-handed investigation of the 1910 bombing of the *Los Angeles Times* building, the agency prospered and in 1921 Burns returned to government service to head the fledgling Bureau of Investigation, the precursor of the Federal Bureau of Investigation (FBI).* Burns faced his heaviest criticism during the administration of President Warren G. Harding, when he seemed reluctant to prosecute the Teapot Dome scandal (involving the sale of federal oil leases to private interests for profit). Although he had successfully prosecuted the Ku Klux Klan in the 1920s, the stigma of Teapot Dome forced Burns to resign in 1924 and return to private life. During his career Burns wrote numerous articles and books, including *The Masked War* (1913), *The Argyle Case* (1913), and *The Crevice* (1915). He died of a heart attack at home in Sarasota, Florida.

SOURCES: Gene Caesar, *Incredible Detective: The Biography of William J. Burns*, 1968; Charles Phillips and Alan Axelrod, *CCC*, 1996.

BURNS NATIONAL DETECTIVE AGENCY. *See* WILLIAM JOHN BURNS.

BURT, LEONARD. (1892–1983) Burt rose to prominence during his early years as a detective in the Scotland Yard* Criminal Investigation Department (CID).* Following a successful career battling drugs, homicide, and vice from 1919 to 1940, the British detective was promoted to chief superintendent. During World War II he commanded MI5 in the British Army Intelligence Corps. Among his most famous cases was the capture of William Joyce, aka "Lord Haw Haw," who made propaganda broadcasts for the Nazis. After the war Burt was credited with cracking the Klaus Fuchs–Allan Nunn May spy ring, which was passing information on atomic weaponry. Compared to his earlier career, his final duties as head of the Special Branch of the Metropolitan Police,* responsible for the protection of the royal family and foreign luminaries such as Marshal Tito and Nikita Khruschev, must have seemed rather anticlimactic.

SOURCE: Leonard Burt, *Commander Burt of Scotland Yard*, 1959.

BURTON, BOB. One of the best-known modern-day bounty hunters, Burton chronicled his exploits in his 1984 book *Bounty Hunter*. Formerly a Marine and soldier of fortune, later became the president of the Bail Enforcement Agents Association.

SOURCES: Bob Burton, *Bounty Hunter*, 1984; Jacqueline Pope, *Bounty Hunters, Marshals, and Sheriffs*, 1998.

BURTON, ISAAC. (prominent 1830s) Little is known about this early Ranger's career except that he was appointed one of the first captains of the Texas Rangers* in 1835. Charged with guarding the Texas coast from Mexican invaders during the territorial conflict with Mexico, Burton's men boarded and seized several Mexican vessels, earning his Rangers the sobriquet "horse marines."

SOURCE: Walter Prescott Webb, *The Texas Rangers*, 1935.

BURTON, MARVIN "RED." (b. 1885) Born outside Mart, Texas, Burton worked on his family farm and then in construction before joining the Waco,

Texas, police force in 1917. Unsettled by the corruption of his colleagues during the early years of Prohibition, he left the force and was hired as sheriff's deputy for McLennan County in 1921. Burton rose to prominence in 1921 when he and another lawman faced down the Ku Klux Klan in Lorena, just south of Waco. During the subsequent confrontation, both men were wounded and Burton was credited with saving his partner's life, shooting several Klan members in the process. Five other local citizens and peace officers were severely wounded while standing up to the Klan. In 1922 Burton joined the Texas Rangers,* beginning an eleven-year pursuit against bootleggers, Klansmen, and oil field roughnecks. After leaving the Rangers in 1933 he returned to Waco and was eventually promoted to police chief. He ended his thirty-five-year law enforcement career in 1951.

SOURCE: Ben Proctor, *Just One Riot*, 1991.

BUSSELL, WILLIAM. (c. 1830–1869) Born in London, Bussell joined the Cape Town, South Africa, police in 1854, was promoted to subinspector in 1856, and in 1859 succeeded John King* as head of the Cape Town Police Force. In 1867 Bussell's career came to a halt when he was accused of misappropriating public funds and placed under arrest. He was subsequently tried, convicted, and sentenced to prison on Robben Island, where he died two years later.

SOURCE: Alan F. Hattersley, *The First South African Detectives*, 1960.

BUTE'S BOBBIES. One of the first, and largest, private police forces in Great Britain, Bute's Bobbies employed more than seventy men in its busiest years. Decked out in green uniforms with gilt buttons, they policed the Bute Docks in Cardiff, Wales, beginning in 1865. Construction on these docks began in 1835, and by the time the job was completed in 1907, that city had become the largest coal-exporting port in the world. With the familiar docklands environment swarming with the usual suspects, longshoremen, prostitutes, vagabonds, and immigrants, it took on an increasingly lawless ambience. In 1865 pressures by local citizens led the marquess of Bute to seek permission to recruit a private law enforcement force. That year, the Bute's Bobbies were born. Within months of their inauguration, the force was credited with reducing crime and civil disorder along the docks.

SOURCE: Pauline Appleby, *A Force on the Move: The Story of the British Transport Police, 1825–1995*, 1995.

BUTLER, SMEDLEY DARLINGTON. (1881–1940) Born into a prominent Quaker family in Chester County, Pennsylvania, over his parents' objections Butler left school at sixteen to fight in the Spanish-American War. Despite his youth and the reluctance of his family, his father's position on the Naval Affairs Committee actually facilitated the enlistment of the underaged Smedley into the

U.S. Marines. Although he missed the action in Cuba, Butler more than made up for it in the following years as he participated in the Philippines insurrection and then the Boxer Rebellion, where he was recommended for the Medal of Honor. (The award was denied since he was a captain and officers were not eligible during this era.)

Butler was awarded the Congressional Medal of Honor in 1914 for his performance during the storming of Vera Cruz. He went on to a brilliant military career and participated in virtually every military engagement between 1898 and 1929. He would eventually garner a second Congressional Medal of Honor, a very rare achievement.

In the 1930s Butler took a two-year leave of absence from the Marines to serve as Philadelphia's director of public safety. Butler's attempts to introduce a military-style discipline to the disreputable police department and to enforce Prohibition in the City of Brotherly Love proved a dismal failure. Taking the reins of police chief in January 1934, Butler ordered all vice to desist within two days. Constitutional law and due process were abandoned, and within forty-eight hours, three-quarters of the city's saloons had been shut down. His attempts at law enforcement included the organization of a "bandit patrol" composed of shotgun-toting roughnecks and armored vehicles ordered to crack down on lawbreakers. Butler reportedly proclaimed, "Shoot a few of them, and make arrests afterward" (Phillips and Axelrod).

The "Fighting Quaker" became an albatross around the neck of the mayor of Philadelphia after he abolished the police academy along with accepted procedures of promotion. Butler's behavior became increasingly erratic, and he was forced to resign as soon as the two-year term ended—but not before complaining, "Sherman was right about war, but leading the Philadelphia police department was worse." Butler's attempts at introducing constabulary methods were unworkable under current political conditions. His last years were no less contentious, as he became a zealous teetotaler and, in 1931, the first American general since the Civil War to be arrested: he was court-martialed for slandering dictator Benito Mussolini in a public speech. The embittered ex–police chief apologized and the charges were dropped. As World War II loomed on the horizon, the former war hero became a fanatical anti-imperialist and pacifist.

SOURCES: Charles Phillips and Alan Axelrod, *CCC*, 1996; Thomas A. Reppetto, *The Blue Parade*, 1978.

BUTLER, THOMAS. (1913–1970) Butler was born in London and joined the London Metropolitan Police* in 1925. Within four years he had risen to detective, beginning a meteoric ascent through the ranks to, finally, detective chief superintendent in 1963. The Scotland Yard* sleuth earned the moniker "Grey Fox" for his relentless pursuit of the fifteen-member gang responsible for the 1963 "Great Train Robbery," which netted the greatest cash theft in history. Butler's dogged five-year pursuit led him throughout Europe and even resulted in his arrest as a Peeping Tom for viewing sunbathers through binoculars in France while looking for his prey. Butler achieved further prominence in 1968 when he apprehended James Earl Ray, the suspected assassin of Martin Luther King Jr., at Heathrow Airport. He retired later that year and died of lung cancer in 1970.

SOURCE: Charles Phillips and Alan Axelrod, *CCC*, 1996.

BYRNE, EDWARD. (d. 1988) New York City police officer Ed Byrne was sitting in his squad car, guarding the home of a police informant who had recently testified against a drug dealer, when he was shot to death by drug dealers in 1988.

SOURCE: William Bratton, *Turnaround*, 1998.

BYRNES, THOMAS F. (1842–1910) Born in Ireland, Byrnes immigrated with his family to America during childhood. Following stints as a gas fitter and a soldier in the Union Army during the Civil War, Byrnes joined the New York City Police Department (NYPD)* in 1863. Five years later he was promoted to roundsman (SEE ROUNDSMEN), before rising to captain in 1870. Byrnes rose to prominence in 1878 following his apprehension of notorious bank robber George Leonidas Leslie and his associates after a three-million-dollar Manhattan bank robbery.

Byrnes was appointed chief of the Detective Bureau in 1880 and introduced a no-tolerance policy for known criminals in the Wall Street financial district. By most accounts Byrnes exemplified the paradoxical nature of nineteenth-century American policing. While he vigorously pursued lawbreakers, he probably paid bribes to move up the police hierarchy, an accepted tradition according to the customs and unwritten rules of urban politics. There is also evidence that the barons of Wall Street rewarded him with the profits of investments made on Byrnes's behalf in gratitude for his protection of the jewelry and financial districts of lower Manhattan from professional criminals. In many respects Byrnes shared many of the virtues and weaknesses of his era's urban peacekeepers.

Byrnes is probably best remembered for the collaborative effort that resulted in the publication of the best-selling *Professional Criminals of America* in 1886. One of the first police officials to use the Bertillon system,* Byrnes was an advocate of modern identification systems, and he zealously created a collection of tintype daguerreotypes of every criminal collared. Each mugshot in the volume was accompanied by detailed descriptions of the modus operandi of the various criminals. A large, charismatic man, Byrnes was not averse to resorting to the third degree* when the need arose. His interrogation room doubled as his "Mystery chamber," a personal museum filled with crime memorabilia, including a hangman's noose.

In 1888 Byrnes assumed the newly created position of chief inspector, ranked second only to the acting superintendent, and four years later Byrnes replaced William Murray as superintendent. However, the mood in New York City was changing, as reformer Charles H. Parkhurst* led a campaign against police corruption and then, in 1895, Theodore Roosevelt* became police commissioner. Byrnes was pilloried by accusations of corruption during the 1894 Lexow Committee (see LEXOW, CLARENCE) hearings, and his wealth came under investigation when he was reported to have accumulated assets of more than $350,000 on a salary of $5,000 a year. Pressured to resign by Roosevelt, Byrnes left law enforcement for good in 1895.

SOURCES: Carl Sifakis, *The Encyclopedia of American Crime,* 1982; James F. Richardson, *The New York Police,* 1970.

BYRNES, WILLIAM WALLACE. (1824–1874) Born in Maine, Byrnes grew up in Missouri where, according to some reports, he studied for the priesthood for a short time at Saint Louis University. Byrnes served in the Mexican War and then hunted Apache scalps with mountain men such as Jim Beckwourth in response to the Mexican government's offer of up to two hundred dollars per scalp. Following the discovery of gold, Byrnes moved on to California for several years before ending up in the Utah Territory. In 1851 he entered law enforcement when he was elected sheriff* of what is now Carson Valley, Nevada.

After recovering from gunshot wounds, Byrnes returned to California and joined the recently created California Rangers in 1853. During his tenure with the Rangers, Byrnes was credited with killing the legendary outlaw Joaquin Murrieta. As proof of his exploits, Byrnes cut off the bandit's head and the hand of one of his henchmen. The trophies were carried to Fort Miller, to be preserved for posterity in an alcohol solution. However, Byrnes was informed that the whiskey on hand would not suffice and that the trophies needed pure alcohol for preservation. Byrnes left the body parts with a colleague, instructing him to change the whiskey regularly until he returned. Upon his return, however, Byrnes found that his friend had finished the whiskey himself and the trophies were now unrecognizable. The head was then discarded, but the withered hand was saved for future reference.

Although it has never been firmly established who killed Murrieta, since Byrnes reportedly knew the outlaw, his word was accepted when he claimed the reward. For a short time afterward Byrnes served as a prison guard at San Quentin penitentiary, and he later fought in several Indian conflicts. His daughter claimed that Byrnes had been wounded more than thirty times during his frontier career, and in his later years he sought solace in the bottle, in part because of the pain of old wounds. In 1873 he lapsed into senility, dying in the Stockton, California, Asylum the following year.

SOURCES: Angel T. Myron, *History of Nevada,* 1881; Sardis W. Templeton, *The Lame Captain,* 1965; William B. Secrest, *Lawmen and Desperadoes,* 1994.

C

CAFFREY, RAYMOND J. (1903–1933) Born in McCook, Nebraska, Federal Bureau of Investigation (FBI)* agent Caffrey was killed in the so-called Kansas City Massacre* on June 17, 1933. Working out of the Oklahoma City field office, Caffrey was assigned to escort mobster Frank Nash from McAlester, Oklahoma, to the Leavenworth Penitentiary in Kansas. Nash, Caffrey, and three police officers were killed during the subsequent ambush at the Kansas City railroad station. The incident was instrumental in convincing Congress, beginning in 1934, to authorize FBI agents to carry guns and make arrests.

SOURCE: Robert Unger, *The Union Station Massacre: The Original Sin of J. Edgar Hoover's FBI*, 1997.

CAGOULARDS. During the reign of Haiti's dictator "Papa Doc" Duvalier, the Tonton Macoutes* made the transition from an unofficial gang of hooded vigilantes, known as the *cagoulards*, to their better known incarnation as a secret police organization. The *cagoulards* were spreading their particular brand of terror well before Duvalier's 1957 rise, but it was Duvalier who organized them into the nucleus of what would become the Macoutes.

SOURCE: Thomas Plate and Andrea Darvi, *Secret Police*, 1981.

CAIRNS, JAMES. (1851–1934) Born in Scotland, Cairns moved to Wichita, Kansas, from Indiana in 1871. Four years later he began several stints as peace officer there, and beginning in 1879 he began an eleven-year term as Wichita town marshal. During his thirty years on the force he worked with Wyatt Berry Stapp Earp* and other Western luminaries. Some Earp authorities cite Cairns as the source for much of the information and misinformation concerning Earp's Wichita years.

SOURCES: Dan L. Thrapp, ed., *EFB*, Vol. 1, 1988; Ed Bartholomew, *Wyatt Earp, The Untold Story*, 1963.

CALAMITY JANES. In central Oklahoma an informal women's group that calls itself the "Calamity Janes" aids the sheriff* during calamities such as floods and major accidents, offering first aid and support to the injured and homeless.

SOURCE: James Cramer, *The World's Police*, 1964.

CALIFORNIA HIGHWAY PATROL. This is one of the most famous highway patrol* units in the world, in part due to the recent pursuit of O. J. Simpson on the Santa Monica Freeway and the popular television show *CHiPs*, which ran from 1977 to 1983. The California Highway Patrol (CHP) was established in 1929. Initially composed of 280 uniformed officers and equipped with 8 automobiles and 224 motorcycles, in 1947 the CHP was renamed and reorganized as the Department of California Highway Patrol.

SOURCE: John P. Kenney, *The California Police*, 1964.

CAMARENA, ENRIQUE "KIKI." (1948–1985) Born in Mexicali, Mexico, and raised in California, Camarena came to international attention in 1985 when, while employed by the U.S. Drug Enforcement Administration (DEA), he was kidnapped and tortured to death by Mexican drug kingpin Rafael Caro Quintero. Camarena was kidnapped on February 5, 1985, and was tortured to death sometime before his body was found a month later.

Following this incident the DEA embarked on an intensive manhunt, called Operation Leyenda, which resulted in twenty-two indictments. Seven people, including three major Mexican drug kingpins, are serving life sentences in the United States for the crime. Among them is the brother-in-law of the former Mexican president. Camarena's story was chronicled in the 1990 television miniseries "Drug Wars: The Camarena Story."

SOURCE: National Law Enforcement Officers' Memorial Fund, *To Serve and Protect*, 1995.

CAMPBELL, GEORGE WASHINGTON. (1850–1881) Born in Greenup County, Kentucky, Campbell moved to Texas in the 1870s and worked in ranching until entering law enforcement as a deputy sheriff* in Clay County in 1876. Four years later he resigned and moved to New Mexico, where he worked as a cattle association's detective. That same year he was appointed the city marshal of El Paso, Texas, but resigned over a salary dispute before the year was out. On April 14, 1881, he was killed in a gunfight with Dallas city marshal Dallas Stoudenmire.*

SOURCES: Fred R. Egloff, *El Paso Lawman: G. W. Campbell*, 1982; Leon Metz, *Dallas Stoudenmire: El Paso Marshal*, 1979.

CAMPBELL, SIR GEORGE WILLIAM ROBERT. (1835–1905) Campbell is best known for his contributions to the Ceylon police and the British Colonial Police system. Campbell entered colonial law enforcement following military service in India. Assigned the task of reorganizing the Ceylon Police Force in 1866, he followed the military model exemplified by the Royal Irish Constabulary.* Among the innovations implemented by Campbell was a compound-style arrangement whereby police lived together with their families in virtual military enclaves to ensure easy mobilization in the event of emergencies. Campbell also instituted proficiency exams, procedure directives, and an impartial program of promotion and reward.

SOURCE: Charles Phillips and Alan Axelrod, *CCC*, 1996.

CAMPBELL, MALCOLM. (1839–1932) Born near London, Ontario, Canada, Campbell arrived in Nebraska in the mid-1860s. He worked in the freighting business and a series of other occupations until 1882, when he was appointed deputy sheriff* in Albany County, Nebraska. The following year he was instrumental in the arrest of the fugitive Colorado killer and reputed cannibal Alferd G. Packer. With his newfound fame, Campbell was elected sheriff of Converse County, Wyoming. Although his jurisdiction was bounded by Johnson County, he reportedly stayed out of the conflict between the cattlemen and settlers. Except for a stint as marshal of Douglas, Wyoming, Campbell left law enforcement for politics and business following his tenure as sheriff.

SOURCES: Dan L. Thrapp, ed., *EFB*, Vol. 1, 1988; Ervan Kushner, *Alferd G. Packer: Cannibal! Victim?* 1980.

CAMPS, FRANCIS EDWARD. (1905–1972) Born in Teddington, England, Camps attended Guys Hospital Medical School and several other institutions and then specialized in forensic medicine. During his career he took part in the investigation of some of the most famous murders of the twentieth century, including the Christie, Coventry, Hume, and Emmett-Dunne cases. His work on the Reginald Halliday Christie murders incorporated methods of criminal investigation that were not made public until they were revealed in his book on the case in 1953. Camps died of cancer in 1972. His books chronicling these murder cases include *The Investigation of Murder* (1966) and the classic *Medical and Scientific Investigations in the Christie Case* (1953).

SOURCES: Francis E. Camps, *The Investigation of Murder*, 1966; Richard Whittington-Egan and Molly Whittington-Egan, *The Bedside Book of Murder*, 1987.

CANINE UNITS. The earliest recorded use of dogs for detective work can be traced to fourteenth-century France, where an organized canine unit patrolled the streets of Saint-Malo for citizen protection until the 1770s, when the dogs fatally attacked a pedestrian and the force was disbanded. In 1889, Ghent, Belgium, became the first urban entity to create a police-dog training academy, preparing thirty-seven dogs to patrol the city of 175,000 from 10 P.M. to daybreak under the watchful eyes of ten constables.*

By the end of the first decade of the twentieth century, other European cities had introduced similar units, with six hundred such units in Germany alone. The first canine unit in the United States was established in South Orange, New Jersey, in 1907, and New York City quickly followed. In 1935 the Royal Canadian Mounted Police (RCMP)* initiated Canada's first program, introducing the longest continuous running program in North America. Experience has demonstrated that the German shepherd is one of the best-suited breeds for this work, although at least seventeen other dogs, including Airedales, Akitas, Labradors, mastiffs, and poodles, have seen service in canine units.

SOURCES: Samuel G. Chapman, *Police Dogs in North America*, 1990; Samuel G. Chapman, "Canine Units," *Encyclopedia of Police Science*, ed. William G. Bailey, 1995.

CANTON, FRANK M. (JOE HORNER). (1849–1927) Canton was born Joseph Horner in Richmond, Virginia. His family moved to Missouri shortly before the outbreak of the Civil War. After his father died in the conflict, his mother moved the family to Denton County, Texas, where Horner became a cowboy and participated in several trail drives to Kansas and Nebraska. In 1870 he entered law enforcement as a deputy sheriff* in Jacksboro, Texas. Soon after he returned to cattle ranching and then drifted into crime over the next several years. In 1874 he killed a black soldier over a remark concerning a white woman, and three years later he was arrested for bank robbery. Escaping from jail, he returned to cow punching and changed his name to the more familiar Frank Canton.

By 1877 he was wanted for a number of crimes and was arrested by a member of the Texas Rangers,* "Jesse' Leigh (Lee) Hall.* After obtaining his release the next year, he left his criminal behavior behind for the next half century and transformed himself into a reliable lawman. In Wyoming he was employed as a range detective for the local stock growers' organization, and in 1882 he was elected sheriff* of Johnson County, leading a contingent of eighteen deputies. In 1891 Canton is suspected of having ambushed Orley E. Jones and a former associate from Texas, John A. Tisdale. He was involved in the 1892 Johnson County War and reportedly took part in the killing of Nate Champion and Nick Ray in that year. Canton was with the besieged regulators who were rescued by army troops.

Canton left Wyoming following the Johnson County debacle and worked in a factory in Nebraska before returning to law enforcement as undersheriff in Pawnee, Oklahoma, in 1894 and then as deputy U.S. marshal (see U.S. MARSHALS SERVICE) for Evett Dumas Nix.* After helping to clean out much of the outlaw menace from the Indian Territory, Canton prospected for gold in the Yukon for several years. He returned to Pawnee and policing in 1900 and, seven years later, upon statehood, was appointed Oklahoma's first adjutant general. Much of Canton's career is shrouded in mystery, including his unsubstantiated claims of having fought in the Chinese Boxer Rebellion and suppressing the Crazy Snake uprising by himself. While in Alaska, Canton befriended novelist Rex Beach and was reportedly the inspiration for many of Beach's western heroes. In his last years he completed his autobiography, *Frontier Trails*, which did little to clear up any speculation about Canton's past.

SOURCES: Robert K. DeArment, *Alias Frank Canton*, 1996; Jack DeMattos, "Frank Canton," *Real West*, May 1979.

CARBALLEDA, LUIS. (b. 1826) Carballeda joined the Mexican army in 1847 and served under General Antonio Lopez de Santa Ana during the war between Mexico and the United States. Following his distinguished military career Carballeda traveled to Europe before returning to the military and completing a thirty-year career in 1877. In 1878 he was appointed inspector general of the city of Mexico and the federal district.

SOURCE: George W. Hale, *Police and Prison Cyclopaedia*, Vol. 2, 1893.

CARBINIERI. This Italian police armed force was formed in the Savoy States in 1814. Initially this military organization was composed of the army's elite. With the unification of Italy in 1861, the Carbinieri became a branch of the army and took the place of local *gendarmes*.* Today it still adheres to its military origins. Subordinated to the Ministry of Defense, during peacetime it is charged with protecting citizens and property and enforcing laws and special state regulations. The Carbinieri is subordinate to the Ministry of the Interior and serves as an executive organization for the detection of crime. As of 1989 it consisted of over 91,239 men who bear ranks and badges identical to those of their military counterparts.

SOURCES: Roy D. Ingleton, *Police of the World*, 1979; James Cramer, *The World's Police*, 1964; George Thomas Kurian, *World Encyclopedia of Police Forces & Penal Systems*, 1989.

CARR, THOMAS JEFFERSON. (b. 1842) Born in Pennsylvania, in his youth Carr moved with his family to Ohio, where he worked as a clerk, taught school, and joined the Union Army during the Civil War. Following his service he attended college and relocated to Colorado. He worked at several jobs in Colorado and then Wyoming in rapid succession, including a stint as a Central City, Colorado, police officer, before winning a term as sheriff* of Laramie County, Wyoming, in 1869. He directed the territory's first legal execution in 1870, survived several gunfights, and ended up spending three terms as sheriff during the 1870s. Local Indians referred to Carr as "Red Cloud" in deference to his wild, flowing beard. Carr distinguished himself as a lawman and, after losing a race for reelection, won appointment as city marshal of Cheyenne for three years. During this era he continued an affiliation with the Rocky Mountain Detective Association and for many years served as detective and assistant supervisor in Wyoming. During his tenure as a peace officer he was well compensated through numerous real estate investments. A stalwart member of the community, Carr was selected by President Grover Cleveland as federal marshal for the Wyoming Territory.

SOURCE: Frank Richard Prassel. *The Western Peace Officer*, 1981.

CARSON, THOMAS. (prominent 1870s) It is unsubstantiated as to whether Carson was a nephew of Kit Carson as he claimed, but in 1871 he served as an Abilene, Kansas, peace officer under James Butler "Wild Bill" Hickok.* Carson reportedly confronted noted Texas gunman John Wesley Hardin for violating the Abilene weapons policy, but no gunplay resulted. Later that year he served as a peace officer in Newton, Kansas, and then in Abilene. He was fired after wounding a bartender in a gunfight. He was subsequently arrested, broke out of jail, and probably fled to Texas, where he vanished into obscurity.

SOURCES: Nyle Miller and Joseph W. Snell, *Great Gunfighters of the Kansas Cowtowns*, 1967; Dan L. Thrapp, ed., *EFB*, Vol. 1, 1988.

CHADBORN, DANIEL J. (1879–1966) Born in Bastrop, Texas, Chadborn moved with his family to the Fort Davis area in his youth, where his father served as sheriff* from 1891 to 1903. Chadborn is best remembered for killing noted West Texas shootist Barney Riggs in a gunfight in 1903. "Buck" Chadborn was soon acquitted of the killing and moved to the Ysleta, Texas, region, where he reportedly assisted the Texas Rangers* on several occasions. While this has not been substantiated, Chadborn's biographer suggests that it is entirely likely since many Special Rangers assisted the understaffed Rangers in that era.

In 1909 he relocated his family to Columbus, New Mexico, where he worked as a deputy sheriff and cattle inspector. He also was engaged as a government intelligence agent along the Mexican border during World War I. He was in Columbus in March 1916, during Pancho Villa's bloody raid on the town, although he was convinced Villa did not personally lead the attack. Chadborn organized a posse to chase down Villa's followers, the Villistas, and following a skirmish, he turned back with several wounded prisoners in tow. The raid on Columbus precipitated General John J. Pershing's punitive expedition across the border.

During the Depression and Prohibition years, Chadborn battled bootleggers as he sporadically worked as deputy sheriff, cattle inspector, and U.S. Customs Service* inspector. He retired from law enforcement in 1941.

SOURCE: Bill C. James, *Buck Chadborn: Border Lawman*, 1995.

CHADWICK, EDWIN. (1800–1890) Formerly a barrister, Chadwick complemented his income by writing editorials on the plight of human suffering in
England. Like Patrick Colquhoun* and Jeremy Bentham, Chadwick was a util-
itarian reformer devoted to police and criminal justice reform throughout his
long life. Chadwick had been a disciple of Bentham and became an exponent
of preventative policing. Since the 1820s he had advocated police reform based
on the French centralized model. In 1836 Chadwick was appointed to the British
Royal Commission on a Constabulary Force to investigate the need for a constabulary in England's fifty-six counties and Wales. Of the three members of
the commission, which included Sir Charles Rowan* and Charles Shaw-Lefevre,
it is generally agreed that Chadwick did most of the work. In particular, the
intrepid Chadwick did most of the legwork, interviewing criminals about their
lifestyles and listening as they critiqued the current state of the parish constables.
The publication of the commission's first report in 1839 is credited with destroying the belief that poverty caused crime; moreover, it proposed the creation of
a police force for the whole country.

According to some of the commission's proposals, the constabulary would be
modeled on the London Metropolitan Police* and financed mostly through
county taxes. Going against British tradition, the report also wanted the force
to be managed and deployed centrally. However, the response to these ideas
was underwhelming and the proposals were not implemented. It seemed too
radical a proposition to introduce a centralized constabulary to the land of the
Magna Carta.

By the 1830s Chadwick was advocating policing in the context of public
service; that the role of the police should not only include preventative policing
but also services that did not require force, such as protecting public health and
assisting accident victims. Despite the fact that Chadwick had an annoying predilection for claiming to be the originator of every police reform with which he
was associated, the Police Act of 1839, which expanded police powers to cover
minor offenses, and the Metropolitan Streets Act of 1867 were partially inspired
by Chadwick's views.

SOURCES: Clive Emsley, *Policing and Its Context, 1750–1870*, 1983; Charles Reith,
A New Study of Police History, 1956.

CHAMBERLAIN, PAUL. (b. 1941) Chamberlain gave up plans for a medical
career and entered law enforcement as a part-time clerk for the Federal Bureau
of Investigation (FBI)* in the early 1960s. Shortly afterwards he entered the
FBI academy at Quantico, Virginia,* graduating in 1965. After postings in
Tulsa, Oklahoma, and San Antonio, Texas, Chamberlain's career received its
greatest boost when he safely recovered the kidnapped son of a Beverly Hills,
California, banker. To express his gratitude, in 1981 the wealthy financier bank-
rolled Chamberlain's one-man investigative consulting firm, Paul Chamberlain
International, to the tune of a half-million dollars.

Over the following decade the one-time FBI agent expanded his operations to almost three dozen employees and fifty field consultants, earning close to ten million dollars annually. The firm specializes in solving corporate kidnappings and extortion and was most prominent when collaborating with the FBI during the savings and loan fraud cases of the 1980s.

SOURCE: Charles Phillips and Alan Axelrod, *CCC*, 1996.

CHAN, CHARLIE. The fictional detective sergeant of the Honolulu Police Department was the creation of writer Earl Derr Biggers (1884–1933). Of Chinese-Hawaiian descent, the assimilated Chan was married, with eleven children. The best detective on the force, Chan is later promoted to inspector. Biggers introduced his sleuth in *The House without a Key* (1925), the first, and generally acknowledged as the best, of the popular six-book series. Biggers's creation was apparently inspired by an article he read about two "Oriental" Hawaiian detectives named Chang Apana and Lee Fook, who solved a perplexing murder case.

Chan's transition to the big screen took some time to become popular because earlier films minimized his role as detective. In the 1926 film adaptation of the first book, Chan is listed twelfth in the credits. Of the actors who portrayed Chan in more than fifty films, none were Asian. The most familiar actors were Caucasian, including the Swedish-born actor Warner Oland, Sidney Toler, and Roland Winters.

SOURCES: Otto Penzler, *The Private Lives of Private Eyes*, 1977; Chris Steinbrunner and Otto Penzler, *EMD*, 1976.

CHANCEMEN. During the nineteenth century, chancemen were temporary police officers who were paid the same amount as regular police officers while performing their duties during their absence.

SOURCE: George W. Hale, *Police and Prison Cyclopaedia*, Vol. 2, 1893.

CHANDLER, GEORGE FLETCHER. (1872–1964) Born in New York State, Chandler attended Syracuse University and then Columbia University, where he received a medical degree in 1895. Eleven years later he entered the New York National Guard, rising to captain by 1910. He participated in the 1916 Pershing expedition, which pursued Mexican bandit and revolutionary Pancho Villa into Mexico, and during World War I, he taught medical skills in Chatanooga, Tennessee.

Chandler gravitated to law enforcement in 1917 when he was appointed the first superintendent of the New York State Police* in 1917. Before resigning six years later to return to his medical practice, he made solid contributions to the fledgling state police force by writing training manuals and developing field policy.

SOURCE: Charles Phillips and Alan Axelrod, *CCC*, 1996.

CHARLEYS. London watchmen became known as Charleys after the reign of Charles I, who has been credited with improving the London night watch* system. Poorly paid and usually rather long in the tooth, these night watchmen were typically individuals who could not find employment elsewhere. During their patrols they were each assigned a specific route, and on the hour, they left their sentry box to see that all was well. In the 1730s the watchmen were often targets of youthful practical jokes. Occasionally bands of young men would espy sleeping Charleys in their sentry boxes and wake them up with loud noises or push their boxes over, trapping them inside. Charleys responded by adopting the use of heavy wooden clubs for protection as well as an assortment of lanterns and rattles* to raise an alarm.

SOURCE: Michael Billett, *Highwaymen and Outlaws*, 1997.

CHEKA, THE. The Cheka was founded in the days following the 1917 October Revolution in Russia and was disbanded in 1922. This repressive police agency, led by Felix Edmundovich Dzerzhinsky,* was called the Cheka, based on the acronym VECHEKA, from the initials of the Russian name for the All-Russian Extraordinary Commission. An offshoot of the military revolutionary committee of the Petrograd Soviet, it was ordered to work closely with the People's Commissariat of Internal Affairs (NKVD)* and the People's Commissariat of Justice. Joseph Stalin once compared the Cheka to the Committee of Public Safety during the French Revolution. It was primarily responsible for tracking down and punishing bandits, black marketeers, terrorists, spies, and counterfeiters. Rather than a prototypical preventative police force, it was more akin to a military-style tribunal assigned to protect the Revolution from enemies of the state. According to one estimate, during the Cheka's four-year reign it executed fifty thousand people and sent thousands to prisons and work camps.

SOURCE: Robert Conquest, ed., *The Soviet Police System*, 1968.

CHENEVIER, CHARLES. (b. 1901) Born in Montelimar, France, the son of a career army officer, Chenevier was drawn to the world of policing at an early age and immersed himself in newspaper and magazine accounts of fabulous police exploits. He attended college and began a journalism career, but in 1925 he decided to live out his childhood fantasies and joined the Sûreté.*

He initially worked with the special railway police, where his talents for criminal investigation were first discovered. Within a few years he was appointed to the judicial branch of the Sûreté, which specialized in more serious offenses, such as murder and robbery. His most famous quarry was Emile Buisson, whom Chenevier arrested in 1938 but who escaped from prison in 1941. He was recaptured and escaped again in 1947, this time from an insane asylum. Buisson led a gang that committed twenty-four robberies between 1947 and 1950, making off with close to sixty million francs. He was also responsible for numerous homicides, mostly witnesses to his crimes. Chenevier led the team that captured Buisson in the early 1950s. (Buisson was executed by guillotine in 1956).

SOURCE: Bruce Henderson and Sam Summerlin, *The Super Sleuths*, 1976.

CHENKIN, GEORGE. (1897–1962) Born in New York City, the diminutive Chenkin was drawn to police work at an early age. At five feet, five inches, he was unable to meet the height requirements of the New York City Police Department (NYPD)* and instead found employment as a parole officer. Chenkin became one of the most respected parole officers of his era. To his credit, he went beyond the call of duty in supervising his charges, and in the process gave a dramatic boost in the amount of parole convictions, which led to a $5,000 bounty being placed on his head. During his tenure as a parole officer Chenkin solved 256 cases, including several murders, narcotics rings, and a movie theater robbery ring.

Following World War II, Chenkin was approached by an insurance company to investigate insurance fraud, and in the subsequent years he became the leading investigator in the field of insurance fraud. By the 1950s he was also investigating cases for the Queens County, New York, district attorney on a regular basis as a special county detective.

SOURCE: Charles Phillips and Alan Axelrod, *CCC*, 1996.

CHEROKEE LIGHTHORSE. In 1808 the Cherokee nation passed a resolution creating a mounted regulator force to suppress horse stealing, robbery, and other criminal acts. A precursor to the lighthorse* units of the Indian Territory, the Cherokee Lighthorse was authorized in November 1844. Composed of a captain, lieutenant, and twenty-four mounted officers, the force was charged with the pursuit and arrest of lawbreakers. However, it would have little impact until after the Civil War as, in the years leading up to the conflict, law enforcement was typically handled by federal sheriffs (see SHERIFF) and their deputies.

The other tribes of the Indian Territory would eventually use the Cherokee Lighthorse as a prototype for creating their own units. The mounted force was often at odds with U.S. law enforcement agencies because of jurisdictional conflicts. However, in the 1870s the lighthorse became more prominent with the passage of treaties giving the Cherokee courts jurisdiction over tribal members. Nonetheless, more serious felonies, such as murder and robbery, remained the responsibility of the court of Judge Isaac Charles Parker* at Fort Smith, Arkansas.

SOURCE: Art Burton, *Black, Red, and Deadly,* 1991.

CHERRILL, FRED. (1892–1964) Born in London, Cherrill developed an interest in fingerprinting* while still in his youth. After a false start pursuing an art degree at Oxford, Cherrill withdrew because of illness. Drawn to police work while sharing a hospital room with a veteran police officer, Cherrill resolved to shift career paths, and in 1914 he was made constable (see CONSTABLES) in the London Metropolitan Police.*

Cherrill quickly became disenchanted with the patrol work but found a more attractive outlet in 1920 when he was able to put his childhood hobby to use after being promoted to the Scotland Yard* fingerprint department. Over the next three decades Cherrill contributed to the developing science of fingerprinting, introducing the single fingerprint method in 1930. Promoted to bureau chief of the fingerprint division in 1938, he retired from that position fifteen years later, having supervised the collection of over two million fingerprints for Scotland Yard.

SOURCE: Charles Phillips and Alan Axelrod, *CCC,* 1996.

CHICAGO DEMOCRATIC CONVENTION RIOTS. *See* WALKER REPORT OF THE CHICAGO DEMOCRATIC CONVENTION.

CHICAGO POLICE DEPARTMENT (CPD). One of America's most storied police departments, the CPD can trace its origins to 1837, when Chicago was first incorporated as a city. The city charter provided for the election of a high constable and the appointment of one constable for each of the city's six wards (see CONSTABLES). By 1850 the city police force was expanded to nine officers. Following the election of Know-Nothing candidate Levi D. Boone to the mayor's office in 1855, more ordinances were passed by the new city council, inaugurating the creation of a police department composed of almost ninety officers. New guidelines by the nativist city council, however, stipulated that policemen had to be American-born, despite the fact that half the city's population was not. As the decade came to a close, the nativist uproar diminished.

To confront a growing crime problem, in 1860 the department created its first detective force, comprised of only the finest officers. As a result, a basic split in the esprit de corps developed between the patrol and detective divisions, which remains today. By 1861 the city had been divided into three police precincts. That same year the state legislature passed into law the creation of a police board as an executive department of the city government. Bypassing the power of the mayor's office, control of the police now lay firmly in the hands of three police commissioners. During this era, the appellation "superintendent of police" was introduced in reference to the head of the police force. The year 1861 also saw the introduction of the police patrol and signal service.

Rampant police corruption in the 1860s convinced the state legislature in 1875 to rescind the 1861 law and return the power over the police to the mayor's office. Henceforth, the mayor would appoint a police commissioner following approval by the city council. Policewomen* were first employed by the department in 1885 when two police matrons* were assigned to each precinct station, mainly to handle female prisoners. In 1884 the CPD created an identification bureau, which set up a rogues' gallery and relied on the Bertillon system.* Although fingerprinting* was introduced to the department in 1905, it would take five years for the Illinois Supreme Court to validate fingerprints as admissible evidence.

The uniforms, equipment, and identification of CPD officers evolved from early leather badges, heavy batons, and precursors to the whistle called "creakers" to the introduction of police uniforms in 1858. Initially, uniforms included a short blue frock coat, a blue navy cap with gold band, and a plain brass star. In 1862, leather badges were replaced by silver stars. In 1904 the badge included the city seal and a number, much like those in current use except smaller.

Although police officers initially walked their beat, they were supplemented by horse-drawn patrol wagons after 1880, and in 1906, as traffic became more congested, a mounted patrol was established, composed of forty men and horses. In 1948 the horse mounted police* force was eliminated, but twenty-six years later it was reintroduced, a reminder of the cyclical nature of police work. The CPD first introduced the automobile in 1906, and within a decade the department was completely motorized. In 1929, one-way radio transmitters were added to several squad cars, leading the department to set up its own radio-broadcasting system the following year.

The police department was completely reorganized following the 1960 "Summerdale Scandals." Mayor Richard Daley appointed a committee, led by Orlando Winfield "O. W." Wilson,* to recommend new methods to improve the CPD and select police superintendents. The committee recommended the creation of a five-member police board, which would nominate candidates for superintendent and provide oversight for other police matters. Wilson was nominated by his fellow committee members to be the next police superintendent. This professor of police administration and dean of the School of Criminology at the University of California accepted the nomination and, over the next seven years, led the transformation of the CPD into a highly centralized organization. Today the 13,000-member force is commanded by Superintendent Terry G. Hillard.

SOURCES: John J. Flinn, *History of the Chicago Police*, 1887; revised, 1973; Raphael W. Marrow and Harriet I. Carter, *In Pursuit of Crime*, 1996.

CHILDS, SIR WYNDHAM. (1876–1946) Born in Cornwall, England, Childs served an apprenticeship under a solicitor before enlisting in the army to fight in the Boer War. He left the military during World War I, but he had already made his mark on the criminal justice system by designing the army's Suspension of Sentences Act, which prevented soldiers from committing crimes in order to be sent back from the frontlines.

Childs was appointed assistant commissioner of police in 1921, and, as commander of the Scotland Yard* Special Branch, was responsible for countering terrorism and espionage. Much of his concentration focused on England's illegal domestic gun trade. Embroiled in controversy, Childs ended his Scotland Yard career in 1928, after only seven years.

SOURCE: Rupert Allason, *The Branch*, 1983.

CHOCTAW LIGHTHORSE. In 1818 lighthorse* police forces were established in each district of the Choctaw Nation, shortly after the tribe was banished to the Indian Territory. The Choctaw Lighthorse was responsible for arresting lawbreakers and settling conflicts between Choctaw factions. According to tribal law, the mounted police served as sheriff,* judge, and jury. Often targeted by the vigilant officers were white whiskey traders. Following apprehension, prisoners were ordered to appear at a designated site for a whipping doled out by the lighthorse. Any murder perpetrated by tribal members resulted in capital punishment administered by a firing squad, much as with the Creek Lighthorse.*

SOURCE: Art Burton, *Black, Red, and Deadly*, 1991.

CHRISTOPHER COMMISSION. In 1991 Los Angeles Mayor Tom Bradley* created an Independent Commission on the Los Angeles Police Department (LAPD)* in the wake of the Rodney King* beating. Chaired by Warren Christopher, the 1991 Christopher Commission report devoted much of its attention to the excessive use of force by the LAPD and recommended that the department abandon the professional model of policing in favor of a community policing approach. The report also concluded that policewomen* were better at averting potential violence than policeman but that male officers still found it difficult to accept their female counterparts because of an emphasis on physical prowess. The Christopher Report recommended hiring more women to alleviate the rising number of brutality complaints by male officers. According to police records, there were no cases of brutality in Los Angeles involving a female officer prior to 1991.

SOURCES: Independent Commission on the Los Angeles Police Department, *Report of the Independent Commission on the Los Angeles Police Department*, July 9, 1991; William P. Bloss, "Police Misconduct: The Rodney King Incident," in *The Encyclopedia of Police Science*, ed. William G. Bailey, 1995.

CHURCHILL, ROBERT. (1886–1958) Following an apprenticeship as a gunsmith, Churchill inherited his own shop in 1910. During his lifetime he introduced scientific ballistics into the Old Bailey (England's most important Crown court, also known as central criminal court) and became one of the leading experts. Churchill became prominent in 1927 when he used a modified microscope to identify the weapon and bullets used in a murder case. The ensuing trial introduced modern ballistics into the criminal courtroom.

SOURCE: Macdonald Hastings, *The Other Mr. Churchill,* 1963.

CHUT CHAI. Chut Chai is Chinese Triad (secret criminal societies) slang for "policeman." Its English translation means "pawn."

SOURCE: Bill Waddell, *The Black Museum,* 1993.

CHUZAISHO. See KOBAN.

CITY OF LONDON POLICE. The City of London Police force remains independent from the London Metropolitan Police.* When the Metropolitan Police Act of 1829* was passed it provided a single police force for the metropolis and proclaimed that policing would cover a radius of approximately seven miles from the town center.

The discomfiting relationship between the London Police Force and the Metropolitan Police, two forces that, common sense argues, should be one and the same, has developed from a centuries-old tradition. The heart of the city of London is about one mile square, with its own lord mayor and aldermen elected by businessmen. Historically, this city corporation was answerable only to the king. The most powerful bankers and traders resided in this quarter and acted as patrons to their supporters in Parliament, whom they expected to look after their best interests in the city of London. Therefore, Sir Robert Peel* was forced to leave the city center out of his police bill, and once more the Metropolitan Police held no jurisdiction in this area.

The police history of London can be traced back to Anglo-Saxon tithings (see TITHING SYSTEM) and sheriffs (see SHERIFF) and to innovations following the Norman conquest of 1066. Prior to the nineteenth century, significant attempts at police regularization were introduced by the Statute of Winchester* in 1285, which commanded cities and towns to establish a watch and ward (see WATCH AND WARD SYSTEM). In 1737 an act of Parliament laid out the duties of night watchmen (see NIGHT WATCH) and constables,* and essentially established the city's first paid police force. In 1832 the London City Force was reorganized, although other unsuccessful attempts at updating the force had been made prior to the passage of the City of London Police Act in 1839.

The City of London Police Act elucidated the regulation of the police force as well as the rights and privileges of the citizens. The boundary between the city of London and Metropolitan London is less easy to recognize than the distinctive uniforms worn by the two police forces. Like its counterpart, the City of London Police operated in a similar manner and maintained sharp discipline; occasionally, the two forces even collaborated with each another.

SOURCE: Philip John Stead, *The Police of Britain*, 1985.

CIZANCKAS, VICTOR I. (1937–1980) Cizanckas was the police chief of Menlo Park, California, in 1977 when he was selected to head up the Stamford, Connecticut, police force, an agency rife with corruption and graft. In order to protect him from political influence, he was given his position "for life." Although he would tragically die in his sleep three years later, during his tenure Cizanckas made great strides in cleaning up the agency by forcing implicated officers to retire early; eliminating the traffic division, which was the main source of police corruption; and hiring citizens to man non–law enforcement positions such as dispatcher and mail clerk. Despite the opposition of the patrolman's union, Cizanckas successfully implemented his reform agenda.

SOURCE: Charles Phillips and Alan Axelrod, *CCC*, 1996.

CLARKE, GEORGE C. (1826–1846) Mysteriously murdered on June 29, 1846, Constable George Clarke had been posted to the Four Wants beat on the outskirts of London, a hotbed of criminal activity. After he failed to show up the next morning following his rounds, a search party found his mutilated corpse in a potato orchard. Clarke had been viciously assaulted, having had his forefinger cut off and his head nearly severed from his shoulders. His weapons were found broken nearby, indicating a furious struggle. An investigation uncovered discrepancies in the stories given by his fellow police squad colleagues, and several were soon taken into custody. Although the suspected constables* were acquitted due to lack of evidence, they were nonetheless cashiered from the force. The crime was never solved.

SOURCES: John Lock, *Dreadful Deeds and Awful Murders*, 1990; Paul Begg and Keith Skinner, *The Scotland Yard Files*, 1992.

CLARKE, JOHN R. (c. 1885–1982) When Clarke died in 1982, he was the last surviving member of the Arizona Rangers.* Originally a blacksmith and cowhand, he joined the Rangers in 1906 but quit in 1908, citing political infighting. He returned to cattle punching and then worked for a bus company in Fresno, California, for thirty years.

SOURCES: Bill O'Neal, *The Arizona Rangers*, 1987; Dan L. Thrapp, ed., *EFB*, Vol. 1, 1988.

CLARKE, WILLIAM JAMES. Soon after arriving in South Africa at the age of eighteen, Clarke joined the Natal Mounted Police* and distinguished himself in the Zulu War. A student of police history, he recommended the merging of all South African Police (SAP)* forces into a single entity, in much the same way as Sir Charles Rowan* had created the London Metropolitan Police* in 1829. He also argued for the creation of a criminal investigation department (CID).* His suggestions provided the groundwork for what would become Act Number 1 of 1894, better known as the "Police Act." In 1902 he visited Scotland Yard* and is credited with gaining enough expertise to introduce fingerprinting* to South African policing. Clarke left CID to accept the position of assistant commissioner and then, in 1906, chief commissioner of police. During his eleven years with CID, his most perplexing case was the disappearance of Gustave Labistour, the attorney general of Natal, during a hunting trip. Although Clarke concluded that crocodiles probably killed Labistour, the case was left open because of unanswered questions.

SOURCE: Alan F. Hattersley, *The First South African Detectives*, 1960.

CLEMENTS, EMMANUEL, JR. (1869–1908) The son of Western cowman and gunman Emmanuel Clements Sr., "Manny" Clements was raised in Runnels County, Texas. He was a cousin of John Wesley Hardin, and his sister was married to "Killin' " Jim Miller. Clements worked as a deputy under Sheriff William David Allison* in Pecos City, Texas, before moving to El Paso in 1894, where he was appointed deputy constable (see CONSTABLES) and then deputy sheriff.* Clements was ambushed by a former Pecos City constable named Joe Brown in an El Paso saloon. According to some reports, his killing was in retaliation for Clements's blackmailing of Albert Fall over his complicity in the killing of Patrick Floyd Jarvis "Pat" Garrett.* Others suggest it was over a personal affair between Clements and his killer, who was working as a bartender in the saloon. No one was ever charged in the slaying.

SOURCES: Leon Metz, *Pat Garrett*, 1974; Dan L. Thrapp, ed., *EFB*, Vol. 1, 1988.

CLUM, JOHN PHILIP. (1851–1932) Born outside Claverack, New York, Clum attended Rutgers College briefly before moving to New Mexico, where he served as a weather observer. In 1874 he was appointed as an Indian agent and posted to the San Carlos Apache Reservation in Arizona. According to most accounts, Clum created the Indian police* concept. The Indian police were usually formerly employed army scouts. Unlike the stereotypical corrupt Indian agent, Clum is credited with having been fairly evenhanded. Clum rose to prominence in 1877 when he brought Apache leader Geronimo back to the reservation. He resigned his position that same year and eventually arrived in Tombstone, Arizona, where he founded the famous *Tombstone Epitaph* newspaper. A supporter of Wyatt Earp* during the controversial O.K. Corral incident, Clum left Tombstone in 1882 and later met up again with Wyatt Earp while working as a postal inspector during the Alaskan gold rush. He joined Earp again in retirement in Los Angeles, where he died of a heart attack in 1932.

SOURCES: Woodworth Clum, *Apache Agent: The Story of John P. Clum*, 1936; Dan L. Thrapp, ed., *EFB*, Vol. 1, 1988.

COBB, GAIL A. (d. 1974) Washington, D.C., police officer Gail Cobb was killed while attempting to apprehend a bank robbery suspect, becoming the first African-American policewoman killed in the line of duty.

SOURCE: Craig W. Floyd and Kelley Lang Helms, eds., *To Serve and Protect*, 1995.

COETZEE, JOHANN. (b. 1929) Raised in rural South Africa, Coetzee entered law enforcement as a member of the mounted police in 1946. He later enlisted in the security police and worked clandestinely to infiltrate the Communist party in South Africa. Coetzee stood out due to his erudition. An expert on communism and ancient Greek philosophy, his doctoral dissertation in political science was a study of Leon Trotsky.

Coetzee was appointed South African commissioner of police in 1983, a position that had traditionally been selected from the members of the Security Police. As head of the 44,000-member police force, Coetzee was responsible for enforcing the apartheid system. Under his command the police department earned a reputation for brutality in its quest to preserve South Africa's segregationist hierarchy. In 1985 Coetzee was given emergency powers, allowing his secret police to embark on a campaign of intimidation, mass detention, torture, and assassination. With the collapse of apartheid in 1991, he left the police service and, since the ascendence of Nelson Mandela, has not returned to law enforcement.

SOURCE: Charles Phillips and Alan Axelrod, *CCC*, 1996.

COINTELPRO. COINTELPRO was a clandestine Federal Bureau of Investigation (FBI)* program established along the lines of a "department of misinformation" in order to create a climate of confusion among the myriad left-wing organizations in America during the 1960s. A special target was the Black Panther party. However, under the administration of FBI director William H. Webster* in the 1980s, this type of secret police tactics was diminished, if not discarded.

SOURCE: Athan G. Theoharis, ed., *The FBI*, 1999.

COLBURN, WAYNE B. (1907–1983) A twenty-five-year police veteran, Colburn was selected as U.S. marshal for the southern district of California in 1962. Eight years later he was appointed head of the U.S. Marshals Service* after controversial director Carl Turner was forced to resign. During his six-year tenure, Colburn reformed the once scandal-plagued organization and deflected criticism in its handling of the 1973 Native American Indian protests at the Wounded Knee Siege* in South Dakota.

Among Colburn's primary goals was obtaining bureau status for the U.S. Marshals Service to place it on the same level as other law enforcement agencies within the Department of Justice. After several years of lobbying, Colburn's efforts paid off in 1973 following the resignation of his antagonist Attorney General John Mitchell. The impetus for the change in status was provided by the professional response of the U.S. marshals during the American Indian Movement occupation of Wounded Knee, the longest civil uprising since the Civil War.

Colburn's restructuring of the U.S. Marshals Service hinged on the creation the Special Operations Group (SOG) in 1971 in response to the civil disturbances of the previous decade. The unit was composed of an elite force of one hundred specially trained deputies who would be available in the event of civil or national emergencies. SOG exemplified the image of the paramilitary model of policing and would pay dividends with its patient handling of the Wounded Knee occupation in 1973. During the seventy-one-day siege, two Indians were killed and one marshal was paralyzed by a gunshot wound. Colburn continued to update and professionalize the U.S. Marshals Service over his last three years before retiring in 1976.

SOURCES: Frederick S. Calhoun, *The Lawmen: United States Marshals and Their Deputies, 1789–1989*, 1991; Charles Phillips and Alan Axelrod, *CCC*, 1996.

COLDBATH FIELDS RIOT. In the early 1830s the London Metropolitan Police* became embroiled in several controversies. In 1833 the force came under fire from Parliament for its use of brutal tactics during a public demonstration organized by the National Political Union at Coldbath Fields. The subsequent clash between the police and the Political Union supporters is considered the first major melee between the police and a London mob. The prime minister had ordered that, if the demonstration took place, the ringleaders should be arrested. However, things got out of control quickly and Sir Charles Rowan* led several baton charges* (see BATON CHARGE, ORIGINS OF) into the rock-throwing mob. Three policemen were stabbed, one fatally. It would seem that the force had yet to win the support of the public since the following trial exonerated those charged with the officer's death, rendering a verdict of justifiable homicide. It would not be long, however, before the Metropolitan Police would become one of the most exalted police forces in the world.

SOURCE: T. A. Critchley, *A History of Police in England and Wales*, 1967.

COLD STORAGE. This term refers to unlawful incommunicado imprisonment. During the 1920s and 1930s, Philadelphia's police force was a known practitioner of this incarnation of the third degree.* This method involved constant interrogation of prisoners in between stints in solitary confinement. The duration of confinement reportedly ranged from a week to a month.

SOURCE: Ernest Jerome Hopkins, *Our Lawless Police*, 1931.

COLEMAN, WILLIAM TELL. (1824–1893) Born in Kentucky, Coleman's father was a prominent legislator and reportedly distantly related to George Washington. Coleman arrived in Sacramento, California, in 1849 but the following year he relocated to San Francisco, where he established his mercantile business, William T. Coleman & Company. Over the next few years he became one of the city's leading importers.

San Francisco faced a growing crime problem during the social and economic upheaval that accompanied the gold rush. The police force proved ineffective in the face of such highly organized criminal enterprises as the notorious Hounds. Aspiring to bring law and order to the Bay City, in 1851 Coleman organized the first San Francisco Vigilance Committee.* This vigilante committee was short-lived, but five years later a new outbreak of violence led to the formation of another Committee of Vigilance. As leader of the committee, Coleman organized twenty-five armed groups of vigilantes and was instrumental in activity that led to the public hanging of several prisoners.

Coleman once again led a vigilance group in 1877, organizing almost six thousand men into the "Pick Handle Brigade." Armed with pick handles, they attempted to put an end to the anti-Chinese fervor sweeping San Francisco. Through his vigilante leadership, Coleman reached national prominence, and in 1884 he was even mentioned as a presidential candidate. However, a series of business failures sent him into bankruptcy. To his credit, while he was only responsible for paying less than half his debt to creditors, he paid them back in full before his death. He was referred to as the "Lion of the Vigilantes" by Robert Louis Stevenson, and author James A. B. Scherer borrowed the phrase as the title for his 1939 biography of Coleman.

SOURCES: Robert M. Senkewicz, *Vigilantes in Gold Rush San Francisco*, 1985; James A. B. Scherer, *Lion of the Vigilantes*, 1939.

COLLINS, BEN. (d. 1906) While his early life is clouded in obscurity, Collins came into prominence when he became the first Native American selected to serve as a U.S. marshal (see U.S. MARSHALS SERVICE) in the Indian Territory (later Oklahoma). Following a stint as marshal, Collins was appointed deputy U.S. marshal for Emet, Oklahoma. Collins's meteoric rise faced its greatest hurdle when he was ordered to arrest Port Pruitt, one of the area's leading citizens. An ensuing gunfight left Pruitt crippled for life. Vowing revenge, Pruitt hired noted assassin "Killin' " Jim Miller to assassinate Collins. Miller lived up to his moniker on August 1, 1906, when he shotgunned Collins to death at close range in front of his wife.

SOURCE: Jay Robert Nash, *EWLO*, 1994.

COLQUHOUN, PATRICK. (1745–1820) Born in Scotland, Colquhoun moved to America for several years before returning to Glasgow. He was elected chief magistrate in 1782 before moving to London in 1789, where he was made justice of the peace* in 1792. Colquhoun became interested in police reform through the work of the Fielding brothers (see FIELDING, SIR HENRY; FIELDING, SIR JOHN) and, after detailed discussions with English philosopher and criminal justice reformer Jeremy Bentham, set to work on *Treatise on the Police of the Metropolis*, which was published in 1797. Among the important police concepts introduced in the book was the idea of crime prevention, a radical departure for the traditionally reactive police establishment. Colquhoun was perhaps one of the greatest influences on Sir Robert Peel,* credited with creating the first modern police force in 1829.

Colquhoun was also credited with the creation of the Thames River Police in 1789. In 1800, his *Treatise on the Commerce and Police of the River Thames* saw publication. His writings led to improved police professionalism and the first systematic examination of crime costs and origins. An advocate of paid professional policing and of recruitment and management under a central authority free of political interference, he spurred police reform and introduced new solutions to maintaining public order in an era of urbanization and industrialization. Colquhoun retired in 1818, two years before his death.

SOURCES: David Yates Grant, *A Biographical Sketch of the Life and Writings of Patrick Colquhoun*, 1818; David R. Johnson, *American Law Enforcement: A History*, 1981.

COLT .45. The Colt .45 revolver was invented in 1837 by Samuel Colt (1814–1862). Prior to the 1830s, peace officers relied on nightsticks and unwieldy muskets to enforce the law. Despite forming a company to manufacture the weapon, Colt found few lawmen outside the Texas Rangers,* interested in purchasing his product. The Colt .45 proved so popular among Texas Rangers during the Mexican War that General Zachary Taylor convinced the army to order one thousand revolvers. Its association with the mounted Rangers and the successful resolution of the war increased the Colt's popularity and led to its acceptance among fighting men in the army and in law enforcement. By 1860 it had become the weapon of choice among Western lawmen and remained so until the introduction of the .38 caliber Smith and Wesson in the twentieth century.

SOURCE: Jack Rohan, *Yankee Arms Maker: The Story of Sam Colt and His Six-Shot Peacemaker*, 1953.

CONLIN, PETER. (1841–1905) Born in New York City, Conlin was a member of the Twelfth New York Regiment and then the Irish Brigade during the Civil War. Conlin joined the New York City Police Department (NYPD)* in 1869 and was promoted to roundsman* (see ROUNDSMEN) three years later, steadily rising through the ranks to become inspector in 1889. Conlin was appointed acting chief of police in 1895, replacing Thomas F. Byrnes,* who had been forced out by scandal and the investigation headed by Clarence Lexow.* In October of that year he reported to the police board that liquor dealers were in full compliance with the Sunday liquor law. What was most noteworthy about this was that it was the first time in the history of the force that a chief of police offered his supervisors an accounting of his stewardship. In December of 1895 Conlin was named permanent chief of police with the support of police commissioner Theodore Roosevelt.* He retired in 1897.

SOURCES: James F. Richardson, *The New York Police*, 1970; H. Paul Jeffers, *Commissioner Roosevelt*, 1994.

CONLISK, JAMES B., JR. (1899–1984) The scion of a police officer, Conlisk was born in Illinois. He achieved his dream of joining the Chicago Police Department (CPD)* in 1946 and rose through the ranks until appointed superintendent by Mayor Richard J. Daley twenty-one years later. During the turbulent 1960s Conlisk and the Chicago police became a popular target for the national media and the liberal establishment. Criticism reached a crescendo during the "police riot" at the 1968 Chicago Democratic National Convention.

During the convention proceedings, thousands of antiwar demonstrators were drawn to Chicago. With the support, and probably under the direction, of Mayor Daley, the protests degenerated into a riot as the news media chronicled Chicago police officers chasing down and indiscriminately beating numerous demonstrators. Although Conlisk weathered the subsequent inquiry, he was forced to resign in 1973 following the indictment of dozens of officers for criminal impropriety.

SOURCE: Charles Phillips and Alan Axelrod, *CCC*, 1996.

CONNELLEY, EARL J. (b. 1892) Born in Columbus, Ohio, Connelley served in the army during World War I before earning his law degree. In 1920 he joined the Federal Bureau of Investigation (FBI),* and seven years later he was elevated to special agent in charge of the St. Louis, Missouri, field office. During his thirty-four-year career he worked in a variety of field offices and on numerous high-profile cases, including the 1948 Alger Hiss Case. During the 1930s he pursued gangsters as a member of the "flying squad," and in the 1940s he directed counterespionage strategy. In 1940 John Edgar Hoover* promoted Connelley to assistant director of major investigations in the field. He retired in 1954.

SOURCE: Athan G. Theoharis, ed., *The FBI*, 1999.

CONNELLY, CHARLES T. (1845–1892) Born in Indiana, Connelly relocated to Kansas following the Civil War. A teacher and the town marshal, Connelly was killed by Grattan Dalton during the famous Dalton raid on Coffeyville, Kansas.

SOURCE: Robert Barr Smith, *Daltons! The Raid on Coffeyville*, 1996.

CONNOR, THEOPHILUS EUGENE "BULL." (1897–1973) Born in Selma, Alabama, Connor was the second of five children. As a young boy he was acccidentally blinded in one eye when a friend shot him with an air rifle. Connor rose to prominence as a segregationist police commissioner in Birmingham, Alabama, during the civil rights era of the 1950s and 1960s. First elected police commissioner of Birmingham in 1937, he served four consecutive terms before stepping down in 1953 to run unsuccessfully for political office. Returning to police commissioner in 1958, Connor rose to national prominence in the spring of 1963 when he authorized the use of power hoses and police dogs against black demonstrators led by Martin Luther King Jr. on the streets of Birmingham. Connor refused to protect the "Freedom Riders," resulting in numerous high-profile incidents of race violence. After watching television reports of the Birmingham incident, President John F. Kennedy reportedly turned to an aide and commented: "The civil rights movement should thank God for Bull Connor. He helped it as much as Abraham Lincoln." That same year Connor was ousted as police commissioner, ending twenty-two years in this position, but he continued his anti–civil rights crusade as president of the Alabama Service Commission, his first successful statewide bid for office.

SOURCE: William A. Nunnelley, *Bull Connor*, 1991.

CONNOR, THOMAS. (1906–1997) Connor grew up in Washington, D.C., where he received his law degree at Catholic University. While working his way through law school he caught the eye of John Edgar Hoover,* who convinced him to join the Federal Bureau of Investigation* (FBI)* upon his graduation in 1932. Connor had initially longed for a baseball career but he never rose higher than the high minor leagues, so he jettisoned his dreams for law in 1929. When Hoover found out about Connor's baseball abilities he hired him with the intention of winning the government league championship.

In 1932 Connor led the FBI team to the championship, and in the process became a Hoover favorite. For the meantime, Connor was assigned to discuss sports with Hoover, a noted sports fan, for an hour each week. When the baseball team finished in second place the following year, Connor was reassigned to the Midwest, where he pursued Depression-era desperadoes such as "Pretty Boy" Floyd, "Baby Face" Nelson, and the Barker gang.

Connor was among the eighteen agents hunting the elusive John Dillinger in July 1934. He was positioned in an alley at the side entrance of the Biograph Theater the night John Dillinger was killed and did not see the actual shooting, although he did espy the unidentified woman who dipped her handkerchief in Dillinger's blood for a souvenir. Ironically, the description of the quarry was almost an exact description of Connor, who narrowly escaped with his life when he attracted the attention of several Chicago policemen that night. Fortunately, he was able to convince them of his identity.

In November 1934 Connor took part in the hunt for Baby Face Nelson and was present for Nelson's demise, but only after he had killed three agents, including a close friend of Connor. Connor resigned from the FBI in 1935 after three stress-filled years that must have seemed like a lifetime. He went on to work for Naval Intelligence during World War II and then served eighteen years with the Central Intelligence Agency (CIA) before joining Radio Free Europe as a supervisor. ·

SOURCE: Robert Thomas Jr., "Thomas Connor, 91, Last of FBI's Dillinger Detail," *New York Times*, April 21, 1997.

CONSER, PETER. (1852–1934) The son of a white trader and a Choctaw woman, Conser was born Peter Coinson near Eagletown, Oklahoma. In 1862 he left the Indian Territory with Confederate forces following the invasion by federal troops. He settled on the Red River near the Texas border for the remaining years of the conflict. In 1877 he was appointed deputy sheriff (see SHERIFF) in Sugar Loaf County and then joined the Choctaw Lighthorse* as captain in the Moshulatubbee District. Conser served with distinction with the Lighthorse and was credited with maintaining the integrity of the unit after it was stripped of its judicial powers.

SOURCE: Art Burton, *Black, Red, and Deadly*, 1991.

CONSTABLES. The word *constable* is derived from the Latin *comes stabuli*, which means "head of the stables." Roman constables, really just glorified servants, were given this moniker because they had demonstrated honesty while protecting the royal stables. By the time of the Norman invasion of Britain in 1066, however, the position of constable had become a position of high prestige under the French kings.

The constable became more identifiable as a peacekeeping officer in England following the Norman era. Tasks included collecting taxes, arresting malefactors, transporting prisoners, and serving legal papers. The position of constable was brought to the American colonies in the early 1600s, where constables were responsible for regulating weights and measures, surveying land, and delivering warrants. Early records credit Joshua Pratt of the Plymouth Colony in 1634 as the first constable in America.

Early American constables were required to supervise the watch and ward system* (night and day police). Constables were most in evidence in more populous cities such as New York City, where Jacob Hays* carved out a forty-year career as high constable. Constables have diminished in importance in the law enforcement network, and in 1976 the word *Police* was dropped from the title of the National Police Constables Association, which is now headquartered in Pennsylvania.

SOURCE: National Constables Association, "Constable," in *Encyclopedia of Police Science*, ed. William G. Bailey, 1995.

CONTINENTAL OP, THE. Created by former Pinkerton's National Detective Agency* operative and mystery writer (Samuel) Dashiell Hammett,* the Continental Op is a nameless detective employed by San Francisco's Continental Detective Agency. As Hammett's first private eye,* the Continental Op served as the model for Sam Spade and the other detective heroes that would follow. As one of Hammett's earliest major literary endeavors and a precursor of the "tough guy" school of detective fiction, the Op solves many cases based on Hammett's short-lived career with the Pinkertons. However, the Op himself was probably inspired by Hammett's former boss, James Wright of the agency's Baltimore office. The Continental Op appears in eleven books published between 1929 and 1962.

SOURCE: Chris Steinbrunner and Otto Penzler, *EMD*, 1976.

COOK, DAVID J. (1842–1907) Born in Indiana, Cook was drawn west in 1859, where he joined the Colorado cavalry during the Civil War. During his military career he demonstrated detective skills that were put to use tracking smugglers, spies, and deserters. Following the war he was elected city marshal of Denver, and in 1869 he was elected Arapaho County sheriff.* Cook rose to prominence after he captured the Musgrove-Franklin gang in 1868, leading to his appointment as deputy U.S. marshal (see U.S. MARSHALS SERVICE).

He returned to the military in 1873 when he was appointed major general of the Colorado militia. Over the next decade he successfully responded to riots and civil disorder, most notably during the 1880 Chinese riot. While his name does not conjure up the deeds of Wyatt Berry Stapp Earp* or James Butler "Wild Bill" Hickok,* Cook's record as a lawman should have overshadowed them, as he arrested more than three thousand culprits while finding time to write one of the most engaging accounts of a Western lawman in *Hands Up! or Twenty Years of Detective Work in the Mountains and on the Plains*, published in 1897. Like most autobiographies it suffers historically when placed under a microscope, but it is still considered a frontier classic. Cook was physically impressive at six feet, three inches, tall. During his career, he was criticized for losing several prisoners to lynch mobs.

SOURCES: Carl Sifakis, *The Encyclopedia of American Crime*, 1982; D. J. Cook, *Hands Up!*, with introduction by Everett L. DeGolyer Jr., reprint, 1971.

COOK, THALIS T. (1858–1918) Born in Uvalde County, Texas, Cook left Bible study in 1874 to join Company F of the Texas Rangers* Frontier Battalion. Suffering from epilepsy, he left the Rangers in 1879 and turned to ranching. In 1889 he returned to the Rangers for a brief stint and then accepted the position of deputy under Sheriff* James Buchanan Gillett* in Brewster County. Cook survived numerous gunfights, including one in which he was shot through the kneecap by Fine Gilliland in 1891. As legend has it, his leg did not heal properly, so Cook had a doctor break it and then set it so he could ride a horse more comfortably. He continued his law enforcement career until the turn of the century.

SOURCES: Robert W. Stephens, *Texas Ranger Sketches*, 1972; Ed Bartholomew, *Biographical Album of Western Gunfighters*, 1958.

COOLEY, SCOTT. (1852–1876) A native Texan, Cooley joined the Texas Rangers* for a brief stint with Captain Cicero Perry's D Company, but he resigned in 1875 and turned to farming. Later that year he killed and scalped Deputy Sheriff John Worley, precipitating the Mason County War. This feud matched German cattlemen against their Texan counterparts, with whom Cooley was affiliated. Cooley blamed the lawman for allowing the Germans to lynch a friend of his who had been in the local jail. The former Ranger killed several others and was able to evade several manhunts because his former Ranger colleagues kept him apprised of the posses' whereabouts. Cooley died in Blanco County in 1876, either from poison or brain fever.

SOURCES: James B. Gillett, *Six Years With the Texas Rangers*, 1925; Dan L. Thrapp, ed., *EFB*, Vol. 1, 1988.

COOPER, IRA. (d. 1939) Credited as the "most significant African-American police officer" of his era, Cooper was initially hired as a "Negro special" by the St. Louis Police Department in 1906. The first college-educated policeman on the force, Cooper earned accolades as one of its most distinguished crime fighters during his tenure on the force, and if not for the color barrier, probably would have become chief of police. Among his greatest accomplishments were the cracking of a 1917 bank embezzlement case and the 1930 solution of the Jacob Hoffman kidnapping along with the subsequent exposure of a local kidnapping ring. In 1911 he became prominent for courageously facing down a lynch mob intent on hanging a prisoner. His achievements led to his inclusion in *Who's Who in Colored America* and to his elevation to sergeant, the first African-American on the force to do so. He later was promoted to lieutenant and put in charge of a unit of black detectives.

SOURCE: W. Marvin Dulaney, *Black Police in America*, 1996.

COOPING. The term *cooping* refers to police officers sleeping on duty. According to a New York City study conducted in 1969, the custom was so prevalent that officers brought alarm clocks and pillows to work. While the term is most identified with New York City, the problem is widespread and known by different euphemisms in other cities. It is "holing" in Boston and "huddling" in Washington, D.C., while Atlanta police search for "pits" to catch some rest. This problem is as old as policing, and there is plenty of evidence that night watchmen (see NIGHT WATCH; WATCH AND WARD SYSTEM) in the colonial era were practitioners. One critic of two-man squad cars suggests that this is a recipe for cooping, since one officer can drive while the other sleeps.

SOURCE: Carl Sifakis, *The Encyclopedia of American Crime*, 1982.

COP. The earliest reference to the word "cop" as synonymous for police officer can be found in "A Hundred Stretches Hence" (1859) by George W. Matsell.* It is also possible the word *copper** was shortened to *cop* after 1846. Many references to *cop* can be found in the 1860s, including *copp* in Horatio Alger's *Ragged Dick* (1867). In 1885 Augustine Costello noted, in *Our Police Protectors*, that in the 1840s the wearing of a star-shaped copper shield led to the use of the word *cop*, although this is not substantiated by any contemporary literary references.

SOURCES: Augustine E. Costello, *Our Police Protectors*, 1885; reprint, 1972; J. E. Lighter, *Historical Dictionary of American Slang*, Vol. 1, 1994.

COPPER. According to Burchfield's *Oxford English Dictionary Supplement*, the term *copper* as a pejorative word for police officer can be traced back to 1846 when it first appeared in the February 21 issue of the *National Police Gazette*.

SOURCE: J. L. Lighter, *Historical Dictionary of American Slang*, Vol. 1, 1994.

CORDES, JOHN H. F. (1890–1966) The first New York City police officer to win two Medals of Honor, Cordes, nicknamed the "Dutchman," joined the department after taking the police exam on a bet in 1915. During his more than three decades on the force, the enigmatic Cordes carved out an unrivaled reputation for humanitarianism and courage under fire.

He was awarded his first Medal of Honor in 1923, when he interrupted a drugstore robbery in progress. During the ensuing struggle the off-duty police officer subdued the two perpetrators, suffering five gunshot wounds in the process, including two from a police officer who mistakenly shot him in the face. Following this shoot-out Cordes never carried a gun on duty again.

Cordes eschewed traditional methods of policing, often preferring to work alone in disguise. At five feet ten inches and less than 150 pounds, Cordes possessed a boyish countenance. In 1927 he won his second medal when the unarmed Cordes was wounded while apprehending two kidnappers.

In 1931 Cordes assisted officer John "Johnny" Broderick* in the capture of a cop killer, "Two Gun Crowley." The "Dutchman" was a complex individual, who never avoided the use of violence but at the same time did not carry a revolver and reportedly helped find jobs for men he arrested after they left prison. He retired in 1949, having risen to acting lieutenant of detectives.

SOURCES: *New Yorker*, September 5, 1953; September 12, 1953; Charles Phillips and Alan Axelrod, *CCC*, 1996; Thomas A. Reppetto, *The Blue Parade*, 1978.

COSSACKS. Inaugurated in 1905, the Pennsylvania State Police* quickly became unpopular among nonnativeborn Pennsylvanians, local peace officers, and civil libertarians as they brutally suppressed labor strikes and conducted search and seizure operations in immigrant communities. Inspired by military models of policing such as the Royal Irish Constabulary* and the Philippines Constabulary,* the ranks were filled by nativeborn Americans with military experience. With the rising social and industrial order during the first decade of the twentieth century, Pennsylvania Governor Samuel Whitaker Pennypacker* gave the state police carte blanche to stem the tide of union strikes. In one notable incident, troopers shot twenty strikers in Mount Carmel only to be exonerated by the governor. During its first decade of existence, the new force was referred to by critics as the Cossacks.

SOURCES: Thomas A. Reppetto, *The Blue Parade*, 1978; Katherine Mayo, *Justice to All*, 1917.

COSTELLO, AUGUSTINE. Costello was a former Irish revolutionary who became a New York City police reporter in the 1880s. He is best remembered for *Our Police Protectors* (1885), his reverent study of the New York City Police Department. On one memorable occasion Alexander S. "Clubber" Williams* became miffed when he was apprised that Costello had named him as the source for the term *tenderloin** and even though Costello had been well-praised for the earlier publication of his book, Williams brought him back to the station, where he was beaten with brass knuckles. Despite his rude treatment at the hands of the police, in 1891 Costello wrote another respectful treatment of a police force, *History of the Police Department of Jersey City*.

SOURCE: Thomas A. Reppetto, *The Blue Parade*, 1978.

COURTRIGHT, TIMOTHY ISAIAH "LONG-HAIRED JIM." (1845–1887) Born in rural Illinois, Courtright fought in the Union Army for General John A. Logan during the Civil War, beginning a lifelong friendship. Following the war Courtright served as an army scout in Texas, Arizona, and New Mexico before entering law enforcement by winning election as city marshal of Fort Worth, Texas, in 1876. During his tenure as city marshal he led a posse in pursuit of noted outlaw Sam Bass. Courtright was pressured to resign in 1879 for drinking too much.

Courtright moved to the mining camp of Lake Valley, New Mexico, in 1883 and found employment as a mine guard, but after killing two ranchers he fled with a five-hundred-dollar reward on his head to Fort Worth, where he began his own detective agency. Captured and acquitted three years later in Socorro, New Mexico, Courtright reopened his T.I.C. Commercial Detective Agency in Fort Worth for a brief spell before closing down to pursue a different money-making strategy: supplying protection to various vice interests. Saloon owner

Luke Short's failure to pay his share led to their gunfight, in which Courtright was killed. Short was exonerated.

SOURCES: F. Stanley, *Longhair Jim Courtright: Two Gun Marshal of Fort Worth*, 1957; Ed Bartholomew, *Biographical Album of Western Gunfighters*, 1958.

COWLEY, SAMUEL P. (1899–1934) Born in Franklin, Idaho, following Mormon missionary work in Hawaii Cowley earned a law degree from George Washington University in 1923. The following year he joined the Federal Bureau of Investigation (FBI)* and, over the next four years, served in the Los Angeles; Detroit; Washington, D.C.; Butte Montana; and Salt Lake City, Utah; field Offices. In 1934 Cowley was assigned to direct the pursuit of the John Dillinger gang in the Midwest. Promoted to inspector, he led the FBI's "flying squad," which, in the Depression era, was charged with pursuing roving gangs of gangsters. Cowley led the hunts for the kidnappers of wealthy businessman Edward Bremer and the Kansas City Massacre* gunmen and was credited with killing Charles Arthur "Pretty Boy" Floyd.

On November 27, 1934, Cowley met his untimely end. He and special agent Herman E. Hollis were tipped off to the whereabouts of the killers of fellow agent W. Carter Baum.* Almost immediately after arriving at the scene, Cowley and Hollis were gunned down as they left their car to pursue Lester "Baby Face Nelson" Gillis's gang members Although mortally wounded, both agents continued to fire at the bandits, and in the process killed Gillis. Hollis died at the scene, and Cowley succumbed to his wounds the next day.

In a postscript to this story, after Chicago Special Agent Melvin Purvis* incurred the wrath of John Edgar Hoover * because of his growing popularity after the killing of John Dillinger at the Biograph Theater, Hoover attempted to diminish Purvis's accomplishment by giving credit to Cowley for planning the campaign that ended Dillinger's career.

SOURCES: Athan G. Theoharis, *The FBI*, 1999; Curt Gentry, *J. Edgar Hoover: The Man and His Secrets*, 1991.

COZZER. Derived from the Hebrew word *chazer*, which means pig, this slang for *policeman* was used by English barrow boys after the 1930s.

SOURCE: Bill Waddell, *The Black Museum*, 1993.

CRANE, STEPHEN. (1871–1900) In September 1896, Crane was beaten up by the aggressive police detective and future death row inmate Charles Becker.* An habitué of prostitutes, Crane came to the aid of a prostitute who was being harassed by police. In the resulting melee, Crane was assaulted and then pressed police brutality charges against the burly Becker. Becker was exonerated when Crane's fondness for opium and prostitutes was introduced into evidence. Uncomfortable now that his foibles had become public knowledge and eager to escape the eye of the law, Crane left New York City soon after the incident.

SOURCE: R. W. Stallman, *Stephen Crane*, 1968.

CREEK LIGHTHORSE. The Creek Lighthorse horse mounted police* enforced laws according to the tribal law code adopted in 1840. For the most part the force was charged with enforcing judgments handed down by the Creek town councils in the Indian Territory. However, it was not until the 1860s that it was actually designated as lighthorse. Among its most important tasks was the suppression of the liquor trade and of horse stealing. Each of the six Creek districts was furnished with a company of lighthorse composed of one officer and four privates, each elected to two-year terms. The Creek Lighthorse was prominent in the capture of the Buck gang.

SOURCE: Art Burton, *Black, Red, and Deadly*, 1991.

CRIMINAL INVESTIGATION DEPARTMENT (CID). The largest and best known branch of Scotland Yard,* the CID was established in 1878 as a special branch that would lead the police force in its transition into a new era of scientific crime fighting. This branch of the Yard developed extensive criminal files, a forensic laboratory, and a fraud squad, and used fingerprinting* and photography. Later it introduced a detective school.

The CID grew out of one of Scotland Yard's most embarrassing moments. The precursor to the CID was called the Detective Branch, and in 1877 three out of its four chief inspectors were found guilty of corruption following a trial at the Old Bailey. The Home Office, a government department responsible for internal affairs in England and Wales, directed an inquiry, which resulted in the groundwork for the new detective branch called the Criminal Investigation Department.

As director of criminal investigations, Sir Howard Vincent* initially led the department and directed its early reorganization. In 1884 Vincent formed a Special Irish Branch of the CID to combat Irish terrorists. In time it evolved into what is now known as the Special Branch. In the early years there was tension between the detectives of CID and the uniformed police because the detectives were paid more and had a better pension plan. The public also opposed the clandestine nature of the plainclothes officers* squad. Starting out with 250 men, the force more than tripled in size during its first six years. By the 1960s it employed more than 1,700 officers.

SOURCES: Bill Waddell, *The Black Museum: New Scotland Yard*, 1993; Paul Begg and Keith Skinner, *The Scotland Yard Files*, 1992.

CROSNE, LOUIS THIROUX DE. (1739–1794) Born in Paris, Crosne had served as a judge, a royal proctor, and intendant (see INTENDANCE OF PO-

LICE) of a province when he was appointed fourteenth, and last, lieutenant-general of police* of Paris in 1785. Shortly after assuming power, Crosne requested additional funding for the police. Among his most pressing concerns was increasing the number of sanitation inspectors and expanding the system of paid informants. Crosne intended to improve life in Paris by concentrating more focus on functions that had been previously neglected, such as waste removal and intelligence gathering. In addition, he requested funds to increase the number of guardposts and fire stations.

During his four-year stint, traditional officials of the ancien régime, including the lieutenant-general, inspectors, and knight of the watch, were discarded as Paris attempted to cope with social disorder, including mobs breaking into the prisons and looting the markets. Although Crosne was blamed for the inefficiency of crowd control and of the courts, he had little control over the powerful political and historical forces sweeping across France as the Bastille fell on July 14, 1789. It was then left up to the municipal authorities to restore order. Armed citizens were transformed into a civilian militia 12,000 strong and led by the Marquis de Lafayette, and on July 16 Crosne resigned, ending the lieutenancy-general of Paris, an institution that had existed since the 1660s. Crosne would be guillotined six years later, one of thousands who perished during the Reign of Terror.

SOURCES: Philip John Stead, *The Police of Paris*, 1957; Alan Williams, *The Police of Paris, 1718–1789*, 1979.

CROWDER, RICHARD R. (b. 1901) Crowder was born in rural Rusk County, Texas. Following service in the U.S. Marines, in 1925 he entered law enforcement with the Dallas Police Department. Five years later he joined the newly created Texas Highway Patrol, before moving over to the Texas Rangers* in 1937 in response to the urgings of Captain Manuel Trazazas "Lone Wolf" Gonzaullas.* He would subsequently carve out a Ranger career and add to the luster of the Ranger mystique in the twentieth century. His most memorable exploit occurred on April 16, 1955, when eighty-one inmates in the Maximum Security Unit of the Rusk State Hospital rioted, stabbing five guards and taking the superintendent and two employees hostage. The mental institution was soon surround by members of the Texas Highway Patrol, prison guards, and local law enforcement officers. One of the rioters threatened that they would take the lives of the hostages if an attempt were made to intervene. Subsequently, Crowder took the initiative and telephoned the suspected riot leader, Ben Riley, and arranged to meet him. Warning Riley not to resort to any "funny business," the Ranger let him know that he was "not going to lose when I come up there" (Proctor). Crowder approached the asylum, armed only with his holstered pistol. After a brief exchange in which Riley repeated a litany of inmate complaints and Crowder replied that they were breaking the law and should surrender peacefully, the hostages were freed and the inmates capitulated. Crowder retired in 1970, having reached the exalted rank of senior captain of the Texas Rangers.

SOURCES: Ben Proctor, *Just One Riot*, 1991; Mitchel Roth (historical text by), *Courtesy, Service, and Protection*, 1995.

CUNNINGHAM, THOMAS. (1838–1900) Born in County Longford, Ireland, in his youth Cunningham moved with his family to America, finally settling in Stockton, California, in the 1850s. He worked as a harness maker for several years and in a variety of elected offices before successfully running for sheriff* of San Joaquin County in 1871. Although at first he was derided for his trade as a harness maker and initially not taken seriously as a peace officer, within a few years he had earned a reputation as one of the top lawmen of his era.

Cunningham first came to prominence in 1874, when he helped Alameda County Sheriff Henry Nicholson "Harry" Morse* track down Tiburcio Vasquez and his gang following a sixty-one-day pursuit covering close to 2,700 miles. In 1881 Cunningham helped capture Bill Miner following a stagecoach robbery, and two years later he played an important role in the apprehension of Black Bart.

During his storied career Cunningham compiled a voluminous record documenting his life as a manhunter. It was estimated that by 1898 he had assembled a rogues gallery of 42,000 photographs and had collected over a thousand weapons and crime souvenirs, which that he displayed in his own museum. Cunningham retired in 1899 and died of a heart attack the following year.

SOURCES: Frank T. Gilbert, *History of San Joaquin County*, 1879; Robert Greenwood, *The California Outlaw*, 1960; William B. Secrest, *Lawmen and Desperadoes*, 1994.

CURRAN COMMITTEE. In 1911, following the murder, in New York City's Times Square, of a gambler who had reported police malfeasance to the press, the New York City Board of Aldermen convened a committee led by Henry Curran to launch an investigation of the New York City Police Department (NYPD).* The committee uncovered a pattern of corruption and inefficiency that stemmed from administrative methods that made any accountability impossible. The committee blamed the systematic, monthly police extortion of brothels and gambling operations on poor supervision and weak discipline. In addition, it found that the NYPD was hostile to citizen complaints. The Curran Committee recommended the creation of an internal security squad comprised of nonpolice personnel. Although the investigation led to the conviction of a captain and four inspectors, its overall impact was negligible.

SOURCES: Thomas A. Reppetto, *The Blue Parade*, 1978; Whitman Knapp, chairman, *The Knapp Commission Report on Police Corruption*, 1972.

CURRY, JESSE E. Born in Hamilton, Texas, while in infancy Curry moved to Dallas with his family. He joined the Dallas Police Department in 1936, beginning a thirty-year career that would lead to his promotion to chief of police in 1960. Curry attended the Traffic Officers Training School at Texas A&M

College in 1944 and shortly afterward was elevated to detective and then sergeant. After winning a Kemper Fellowship, he attended the Northwestern University Traffic Institute and then completed his police science education at Southern Methodist University. In 1946 he was placed in charge of the Dallas police motorcycle division and rapidly moved through the ranks. His most controversial years as chief coincided with the assassination of President John F. Kennedy in Dallas in 1963 and its aftermath. Curry retired from the force in 1966 and went into the bank security business.

SOURCE: Jesse Curry, *Retired Dallas Police Chief Jesse Curry Reveals His Personal JFK Assassination File.* 1969.

CURTIS, EDWIN UPTON. (1861–1922) Born in Roxbury, Massachusetts, and educated at Bowdoin College and then Boston University Law School, Curtis developed an early affinity for politics, and in 1894, he won the Boston mayoral election. Returning to his law practice following his stint as mayor, he remained active in municipal affairs and in 1918 was appointed Boston police commissioner.

Curtis inherited a department in turmoil. Wages had been stagnant as the economy entered a period of inflation. Despite his attempts to improve conditions, the city council refused to go much further than an annual salary increase of two hundred dollars. Earning half the wage of other workers during the postwar years, disgruntled officers attempted to unionize. After they applied to the American Federation of Labor (AFL) for a charter, Curtis came down hard on union supporters. Although there were no rules forbidding them to unionize, Curtis threatened disciplinary action for any member of the force who attempted to join the union.

Formal charges were brought against nineteen policemen, and when Curtis refused to compromise and fired the offenders, the police force took the unprecedented action of voting to go out on strike, on September 8, 1919. Curtis inflamed the force even further by threatening all strikers with dismissal: thus ended the careers of three-quarters of the force. Despite the presence of amateur volunteer replacements, Boston streets were soon in the throes of a wave of looting, robbery, and vandalism. With pandemonium running supreme, Massachusetts Governor Calvin Coolidge brought in state troops to restore order.

Curtis was vindicated by the Boston media for standing up against the "Bolshevik" unionizers with his hard-line attitude. He kept his job and set about resurrecting the police force by hiring new officers; Shortly before his death in 1922, Curtis had rebuilt the city police force.

SOURCES: Charles Phillips and Alan Axelrod, *CCC*, 1996; Francis Russell, *A City in Terror*, 1975.

CUTHBERT, CYRIL. (d. 1984) Cuthbert is credited with founding the Scotland Yard* Forensic Science Laboratory. A Devon police constable (see CON-

STABLES) with a unique background, Cuthbert had taken several college courses in dentistry and chemistry and had apparently cut short his medical career to enter law enforcement. He naturally gravitated toward criminal medicine, although he was initially ensconced in the Criminal Records Office. While his superiors remained unaware of his predilection for scientific investigation, Cuthbert assisted his colleagues in their more perplexing cases.

In the 1930s Cuthbert found himself in the awkward position of having to testify in court as a representative of the "Metropolitan Police Laboratory," although it did not yet exist. Despite the outrage of the assistant commissioner, Cuthbert's evidence secured a conviction, which brought him to the attention of the police commissioner, Viscount Hugh Montague Trenchard.* However, Cuthbert was temporarily stumped when the commissioner asked for a tour of the "laboratory." Cuthbert quickly gathered as many accoutrements as possible to give the impression of such a facility and even borrowed a white hospital coat to lend some authenticity to his claims. Trenchard was so outraged by the dearth of equipment in the so-called laboratory that he immediately pushed through appropriations for an ultra-modern facility, replete with lecture halls, dark rooms, and laboratories. Erstwhile Criminal Records clerk Curtis was quickly selected to supervise the laboratory, which was to be equipped with the latest technology, including microscopes, epidiascopes, centrifugal separators, and X-ray machines, when it opened in April 1935. Despite the advances heralded by the laboratory the old guard on the police force took many more years to appreciate the value of forensic science.

SOURCE: Oliver Cyriax, *Crime: An Encyclopedia*, 1993.

D

DAKE, CRAWLEY P. (1827–1890) Born in Kentfield, Ontario, Canada, and raised in Ogdensburg, New York, Dake operated businesses in Michigan and fought in the Civil War. He left the military in 1864 to recuperate from a serious battle injury and then spent a stint with the Internal Revenue Department. Dake served as chief deputy marshal in Detroit prior to his appointment to U.S. marshal for the Arizona Territory in 1878, succeeded Wiley W. Standefer.* He appointed eight new deputies, including Virgil Earp,* and was charged with ending the bandit scourge along the Mexican border. However, what started out as a cooperative arrangement with Mexican peace officers soon disintegrated into animosity between the two forces.

Dake was roundly criticized when Virgil Earp participated in the 1881 gunfight at Tombstone's O.K. Corral. Subsequently, Dake was ordered by the acting attorney general to take action against the local "cowboy" faction. After Virgil Earp was ambushed by the cowboy faction in December 1878, his brother, Wyatt Berry Stapp Earp,* reportedly sought appointment as deputy under Dake. According to most sources, the ensuing vendetta ride following the slaying of Morgan Earp* the following year did much to tarnish the image of the Arizona federal marshal's office. More political bureaucrat than Western lawman, Dake was ineffective in reducing the conflict between the Earp and Clanton factions. Dake left office in 1882, having been replaced by Zara L. Tidball, but three years later he was later charged with misappropriating federal funds while in office. Dake was exonerated the following year and spent the remainder of his life as a merchant and in the mining business in Prescott, Arizona.

SOURCES: G. L. Seligmann Jr., "Crawley P. Dake, U.S. Marshal," *Arizona*, Spring 1961; Larry D. Ball, "Pioneer Lawman: Crawley P. Dake and Law Enforcement on the Southwestern Frontier," *Journal of Arizona History* 14, Autumn 1973.

DALTON, FRANKLIN. (c. 1858–1887) Of the fifteen Dalton children, only four turned to crime. Frank, the oldest son, began his law enforcement career in 1884 when Judge Isaac Charles Parker* appointed him a U.S. marshal at Fort Smith. He was killed not far from Fort Smith in a gun battle with the Smith-Dixon gang, which specialized in horse theft and whiskey smuggling. Soon after, his three youngest brothers, Grat, Bob, and Emmett, applied for, and received, silver stars from Parker as either marshal or deputy marshal. However, the brothers soon turned to crime and Parker rescinded their appointments.

SOURCES: Jay Robert Nash, *EWLO*, 1994; Ed Bartholomew, *The Dalton Gang and the Coffeyville Raid*, 1968.

DANIELS, BENJAMIN F. A longtime friend of Theodore Roosevelt* and a fellow Rough Rider, Daniels was appointed U.S. Marshal for Arizona in 1901 following the assassination of President William McKinley. Ever the frontier enthusiast, Roosevelt was impressed by Daniels's credentials as buffalo hunter, gambler, and assistant city marshal of Dodge City, Kansas, in the 1880s. Daniels was no stranger to violence, having taken part in the county seat feud in Gray County, Kansas. Daniels joined the Rough Riders of the Spanish-American War after working as gambler and policeman in Colorado's Cripple Creek boomtown. On returning to Arizona after the war, Roosevelt remembered his intrepid comrade, who was always at the front. However, Daniels failed to disclose a previous term in prison for horse theft, and when this was revealed, Roosevelt was forced to ask for his resignation. Two years later Daniels was appointed superintendent of the territorial prison, and by 1906 Roosevelt felt that Daniels had atoned for his past and reappointed him marshal. During his tenure in office, Daniels contended with Mexican revolutionaries, served process on Indian reservations, and championed Roosevelt's strategy to bring Arizona and New Mexico into the Union as one state. With Roosevelt leaving office in 1909, President Taft replaced Daniels with Charles A. Overlock, a proponent for separate statehood for Arizona.

SOURCE: Larry D. Ball, *The United States Marshals of New Mexico and Arizona Territories, 1846–1912*, 1978.

DAUGHTRY, SYLVESTER, JR. (b. 1945) Daughtry began a distinguished career with the Greensboro, North Carolina, police in 1968. Over the next two decades he rose through the ranks to become the department's police chief. He was instrumental in modernizing the police force and improving professional standards for police departments around the country. Under his direction, his department became the first North Carolina police department to be accorded national recognition. Daughtry received perhaps his greatest honor when he became the second African-American president of the International Association of Chiefs of Police (IACP)* in 1993.

SOURCE: Charles Phillips and Alan Axelrod, *CCC*, 1996.

DAVIDSON, ALASKA P. (b. 1868) In 1922 Bureau of Investigation Director William John Burns* selected the fifty-four-year-old Davidson as the Bureau's first female agent. Due to the proscribed notions of women in policing during this era, Davidson was used in a limited capacity, mainly pursuing investigations related to the Mann Act. When John Edgar Hoover* was appointed director in 1924 he was intent on eliminating all unqualified agents. Although Davidson was considered a refined individual, her limited education (three years of public school) was deemed inadequate, and she was forced to resign in June 1924.

SOURCE: Athan G. Theoharis, ed., *The FBI*, 1999.

DAVIS, EDWARD M. (b. 1916) Born in Los Angeles, Davis joined the Los Angeles Police Department (LAPD)* in 1940. Prior to his appointment as police chief in 1969, Davis held commands in the Technical Services Bureau, Newton Street Division, and Records and Identification Division. Except for a three-year stint in the Navy during World War II, Davis served the LAPD from 1940 until his retirement in 1978.

Davis acquired a reputation as a tough law-and-order police chief and was often prominent in the media for his outspoken statements, leading hippies and radicals to refer to him as "Crazy Ed." During his tenure as chief he instituted the basic car plan concept, which was designed to bring citizens and police officers closer together. The Davis era saw new technological advances that increased officer efficiency, ranging from the automated want and warrant system, which informed officers if an individual was wanted, to the ASTRO program (designed for surveillance operations). In addition he championed team policing and the special weapons and tactics (SWAT)* team. Among his most important contributions to the force was his revamping of the department manual, which would serve as a model for police forces throughout the nation.

The LAPD began to develop a siege mentality during the turbulent 1960s and 1970s after such highly publicized violent encounters as the December 9, 1969, shootout with Black Panthers; the Devonshire Downs riots (1969); the Venice Beach riots (1969); and the 1974 Symbionese Liberation Army shootout. Together with a severe earthquake and the Alphabet Bomber case, Davis's team concept of policing was continually tested. Following his retirement in 1978, he successfully ran for state senator.

SOURCES: Arthur W. Sjoquist (historical text by), *Los Angeles Police Department Commemorative Book, 1869–1984*, 1984; Joe Domanick, *To Protect and Serve*, 1994.

DAVIS, JAMES EDGAR. (b. 1889) Born in Texas, Davis saw army service in the Philippines before arriving in Los Angeles in 1911. Within a month he was a member of the Los Angeles Police Department (LAPD).* An ambitious police officer, the five-foot-seven, 220-pound Davis was promoted to police chief in 1926 after eight years as a patrolman. Just prior to his promotion, the mayor had slashed his budget by almost 30 percent, leading to the elimination

of the police school and other innovations inaugurated by August Vollmer.*
Vastly undermanned, Davis targeted the usual suspects of the 1920s, namely
vice, radicals, bootleggers, and vagrants. In response he assembled a fifty-man
"Gun Squad" to prowl the streets, searching for these enemies of the state.

During his tenure as police chief, Davis introduced the LAPD to the use of
"hotsheets," lists of license plates of stolen cars. Every motorcycle officer and
patrol car officer carried these sheets with them, leading to a 900 percent increase in the arrest of car thieves. He also implemented the dragnet system for
hunting down fugitives and campaigned to control the transient problem in Los
Angeles during the winter months. Davis's fondness for crime statistics and flow
charts allowed him to revel in his city's decreasing crime rate.

In the 1920s the LAPD came under increasing scrutiny due to accusations of
police corruption. Davis attempted to head off further damage and investigation
by dismissing 250 officers. However, the Police Commission could not be pla-
cated after 62 policemen were implicated in corruption activities, and public
opinion no longer supported the police chief. Following the 1929 testimony by
a major bootlegger that he had paid $100,000 per year for police protection,
Davis was charged with incompetence and neglect of duty, and to protect his
pension he accepted a demotion to deputy chief in charge of traffic.

SOURCES: Joe Domanick, *To Protect and Serve*, 1994; Arthur W. Sjoquist (historical
text by), *Los Angeles Police Department Commemorative Book, 1869–1984*, 1984.

DAWSON, MARGARET DAMER. (1874–1920) Born in Sussex, England, at
an early age Dawson was drawn to a musical career and studied music composition at London's Royal Academy of Music. Although she came from a
wealthy family, Dawson developed a benevolent streak that led her to relent-
lessly campaign for the better treatment of animals, earning several prestigious
medals in the process.

Shortly before the outbreak of World War I, Dawson joined the Criminal Law
Amendment Committee, one of the first organizations to lobby for female peace
officers in Great Britain. With the outbreak of hostilities in 1914 she helped
establish a female police auxiliary in London. As numerous expatriates from the
Continent descended on England, they became easy targets for an army of root-
less criminals and con men plying their trades on the dark streets of London.

Dawson organized a coterie of progressive-thinking women into a benevolent
group that met refugees at the train station and helped them become safely
situated. After meeting with London police commissioner Sir Edward Richard
Henry,* Dawson was authorized to establish the Women's Police Volunteer unit.
Although uniformed and official looking, they were without powers of arrest.
Foremost among their goals was the abatement of prostitution. Dawson came
into conflict over leadership issues and resigned in 1915 to form the Women's
Police Service. Affiliated with local constabulary stations, this organization, like
its counterpart in America, the police matrons,* was charged with supervising

delinquent children and prostitutes. Over time, more duties would be added. She led the agency until her death five years later.

SOURCE: Charles Phillips and Alan Axelrod, *CCC*, 1996.

DEBELLEYME, LOUIS-MARIE. As prefect of police for Paris from 1828 to 1829, Debelleyme put one hundred uniformed policemen on the streets, predating Peel's London force by several months and the New York City Police Department (NYPD)* by almost sixteen years. The police uniforms* were a dramatic blue and complemented by a cocked hat. Weapons included sabers at night and canes by day. Although his prefecture lasted only eighteen months, Debelleymes' accomplishments were many. None, however, was more long lasting than the introduction of uniformed police officers to the streets of Paris. During his brief tenure he also created the post of chief of the municipal police, instituted a fixed schedule for the Paris omnibus service, designated patrol routes, abolished the monthly tax charged to prostitutes, and created the commissioners of police, who were remanded to the judicial authority in order to conduct investigations. Debelleyme resigned in 1829 and was replaced by Jean Mangin.

SOURCES: Philip John Stead, *The Police of France*, 1983; Philip John Stead, *The Police of Paris*, 1957.

DEETZ, OLLIE. (c. 1850–1839) While marshal of Manhattan, Colorado, in 1887 Deetz killed three men for the hundred dollars apiece offered by the city fathers. His killing did not stop here, and he was suspected of sometimes planting evidence on victims before he killed them. In 1889 Deetz was unceremoniously lynched after he participated in a bank robbery in Rock Creek, Wyoming.

SOURCE: Larry Rolfe, "The Renegade Marshal Wrote His Memoirs in Blood," *Frontier West*, October 1974.

DEGER, LARRY. (prominent 1870s) The three-hundred-pound Deger came to prominence as marshal of Dodge City, Kansas, in the late 1870s. Deger soon found himself on the outs with the popular William Bartholomew "Bat" Masterson,* whose brother Edward J. Masterson* worked as Deger's assistant marshal. In 1877 Masterson won the support of local leaders, who championed him in a race against Deger for undersheriff of Ford County. Masterson won by three votes, and soon after the city council replaced Deger as city marshal with Ed Masterson.

SOURCE: Robert K. DeArment, *Bat Masterson*, 1979.

DEITSCH, PHILIP M. (1840–1903) Immigrating to America with his family to Cincinnati, Ohio, from Germany, Deitsch entered law enforcement as a member of the Cincinnati Police Department in 1863. Within three months he was promoted to lieutenant (probably through the political patronage system). In 1873 he left the force and joined the U.S. Revenue Service.

When the scandal-ridden Cincinnati Police Department was reorganized in 1886, Deitsch was selected to become the new police chief. Embarking on a campaign of reform, Deitsch introduced paramilitary standards to improve discipline and professionalism. He instituted a three-man platoon system, which reduced the traditional twelve-hour duty by four hours. His impact was influential across America as many departments followed his lead by setting higher standards, including better fitness and training for police officers. Deitsch rose to prominence as the International Association of Chiefs of Police (IACP)* endorsed his strategy in its annual meetings.

SOURCES: Charles Phillips and Alan Axelrod, *CCC*, 1996; George M. Roe, ed., *Our Police: A History of the Cincinnati Police Force, from the Earliest Period to the Present Day*, 1890.

DELOACH, CARTHA DEKLE. (b. 1920) Born in Georgia and educated at Stetson University, "Deke" DeLoach joined the Federal Bureau of Investigation (FBI)* in 1942. After a stint as a field agent, he was transferred to Washington, D.C., where he began his public relations career. Affiliated with the Security Division (the precursor of the controversial Domestic Intelligence Division), in 1959 DeLoach was chosen to head the Crime Records Division. Over the next thirteen years he functioned as the voicepiece of John Edgar Hoover* in the supposed war against the communist infiltration of the American government.

In 1964 DeLoach headed up a special surveillance and wiretapping unit to monitor the activities of Martin Luther King Jr. during the Democratic National Convention meeting. In 1965 he was promoted to assistant director of the FBI and subsequently developed a close professional and personal relationship with President Lyndon B. Johnson. "Deke" DeLoach was reportedly the only member of the FBI to have a direct telephone connection to the White House.

DeLoach was also responsible for the campaign to disparage King by leaking details of his alleged extramarital infidelities to the newspapers. Johnson soon distanced himself from DeLoach, who managed to hold his post as the chief FBI intermediary with the White House into the Richard Nixon administration. He retired from the FBI in 1970 and chronicled his FBI career in his 1995 book, *Hoover's FBI: The Inside Story by Hoover's Trusted Lieutenant*.

SOURCES: Curt Gentry, *J. Edgar Hoover: The Man and His Secrets*, 1991; William W. Turner, *Hoover's FBI*, 1970; reprint, 1993.

DENNY, CECIL EDWARD. (1850–1928) Born in Hampshire, England, and educated in France and Germany, Denny emigrated to the United States in 1869. He initially worked as a farmer on the outskirts of Chicago and was staying in the city at the time of the great Chicago fire in 1871. In 1874 he moved to Ontario, Canada, and joined the North-West Mounted Police. Commissioned as captain in what was to be the precursor to the Royal Canadian Mounted Police

(RCMP),* he was one of the first three hundred officers. During his first year he was engaged constructing forts and commanded a "Mountie" unit at Fort Calgary. In 1882 he resigned from the force and became an Indian agent for the Cree and Assiniboine Indians near Fort Walsh in the Northwest Territories. Three years later he was operating a ranch when the Riel Rebellion broke out, and he was placed in charge of the local tribes during the rebellion. Denny sporadically engaged in scout work for the police but never returned to active duty.

SOURCE: Cecil E. Denny, *The Law Marches West*, 1939; reprint, 1972.

DENVER, COLORADO, POLICE DEPARTMENT. Settled in 1858, Denver elected its first peace officers the following year, following its incorporation as a city. William E. Sisty was elected as Denever's first city marshal. Between 1859 and 1871, eight different men held the position of city marshal (sometimes referred to as chief of police). George E. Thornton became Denver's first police chief in 1862 after the city council authorized the position. In 1864 officers adopted a bright metallic star as their first police badge after a city ordinance was passed requiring them to do so. The badges were engraved with each officer's title, including "police" or "Chief of Police."

Policemen were identified by police hats beginning in 1871 and around that time began carrying batons, but they still did not wear characteristic police uniforms.* Into the twentieth century, few Denver citizens considered policing a viable career path as officers were either appointed or elected and were subject to the whims of politicians and constituents. In 1873 the Denver City Council established a police force modeled after the New York Metropolitan Police, which included standard uniforms and badges. The inauguration of a policeman's ball in 1873 gave officers the opportunity to showcase their fancy new uniforms and raise money to pay for them. Early the next year the city introduced its first book of police guidelines. During the 1870s the city council authorized the construction of a rogues' gallery, horse mounted police* patrols, and a rotation system that allowed each officer to become acquainted with detective work for a month at a time.

In 1886 the Denver police introduced its first patrol wagon and added thirty callboxes to strategic locations throughout the city. With this new system in place, officers could check in with headquarters periodically rather than wasting time making repeated visits to the station in person. In 1888 the first police matrons* were hired to supervise female prisoners at the local jail. One of Denver's most prominent and longest serving chiefs of police was Hamilton Armstrong, who served four nonconsecutive terms between 1894 and 1921.

During the first two decades of the twentieth century, Denver experimented with Home Rule in an attempt to eliminate interference from state government. Under this system the police and fire departments were controlled by the mayor and a civil service system. During the tenure of police chief Michael Delaney, the force was bombarded by lawsuits due to his fondness for police brutality and the third degree.* The first traffic squad was created in 1910, made up of the most physically impressive men in the department. Popular wisdom suggested that a 220-pound man could be more easily seen than a smaller one when conducting traffic in a busy intersection. Labor violence and urban disorder in 1920 required the mayor to call in the militia to help the understaffed police force. Following this episode, one hundred officers were added to the force.

In 1921 Herbert S. "Rugg" Williams was promoted to police chief. His sixty-two-year tenure on the Denver police force is considered the longest of any member of a metropolitan police force in the United States. In 1930 the Denver police introduced the airplane to its crime-fighting arsenal. Two years later, police radios were installed in a number of patrol cars, heralding myriad technological innovations in the burgeoning force.

At forty-four years of age, Herbert Forsyth became the youngest Denver police chief and, during the 1950s, he was credited with modernizing the police force and reducing the crime rate. In 1972 Arthur G. Dill began his term as police chief, and by the time he left office almost eleven years later, he could boast of having served the longest continuous term as police chief. During his watch, the Denver police moved to a new facility and police officers began carrying handheld radios. By the 1990s the Denver Police Department had grown to a force of 1,364 officers.

SOURCE: William G. Bailey, "Denver Police Department," in *The Encyclopedia of Police Science*, ed. William G. Bailey, 1995.

DE VEIL, SIR THOMAS. (1684–1748) Born in St. Paul's Churchyard, De Veil's father was an impoverished clergyman. After being home schooled, he was apprenticed to a mercer in 1700. The following year De Veil enlisted in the army. As he rose through the ranks to captain, he developed champagne tastes, which, following his release from the service, would lead him into bankruptcy. He salvaged his reputation when he was appointed magistrate in 1729. In an era before the existence of a full-time police force the magistrate was responsible for law enforcement personnel, who were typically the masses.

Over the next two decades De Veil rose to prominence through his enforcement of the 1736 Gin Act and the destruction of one of London's most powerful criminal organizations. De Veil also established what would become the Bow Street headquarters under Sir Henry Fielding* and Sir John Fielding, considered the cradle of the modern police force. The only chink in his armor was his participation in a patronage system that allowed him to collect bribes from brothels and gambling house keepers, as well as fees and fines. He claimed he needed the extra income to support more than twenty children fathered with at least four different wives.

As the leading magistrate and the most important early figure in British policing, De Veil was unable to persuade the London populace that having a police organization would be in their best interests, and on several occasions mobs attacked the Bow Street house. The first Bow Street police-magistrate, he kept his position until his death in 1748. He also authored *Observations on the Practice of a Justice of the Peace* (1747).

SOURCES: Patrick Pringle, *Hue and Cry: The Story of Henry and John Fielding and Their Bow Street Runners*, 1955; Percy H. Fitzgerald, *Chronicles of the Bow Street Police Office*, 1888.

DEVERY, WILLIAM. (1855–1919) Just one in a long line of corrupt New York City Police Department (NYPD)* officials, as a boy Devery brought his father lunch while he worked as a bricklayer during the construction of Tammany Hall, beginning an affiliation with the center of city corruption that would last for a half century.

Devery grew to 250 pounds, earning him the moniker "Big Bill," and in his twenties he won a reputation as a fearless brawler when he worked as a Bowery bartender. He joined the police in 1878 after paying the traditional bribe to win appointment. He continued to pay as he climbed the ladder to sergeant in 1884 and then captain seven years later. As First Precinct captain, he was rewarded with control of the notoriously corrupt Eldridge Street Station, a lucrative tenderloin* area replete with bribe-paying whorehouses.

Virtually born into the Tammany machine system, Devery brought out the vote early and often on Election Day, leading to his selection as police chief in 1898. Devery found himself in control of a greatly expanded New York City, since the year before, Brooklyn, Queens, and Staten Island had been added to Manhattan to create the familiar metropolis of today. With expansion came new opportunities for graft, since new police districts created more offices to be purchased.

Although he was turned out of office in 1894 following revelations disclosed by the committee chaired by Clarence Lexow,* he returned to his position in 1896. Devery successfully helped the unscrupulous Robert Van Wyck win the mayorship, an accomplishment that would not protect Devery from being forced out of office by the state legislature in 1901. The deposed police chief was undeterred and campaigned for district leader on his home turf of Chelsea, winning handily in 1902. However, in his campaign for reelection the following year he suffered a reversal and retired from public life.

SOURCES: Thomas A. Reppetto, *The Blue Parade*, 1978; H. Paul Jeffers, *Commissioner Roosevelt*, 1994; Charles Phillips and Alan Axelrod, *CCC*, 1996.

DE VILLIERS, ISAAC PIERRE. Born and raised in the Cape region of South Africa, de Villiers could trace his roots back to the early French Huguenot settlers who, together with the Dutch colonists, created South Africa's rich Afrikaner community. Following service in World War I, he practiced law in Cape Town and then in 1928 was appointed lieutenant colonel, and, later, commissioner, of the South African Police (SAP).* De Villiers was expected to guide the transition of the force to one that was more centrally controlled and featured military-style discipline. In addition he was charged with ensuring that the officers came from the Afrikaner class. De Villiers earned the monikers "Mussolini" and "Roman Centurion" for his imposition of military discipline. As a result of the new, demanding regimen, many police officers resigned rather than adhere to the physical training. By 1938 most officers spoke the Afrikaans language, a prerequisite for advancement while the conservative Afrikaners were in power.

Credited with modernizing the SAP, de Villiers was also vilified for purging much of the English-speaking officer class from the upper ranks. In 1940 de Villiers was transferred from the SAP to become major general of the defense force preparing for action during World War II. His military experience in the earlier war made him a prime candidate to lead an infantry division composed partly of police battalions. In 1944 de Villiers returned to take charge of the SAP. He retired the next year, having fulfilled his mandate to militarize the police force.

SOURCES: John D. Brewer, *Black and Blue*, 1994; F. Cooper, *The Police Brigade*, 1972.

DEW, WALTER. (1863–1947) The Scotland Yard* veteran Dew first came to prominence during the unsuccessful search for Jack the Ripper in 1888. Twelve years later he was promoted to chief inspector, and in the new century he would become universally prominent when he tracked down the notorious poisoner Dr. Hawley Harvey Crippen, following a three-thousand-mile manhunt.

Crippen had killed his wife in order to live with another woman, a familiar pathology but, nonetheless, one that grabs the public's attention. Crippen parried with the investigators looking for his wife, explaining that she had left for America. Shortly after interrogation by Dew, Crippen and his secretary, Ethel Clara LaNeve, boarded a steamship bound for Canada. In the meantime, Dew found the remains of Crippen's wife buried in the coal cellar of their home. A warrant was then issued for Crippen's arrest. While boarding the steamship *Montrose*, Crippen was recognized by the captain, who telegraphed Scotland Yard, apparently the first time telegraphy was used in a criminal case.

Chief inspector Dew caught up to the ship shortly before it docked in Canada, and when he approached his familiar prey, Dew reportedly commented: "Good morning, Dr. Crippen. I am Chief Inspector Dew of Scotland Yard. I believe you know me" (Begg and Skinner). Crippen was returned to England for trial and was executed on November 23, 1910. Dew went on to chronicle his career in *I Caught Crippen* (1938).

SOURCES: Sir Harold Scott, ed., *The Concise Encyclopedia of Crime and Criminals*, 1961; Paul Begg and Keith Skinner, *The Scotland Yard Files*, 1992.

DEWEY, THOMAS E. (1902–1971) Born in Owosso, Michigan, Dewey attended the University of Michigan. Probably best remembered for losing the presidential election to Harry Truman in 1948, as special prosecutor in New York City during the 1930s he attacked police corruption and organized crime with relentless energy. Not only did he restore integrity to the New York City Police Department (NYPD),* he engineered the demise of criminals such as Lucky Luciano and Dutch Schultz as well as Tammany Hall boss James J. Hines. Often compared with New York City mayor and law-and-order spokesman Rudy Giuliani, Dewey became a national hero and revered racket-buster in his time, survived death threats from Dutch Schultz, and served as governor of New York state three times.

SOURCES: Stanley Walker, *Dewey: An American of This Century*, 1944; Thomas A. Reppetto, *The Blue Parade*, 1978.

DICK. American and Canadian slang for *detective*, this term originated in the late 1890s.

SOURCE: J. E. Lighter, *Historical Dictionary of American Slang*, 1994.

DICKENS, CHARLES. (1812–1870) The noted Victorian novelist Dickens is credited with coining the word *detective*, introducing the term in "On Duty with Inspector Field*," a journalistic contribution to *Household Words* in 1850. He introduced the first fictional detective, Inspector Bucket, in his novel *Bleak House*, reputedly based on Inspector Charles Frederick Field, who led Dickens on his rounds on the London docks. As an early Scotland Yard* detective, Field helped Dickens gather material for his *Household Words* articles. Dickens chronicled the state of policing in England through characters in such books as *Oliver Twist* (1837–1839), *Our Mutual Friend* (1864–1865), *Martin Chuzzlewit* (1843–1844), *Dombey and Son* (1846–1848), *Bleak House* (1852–1853), and *Great Expectations* (1860–1861).

SOURCES: Oliver Cyriax, *Crime*, 1993; Philip Collins, *Dickens and Crime*, 1962.

DICKLESS TRACY. Derived from the name Dick Tracy, this contemptuous slang refers to policewomen.* Reference to this term can be traced back to 1963. Joseph Aloysius Wambaugh, Jr.* used the term in his 1983 novel, *Delta Star*.

SOURCE: J. E. Lighter, *Historical Dictionary of American Slang*, 1994.

DODGE, FRED JAMES. (1854–1938) Born in Spring Valley, California, Dodge was reportedly already an undercover agent for the Wells Fargo Detective Bureau* when he arrived at Tombstone, Arizona, in late 1879. He was instrumental in the appointment of Wyatt Berry Stapp Earp* as a messenger and guard for the stage company. Dodge was aligned with the Earp faction during its conflict with the "cowboys faction," which culminated in the O.K. Corral incident.

Dodge is credited with playing a major role in the solution of the 1883 Bisbee massacre, involving the deaths of four citizens in a holdup. Six perpetrators would hang for this crime. Dodge used his law enforcement position as Tombstone constable (see CONSTABLES) as a cover for his clandestine work for Wells Fargo. In 1890 Dodge "came in from the cold" and began publicly working for Wells Fargo out of Houston, Texas. He collaborated with numerous frontier lawmen, including Henry Andrew "Heck" Thomas.* Dodge was responsible for the solution of several train robberies, including some committed by the noted Dalton and Doolin gangs. An intrepid investigator, Dodge often worked several cases at a time, and he survived at least one assassination attempt. On one occasion, after he spent over two years solving a $35,000 case, Wells Fargo awarded him a gold watch. He died at his ranch in Boerne, Texas.

SOURCE: Fred Dodge, *Under Cover for Wells Fargo*, ed. Carolyn Lake, 1969.

DODGE CITY PEACE COMMISSION PHOTOGRAPH. In June 1883, Wyatt Berry Stapp Earp,* Luke Short, William Bartholomew "Bat" Masterson,* W. H. Harris, W. F. Petillon, Charles E. Bassett,* Frank McLain, and Neal Brown sat for one of the most famous photographs in the history of the American West. In reality Earp and several friends had been summoned by Short to help him out of a bit of trouble. Conflict was brewing between the Short-led faction and a group led by the new mayor, former marshal Larry Deger.* He summoned Earp, Masterson, and friends to intervene on his behalf. The subsequent conflict had more bark than bite, and after matters were amicably settled between the participants, Earp and some seven colleagues sat for the photograph, which was later labeled, somewhat facetiously, "Dodge City Peace Commission." Widely reprinted after first appearing in the *National Police Gazette* six weeks later, the portrait has given many historians the false impression that it was taken during the earlier heyday of the Kansas cowtown.

SOURCES: Allen Barra, *Inventing Wyatt Earp*, 1998; Casey Tefertiller, *Wyatt Earp: The Life behind the Legend*, 1997.

DOGBERRY. A precursor to the Keystone Kops* of the silent film era, William Shakespeare introduced a group of bumbling comic constables,* the Messina night watch* led by Dogberry, in his play *Much Ado about Nothing* (c. 1599). Violating English syntax at every opportunity, these comic foils epitomized the cowardly cop, unwilling to apprehend a lawbreaker if there any risk was involved. At one point a watchman (see NIGHT WATCH; WATCH AND WARD SYSTEM) queries whether they could arrest any thieves they meet up with and Dogberry answers with his typical aplomb, "Truly, be your office you may; but I think they that touch pitch will be defiled" (Boyce). This badinage was reportedly a parody of a sixteenth-century London statute that attempted to control nighttime activity in the city.

The laughable policeman is considered an ancient theatrical type, and Shakespeare used a similar figure, Constable Dull, in *Love's Labor's Lost*. During the Elizabethan era London law enforcement was viewed as inadequate, if not inept. Indeed, 230 years would pass before London policemen attained a measure of respect.

SOURCES: Isaac Asimov, *Asimov's Guide to Shakespeare*, 1978; Charles Boyce, *Shakespeare A to Z: The Essential Reference to His Plays, His Poems, His Life and Times, and More*, 1990.

DOUGLAS, JOHN E. (b. c. 1945) Born in Brooklyn, New York, and educated at Montana State University and Eastern New Mexico University, Douglas joined the Federal Bureau of Investigation (FBI)* in 1970 and initially worked out of the Detroit, Michigan, and Milwaukee, Wisconsin, field offices. While attending a 1975 in-service class on hostage negotiation, he came under the influence of Howard Teton* and Patrick J. Mullaney,* reportedly the originators of criminal profiling. Two years later Douglas was assigned to replace Mullaney at the Behavioral Science Unit at Quantico, Virginia.* Douglas came to prominence, along with colleague Robert Ressler, for creating a database on serial killers based on prison interviews. This research was instrumental in the development of various profiling techniques.

Douglas came to national attention following the success of the Thomas Harris book *Silence of the Lambs* and the subsequent Academy award-winning film. One of the main characters in this story was reportedly inspired by Douglas. He was promoted to unit chief of the Behavioral Science Investigative Support Unit in 1990. Five years later he retired but has continued to work as a consultant for the FBI. In addition to several books on criminology written while with the FBI, Douglas's books include *Mind Hunter* (written with Mark Olshaker) (1995), *The Unabomber* (1996), *Journey into Darkness* (1997), and *Obsession* (1998).

SOURCE: Athan G. Theoharis, ed., *The FBI*, 1999.

DOVE, JERRY L. (1956–1986) Born in Charleston, West Virginia, Dove received a J.D. degree from West Virginia University in 1981. He joined the Federal Bureau of Investigation (FBI)* in 1982 and served in the Pittsburgh, Pennsylvania, and San Diego, California, offices. After two years with the Miami, Florida, office, on April 11, 1986, he was killed in action, along with FBI agent Benjamin P. Grogan,* during a shoot-out with better-armed bank robbers. The bloodiest day in FBI history resulted in the wounding of five other agents and the killing of both suspects. The tragedy in Miami spurred the agency to introduce new weapons for agents and better firearms training. This incident inspired the 1992 TV movie *In the Line of Duty: The FBI Murders.*

SOURCE: Athan G. Theoharis, ed., *The FBI*, 1999.

DOWBIGGIN, SIR HERBERT. (1880–1966) Credited with being one of the founders of the British Colonial Police, Dowbiggin enlisted as an inspector in the Ceylon Police Force in 1901. Following promotion to superintendent four years later, he set to reorganizing the force along the lines of the London Constabulary model. In 1913 his accomplishments led to his appointment as inspector general, a position he would hold for the next twenty-four years. During his tenure he oversaw the transition of the force from a military-style militia to a preventative police organization. Over the next twelve years he introduced the Criminal Investigation Department (1915), a photographic unit, and better weapons training.

In 1925 Dowbiggin instituted a police training academy as well as a volunteer Police Boy's Brigade. His prominence as a police innovator with the Ceylon police led to stints on special duty with the Cyprus Police (1926), the Palestine Police (1930), and the Northern Rhodesia Police (1937). When Dowbiggin stepped down as inspector general of Ceylon in 1937, he left a legacy that included an unarmed civil police force and training facilities that surpassed most of those in Great Britain.

SOURCES: Charles Phillips and Alan Axelrod, *CCC*, 1996; Philip John Stead, *The Police of Britain*, 1985.

DOYLE, SIR ARTHUR CONAN. (1859–1930) Doyle, the creator of fictional detective Sherlock Holmes,* had initially aspired to a medical career. Unable to muster much of a practice, Doyle whiled away his spare time writing fiction. The creation of Sherlock Holmes was perhaps inspired by Edgar Allan Poe's 1840s detective story *The Murders in the Rue Morgue*, featuring detective Auguste C. Dupin.*

Doyle's creation was at least as inventive as he was derivative, since many of Holmes's procedures had little analogy in the real world of forensics at that time. The detective's use of the trademark magnifying glass, his tape measure, and monographs on varieties of cigarette ash and composition of different clays and muds were all products of Doyle's imagination. The use of fingerprinting* and anthropometry* in *A Study in Scarlet* (1887) clearly presaged their appearance in the criminologist's arsenal.

Doyle occasionally left his world of fiction and participated in several true-life police cases, most memorably in 1908, when a German Jew by the name of Oscar Slater was wrongfully convicted of bludgeoning to death an elderly woman during a robbery. The only evidence linking the immigrant to the murder was the testimony of several eyewitnesses. After examining the trial transcripts, Doyle found numerous discrepancies in the case that should have led to an acquittal. The pulbication of his booklet *The Case of Oscar Slater* ignited a firestorm of protest over the miscarriage of justice leading to the release of Slater in 1928. Doyle also contributed to the avalanche of material on Jack the Ripper with his theory of "Jill the Ripper," a midwife who could kill without garnering much attention in the shadowy streets of London's East End.

SOURCES: John Dickson Carr, *The Life of Sir Arthur Conan Doyle*, 1949; Trevor H. Hall, *Sherlock Holmes: Ten Literary Studies*, 1969.

DRAGNET. Best known as a television series, *Dragnet* originally debuted as a radio show in June 1949. Creator Jack Webb had received the cooperation of Los Angeles Police Department (LAPD)* Chief William Henry Parker,* who reportedly viewed the show with a bit of trepidation. When the show premiered on television on January 3, 1952, it revolutionized the way in which fictional police officers were portrayed. The opening was the familiar, terse Jack Webb voice-over: "This is the city. Los Angeles, California. I work here. I carry a badge." The original cast included Jack Webb as Sergeant Joe Friday and Ben Alexander as Officer Frank Smith.

When the radio show moved to television, the LAPD introduced new ground rules. LAPD advisor's initially were paid $125 per week and worked during their shifts. Parker was against this from the start and insisted they would now have to consult on vacation time. Another important rule was that the advisors for each story would have to come from the division being portrayed (i.e., a homicide story must have a Homicide Squad consultant). Webb's quest for authenticity made this compromise an easy one. Chief Parker also required script control, insisting that each one be approved by the Public Information Division. This meant no sexual connotations or derogatory language. When Webb mistakenly used the word *cop* in one show, Parker let him know it would be unacceptable.

Unlike the silly 1960s version of the show, with Webb and Harry Morgan, the 1950s series was gritty and more authentic. Most television critics credit the show with introducing the drama series to television following the avalanche of variety shows that characterized the early television years.

Jack Webb is credited with most of the innovations of the show, including using realistic criminal cases and police procedures. Most episodes emphasized the more mundane aspects of policing rather than the typical thrill-a-minute fare that the public expected. By 1954 the number two–ranked television show had made Webb a player in Hollywood and had won two Emmys. Music lover Jack Webb was reportedly thrilled when the theme from his show became the first TV theme to break into radio's Top 10.

SOURCES: Jeff Siegel, *The American Detective: An Illustrated History*, 1993; Joe Domanick, *To Protect and Serve: The LAPD's Century of War in the City of Dreams*, 1994.

DRUMMOND, THOMAS. (1797–1840) Born in Edinburgh, Scotland, the precocious Drummond attended the University of Edinburgh at the age of thirteen.

Graduating with a degree in engineering, he went on to patent two inventions. One, the Drummond light, would be used to illuminate lighthouses for years. Moving to Ireland in 1824, Drummond developed friends in high positions, and by 1835 he had been appointed chief administrator of Ireland. At the time of his appointment, Ireland was racked by internecine conflict between Catholics and the Protestant government. Dublin was policed by a force of four-hundred Protestant watchmen (see NIGHT WATCH; WATCH AND WARD SYSTEM), Protestant watchmen who were described as lazy drunks by one observer. In response Drummond disbanded the watchmen and created the Irish Constabulary (later the Royal Irish Constabulary).*

In order to properly reflect the nation's demographics Drummond's constabulary was composed of ten thousand, mostly Catholic, men, who represented the country's majority. Despite resistance from England, Drummond's strategy proved successful and staved off the religious conflict that would explode in the twentieth century.

SOURCE: Charles Phillips and Alan Axelrod, *CCC*, 1996.

DRUSCOVICH, NATHANIEL. (1842–c. 1880) Of Polish heritage and fluent in several languages, Druscovich joined the London Metropolitan Police* in 1864. He rapidly earned a reputation for intelligence and was promoted to inspector within five years. In 1877 he was implicated, along with Inspector John Meiklejohn and Chief Inspector William Palmer,* in the Turk Fraud Scandal, in which, for a variety of reasons, the three had become involved with a fraudulent bookie operation. All three men were found guilty and sentenced to two years of hard labor. Druscovich's health suffered in prison, and he died soon after his release.

SOURCES: Belton Cobb, *Critical Years at the Yard*, 1956; Joan Lock, *Dreadful Deeds and Awful Murders*, 1990.

DUFFIELD, MILTON B. (1810–1874) Born in Wheeling, Virginia (now West Virginia), Duffield tried his hand in the mercantile business, but in 1851 he left his family to pursue more lucrative prospects, first in Texas and then in California. Settling in Tuolumne County, Duffield spent almost a decade engaged in ranching, prospecting, and land acquisition. In 1854 he narrowly survived an ambush by three assassins. After a brief respite in the East he returned to the West, and on March 6, 1863, he was appointed the first U.S. Marshal (see U.S. MARSHALS SERVICE) in the Arizona Territory, a position he would hold for two years.

After a stint as a special postal agent for Colorado, Arizona, Colorado, and New Mexico, Duffield was involved in numerous violent skirmishes with well-armed adversaries. Not one to go unencumbered with weapons, in one engagement he reportedly wore eleven firearms and a knife at the same time. He survived an assassination in a courtroom and then was stabbed thirty-one times by Mexican assailants. Judging by the sheer number of attempts on his life even after he left law enforcement, it appeared that Duffield was not very well liked. In 1874 he was killed by James T. Holmes during an argument over a mining claim. Holmes escaped jail prior to his trial and was never recaptured.

SOURCES: Benjamin Sacks, *Arizona's Angry Man: United States Marshal Milton B. Duffield*, 1970; Dan L. Thrapp, ed.. *EFB*, Vol. 1, 1988; Larry D. Ball, *The United States Marshals of New Mexico and Arizona Territories, 1846–1912*, 1978.

DULLEA, CHARLES. (b. 1888) Born in San Francisco, California, Dullea joined the San Francisco Police Department* in 1914 following a stint in the U.S. Marines. Dullea was promoted to chief of detectives in 1929 and then city police chief in 1940. After seven years as chief he resigned but stayed active in policing, serving as president of the International Association of Chiefs of Police (IACP)* from 1947 to 1948 and then on the California parole board. Chief of the Berkeley, California, Police Department* August Vollmer* earned Dullea's ire when he referred to the San Francisco police force as staffed by "morons." Dullea was so irked by this comment that he instructed his chauffeur to always avoid Berkeley when driving him.

SOURCE: Thomas A. Reppetto, *The Blue Parade*, 1978.

DUPIN, AUGUSTE C. The fictional detective Dupin appeared in Edgar Allan Poe's *The Murders in the Rue Morgue* (1841); *The Mystery of Marie Roget* (1842–1843), based on the Mary Cecilia Rogers* murder case; and the *Purloined Letter* (1845). Poe's detective was reportedly inspired by either Paris police chief Jesquet during the reign of Louis Phillippe or Eugene François Vidocq,* with whose memoirs Poe was familiar.

SOURCE: William Amos, *The Originals*, 1985.

DURK, DAVID. (b. c. 1937) Born in New York City and educated at Amherst College and Columbia University, Durk joined the New York City Police Department (NYPD)* in 1963. A model police officer, he soon became a pariah in the department as he discovered rampant corruption that reached into the highest levels of the police administration. Rebuffed in his attempts to put an end to the environment of corruption that flourished in city government, he went to the press with fellow officer Frank Serpico.* Their efforts were instrumental in forming the Knapp Commission,* which launched the largest investigation of police corruption in American history. Following the trial both officers became media celebrities. Durk appeared on *The Tonight Show*, taught a course on "The Police and Social Change" at Yale University, and turned down a host of offers in order to stay with the department. In 1972 he left the force to work for the deputy commissioner for organized crime control.

SOURCES: James Lardner, *Crusader: The Hell-Raising Police Career of Detective David Durk*, 1996; Whitman Knapp, chairman, *The Knapp Commission Report on Police Corruption*, 1972.

DZERZHINSKY, FELIX EDMUNDOVICH. (1877–1926) Dzerzhinsky was born in Vilna, Poland (now Lithuania); otherwise, little is known about his early years. By the late 1890s he was drawn into the orbit of radical politics and was arrested and exiled to Siberia. Following several escape attempts, he made it to Berlin in 1902 and took part in the Polish Revolution three years later. Exiled and sentenced to hard labor, he was released during the Russian Revolution. His contributions to the movement led to his appointment as head of the Cheka,* the first Communist government secret police.

Under Dzerzhinsky, the Cheka controlled subversion within the Communist party through a campaign of terror. Following the end of the Russian Civil War in 1921, Lenin abolished the Cheka and created the OGPU (Unified State Police Administration), through which he felt he controlled the country better. Dzerzhinsky kept his post but his power over the organization was considerably diminished.

SOURCE: John J. Dziak, *Chekisty: A History of the KGB*, 1988.

E

EARP, MORGAN. (1851–1882) Born near Pella, Iowa, Earp entered law enforcement as deputy town marshal of Dodge City, Kansas, in 1876, where he developed a reputation as a proficient gunman, leading to his stint as a "town tamer" in Butte, Montana. Reportedly the handsomest and most reckless of the Earp brothers, Morgan joined his brothers Wyatt Berry Stapp Earp* and Virgil Earp* in Tombstone in 1880 and worked as a special deputy, gambler, occasional prospector, and shotgun guard on Wells Fargo stagecoaches. Perhaps it was a case of serendipity, but as soon as he left Wells Fargo, a series of stage robberies ensued. Morgan is probably best remembered for his participation in the 1881 gunfight at the O.K. Corral, in which he supposedly killed Billy Clanton and then suffered a serious gunshot wound to the shoulder. Following his recovery he was ambushed and killed the following year while playing billiards at R. S. Hatch's Bank Exchange Saloon. Subsequently, Wyatt hunted down several men whom he suspected were involved in the killing.

SOURCES: Casey Tefertiller, *Wyatt Earp: The Life behind the Legend*, 1997; Dan L. Thrapp, ed., *EFB*, Vol. 1, 1988.

EARP, VIRGIL. (1843–1906) Born in Ohio County, Kentucky, Earp served in the Union Army during the Civil War. Following the war, he traveled West and worked as a freighter teamster, railroad worker, and sawmill operator before entering law enforcement as an unpaid deputy marshal in Yavapai County, Arizona, in 1877. The following year he was appointed nightwatchman (see NIGHT WATCH) of Prescott, Arizona, and shortly after was elected constable (see CONSTABLES). In 1879 Virgil was appointed deputy U.S. marshal for the Arizona Territory in Prescott. The next year saw him move to Tombstone, the town forever linked with the Earp family name, where he was selected as assistant village marshal. He subsequently lost elections for village marshal and city chief of police, but in June 1881 he was appointed acting city marshal (chief of police), a position he would hold until suspended after his participation in the gunfight at the O.K. Corral, where he was wounded.

Virgil was ambushed and his left arm permanently injured by a shotgun blast, but he survived the shooting and left the territory for California and won election as marshal of Colton, California, in 1887. He later returned to Prescott, Arizona, and, over the last seven years of his life, was employed as a special court constable in Prescott and as deputy sheriff of Esmeralda County, Nevada, where he died of pneumonia ten months after his appointment. In one of his most controversial acts, Virgil reportedly hunted down the killer of his brother Warren in 1900. While Wyatt is the Earp most linked with law enforcement, Virgil actually had the more stellar career.

SOURCES: Don Chaput, *Virgil Earp: Western Peace Officer*, 1994; Casey Tefertiller, *Wyatt Earp: The Life behind the Legend*, 1997.

EARP, WYATT BERRY STAPP. (1848–1929) One of the legendary figures from America's frontier past, Earp was born in Hartford, Kentucky. Following several years of farming in Iowa, the Earp family emigrated to California. In the mid-1860s Wyatt left home for a peripatetic career as buffalo hunter, wagon train scout, and railroad worker. Earp apparently entered law enforcement in 1873 when he was recruited as deputy marshal in Ellsworth, Kansas. In 1874 he served as deputy marshal in Wichita, Kansas. Two years later he was appointed chief deputy of fabled Dodge City, where he was assisted by his brother Morgan Earp,* and brothers William Bartholomew "Bat" Masterson* and James "Jim" P. Masterson.*

In 1879 Wyatt left for the boomtown of Tombstone, Arizona, hoping to strike it rich in the saloons and gambling halls rather than in the silver mines. On October 26, 1881, Earp took part in the gunfight at the O.K. Corral, probably the most famous gunfight in Western lore. After the well-chronicled events that followed the bloody gunfight, Earp left Arizona for California. The remaining half century of his life was rather uneventful compared to the years leading up to Tombstone. When not hanging around the fledgling motion picture community in Los Angeles, Earp raised horses, prospected for gold in Alaska, ran a saloon, served as a boxing referee, and told his story to Stuart Lake, who re-invented the "legendary" shootist in the 1931 biography *Wyatt Earp: Frontier Marshal*.

SOURCES: Allan Barra, *Inventing Wyatt Earp*, 1998; Casey Tefertiller, *Wyatt Earp: The Life behind the Legend*, 1997.

EASTMAN, GEORGE DANIEL. (1912–1991) Educated at the University of Washington and Michigan State University, Eastman served as chief of the Seattle, Washington, Police Department from 1946 to 1952. After a stint as consultant to the U.S. Treasury Department,* he was appointed as superintendent of the Port of New York Authority police in 1957, a position he would hold until he accepted appointment as director of public safety for Pontiac, Michigan, in 1960. That same year he began teaching police administration at Michigan State University, and in 1971 he coedited *Municipal Police Administration*. Eastman earned a reputation as an expert in police training and was consulted on police matters by more than forty American cities prior to his retirement in 1987.

SOURCE: Charles Phillips and Alan Axelrod, *CCC*, 1996.

EAVES, A. REGINALD. A graduate of Morehouse College and a former Boston prison commissioner, in 1974 Eaves became the first African-American appointed public safety commissioner of Atlanta and the first public safety director of a major southern city. He was credited with leading Atlanta to an 8 percent decrease in the major crime rate during his first year of office. His success was in part due to Eaves's inauguration of Atlanta's first team policing program, which was designed to improve relations between police and the black community. He was also credited with improving the diversity of the force to conform with the racial demographics of the city, increasing the number of black officers from 23 to 35 percent. However, in order to do this he had to overcome charges of reverse discrimination from white officers. After four years on the job, Eaves left the force, embattled by critics who charged he was unqualified and by his own scandalous mistakes, which included hiring a relative for a city job and employing a convicted felon as his personal secretary. Following his resignation he was hired as a Fulton County, Georgia, commissioner. He was succeeded as police chief by Lee Patrick Brown.*

SOURCE: W. Marvin Dulaney, *Black Police in America*, 1996.

EGAN, EDWARD "EDDIE." (1929–1984) Egan may be best remembered as "Popeye Doyle," and his exploits as a New York City Police Department (NYPD)* officer inspired the film *The French Connection*. Born in the Bronx, New York, as a teenager he played pro baseball for the Yankee Triple-A farm team. (When Egan left the team to join the U.S. Marines, he was replaced in center field by a young prospect named Mickey Mantle.) Egan joined the New York City Police Department (NYPD)* following his stint with the Marines and rose from beat officer to detective first grade. Along with his partner, Salvador "Sonny" Grosso,* he rose to prominence in 1962 after coordinating one of the largest heroin busts in New York City history. The arrest of the "French Connection" and the seizure of 120 pounds of heroin worth $32 million led author Robin Moore to chronicle the story in *The French Connection*, which was made into a blockbuster movie. In the movie based on this episode, Egan played his own boss. He spent ten more years on the force before being demoted in 1971 for violating evidence procedures in another drug case.

Egan left the force and became a familiar fixture in Hollywood as a consultant for crime films, an actor in films such as *Badge 373* and the *Seven-Ups*, and in numerous television appearances. Splitting his last years between Fort Lauderdale, Florida, and Los Angeles, ever the entrepreneur, Egan started a detective agency in Florida called Security Limited and opened the "Lauderdale Connection" restaurant. In 1984 he died in Miami, Florida, after a long battle with cancer.

SOURCE: John Slate and R. U. Steinberg, *Lawmen, Crimebusters, and Champions of Justice,* 1991.

EGAN, WILLIAM F. "DAD." (c. 1832–c. 1924) Born in Kentucky, Egan moved to Denton, Texas, in 1859, where he began his affiliation with Sam Bass. Following service in the Confederate cavalry during the Civil War, he was elected sheriff* of Denton. Egan remained friends with Bass even as he began his turn to crime, and after a train robbery in 1878, Egan began cooperating with the Texas Rangers* in pursuing Bass for a series of robberies. The two men maintained mutual respect while Egan continued to hunt Bass and his crew. Egan probably breathed a sigh of relief when Bass was killed at Round Rock, far from his jurisdiction. Soon after this affair, Egan resigned his position.

SOURCE: Wayne Gard, *Sam Bass,* 1969.

EINSTEIN, ISADORE "IZZY." *See* IZZY AND MOE.

ENRIGHT, RICHARD EDWARD. (1871–1953) Born in Campbell, New York, Enright worked as a telegrapher in Elmira and Queens, New York, before joining the New York City Police Department (NYPD)* in 1896. During his first two decades on the force, his strident pro-union views and position as president of the Police Lieutenants' Benevolent Association thwarted any attempt that he may have made to rise above the rank of lieutenant. However, with the election of Mayor John F. Hylan in 1918, Enright won the allegiance of a more enlightened administration and became the first New York City police commissioner to be appointed from within the ranks of the police force.

Upon his elevation to commissioner, Enright implemented several reforms, including giving one day off to the rank and file for every six days on the line. In addition he hired several policewomen* to appease the suffragist constituency. Other improvements included lobbying the government to exempt police officers from the draft, improving the police pension system, introducing a convalescent home for police officers injured in the line of duty, and increasing the police relief fund.

Among Enright's reorganization efforts were attempts to reduce the number of police precincts for better management; creating a twenty-four-hour Missing

Persons Bureau; revising the department merit system, which was arrest-quota based; and a scheme to suppress illegal gambling. Enright was at constant loggerheads with police administration as he attempted to rid the department of corruption and unproductive employees.

The 1920s were characterized by the challenges posed by Prohibition and the concomitant crime wave it produced. Enright weathered several libel suits and continued to fight the corrupt hegemony of the police bureaucracy by instituting charges against various captains and inspectors for noncompliance with Prohibition laws. Prior to his retirement, Enright helped create the International Police Conference to further cooperation between international police organizations. His platform for reform promoted international fingerprint registration. His promising career as a detective novelist began with his 1925 effort, *Vultures of the Dark*, but his sophomore effort, *The Borrowed Shield*, fell short, effectively ended his writing career that same year. Enright also published the *Syllabus and Instruction Guide of the Police Academy* in 1925.

During his retirement Enright flirted with the pulp magazine trade, but with little success, and in 1933 he lent his hand to the New Deal's National Recovery Administration by organizing its law enforcement service. At his death from a serious spinal cord injury he was director of the United States Detective Bureau.

SOURCES: "Richard Edward Enright," in *The Encyclopedia of Police Science*, ed. William G. Bailey, 1995; Richard E. Enright, "Everybody Should Be Fingerprinted," *Scientific American*, October 1925.

EVANS, JOSEPH W. (1851–1902) Born in Fayetteville, North Carolina, Evans moved to Phoenix, Arizona, in 1872, where he worked as a supervisor for the Arizona Stage Company for several years before entering law enforcement as a special agent for the Wells Fargo Detective Bureau* in 1877. Three years later, U.S. marshal Crawley P. Dake* appointed him deputy U.S. marshal (see U.S. MARSHALS SERVICE) out of Tucson, Arizona. An Earp (see EARP, MORGAN; EARP, VIRGIL; EARP, WYATT BERRY STAPP) supporter he reportedly witnessed the gunfight at the O.K. Corral. He left law enforcement for a distinguished career in the real estate business.

SOURCES: Larry D. Ball, *The United States Marshals of New Mexico and Arizona Territories, 1846–1912*, 1978; Dan L. Thrapp, ed., *EFB*, Vol. 1, 1988.

EVERT, ANGHELOS. (1895–1971) Following graduation from Athens University with a law degree in 1930, Evert joined the Athens, Greece, police and, within a decade, rose to police chief. During World War II he rose to prominence by helping the Greek resistance and saving many Greek Jews from deportation to the German concentration camps. In 1969 the Israeli government recognized his heroic efforts as thousands of Greek Jews paid homage to him by brandishing the fake documents he had supplied, which had allowed them to escape the camps.

SOURCE: Charles Phillips and Alan Axelrod, *CCC*, 1996.

F

FABIAN, ROBERT. (b. 1901) Fabian joined Scotland Yard* in 1921 as one of the regular constables* and gradually worked his way up to the Vice Squad (1926) and, finally, to superintendent of the Criminal Investigation Department (CID).* During his stellar twenty-eight-year career, he played a prominent role in numerous high-profile cases including the murder of Alex de Antiquis (1947) and the "Black Butterfly" murder (1939). Fabian retired in 1949.

SOURCE: Robert Fabian, *Fabian of the Yard*, 1953.

FALLON, MALACHI. (1814–1899) Born in Athlone, Ireland, Fallon came to New York while still a young boy. Following an apprenticeship to a saddler, he entered law enforcement as a member of the New York City Police Department (NYPD).* Lured to California under the spell of gold fever, Fallon arrived in San Francisco in 1849 and immediately set out for the gold fields.

Later in 1849 Fallon was asked to become San Francisco's first police chief by merchants who had been apprised of his law enforcement experience. He accepted and subsequently appointed an assistant chief, three sergeants, and thirty officers. However, in 1851, when crime continued to rise unabated, newspaper editors and public opinion went against the police chief and the San Francisco Vigilance Committee* took over many of the police department's duties. In 1851 Fallon was resoundingly defeated in the race for city marshal. Following his fall from grace, the ex-marshal came under scrutiny by the vigilance committee, which examined his term in office. Although exonerated of corruption charges, Fallon never worked in law enforcement again. He later opened a saloon, where he regaled customers with stories of the California gold rush.

SOURCES: Kevin J. Mullen, "Malachi Fallon: San Francisco's First Chief of Police," *California History*, Summer 199?; Mary Floyd Williams, ed., *Papers of the San Francisco Committee of Vigilance of 1851*, 1919.

FARRELL, THOMAS J. (b. 1856) Born in Ireland, Farrell was brought to New Orleans as a youth, where he was educated and first entered police work while employed by his uncle's detective agency. One of his most perilous assignments was the nighttime patrolling of the Mississippi River waterfront to search for smugglers and wharf thieves.

Following the death of his uncle, Farrell joined the Pinkerton's National Detective Agency* in 1883. During his years with the Pinkertons, he won acclaim for ending the careers of noted Alabama train robber Rube Burrows and highwayman Eugene Bunch of Louisiana. In one of his most celebrated cases, Farrell solved the 1890 murder of four members of the Drake family of Viroqua, Wisconsin, in forty-eight hours. He is also credited with solving the murder of Dr. Cronin by Clan-na-Gael members and a controversial tally-sheet forgery case in Columbus, Ohio. In the early 1890s, Farrell was appointed superintendent of the seventy-nine-member Dayton, Ohio, police force.

SOURCE: George W. Hale, *Police and Prison Cyclopaedia*, 1893.

FAUROT, JOSEPH A. (1872–1942) Faurot is considered the father of American fingerprinting.* After witnessing a demonstration of fingerprinting by Scotland Yard* at the 1904 Louisiana Purchase Exposition held in St. Louis, Missouri, Faurot implored his superiors in the New York City Police Department (NYPD)* to adopt the system With the support of then-commissioner William McAdoo,* Faurot went to London to study fingerprinting; however, when he returned, McAdoo had been replaced by a new commissioner with little interest in new identification techniques. While St. Louis became the first American city to adopt fingerprinting, Faurot continued to petition for the system. After solving a high-profile theft and a murder using the new technique, Faurot was still left with little support since the suspects were convicted on the basis of confessions rather than of fingerprinting. Faurot would finally win his crusade in 1911 when he had fifteen court employees place their prints on a piece of paper along with those of a suspect in custody for a burglary. When, on his first attempt, he successfully matched one of the prints to its exact duplicate on a glass, he won the conviction of the burglar and, in the process, established the value of the system. Faurot was placed at the head of the New York Police Department's fingerprint bureau, a position he would hold until his retirement in 1930.

SOURCE: Carl Sifakis, *The Encyclopedia of American Crime*, 1982.

FAY, FRANCIS X. (d. 1990) Fay served in the U.S. Cavalry during World War I and in 1922 joined the Federal Bureau of Investigation (FBI)* as an agent. Working out of the Pittsburgh, Pennsylvania, office, he was instrumental in settling the famous Hatfield and McCoy feud in West Virginia. Later, based in the New York City office, he worked on the Lindbergh kidnapping and received much of the credit for starting the FBI laboratory and its firearms program. He retired in 1935 and became supervisor of security for Macy's New York City Department Store. Fay later founded the Society of Former Special Agents of the FBI.

SOURCE: Athan G. Theoharis, ed., *The FBI*, 1999.

FEDERAL BUREAU OF INVESTIGATION (FBI). Prior to the twentieth century, with no federally designated crime-fighting bureau in place, the U.S. Treasury Department* and the Department of Justice investigated federal crimes. In 1901, former New York City police commissioner Theodore Roosevelt* became president. A stalwart proponent of centralized law enforcement, he chose the Treasury Department's Secret Service as the preferred agency for launching federal crime investigations. However, Congress demurred and enacted a law prohibiting Treasury detectives from being employed by other government departments, including the Department of Justice. In response, the intrepid former Rough Rider ordered Attorney-General Charles Joseph Bonaparte* to "create an investigative service within the Department of Justice subject to no other department or bureau and which will report to no one except the Attorney General" (Theoharis). On July 26, 1908, the Bureau of Investigation was created. However, it would be another twenty-seven years before it was renamed the Federal Bureau of Investigation.

The Bureau grew gradually over its first decades. The Mann Act of 1910, World War I, and the Russian Revolution saw the expansion of the Bureau's role in federal law enforcement. During its early years the bureau investigated white slavery, espionage, sabotage, and draft violations, and in 1919 the force was empowered to investigate motor vehicle theft with the passage of the National Motor Vehicle Theft Act (Dyer Act).

The Bureau underwent growing pains in the 1920s and, to lead the organization into the new era, John Edgar Hoover* was selected as director in 1924. Hoover brought professionalism to the agency, establishing rigid codes of conduct and replacing the seniority-based system of promotion with one based on merit. Under Hoover's direction, special agents were required to be college educated, with degrees in law or accounting.

In 1924 Congress approved the transfer of fingerprint records at Leavenworth Federal Prison and the criminal records maintained by the International Association of Chiefs of Police (IACP)* to the FBI. The collection of over 810,000 records became the nucleus of the FBI Identification Division, created in July 1924. In 1932 the FBI laboratory was established to aid federal and local investigations through the scientific analysis of blood, hair, firearms, handwriting, and other types of evidence. By the 1990s, the laboratory was conducting over a million examinations per year for close to fifteen thousand investigations.

Rising crime and repercussions from the 1933 Kansas City Massacre* led Congress to enact a wave of legislation in 1934 that increased the power and prestige of the FBI. Agents were given full arrest powers and the authority to carry firearms, and new laws significantly expanded the number of federal crimes as well as the FBI's jurisdiction. Subsequently, it became a federal crime to cross state lines to avoid prosecution, to extort money with telephones or other federally regulated methods, to rob a federal bank, or to transport stolen property valued at over five thousand dollars across state lines.

During the Prohibition and Depression years, the FBI focused much of its attention and energies on the pursuit of public enemies* such as John Dillinger, the Barker gang, Pretty Boy Floyd, Machine Gun Kelly, and other media sensations. Although Kelly was credited with introducing the G-men* moniker, its origins can be traced to other sources. All the Bureau's functions were consolidated and transferred to the Division of Investigation in 1933, and on March 22, 1935, it was renamed the Federal Bureau of Investigation.

SOURCES: Athan G. Theoharis, ed., *The FBI: A Comprehensive Reference Guide*, 1999; David R. Johnson, *American Law Enforcement: A History*, 1981.

FELT, MARK W. (b. c. 1918) Raised in Twin Falls, Idaho, and educated at George Washington University Law School, Felt joined the Federal Bureau of Investigation (FBI)* in 1942. During the war years he worked for the Espionage Section out of the Houston and San Antonio, Texas, and Washington, D.C., field offices. Following the war he shifted his attention toward communist surveillance and conducting security investigations of prospective employees for the U.S. Atomic Energy Commission. In the 1950s he investigated organized crime activities out of the Nevada and Kansas City offices.

With the death of John Edgar Hoover* in 1972, new director Louis Patrick Gray III* promoted Felt to associate director, the number two position in the agency. During the 1970s Felt was assigned to supervise the investigation of the domestic terrorist group known as the Weather Underground, and in 1980 he was convicted of authorizing illegal surveillance of friends and family members of that group. The following year President Ronald Reagan pardoned Felt and the former assistant director of the FBI Domestic Intelligence Division Edward S. Miller. The two men had been the first senior FBI officials ever to be indicted. Felt retired from the FBI in 1973, and 1979 saw the publication of his autobiography, *The FBI Pyramid: From the Inside*.

SOURCE: Curt Gentry, *J. Edgar Hoover: The Man and His Secrets*, 1991; Athan G. Theoharis, ed., *The FBI*, 1999.

FIELD, CHARLES FREDERICK. Field joined the Metropolitan Police in 1829, the same year it was created. Promoted to Inspector of L Division, he would become one of the most famous detectives of the early Peelers.* The Charles Dickens* character Inspector Bucket was reportedly based on Field.

SOURCES: Paul Begg and Keith Skinner, *The Scotland Yard Files*, 1992; Joan Lock, *Dreadful Deeds and Awful Murders*, 1990.

FIELDING, SIR HENRY. (1707–1754) The son of an army officer, Fielding was born near Glastonbury, England. An impressive physical specimen at over six feet tall, Fielding is best remembered as a novelist and playwright and author of the picaresque novel *Tom Jones*. Fielding left the literary world in 1748 because of censorship restrictions and began work as a magistrate. During his six-year tenure at this post, he implemented several policies that led to increased safety on the streets of London. Fielding introduced the Bow Street Runners* (initially "Mr. Fielding's People"), a specially formed group of six to eighty constables* who ran to the aid of crime victims and pursued the perpetrators. Fielding quickly developed a reputation for honesty as his Bow Street Runners flourished, successfully capturing fugitives, who were unaccustomed to such pursuit on their familiar stomping grounds.

Fielding demonstrated his foresight in police matters in his 1749 essay, *An Enquiry into the Causes of the Latest Increase of Robberies*, which called for a professional, full-time police force. One of his first goals as magistrate was to stem the corruption emanating from the Bow Street office. Fielding funded the publication of *The Covent-Garden Journal*, a precursor to the Scotland Yard* *Police Gazette*, which was dedicated to educating the public about the rising crime problem.

Despite the reluctance of the public to welcome a professional police force, Fielding persisted in his attempts to win support from the government for a full-time force. In 1753 he was thrown a bone when he was awarded a grant, which he used to establish a twelve-man murder investigation team. Sir Henry was succeeded by his half-brother, John Fielding, the following year upon Sir Henry's death. As tribute to his efforts, John kept the Bow Street Runners alive.

SOURCES: Patrick Pringle, *Hue and Cry: The Story of Henry and John Fielding and Their Bow Street Runners*, 1955; F. H. Dudden, *Henry Fielding: His Life, Works, and Times*, 1966.

FIELDING, SIR JOHN. (1721–1780) The son of an army general and the half-brother of Sir Henry Fielding,* John was blind from birth. He served as a magistrate for several years and, upon his brother's death in 1754, succeeded him as Westminster magistrate and head of the Bow Street Runners.* His 1755 pamphlet, *Plan for Preventing Robberies within Twenty Miles of London*, explained his strategy for breaking up organized gangs of robbers, which plagued the outskirts of the city. Three years later he published a similar pamphlet, "An Account of the Origin and Effects of a Police Set on Foot in 1753 by the Duke of Newcastle on a Plan Suggested by the Late Henry Fielding."

An astonishing detective, regardless of his blindness, Fielding (sometimes referred to as the "Blind Beak") reportedly could identify thousands of criminals by voice alone. During his tenure with the Bow Street Runners, he made Bow Street the official police headquarters, with two horses always posted at the ready to pursue highwaymen. As a police reformer, John, like his half-brother Henry, was ahead of his times as he argued for a full-time force engaged in preventive policing techniques. However, it would be another fifty years before the policing strategies of the Fieldings would see fruition.

SOURCES: Patrick Pringle, *Hue and Cry: The Story of Henry and John Fielding and Their Bow Street Runners*, 1955; F. H. Dudden, *Henry Fielding: His Life, Works, and Times*, 1966.

FINCH, STANLEY WELLINGTON. (1872–1951) Born in Monticello, New York, and educated at Baker University in Kansas and then at the Washington, D.C., Corcoran Scientific School, Finch joined the U.S. Department of Justice* in 1893. As Finch continued his ascent through the department to chief examiner of the U.S. courts, he earned his law degree at National (now American) University. Following graduation in 1908, he was appointed the first chief of the Bureau of Investigation by Attorney General Charles Joseph Bonaparte.*

Following his appointment Finch began professionalizing the new agency, liberally borrowing administrative and organizational procedures from other agencies such as the U.S. Secret Service.* During his tenure as chief, he vigorously crusaded against "white slave trafficking" and other methods of forcing women into prostitution. With the assistance of progressive reformers, Finch directed the creation of a chain of halfway houses to rehabilitate those that had been rescued from a life of vice. Finch's efforts against prostitution inspired Congress to pass the 1910 Mann Act, which made it a federal crime to transport women over state lines for "immoral" purposes. This act enhanced the jurisdiction of the Bureau after 1910, and in 1912 Finch was appointed by the (Department of Justice) to direct the national campaign against white slave traffic. Finch stepped down from this position the following year. The rest of his career included stints with the Department of Justice as an inspector of the Bureau of Prisons, audit clerk, and as special assistant to the attorney general in the Anti-Trust Division.

SOURCES: Charles Phillips and Alan Axelrod, *CCC*, 1996; Athan G. Theoharis, ed., *The FBI*, 1999.

FINGERPRINTING. Fingerprinting has existed as a form of signature in China and Japan for many years, and as early as the 1820s an anatomy professor named Johann Purkinje noted that every person's fingerprints were unique. However, without any type of classification system, this method of identification was useless. By the late 1850s, fingerprints were being used by British magistrate William Herschel to prevent the wrong people from fraudulently collecting money on the dole. In 1880, Henry Faulds, a Scottish physician working in Tokyo, exonerated a suspected thief by comparing fingerprints left at the crime scene with those of the suspect.

In the late 1880s, Sir Francis Galton attempted to create a classification system and wrote the book *Fingerprints* (1892). However, it would be left to Sir Edward Richard Henry,* inspector general of the Nepal Police, to grapple with the problem, and in 1896 he experienced an epiphany while on a railway journey. Henry noted that every fingerprint has a delta, a roughly triangular space around the central whorl formed by the lines running off to either side. Henry reasoned that the size of this area has an exact numerical quantity, consisting of its width in terms of the number of papillary lines. These lines could be counted with the help of a needle and then classified according to whether they were whorls or one of the four basic types of arches and loops. In 1896 Argentina became the first country to base its identification system on fingerprinting. The next year, fingerprint identification replaced bertillonage (see BERTILLON SYSTEM) in India and was credited with snaring its first criminal soon after.

In 1902 Henry was appointed assistant commissioner of Scotland Yard,* and the following year he introduced the Yard's Central Fingerprint Branch. America would continue to lag behind in implementing the new system, with St. Louis, Missouri, becoming the first city to adopt the system, following a demonstration at the World's Fair.

In 1924, American fingerprint efficiency was given a boost when fingerprint files maintained at the Federal Prison at Leavenworth and the files kept by the International Chiefs of Police (IACP)* were combined and relocated to the Federal Bureau of Investigation (FBI)* in Washington, D.C. Today, new fingerprint technology allows the FBI to check prints via computer, and other advances allow matches to be made using only a portion of a fingerprint.

SOURCES: Douglas G. Browne and Alan Brock, *Fingerprints: Fifty Years of Scientific Crime Detection*, 1953; George W. Wilton, *Fingerprints: History, Law, and Romance*, 1938.

FISHER, JOHN KING. (1854–1884) Born in Upshur County, Texas, Fisher regularly moved throughout Texas with his rancher father before settling in Goliad, Texas. An expert horseman, Fisher was sentenced to the state penitentiary for two years for burglary in 1870 but pardoned four months later. Following his release he moved to the Pendencia River country and developed a reputation as a hired gun. By 1878 he claimed to have killed seven men, "not counting Mexicans" (Thrapp). By the late 1870s Fisher had been exonerated for several killings and seemed to have made the transition to lawman, having been appointed deputy sheriff of Uvalde County in 1881. Two years later he was acting sheriff* of the county.

While visiting Austin, Texas, in 1884 Fisher ran into his old friend Ben Thompson.* After visiting several saloons, they traveled together to San Antonio. It is unknown whether Fisher knew that Thompson had killed Jack Harris, the proprietor of the Turner Hall Opera House, two weeks earlier. In any case, both men were assassinated while watching a play at the same opera house, on the night of March 11, 1884, by associates of Harris.

SOURCES: O. C. Fisher and J. C. Dykes, *King Fisher: His Life and Times*, 1966; Dan L. Thrapp, ed., *EFB*, Vol. 1, 1988.

FLAKE. To *flake* or *flake out* is police slang that refers to the age-old technique of planting incriminating evidence, such as illegal drugs or weapons, on a suspect or in his or her lodgings. The term's origins can be traced back to the early 1970s.

SOURCE: J. E. Lighter, *Historical Dictionary of American Slang*, Vol. 1, 1994.

FLATFOOT. Although this slang word referred to enlisted sailors in the 1830s and staunch supporters of political parties in the 1880s, its best-known usage is associated with police patrolmen or detectives beginning in the second decade of the twentieth century and refers to the bipedal gait of the patrolman. It entered the British lexicon in the 1930s. Similarly, *flatties* is derivative slang for policeman.

SOURCE: J. E. Lighter, *Historical Dictionary of American Slang*, 1993.

FLATT, GEORGE W. (c. 1853–1880) Born in Tennessee, Flatt served as deputy constable in Caldwell, Kansas, and participated in several deadly gunfights prior to his appointment as town marshal after Caldwell became incorporated in August 1879. He was succeeded in office the following year by William Horseman. After Flatt was ambushed and killed that same year, Horseman was tried but exonerated for his killing.

SOURCE: Nyle H. Miller and Joseph W. Snell, *Great Gunfighters of the Kansas Cowtowns, 1867–1886*, 1967.

FLA YIU. Meaning "flowery waist" in Chinese, this term is Triad (Chinese secret criminal societies) slang for police officer.

SOURCE: Bill Waddell, *The Black Museum*, 1993.

FLIC. The term *flic* is French slang for police officer.

SOURCE: Jay Robert Nash, *Dictionary of Crime*, 1992.

FLYING SQUAD. Scotland Yard* introduced a mobile unit called the Flying Squad after World War I as criminals adapted readily to the automobile. Scotland Yard responded by dividing London into four detective districts in 1919, each commanded by a detective superintendent who was given the authority to go into action without prior approval from headquarters. The Flying Squad initially referred to two policemen who each patrolled two of the four districts with wireless receivers. Initially the Flying Squad used a horse-drawn, covered van in which twelve policemen observed certain neighborhoods through peep-holes. As soon as a suspect was spotted, an officer would leap out and apprehend the quarry.

In short order, two powerful Crossley motor vehicles as well as ordinary cars replaced the horse-drawn carriage. Originally known as "Q-cars," in reference to wartime "Q" ships, which were disguised as merchantmen, the newspapers began referring to the new mobile unit as the Flying Squad. By the 1920s, the only missing ingredient was adequate communication between the cars and headquarters, which was remedied in 1922 with the introduction of car radios. Although the activities of the Flying Squad captured the public's imagination, it had little effect on the overall crime problem.

SOURCES: Angus Hall, ed., *The Crime Busters*, 1976; Sir Basil Thomson, *The Story of Scotland Yard*, 1936.

FLYNN, WILLIAM JAMES. (1867–1933) Born in New York City, Flynn began a twenty-year career with the U.S. Secret Service* in 1897. In 1910 he took a two-year leave of absence to direct the reorganization of the New York City detective unit. Upon his return to the Secret Service in 1912, he was pro-moted to chief. In 1919 he accepted the appointment of director of the Bureau of Investigation. During his two-year reign as Bureau chief, Flynn was promi-nent in the Bureau's campaign against radical activists, which resulted in the Palmer Raids in 1920. Flynn was succeeded as director by William John Burns* in 1921.

SOURCES: Curt Gentry, *J. Edgar Hoover: The Man and His Secrets*, 1991; Athan G. Theoharis, ed., *The FBI*, 1999.

FOOTPRINTS. In the industrialized nations, footprints have seldom been used to solve criminal cases because most people wear shoes. However, in Third World countries, the opposite is true. In 1946, a body was found sans head and hands but was identified by a chiropodist who had treated the woman's feet for bunions. Like fingerprints (see FINGERPRINTING) the ridges of the soles of the feet are unique for each individual. In 1992 the *Journal of Forensic Science Society* unveiled the pedobarograph, an apparatus that encodes images into a computer in order to show the pressure patterns on a shoe during a complete step. This facilitates the comparison between a suspect and his or her footwear and allows an assessment of the individual's gait and build from the resulting tread pattern.

SOURCES: Oliver Cyriax, *Crime*, 1993.

FORAKER, CREIGHTON M. (b. 1861) Born in Hillsboro, Ohio, as a young man Foraker sought his fortunes as a prospector in Colorado. By 1887 he had relocated to Grant County, New Mexico, where he became the first U.S. marshal (see U.S. MARSHALS SERVICE) to serve under the recently implemented salary system in 1896. Prior to that year, marshals were forced to subsist on an outdated fee system that had been introduced in the eighteenth century.

Foraker was instrumental in professionalizing his deputies, requiring them to be conversant in Spanish and to act professionally. In return he granted them fixed salaries and put an end to the old system of patronage, which saw politically motivated local sheriffs hindering investigations. Foraker's men faced one of their greatest challenges in the decade following 1896 when a series of train robberies forced cooperation between the traditionally competitive federal and local law enforcement organizations. In 1897 Foraker's men hunted down William "Black Jack" Christian, who had killed a deputy a few years previously, and later his deputies brought in train robber Thomas "Black Jack" Ketchum for trial. Hanged in 1901, Ketchum has the dubious honor of being the only man hanged for violating New Mexico's draconian train-robbing laws. Foraker was reappointed to office four times but was forced out in 1912 when a new administration took charge in Washington, D.C.

SOURCES: Jay Robert Nash, *EWLO*, 1994; Frederick S. Calhoun, *The Lawmen: United States Marshals and Their Deputies, 1789–1989,* 1989.

FORD, JOHN SALMON "RIP." (1815–1897) Born in Greenville, South Carolina, Ford arrived in Texas in 1836 and, during his long life in the state, worked at a series of professions including physician, newspaper editor, surveyor, explorer, Indian fighter, Confederate general, mayor, and captain in the Texas Rangers.* Ford received his moniker "RIP" during the Mexican War, when he was responsible for notifying the next-of-kin of those killed in battle. In reverence for the deceased, he closed each letter with the expression "Rest in Peace." However, as casualties mounted during the Mexico City campaign, Ford resorted to writing "RIP" to save time on paperwork.

Between service in the Mexican and Civil Wars, Ford entered law enforcement as a Texas Ranger. During the Mexican War he served as adjutant under Texas Ranger John Coffee "Jack" Hays*; this was the only time the force would serve together as a unit in the U.S. armed forces during a major conflict.

Following the Mexican War in 1848, Ford left the Rangers and pursued other interests. During the following winter Ford was authorized to raise a Ranger company to protect settlers from Comanches and bandits between the Nueces and Rio Grande Rivers. His company became known as "Ford's Old Company," and during its two-year existence it saw numerous skirmishes before being disbanded in 1851. In 1857 Ford was promoted to major and senior captain of the Rangers, with command over the remaining companies in the field. Ford's force participated in the largest Indian battle in Ranger history in 1858.

Ford's Ranger career included many high points in the history of the force. He saw his last action in the law enforcement group and frontier defense in the Cortina War in 1859–1860 before leaving the Rangers for good in 1860. He went on to serve in the Confederacy during the Civil War, taking part in the battle of Palmito Ranch, the last battle of the war, and later was elected mayor of Brownsville, Texas. He died in San Antonio.

SOURCES: W. J. Hughes, *Rebellious Ranger: Rip Ford and the Old Southwest*, 1964; John Salmon Ford, *Rip Ford's Texas*, edited by Stephen Oates, 1963; Walter Prescott Webb, *The Texas Rangers*, 1935.

FORDING, ADDISON. In 1960 Fording was appointed as Berkeley, California, Police* Chief. He had joined the police force in 1936 and had earned a degree in mechanical engineering at the University of California in 1931. His rise through the ranks began at sergeant in 1939, lieutenant in 1943, and then captain in 1953. During his tenure with the force he graduated from the FBI National Academy, took courses under August Vollmer* at Berkeley, and was appointed chief of the Detective Division. Fording rose to prominence in 1964, while contending with student demonstrations resulting from Berkeley's Free Speech Movement. According to agreements between the University of California and the Berkeley Police Department, Fording's force was required to provide assistance on campus when called upon by the University Police. Fording described the campus demonstrations of December 3, 1964, as "one of the most serious cases of mass civil disobedience in the history of the State of California." The force was credited with the arrest of 773 demonstrators without any serious injuries. In 1965 and 1966 the Berkeley force weathered several large anti–Vietnam War protests, including one in which the Hell's Angels motorcycle group threatened the peace march. Weary of the civil unrest of the 1960s, Fording retired in July 1966.

SOURCE: Alfred E. Parker, *The Berkeley Police Story*, 1972.

FORNOFF, FREDERICK. (1859–1935) Born in Baltimore, Maryland, Fornoff arrived in Albuquerque, New Mexico, in 1880 following a stint as a miner in Colorado. He joined the city police and rose to the rank of police chief. Following service in the Rough Riders during the 1898 Spanish-American War, Fornoff served as a deputy U.S. marshal and then deputy sheriff* of Bernalillo County.

As captain of the New Mexico Mounted Police* he investigated the murder of Patrick Floyd Jarvis "Pat" Garrett* in 1908, and concluded that "Killin' " Jim Miller had been hired by wealthy El Paso cattlemen. This conclusion remains unsubstantiated since his report has disappeared, reputedly destroyed by the attorney general's office.

SOURCES: James Madison Hervey, "The Assassination of Pat Garrett," *True West*, March–April 1961; Los Angeles Westerners, "The Key to the Mystery of Pat Garrett," *Branding Iron*, June 1969.

FORT APACHE. Although Fort Apache usually brings to mind the military outpost on the Apache frontier, in the 1970s the term was popularly applied to the crime ridden Forty-First Police Precinct in the Bronx, New York City. Some sources indicate that the term was used as early as the 1950s.

SOURCE: J. E. Lighter, *Historical Dictionary of American Slang*, Vol. 1, 1994.

FOSDICK, RAYMOND BLAINE. (1883–1972) Fosdick was born in Buffalo, New York, and educated at Colgate College and Princeton University before receiving a law degree from the New York Law School in 1908. While Fosdick could cite numerous accomplishments in the public sector, he is best remembered in law enforcement circles for a groundbreaking series of books on policing.

At the urging of John D. Rockefeller Jr., Fosdick embarked on a study of European police organizations that resulted in the 1915 publication of *European Police Systems*. His study of virtually every major European police force fostered an image of a professional brand of policing that outshone the decentralized and more amateurish American counterparts. In 1920, again at the behest of Rockefeller, Fosdick completed a complementary volume on American policing, titled *American Police Systems*. After visiting seventy-two cities, Fosdick concluded that American policing was victimized by lack of professionalization and rife with political corruption. The publication of his findings created a backlash from the American police establishment but also led to reform efforts in many cities.

Fosdick's police studies offer only one facet of a fascinating life. He joined the Pershing expedition against Pancho Villa in Mexico in 1917 and compared military training methods in Canada, England, and France. He went on to serve in numerous public service organizations funded by the Rockefeller family, was chosen to by Woodrow Wilson to represent the United States at the ill-fated League of Nations meeting, and wrote fourteen books. Tragically, in 1932, Fosdick's wife killed both their children before committing suicide. Fosdick would remarry in 1936.

SOURCES: Raymond Blaine Fosdick, *Chronicle of a Generation: An Autobiography*, 1958; William G. Bailey, ed., *The Encyclopedia of Police Science*, 1995.

FOSTER, GEORGE, AND LAURIE, ROCCO. (d. 1972) On January 27, 1972, rookie New York City Police Department (NYPD)* officers and Vietnam veterans George Foster and Rocco Laurie were ambushed and killed by the Black Liberation Army terrorist faction. These highly publicized killings were chronicled in Al Silverman's book *Foster and Laurie* (1974).

SOURCE: Al Silverman, *Foster and Laurie*, 1974.

FOUCHÉ, JOSEPH. (1759–1820) Born near Nantes, France, and educated at the Nantes Oratory, Fouché initially studied for the priesthood and taught mathematics and physics at the Oratory following graduation. As a member of the 1793 Committee of Public Safety during the Reign of Terror following the French Revolution, Fouché was ordered to regain the support of the city of Lyons. Fouché was castigated for using cursory trials, the guillotine, and then a mass execution with a cannon barrage to convince them to support the revolutionary government. Following this fiasco, Fouché barely survived with his head. Subsequently, he fell from grace and sank into obscurity for several years.

By 1798 Fouché was considered rehabilitated and was appointed to several high positions. On July 29, 1799, Fouché was appointed as the tenth minister of the general police of the Republic of France. His ministry was mostly political in nature and he was reportedly unconcerned with ordinary police concerns such as vice and street lighting. He created a secret police force and won the support of the emergent Napoleon Bonaparte, who confirmed him as minister of police. Fouché's career as minister of police roughly coincided with Napoleon's career as emperor; he served from 1799 to 1802, from 1804 to 1810, and then in 1815 following Napoleon's last return from exile.

From the start Fouché demonstrated an acumen well suited to police work. Considered the father of police intelligence operations, during his tenure he reorganized the Paris police, initiating the prefecture system that exists to this day. Fouché is credited with establishing a centralized police force that was responsible to the national government. His administrative innovations included setting up police departments that were proportional to the populations of various urban units. Over time he became a proponent of preventive policing and was successful in eliminating much of France's bandit scourge.

SOURCE: Philip John Stead, *The Police of Paris*, 1957.

FOX, JAMES MONROE. (1937–1998) Born in Chicago, the son of devout Baptists, Fox was so impressed by the visit of a Federal Bureau of Investigation (FBI)* agent to his church camp when he was thirteen that he set as his own career goal to become an FBI agent. At the age of twenty-five Fox joined the Bureau. During his stellar career he hunted communist spies, pursued mobsters, and tracked down modern terrorists. The top man at the FBI's New York bureau, Fox ingratiated himself with Salvatore "Sammy the Bull" Gravano when he testifying against crime boss John Gotti and, after the successful prosecution, when he gave Gravano his own FBI lapel pin for helping cinch the case. Fox drew widespread attention following the World Trade Center bombing in 1993 when he assured Americans that this was not the beginning of a jihad on his home turf. He would subsequently lead the hunt that tracked down the bombers. In December 1993 Fox was suspended by Director Louis J. Freeh* for violating a gag order by publicly supporting agents who had been criticized on the World Trade Center case. Fox retired the following month.

SOURCE: Gene Mustain, "Some of His Best Friends Were Crooks," *New York Times Magazine*, January 4, 1998, pp. 34–35.

FRANCE, JOHN "JOHNNY." (b. 1940) Born and raised in Madison County, Montana, France rose to prominence as the "mountain man sheriff" in 1984 when he captured the kidnappers of world-class athlete Kari Swenson in the Montana backcountry. Swenson had been training near the Big Sky Resort when a father and son by the name of Don and Dan Nichols abducted her. In the process of being taken prisoner, Swenson was seriously injured by a gunshot. As searchers pursued the duo, one attempted to rescue Kari but was shot to death. France tracked the duo for five months and arrested them peacefully. His tenure as sheriff* ended when he lost reelection in 1986.

SOURCE: Johnny France, *Incident at Big Sky: The True Story of Johnny France and the Capture of the Mountain Men*, 1986.

FRANK, ANTOINETTE. On March 3, 1995, New Orleans police officer Antoinette Frank and an eighteen-year-old friend visited a restaurant where Frank sometimes moonlighted as a security guard along with fellow cop Ronald Williams. Adding another sordid page to the history of one of America's worst police departments, her colleague, Williams, let the two in. Frank and the teenager then shot Williams and killed two of the restaurant owner's children as they begged for their lives. Unknown to the killers, a third child witnessed the murders as she hid in a storage cooler. The two killers then robbed the business of ten thousand dollars. Frank returned to the police station to get her squad car after word filtered back that a cop had been killed. As Frank pulled up to the restaurant, she appeared nonplussed when the survivor accused her of committing the murders. Frank confessed and sits on death row in the women's prison in St. Gabriel, Louisiana. Since the killing she has also been linked to the killing of her father, whose bones were uncovered by an inquisitive dog.

SOURCE: David Remnick, "The Crime Buster," *New Yorker*, February 23, 1997; March 3, 1997.

FRANKLIN, BENJAMIN. Franklin headed the detective unit of the Philadelphia police force during the Civil War but was dismissed from the department because of his weakness for alcohol. While serving as the Philadelphia superintendent of Pinkerton's National Detective Agency* in 1873, Franklin came to prominence when he was approached by the Philadelphia and Reading Railroad to help suppress the Molly Maguires. (This secret labor terrorist organization, composed chiefly of Irish immigrant miners, conducted a campaign of sabotage and murder against mine owners prior to the involvement of the Pinkertons.) Franklin later investigated the famous Charlie Ross kidnapping case. Hired by Allan Pinkerton, Franklin would be fired once more for drinking in 1879. Following his dismissal he formed his own detective agency in Philadelphia.

SOURCES: Frank Morn, *"The Eye That Never Sleeps,"* 1982; James Mackay, *Allan Pinkerton: The First Private Eye*, 1996.

FREE, MICKEY. (1847–1915) Born in Santa Cruz, Sonora, Mexico, Free was abducted in his youth by Apache Indians, an incident that led to a famous confrontation between Cochise and Second Lieutenant George N. Bascom. Free was then taken by the Apaches to the San Carlos area, where he was adopted into the Western White Mountain Apache family.

In the 1870s Free joined the Apache Scouts and by 1874 had begun a long association as an interpreter with frontier legend and Indian fighter Al Sieber. Although he was reputed to have a checkered background, there is no substantiation that he ever killed anyone. Following the Apache campaigns of the 1880s, Free was often hired by Arizona lawmen as a manhunter and for a time rode with Thomas "Tom" Horn.* In 1898 Free led a man-hunting unit of ten Apaches.

SOURCE: Kinney Griffith, *Mickey Free: Manhunter*, 1969.

FREEH, LOUIS J. (b. 1950) Born in Jersey City, New Jersey, Freeh was educated at Rutgers University, graduating from its law school in 1974. The following year he joined the Federal Bureau of Investigation (FBI).* During the next six years he was mainly involved in organized crime investigation. He is credited with having made great strides in moderating racketeering in the longshoreman's union and prosecuting the Sicilian Mafia in the "Pizza Connection" case. In 1981 Freeh moved to the U.S. Attorney General's Office, again targeting organized crime kingpins.

Following the 1993 resignation of William Steele Sessions,* President Bill Clinton appointed Freeh as director of the FBI. Although initially viewed as an exceptional choice by both parties, his tenure as chief has been mired in controversy. Having brought a decisive and aggressive style to the agency, which had been struggling to restore its prestige since the John Edgar Hoover* era, few suspected the number of high-profile embarrassments that would mar Freeh's administration. The most glaring incidents have included the botched interview with falsely accused Olympic bombing suspect Richard Jewell; the investigation of the Pan-Am plane crash; a series of domestic bombing cases; inefficiency in the FBI crime lab; the Waco, Texas, and Ruby Ridge, Idaho, shoot-outs, and security lapses in the atomic weapons labs. Many critics blame Freeh's problems on his previous lack of high-level managerial experience in Washington.

SOURCE: Athan G. Theoharis, *The FBI*, 1999.

FREY, JACOB. (b. 1835) Born in Baltimore, Maryland, Frey was appointed captain of the Baltimore Police Department* in 1867. Three years later he rose to deputy marshal. In 1885 Frey was promoted to marshal of police (police chief), commanding a force of 809, including officers, police matrons,* clerks, and supervisors.

SOURCE: George W. Hale, *Police and Prison Cyclopaedia*, 1893.

FROEST, FRANK. One of the leading detectives in Scotland Yard* in the late 1880s, in 1907 Froest was appointed the first chief of Scotland Yard's "Murder Squad." Three years later he played a prominent role in the apprehension of noted wife-killer Dr. Hawley Harvey Crippen, who was captured during a trans-Atlantic chase.

SOURCE: Paul Begg and Keith Skinner, *The Scotland Yard Files*, 1992.

FULD, LEONHARD FELIX. (1883–1965) Born in New York City and educated at Columbia University, the precocious Fuld earned five degrees in seven years. Although he lacked law enforcement experience, he is remembered in police circles for the publication of his doctoral dissertation, "Police Administration: A Critical Study of Police Organizations in the United States and Abroad." His 551-page book, *Police Administration*, is probably the first comprehensive and readable study of American police administration. In this book the perspicacious lawyer forecast many of the progressive reforms that would characterize policing in the coming years, including a better use of police discretion while performing daily duties, more stringent hiring requirements, and a recognition of the dangers of political patronage. Fuld also recommended better police training in the proper use of deadly force and better systems for scrutinizing police misconduct.

Fuld devoted the rest of his life to public service and lucrative financial investing. At his death the lifelong bachelor left twenty-five million dollars in trust to a nursing foundation. Despite all his wealth, Fuld lived frugally in one of his own Harlem tenement properties with his sister, and could often be seen performing janitorial duties in the building.

SOURCES: William G. Bailey, "Leonhard Felix Fuld," in *The Encyclopedia of Police Science*, ed. William G. Bailey, 1995; *New York Times*, September 1, 1965, p. 1.

FUZZ. This slang term for policeman can be traced back to at least 1929. It is also used to refer to prison guards or turnkeys. It was first used in Canada in the 1950s and Great Britain in the 1960s. According to Bill Waddell in *The Black Museum* (1993), it is derived from the similarity between police whiskers, once in vogue, and the parasitic mold found on rotten fruit.

SOURCES: J. E. Lighter, *Historical Dictionary of American Slang*, 1994; Bill Waddell, *The Black Museum*, 1993.

G

GAMEWELL POLICE SIGNAL SYSTEM. Headquartered in Newton, Massachusetts, the Gamewell Company was one of the early manufacturers of call boxes, first for fire departments and then for police. Beginning in the 1860s the Gamewell Company furnished fire alarm and police signal Telegraphs. The Chicago Police Department (CPD) Department (CPD)* pioneered the police signal system in 1881, and by the end of the decade most large cities had followed suit. In 1888 Boston selected the Municipal Police Signal System. Three years later Atlanta introduced that city's first call box system.

By the twentieth century a typical Gamewell Box was a street box with a light on the top and a phone inside for officers to use. It had a large bell or horn attached to it on the top of the pole that extended from the box. If the call was received during the daytime, either the bell or horn would sound, and the nearest officer would respond by going to that box and opening it with his brass key to receive word of a police call in the area.

SOURCE: William G. Bailey, ed., *The Encyclopedia of Police Science*, 1995.

GARD, GEORGE E. (1843–1904) Born and educated in Warren County, Ohio, Gard moved to California in his late teens after accompanying his uncle there on a cattle drive. Following service in the Civil War, he returned to California, joining the Los Angeles Police Department (LAPD)* force in 1871. As one of only six peace officers on the force, Gard was bedeviled by lack of support during anti-Chinese riots and probably was forced to resign from the force after a new police chief failed to reappoint him.

Between 1875 and 1884 Gard served as Los Angeles county chief deputy recorder, chief of police, and sheriff,* all the while pursuing various business interests in the Asuza Valley. In 1890 he was appointed U.S. Marshal (see U.S. MARSHALS SERVICE) for the southern district of California. Over the next four years he participated in several gunfights, including the shoot-out with noted train robbers Chris Evans and John Sontag in 1893.

In 1895 Gard accepted an offer to become chief of detectives for the Southern Pacific Railroad and shortly after also established his own private detective agency. In 1903 Gard was stricken with pneumonia while investigating a murder case and, after three months in bed, died at home, in Los Angeles.

SOURCES: Harris Newmark, *Sixty Years in Southern California*, 1930; William B. Secrest, *Lawmen and Desperadoes*, 1994.

GARRETT, BUCK. (1871–1929) Born in Tennessee, Garrett grew up in East Texas and at a young age was appointed deputy U.S. marshal. In 1892 he was recruited, along with twenty-one others to serve warrants on "dangerous outlaws" in Wyoming, in what became known as the Johnson County War. He was present during the killing of Nick Ray and Nate Champion and was later apprehended with fellow Texans following the siege of the TA Ranch. They were soon released and left Wyoming.

After his release, in 1905, Garrett was elected police chief of Ardmore, Oklahoma, and five years later became sheriff* of Carter County, Oklahoma. Garrett had a reputation for rarely carrying a gun, although he never wavered when confronted with a potentially violent encounter. A large man and master horseman, Garrett lost his 1922 reelection bid due to his campaign against the Ku Klux Klan.

SOURCES: Louise Riotte, "Buck Garrett, Man and Legend," *True West*, January–February 1970; Helena Huntington Smith, *The War on the Powder River*, 1966.

GARRETT, PATRICK FLOYD JARVIS "PAT." (1850–1908) Born into a farm family in Chambers County, Alabama, as a child Garrett moved with his family to Louisiana. By the age of nineteen he was hunting buffalo in Texas and New Mexico, where he killed another hunter in an argument. Exonerated at Fort Griffin, Garrett relocated to Fort Summer, New Mexico, and found employment under cattleman John Chisum. In 1880 he married and began a family that would include eight children. He was particularly fond of his blind daughter, Elizabeth, who became close friends with Helen Keller and wrote the official state song of New Mexico.

Garrett arrived in New Mexico following the Lincoln County War, and except for Billy the Kid, most of the participants were either dead or had left the scene. While legend has it that Garrett and the Kid had developed a fast friendship, there is no historical evidence to support such claims. Thanks to Chisum's patronage, the ambitious Garrett was elected sheriff* in 1880 on a pledge to drive out the remaining desperadoes. Later that year Garrett led the posse that tracked down and killed Billy the Kid's associates Tom O'Folliard and Charlie Bowdre.

After the Kid surrendered, he was convicted of murdering Sheriff William Brady* and sentenced to the Lincoln gallows. The Kid enhanced his reputation when he killed two guards at the jail while making a successful escape. Garrett tracked him down to the home of Fort Sumner community leader Pete Maxwell and shot the Kid on July 14, 1881.

The rest of Garrett's life was rather anticlimactic. Pilloried for his ambush of Billy, the Kid, Garrett became somewhat of a pariah while Billy was elevated to mythic frontier hero. Garrett lost his reelection for Lincoln County sheriff and collaborated with journalist Ash Upson on the dreadful *The Authentic Life of Billy, the Kid*. Upson claimed that Garrett contributed nary a word to the tome. During Garrett's remaining years, he organized the short-lived "Pat Garrett Rangers" near Tascosa, Texas, and fostered irrigation projects in eastern New Mexico.

Returning to New Mexico, Garrett was made Dona Ana County sheriff and charged with investigating the murder of Colonel Albert Jennings Fountain. Although several suspects were eventually arrested, all were acquitted. President Theodore Roosevelt* appointed Garrett collector of customs for El Paso, Texas, in 1901 but four years later he lost the president's support when he falsely introduced one of his nefarious associates as a local cattleman. Returning to his ranch in New Mexico, Garrett was later shot by one of three men with whom he was transacting a business deal as he walked off to urinate on the side of the road. Accused of his murder, Wayne Brazel claimed it was in self-defense and was acquitted. Although Garrett authority Leon Metz asserts that Brazel was indeed the killer, most scholars believe it was noted assassin James B. "Killin' Jim" Miller.

SOURCES: Leon C. Metz, *Pat Garrett: The Story of a Western Lawman*, 1974; Dan L. Thrapp, ed., *EFB*, Vol. 1, 1988.

GARRISON, HOMER, JR. (1901–1968) Born in Kickapoo, Texas, Garrison began his law enforcement career as a deputy sheriff in East Texas while still in his teens. In 1929 he entered state law enforcement as an inspector with the Texas License and Weight Division. The following year he joined the newly established Texas Highway Patrol. In 1931 he was promoted to captain and thus began a long career of accomplishments in Texas state law enforcement that would lead him to the directorship of the Texas Department of Public Safety* (DPS) in 1938, following the death of Colonel H. H. Carmichael. For almost thirty years he would lead the DPS and Texas Rangers,* longer than any former director. The success of Garrison's management style led the governor of New Mexico to ask for his guidance in organizing a state highway patrol. During his tenure Garrison is credited with developing the first driver-licensing program in the country, reducing traffic fatalities, and augmenting the patrol's communications system to better coordinate with other law enforcement agencies.

SOURCE: Mitchel Roth (historical text by) *Courtesy, Service, Protection: The Texas Department of Public Safety's Sixtieth Anniversary*, 1995.

GATES, DARYL F. (b. 1926) Born in Glendale, California, Gates attended the University of Southern California but left school prior to graduation to join the Los Angeles Police Department (LAPD)* in 1949. He quickly become a favorite and protégé of reformer police chief William Henry Parker.* Gates transferred to the juvenile division and then to Vice after serving as an assistant to Parker for fifteen months, and in 1954 he was promoted to sergeant. (According to one source, because Gates was of average height he fit one of Parker's unspoken rules, which was that none of his assistants could be taller than he.)

In 1963 Gates was selected as captain and head of the intelligence division and was instrumental in infiltrating student radical groups and organized crime as the 1960s wore on. In 1965 Gates supervised the police during the Watts riot and was struck by their incapacity to handle urban insurrections. His examination of riot control strategies led him to write two manuals dealing with the subject. During the Vietnam War years, Gates applied guerrilla warfare and Marine tactics to police work. After creating the antisniper D Platoon, consisting of the department's best marksman, Gates suggested to Chief Parker that it would be appropriate to call it the Special Weapons Attack Team (SWAT). Parker opposed the word *attack*, but Gates remained so taken with the acronym that he changed the title to Special Weapons and Tactics (SWAT).*

In 1978 Gates was appointed Los Angeles's forty-ninth police chief, succeeding Edward M. Davis.* His term as chief was tarnished by controversy. A siege mentality had developed among a force that had fewer officers per capita than any other major American city. Consistently in conflict with Mayor Tom Bradley,* Gates came under fire for putting the African-American mayor under surveillance and for a series of public gaffes including most notably his notion that blacks died more often from choke holds because their "veins or arteries do not open as fast as they do in normal people" (Domanick).

The ascension of Daryl Gates came to an ignominious conclusion in the 1990s following the videotaped beating of Rodney King* and the ensuing Los Angeles riots. During Gates's reign, the LAPD seemed to be perpetually under fire. In the first half of the 1980s alone, the city of Los Angeles paid close to $13 million to settle police misconduct suits. Gates retired in 1992 following accusations that his police force was slow to respond to the rioting in South-Central Los Angeles.

SOURCES: Daryl F. Gates, with Diane K. Shah, *Chief: My Life in the LAPD*, 1992; Joe Domanick, *To Protect and Serve: The LAPD's Century of War in the City of Dreams*, 1994.

GAULT, BENJAMIN MANNY. (1886–1947) Born in Travis County, Texas, Manny Gault worked in a furniture-manufacturing plant before joining the Texas Rangers* at the behest of Frank Hamer* in 1929. During the 1930s he saw action during the 1930 Sherman race riot and in the oil field boomtowns of East Texas. Like many of the oldtime Rangers, Gault resigned in 1933 after Miriam

"Ma" Ferguson took office as Texas governor. Gault rose to prominence in 1934 when he joined Hamer in the pursuit of outlaws Bonnie and Clyde into Louisiana. He was one of six posse members who participated in the final ambush of the killer couple on May 23, 1934. Following this incident Gault returned to the Rangers and was soon an employee of the reorganized force within the Texas Department of Public Safety.* In 1938 he was promoted to sergeant, and then captain, of Company C in Lubbock. In the early 1940s Gault focused his attentions on illegal gambling operations, cattle theft, bank robberies, and the sporadic murder cases.

SOURCE: Mike Cox, *Texas Ranger Tales*, 1997.

GAYNOR, WILLIAM JAY. (1849–1913) Born in upstate New York, Gaynor had originally prepared for the priesthood but instead traveled West for a brief time and, for some reason, renounced Catholicism, explaining that he thought it was too conservative. He returned to New York, opened a law practice, and jumped on the police reform bandwagon, leading to his appointment as police commissioner. Following his term as commissioner, Gaynor devoted the rest of his career to public service, serving as state Supreme Court justice and mayor of New York beginning in 1909. During his tenure as mayor he continued his campaign of police reform. In 1910 he barely survived an assassin's bullet. He died three years later.

SOURCE: Thomas A. Reppetto, *The Blue Parade*, 1978.

GENDARME. The term *gendarme* is derived from the French phrase *gens d'armes*, referring to soldiers or armed men used for peacekeeping before the advent of professional policing.

SOURCE: Patrick Pringle, *Hue and Cry*, 1955.

GENDARMERIE NATIONALE. This French police force can trace its origins back to the twelfth century. Three hundred years later, mounted *gens d'armes* and archers were consolidated to form the nucleus of what eventually became known as the *gendarmerie*. During the French Revolution, this unit became known as the national *gendarmerie* and was entrusted with maintaining internal and external security in France. During the Napoleonic Wars, many countries within the French orbit adopted similar police units. Over time Napoleon increasingly employed the Gendarmerie Nationale in civil police work. Today this force is responsible for enforcing the law in the more rural areas of France and in communities of less than 10,000 inhabitants. Since France has few densely populated metropolitan areas, it is estimated that the force is responsible for 95 percent of French territory and almost half the population.

The Gendarmerie Nationale is controlled by a director general who is responsible to the minister of defense. The Gendarmerie Nationale has divided

France into three regions, each headed by a general. There are two specialized branches that make this force distinct. The Gendarmerie Mobile is trained in paramilitary tactics and employed as a public order unit. Its members are housed in barracks around the country and can be quickly deployed. Highly mobile, they are equipped with armored vehicles, light tanks, and helicopters. The other unit is the Republican Guard, which is used for ceremonial occasions.

SOURCES: Christine Horton, *Policing Policy in France*, 1995; James Cramer, *The World's Police*, 1964.

GENDARMES. Most foreigners are under the false impression that all French police are *gendarmes*. The confusion stems from the similarity of French police uniforms and the higher visibility of the members of the Gendarmerie Nationale,* who are the most prominent officers in France, numbering 125,000 members as of 1983. The term *gendarmes* is also used as slang in reference to police officers.

SOURCE: Philip John Stead, *The Police of France*, 1983.

GESTAPO. Following the ascendance of the Nazi party in Germany in 1933, German police forces were reorganized and a new national system of police was created under the Reich minister of the interior. Three years later the position of chief of the German Police was established. The police force was reorganized into two units, the *Ordnungspolizei*, or uniformed police, and the *Sicherheitspolizei*, or security police. Besides these two groups, a new force called the *Geheimestaatspolizei* (better known by its acronym, Gestapo) was created.

The Gestapo was essentially the state secret police force. Unobstructed by outside interference, the Gestapo used the concentration camp system to incarcerate anyone whose activities, interests, associations, or origins were deemed harmful to state security. These broad powers allowed this nefarious unit to restrict rights of assembly and freedom of speech. With a mandate to prevent and detect political crimes, there was little interference from the courts of law. Combining the powers of the judiciary and executive branches, the Gestapo controlled the fate of suspects from arrest and detention to the concentration camps and the firing squad.

SOURCES: Edward Crankshaw, *The Gestapo*, 1956; Louis L. Snyder, *Encyclopedia of the Third Reich*, 1989.

GILLETT, JAMES BUCHANAN. (1856–1937) Born in Austin, Texas, Gillett became a cowboy after his family moved to Lampasas, Texas, in 1872. In 1875 he joined Texas Rangers* Company D, commanded by Captain Daniel Webster Roberts.* During his first year he participated in a skirmish with Apaches and tried to suppress the Mason County feud. After distinguishing himself against rustlers, Mexican bandits, and hostile Indians, Gillett was handpicked for the elite Company E. Gillett was on the detail that transported John Wesley Hardin to the Huntsville Penitentiary.

Gillett campaigned against the Apaches near El Paso following the Salt War, and was nearby, but did not witness, the deaths of Sam Bass at Round Rock and Victorio near the Mexican border. In 1881 he resigned from the Rangers and served four years as El Paso city marshal. He entered ranching after retiring from law enforcement and is credited with writing a classic account describing his life in the Texas Rangers.

SOURCES: James B. Gillett, *Six Years with the Texas Rangers*, 1925; Dan L. Thrapp, ed., *EFB*, Vol. 2, 1988.

GLAISTER, JOHN. (1892–1971) Born in Glasgow, Scotland, Glaister traded his acting ambitions for a medical career. Following service in the Royal Army Medical Corps during World War I he worked in forensic medicine at Glasgow University. Then, in 1926, he was called to the bar. As both a doctor and a barrister, Glaister possessed unique qualifications as a crime investigator. Following in the footsteps of Sir Sydney Alfred Smith* who had just returned from Cairo, in 1927 Glaister accepted an appointment as a medico-legal consultant to the government of Egypt. He returned to Great Britain in 1931 and spent the next thirty-two years at Glasgow University. During his career as a forensic scientist, he investigated thousands of cases, but the most prominent was the Ruxton murder case of 1935. Glaister supervised an amazing reconstruction of the dismembered bodies of two victims and was one of the first individuals to superimpose the negative photograph of a skull over a positive portrait of the victim. The perpetrator was arrested, convicted, and hanged. Besides writing several medical textbooks Glaister, coauthored with James Couper Brash, *Medico-Legal Aspects of the Ruxton Case* (1937), a classic account of the investigation. Erle Stanley Gardner claimed that Glaister was the inspiration for the fictional Perry Mason, due to his scientific know-how.

SOURCE: Richard Whittington-Egan and Molly Whittington-Egan, *The Bedside Book of Murder*, 1987.

GLASS, JOHN M. (1843–?) Born in Tennessee, Glass entered law enforcement as an officer with the California state prison system. After a six-year stint in this capacity, he served two terms as city marshal of Jeffersonville, Indiana. He moved to Los Angeles in 1885 and joined the Los Angeles Police Department (LAPD)* the following year; in 1889 he was appointed police chief of the seventy-two-member force. Over the next several years he earned a reputation as a strict disciplinarian and is credited with systemizing police work in Los Angeles. Glass was recognized for introducing the first timebook, dividing the city into four police districts, which were then split and numbered from one to eight. Roundsmen,* better known today as sergeants, were able to keep a record of their patrolmen's beats that way.

Glass organized the city's first detective bureau under Charles O. Moffett shortly after taking charge of the department. The LAPD in the 1880s was military in appearance, with policemen equipped with Winchester rifles, handcuffs, whistle, and baton, and crowned with a quasi-military hat. Chief Glass was the first California police chief to adopt the use of the Bertillon system.* Other firsts credited to Glass include the first police matrons,* patrol wagon, substation, alarm system, and entry-level standards for new recruits.

SOURCES: Arthur W. Sjoquist (historical text by), *Los Angeles Police Department Commemorative Book, 1869–1984*, 1984; George W. Hale, *Police and Prison Cyclopaedia*, 1893.

GLASSFORD, PELHAM DAVIS. (1883–1959) Born in Las Vegas, New Mexico, Glassford graduated from West Point in 1904. During World War I he served in France, fighting in the battles of the Marne and Saint-Mihiel. In October of 1918 Glassford became the country's youngest general when he took command of the Fifty-First Field Artillery Brigade. Following the war he served in the army in various capacities until retiring in 1931. That same year he was appointed superintendent of the Washington, D.C., police.

As an outsider and a military man, from the start Glassford was viewed with suspicion by liberals and the rank and file. However, the liberal constituency was surprised by Glassford's reluctance to harass procommunist demonstrations during a 1931 hunger march. Glassford developed a reputation as a sympathetic official, which countered his paramilitary image. During the 1932 bonus march (veterans descended on Washington, D.C. with their families asking for the "bonus" promised them in 1924 and scheduled for payment in 1945) he was reportedly one of the few officials to support the marchers' right to set up encampments in the city parks and even arranged for public donations for food and shelter. However, on July 28, 1932, Glassford was forced to enforce President Herbert Hoover's directive to evict the squatters. In the ensuing turmoil, several marchers were killed. Soon after, army troops under Douglas MacArthur drove off the remaining bonus marchers.

Glassford resigned on October 30, 1932, and wrote a series of newspaper articles that suggested Hoover's treatment of the protestors had resulted in his loss to Franklin D. Roosevelt in the 1932 presidential election. In 1936 Glassford served in law enforcement for the last time as police chief of Phoenix, Arizona.

SOURCES: Roger Daniels, "Pelham Davis Glassford," *ANB*, Vol. 9, 1999; Irving Bernstein, *The Lean Years*, 1960.

GLOVER, JOHN D. (b. 1939) Born in Miami, Florida, and educated at Florida A&M University, Glover joined the Federal Bureau of Investigation (FBI)* in 1966. After stints in the Kansas City, Missouri, and Washington, D.C., field offices, Glover served as a firearms instructor at Quantico, Virginia.* He served in a variety of capacities before FBI director William H. Webster* appointed him to executive assistant director in 1982, making him the highest-ranking African-American in the Bureau. Glover was most prominent when he supervised the FBI investigation of the Atlanta child murders.

SOURCE: Athan G. Theoharis, ed., *The FBI*, 1999.

G-MEN. George "Machine Gun" Kelly reputedly coined this moniker for government men or Federal Bureau of Investigation (FBI)* agents when he was captured while still in bed. As the FBI agents burst into his room, he reportedly shouted "Don't shoot, G-men!" According to debunkers, the term was already in the American lexicon and Kelly never uttered this response but rather responded, "I've been waiting for you all night." Then, ever the publicity machine, FBI Director John Edgar Hoover* invented the apocryphal story to gain publicity. According to some sources, some nineteenth-century gangsters alluded to Secret Service agents and other government law enforcers as G-men.

SOURCE: Carl Sifakis, *The Encyclopedia of American Crime*, 1982.

GODDARD, HENRY. (1800–c. 1870) One of the most famous members of the early Bow Street Foot Patrol, Goddard joined the force in 1824 and two years later was promoted to runner for the Great Marlborough Street Police Office, officially making him a detective. In 1834 he was brought into the Bow Street Runners* and stayed with them until they were abolished five years later. In 1840 Goddard was hired as Northamptonshire's first chief constable, a position he would hold until forced into retirement for health reasons in 1849. Goddard's *Memoirs of a Bow Street Runner*, published for the first time in 1956, offers valuable insight into this little-chronicled era.

SOURCES: P. F. Speed, *Police and Prisons*, 1977; Anthony Babington, *A House in Bow Street*, 1969.

GONZAULLAS, MANUEL TRAZAZAS "LONE WOLF." (1891–1977) Born in Cadiz, Spain, Gonzaullas was the only captain in the Texas Rangers* who was of Spanish descent. Gonzaullas was drawn to law enforcement while still a youth when his two brothers were murdered by bandits. He joined the Rangers in 1920 and, over his thirty-one-year career, battled bootleggers during Prohibition and pursued the Phantom Killer of Texarkana and outlaws Bonnie and Clyde. Gonzaullas also was present during the courthouse burning and lynching in Sherman, Texas, and the Beaumont, Texas race riots.

In 1935, during the reorganization of the Rangers, Gonzaullas was promoted to chief of the Bureau of Intelligence and is generally credited as the first Ranger to make the transition to modern, scientific methods of crime detection. After retiring from the force in 1951, he served as a technical advisor in Hollywood.

SOURCE: Brownson Malsch, *Captain M. T. "Lone Wolf" Gonzaullas: The Only Texas Ranger Captain of Spanish Descent*, 1980.

GOODWIN, ISABELLA. After the death of her patrolman husband in 1895 Goodwin took a civil service exam and won appointment as one of the police matrons* working with the New York City police. From 1896 to 1910 she worked out of the Mercer Street Station and was gradually involved in detective work. After uncovering various extortion rackets and banking scams, Goodwin rose to prominence in 1912 after she solved a $25,000 robbery. That same year she was appointed detective first grade, more than doubling her previous salary to $2,250. She is often recognized as one of the world's first female detectives. Goodwin also served as New York City's deputy commissioner of police for several months following the abrupt resignation of Ellen O'Grady.*

SOURCES: Kerry Segrave, *Policewomen: A History*, 1995; Dorothy Moses Schulz, *From Social Worker to Crimefighter*, 1995.

GORDON RIOTS. The Gordon Riots broke out in London in 1780. In this era before professional policing, little could be done to control mobs intent on destruction. The riots initially began as a protest against the repeal of specific anti-Catholic laws. The rioters were soon joined by almost every member of London's notorious underworld. During a six-day binge, the mob set fire to countless buildings and looted with abandon, and, in certain instances, its members even drank themselves to death; however, it never killed anyone. It was not until troops were called in that the riot was quelled. Over two hundred people were killed by the militia and hundreds were wounded. The insufficiency of civil power was immediately apparent, but the British government's use of military force came under even greater criticism. This incident and subsequent riots would spur the government and citizenry toward accepting the inevitable development of an official police organization.

SOURCES: Philip John Stead, *The Police of Britain*, 1985; Elaine A. Reynolds, *Before the Bobbies*, 1998.

GORON, MARIE-FRANÇOIS. (1847–1933) Born in Rennes, France, Goron joined the Paris Police in 1881 after serving in the French Army. His rise through the ranks was meteoric, and he reached commissioner of police for the Partin district by 1885. Three years later he was promoted to deputy chief of the Sûreté.* Short, fat, and pink-skinned, Goron was nicknamed "the Pig." Nonetheless, his unorthodox detective methods elevated him to the pantheon of great detectives. His most famous case was his solution of the 1889 Gouffe murder and the manhunt for the suspects, which took Goron across the Atlantic Ocean. In 1890 the final suspect in this case was arrested in Cuba and returned to France for a date with the guillotine.

SOURCE: Frank Smyth and Myles Ludwig, *The Detectives: Crime and Detection in Fact and Fiction*, 1978.

GRASS-EATERS. In police parlance, corrupt policemen come in two forms, meat-eaters* and grass-eaters (the latter, according to the 1972 Knapp Commission,* is the more common of the two types). The Knapp Commission reported that most police who accept payoffs are grass-eaters, meaning that they are willing to accept gratuities from gamblers and small payments from contractors but do not aggressively seek out payments.

SOURCE: Whitman Knapp, chairman, *Knapp Commission Report on Police Corruption*, 1972.

GRAY, LOUIS PATRICK, III. (b. 1916) Born in St. Louis, Missouri, Gray was educated at Rice University and the U.S. Naval Academy. Following service in World War II, Gray was chosen to attend the Navy postgraduate program to study law at George Washington University. Following graduation he served in the Korean War as a captain and was named to the Joint Chiefs of Staff in 1958.

In 1960 Gray affiliated himself with Richard Nixon's unsuccessful presidential campaign. His support would earn him dividends when Nixon won the presidency in 1968 and he was appointed to a high executive post. During the early 1970s Gray worked for the U.S. Department of Justice* Civil Division and, at Nixon's direction, spent considerable effort prosecuting antiwar demonstrators.

Grays allegiance to Nixon led to his selection as the successor to John Edgar Hoover* following Hoover's death in 1972. Gray proved a breath of fresh air to Federal Bureau of Investigation (FBI)* employees, who had chafed under Hoover's micromanagement. Gray relaxed many of the strict regulations, including the dress code, and championed the appointment of women as field agents. Gray's record as director was tarnished by his peripheral participation in the Watergate cover-up and other "dirty tricks." He resigned in 1973 after admitting he had had evidence of the break-in destroyed.

SOURCE: Athan G. Theoharis, *The FBI*, 1999.

GREENING, JOHN. In 1932 John Greening succeeded August Vollmer* as chief of the Berkeley, California, Police Department.* During his tenure as chief he continued to follow the policies set by his predecessor. Police officers were expected to offer suggestions for improving their performance and efficiency. He warned his officers not to give the names of juveniles to journalists and took surveys of local merchants to help improve security measures. As police chief during the Depression years, he had to contend with rising suicide rates and juvenile crime. He also supported a fingerprinting* campaign and was an advocate of universal fingerprinting. His voluntary campaign led sixteen thousand Berkeley residents to provide their fingerprints, amounting to almost one-quarter of the population. Greening retired as chief in 1944.

SOURCE: Alfred E. Parker, *The Berkeley Police Story*, 1972.

GRIMES, AHIJAH W. (1855–1878) Born in Bastrop, Texas, Grimes, who went by the monikers "High" and "Caige," was trained in the printing trade before entering law enforcement as Bastrop city marshal in 1874. Two years later he was appointed constable (see CONSTABLES), but the following year he joined the Texas Rangers* for a three-month stint, beginning in December 1877. Soon after he resigned from the Rangers he was appointed deputy sheriff in Georgetown, Texas. Grimes was among the party of lawmen who tracked Sam Bass to nearby Round Rock. When Grimes and another peace officer attempted to apprehend Bass and his two accomplices, they were met with gunfire. Grimes was mortally wounded by six gunshot wounds before he could even unsheathe his gun. When Bass was later mortally wounded he reportedly confessed that if his bullets had killed Grimes, this was the first man he had killed.

SOURCES: Wayne Gard, *Sam Bass*, 1969; Robert W. Stephens, *Texas Ranger Sketches*, 1972; Mike Cox, *Texas Ranger Tales*, 1997.

GROGAN, BENJAMIN P. (1933–1986) Born in Atlanta, Georgia, Grogan joined the Federal Bureau of Investigation (FBI)* in 1953, serving in a variety of field offices before being assigned to Miami, Florida, in 1966. On April 11, 1986, he was killed, along with agent Jerry L. Dove,* while attempting to arrest heavily armed bank robbers. Five other agents were wounded in the bloodiest day in FBI history, and the incident led to better firearms training and the adoption of new weapons by field agents. It also inspired the 1992 TV movie *In the Line of Fire: The FBI Murders*.

SOURCE: Athan G. Theoharis, ed., *The FBI*, 1999.

GROOME, JOHN C. (1860–1930) Born in Philadelphia, Groome joined the Pennsylvania National Guard, beginning a lifelong career in the military and law enforcement. He commanded his unit in the Spanish-American War and returning home to help suppress the 1902 Anthracite Coal Strike. Three years later he was appointed to lead the newly created Pennsylvania State Police* after the governor agreed there would be no political tampering. Under Groome's direction, the paramilitary-oriented state police force became a model for similar units. Groome resigned in 1917 to serve in World War I. Following the war he was made warden of Pennsylvania's Eastern State Penitentiary.

SOURCES: Katherine Mayo, *The Standard-Bearers: True Stories of Heroes of Law and Order*, 1918; H. Kenneth Bechte, *State Police in the United States*, 1995.

GROSS, HARRY. (1916–1986) The arrest of New York City gambling syndicate kingpin Harry Gross on September 15, 1950, led to one of the biggest police scandals in city history. After agreeing to cooperate with the district police, Gross recounted in detail how police officers protected his book making operation beginning in the 1940s. Gross reported paying officers over a million dollars a year in cash and personal gifts. His grand jury testimony in 1951 led to the indictment of twenty-one officers for conspiring to protect the Gross gambling operations. In addition, over fifty patrolmen were listed as co-conspirators but were not indicted due to lack of evidence. Gross committed suicide at age 71 in 1986.

SOURCE: Whitman Knapp, chairman, *The Knapp Commission Report on Police Corruption*, 1972.

GROSSO, SALVADOR "SONNY." (b. 1935) Grosso caught the attention of the public along with partner Edward "Eddie" Egan* when they busted the "French Connection" drug operation in 1962. A street-smart New York City police undercover detective, Grosso and his partner made headlines and became media celebrities with the high-profile seizure of fifty kilos of heroin worth $32 million, the biggest heroin bust up to that time. Becoming star struck, Grosso subsequently left the force to act as a technical consultant for the book and movie accounts of *The French Connection*. He later consulted for the films *The Godfather* and *The Seven-Ups* and for detective television shows such as *Kojak*, *Baretta*, and the *Rockford Files*. In 1980 he cofounded a production company to make reality-based television programs.

SOURCE: Charles Phillips and Alan Axelrod, *CCC*, 1996.

GRUNTER. This term is British slang for policeman.

SOURCE: Bill Waddell, *The Black Museum*, 1993.

GUARDIA CIVIL. The oldest national police in Spain, the Guardia Civil (Civil Guard) was patterned after the French Gendarmerie Nationale.* Organized along the lines of the military model, today it is responsible for policing rural Spain, the highway patrol, guarding security installations, controlling weapons trafficking, and protecting the frontiers, ports, and airports. Affiliated with the armed forces, the Civil Guard has yet to overcome its negative image as an ultraconservative link to the Franco past. The Civil Guard has been tarnished of late by incidents of corruption, and it has been targeted by Basque and Cataluna terrorist groups because of its close association with the national government.

SOURCES: George T. Kurian, *World Encyclopedia of Police Forces and Penal Systems*, 1989; Ian R. MacDonald, "Spain's 1986 Police Law: Transition from Dictatorship to Democracy," *Police Studies* 10, (1987), pp. 16–22.

GUARDIAN ANGELS. Combining the traditions of vigilantism and auxiliary policing, the Guardian Angels came to national prominence in the 1970s. By the mid-1980s they claimed a national membership of almost five thousand, with chapters in forty-three cities. The Guardian Angels relied on private donations for support, paid their own transit fares, and wore the now-familiar red berets. Founded by Curtis Sliwa,* this controversial auxiliary police force earned a controversial reputation for their crime-fighting techniques and lack of peace officer status. The Angels typically patrol city streets, subways, and public housing projects in groups of ten or more people. Although criticized for interfering with professional police services, they remained popular in communities with little police protection. Prospective members must agree to attend a three-month training program, and the first 50 members of any new chapter must have a crime-free record. When the New York City Police Department (NYPD)* conducted a screening of 550 local members, they found that only 6 had criminal records.

According to the scanty information available, most patrol members reside in high-crime and low-income neighborhoods and, compared to police departments, have a disproportionately higher Hispanic, African-American, and female membership. An extralegal law enforcement organization, the Guardian Angels find their strongest support among the elderly and the poor. There have been incidents in which Angels have been arrested and even killed by police officers. One observer described the Guardian Angels as "a cross between a Special Forces military squad and a street gang" (Greenberg).

SOURCES: Martin Alan Greenberg, *Auxiliary Police*, 1984; James Haskins, *The Guardian Angels*, 1983.

GYLAM, LEWIS J. (d. 1873) Born in Texas, Gylam relocated to Lincoln County, New Mexico, around 1872. That year he succeeded William Brady* as the county's second sheriff.* Gylam apparently had a falling out with Lawrence G. Murphy, who had supported him in his election campaign. When Gylam lost his reelection bid, he blamed his former supporters and threatened to kill Murphy and his partner. By the fall of 1873 Gylam had fallen in with the notorious Horrell brothers, who had escaped jail in Texas and moved to Lincoln County. Gylam and two others rode into Lincoln on December 1, seeming intent on disturbing the peace. In the course of a drinking binge accompanied by random gunshots, they were confronted by Lincoln County constable (see CONSTABLES) Juan Martinez and four police officers, who demanded that Gylam and his friends surrender their guns. In the ensuing gunfight, Martinez and the three carousers, including Gylam, were shot dead.

SOURCE: Don Bullis, *New Mexico's Finest*, 1996.

H

HALE, GEORGE W. (b. 1855–) Born and educated in Lawrence, Massachusetts, Hale moved to Illinois in 1872. Following stints farming and then steam-
boating on the Mississippi and Arkansas Rivers, Hale returned East to recuperate
from a bout of malaria. In 1875 Hale took passage on a steamer bound for
California, where he would spend several years raising sheep. In 1878 he survived a serious wagon accident while employed as a teamster. The following
year he enlisted in the Sixth U.S. Cavalry and participated in field action against
Apaches in Arizona. Hale spent his last years on the Western frontier in the
Arizona Territory as a member of General George Crook's 1883 expedition
against the Apaches in Mexico and then in a series of dead-end jobs.

In 1884 Hale returned to Massachusetts. Following his honorable discharge
from the military in 1887, he joined the Lawrence, Massachusetts, police force.
Beginning in 1891 Hale began compiling what would become his groundbreaking *Police and Prison Cyclopaedia* (1892). Hale's last years are shrouded in
mystery. No one knows what spurred him to compile his police and prison
reference work, but it is evident that he meant to follow it up with additional
volumes. His work demonstrates painstaking research and a methodology that
included sending questionnaires to police chiefs around the world in order to
enumerate their various duties and legal procedures. Written over close to a
year, the book is a fabulous compendium of details, listing such data as the
statistics of all police departments in cities of over 100,000 population in 1890,
crime definitions, and U.S. civil service regulations, as well as civil service
regulations and police procedures around the world. What little is known about
the enigmatic Hale is derived from *Lawrence Evening Tribune* editor William
T. Sellers's biographical depiction of him, which was published in the *Cyclopaedia*.

SOURCES: George W. Hale, *Police and Prison Cyclopaedia*, 1893; William G. Bailey, "George W. Hale," in *Encyclopedia of Police Science*, ed. William G. Bailey, 1995.

HALL, JESSE LEIGH (LEE). (1849–1911) Born in Lexington, North Carolina, Hall moved to Texas in 1869 and changed the spelling of his middle name to the more familiar Lee. He entered law enforcement as a city marshal in Sherman, Texas, and two years later became the deputy sheriff of Denison, Texas. Following several shoot-outs and himself suffering a serious gunshot wound, Lee left local policing to become lieutenant of the Texas Rangers* Special Force in 1876. His early career received a boost when he helped end the Sutton-Taylor feud and later arrested John King Fisher.* Hall rose to captain during his four-year career with the Rangers and was credited with more than four hundred arrests. He was also involved in the events surrounding the death of Sam Bass at Round Rock.

Hall left the Rangers in 1880 to marry and start a cattle ranch and soon after became friends with the young William Porter (O. Henry). Porter later published an account of his ranching days with Hall under the O. Henry moniker. Hall was appointed an Indian agent in the Oklahoma Indian Territory but was forced to retire two years later when he was suspected of malfeasance. (He was eventually cleared of all charges.) He continued to work sporadically as a peace officer, most prominently as deputy sheriff in San Antonio. During the Spanish-American War, Hall raised several regiments of soldiers and then fought in the Philippines campaign, where he was commended for gallantry. He left the service in 1900 and spent his remaining years guarding gold mines south of the border and prospecting for oil leases.

SOURCES: Dora Neill Raymond, *Captain Lee Hall of Texas*, 1940; Walter Prescott Webb, *The Texas Rangers*, 1935.

HAMER, FRANK. (1884–1955) Hamer was born near Fairview, Texas, and grew up in San Saba County, where he developed an early interest in the outdoor life. At well over six feet tall, in 1906 he was a perfect fit for the Texas Rangers,* the law enforcement agency with which he would be forever identified. During his storied career he participated in more than fifty gunfights and was wounded twenty times. His Ranger years saw the transition between two eras as he fought mounted bandits and tommy gun–bearing bank robbers in automobiles. He was estimated to have killed between fifty and one hundred men as a lawman.

His first assignment with the Rangers was bringing law and order to the Texas oil boomtown of Doran, which he accomplished with great aplomb. Hamer took particular pleasure in hunting down bank robbers and, in perhaps his most complicated case, he investigated the killing of innocent men as bank robbers in return for the five-thousand-dollar rewards offered by the Texas Bankers Association. His solo investigation resulted in the arrest of the murder ring leaders (local peace officers) and subsequently brought an end to scandal.

Hamer resigned from the force in 1934 during the reign of Governor Miriam "Ma" Ferguson to protest the patronage system that rewarded friends of the governor with special ranger commissions. It was during this period that Hamer came to national prominence when he was hired to track down outlaws Bonnie and Clyde. The killer couple had killed eight law enforcement officers and generally eluded Texas peace officers. Hamer led the posse that ambushed and killed the couple in northwest Louisiana after a 102-day pursuit. Hamer's portrayal as an incompetent lawman in the 1967 film *Bonnie and Clyde* was libelous, since in reality he easily stands in the pantheon of the greatest Rangers. Hamer returned to the Rangers following Ferguson's retirement, and he himself retired in 1949.

SOURCES: Walter Prescott Webb, *The Texas Rangers*, 1935; H. Gordon Frost and John H. Jenkins, *"I'm Frank Hamer,"* 1968.

HAMILTON, MARY. Hamilton joined the New York Police Department's Missing Person's Bureau in 1917 as a volunteer. She was one of the earliest policewomen* in New York City, although she only enjoyed secondary status, mainly being responsible for cases that fit her socially prescribed role as a caregiver and included women and children. In 1918, When Ellen O' Grady was promoted to deputy commissioner of police, the women's movement in policing received a great boost. In 1924 Hamilton became the city's first female police field supervisor when she was appointed director of the recently created Women's Police Bureau. In January 1926 she resigned, believing that policewomen could never match their male counterparts in the field and therefore should stay relegated to preventative and protective tasks dealing with children and women. She published several articles on policing and penned her autobiography, *The Policewoman: Her Service and Ideals* (1924), which chronicled the development of the policewoman's movement.

SOURCES: Kerry Segrave, *Policewomen: A History*, 1995; Dorothy Moses Schulz, *From Social Worker to Crimefighter*, 1995.

HAMMETT, (SAMUEL) DASHIELL. (1894–1961) Born in St. Mary's County, Maryland, Hammett dropped out of school and later joined Pinkerton's National Detective Agency* in Baltimore. Best known as the creator of some of literature's most memorable mysteries and of fictional detective Sam Spade, Hammett gained much of his insight and inspiration from his stints as a Pinkerton in cities such as San Francisco. (His first arrest resulted in the apprehension of a suspect for stealing a Ferris wheel.) Hammett also investigated gambler Nick Arnstein and the famous Fatty Arbuckle rape case. A careful examination of his eight years as a Pinkerton reveals many parallels with his fiction. Following service during World War I, Hammett returned to detective work for a brief time, but his chronic tuberculosis hampered his effectiveness, and he turned to writing and alcohol.

SOURCES: Chris Steinbrunner and Otto Penzler, *EMD*, 1976; Jeff Siegel, *The American Detective: An Illustrated History*, 1993.

HANKEY, RICHARD O. (1915–1979) Born in Illinois, Hankey studied criminology at the University of California, Berkeley, where he came under the influence of noted police reformer August Vollmer.* Following graduation in 1939, Hankey joined the Berkeley, California, Police Department* and rose to sergeant under Vollmer before joining the army during the closing days of World War II. Stationed in Germany, Hankey was instrumental in reconstructing and reorganizing German civil law enforcement in the postwar years. Hankey moved into academia on his return to the United States and, after several appointments, developed the Department of Police Science and Administration at the University of California at Los Angeles, which would become a training ground for the Los Angeles Police Department (LAPD).* At his death Hankey was a nationally recognized leader in the police professionalization movement.

SOURCE: Charles Phillips and Alan Axelrod, *CCC*, 1996.

HANSEN, HARRY. Nicknamed "Mr. Homicide," Hansen was one of the most formidable detectives on the Los Angeles Police Department (LAPD)* in the 1940s. Hansen joined the LAPD in 1926, quickly earning a reputation as fingerprinting* expert in the Records Bureau. He ascended the police hierarchy to auto theft, robbery investigation, and the burglary squad, and in 1936 he was promoted to the homicide squad.

During his forty-two-year career, Hansen solved hundreds of murders, but he is probably best remembered for his investigation of the 1947 "Black Dahlia" case. On January 15 the body of twenty-two-year-old Elizabeth Ann Short was discovered in a vacant lot. Her body had been cut in half with almost surgical precision. A known habitue of the local bar scene, Short was given the moniker "Black Dahlia" for her predilection for dressing in black.

Hansen was teamed with Jack McCreadie, who was awarded the sobriquet "Father McCreadie" for his ability to get suspects to confide in him. Despite innumerable investigations and follow-up on countless clues without success, the detectives persisted for several decades. When Hansen retired in 1968, the Black Dahlia case was still unsolved, and it remains so to this day.

SOURCES: John Gilmore, *Severed: The True Story of the Black Dahlia Murder*, 1994; Bruce Henderson and Sam Summerlin, *The Super Sleuths*, 1976.

HARPER'S POLICE. In 1844, prior to the creation of the New York City Police Department (NYPD) the next year, an ephemeral nativist police force known as "Harper's Police" patrolled the city in 1844. This force was notable for its early use of police uniforms,* in this case a blue uniform with the letters M. P. signifying Municipal Police, on the collar. Police could fold the collar down to obscure their identities. Reviled by the public, the short-lived force was a frequent target of stonings and verbal abuse and early on demonstrated the unpopularity of uniformed policing.

SOURCE: Wilbur R. Miller, *Cops and Bobbies*, 1973.

HARRINGTON, PENNY. (b. 1949) Harrington was born in Michigan and educated at Michigan State University. Following graduation from the criminal justice program in 1964, she moved to Portland, Oregon, where she was rejected in her attempts to join the local police force. Over the next two years she petitioned the mayor to increase the number of policewomen* on the force. In 1966 her lobbying paid off when she was appointed to the Women's Protective Division, which handled juveniles and rape victims.

After a static six years with the division, Harrington filed the first of dozens of complaints demanding equal opportunities for women in other areas of policing. Shortly afterward she became the city's first female police detective. Over the next sixteen years she was promoted through the ranks, but not without having to file a suit at each stage. In the process she earned a series of firsts: first female sergeant, first female lieutenant, and first female captain. In 1985 her persistence paid off when she became the first female police chief of a major American city. Although she was responsible for improved relations with the minority communities, her eighteen months as chief were marked by rancor and criticism over her restructuring of the department. Harrington resigned less than two years into her term. She filed an unsuccessful sexual harassment suit to win back her job, but to no avail.

SOURCE: Charles Phillips and Alan Axelrod, *CCC*, 1996.

HARRIOT, JOHN. (1745–1817) A legal expert and former British naval officer, Harriot collaborated with Patrick Colquhoun* in developing one of the earliest blueprints for preventive policing. Together they formulated a river police for the Thames River, in part to suppress the rampant theft plaguing West India Company merchants. Their strategy included the creation of a new magistrate's court supported by clerks and constables, a preventive police force to patrol the Thames River environs, the introduction of ship guards, and a system for hiring men of good character as dock laborers. By 1799 their strategy was in place and, within its first eight months of operation, it was paying huge dividends as theft dropped almost 95 percent. In 1839 the river police officially became the Thames Division of the London Metropolitan Police.*

SOURCES: George Howard, *Guardians of the Queen's Peace*, 1953; Philip John Stead, *The Police of Britain*, 1985.

HARRIS, EMIL. (1839–1921) Born in Prussia, Harris immigrated to the United States in his mid-teens. He worked at a variety of jobs in New York City, San Francisco, and Los Angeles before joining the Los Angeles Police Force (LAPD)* in 1870. Described as a "natural-born lawman," Harris was one of only seven members of the fledgling police force. He was with the force when it unsuccessfully attempted to thwart an anti-Chinese riot that resulted in nineteen lynchings.

Harris was defeated in his run for city marshal in 1874 and later that year participated in the capture of the noted outlaw Tiburcio Vasquez. After several years as deputy sheriff, he was appointed LAPD chief in 1877, a rare feat in this era for someone of Jewish heritage. However, his success was short-lived since the new city council voted to oust him the following year.

Harris continued to work in law enforcement and in 1879 he started the first private detective agency in Los Angeles. During the next decade he was appointed constable (see CONSTABLES) and then rejoined the Los Angeles police, rising to chief of detectives in 1888. He retired from policing in 1918 and died in Los Angeles three years later.

SOURCES: Harris Newmark, *Sixty Years in Southern California*, 1930; Norton B. Stern and William M. Kramer, "Emil Harris: Los Angeles Jewish Police Chief," *Southern California Quarterly*, 1973; William B. Secrest, *Lawmen and Desperadoes*, 1994.

HARRIS, LEONARD. (1827–1894) Born in New York City, Harris came to California during the 1849 gold rush. During the 1860s he served as the warden of the Sacramento County jail and later as deputy sheriff. His primary duties included transporting prisoners to San Quentin Prison, where he himself would later find employment as a prison guard. He joined the Sacramento police force in 1872 and, over the next five years, helped capture several stagecoach robbers and murderers. In 1879 he left the police force to serve as a detective for the Central Pacific Railroad. In 1887 he pursued train robbers into Mexico and the following year assisted Wells Fargo Detective Bureau* detective James Bunyan Hume* in the investigation of a series of train robberies. Five years later Harris suffered a severe neck wound during an attack on a train that he was guarding. In 1894 he was mortally wounded while apprehending Alexander Azoff during the robbery of a railroad station in Santa Cruz County. (Azoff was captured several days later and hanged in 1895.)

SOURCES: Richard Dillon, *Wells Fargo Detective*, 1969; William B. Secrest, *Lawmen and Desperadoes*, 1994.

HART, CALEB LAWSON. (1862–1934) Born in Park County, Texas, "Loss" Hart moved to the Indian Territory with his family in 1879 and, over the next fifteen years, worked as a blacksmith and cattle rancher, and then as a deputy U.S. marshal for eleven years. He is best remembered for killing Bill Dalton near Ardmore, Oklahoma, on June 8, 1894. Subsequently he barely survived a smallpox attack and then worked in the merchandising field.

SOURCE: Charles J. Mooney, "The Man Who Killed Bill Dalton," *Golden West*, January 1974.

HATHERILL, GEORGE. (b. 1898–?) Born in London, Hatherill served in France and Flanders during World War I. His proficiency with foreign languages led to his hiring by the Special Branch of the London Metropolitan Police* and then Scotland Yard.* From 1931 to 1939 he investigated many cases on the European continent and collaborated with police forces to suppress drugs and arms smuggling, as well as counterfeiting. His forty-five-year career with Scotland Yard culminated in his investigation of the Great Train Robbery case, which involved one of the largest cash heists in history.

SOURCE: George Hatherill, *A Detective's Story*, 1971.

HAYMARKET RIOT. On March 4, 1886, in one of the most tragic episodes of labor-related violence, fifteen thousand laborers held a rally for improved working conditions and against police brutality at Chicago's Haymarket Square. While a teamster spoke to the crowd, 180 police officers appeared on the scene and demanded that the protestors disperse. As the speaker dismounted the podium, which was mounted in a truck, someone from the crowd threw a dynamite bomb into the police, killing seven police officers. The police returned fire, killing two civilians and injuring dozens. This tragedy led to a public backlash against the labor movement, branding members as anarchists and Reds (communists). Nine speakers were indicted for murder.

The prosecution presented a weak case, with no evidence as to who threw the bomb. However, with a jury devoid of industrial workers, it seemed like the deck was stacked against the defendants, who were all convicted. Eight received the death penalty and one was sentenced to twenty years' imprisonment. While the verdict initially was popular in the United States, public opinion wavered as a movement began to commute the sentences to life imprisonment. However, only three of the prisoners would live. The day before the executions, one of the prisoners blew his face off with a bomb and died later in the day. The other four mounted the gallows steps to their deaths the next day. Six years after the Haymarket incident, a new governor examined the incident, pardoned the survivors, and declared the executed men innocent.

SOURCES: Carl Sifakis, *Encyclopedia of American Crime*, 1982; Thomas A. Reppetto, *The Blue Parade*, 1978; Bernard Kogan, *The Chicago Haymarket Riot*, 1959.

HAYNES, SAMUEL JONATHAN. (1857–1948) Born in what was then Longtown in the Indian Territory, Haynes became one of the best-known members of the Creek Lighthorse* horse mounted police* unit. As captain he was prominent in several skirmishes during the Esparchecher War. For a time he also worked as a deputy U.S. federal marshal and participated in the capture of the Buck gang. After leaving the Lighthorse he served as an interpreter and delegate for the Cherokee Nation and represented his tribe in Washington, D.C., on numerous occasions.

SOURCE: Art Burton, *Black, Red, and Deadly*, 1991.

HAYS, JACOB. (1772–1850) Born in Bedford Village, New York, following a stint working in the family business, Hays procured an appointment as a member of New York City's "Mayor's Marshals" in 1798. Three years later he was chosen to lead the constabulary force (see CONSTABLES) a position he would hold for the next forty-nine years. His reputation for toughness and stern discipline earned him such monikers as "Old Hays" and the "terror of evil-doers."

Over the ensuing decades Hays's reputation reached almost mythical proportions in Europe. Seldom seen without his gold-headed baton, Hays is credited with introducing the familiar policing tactic of patrolling in pairs for protection and to guard against corruption. Among his more noteworthy innovations was the "loss book," which inspired better record keeping by requiring the recording of thefts, criminal descriptions, and stolen goods. He also developed an extensive network of informers and was unusually skilled at crowd control.

In the 1840s Hays escorted English novelist Charles Dickens* through the crime-ridden environs of New York City. Dickens's account of the odious conditions and the dangers of policing added further luster to the Hays legend back in England. As tribute to his legendary status, when the New York City Police Department (NYPD)* was reorganized in 1844, although Hays's position of high constable was eliminated, out of respect, the city fathers allowed him to keep his title and awarded him benefits for life. Often referred to him as "the first of the modern detectives," in his own lifetime Hays was accorded such respect that parents warned their obstreperous offspring to "be good, or Old Hays will get you!" In 1935, his descendant Arthur Hays Sulzberger became the publisher of the *New York Times*.

SOURCES: Sutherland Denlinger, "Old Hays—There Was a Cop," *New York World Telegram*, March 1–6, 1937; *National Cyclopaedia of American Biography*, Vol. 12, 1904, p. 354; Augustine E. Costello, *Our Police Protectors*, 1885; reprint, 1972.

HAYS, JOHN COFFEE "JACK." (1817–1883) Born in Cedar Lick, Tennessee, Hays moved to San Antonio in 1836 and promptly joined the army of the Texas Republic in the war for independence. At the behest of President Sam Houston, he joined a company of Texas Rangers* captained by Erasmus "Deaf" Smith. Described as shorter than five feet, nine inches, with reddish brown hair and hazel eyes, Hayes soon became popular among his colleagues.

Over the years Hays became one of the most indomitable Rangers. In 1840 he was appointed to the Ranger company that patrolled from San Antonio south. (It would be during his tenure with the Rangers that the force would establish its enduring reputation.) Two years later he was promoted to major and assigned the two companies on the southwest frontier. He was given incredible autonomy—the power to declare martial law, keep law and order along the border, and trade prisoners of war with Mexico. By 1845 his authority was increased, putting him in command of four frontier Ranger companies. Under Hays's leadership, the Rangers were rarely defeated, emerging victorious in a host of clashes, such as at the battles of Walker's Creek, Canon de Ugalde, and Painted Rock. Hays would also command Rangers in the Mexican War. Following the War Hays left the force for an even more successful career in gold rush California, where he became sheriff* of San Francisco County and eventually founded the city of Oakland.

SOURCES: James K. Greer, *Colonel Jack Hays: Texas Frontier Leader and California Builder*, 1952; Walter Prescott Webb, *The Texas Rangers*, 1935.

HEINRICH, EDWARD OSCAR. (1881–1953) Born in Clintonville, Wisconsin, following graduation from the University of California in 1908, Heinrich relocated to Tacoma, Washington. Considered an excellent chemist, he was often called to testify as an expert witness. His investigative background led to his appointment as police chief of Alameda, California. A year later he accepted the city manager position in Boulder, Colorado. Returning to the Bay area, he began lecturing at the University of California at Berkeley, where he carved out a reputation as a master of ballistics.

Among the most prominent cases Heinrich solved during his career were the Black Tom bombing in Jersey City and the Fatty Arbuckle rape case. However, the incident that initially drew the most attention was the D'Autremont train robbery, which left four dead. Putting his investigative acumen to work, Heinrich determined that the perpetrator was a left-handed lumberjack from the Northwest, in his early twenties, and a meticulous dresser. His description led to the arrest of the killer.

SOURCE: Eugene B. Block, *The Wizard of Berkeley*, 1958.

HELLDORF, WOLF HEINRICH GRAF VON. (1896–1944) Born in Merseburg, Germany, Helldorf won two Iron Crosses while serving in the German Army during World War I. He joined the Sturmabteilung (SA), or Storm Detachment, during the early years of the Nazi party and following Adolf Hitler's ascension to chancellor. Helldorf was promoted into the Nazi hierarchy. He was made police president of Potsdam in 1933 and then assumed the same position two years later in Berlin. A man of contradictions, he would admonish his officers for taking part in anti-Jewish mayhem yet participate in the confiscation of Jewish passports, which were then sold back to their owners for profit. In 1944 Helldorf was arrested and convicted for the bombing attempt on Hitler's life. He was tortured and then hanged with a piano wire, along with his fourteen coconspirators, on August 15, 1944.

SOURCE: Louis L. Snyder, *Encyclopedia of the Third Reich*, 1989.

HELM, JACK. (c. 1838–1873) Little is known about Helm's early life except that he worked as cowboy in Texas before serving in the Confederate Army during the Civil War. A notoriously violent man who was described by one source as "the most cold-blooded murderer ever to wear a badge" (Sifakis), he reportedly killed a man simply for whistling a Yankee tune. Following the Civil War, Helm returned to Texas and participated in the Sutton-Taylor conflict on the Sutton side, leading a force of 200 regulators. In 1869 he was appointed a captain in the Reconstruction-era Texas State Police. He was dismissed from the force after killing two Taylor supporters in a vigilante action. Helm met his end when noted gunman John Wesley Hardin, a distant relative of the Taylors, appeared on the scene. Hardin killed Helm with a shotgun blast during a pitched gunfight in a blacksmith's shop.

SOURCES: Jay Robert Nash, *EWLO*, 1994; Carl Sifakis, *Encyclopedia of American Crime*, 1982.

HENDERSON, SIR EDMUND. (1821–1896) Henderson succeeded Sir Richard Mayne* as chief commissioner of the London Metropolitan Police* in 1869. Formerly with the Royal Engineers, Henderson had spent the previous thirteen years supervising convicts in Australia Returning to London, he inherited a well-established police force, which he modified by expanding the central detective force and introducing permanent divisional detectives. He also abolished the requirement that men wear their police uniforms* off duty and instituted fixed posts where an officer could be found at all times. Henderson is credited with reorganizing the police organization, creating the elite Criminal Investigative Division (CID),* and streamlining the headquarters at Scotland Yard.* Throughout his tenure Henderson was a target for criticism. As London weathered a series of strikes and political upheaval, he increasingly came under fire. He resigned from the force in 1886.

SOURCES: Wilbur R. Miller, *Cops and Bobbies: Police Authority in New York and London, 1830–1870*, 1973; David Scoli, *The Queen's Peace*, 1979.

HENDERSON, WILLIAM. Henderson began his law enforcement career as a lieutenant in Glasgow, Scotland, in the 1860s. After promotion to chief detective, he transferred to the Manchester, England, police and was instrumental in the suppression of the Fenian conspiracy, which was centered in that town. Henderson played an integral role in the arrest of the Fenians responsible for the attack on a police van that resulted in the killing of a police sergeant. As chief inspector of detectives, he was a central figure in crushing the Murphy Riots.

Following his nine-year stint as chief of the Manchester Detectives, he was appointed chief constable of Leeds (see CONSTABLES), where he flourished for three years before being elevated, in 1878, to chief constable of Edinburgh, in his homeland. Henderson recounted his most prominent exploits in *Clues, or Leaves from a Chief Constable's Note Book.*

SOURCE: George W. Hale, *Police and Prison Cyclopaedia*, Vol. 2, 1893.

HENNESSEY, DAVID PETER. (d. 1890) Hennessey served as a New Orleans, Louisiana, detective until he was dismissed from the force in 1881 after a controversial gunfight. He was later exonerated and was reappointed to the force as a detective. He resigned to open his own private detective agency until he was appointed police chief of New Orleans in 1888. One of his first acts was to proclaim that he would investigate a spate of shootings in the Italian-American community. In the prior eighteen months there had been forty murders connected to mob warfare between the Provenzano and Matrangas families. When Hennessey identified members of the Provenzano crime family as Mafia members, he reportedly telegraphed Rome for their criminal records. Worried about the potential ramifications of Hennessey's crusade, the two families temporarily banded together and put out a contract on the police chief's life.

On October 15, 1890, Hennessey was gunned down a half-block from his home. With the acquittal of sixteen defendants in what proved to be a sham trial on March 12, 1891, the city's Italian community turned out for a huge celebration. Two days later a huge mob led by some of New Orleans's leading citizens stormed the jail where the defendants were still confined. In the resulting melee, two men were hanged from lightposts, seven shot by a firing squad, and two hunted down and shot.

SOURCES: Dennis C. Rousey, *Policing the Southern City: New Orleans, 1805–1889*, 1996; Richard Gambino, *Vendetta*, 1977.

HENRY, SIR EDWARD RICHARD. (1850–1931) During a career in the Indian Civil Service that began in 1873, Henry was promoted through a series of appointments and rose to inspector general of police in the province of Bengal, India, in 1891. In 1893 he implemented the Bertillon system* of identification but found it time-consuming and inexact. Building on recent innovations introduced by fingerprinting* experts Henry Faulds, William Herschel, and Francis Galton, Henry sought to create a practical system for filing fingerprints that could be used for crime detection.

In 1896 Henry made a breakthrough in fingerprint identification based on five basic geometric patterns and certain subpatterns. He created a simple formula that utilized a letter and number system to produce a code for identifying individual prints. With the support of the governor general, Henry implemented the system in Bengal, where it was an overwhelming success, demonstrating its superiority over the older Bertillon system. Henry published his findings in *Classification and Uses of Fingerprints*.

By 1901 Scotland Yard* had adopted Henry's system of dactyloscopy, which relied on the classification of patterns and numbers of ridges in a person's fingerprints. Soon after, Henry was appointed acting commissioner of the London Metropolitan Police* and commander of the Criminal Investigative Department (CID).* Over the next decade the Henry system was implemented in the United States and much of Europe. He later established the Peel Training School and survived an assassination attempt as he entered his house. Henry retired from law enforcement in 1918.

SOURCE: Philip John Stead, *The Police of Britain*, 1985.

HERAULT, RENÉ. (1691–1740) Born in Rouen, France, Herault served as lieutenant-general of police* of Paris from 1725 to 1740. While not in the pantheon of great Paris police chiefs, Herault was limited in what he accomplished by his own religious convictions. However, he is credited with directing the placing of street names at Paris street intersections.

SOURCES: Alan Williams, *The Police of Paris*, 1979; Philip John Stead, *The Police of France*, 1983.

HEWITT, CECIL ROLPH. (b. 1901) Born in London, Hewitt followed his father into the City of London Police as constable (see CONSTABLES) in 1921. He received numerous promotions, reaching chief inspector in 1938. Eight years later he left law enforcement to establish a writing career, which was mainly focused on policing and crime. Among his more police-oriented works are *Commonsense about Crime and Punishment* (1961), *The Police and the Public* (1962), *Law and the Common Man* (1967), and *The Queen's Pardon* (1978). A prolific writer, he also is well known for his journalism and wrote under the pseudonyms R. H. Cecil, Oliver Milton, and C. H. Rolph.

SOURCE: Charles Phillips and Alan Axelrod, *CCC*, 1996.

HICKMAN, TOM. (1886–1962) Born in Cooke County, Texas, Hickman entered law enforcement as a deputy constable in Gainesville, Texas, in 1908. In 1919 he joined the Texas Rangers* and was assigned to patrol along the Rio Grande and in the Big Bend region. Promoted to captain in 1921, he took part in the Texas-Oklahoma boundary dispute, Ku Klux Klan incidents in Waco and Corpus Christi, and the restoration of order to various boomtowns, including Borger, Eastland, Mexia, and Kilgore. Hickman was prominent in the killing of two bank robbers when they resisted arrest following the robbery of the Red River National Bank in Clarksville. He also led the manhunt for the "Santa

Claus" bank robbers, so named because their leader wore a Santa Claus costume during the robbery of a West Texas bank.

Hickman retired from the Rangers in the mid-1930s and, over his remaining years, served as deputy sheriff of Gainesville, Florida; chief of security for Gulf Oil Corporation; and, in 1961, chairman of the Texas Public Safety Commission.

SOURCES: Mitchel Roth (historical text by), *Courtesy, Service, Protection: The Texas Department of Public Safety's Sixtieth Anniversary*, 1995; Mike Cox, *Texas Ranger Tales II*, 1999.

HICKOK, JAMES BUTLER "WILD BILL." (1837–1876) Born into a farming family in Homer, Illinois, Hickok moved west to the Kansas Territory following the death of his father in the mid-1850s. In the years leading up to the Civil War, he joined General James Lane's Free State Army during the conflict in "Bleeding Kansas."

Hickok became a national figure in 1861 after killing David McCanles at Rock Creek, Nebraska, in a dispute over money. Hickok was not involved directly in the dispute but intervened when a mutual acquaintance was threatened, and in the ensuing gunfight shot McCanles and one of his employees. The story served as grist for the developing dime novel industry. Four years later Hickok killed Dave Tutt in a celebrated walkdown gunfight on the streets of Springfield, Missouri. Following the Civil War, Hickok served as a scout and guide and developed an amazing proficiency in marksmanship.

Although he had served a short stint as a constable (see CONSTABLES) in Monticello Township, Johnson County, and as deputy U.S. Marshal (see U.S. MARSHALS SERVICE) at Fort Riley, Kansas, in 1871, Hickok's law enforcement reputation rests on his appointment as marshal of Abilene, Kansas, in 1871. During his eight-month term in office, he managed to bring order to this cattletown. However, his tenure was not without tragedy. On October 5, 1871, after a shoot-out with Texas gamblers Phil Coe and Ben Thompson* in which Coe was killed, Hickok mistakenly turned and fired as a figure came at him from behind, tragically killing Mike Williams, his own deputy. Hickok was dismissed after the cattle trade began to bypass Abilene for other Kansas terminals and as the town wearied of the peace officer with a propensity for gunplay.

Over the remaining five years of his life, Hickok acted in Wild West shows and patronized gambling saloons. In 1876, with his eyesight failing but his gambling skills improving, he married Agnes Lake Thatcher but then left for Deadwood, South Dakota, following the Black Hills gold discovery. Here he met Calamity Jane, and their casual, but probably platonic, relationship added a romantic dimension to his growing legend. On August 2, 1876, Hickok was shot and killed by Jack McCall while playing poker. He died holding two black aces and two black eights, a "dead man's hand." McCall was hanged for the murder the following year.

SOURCES: Joseph G. Rosa, *They Called Him Wild Bill: The Life and Adventures of James Butler Hickok*, 1964; Joseph G. Rosa, *Wild Bill Hickok: The Man and His Myth*, 1996.

HIGHWAY PATROL. Prior to the 1920s, laws governing the movement of motor vehicles were typically enforced by either county or municipal police, depending on the jurisdiction. With the growing popularity of the automobile in the first two decades of the twentieth century, several states established law enforcement agencies specifically to deal with traffic problems. In 1916 Maryland became the first state to introduce such a force. Five years later Delaware, Illinois, Indiana, Maine, Oregon, and Washington followed suit in establishing agencies to enforce traffic laws. Initially, the highway patrols were small, unarmed, and restricted to motor vehicle related infractions.

Most of the state police forces created between 1923 and 1927 were of the highway patrol variety, including Illinois (1923), Utah (1923), Virginia (1924), Vermont (1925), and Louisiana (1928). The Illinois force differed somewhat from the other units. Known as the "highway maintenance police," its role was expanded to include a larger contingent of officers and an increased mandate, which allowed for the arrest of all violators of state laws.

Between 1929 and 1941, fifteen states created state law enforcement agencies. Of these, only the agencies in Missouri, Oklahoma, and New Hampshire were imbued with total police powers. The other twelve were limited to highway patrol duty. Although the highway patrol movement peaked in 1921, during the Depression years there was an increased emphasis on highway patrols over the earlier, paramilitary-constabulary models. According to one authority on state policing, over three-quarters of the state police forces that were established during this era were modeled on the highway patrol.

Today most highway patrol agencies do not employ plainclothes officers* and do not investigate criminal cases throughout the state. The Washington Highway Patrol is an exception to the rule: it has wide-ranging criminal and traffic enforcement authority and employs plainclothes criminal investigators.

Currently, twenty-six states utilize highway patrols. These units range in size, with the largest in California and the smallest in Wyoming. Patrol officers typically have statewide powers of arrest for traffic or criminal offenses committed on state highways or property. The highway patrols operate under a variety of organizational schemes. In states such as Kansas, Nebraska, North Dakota, and Washington, they operate directly under the governor. Some highway patrols perform traffic and criminal investigative duties under a larger umbrella organization, including those in Alaska, Arkansas, Connecticut, Delaware, Indiana, Kentucky, Louisiana, Maine, Maryland, Massachusetts, New Hampshire, New Jersey, Vermont, and West Virginia. However, other states have a highway patrol that is separate from a state bureau of investigation.

SOURCES: H. Kenneth Bechtel, *State Police in the United States*, 1995; Donald A. Torres, *Handbook of State Police, Highway Patrols, and State Investigative Agencies*, 1987.

HINES, WILLIAM. (1897–1952) "Red" Hines joined the Los Angeles Police Department (LAPD)* at the age of twenty-four and distinguished himself while working undercover investigating the Industrial Workers of the World (IWW). Subsequently, he spent fifteen years as head of the LAPD Red squad. He was demoted to patrolman in 1938 when a new reform-oriented police administration cleaned house, and five years later he retired to work as a private security consultant.

SOURCE: Thomas A. Reppetto, *The Blue Parade*, 1978.

HITCHEN, CHARLES. (c. 1675–1727) Hitchen purchased the law enforcement position of London Under-City-Marshal in 1712 and within a short time was a familiar habitué of taverns and acquainted with numerous members of London's underworld, leading many to suspect he had been involved in illicit activity prior to gaining office. During his first year in office he was accused of charging usurious sums for the return of stolen items and consorting with known criminals. To his credit, in 1713 Hitchen wrote a pamphlet outlining crime-fighting measures, which included making lists of brothels, pawnbrokers, and fences. He also proposed separating potential criminal informants from other prisoners at Newgate Prison.

In 1713 Hitchen hired Jonathan Wild,* the future thief-taker general,* as his deputy, a relationship that would last only a year. His protégé surpassed his superior, not only in thief-taking skills, but in elan and finesse as well. Although married, Hitchen was a notorious homosexual who was often at odds with his superiors as he gallivanted around London with young men in tow; moreover, he was a frequent visitor to the area known as "Sodomites' Walk." Hitchen and Wild parted ways in 1714 as Wild scaled the heights of fame and fortune and earned his reputation as thief-taker general. Hitchen, by all accounts was jealous of the ascendence of his former protégé, and in his new role as reformer, vigorously mounted a campaign against Wild. Following Wild's arrest and conviction, Hitchen accompanied the procession to Tyburn Hill where Wild's execution took place.

Hitchen was sporadically barred from acting as under-city-marshal for misbehavior but was always reinstated until being caught in a compromising position. His career in law enforcement ended somewhat ignominiously in April of 1727 when he was caught, flagrante delicto, committing sodomy at a Charing Cross tavern. As this was a much-stigmatized crime at the time, Hitchen was sentenced to pay a fine, a stint in the pillory, and then six months in the infamous Newgate Prison. His time in prison apparently broke his health, and he died shortly after his release.

SOURCES: Gerald Howson, *Thief-Taker General*, 1970; Donald Rumbelow, *I Spy Blue*, 1971.

HOGUE, EDWARD O. (c. 1847–1877) Born in France, Hogue joined the Ellsworth, Kansas, police force in 1872, eventually rising to the rank of city

marshal and then deputy sheriff (see U.S. MARSHALS SERVICE; SHERIFF).*
In November 1873 he lost the race for sheriff, but two years later he returned
to peacekeeping as a deputy sheriff in Dodge City.

SOURCE: Nile H. Miller and Joseph W. Snell, *Great Gunfighters of the Kansas Cowtowns, 1867–1886*, 1967.

HOLLISTER, CASSIUS M. (1845–1884) Born in Ohio, Hollister migrated to
Kansas in 1877 and lived in several cities before winning the 1879 mayoral
election in Caldwell, Kansas. In 1883, "Cash" Hollister was appointed deputy
U.S. marshal (see U.S. MARSHALS SERVICE). That same year he participated
in several deadly gunfights that resulted in the deaths of several rustlers and
Chet Van Meter. The following year he resigned his position but stayed in law
enforcement as deputy sheriff (see SHERIFF) of Sumner County. In 1884 he
was killed while trying to arrest Texas badman Robert Cross.

SOURCE: Wayne T. Walker, "Cash Hollister—Border Lawman," *Real West*, March
1982.

HOLMES, ROBERT H. (d. 1917) Holmes joined the New York City Police
Department (NYPD)* in 1913. Four years later he was killed after surprising a
burglar, becoming the first African-American policeman killed in New York
while on duty. Over twenty thousand people attended his funeral, which was
reportedly the first to display flags at half-mast for a fallen police officer.

SOURCE: Craig W. Floyd and Kelley Lang Helms, eds., *To Serve and Protect*, 1995.

HOLMES, SHERLOCK. Originally named Sherrinford Holmes, the fictional
creation of Sir Arthur Conan Doyle* played center stage in numerous Doyle
stories between 1887 and 1927. Although no less than five prototypes have been
considered as the basis for Holmes, Doyle admitted that his inspiration was
derived from the career of Dr. Joseph Bell, a surgeon and Edinburgh professor,
whose reputation for deduction in medical matters was legendary. While a medical student under the direction of Bell, Doyle reportedly observed Bell correctly
deduce that a patient had been a recently noncommissioned officer earlier posted
to Barbados. Bell explained that despite good manners and an air of authority,
the patient did not remove his hat, as is customary in the army. However, if he
had been out of the service long he would have acclimated to civilian life and
would have removed the hat. As for the patient's complaint of elephantiasis, it
was endemic in the West Indies but not the British Indies.

Other prototypes suggested as the inspiration for Holmes include a private
consulting detective named Wendel Scherer, anatomy professor Oliver Wendell
Holmes, and Edinburgh toxicologist Professor Sir Robert Christenson, a medical
witness in the trial of body-snatchers Burke and Hare. As for his trademark
deerstalker hat and curved pipe? The deerstalker, which does not appear in any

Holmes story, was added by illustrator Sidney Paget. Similarly, the pipe was added by illustrator Frederick Dorr after Paget died.

SOURCES: Owen Dudley Edwards, *The Quest for Sherlock Holmes*, 1982; William Amos, *The Originals*, 1985.

HOLSTROM, JOHN. (b. 1910) Holstrom succeeded John Greening* as Berkeley, California, Police Chief* in 1944. The first college-educated man to assume this position, he joined the force in 1931 following graduation from the University of California, Berkeley. A student of the policing methods of August Vollmer,* Hollstrom advocated a modern, scientific approach to policing. Following stints as sergeant and lieutenant he was appointed police chief after a rigorous competition. In the 1930s and 1940s he often contended with student riots emanating from college sporting events. While the jurisdiction of the police did not include the local campus, once the students left campus they were in the city of Berkeley.

The year Holstrom became police chief saw the city's major crimes climb to an all-time high of 1,714. In order to counter this trend he began to seek better-caliber police officers and to increase their effectiveness by maintaining round-the-clock police beats. He also established an emergency police unit composed of local community members who volunteered to work four-hour shifts every five days. This allowed the regular police force to concentrate on more serious matters.

By 1950 police officials from around the world were visiting Berkeley to study its traffic control and police methods. Hollstrom was credited with creating a new set of department regulations that made an important contribution to police administration. He was also an advocate of better pay for police officers and helped develop a code of ethics for the Peace Officers Research Association in the early 1950s. A leading voice in the police professionalization movement, he was a member of the University of California faculty beginning in 1945. In 1957 he was elected president of the International Association of Chiefs of Police (IACP).* He resigned from the force in 1950.

SOURCE: Alfred E. Parker, *The Berkeley Police Story*, 1972.

HOMESTEAD STRIKE. One of the most notorious incidents in the history of Pinkerton's National Detective Agency* took place in the small town of Homestead, Pennsylvania. Located just seven miles away, the Carnegie, Phipps Steel Company was the main employer for the Homestead community. In 1889, striking steel workers chased off one hundred sheriff's deputies who been summoned to protect the steel plant. Three years later a new strike erupted over poor wages and other concerns, and the plant manager Henry Clay Frick eschewed local law enforcement for the Pinkertons. Shortly after July 4, 1892, almost four hundred Pinkertons from Chicago, New York, and Philadelphia converged on Homestead by barge. Unsure who their opposition was, strikers mistook the approaching detective force as an army of strikebreaking scabs and opened fire on them. Subsequently, a twelve-hour siege ensued, involving a heated exchange of gunfire. Ten workers and three Pinkertons were killed and Homestead entered the American consciousness as a terrible reminder of the class struggle that accompanied industrialization during the late nineteenth century. Investigation into the Homestead affair awakened Americans to the growth of the private police industry in America and tarnished the image of the Pinkertons. The antidetective mood that resulted from the carnage led to the passage of several anti-Pinkerton laws in the 1890s.

SOURCES: Frank Morn, *"The Eye That Never Sleeps,"* 1982; James D. Horan, *The Pinkertons,* 1968.

HOOVER, JOHN EDGAR. (1895–1972) Hoover was born in Washington, D.C., Hoover's father was a career civil servant who became superintendent of engraving and printing in the Coast and Geodetic Survey. His mother read the Bible daily and taught Hoover the value of Calvinism and the sinfulness of the human condition. After graduation as valedictorian of his high school class, Hoover planned to enter a seminary but instead opted for George Washington University, earning a law degree in 1917. That same year he went from college to the U.S. Department of Justice,* to which he would devote the next fifty-five years of his life, with forty-eight years as head of the Federal Bureau of Investigation (FBI).*

Hoover first came to prominence as head of the Justice Department's General Intelligence Division under Attorney General Mitchell Palmer. Over the next several years, at Palmer's direction, Hoover oversaw a campaign of persecution against foreigners who had been identified as communist sympathizers. Mass arrests and the trampling of constitutional protections resulted in hundreds of deportations and illegal searches and seizures. However, this was only the prelude to the 1919 Palmer raids, which resulted in several thousand more arrests. Here Hoover developed his predilection for maintaining secret files on individuals under investigation, a practice that would haunt America for the next half-century.

In 1921 Hoover was transferred to the Bureau of Investigation (it became the Federal Bureau of Investigation in 1935), where he served as assistant director. Following a series of scandals, bureau director William John Burns* decided to retire, and on May 10, 1924, Hoover was handed the reins of the Bureau. Hoover's appointment inaugurated a new era in professionalism, which introduced the latest scientific methods of detection, expanded the fingerprinting* bureau, and began the hiring of lawyers and public accountants as special agents.

In 1930 a congressional act required police agencies to compile crime statistics that would be disseminated through the FBI *Uniform Crime Reports (UCR).** Throughout the 1930s, Hoover concentrated his war on crime on bank robberies and high-profile crimes targeting such "public enemies" as Pretty Boy

Floyd, Baby Face Nelson, and John Dillinger. A genius at public relations, Hoover convinced Hollywood to produce a series of films creating the traditional image of the FBI agent as incorruptible and professional. In 1935 alone, more than sixty films fostered this portrait, including the James Cagney vehicle *G-Men*.*

In the 1930s federal legislation increased the power and prestige of the FBI, as the National Kidnapping Act, the National Extortion Act, and the Bank Robbery Act increased the organization's mandate. In 1935 the Bureau officially became the Federal Bureau of Investigation, and that same year, the FBI Academy was opened in Quantico, Virginia.*

During World War II Hoover shifted the focus of the Bureau toward fighting the activities of the communists and fascists, and in 1939 President Franklin D. Roosevelt placed Hoover in charge of domestic counterintelligence. Hoover solidified his public support by collaborating on books and films such as *The FBI in Peace and War* (1943) and *The House on 92nd Street* (1945). He took credit for the capture of German saboteurs off Long Island in 1942, although recent research indicates that one of the Germans gave up his comrades.

Although Hoover's FBI performed admirably in the war years, during the post–1945 Cold War years Hoover once again reverted to Red-baiting hysteria as the FBI's war against the Communist party led to his veneration among conservatives and loathing and fear among liberals. In the 1950s the FBI gathered evidence that uncovered the Klaus Fuchs atomic spy ring and led to the execution of Julius and Ethel Rosenberg for espionage activities. Hoover allied his organization with his close friend Senator Joseph McCarthy during the communist witch-hunt of the 1950s and wrote the book *Masters of Deceit: The Story of Communism in America and How to Fight It* (1958), which detailed his strategies for defeating communism and contributed to the growing hysteria over Soviet expansion. A bestseller, it sold two and a half million copies.

Continuing Hoover's masterful manipulation of popular entertainment, the 1950s saw the release of the hagiographic James Stewart vehicle *The FBI Story* (1959) and the publication of the bestselling book of the same name (1959) by Don Whitehead. In 1965 television introduced *The FBI*, a television series starring Efrem Zimbalist that ran until 1974 and was enormously popular.

With the election of John F. Kennedy and the ascendancy of his brother Robert to attorney general, it seemed that Hoover's days were numbered. It has been speculated that despite the rancor between Hoover and the Kennedys, he kept his job because he had secret files on the two brothers. Waiving the mandatory retirement age of seventy, Hoover was reappointed by Presidents Lyndon Johnson and Richard Nixon. Hoover had created a Counter Intelligence Program (generally called by its acronym, COINTELPRO*), to investigate communists but expanded it in the 1960s and 1970s to target radical student groups, the Black Panthers, and civil rights leaders such as Martin Luther King, Jr.

Hoover developed a particular aversion for Martin Luther King, Jr., whom he called "the most notorious liar in the country" (Powers). Escalating his campaign to destroy the career of the civil rights leader, Hoover's smear tactics included making tape recordings of King in sexually compromising situations and threatening to make them public, hoping to push him to suicide.

The remainder of Hoover's tenure as FBI chief became increasingly bizarre, and although he is credited with creating the professional FBI, suppressing kidnapping and bank robbery in the 1930s, and containing the espionage menace during World War II, Hoover will probably be remembered for violating constitutional protections and keeping secret files. His relationship with protégé Clyde Anderson Tolson* led many people to conjecture about his sexual preferences; this and his reluctance to recognize organized crime have tarnished his reputation and been the subjects of numerous exposés of Hoover's well-chronicled life. Unfortunately future historians will only be able to presume what was in his personal files since his secretary, Helen Gandy, was directed to destroy them following his death in 1972.

SOURCES: Richard Gid Powers, *Secrecy and Power: The Life of J. Edgar Hoover*, 1987; *New York Times*, May 3, 1972; Jay Robert Nash, *Citizen Hoover: A Critical Study of the Life and Times of J. Edgar Hoover and His FBI*, 1972.

HOOVER, LARRY T. (b. 1945) Born in San Francisco, California, and educated at Michigan State University, Hoover entered law enforcement with the Lansing, Michigan, police department but turned to academics and police training in the 1970s. He served on the faculty at Michigan State University and as training coordinator with the Michigan law Enforcement Officer's Training Council. A past president of the Academy of Criminal Justice Sciences, since 1977 he has served on the criminal justice faculty of Sam Houston State University and is director of the school's Police Research Center.

SOURCE: Mitchel Roth, *Fulfilling a Mandate*, 1997.

HOPE, ALEXANDER W. (c. 1826–1856) Born in Virginia, Hope arrived in California during the gold rush and following service in the Mexican War. Hope was one of the earliest physicians in southern California and a member of the first California state senate. Following the discovery of gold crime was rampant in Los Angeles and throughout most of the state. Hope offered his services to the law-and-order sector and in 1851 was appointed Los Angeles Police Department (LAPD)* chief. During his tenure as police chief he led a force of ninety unpaid police comprising the city's leading citizens. Each wore a white ribbon badge emblazoned with "City Police" in both Spanish and English. However, despite their good efforts, crime persisted in the outlying areas, requiring the formation of a horse mounted police* force in 1853. In August the Los Angeles Rangers was created. Like the legendary Texas Rangers,* they were required to supply their own weapons until the following year, when they received state support. The Rangers successfully controlled the crime problem for several years but only were in action sporadically, when their services were required. Dr. Hope, lawman, politician, and physician, died in the early years of the mounted force.

SOURCE: William B. Secrest, *Lawmen and Desperadoes*, 1994.

HORN, THOMAS "TOM." (1860–1903) Born near Memphis, Scotland County, Missouri, Tom Horn ran away from home at fourteen and made his way to Santa Fe, New Mexico, a region with which he would become familiar over the next two decades. Fluent in Spanish, Horn worked as a scout and army packer in the Arizona territory and in 1882 participated in the Apache campaign that followed the breakout from the San Carlos Reservation. Over the next few years Horn worked as a scout for General George C. Crook and then for Al Sieber. In 1886 Horn acted as a Spanish-English interpreter (although in his autobiography he claimed fluency in Apache, this is unsubstantiated) and was wounded during the final capture of Geronimo.

Horn left the army soon after the Geronimo campaign and prospected for gold in Arizona and was employed as a gunman for the Tewksburys in the Pleasant Valley War of 1886–1892. He began his short-lived law enforcement career at Pinkerton's National Detective Agency* from 1890 to 1894. Preferring to work alone, he tracked outlaws in the Denver area before leaving the agency to work as a stock detective for the Swan Land and Cattle Company. During the mid-1890s Horn worked as a hired gun and reportedly killed several Wyoming ranchers for six hundred dollars a piece each.

Although Horn claimed to have participated in the Spanish-American War, it appears only that he worked as a packer for several months in Tampa, Florida. Two years later he was employed as a glorified hitman in Colorado using the alias James Hicks. After he killed several ranchers suspected of stealing cattle, rustlers seemed to take their trade to better climes. The following years saw Horn working as a stock detective in Wyoming, where, almost immediately, he became a suspect in the shooting death of a fourteen-year-old boy. With no conclusive evidence, it took subterfuge on the part of deputy U.S. marshal (see U.S. MARSHALS SERVICE) Joe LeFors* to get Horn to sign his own death warrant. Apparently, after several libations LeFors induced Horn to brag about his long-range marksmanship and state that he could have killed the boy from three hundred yards. In the next room a court stenographer recorded the "tarnished" confession of the drunken killer. Horn later accused the stenographer of embellishing his words, but he was convicted for the crime and hanged. This case is still a matter of some conjecture.

In recent years Hollywood has attempted to rehabilitate the image of the hired killer through movies such as Steve McQueen's *Tom Horn* and the David Carradine vehicle *Mr. Horn*. Horn himself contributed to his own legend by penning his autobiography while awaiting execution. One critic of this self-serving project, which was probably later edited and partly ghost-written by someone else, reported, "whether Horn was guilty or not, a good case could be made for hanging anyone who wrote that book" (Thrapp).

SOURCES: Dan L. Thrapp, ed., *EFB*, Vol. 2, 1988; Joe LeFors, *Wyoming Peace Officer: The Autobiography of Joe LeFors*, 1953; Tom Horn, *Life of Tom Horn Written by Himself: A Vindication*, 1904.

HORSE MOUNTED POLICE. While it is unknown when the first horse was used in a police action, most historians trace the utilization of mounted forces in peacekeeping activities to King Charles's *Articles of War* (1629), which ordered that the provost be allowed a horse "for he must be riding from one garrison to another correcting many, lest the soldiers scathe the country and frighten the people." Although Australia and Texas implemented mounted police forces by the 1820s, credit should be given to London's 1895 Horse Patrol as the earliest formal mounted police force.

Beginning in 1758 the London Bow Street Runners* police established the mounted branch of the London Metropolitan Police.* Over the ensuing years, Sir John Fielding* implemented his *Plan for Preventing Robberies within Twenty Miles of London*, which included a regular force of mounted men charged with crime prevention and criminal apprehension stationed along the turnpikes leading into London proper. By the time the Horse Patrol began operations in October 1763, its size had quadrupled to eight. Nevertheless, although the mounted patrol was considered an immediate success, on the roads leading into London, crime persisted into the nineteenth century.

In 1805 the Bow Street Horse Patrol consisted of fifty-two men and mounts, who were charged with patrolling main roads up to twenty miles distant from London. Like most twentieth-century incarnations of the mounted police, officers came from the military, typically the cavalry. Like the Pennsylvania State Police,* they were housed in cottages near the patrol routes. Each man was equipped with a sabre, pistol, handcuffs, and a truncheon,* and with their scarlet waistcoats, white leather coats, and steel-spurred Wellington spurs, they were an elegant sight. Not surprisingly, they were given the names "Redbreasts" and "Robin Redbreasts."

Mounted police forces in the British tradition appeared throughout the empire over the next 150 years. Founded in 1825, Australia's New South Wales Mounted Police Division considers itself the oldest continuous mounted police unit in the world. Horses played a critical role in policing in South Africa, New Zealand, India, and, of course, Canada, where the Royal Canadian Mounted Police (RCMP)* remains the country's most enduring symbol. In the United States a ranging tradition can be found with the Texas Rangers,* the Arizona Rangers,* and the New Mexico Mounted police. The Mexican Rurales* and the Jordanian desert patrol, which uses camels, are two other incarnations of the mounted police tradition, which exists throughout the world.

Ever since the advent of policing it has been obvious that an officer on horseback has advantages over his bipedal counterpart, particularly in controlling crowds. By the end of 1982, eighteen British police forces had mounted branches. In one of the largest peacetime policing operations in the Great Britain, three thousand police confronted twelve thousand picketers during an industrial dispute at a coking plant near Sheffield. Horses proved indispensable in this action.

There are no accurate statistics on the number of horse mounted police forces in the world today, but it is clear that their numbers are on the increase. Over the past several decades, mounted patrols have become a familiar presence in most large cities, in downtown areas, in shopping malls, and even in vice-ridden districts. The main disadvantages associated with horse patrols are their limitations in inclement weather, restrictions on response availability (a mounted unit has greater mobility than a foot officer but, obviously, far less than an automobile), vulnerability of a horse, limited carrying capacity (there is no trunk), and the horses tendency to litter the streets. Nevertheless, mounted patrols persist and are considered advantageous for riot control, community relations, high visibility, and the touch of pageantry they bring to events such as parades and funerals.

SOURCES: Mitchel Roth, "Mounted Police Forces: A Comparative History," *Policing* 21, Fall 1998; William E. Carfield, *Comparative Analysis of Twenty-Five Horse Mounted Police Units in the United States*, 1982; Patrick Pringle, *Hue and Cry*, 1955; Judith Campbell, *Police Horses*, 1968.

HOUGHTON, ROBERT A. (1914–1998) Houghton served as deputy chief and chief of detectives for the Los Angeles Police Department (LAPD).* He is best remembered as the lead investigator of the assassination of Robert F. Kennedy at the Ambassador Hotel on June 5, 1968. Houghton chronicled his investigation in the 1970 book *Special Unit Senator*. His exhaustive ten-volume report included close to five thousand interviews and interrogations and more than fifty thousand pages of documentation. Determined not to repeat the mistakes made by the Dallas police following the 1963 presidential assassination of John F. Kennedy, according to *Los Angeles Times* writer Robert Kirsch, Houghton conducted "the longest, largest, and most expensive criminal investigation ever undertaken" by the LAPD. The investigation concluded beyond a reasonable doubt that Sirhan Sirhan had acted alone. He was quickly convicted of the murder and sentenced to life in prison.

The following year Houghton was one of the lead investigators in the Manson Family murders of Sharon Tate and four of her houseguests as well as the killings of Leno and Rosemary LaBianca. Following an arduous investigation, Charles Manson and several of his followers were convicted of the crimes and sentenced to life in prison.

SOURCE: "Chief Investigator on RFK Assassination, Manson Murders, Dies," *American Police Beat*, September 1998, p. 5.

HOUSTON, LENORE. (b. 1879) Houston was the first and only woman appointed as special agent by Federal Bureau of Investigation (FBI)* director John

Edgar Hoover.* Hired in 1924 at the relatively advanced age of forty-five, Houston had attended college for three years. She was assigned to the Philadelphia field office, where her law enforcement duties focused mainly on Mann Act violations. She resigned in 1928 and in 1930 was committed to a mental hospital after suffering hallucinations and threatening to kill Hoover.

SOURCE: Athan G. Theoharis, ed., *The FBI*, 1999.

HOUSTON, TEXAS, POLICE DEPARTMENT. The earliest attempts at establishing a law enforcement presence in this Texas bayou city occurred in 1832 while still a domain of the Mexican government. As *alcalde*, or mayor, John W. Moore was charged with performing the duties of sheriff.* Five years later city leaders took tentative steps toward establishing a city patrol, but it would not be until the years following the Civil War that serious consideration was given to the creation of a police force. In 1865 the city council authorized the marshal to increase the size of the police department, although it was still limited to forty officers. The following year local merchants, won support to create a "special merchants' police force" to preserve law and order and protect their property, although it was controlled by the city marshal.

The Houston police force hired its first African-American officers in 1875 and, as in other American communities during this era, they were assigned to patrol black communities. By the 1880s the city had not yet escaped its provincial roots, and police records indicate that as late as 1885 two officers were engaged as "cow catchers." Assigned to capture wandering livestock on city streets, these officers were apparently the predecessors to the city's mounted traffic officers.

Houston police officers did not adopt official uniforms until 1891. During the next decade the first detective unit was established and a patrol wagon was added to the force, which, by 1900, consisted of twenty-four men. The Houston police force emerged as a more modern police apparatus by the turn of the century with the ascendance of J. G. Blackburn to chief in 1898. He was credited with eschewing the political patronage system and basing promotion on merit. He also implemented patrol beats of two-man police teams and established an identification system based on the Bertillon system* and necessitating the purchase of measurement and photographic equipment.

In the early 1900s police matrons* were hired at the behest of the local temperance committee. In 1907 the city council passed its first motor vehicle ordinance, which required night lights, vehicle registration, and speed limits under fifteen miles per hour. The police department purchased motorcycles to keep up with the growing traffic problems. By 1915 the department was recognized as possessing one of the leading identification systems in the country. In 1917 the department hired Eva J. Bracher as its first female police officer (see POLICEWOMEN). Later, she would become its first female detective. Unfortunately, 1917 is remembered for race riots that resulted in the deaths of five police officers and four soldiers. As a result, thirteen men were hanged the next year by the army following the largest military court-martial in American history.

During the 1920s the department continued to modernize, adopting car radios and Gamewell Police Signal system* boxes. In 1933 the police department was renamed the Department of Public Safety, and three years later introduced its first airplane. In 1950 the force opened the most modern police facility in the South using state-of-the-art electronic surveillance equipment. By the 1960s women became a larger presence in the department, but they were typically employed in clerical positions. The appointment of Herman B. Short to chief in 1964 began a nine-year tenure that saw the creation of what would become the largest helicopter patrol squad in the world and other innovations. During this contentious decade the Houston police faced antiwar protests and various racial incidents that occasionally escalated into violence.

When Lee Patrick Brown* took over the police force in 1982, he was faced with a jurisdiction larger than New York City and Chicago combined. With the downturn of the local economy spurred on by plunging oil prices in the 1980s, Houston faced a rising crime problem that would take another decade to reverse. In 1990 Houston made history when the police force hired Elizabeth M. Watson as its first female police chief. By 1992 Houston's 18 percent crime drop made it first among the nation's fifty largest cities.

SOURCES: Linda J. Nanfria, *The Houston Police Department*, 1983; William G. Bailey, "Houston Police Department," in *Encyclopedia of Police Science*, ed. William G. Bailey, 1995.

HOWIE, NEIL. (c. 1834–1874) Born in Scotland, Howie immigrated with his family to the United States in his childhood. After a peripatetic youth spent in Wisconsin and Colorado, he reached southwestern Montana in 1863, where William Henry Handy Plummer* tried, without success, to enlist him in his outlaw gang. Howie's first ventures in law enforcement involved vigilante activities, including the capture of Dutch John Wagner in 1864. Later that year he was appointed sheriff* of Madison County, Montana. Following his stint as sheriff, he was selected as the first deputy U.S. marshal (see U.S. MARSHALS SERVICE) for Montana. In 1867 he was commissioned a colonel in the Montana Territorial militia and successfully completed the construction of Fort T.F. Meagher and Fort Howie. Subsequently, Howie led an increasingly unsettled life. In 1872 he helped his brother get a pardon for murder in Colorado and then moved to Utah. Two years later, Howie took a management position with a mining company on the tropical island of Trinidad. He was involved in several deadly gunfights in Trinidad before succumbing to malaria in March 1874.

SOURCES: Nathaniel Pitt Langford, *Vigilante Days and Ways*, 1957; Dan L. Thrapp, ed., *EFB*, Vol. 2, 1988.

HUE AND CRY. According to ancient Anglo-Saxon law, when a felon was observed leaving a crime scene, everyone was supposed to join in the chase. Anyone who hesitated would be fined. The medieval equivalent of yelling "Stop, thief!" the hue and cry required the pursuit of the culprit "with horn and voice" from town to town until apprehended. According to the Statute of Winchester* of 1285, the hue and cry was to be strictly adhered to so that criminals could be captured swiftly. However by the sixteenth century few citizens took the hue and cry seriously.

SOURCES: Patrick Pringle, *Hue and Cry*, 1955; James Cramer, *The World's Police*, 1964.

HUGHES, EDWARD ARTHUR ST. GEORGE. (b. 1847–) Born in Three Rivers, Quebec Canada, Hughes was drawn to a military career while still in his teens. After attending military school in Quebec, he served on the Canadian frontier in 1864 during the Fenian incident. Hughes rose through the ranks to brigade major in 1883. He left the military, and in 1884 practiced law in Montreal. Two years later he returned to his battalion and took part in the North West rebellion. In April 1888, Hughes was appointed chief of police for Montreal. During his tenure he increased the force from 228 officers to 375 while increasing pay and introducing better discipline.

SOURCE: George W. Hale, *Police and Prison Cyclopaedia*, Vol. 2, 1893.

HUGHES, JOHN REYNOLDS. (1855–1947) Born in Cambridge, Illinois, Hughes moved to Texas at the age of fourteen. A rancher until 1886, the following year Hughes joined the Texas Rangers,* inaugurating a twenty-eight-year career, which established a record for Ranger longevity. During his long tenure he served in every Texas county along the Rio Grande River. He was promoted to corporal in 1889 and captain in 1893.

In 1871 Hughes was wounded in the right arm during a skirmish with Choctaw Indians. Over the following years he developed dexterity with his left hand. During the Mexican Revolution the Mexican government put a bounty on him for arms smuggling. Hughes was credited with wiping out the Ybarra, Fiar, and Massey gangs. He was also credited with capturing Catarina Garza, who was blamed for the 1888 "Garza War"; New York criminal Charles F. Dodge; and Juan Perales. Known as "the border boss," Hughes met some of the best-known figures of the West, including John Wesley Hardin, Pancho Villa, and Patrick Floyd Jarvis "Pat" Garrett. After James E. Ferguson became governor, Hughes retired (in 1915). At 92, ill and despondent, on June 3, 1947, the old Ranger killed himself with his .45 in his sister-in-law's garage.

SOURCES: Jack Martin, *Border Boss: Captain John R. Hughes, Ranger*, 1942; Walter Prescott Webb, *The Texas Rangers*, 1935.

HUGHES, MICHAEL. (b. 1870) Born in Ireland, Hughes arrived in Chicago in 1888 and three years later joined the Chicago Police Department (CPD).* He rose to sergeant and then to lieutenant of detectives by 1920. Promoted to captain in 1921, he was described by one contemporary as "the best thief-catcher Chicago ever knew." He then served as chief of detectives until 1924, but was demoted the following year for a minor indiscretion. He took a leave of absence rather than resigning. A favorite of both the mayor and journalists, he was given the moniker "Go get 'em Mike" for his zealous pursuit of criminals. As chief of detectives, Hughes commanded a unit of 193 men. In 1927 he was appointed general superintendent of the entire force. As police chief he kept the pressure on the Al Capone syndicate by raiding Capone's breweries, gambling houses, and brothels. As a result, Capone moved his family out of Chicago. In 1928 Hughes resigned as police commissioner due to medical problems. Although he closed over fifteen hundred gambling establishments, some authorities linked his resignation to his inability to suppress vice in Chicago.

SOURCE: Raphael W. Marrow and Harriet I. Carter, *In Pursuit of Crime*, 1996.

HUME, JAMES BUNYAN. (1827–1904) Born in Delaware County, New York, Hume moved with his family to Indiana as a youth, where he worked on the family farm until lured to California by gold fever in 1849. Over the next decade Hume prospected with varying degrees of success. He first entered law enforcement in 1862 when he was appointed city marshal and chief of police of Placerville, California. Two years later he was selected undersheriff at a most opportune time, when he participated in the tracking and apprehension of stagecoach robbers who took part in one the most dramatic stagecoach robberies of Western lore. On July 1, 1864, Confederate soldiers plundered two stages in the Placerville area, stealing thirty thousand dollars and leaving behind a receipt for the theft. When Hume came on the scene, one deputy had already been killed during pursuit of the bandits. Hume is credited with tracking down the responsible culprits.

Hume was elected sheriff* of El Dorado County in 1867 but was defeated in a second attempt in 1871. After leaving law enforcement to serve as an administrator at the Nevada State Prison, he was lured by the Wells Fargo Detective Bureau* into taking charge of its first office in 1873. Understaffed, Hume had to contend with a low conviction rate and with wide-ranging outlaw gangs. Although he captured noted stage robber Dick Fellows in 1875, out of 31 robberies, only 6 resulted in convictions. In 1883 Hume was instrumental in the capture of the noted highwayman Black Bart. When it came time to enumerate his success with Wells Fargo in 1884, records indicate that since 1870 he had secured 240 convictions out of 313 stage robberies, 23 burglaries, and 8 train robberies. Hume later participated in the capture of the Dalton brothers in Oklahoma, but as time took its toll on the storied lawman, he began to turn over many of his responsibilities to his assistant, John Nelson Thacker.* Hume died in San Francisco in 1904.

SOURCES: Richard Dillon, *Wells Fargo Detective*, 1969; William B. Secrest, *Lawmen and Desperadoes*, 1994.

HUNDRED SYSTEM. Anglo-Saxon England was divided into shires, the modern equivalent of counties. Under the tithing system,* inhabitants were organized into groups of ten, each including a leader who was responsible for assigning duties to the other nine. This group was known as a tithing, and its leader as the tithingman. Each member was responsible for the behavior of the others, and if one broke the law, the others were responsible for either apprehending the culprit or themselves paying a fine. Every ten tithings were organized into a "hundred," which was led by the hundred-man. In an era before professional policing, communities policed themselves; thus, the tithings and hundreds demonstrated the importance of community responsibility and cohesion.

SOURCE: Charles Reith, *The Blind Eye of History*, 1952.

HUNT, NICHOLAS. (b. 1848–) Born in Ireland, Hunt joined the Hyde Park, Illinois, police force in 1871, where he rose to sergeant in 1878 and then, a year later, to captain. One of his lieutenants, Patrick J. Lavin,* would make his mark in Chicago policing. In 1899 Hyde Park was annexed by Chicago and both men became captains on the Chicago Police Department (CPD)* force. Hunt solved numerous high-profile murder cases, including the Reniger-Purdy and Sena-Conti murders, and he captured killer Alex Rice. In 1890 Hunt made inspector, and four years later he solved the murder of Alfred Barnes in the notorious Flats Horror case.

In 1901 Hunt came under fire by the Hyde Park Protective Association for his reluctance to suppress gambling and vice in the Hyde Park area. In 1903, at the age of fifty-seven, he was dismissed from the department, seven years after having passed retirement age. Hunt was soon offered a job by the Pinkerton's National Detective Agency, but he turned it down and in late 1915 was rehired by the force as chief of detectives. During his brief tenure in this post, his most important case was the Washington Park Bank robbery, reportedly Chicago's first daylight bank robbery using an automobile. Hunt resigned from the force for good in 1916.

SOURCE: Raphael W. Marrow and Harriet I. Carter, *In Pursuit of Crime*, 1996.

HUTZELL, ELEONORE. One of the earliest policewomen,* Hutzell served on the Detroit police force beginning in the 1920s. An advocate for policewomen,* but not for equality with her male counterparts, she was promoted to deputy commissioner of the Detroit Police Department in the early 1930s. In 1933 she published a policewoman's manual entitled *The Policewoman's Handbook*. Hutzel, however, subscribed to the notion that policewomen should be limited to dealing with juveniles, females, and cases that did not require court actions, and that they should fill a social service role rather than be crime fighters. While Hutzell was deputy commissioner and director of the Women's Division of the Detroit Police Department, the police department employed thirty-nine women, three as sergeants.

SOURCES: Dorothy Moses Schulz, *From Social Worker to Crimefighter*, 1995; Kerry Segrave, *Policewomen: A History*, 1995.

I
_____

IGII, TAMEGORO. (b. 1905) Tokyo Metropolitan Police Sergeant Igii is credited with the apprehension of mass murderer Sadamichi Hirasawa in 1948. On January 26, 1948, Hirasawa entered a branch of Tokyo's Teikoku Bank. He was wearing an official-looking sanitation uniform and he told the bank officers he had been ordered to immunize the bank employees against an outbreak of dysentery. He injected a dose of purported antidysentery medication into each employee's teacup, whereupon they drank the potion and were soon writhing in agony on the floor. Hirasawa proceeded to ransack the bank and escaped with 164,400 yen in cash. Twelve of the employees died from what turned out to be potassium cyanide. This massacre and robbery was the most prominent crime to occur in Japan during the postwar era. A nationwide manhunt ensued but made little headway until Igii was brought into the case. His knowledge of calling cards, an old Japanese tradition in which professionals and businessmen exchange business cards on their first meeting, led Igii to the suspect seven months after the crime was committed.

The subsequent trial was the first major case brought before the Japanese court system since General Douglas MacArthur abolished the French system of jurisprudence that had been adopted earlier in the century. Sentenced to death, Hirasawa was still sitting on death row in the late 1970s. According to the *Guiness Book of World Records*, this was the slowest execution in history. Following the conclusion of the case, Igii was promoted from sergeant to police inspector. In 1949 he became an instructor at the police academy, and three years later he returned to the Metropolitan Police Department's homicide division. He retired in 1964.

SOURCE: Bruce Henderson and Sam Summerlin, *The Super Sleuths*, 1976.

ILLINOIS CRIME SURVEY. In the 1929 *Illinois Crime Survey*, August Voll-mer* denounced "the corrupt political influence exercised by administrative officials and corrupt politicians" over the Chicago Police Department (CPD).*

SOURCE: Samuel Walker, *Popular Justice*, 1998.

INDIAN POLICE. In the 1860s and 1870s, Indian police forces were developed to handle disorder and criminal activities on the reservations. Reservation agent John Philip Clum* was instrumental in demonstrating that Indian police officers could effectively maintain order. When Clum arrived at the Apache reservation at San Carlos in the Arizona Territory, he hired four Apaches to police the reservation. Despite an initial reluctance by neighboring whites to allow the Indians to police themselves, within six months, order had been restored on the reservation. As the reservation increased in population, Clum's Indian police force grew to twenty-five members. The U.S. government soon took notice of this successful experiment and in 1878 authorized the establishment of Indian police on most frontier reservations. By 1890, fifty-nine reservations could boast Indian police units, totaling seventy officers and seven hundred privates.

The Indian police were chiefly responsible for keeping the peace; protecting property; discovering and returning stolen property; and arresting drunk and disorderly individuals, horse and cattle thieves, and whiskey sellers. Indian police were poorly paid and equipped and were often unwilling to wear police uniforms.*

SOURCES: William T. Hagan, *Indian Police and Judges*, 1966; John P. Clum, "The San Carlos Apache Police," *New Mexico Historical Review*, July 1929.

INFORMANTS. *See* SUPERGRASS.

INTENDANCE OF POLICE. Based on the French model of policing, the office of intendant of police was created in Lisbon, Portugal in 1762. Rio de Janeiro adopted the position in 1808 and, together with a militarized police force, it became the foundation for the development of the Rio de Janeiro police. The police intendance was responsible for maintaining public order, apprehension of criminals, surveillance, and crime investigation. The first intendant of the Rio de Janeiro police was Paulo Fernades Viana.*

SOURCE: Thomas H. Holloway, *Policing Rio de Janeiro*, 1993.

INTERNATIONAL ASSOCIATION OF CHIEFS OF POLICE (IACP). Steps were taken toward creating a national police association in the United States following the 1871 National Police Convention held in St. Louis, Missouri. Although police executives recognized the need for a forum to share new strategies for policing as well as to discuss new scientific investigative techniques, it would be another twenty-two years before police executives would again meet en masse. During a perfunctory meeting held in Chicago to coincide with the 1893 Columbian Exposition, the National Police Chiefs Union concentrated on organization rather than issues. However, by 1901 the union had established itself as a strong force for police professionalization.

As president of the nascent organization, Washington, D.C., police chief Richard Sylvester* introduced a program of educational meetings and publications. In 1915 the National Police Chiefs Union made the transition to the International Association of Chiefs of Police (IACP), and over the past eight decades it has been instrumental in implementing numerous police reforms.

Important police reformers such as August Vollmer* and Fred Kohler* have used the meetings of the IACP to launch important reform agendas. In 1907 Kohler delivered a speech on how best to suppress the "social evil" of prostitution, and at the 1919 meeting Vollmer argued for better preventive policing. However, the IACP has dropped the ball on many occasions as well. In 1919, following a series of urban race riots, officials at the national meeting ignored race issues and did not even address the paucity of African-American police officers. Along with the Bureau of Investigation and leading criminologists, the IACP developed the *Uniform Crime Reports (UCR)* system in 1930.

SOURCES: Samuel Walker, *Popular Justice*, 1998; William G. Bailey, ed., *The Encyclopedia of Police Science*, 1995.

INTERNATIONAL ASSOCIATION OF POLICEWOMEN (IAP). The International Association of Policewomen was founded by Alice Stebbins Wells* in 1915. With the support of the International Association of Chiefs of Police (IACP),* she formed the organization as a clearinghouse for setting standards for policewomen* and "placing special emphasis upon crime prevention and protective measures for women and children." Its first meeting in 1916 attracted policewomen from fourteen states. In 1919 Mina Van Winkle* from the Washington, D.C., police department's Woman's Bureau succeeded Wells as head of the IAP. However, the organization was short-lived and was disbanded following the death of Van Winkle in 1932, its chief financial contributor and president. In 1956 the organization was resurrected as the International Association of Women Police.

SOURCES: Kerry Segrave, *Policewomen: A History*, 1995; Dorothy Moses Schulz, *From Social Worker to Crimefighter*, 1995.

INTERNATIONAL CRIMINAL POLICE ORGANIZATION (INTERPOL). Interpol was largely the brainchild of Dr. Johann Schober,* the head of the Vienna, Austria, police and the country's former chancellor. Schober envisioned Interpol as a panacea for the international crime problem. He believed that if disparate police forces cooperated with each other, they could be more effective in deterring crime within their borders and catching offenders as the crimes occurred. In 1923 Schober sponsored a world conference of law enforcement officers in Vienna. In the years prior to the outbreak of World War II, the organization would continue to add new members. Initially headquartered in Vienna, with the ascendence of Nazi Germany and the annexation of Austria in 1938, the organization was disbanded.

Following the war, Interpol was resurrected at a 1946 conference in Brussels, Belgium. In the intervening years, Interpol's central offices were relocated to Paris and then Lyons, France. Contrary to popular notions, Interpol officers do not make arrests or participate in the apprehension of criminals. Instead, the organization serves as a clearinghouse for information, which it disseminates to over 177 police forces around the world as of 1998. Interpol houses millions of files, including mugshots and fingerprints. Although it keeps a low profile, Interpol played a prominent role in exposing the 1980s Pizza Connection, a drug-trafficking and money-laundering operation involving several Mafia families. Between 1984 and 1989, John Simpson, an American and chief of the U.S. Secret Service,* presided as president of Interpol.

SOURCES: Iris Noble, *Interpol: International Crime Fighter*, 1975; Trevor Meldal-Johnson and Vaughn Young, *The Interpol Connection*, 1979.

IREY, ELMER LINCOLN. (1888–1948) Irey joined the U.S. Internal Revenue Service (IRS) enforcement branch in 1919. Over the next two decades he would set up one of the best investigative teams in the history of the U.S. Treasury Department.* His unit, dubbed the "T-men," included Frank J. Wilson,* who successfully infiltrated the Capone mob, leading to the conviction of the mob boss in 1931 for tax evasion. Irey pursued other high-profile cases as well, including tax cases involving Louisiana Governor Huey Long and publisher Moe Annenberg. He also recorded the serial numbers from the Lindbergh ransom that resulted in the arrest of Bruno Richard Hauptmann. Irey's T-men were credited with apprehending 15,000 tax swindlers during his twenty-seven-year career. Promoted to chief coordinator of the IRS law enforcement team in 1937, he retired four years later.

SOURCE: Frank Spiering, *The Man Who Got Capone*, 1976.

IRISH POLICEMEN. A staple of 1940s films noir, the Irish policeman was a familiar component of urban policing in America throughout the second half of the nineteenth century. With the heavy influx of Irish immigrants in the 1840s and 1850s, there were few opportunities available to the undercapitalized newcomers. The political bosses of New York City and other cities quickly saw the immigrants as a source of votes. Hundreds, if not thousands, of Irishmen would enter the police force through political patronage. According to extant records for 1855, there was almost an even correlation between New York's Irish population (28 percent) and the number of Irish policemen (27 percent).

Irishmen were better represented on the New York City Police Department

(NYPD)* force than they were on the London force. This was in part due to the 1837 proclamation of commissioner Sir Richard Mayne* that the notoriously prolific Irishmen would be barred from serving on the force if they had more than three children, since he was worried that the pay would be inadequate to support the family. By 1860, this number was reduced to two children. Following this directive, the number of Irishmen on the London force (see LONDON METROPOLITAN POLICE) dropped from 16 percent in 1834 to 7 percent in 1855. According to historian Wilbur Miller, the Irish policeman was a much less familiar local figure in London than in New York City. The 1863 New York City Draft Riots* served as a turning point in the relationship between the Irish New York policemen and their constituents. During this episode their heroic stance against the Irish mobs served as a crucible which tested their mettle and demonstrated that the force came before their countrymen.

SOURCES: Wilbur R. Miller, *Cops and Bobbies*, 1973; James F. Richardson, *The New York Police*, 1970.

IZZY AND MOE. Isadore "Izzy" Einstein and Moe Smith were two of the most successful and honest Prohibition agents* at a time when 706 agents were dismissed from the force for corruption and incompetence between 1920 and 1928. Both agents weighed well over 200 pounds, leading the media to refer to them as "Tweedledum" and "Tweedledee." Izzy and Moe made great newspaper copy during a time when there was little good news to report. Disguised as rabbis, bootleggers, or football players Izzy and Moe were credited with making over five thousand arrests and confiscating five million bottles of contraband liquor. In order to successfully prosecute liquor scofflaws it was necessary to produce samples of evidence in court. The pair's modus operandi began with gaining entry to a speakeasy. After ordering a drink, they would pour the illegal beverage into a funnel connected by a tube to a flask hidden in one of the agent's back pockets.

Following stints as a dry goods salesman and then as a clerk for the New York Post Office, Einstein offered his services to the Federal Prohibition Bureau. Fluent in Yiddish and other eastern European dialects, the stocky, rotund civil servant began his career as a revenue agent in 1920. Several weeks later he brought his friend Moe Smith in as his partner. They proved so effective as a team that some speakeasies mounted photos of the agents on the wall. Their most eventful day on the job included sixty-five raids.

During the 1920s the exploits of Izzy and Moe were often captured in catchy newspaper headlines, such as 'Izzy is Bizzy and So Is Moe." Cities such as Atlanta, St. Louis, and Chicago soon coveted the duo, The two were immediate successes wherever they went, but they set the record for their quickest bust in New Orleans, where they made their first arrest thirty-five seconds after their arrival. In the end, their careers were short-circuited because of their predisposition for publicity. In November 1925, they resigned from the bureau, with Izzy explaining, "I fired myself." Friends for life, they subsequently entered the insurance business. Izzy would also write his autobiography, titled *Prohibition Agent Number 1*.

SOURCE: Carl Sifakis, *The Encyclopedia of American Crime*, 1982.

J

JACKSON, FREDERICK EUGENE. (1861–1949) Born in Wyaslung, Wisconsin, Jackson could reported_y trace his lineage back to the American icon Andrew Jackson. He moved to California with his family in the 1870s and earned a reputation as a fair marksman. He entered law enforcement in Nevada sometime in the 1880s. He served as deputy sheriff in Fresno and was selected by the Wells Fargo Detective Bureau* to assist in the apprehension of train robbers Chris Evans and John Sontag in 1893. During the gunfight, Jackson received a serious gunshot wound to his leg, which necessitated amputation. After a brief convalescence he joined Wells Fargo as a shotgun guard (reportedly, he was its only one-legged guard). In 1899 he left Wells Fargo to start a family, but the following year saw him appointed deputy sheriff in Amador County. Over the next thirty-six years, Jackson continued to sporadically work as a lawman when not prospecting for gold. He served his last stint with a badge in 1935 at the age of seventy-four, a full forty-two years after losing his leg.

SOURCES: William B. Secrest, *Lawmen and Desperadoes*, 1994; C. B. Glasscock, *Bandits and the Southern Pacific*, 1929.

JACKSON, SIR RICHARD LEOFRIC. (1902–1975) Born in Calcutta, India, and educated at Eton and Trinity College in England, Jackson entered the legal profession in 1927 in India but returned to England during the troubles of the Indian independence movement. Specializing in criminal law, Jackson initially worked as a prosecutor but joined Scotland Yard* as an administrator in 1945. In 1952 he was promoted to assistant commissioner of the Criminal Investigation Department (CID),* in charge of 1,650 investigators. During his tenure with CID he earned a reputation as an incredibly efficient administrator, who could cite an 80 percent conviction rate in murder cases. His success earned him the presidency of Interpol* from 1960 to 1963, when he retired.

SOURCE: Charles Phillips and Alan Axelrod, *CCC*, 1996.

JEFFREYS, ALEC. (b. 1950) In 1985 Jeffreys was credited with making one of the greatest advances in the history of forensic science when he discovered DNA fingerprints while conducting research at the University of Leicester, England. Initially, genetic fingerprinting was used to resolve paternity and immigration suits. In 1987 British police used DNA evidence to secure the conviction of the British rapist and murderer Colin Pitchfork. Joseph Aloysius Wambaugh Jr.* chronicled this case in his best-selling book *The Blooding*. DNA evidence was first used successfully in the United States the following year with the conviction of a rapist.

SOURCE: Dick Thompson, "A Trial of High-Tech Detectives," *Time*, June 5, 1989.

JOB, THE. This term is British police slang for the London Metropolitan Police* organization, which is usually used in reference to the more detestable aspects of "the job." It also happens to be the title of the fortnightly newspaper of the London Metropolitan Police.

SOURCE: Peter Laurie, *Scotland Yard*, 1970.

JOCKS OR JOCKEYS. These terms are eighteenth-century British slang for detective.

SOURCE: Bill Waddell, *The Black Museum*, 1993.

JOHNSON, EDWIN W. (1853–1931) Born in Clark County, Arkansas, Johnson entered law enforcement as a deputy sheriff in Arkadelphia in 1876. Four years later Johnson was appointed deputy in Clay County, Texas, where he was instrumental in ending the local fence-cutting problem. During the 1880s he served as deputy in Young County, Texas, and as deputy U.S. marshal (see U.S. MARSHALS SERVICE) in Young County, Texas, and in the Indian Territory. In 1888 he lost his right arm in a Wichita Falls, Texas, gunfight with Bob James, but in no time he had developed enough dexterity in his other arm to continue working as a peace officer.

Later that year Johnson helped arrest four of the Marlow brothers, who were wanted for horse theft. It was thought best to move the Marlows out of the community, where feelings ran high against them. Johnson led an eight-member security force in an attempt to move the Marlows to a more secure location sixty miles away. However, they were waylaid by a mob not far from town. In the resulting gun battle, Johnson's one good hand was all but torn up by a gunshot and ten men were killed, including his main deputy and two of the Marlow brothers. (The story of the Marlow brothers ambush was reportedly the inspiration for the 1965 John Wayne vehicle *The Sons of Katie Elder*.) This episode was followed by claims that Johnson was part of the mob, but he was eventually acquitted. He moved to Los Angeles in 1916, where he served as a deputy sheriff for fifteen years.

SOURCES: Edward W. (Ted) Johnson, "Deputy Marshal Johnson Breaks a Long Silence," *True West*, January–February, 1980; Glenn Shirley, *The Fighting Marlows*, 1994.

JOHNSON, GRANT. (d. 1929) Next to Bass Reeves,* Johnson is considered one of the most prominent African-American deputy U.S. marshals (see U.S. MARSHALS SERVICE) ever posted to the Indian Territory. His early life is obscure, but he was most probably born in North Texas. Quiet and reserved and of average size, Johnson became a deputy U.S. marshal in 1887. Judge Isaac Charles Parker* remembered him as one of the foremost lawmen in the Indian Territory. On more than one occasion, Johnson collaborated with Bass Reeves to apprehend desperadoes. He was credited with capturing numerous horse thieves and survived several gunfights, yet he did not kill his first man until 1901. Despite the achievements of black lawmen Bass Reeves, Zeke Miller,* and Grant Johnson, not one African-American was ever appointed U.S. marshal in the Indian Territory. Johnson resigned after a twenty-year career and for a time worked as a policeman in Eufala, Oklahoma.

SOURCE: Art Burton, *Black, Red, and Deadly*, 1991.

JOHNSON, HENRY J. (1818–1875) Born in Glasgow, Scotland, Johnson apparently joined the local police force at a young age and demonstrated intuitive powers that would characterize the new age of policing. After a stint working as a detective in Australia, he moved to San Francisco in 1855, where he joined the local police force, called the Special Police, which was financially supported by the residents of the beat that was patrolled. As he became more involved in detective work he was often paired with Isaiah Wrigley Lees,* head of the San Francisco Police detective department.

In 1859 the two detectives solved the robbery of the Freeman & Company Express by resorting to classic detective skills, whereby they found it to have been an inside job. In 1863 Johnson branched out of the traditional police milieu when he was appointed special officer for the Pacific Mail Steamship Company and the following year was made government detective by the commander of the Department of the Pacific. Four years later Johnson worked freelance for the Wells Fargo Detective Bureau.* Because of the political infighting that was so rampant in the municipal policing of the nineteenth century, Johnson left the San Francisco force to concentrate on private detective work in 1871. He later served short stints as a Wells Fargo detective and deputy U.S. Marshal (see U.S. MARSHALS SERVICE), and again returned to city police work briefly in 1874.

SOURCE: William B. Secrest, *Lawmen and Desperadoes*, 1994.

JONES, FRANK. (1856–1893) Jones joined the Texas Rangers* at seventeen and within a year had made a name for himself as a lawman by killing two horse thieves who had planned to ambush him. In 1880 he hunted down the individuals responsible for the 1875 Mason County War. Never one to shy away from gunplay, he killed several rustlers in barroom frays, including badman Tex Murieta.

Awarded the rank of captain, in 1891 he successfully led rangers in the pursuit of four Southern Pacific train robbers along the Mexican border. Three were killed in a gun battle and the fourth committed suicide. He participated in his last gunfight on June 29, 1893, when he crossed into Mexican territory searching for the Olguin cattle thief gang. Jones died from several gunshot wounds after cornering the gang. His last words to a fellow ranger were, reportedly, "Boys, I am killed" (Nash). Since the killing took place in Mexican territory, no one was brought to justice for his death.

SOURCES: Walter Prescott Webb, *The Texas Rangers*, 1935; Jay Robert Nash, *EWLO*, 1994.

JONES, GUSTAVE T. (1882–1963) Jones served as assistant police chief in San Angelo, Texas, in 1905 and then was appointed assistant sheriff of Tom Green County, Texas. In 1908 Jones began a two-year stint with the vaunted Texas Rangers.* He resigned in 1910 to join the U.S. Customs Service.* Over the next decade he performed a variety of duties along the Mexican border, including inspector for the U.S. Immigration Service. In 1917 Jones joined the Bureau of Investigation and continued his service on the Texas border. He is credited with developing a military intelligence strategy on the border during World War I.

In the 1930s he was instrumental in the capture of George "Machine Gun" Kelly in the wake of the Urschel kidnapping case. Jones assisted in the transportation of Kelly and mob boss Al Capone to the Alcatraz prison in 1934. Jones served as Special Intelligence Service coordinator for the Federal Bureau of Investigation (FBI)* in Mexico from World War II until his retirement in 1943.

SOURCE: Athan G. Theoharis, ed., *The FBI*, 1999.

JONES, JAMES WORMLEY. (c. 1884–1958) Born in Fort Monroe, Virginia, "Jack" Jones attended college for four years prior to joining the Washington, D.C., Metropolitan Police Department in 1905. He served in a variety of capacities and rose to detective before joining the army in 1917. He saw action in France in 1918 and then returned to the Washington, D.C., police force after the end of European hostilities. On November 19, 1919, Jones became the first African-American special agent in the history of the Federal Bureau of Investigation (FBI).* Posted to the New York City and Pittsburgh, Pennsylvania, field offices, Jones proved a savvy undercover operative when he infiltrated Marcus

Garvey's black nationalist organization in the early 1920s. He retired in 1923 after his cover was foiled and he could longer effectively work undercover.

SOURCE: Athan G. Theoharis, ed., *The FBI*, 1999.

JONES, JOHN B. (1834–1881) Born in Fairfield County, South Carolina, Jones emigrated with his farmer family across the South, settling in Corsicana, Texas, in 1838. Jones returned to his roots to study at Mt. Zion College in Winnsboro, South Carolina, before returning to Texas and the cattle business following graduation. During the Civil War he served in the Eighth Texas Cavalry, which was better known as Terry's Texas Rangers. He rose to the rank of captain, and after the war sought homes in Brazil and Mexico for expatriate Confederates.

After a stint as a member of the Texas State Legislature beginning in 1868, Jones entered law enforcement in 1874 when he was appointed major of the Frontier Battalion of the Texas Rangers.* Charged with leading six companies of Rangers with seventy-five men in each, Jones's force was responsible for controlling outlaws and Indian depredations from the Red River to the Rio Grande. His battalion fought over a dozen skirmishes with Indians in 1874 alone. As the Indian threat diminished in the 1870s Jones was drawn more to controlling the bandit problem and stemming civil unrest.

As Ranger captain, Jones was credited with influencing the truce that ended the Horrell-Higgins feud in Lampasas County and ending the Mason County feud. He was also instrumental in tracking down and destroying the Sam Bass–led train-robbing gang at Round Rock, Texas, in July 1878. Jones's reputation was tarnished during his involvement in the 1877 El Paso Salt War. His mishandling of the feud between Hispanics and whites over control of salt-producing lands led to the deaths of several civilians that most felt could have been avoided had Jones not underestimated the depth of animosity in the community.

Following the killing of Sam Bass in 1878, Jones left the field to serve as commander, or state adjutant general, of the Texas Rangers. Physically unreposing at five feet, eight inches, and possessed of temperate habits, Jones has taken his place in the pantheon of legendary Rangers. He died of suppurative hepatitis in 1881.

SOURCES: Walter Prescott Webb, *The Texas Rangers*, 1935; C. L. Sonnichsen, *Ten Texas Feuds*, 1957; Billy Mac Jones, "John B. Jones," in *Rangers of Texas*, ed. Ben Proctor, 1969.

JUDY SCUFFER. This term is British slang for policewoman; it was popular in the Liverpool area.

SOURCE: Bill Waddell, *The Black Museum*, 1993.

JUSTICE OF THE PEACE. The law enforcement position of justice of the peace (JP) can be traced back to its precursors in twelfth-century Norman England, when certain knights were appointed by King Richard I to keep the peace. In the following century they became known as *custodes pacis*, or keepers of the peace. Over time the position evolved so that they were allowed to make arrests and serve warrants. In 1361 the JPs were formally recognized as justices imbued with police, judicial, and administrative authority. Subsequently, the JPs took over many of the responsibilities of the sheriffs (see SHERIFF) and constables.* These unpaid officials were commonly selected from the feudal lords and were allowed to compensate themselves by collecting fees and expenses. The JP's most recognizable weapon was a staff-like baton, which was often placed above his cottage door.

By the 1500s the JPs had come under criticism for granting favoritism and bail to convicted felons. Consequently, they were often derided as "boobies" and "scum of the earth" by their constituents. England removed the property-holding qualifications for office by 1900, and the position was sapped of its ancient powers related to law enforcement. In the United States most of the JP's duties have been taken over by police magistrates. Although the position can still conjure up images of Judge Roy Bean of Texas, in reality it has been diminished to presiding over weddings.

SOURCE: T. A. Critchley, *A History of Police in England and Wales, 900–1966*, 1967.

K

KANSAS CITY MASSACRE. On June 17, 1933, Federal Bureau of Investigation (FBI)* agent Raymond J. Caffrey,* the McAlester, Oklahoma, Police chief Otto Reed, and Kansas City Police detectives W. J. "Red" Grooms and Frank Hermanson were reportedly ambushed and killed by machine-gun fire in what has become known as the Kansas City Massacre. In addition, FBI agents Joseph Lackey, Reed Vetterli, and Frank Smith were wounded by gunfire. Since FBI agents were not yet authorized to carry weapons at this time, the men were unarmed. This incident shocked the nation.

That day FBI agents and policemen were escorting convicted criminal Frank Nash out of Kansas City's Union Station in preparation for his trip to Leavenworth Penitentiary. Nash was an escaped convict wanted for robbing banks and trains. It was common practice at this time for FBI agents to use local police for backup when making arrests. At that time, arrests had to be made by local peace officers before the FBI could take over jurisdiction. As Nash had been captured in Hot Springs, Arkansas, Police Chief Reed was along for the roust because he recognized Nash and because local law enforcement in Hot Springs was notoriously corrupt, which meant that federal agents could not expect much help from local peace officers.

Unknown to the FBI agents, someone in the Kansas City Police Department leaked word of the looming train trip to local underlings of the Pendergast machine, who relayed the news to underworld figures. As the seven law enforcement officers left Union Station, with Nash, they were apparently accosted by three men toting machine guns, one of whom was Charles "Pretty Boy" Floyd. While some authorities suggest the incident was a rescue attempt that failed, others argued that the gunmen were intent on silencing Nash. Nonetheless, what resulted was one of the most infamous attacks on law enforcement officers in American history. Pretty Boy Floyd would be hunted down and killed in 1934, but the identities of the other gunmen have never been uncovered.

A recent book by Pulitzer prize–winning investigative journalist Robert Unger makes a good argument that none of the official accounts are true. After an exhaustive search through the original eighty-nine-volume FBI file on the case, Unger argues that the primary killers in Kansas City were the lawmen themselves. According to Unger, one of the men was unfamiliar with his shotgun and, in the closely confined space of the automobile, unleashed a fusillade of lead in a panic, killing Nash in the front seat and triggering a deadly gunfight that killed five lawmen, several by friendly fire. Unger insists that the evidence in the FBI files indicates that FBI agent Joe Lackey accidentally killed Nash, Caffrey, and Hermanson. In addition, Chief Reed was killed by a .38-caliber bullet, which was probably fired from a lawman's weapon.

Following the "Kansas City Massacre," FBI director John Edgar Hoover* used its consequences to launch a high-profile campaign to hunt down public enemies (such as Pretty Boy Floyd) in the nation's heartland. In 1934 Franklin D. Roosevelt signed into law nine anticrime bills that enlarged the crime-fighting powers and jurisdiction of the FBI. Following the passage of these measures, FBI agents would be responsible for suppressing federal bank robberies, the transportation of stolen property across state lines, and other crimes, and would be allowed to carry and use firearms.

SOURCES: Robert Unger, *The Union Station Massacre: The Original Sin of J. Edgar Hoover's FBI*, 1997; Merle Clayton, *The Union Station Massacre*, 1975; Don Whitehead, *The FBI Story*, 1956; Curt Gentry, *J. Edgar Hoover: The Man and the Secrets*, 1991.

KEELER, LEONARDE. (1903–1949) Born in Chicago, Keeler was educated at Stanford, where he met Dr. John A. Larson,* inventor of the polygraph. With the support of noted Berkeley police chief August Vollmer,* the two academics created the lie detector.*

Following college Keeler worked at Joliet Penitentiary and perfected the new device by testing it on more than five hundred inmates. In 1929 his accomplishments earned him the position of chief psychologist and polygraph examiner at the Northwestern University's Scientific Crime Detection Laboratory. In 1931 his improved lie detector, the Keeler Polygraph, was patented.

Although he was unsuccessful in his attempts to receive permission to use the machine on Lindbergh kidnapper Bruno Hauptmann, Keeler went on to great financial success and was recognized as the leading lie detector authority. In the 1940s Keeler was responsible for screening prospective employees for the government's top secret atomic energy weapons program and interrogating German prisoners of war. Following the war the Keeler Polygraph School was established in Chicago with his involvement.

SOURCE: Eugene B. Block, *Lie Detectors: Their History and Use*, 1977.

KELLEY, CLARENCE MARION (1911–1997) Born in Kansas City, Missouri, and educated at the University of Kansas, Kelley attended law school before joining the Federal Bureau of Investigation (FBI)* as an agent in 1940. After an undistinguished early career, and feeling disenchanted with the policies of John Edgar Hoover* during the civil rights era, he left the agency to become Kansas City police chief in 1961.

During his tenure as chief Kelley updated the force, introducing new crime-fighting techniques such as computers to track criminals and making great strides in civil rights reform. His record was tarnished by what critics described as a "police riot" in 1968 when police used excessive force while attempting to quell the riots that followed the assassination of Martin Luther King Jr.

In 1973 President Richard Nixon appointed Kelley to lead the FBI, making him the first permanent director following the death of Hoover (Louis Patrick Gray* before him was an acting director). Over the next five years Kelley is credited with steering the agency through the turmoil of the post-Watergate era by removing it from political influence, reorganizing it, and developing new crime-fighting strategies such as sting operations. As director, Kelley supervised a number of prominent investigations, including the Patty Hearst kidnapping and the Wounded Knee Siege.* He left the FBI in 1978 and started a private investigation firm. Kelley died following a battle with emphysema and several strokes.

SOURCES: *Houston Chronicle,* August 6, 1997; Athan G. Theoharis, ed., *The FBI,* 1999.

KENDALL, AMOS. (1789–1869) A former journalist and a supporter of Andrew Jackson's presidential campaign, following "Old Hickory's" victory, Kendall was appointed U.S. postmaster general (in 1835). During his tenure, which lasted until 1840, Kendall proved an efficient administrator. Kendall is best remembered in law enforcement lore for establishing the Office of Inspection, the first federal police force within the executive branch of the federal government. The special force was inaugurated in 1836 to protect against postal theft, corruption, and highway robbers and to foil mail swindles and the trafficking of pornographic materials through the mail.

SOURCE: Amos Kendall, *The Autobiography of Amos Kendall,* 1872.

KENNEDY, JOHN ALEXANDER. (1803–1873) The son of Irish immigrants, Kennedy was born in Baltimore, Maryland. A lifelong opposition to slavery led him to serve as secretary of the short-lived Maryland Anti-Slavery Society in 1825. He then became co-editor of an abolitionist newspaper and stayed active in the abolition movement, publishing numerous articles in William Lloyd Garrison's anti slavery newspaper, the *Liberator.*

Kennedy had learned the sign painter's trade in his youth and in 1828 was involved in a related painting business in New York City. A rising politician in the Democratic party, he served in a variety of positions before being named superintendent of the New York Metropolitan Police* in 1860. Despite a lack of police experience, during his ten years as superintendent he improved police discipline and efficiency. As the country moved closer to war, Kennedy was often accused of high-handedness and the infringement of constitutional rights. He was accused of overstepping his authority for intercepting weapons intended for the South before the onset of hostilities. More noteworthy was his dispatching of New York City police officers outside their jurisdiction to Baltimore to investigate potential assassination plots against president-elect Abraham Lincoln. It has never been substantiated that Kennedy was as instrumental as he claimed at uncovering the plot, since credit as always been accorded to Pinkerton's National Detective Agency.*

During the Civil War era Kennedy zealously supported Union and Republican causes and appointed a provost marshal* to apprehend deserters. During the 1863 New York City Draft Riots* he was savagely beaten by rioters and left for dead. Although he recovered he was left permanently lame. He lost any chance of support from the German immigrant community after the war when he strictly enforced the 1866 Metropolitan Act, which banned the sale of liquor on Sundays. Kennedy's days were numbered following the passage of the 1870 Tweed charter for the city, which abolished all state commissions in New York City and replaced the Metropolitan Police with the municipal police department. His last years were spent as president of a street railroad company and a collector of assessments.

SOURCES: James F. Richardson, *The New York Police: Colonial Times to 1901*, 1970; Iver Bernstein, *The New York City Draft Riots*, 1990; *New York Times*, June 21, 1873.

KENNEDY, STEPHEN PATRICK. (1906–1978) Born in Brooklyn, Kennedy left school early and worked at a succession of dead-end jobs before joining the New York City Police Department (NYPD)* in 1928. Eight years later he was promoted to captain. In the meantime he attended law school and earned a degree in 1946. Advancements to inspector and commander of the Waterfront Squad followed, and in 1954 he was made chief inspector.

Kennedy was promoted to police commissioner in 1955. During his five-year tenure he proved a popular and honest leader. Nothing demonstrates his allegiance to the rank and file better than his resignation in 1961 in protest over the mayor's refusal to pay police officers higher wages.

SOURCE: Charles Phillips and Alan Axelrod, *CCC*, 1996.

KEYSTONE KOPS. In the tradition of William Shakespeare's Dogberry* in *Much Ado about Nothing*, the silent film director Mack Sennett combined cops and comedy in a series of short films released in the early 1900s. In a time when police officers were controlled by political machines and often required to purchase their position, Sennett felt that as symbols of dignity and authority, they more than deserved their due as comic foils.

In late 1912 the Keystone Kops made their first appearance in celluloid with the release of *Hoffmeyer's Legacy*. Its success guaranteed that every Sennett comedy after this would feature at least one or more comic cops. The release of *The Bangville Police* proved even more successful, and Sennett began experimenting with the Keystone Kops as the featured characters. In 1914 Sennett unveiled *In the Clutches of a Gang*, a two-reeler that involved the Kops in a kidnap caper and is considered one of the best in the series.

The Keystone Kop films are credited with introducing the chase scene to motion pictures. Every film served up a generous number of careening car chases, man-animal chases, and vehicle-man chases. However, none of these scenes were shot without considerable precision. Some scenes required gaining permission to use certain intersections for filming, although this was not always the case. Often liquid soap would be lathered over a road and stunt drivers would attempt to negotiate the slippery conditions at speeds of fifty miles per hour before applying the brakes. To perform what looked like death-defying railroad crossings, a locomotive and its crew would be hired for the day.

While the stunts seemed remarkable for this time period, many were performed with camera tricks. However, many scenes were so dangerous that insurance companies were reluctant to cover the actors. Camera speed and editing made the tempo seem much faster than in reality. Like Shakespeare's Dogberry, the Kops were caricatures of suburban police officers who provided comic entertainment for the masses and did little to remedy lawlessness.

SOURCE: Kalton C. Lahue and Terry Brewer, *Kops and Custards: The Legend of Keystone Films*, 1968.

KGB. The Committee for State Security, or Komitet Gosudarstvennoy Bezopasnosti (KGB), was one of the Soviet Union's main law enforcement agencies prior to the end of the Cold War. With the diminishment of the MVD* apparatus following the execution of Lavrenti Pavlovich Beria* in 1954, the KGB reemerged as a separate state security organ, taking responsibility for espionage and counterespionage and for counterintelligence services within the Soviet Armed Forces. The MVD and KGB had operated under various names and organizational structures for decades and shared the responsibility for law enforcement within the Soviet Union. The KGB was concerned mainly with internal security, investigating major crimes that threatened the state, both externally and internally. The KGB remained more powerful than the MVD because of its close connection to the Central Committee of the Communist party and its mandate to carry out activities above the law. As the president of the new Russian Republic following the fall of communism, Boris Yeltsin abolished the KGB and replaced it with the Russian Agency for Federal Security. Unlike its predecessor, the new agency was expected to cooperate with foreign police agencies.

SOURCES: John J. Dziak, *Chekisty: A History of the KGB*, 1988; Robert Conquest, ed., *The Soviet Police System*, 1968.

KIDD, ROBERT. (1858–1895) Following a stint in the City of Manchester Police, Kidd joined the London & North Western Railway Police in 1885 and four years later was promoted to detective sergeant. On September 29, 1895, Kidd and another colleague were patrolling a station that was a popular target for thieves when they separated to complete their patrol. Kidd's colleague was ambushed by a gang of thieves, and when he regained consciousness, he found Kidd mortally wounded. The perpetrators were soon caught, and one was hanged. Kidd was the first of the Railway Police* to be murdered in the line of duty.

SOURCE: Pauline Appleby, *A Force on the Move*, 1995.

KIDDER, JEFFERSON P. "JEFF." (c. 1875–1908) Born in South Dakota, Kidder enlisted in the Arizona Rangers* in 1903. Although he made sergeant, his ascension through the ranks was stymied by his fierce temper. On several occasions he was disciplined for brutality complaints. He accompanied Captain Thomas H. Rynning* across the Mexican border on at least one unofficial assignment and in 1906 killed a man in a Douglas, Arizona, gunfight. Two years later he participated in a heated exchange with Mexican police in Sonora, Mexico, that left three of them wounded, one fatally. Kidder initially survived a bullet wound to the stomach, but after his capture he was physically abused in a Mexican jail and died from his wound.

SOURCES: Joseph Miller, *The Arizona Rangers*, 1972; Bill O'Neal, *The Arizona Rangers*, 1987.

KING, JOHN. (1807–1859) Born into a Norwich, England, farming family, King would ultimately make his mark on British policing by transforming the Cape Town, South Africa, police force. In 1824 he joined the British Cavalry and over the next three years was mostly involved with suppressing the civil disorder associated with the early years of England's Industrial Revolution. In 1829 he left Norwich for London, where he found employment in the new London Metropolitan Police.* Within two years he was promoted to sergeant and over the next several years he worked with a protégé of Charles Dickens,* Inspector Charles Frederick Field,* and the young constable Charles Goff (see CONSTABLES). In 1839 King left England for Cape Town after Colonel Sir Charles Rowan* selected him to train local police forces in the South African colony. King implemented street lighting, horse mounted police,* and beat patrols and directed the construction of a police station house. During a two-year period he supervised the collection of a four hundred–volume police library. Within a few short years King had placed the stamp of the Metropolitan Police on the Cape Town force as arrests rose and crime diminished. King died from heart disease in 1859, shortly after resigning from the force.

SOURCE: Alan F. Hattersley, *The First South African Detectives*, 1960.

KING, RODNEY. (b. 1966) The beating of the black motorist Rodney King by Los Angeles Police Department (LAPD)* officers on March 3, 1991, was captured on videotape by witness George Holiday. Its worldwide broadcast focused attention on the excessive use of force by the LAPD and ultimately led to the indictment of several officers, the Los Angeles riots, and the resignation of police chief Daryl F. Gates.*

The incident began, just before 1:00 A.M., when California Highway Patrol* officers engaged in a high-speed pursuit of King, whom they claimed to have witnessed driving well over the speed limit. Other police vehicles joined in the pursuit and, following King's apprehension, claimed to have been threatened by King's resistance. In their attempts to subdue him they used a stun gun before resorting to batons. The videotape footage of the incident captured officers Laurence Powell, Theodore Briseno, and Timothy Wind striking King repeatedly with their batons, at the apparent direction of their commanding sergeant, Stacey Koon.

King sustained a broken cheekbone and right ankle, twenty stitches, and numerous cuts and abrasions. Blood analysis determined that King was legally intoxicated but did not have any residue of illegal drugs in his system. The four officers were charged in California State Court with criminal assault and the use of excessive force. They were able to obtain a change of venue for the court case to the white, middle-class suburb of Simi Valley and were acquitted in April 1992. Almost immediately some of the worst riots in American history broke out in Los Angeles, resulting in fifty-three deaths and millions of dollars in property destruction. Subsequently, the U.S. Department of Justice* conducted its own investigation and indicted the officers for violating federal laws by depriving King of his civil rights. Briseno and Wind were exonerated, but Koon and Powell were found guilty and sentenced to short prison terms.

SOURCES: William P. Bloss, "Police Misconduct: The Rodney King Incident," in *The Encyclopedia of Police Science*, ed. William G. Bailey, 1995; Daryl F. Gates, with Diane K. Shah, *Chief: My Life in the LAPD*, 1992.

KING, WILLIAM. Formerly a fireman, King joined the New York City Police Department (NYPD)* in 1907. After service in World War I he returned to the NYPD in 1926 and was eventually promoted to detective lieutenant in the Bureau of Missing Persons. The New York police detective is credited with almost single-handedly bringing the notorious serial killer Albert H. Fish to justice in 1934. King used a spectroscope to find an almost invisible mark on an envelope sent by Fish to a victim's mother describing how he dismembered and ate her ten-year-old daughter. Fish was executed in the electric chair on January 16, 1936.

SOURCE: Harold Schecter, *Deranged*, 1990.

KIPLEY, JOSEPH. (1848–1904) Born in Patterson, New Jersey, Kipley moved to Chicago in 1865 where he found employment as a picture framer. He joined the Chicago Police Department (CPD)* in 1872 and seven years later was promoted to detective. In 1880 he was elevated to lieutenant and, along with Lieutenant John Shea,* was placed in charge of the detective division. Together they were credited with solving dozens of cases, including burglaries, counterfeiting cases, robberies, and fencing operations. Kipley later made captain, but he was dismissed in 1895 when the Republican mayor purged the force of Democrats. Two years later a new mayoral administration hired Kipley back, this time as chief of police. Kipley in turn discharged 438 Republicans when he returned to office.

SOURCES: John J. Flinn, *History of the Chicago Police*, 1887; Raphael W. Marrow and Harriet I. Carter, *In Pursuit of Crime*, 1996.

KIRCHNER, CARL. (1867–1911) Born in Bee County, Texas, Kirchner began a six-year stint with the Texas Rangers* beginning in 1889. He participated in several gunfights and in 1893 was instrumental in rescuing a group of Rangers during a battle near Tres Jacales, just across the Mexican border. It was here that Ranger Captain Frank Jones* was killed. Kirchner is credited with mediating with Mexican authorities to secure the return of his body to Texas. Following his Ranger career he was hired by Mexican authorities to protect a money shipment being transported to Vera Cruz in 1904. He succumbed to typhus in El Paso.

SOURCES: Robert W. Stephens, *Texas Ranger Sketches*, 1972; Walter Prescott Webb, *The Texas Rangers*, 1935.

KNAPP COMMISSION. Long before the police scandal in the New York City Police Department (NYPD)* became public, Frank Serpico* made numerous allegations of corruption in the department, which were ignored. Serpico felt he had no choice but to go the press with the story, and in April 1970 the *New York Times* printed an exposé of NYPD corruption. Mayor John V. Lindsay was promoted to appoint an interdepartmental committee to investigate the charges, and in turn, the committee recommended that an independent citizen's commission be established to continue the investigation.

Named after its chairman, Wall Street attorney Whitman Knapp, the Knapp Commission investigated police corruption in New York City for two and a half years before releasing its report in 1973. According to the report, more than half the city's 29,600 police officers had participated in some type of corrupt activity.

The Knapp Commission uncovered two types of corrupt officers. It termed meat-eaters* the relatively small contingent of officers who spent their working hours looking for opportunities that they could exploit for financial gain, including gambling and illegal drugs. Grass-eaters,* on the other hand, were the majority of patrolmen who did not necessarily take payoffs but would occasionally accept gratuities from various entrepreneurs. The book *Serpico*, by Peter Maas, and the movie of the same name recounted some of the events leading up to the formation of this commission.

SOURCES: Peter Maas, *Serpico*, 1973; Whitman Knapp, chairman, *The Knapp Commission Report on Police Corruption*, 1972.

KOBAN. Japan is divided into forty-seven prefectures, which closely resemble American countries in size and American states in conception. Prefectures are divided into districts, each having its own police station area, which is under the control of prefectural police headquarters. Each police station's jurisdiction is divided into smaller jurisdictions, each of which is linked to a police box called either a *koban* or a *chuzaisho*. *Kobans* are located in urban areas and are manned by two to twelve officers per shift. *Kobans* vary in size and structure, ranging from kiosks at busy street intersections to a rustic house along a canal. Their two most characteristic features are a red globe hanging over the front door and drab gray interior walls. In contrast to the urban *koban*, the chuzaisho is located in a rural area and built more along the lines of local village homes, replete with accommodations for the officer and his family.

SOURCES: David H. Bayley, *Forces of Order: Policing Modern Japan*, 1991; Walter L. Ames, *Police and Community in Japan*, 1991; Craig L. Parker Jr., *The Japanese Police System Today: An American Perspective*, 1984.

KOEHLER, ARTHUR. (1885–1967) Koehler joined the U.S. Forest Service in 1912 and became the nation's foremost wood identification expert. His skills as an xylotomist, or wood expert, led to his participation in several famous criminal cases. In 1922 his identification of elm fragments from a dynamite bomb led to the conviction of its maker. He helped convict arsonists, tree thieves, and several other bombers. However, his most sensational exploit was his identification of parts of the wood ladder used in the Lindbergh kidnapping as coming from Bruno Hauptmann's home and determining that his tools were used to make the ladder. This evidence was the strongest circumstantial evidence in the 1935 court case.

SOURCES: Carl Sifakis, *The Encyclopedia of American Crime*, 1982; Noel Behn, *Lindbergh: The Crime*, 1994.

KOHLER, FRED. (1869–1933) Kohler, is a former Cleveland, Ohio, street cop, was promoted to city police chief in 1903. The Cleveland police had a well-deserved reputation for corruption and malfeasance when the new reform mayor tapped Kohler to turn things around. Among the reforms implemented by Kohler was a "sunrise court," which allowed minor offenders to get to work on time through quick processing following a minor violation, and therefore to save their jobs.

In 1908 Kohler introduced his "Golden Rule Policy," which dealt more informally with juvenile offenders. By diverting minor offenders out of the formal criminal justice system, courts could concentrate on more serious matters and the offender would be less stigmatized. Kohler's strategies were viewed with skepticism in many quarters; however, president (and former New York City police commissioner) Theodore Roosevelt* thought he was the best police chief in America.

Kohler remained chief for nine years, but in 1913 he was forced to step down after an extramarital affair became public knowledge. This came on the heels of another public embarrassment when it was revealed he had delivered a plagiarized speech to the International Association of Chiefs of Police (IACP)* the previous year. He continued his public service as mayor from 1921 to 1923. Kohler's legacy was further tainted when $500,000 (probably illegal pay-offs) was discovered in his safe deposit box following his death.

SOURCES: Thomas A. Reppetto, *The Blue Parade*, 1978; James F. Richardson, *Urban Police in the United States*, 1974.

KOSTERLITZKY, EMILIO. (1853–1928) Born in Russia, Kosterlitzky immigrated to the United States and joined the army. He enlisted in the Mexican Army in 1873 and rose rapidly through the ranks to commander of *la cordada*, the elite cavalry unit that patrolled along the border with America. During his tenure with the mounted force he often collaborated with his American counterparts such as the Arizona Rangers.*

Kosterlitzky's career in law enforcement is most identified with his leadership of the controversial Rurales* police force, many of whom had been desperadoes at one time or another. As colonel of this unit, he enforced government policies that subjugated peons and fought border bandits and hostile Indians. On many occasions he "informally" extradited criminals (and revolutionaries) to American peace officers. Kosterlitzky fled to America following the Mexican Revolution and later worked for the U.S. Department of Justice* in Los Angeles. In 1917, at the age of sixty-four, Kosterlitzky was appointed a special agent of the Bureau of Investigation. He resigned two years later, but his language proficiency was in such great demand that he was rehired in 1922 and stayed with the Bureau until 1926.

SOURCES: Carl Sifakis, *Encyclopedia of American Crime*, 1982; Athan G. Theoharis, *The FBI*, 1999.

KRIPO. The German criminal police better known as the Kripo, for Kriminalpolizei, are plainclothes officers* similar to their American counterparts. They are imbued with search-and-seizure powers and are entrusted with building cases for court and instituting charges against suspects.

SOURCE: George Thomas Kurian, *World Encyclopedia of Police Forces and Penal Systems*, 1989.

KUSO, FRIEDRICH. (b. 1917) Born in Vienna, Kuso graduated from law school and then served in Erwin Rommel's Afrika Korps in World War II, during which he was captured and spent several years in American prisoner-of-war camps. While incarcerated he developed an interest in law enforcement and became an avid reader of police magazines. Following the war he returned to Vienna and practiced law, but he was drawn to criminal field work. In 1947 he joined the Vienna State Security Office as police commissioner. Within eight years he was selected to lead Vienna's largest police precinct, and in 1959 he was promoted to chief of the investigation division for all capital crimes.

As head of the special branch of the security office, Kuso became prominent for his solution of some of the country's most spectacular murder cases. One of his most famous cases was the killing of a ten-year-old ballet student at the Vienna State Opera House. His investigation led to the arrest and conviction of Joseph Weinwurm in 1963, just three months after the killing. Weinwurm confessed to being responsible for a series of knife attacks on women. To solve this investigation Kuso consulted with psychological and criminological experts to develop a profile of the offender.

SOURCE: Bruce Henderson and Sam Summerlin, *The Super Sleuths*, 1976.

L

LAMBOURNE, ALEXANDRA. (1912–1999) Born in Marylebone, London, Lambourne worked as an embroiderer and dressmaker before joining the London Metropolitan Police* as a police constable (see CONSTABLES) in 1940. During her twenty-seven-year career she was promoted to sergeant in 1947, inspector in 1959, and then chief inspector in 1960.

Lambourne was most prominent in the solution of the notorious acid bath murders, which resulted in the arrest and conviction of John Haigh in 1949. Haigh made the transition from petty criminal to murderer in 1945 when he bludgeoned an entire family to death and disposed of the bodies in a vat of sulfuric acid. Subsequently, he forged his name on various family documents to gain possession of several houses and bank accounts. Having gone through the money within three years during a gambling spree, he killed several other people in similar fashion. However, in 1949 his subterfuge was uncovered when, under questioning about the disappearance of one elderly victim, Sergeant Lambourne became suspicious. Her doubts helped crack the case and led to Haigh's arrest, conviction, and execution in 1949.

SOURCES: *London Telegraph*, May 15, 1999; Bill Waddell, *The Black Museum*, 1993.

LANGFORD, NATHANIEL PITT. (1832–1911) Born in Oneida County, New York, Langford worked as a banker in St. Paul, Minnesota, in 1853 and nine years later went West for health reasons and to prospect for gold. He ended up in Virginia City, Montana. A leading member of the Montana Vigilantes, who were responsible for hunting down the William Henry Handy Plummer* gang in 1864, Langford zealously protected the names of his fellow vigilantes, even leaving them unnamed in his famous two-volume 1890 account of their activities, *Vigilante Days and Ways*, which is now considered a Western classic.

Compared to the 1860s, the last fifty years of Langford's life were rather uneventful. He worked as an Internal Revenue officer and served as first superintendent of Yellowstone National Park (1872–1877). He reportedly made the first recorded climb up the Grand Teton Mountain. Then, in 1885, he returned to St. Paul, Minnesota, to enter business and conduct historical research.

SOURCES: Richard H. Dillon, "Nathaniel Pitt Langford," *ANB*, Vol. 15, 1999; Dan L. Thrapp, ed., *EFB*, Vol. 2, 1988; Thomas J. Dimsdale, *Vigilantes of Montana*, 1915.

LA REYNIE, GABRIEL NICOLAS DE. (1625–1709) Born in Limoges, France, as the first lieutenant-general of police* of Paris, La Reynie is credited with lighting the city to make it safer at night. In order to make this work he was forced to employ at least 370 men just for this undertaking. It would not be until the introduction of new lighting innovations in 1769 that this force of lamplighters would be reduced. By the end of the seventeenth century, Paris would be illuminated by six thousand lanterns, making it the best-lit city in Europe. As lieutenant of police between 1667 and 1697, he implemented resolutions that reduced city fire hazards, including prohibiting citizens from smoking in the vicinity of combustibles. In addition, La Reynie systematically implemented a street-cleaning strategy.

La Reynie began his tenure with a force of 410 foot police and 144 horse mounted police.* Charged with controlling the press, he did not shirk from hanging printers or bookbinders for sedition, and he was instrumental in creating a system of informers known as *mouchards*.* Much to his credit, during his thirty years as lieutenant-general, Paris became a safer and cleaner city. Following his resignation, La Reynie was appointed to the Council of State, a position he would hold until his death.

SOURCES: Philip John Stead, *The Police of Paris*, 1957; Alan Williams, *The Police of Paris: 1718–1789*, 1979.

LARN, JOHN M. (1849–1878) Born in Alabama, Larn moved to Colorado in his youth but left for New Mexico following an altercation in which he killed a rancher. In 1871 he participated in a cattle drive from the fort Griffin area to Colorado, which was marred by rustling, gunfights, and confrontations with the U.S. Cavalry. By 1876 he had developed a friendship with John Henry Selman* while both men were members of a Texas vigilante committee in Shackelford County. His vigilante experience led to his election as sheriff* in February 1876. With a jurisdiction of thirteen counties, the mercurial Larn often resorted to vigilante tactics such as lynchings in his pursuit of cattle rustlers and the like. On several occasions Larn and Selman were suspected of themselves participating in illegal activities. He resigned from office in March 1877 and, along with Selman, apparently worked as a deputy inspector of cattle hides and animals in Shackelford County while putting together an outlaw band of some sixteen men. In 1878 Larn was arrested by his successor, Sheriff William

Cruger, and held in an Albany, Texas, jail. The following night vigilantes executed him in his cell after they were unable to remove his shackles to transport him to the nearest tree for hanging.

SOURCES: Leon Metz, *John Selman: Texas Gunfighter*, 1966; Dan L. Thrapp, ed., *EFB*, Vol. 2, 1988.

LARSEN, HENRY ASBJORN. (1899–1964) Born in Fredrikstad, Norway, following a short career in the Norwegian navy and merchant marine, Larsen immigrated to Canada in his twenties. In 1928 he joined the Royal Canadian Mounted Police (RCMP)* as commander of a police vessel. Putting his maritime training to use, he eventually patrolled more than three million square miles (comprising the largest police beat in the world), from the Yukon to Northern Quebec. He was eventually promoted to superintendent and in 1942 he became the first person to circumnavigate the North American continent.

SOURCE: Charles Phillips and Alan Axelrod, *CCC*, 1996.

LARSON, JOHN A. (1892–1965) Larson collaborated with Berkeley, California Police Department* Chief August Vollmer* at the University of California and invented the first lie detector* in 1921. In 1932 he cowrote, with his protégé Leonarde Keeler* and George Harry, the classic text *Lying and Its Detection*. Although Larson invented the polygraph and went on to a stellar career as a prominent psychiatrist, Keeler is generally credited with perfecting the device.

SOURCE: Eugene B. Block, *Lie Detectors: Their History and Use*, 1977.

LAURIE, ROCCO. *See* FOSTER, GEORGE AND LAURIE, ROCCO.

LAURIE, SIR PERCY. (1880–1962) The Harrow-educated Laurie joined the Royal Scots Greys in 1902 and distinguished himself in combat during World War I, Following the conflict he joined Scotland Yard* and in 1933 was appointed assistant commissioner of the mounted branch. Laurie came to prominence in policing for his innovative techniques for using horse mounted police* for crowd and riot control. He retired in 1936, served as assistant chief constable (see CONSTABLES) to the British War Department, and then was appointed provost marshal* for the United Kingdom. He was exonerated of charges that he had fraudulently obtained food ration coupons in 1943 but resigned his post anyway.

SOURCE: Charles Phillips and Alan Axelrod, *CCC*, 1996.

LAVIN, PATRICK J. (1843–1923) Born in Ireland, Lavin arrived in Chicago in 1868 and joined the Chicago Police Department (CPD) force in 1875. He was present during the Halsted Street Viaduct Riot in 1877 and then during the 1886 Haymarket Riot.* In 1902 he was promoted to captain, but in 1906 he resigned as inspector of police after being accused of graft in a jewelry theft case. Although he was exonerated, his career remained tainted, and although, reinstated as inspector, he resigned the following day. Sources vary as to his demise, some reporting heart disease and others, suicide.

SOURCES: Raphael W. Marrow and Harriet I. Carter, *In Pursuit of Crime*, 1996; John J. Flinn, *History of the Chicago Police*, 1887; revised, 1973.

LAW ENFORCEMENT ASSISTANCE ADMINISTRATION (LEAA). Among the provisions of the 1968 Omnibus Crime Control and Safe Streets Act was the act that created the law Enforcement Assistance Administration, which is designed to support state and local governments crime control measures. The LEAA was initially guided by a supervisor and two assistants appointed by the president with the consent of the Senate. In 1973 a Safe Streets Act amendment transferred authority to one manager.

Beginning with the first appropriation of sixty million dollars in 1968, by the time the program ended in 1982, seven billion dollars had been devoted to criminal justice efforts and police education, in the largest, and probably most criticized, federally funded criminal justice program in American history. Although the program was liquidated in 1982, the existence of the National Institute of Justice, the National Institute of Corrections, the Bureau of Justice Statistics, and the National Institute for Juvenile Justice and Delinquency Prevention, all created by the LEAA, offer ample testimony to the long-range impact of this federal criminal justice program.

SOURCES: Joseph B. Vaughn, "Law Enforcement Assistance Administration," in *Encyclopedia of Police Science*, William G. Bailey, 1995; Twentieth Century Fund, *Law Enforcement: The Federal Role*, 1976.

LEARY, HOWARD R. (1912–1994) Formerly a policeman in Philadelphia, Leary obtained a law degree on his nights off and in 1963 was appointed Philadelphia police commissioner. Three years later he was offered the same post with the more prestigious New York City Police Department (NYPD).* Among his most progressive reforms as police commissioner was the introduction of a 911 police emergency phone number and the NYPD's first computerized dispatch system. Leary worked hard to diversify the racial and ethnic composition of the force, but like most big city police commissioners in the 1960s, he was often overwhelmed by police scandals and social turbulence.

The most controversial episode of his tenure involved the Knapp Commission,* which disclosed a pattern of corruption in the police department. While Leary received some of the blame for the scandals, his 1970 resignation was probably the result of pressures such as low police morale, antiwar and civil rights violence, and poor relations with city hall. Following his retirement he entered business and then taught criminal justice at Trenton State College in New Jersey.

SOURCES: James Lardner, *Crusader*, 1996; Charles Phillips and Alan Axelrod, *CCC*, 1996.

LEASURE, WILLIAM. (b. 1946) Born near Detroit, Michigan, Leasure joined the U.S. Marines in 1966 and served as a military policemen in Vietnam. Following his discharge in 1969 he joined the Los Angeles Police Department (LAPD).* Over the following decade the seemingly mild-mannered Leasure became known as "Mild Bill." What people did not know was that the unassuming traffic cop, who would let motorists off with just a warning, was living a double life as a professional killer, using his badge as a shield for a decade-long spree of adultery, burglary, and murder. Following two 1991 trials he plea-bargained to a sentence of fifteen years to life, which meant he would be up for parole in 2004.

SOURCE: Edward Humes, *Murderer with a Badge*, 1992.

LEATHERHEADS. Prior to wearing official police uniforms* in the 1850s, the early New York City watchmen of the 1820s wore outdated firefighter's leather hats, without the upright front plate. Varnished twice a year, these hats eventually became as hard as iron and the watchmen were given the derogatory sobriquet of leatherhead. These unskilled watchmen often became targets for gangs of street toughs who came upon unsuspecting leatherheads asleep in their watch-boxes and awakened them by jerking the sentry box loose from its mooring with the assistance of a stout rope.

SOURCES: George W. Walling, *Recollections of a New York City Chief of Police*, 1890; Augustine E. Costello, *Our Police Protectors*, 1885; reprint, 1972.

LE COCQ DE OLIVEIRA, MILTON. (1920–1964) Milton Le Cocq de Oliveira was Brazil's preeminent crime investigator in the 1950s. A police legend in his own time, he was the grandson of a Brazilian engineer and an English woman. Le Cocq was often referred to as "the Gringo" for his mixed heritage. After reading a book about the heroic exploits of a famous French police officer, he was inspired, against his parents wishes, to become a detective. At the age of seventeen he joined the Brazilian army and became a military policeman. He soon made the transition to civilian policing, and after coursework in police science, he achieved his childhood goal of becoming a detective.

In the late 1950s the crime problem in Rio de Janiero was skyrocketing out of control. In response, the police department authorized the formation of a special crime-fighting force. Le Cocq and seven colleagues were selected to make up the nucleus of a motorized squad in the special unit. Le Cocq came to prominence when he able to solve cases that nobody else could. In his capacity as detective Le Cocq eschewed police uniforms* and wore a beret. A master of disguise, he looked more like the prey than the pursuer. His most famous case was his killing of Buck Jones, a sadistic killer and rapist. Le Cocq was an intrepid investigator, sometimes spending six months hunting down his quarry.

Considered a Renaissance man, Le Cocq mastered many of the building trades and was reportedly a faithful husband and a teetotaler. However, on August 24, 1964, his luck ran out when he was murdered by a small-time thug. His death inspired the creation of the Scuderie Detective Le Cocq (Detective Le Cocq Emblem). His assailant was killed three months later, suffering over one hundred gunshot wounds. Le Cocq's death is credited with inspiring the creation of Brazil's notorious "Death Squads," motorized police squads that take the law into their own hands and even execute criminals. These Death Squads are particularly active in Rio de Janiero and are responsible for hundreds of killings. It is doubtful Le Cocq would have approved.

SOURCE: Bruce Henderson and Sam Summerlin, *The Super Sleuths*, 1976.

LEDBETTER, JAMES F. (1852–1937) Born in Madison, Arkansas, Ledbetter began his law enforcement career as a deputy sheriff (see SHERIFF) in Johnson County, Arkansas, beginning in 1894. After ten years he moved to Indian Territory, where he worked for an express company and then was appointed deputy U.S. marshal (see U.S. MARSHALS SERVICE) under Morton Rutherford. From 1908 to 1910 he served as Muskogee's police chief, and he would call the town home for the remainder of his life. "Bud" Ledbetter is credited with singlehandedly capturing several members of the Al Jennings gang.

SOURCES: Glenn Shirley, *West of Hell's Fringe*, 1978; Dan L. Thrapp, ed., *EFB*, Vol. 2, 1988.

LEES, ISAIAH WRIGLEY. (1830–1902) Born in Lancaster, England, Lees worked as a mechanical engineer and metalworker in Paterson, New Jersey, prior to trying his hand at mining during the California gold rush in 1849. Disenchanted with the miner's life, he moved to San Francisco, where, in 1852, as an amateur detective, he helped solve a murder that resulted in the first legal execution there under the American government. In October of the following year he joined the San Francisco police department, beginning an almost fifty-year affiliation with the force. Promoted to assistant captain and detective shortly after his initial appointment, he became a proponent of new identification techniques. By 1855 he started a rogue's gallery composed of daguerreotypes paid for out of his own salary, one of the earliest examples in the West. By 1859 his innovations led to his promotion to captain of the San Francisco police force.

Lees was instrumental in solving some of the Bay City's most infamous cases. In 1863 he captured a Confederate vessel attempting to leave the bay to embark on a privateering raid. In 1864 his skills caught the eye of Mark Twain, who heralded his acumen in a local newspaper. During his tenure Lees participated in cases out of his jurisdiction both nationally and internationally. In 1875 he recovered the painting *Elaine*, which had been stolen from a San Francisco art gallery, and in 1895 he succeeded at perhaps his most outlandish murder case when he solved the killing of two girls in a local church, leading to the conviction and execution of Theodore Durrant, despite a paucity of hard evidence. Lees was promoted to San Francisco police chief in 1897 and retired three years later.

SOURCES: William B. Secrest, *Lawmen and Desperadoes*, 1994; Dan L. Thrapp, ed., *EFB*, Vol. 2, 1988.

LEFORS, JOE. (1865–1940) Born in Paris, Texas, Lefors was raised in the Indian Territory and then settled with his family near Mobeetie, Texas. In the late 1870s he trailed cattle to Kansas, worked as a freighter and mail rider, and participated in several Indian skirmishes. Except for a brief interlude ending in 1881, Lefors continued to work as a cowboy between Texas, Kansas, and then Wyoming. Cattle rustling was so endemic in Wyoming that Lefors took a job supplying meat to a Montana Indian reservation just to get away from the rustlers. In 1895 he was hired as a livestock inspector in Montana and Wyoming and began making plans to clear out the rustlers in the Hole-in-the-Wall region. After being thwarted by the rustlers during an 1897 invasion of their hideout, Lefors organized a fifty-four-man force to finish the job. He eventually succeeded in routing the rustlers and rescuing over a thousand head of cattle.

Lefors later was hired as a railroad detective and led a posse after Butch Cassidy and the Sundance Kid following an 1899 train robbery. Although the pair escaped through no fault of his own, his thousand-mile pursuit added to the making of his legend as one of the most relentless manhunters in Western history.

Beginning in 1898 LeFors was appointed deputy U.S. marshal (see U.S. MARSHALS SERVICE) out of Cheyenne. He is probably best remembered for tracking down Thomas "Tom" Horn* and conning him into confessing to the killing of a young boy, a confession that led Horn to the gallows. In 1908 LeFors resigned as deputy marshal and left law enforcement.

SOURCE: Joe LeFors, *Wyoming Peace Officer*, 1953.

LEGUAY, JEAN. (1910–1989) Following the fall of France in 1940, Leguay was appointed deputy police chief for the Nazi-aligned Vichy regime. He initially escaped punishment for his collaborationist behavior and was allowed to continue his career in the French civil service after the 1944 liberation of France. However, thirty-five years later his wartime past came back to haunt him when he was arrested and charged with deporting thirteen thousand French Jews to the Nazi death camps in 1942. Adhering to the typical refrain, that he was just following orders, he was released pending a new trial. Seven years later, in 1986, he was once again prosecuted for a different case involving the deportation of French Jews. The prosecutor had a formidable case that concluded that Leguay had actually instigated the deportation. He evaded trial when he died of liver cancer in 1989.

SOURCE: Charles Phillips and Alan Axelrod, *CCC*, 1996.

LENOIR, JEAN CHARLES. (1732–1807) Born in Paris, Lenoir served as lieutenant-general of police* of Paris from August 1774 to May 1775 and from June 1776 to August 1785. His first term was interrupted by bread riots, which led to his dismissal after he refused to use military troops to curtail the civil disorder. Restored to office, he dedicated his tenure to improving street lighting and cleaning and promoting hygiene in taverns and dairies. His contributions to municipal living conditions included making first-aid equipment available in every commissioner's office, establishing schools for the indigent poor, and inaugurating a bakery school. In addition, he improved sanitation and protected the city's water supply by moving the Innocents Cemetery from its original location within the city boundaries. Lenoir is also credited with establishing the country's system of state pawn shops, considered a precursor to today's Credit Municipal, which provided low-interest loans to citizens. Lenoir was succeeded in office by Louis Thiroux de Crosne.*

SOURCES: Alan Williams, *The Police of Paris*, 1979; Philip John Stead, *The Police of France*, 1983.

LEOPARDS, THE. During the 1970s, Haiti ruler "Baby Doc" Duvalier was pressured to diminish the visibility of the Tonton Macoutes,* which he conveniently transferred to the countryside. To fill the void in the urban environs, the less secretive Leopards force was formed. Highly organized and well disciplined (unlike their predecessors, the Macoutes), the Leopards wore blue uniforms and were thoroughly military but had less autonomy.

SOURCE: Thomas Plate and Andrea Darvi, *Secret Police*, 1981.

LEPINE, LOUIS. Except for a respite between 1897 and 1899, Lepine served as prefect of the Paris Police for almost twenty years. The diminutive Lepine was initially referred to as "the Prefect of the Streets," but he soon won over his constituency by modernizing the force and improving relations between the police and the public. Sartorially resplendent in derby and tailcoat, he became a familiar man about town and the best known prefect of his time. A man of action, he was usually in the thick of operations, whether it be riots, strikes, demonstrations, or bank robberies.

SOURCES: Philip John Stead, *The Police of Paris*, 1957; Philip John Stead, *The Police of France*, 1983.

LEUCI, ROBERT. (b. 1940) Leuci was the hero of Robert Daley's 1978 book *Prince of the City* and the movie of the same name. An eleven-year veteran on the force and a detective and team leader on the New York City Police department (NYPD)* Special Investigating Unit of the narcotics division, in the early 1970s he was enlisted by federal prosecutors to work undercover to root out corruption on the police force. Of the four police officers enlisted (which included William Phillips,* Edward Droge, and Alfonso Janotta), he was the only one not compelled to do so for being caught breaking the law. Leuci's participation in the investigation ended in June 1972 after the *New York Times* revealed his activities. Forced to break the police code of secrecy ("the blue wall of silence"), he helped put together cases against lawyers, bail bondsmen, mob figures, and his own partners. Following the trial he was offered a new name and relocation but chose to remain on the force.

SOURCES: Robert Daley, *Prince of the City*, 1978; Whitman Knapp, chairman, *Knapp Commission Report on Police Corruption*, 1972.

LEXOW, CLARENCE. (1852–1910) Educated in Europe and Columbia Law School, the worldly Lexow, whose name became synonymous with police reform, practiced law before winning a New York State Senate seat in 1893. He came to prominence during his investigation of the New York City Police Department (NYPD)* at the behest of Reverend Charles H. Parkhurst.* Although he is chiefly remembered for his chairmanship of the Lexow Committee, most people considered him a pragmatist who was most interested in furthering his own career. The ensuing commission discovered a menu of bribes for rising through the ranks of New York's Finest* (for example, $300 just to be appointed to the force) and an established system for shaking down illegitimate businesses. Although numerous officers were ultimately dismissed and the Tammany machine was replaced by reform-minded politicians, there were no enduring achievements, and just four years later Tammany was back in the hands of the bosses and the police department had reverted back to a corrupt sink of iniquity.

SOURCES: Thomas A. Reppetto, *The Blue Parade*, 1978; James F. Richardson, *The New York Police: Colonial Times to 1901*, 1970.

LEXOW COMMITTEE. *See* LEXOW, CLARENCE.

LIE DETECTOR. The lie detector, better known as the polygraph, came into existence as the cardio-pneumo-psychogram in 1921 following the publication of William Marston's article advancing his notion that lies affected blood pressure. Shortly afterward, Berkeley California, Police Department* chief August Vollmer* ordered the construction of a machine replete with the familiar blood pressure armband. Vollmer insisted on being the first guinea pig and was impressed at how readily the machine detected his lies during a mock interrogation. The lie detector was given added credibility when it was used to break the high-profile San Francisco murder of Father Patrick Heslin by William Hightower in August 1921.

Over the following decade it became obvious to interviewers that suspects typically had a limited reservoir of adrenalin that, once expended, caused them to fall into an exhausted state allowing for placid-body responses. In response, the three-minute interview was introduced. By the 1950s the polygraph was considered successful 95 percent of the time. An expensive device that is used to clear the innocent as well as to indict the guilty, each lie detector machine costs more than ten thousand dollars. Its findings are inadmissible in a court of law unless both sides agree.

SOURCE: Eugene B. Block, *Lie Detectors: Their History and Use*, 1977.

LIEUTENANT-GENERAL OF POLICE. In 1666 Louis XIV created the police position of lieutenant-general of police for Paris. Originally called the lieutenant of police, the title was changed to lieutenant-general of police in 1674. The fourteen men who held this position between 1666 and 1789 were responsible for a variety of administrative and judicial tasks, including controlling prices, weights, and measures; inspecting markets; apprehending criminals; and the surveillance of suspected traitors. Often tyrannical in nature, the lieutenants-general exercised control over all offenders, both criminal and political. After the French Revolution this position was abolished and Napoleon appointed a minister of police who was more focused on gathering information and state security.

SOURCES: Alan Williams, *The Police of Paris, 1718–1789*, 1979; Philip John Stead, *The Police of Paris*, 1957.

LIGHTHORSE. This term was assigned to mounted Indian police* forces in the Indian Territory. Each of the Five Civilized Tribes referred to this police force in their tribal law books. Lighthorsemen were authorized to not only enforce court decisions but also to use their own discretion in upholding the law. The most noted lighthorse units included the Cherokee Lighthorse,* Choctaw Lighthorse,* Creek Lighthorse,* and Seminole Lighthorse.*

SOURCE: Art Burton, *Black, Red, and Deadly*, 1991.

LINGLE, ALFRED "JAKE." (1892–1930) Lingle worked as a police reporter for the *Chicago Tribune* in the Capone era. He reportedly had ties with both the Capone and Bugs Moran factions while remaining particularly close to police commissioner William P. Russell. On more than one occasion Lingle was referred to as "Chicago's unofficial chief of police" because of his close association with Russell.

On June 9, 1930, Lingle was murdered and elevated to martyr status. Newspapers offered substantial rewards and the police launched an intensive investigation. When investigators found that on a sixty-five-dollar weekly salary, he owned homes in Chicago and Indiana, employed a chauffeur, and kept a room in a luxurious hotel, his status as a hero was tarnished. Soon authorities found that Lingle was leading a double life as a fixer and shakedown artist who had double-crossed Capone and was behind on bribes to various political leaders. A young gangster named Leo V. Brothers was arrested for the crime. On being convicted and sentenced to fourteen years, he replied, "I can do that standing on my head." He was paroled eight years later.

SOURCE: Raphael W. Marrow and Harriet I. Carter, *In Pursuit of Crime*, 1996.

LOCKSTEP SURVEILLANCE. This law enforcement technique is more a harassment technique than anything else. The overt and persistent shadowing of crime figures was most notably used during the round-the-clock surveillance of mobster Sam Giancana by the Federal Bureau of Investigation (FBI)* in 1963. However, in this case Giancana had the last laugh when he challenged this technique in court and won.

SOURCE: Carl Sifakis, *The Mafia Encyclopedia*, 1999.

LONDON METROPOLITAN POLICE. The London Metropolitan Police force was established following Parliament's passage of the Metropolitan Police Act of 1829.* After seven years of opposition from the public and Parliament, British Home Secretary Sir Robert Peel* established a centralized London police force in response to the social upheavals that accompanied industrialization and rising crime. A preventive, rather than reactive, force, it replaced the age-old night watch* with professional, paid, full-time officers. The London "bobbies" patrolled regular beats, wore uniforms, and were paramilitary in structure and discipline. Under the direction of commissioners Colonel Sir Charles Rowan* and Sir Richard Mayne,* the force was able to overcome the trepidation of the public about a strong police force by improving community relations and reinforcing its image as a civilian police force.

SOURCES: Wilbur R. Miller, *Cops and Bobbies*, 1977; Philip John Stead, *The Police of Britain*, 1985.

LONERGAN, THOMAS E. (b. 1844) Born in Lockport, Illinois, and educated at Notre Dame, he fought for the Union in the Civil War. Lonergan worked a short stint for the postal service before joining Pinkerton's National Detective Agency* in Chicago. By 1866 he had won the favor of George Henry Bangs and assisted the superintendent in organizing Pinkerton branches in Philadelphia and New York. He resigned in 1867 and went on to a multifaceted career as editor of the *New York Era* and as a professor of military strategy at a New York college. He continued to work in the newspaper field until accepting a position in the U.S. Secret Service* under H. C. Whitley.

SOURCES: George P. Burnham, *Memories of the United States Secret Service*, 1872; Frank Morn. *"The Eye That Never Sleeps,"* 1982.

LOS ANGELES POLICE DEPARTMENT (LAPD). One of the most storied and controversial police agencies in American history, the LAPD can trace its beginnings to 1850 when Los Angeles was first incorporated as a city. That same year saw the election of the first city marshal and sheriff.* By 1853 the crime problem was out of control, and in June a police force of one hundred volunteers was authorized by the city council. The first police officers wore white ribbon badges bearing the title, "City Police—Authorized by the Council of Los Angeles," in both English and Spanish. This early law enforcement group became known as the Los Angeles Rangers and worked side-by-side with the sheriff and marshal.

In 1855 the Los Angeles Guards was formed to help with local law enforcement duties, and although they are credited as the first uniformed officers in the city, they soon degenerated into little more than a fraternal organization. Fourteen years later the first paid police force was organized and William C. Warren was appointed city marshal. In 1870 the first Board of Police Commissioners was appointed, under a city ordinance, and police enforcement of various ordinances filled the city coffers.

The late 1870s saw the appointment of Jacob F. Gerkins as the city's first police chief as policemen donned regulation police uniforms* consisting of felt hat, a hip-length blue serge coat, and an eight-pointed silver star, which each patrolman was required to purchase at six dollars apiece. Each star was inscribed "Los Angeles Police." By the 1880s, traffic enforcement and the telephone had become part of police work. The most prominent police chiefs of the late nineteenth century included John M. Glass* (1889–1900), who introduced the Bertillon system,* police matrons,* patrol wagons, and substations to the LAPD.

At the turn of the century, the population of Los Angeles stood at 102,000, with only sixty-nine police officers manning the "thin blue line." As the new century dawned, Los Angeles struggled with growing pains and political factionalism. The mayor preferred to appoint police chiefs from outside the department in order to implement his agenda without interference from the rank and file. Between 1900 and 1923, sixteen different police chiefs were hired, resulting in instability and with little impact on the growing crime problem. In 1900, police officers were referred to as patrolmen and were identified by their helmets and silver star badges. By 1903, the force still numbered less than eighty men.

The early 1900s saw the introduction of a Gamewell Police Signal System* and the adoption of a bicycle "Flying Squad" and the first patrol cars. In 1911 a fingerprinting* system was inaugurated to supplement the Bertillon records. The police department could then boast a contingent of 520 members, but the mayor still controlled the position of chief of police. Without civil service protection, inexperienced, nonprofessional police chiefs became the bane of the department's existence. The years 1918 to 1919 saw the highest mortality of police officers in the department's history, with seventeen killed in the line of duty, representing 2 percent of the force.

During the Prohibition era of the 1920s and 1930s, corruption reached into the highest levels of the department, and despite attempts by Chief August Vollmer* (1923–1924) to reform the force, Depression- and Prohibition-related corruption pervaded city politics unabated. Vollmer, however, was credited with reorganizing the department, which included over sixteen hundred police officers and civilian personnel. He implemented drastic changes that led to more efficient administration and scientific investigation, and raised personnel qualifications. One of his foremost innovations was his creation of the "Crime Crusher" division, composed of three hundred mobile officers used to control residential crime and respond to the growing organized crime syndicates.

When Vollmer left after just one year, he had reorganized the LAPD into eleven divisions, each uniting related functions under a single head. These divisions included the uniformed division, property division, detective division, construction and maintenance, jail division, crime prevention division, traffic division, transportation division, record division, vice division, and the Crime Crushers.

Although the 1930s saw the introduction of police radios, improved communications, a border patrol, and a new police academy, the tumultuous years following Vollmer's stint as police chief continued to be characterized by political patronage and corruption. In one of the more unsavory episodes of this period, an ex-LAPD cop named Harry Raymond had been selected to investigate corruption in the mayor's office. While conducting his investigation, he discovered that the Police Intelligence Squad was inextricably linked to corruption in the mayor's office. Subsequently, Raymond barely survived a bombing attempt. While starting his car one day, it exploded, riddling him with shrapnel. Soon after, a captain from Intelligence, who had reputed ties to the underworld, was sent to prison for attempted murder. After a trial revealed corruption in high places, Los Angeles Mayor Frank Shaw became the first mayor in America to ever be recalled. Several months later, police chief James Edgar Davis* resigned.

In 1939, many corrupt high-ranking officers were purged from the ranks, inaugurating an era of reform and professionalism. Police Chief William Henry Parker* (1950–1966) was recognized as a leading exponent of professionalism and made history in 1950 when he appointed the first female African-American sergeant. During the 1960s he began to integrate the department as well with black officers, who formerly were restricted to patrolling only black neighborhoods. Among the more sensational episodes to occur during the Parker era were the incident described in *The Onion Field* (1963), the Bloody Christmas* (1953) scandal, and the 1965 Watts riots.

The 1960s was a turbulent decade for the force, and with the sudden death of Chief Parker in 1966, an era had passed. The late 1960s and the 1970s bore the imprint of the flamboyant Chief Edward M. Davis* (1969–1978), whose tenure saw shootouts with the Black Panthers, the Alphabet Bomber case, riots on Venice Beach, the fiery confrontation with the Symbionese Liberation Army, and the expansion of the Criminal Conspiracy Section, which had been created following the 1968 assassination of Bobby Kennedy in Los Angeles.

When Daryl F. Gates* became the department's forty-ninth chief in 1978, it inaugurated the most controversial era in the history of the LAPD. The media frenzy surrounding the beating of Rodney King* in 1991 and the Los Angeles Riots led to Gates's retirement in 1992. Gates is remembered for his advocacy of the Special Weapons and Tactics Team (SWAT).* Criticism for not responding to the riots in a timely fashion and for the steady decline in public satisfaction contributed to a siege mentality among LAPD officers. Gates was succeeded by Philadelphia Police Commissioner William L. "Willie" Williams.*

SOURCES: Arthur W. Sjoquist (historical text by), *Los Angeles Police Department Commemorative Book, 1869–1984*, 1984; Joe Domanick, *To Protect and Serve*, 1994.

LOVE, EULIA MAE. (1940–1979) The killing of Eulia Mae Love by Los Angeles Police Department (LAPD)* officers on January 3, 1979, was one the most controversial police brutality cases in the history of the department. Love was an impoverished, hard-working mother with three daughters. On the morning of January 3, a meter man from the gas company came to collect payment or shut off the gas, which Love used for cooking meals. In despair Love hit the meter man with a shovel and then went to a market to get the minimum payment for the gas company. Meanwhile, the assault was reported to his supervisor and the LAPD.

Love's children reported that when the gas company vehicles returned, Love had attempted to pay her bill but that company representatives had rolled up their windows, causing her to lose any remaining sense of composure. She went into her house and came back out with a kitchen knife about the same time an LAPD squad car pulled up. In the ensuing confrontation, she cursed at the officers, who were able to knock the knife from her hand. When she reached down to retrieve the knife, she was shot at least six times from only ten feet away. The officers claimed that she was about to throw it. They then handcuffed the dying woman. She was dead less than three minutes after the arrival of the police.

Following the release of the Eulia Love report, the department tightened up its shooting policy. After her killing the *Los Angeles Times* made the transition from police booster to focusing much of its coverage on the day-to-day activities of the LAPD.

SOURCE: Joe Domanick, *To Protect and Serve*, 1994.

LOVE, HARRY. (c. 1810–1868) Born in Vermont, Love was reportedly a descendant of Ethan Allen. He went to sea as a boy and later fought in the

Seminole and Black Hawk Wars before moving West and taking part in the Texas War for Independence and then the Mexican War. In the early 1850s he was in California when he was appointed deputy sheriff (see SHERIFF) for Santa Barbara and Los Angeles. With the creation of the California State Rangers in 1853, Love was selected as a captain and was ordered to recruit a company of twenty men to suppress the bandit menace in the Mariposa region. He was credited with leading an attack on a bandit encampment several months later that resulted in the killings of Joaquin Murrieta and Three Fingered Jack. Love and his men shared a six-thousand-dollar reward. The rest of his life was rather anticlimactic. After several failed business ventures and problems with alcohol, Love got into a gunfight with another man over the affections of his three-hundred-pound wife. In the confrontation, both men were wounded, but Love would die following the amputation of his arm.

SOURCES: William B. Secrest, "Hell for Leather Rangers," *True West*, March–April 1968; Dan L. Thrapp, ed., *EFB*, Vol. 2, 1988.

LUCY, SIR THOMAS. As a justice of the peace* during the late sixteenth century, Lucy reportedly was responsible for fining a young William Shakespeare for poaching. This incident supposedly inspired Shakespeare's creation of Justice Shallow in *The Merry Wives of Windsor*. Lucy had been knighted in 1565 and was generally regarded as a more than adequate peace officer. A strict Protestant, he frequently targeted Jesuits and Catholic landholders for persecution. He later served as a member of Parliament and as sheriff* of Warwickshire in 1578 and then of Worcestershire in 1584. Lucy's son Thomas followed in his father's footsteps, succeeding him as sheriff of Warwickshire in 1600.

SOURCE: Irene Gladwin, *The Sheriff*, 1984.

LYNCH, CHARLES. (1736–1796) Born into a Quaker family in Virginia, Lynch, whose name has become synonymous with "lynch law," served as justice of the peace* of Bedford County beginning in 1767 and later represented the county in the House of Burgesses. During the American Revolution he served in the militia under General Nathanael Greene.

He is best remembered in law enforcement circles for his participation with other leading citizens in local vigilante activities. Along with other justices of the peace and militia officers, Lynch arrested suspects and, following informal trials, punished, anyone who threatened to upset the traditional social order. In a society often on the edge of anarchy, Loyalists, slaves, Indians, and English officials were all viewed with distrust and at one time or another could be found tied to the whipping post, where "Lynch law" justice was administered. Punishment usually consisted of being tied to an oak tree and receiving thirty-nine lashes. The phrase entered the American and English dictionaries in the 1850s, although it has become identified with extralegal hangings. There is still some debate over the inspiration for the term, with some sources indicating it was derived from the actions of vigilante William L. Lynch.*

SOURCES: Brent Tarter, "Charles Lynch," *ANB*, Vol. 14, 1999; Charles Phillips and Alan Axelrod, *CCC*, 1996.

LYNCH, WILLIAM L. (1924–1820) Born in Pittsylvania County, Virginia, in 1780 Lynch led a vigilante movement to purge the county of lawbreakers. The members of the vigilante committee signed a written charter, but the document did not specifically mention hanging as the punishment (although it was typically the punishment for a capital offense). Like fellow Virginian vigilante Charles Lynch,* William has also been cited as the possible inspiration for the term *lynching*, but the origin of the term is still inconclusive.

SOURCE: Charles Phillips and Alan Axelrod, *CCC*, 1996.

M

McADOO, WILLIAM. (1853–1930) Born in Ireland, McAdoo immigrated to the United States and earned distinction as a lawyer and politician. From 1883 to 1891 he served in the New York House of Representatives and then was appointed secretary of the navy by President Grover Cleveland. He served as New York City Police Department (NYPD)* commissioner from 1904 to 1906 and as chief magistrate from 1910 to 1930. McAdoo was credited with reorganizing and reforming the New York City court system. He published *The Procession to Tyburn: Crime and Punishment in the Eighteenth Century* (1927), a series of sketches based on the three-volume *Criminal Recorder* published in 1804.

SOURCES: Thomas A. Reppetto, *The Blue Parade*, 1978; George E. Rush, *The Dictionary of Criminal Justice*, 1994.

McCARTHY, DENNIS V. N. (b. 1935) Born in Baltimore, Maryland, he attended Lynchburg College and, following graduation in 1962, joined the U.S. Treasury Department.* In 1964 he transferred to the U.S. Secret Service* and served as bodyguard to presidents from Lyndon Johnson to Ronald Reagan. During the Reagan assassination attempt in 1981, McCarthy was credited with wrestling assassin John Hinckley to the ground. In 1981, along with fellow agents Jerry Parr, Ray Shaddick, and Tim McCarthy, he was awarded the Secret Service Medal of Valor, the agency's highest award. In 1984, McCarthy retired from the Secret Service after twenty years of service.

SOURCE: Dennis V. N. McCarthy, with Philip W. Smith, *Protecting the President*, 1985.

McCORD, MYRON. McCord moved to Wisconsin from New York in the 1850s and developed a fifty-year friendship with future president William McKinley after serving with him in Congress. McCord moved to Arizona in 1893, and four years later McKinley appointed him governor of the territory. McCord resigned the next year to serve as colonel of an infantry unit during the Spanish-American War. In 1902, following the assassination of his patron, McKinley, McCord was appointed U.S. Marshal (see U.S. MARSHALS SERVICE) for Arizona by President Theodore Roosevelt.* In 1903 McCord arrested lawman-turned-outlaw Burt Alvord* for federal mail robbery. He recaptured Alvord when he led a mass jailbreak from the Tombstone jail. McCord then accompanied Alvord to the territorial prison. While acting as a U.S. Marshal, he became an outspoken advocate for the short-lived Arizona Rangers.* In 1904 McCord suppressed gun running along the Mexican border, the next year he was succeeded in office by Benjamin F. Daniels.*

SOURCE: Larry D. Ball, *The United States Marshals of New Mexico and Arizona Territories, 1846–1912*, 1978.

McCULLOCH, BENJAMIN. (1811–1862) Born in Rutherford County, Tennessee, McCulloch was reportedly friends with David Crockett and just missed accompanying him to Texas and death at the Alamo. McCulloch reached Texas in time to fight in the battle of San Jacinto in 1836. Following the battle, although he was promoted to first lieutenant, he left the army. He distinguished himself at the battle of Plum Creek in 1840, and over the next several years he participated in several skirmishes with Comanches and worked occasionally as a scout for the Texas Rangers.*

McCulloch won a seat in the Texas State Legislature in 1845 but resigned the following year and recruited a Texas Ranger regiment to fight in the war with Mexico. He saw most of his service with the Texas Rangers during the war. Following the war he moved to California and worked as a sheriff* in Sacramento County. He then returned to Texas in 1853 and wore the badge of a U.S. marshal (see U.S. MARSHALS SERVICE) for six years. During the Civil War he fought for the Confederacy and was killed at the battle of Pea Ridge.

SOURCES: Walter Prescott Webb, *The Texas Rangers*, 1935; Ben Proctor, "Ben McCulloch," in *Rangers of Texas*, ed. Roger N. Conger, et al., 1969.

McCULLOCH, HUGH. (1808–c. 1890) Born to Scottish immigrants in Kennebunkport, Maine, he practiced law in Fort Wayne, Indiana, where he began a lifetime association with the financial business. Starting out as a bank branch manager for the State Bank of Indiana, McCulloch eventually would be entrusted with supervising all twenty-six of the company's banks. Earning a reputation as a financial genius, he came to the attention of Treasury Secretary Salmon P. Chase, who, In 1863, appointed McCulloch comptroller of the country's national currency. After a U.S. Treasury Department* investigation determined that one-third of the nation's currency was counterfeit, McCulloch broached the subject of a federal law enforcement agency devoted to the counterfeiting problem with President Abraham Lincoln. Lincoln approved the creation of what would become the U.S. Secret Service* the same day that he was assassinated. In 1865, the U.S. Secret Service came to fruition under President Andrew Johnson. In its first year under director William P. Wood,* several hundred counterfeiters were apprehended and imprisoned.

SOURCES: Walter S. Bowen and Harry E. Neal, *The United States Secret Service*, 1960; Charles Phillips and Alan Axelrod, *CCC*, 1996.

McDONALD, HUGH CHISHOLM. (b. 1913) Born in Hopkins, Minnesota, and educated in Michigan and California, in 1940 McDonald entered law enforcement as deputy in the Los Angeles County Sheriff's Department. During World War II he was assigned to hunt down black marketeers in Europe. Since most did not have criminal records, McDonald had little to go on for identification. He hit on an idea that revolutionized identification techniques when he invented the Identi-kit system. With the system, a collection of prefabricated facial features, an eyewitness could create a composite suspect.

Following the war McDonald returned to California, and after meeting with criminal justice officials and the Townsend Company, he began to market an improved version of the identification kit to police departments across America. The Identi-kit system was first adopted in Great Britain. In 1960 McDonald was promoted chief of detectives in Los Angeles county. Over the years he consulted part-time for the Central Intelligence Agency (CIA),* and in 1968 he left policing to establish his own security company. In 1973 he inaugurated his career as a novelist with *The Auditorium Affair*, followed by five more novels written in the 1970s.

SOURCE: Charles Phillips and Alan Axelrod, *CCC*, 1996.

McDONALD, WILLIAM "BILL." (1852–1918) Born in Mississippi, McDonald moved to Texas with his family when he was fourteen. In 1891, he began his fifteen-year career with the Texas Rangers* after having worked as a grocer, deputy sheriff, and manhunter. It was rumored that he made life so miserable for cattle rustlers that they vowed to shoot McDonald on sight.

McDonald was the very personification of the Texas Ranger to many Texans, especially when he successfully backed down armed black soldiers at Fort Brown in 1906 and then disdainfully told a vengeful mob that they "looked like fifteen cents in Mexican money" (Paine and McDonald). He played the Ranger role to perfection when he arrived alone to enforce legislation against prize fighting in Dallas. Conditions seemed rife for a riot. When the alarmed mayor asked the lone Ranger where his men were, legend has it that McDonald responded: "Hell! Ain't I enough? There's only one prize fight" (Paine and

McDonald). Apparently the often-repeated retort of "One Riot, One Ranger," came from comments attributed to McDonald in the classic Ranger biography *Captain Bill McDonald: Texas Ranger*, written by Albert Bigelow Paine. After his ranger career, McDonald served as a bodyguard for Woodrow Wilson in 1912, then, until his death in 1918, he served as federal marshal for the northern district of Texas.

SOURCES: Ben Proctor, *Just One Riot*, 1991; Walter Prescott Webb, *The Texas Rangers*, 1935; Albert Bigelow Paine and Captain Bill McDonald, *Texas Ranger: A Story of Frontier Reform*, 1909; reprint, 1986.

McDUFFIE, ARTHUR. (1946–1979) On December 17, 1979, Miami Police reported that Arthur McDuffie had sustained mortal head injuries after crashing his motorcycle while fleeing police. McDuffie died four days later. An investigation into the case determined that McDuffie, an insurance salesman, had been pulled over and beaten severely by police officers. Subsequently, four white Miami police officers were acquitted in the death of this black ex-marine by an all-white jury. Following the decision, the worst American race riot in twelve years erupted, leading to fifteen deaths and $200 million in property damage.

SOURCE: George E. Russ, *The Dictionary of Criminal Justice*, 1994.

McGARIGLE, WILLIAM J. Born in Milwaukee, Wisconsin, McGarigle succeeded Simon O'Donnel as general superintendent of the Chicago Police Department (CPD).* College educated, he worked for the United States Express Company and then for the Chicago, Milwaukee & St. Paul Railroad Company before joining the police force in 1872. He soon became a favorite of Superintendent Elmer Washburn and in 1875 was promoted to chief of detectives. Appointed to superintendent in 1880, he resigned two years later to run unsuccessfully for sheriff.* While in office he was viewed as a tool of vice lord Mike McDonald, a relationship that would lead to McGarigle's arrest for a fraud scheme soon after he left office. One of McGarigle's last acts as police chief was to investigate police departments in Europe in 1882. His subsequent report contrasted his department with those in London, Paris, and Vienna.

McGarigle later served as a warden for a county hospital but soon became entangled in illegal transactions that led him to become a fugitive from the law. When confronted with charges of fraud by a local sheriff, he fled to Canada and did not return to Chicago until 1908. He then confessed to participating in the fraud, and after the case was settled, opened a saloon.

SOURCES: Raphael W. Marrow and Harriet I. Carter, *In Pursuit of Crime*, 1996; John J. Flinn, *History of the Chicago Police*, 1887; revised, 1973.

McNELLY, LEANDER H. (1844–1877) Born in Virginia, McNelly moved to Texas with his family in 1860. The following year he enlisted in the Fifth Regiment, Texas Mounted Volunteers, and participated in several campaigns in the Southwest. He was wounded in 1864, and after recuperation was appointed to hunt down deserters. After the war he farmed in Brenham before joining the Reconstruction-era State Police from 1870 to 1873.

When the Texas Rangers* were reorganized in 1874, McNelly was directed to lead a special battalion to put an end to the Sutton-Taylor feud in DeWitt County and suppress outlawry on the Nueces Strip. In 1875 he was assigned to patrol the Mexican border, where he came into conflict with Mexican bandit Juan Cortina. Cortina had been a thorn in the side of border ranchers for fifteen years, and McNelly is credited with ending the menace. Forced to retire because of ill health, he died in 1877 from tuberculosis.

SOURCES: Walter Prescott Webb, *The Texas Rangers*, 1935; Joe B. Frantz, "Leander H. McNelly," in *Rangers of Texas*, ed. Roger N. Conger, et al., 1969.

McPARLAND, JAMES. (1844–1919) McParland immigrated to the United States when he was nineteen. He worked as a wagon driver for a coal company before joining Pinkerton's National Detective Agency* in the 1870s. He rose to prominence and became the enemy of the radical union movement when he was assigned to infiltrate the Molly Maguires, a secret labor society dedicated to terrorizing the coalfields owned by the Reading Railroad.

Posing as James McKenna, an Irish vagrant, McParland gained the confidence of the inside circle of the Mollies in 1873 and made daily reports on their activities, which included murders and sabotage. His testimony would lead to the conviction of more than sixty men and the hanging of eleven. McParland was demonized by the radicals and heralded by the antilabor movement. Arthur Conan Doyle* reportedly based *The Valley of Fear* on McParland's exploits after meeting William Allan Pinkerton* on a transatlantic steamer.

Following his success against the Molly Maguires he became the head of Pinkerton's Denver office. In 1905 he was once again prominent during the investigation into the assassination of former Idaho governor Frank Steunenberg. In this instance he was much less successful. When his suspects were brought to court, defense attorney Clarence Darrow made a shambles of the prosecution's case as well as McParland's subterfuge. Despite confessions and statements implicating several labor leaders, only Harry Orchard was sentenced to death (and his sentence was commuted to life). A footnote to the Molly Maguire case is that in 1979, Molly Maguire chief John "Black Jack" Kehoe was given a full state pardon a century after his execution when it was determined he was probably framed by the detectives.

SOURCES: J. Anthony Lukas, *Big Trouble*, 1997; James D. Horan, *The Pinkertons*, 1968; James Mackay, *Allan Pinkerton: The First Private Eye*, 1996.

McPHAUL, HENRY H. (b. 1867) Born in Waco, Texas, McPhaul joined the Arizona Rangers* in 1905 after a law enforcement career that had already included stints as deputy sheriff of Maricopa and prison guard at the Yuma Territorial Prison. Initially assigned to the Yuma area, he rapidly developed a reputation for his brutal treatment of the local Mexican population, sometimes even resorting to buffaloing* suspects with the barrel of his handgun. After one incident he was brought up on charges of assault. He was exonerated and then transferred to Pima County, Arizona, where he intended to stay following his retirement in 1906.

SOURCE: Bill O'Neal, *The Arizona Rangers*, 1987.

McWEENY, JOHN. (b. 1857–) Born in Manistee, Michigan, McWeeny came to Chicago in 1881 and joined the Chicago Police Department (CPD)* four years later. McWeeny had spent twenty-six years in the CPD before being elevated to chief of police in 1911. He was wounded by the bomb explosion at the Haymarket Riot* and was credited with rescuing another officer despite his own severe wounds. During his tenure as chief, McWeeny contended with industrial disturbances and labor disputes. He almost immediately had an impact on the department by abolishing the old military-style police uniforms* from the Leroy Steward era and returning to more traditional uniforms. McWeeny was credited with establishing a vagrancy bureau to control the transient problem by keeping records of vagrants. However, from the start his tenure was plagued by problems, including the United Police, an organization within the police department modeled that was on New York City's Policeman's Union. McWeeny led a campaign that ultimately saw the organization disbanded. Compounding police problems was an antiquated police telephone system that complicated, if not prevented, police officers from receiving or sending calls. Following a report by the Chicago Vice Commission, McWeeny was forced to resign from the force in 1913.

SOURCES: Raphael W. Marrow and Harriet I. Carter, *In Pursuit of Crime*, 1996; John J. Flinn, *History of the Chicago Police*, 1887; revised, 1973.

MADSEN, CHRIS. (1851–1944) Born in Schleswig, Denmark, Madsen fought in the Danish-Prussian War and then the Franco-Prussian War, where he was wounded at the battle of Sedan. He immigrated to New York City in 1875 and then enlisted in the U.S. Seventh Cavalry. Madsen saw action in several Indian campaigns and reportedly helped bury some of General George Armstrong Custer's men following the Battle of the Little Big Horn. He left the military for law enforcement in 1891, serving as deputy U.S. marshal (see U.S. MARSHALS SERVICE) in El Reno, Oklahoma. He entered Western lore as a member of the "Three Guardsmen" along with Oklahoma lawmen Henry Andrew "Heck" Thomas* and William Matthew "Bill" Tilghman, Jr.*

Madsen was involved in numerous pursuits, but he was notably eager to avoid to gunplay if possible. However, he was deadly when the need arose. In 1895 he led the posse that gunned down Doolin associates Tulsa Jack Blake and Red Buck Waightman, and the following year he killed bank robber Oliver Yountis near Orlando, Oklahoma. Madsen served with the Rough Riders of Theodore Roosevelt* (probably as quartermaster) during the Spanish-American War but was rejected when he tried to enlist during World War I. Madsen formed the Eagle Film Company with fellow lawmen Evett Dumas and Tilghman and began plans to make a film called *The Passing of the Oklahoma Outlaws*, which was released in 1915. His other jobs in law enforcement included chief of police of Oklahoma City and U.S. marshal (see U.S. MARSHALS SERVICE) of Guthrie, Oklahoma.

SOURCES: Glenn Shirley, *West of Hell's Fringe: Crime, Criminals, and the Federal Peace Officer in Oklahoma Territory, 1889–1907*, 1978; Paul I. Wellman, *A Dynasty of Western Outlaws*, 1961.

MAGHOTLA. In the 1940s, South Africa tribal vigilante groups called *maghotla* were established to assist in the policing of black townships. They are considered the precursor to the African township police. Like most vigilante groups, the *maghotla* were criticized for their brutal methods and kangaroo courts. Although not initially sanctioned by the state apparatus, they were given free rein to enforce law and order. However, by the 1980s officials began to back away from the *maghotla* and police barred them from patrolling the streets of Soweto. To fill their place, the community councils were given the power to establish their own police forces.

SOURCE: John D. Brewer, *Black and Blue*, 1994.

MAIGRET, JULES. The fictional creation of Georges Simenon (b. 1903), Inspector Maigret is considered the French equivalent of Sherlock Holmes.* Simenon's creation was reportedly inspired by the French detective Marcel Guillaume, who died in 1963 at the age of ninety-one.

Maigret initially entered police work after an unsuccessful stab at medicine. Working out of the quai des Orfevres,* Maigret patrolled railway stations and worked vice before his elevation to detective work in department stores. He would rise through the ranks to commissioner (*commissaire*), although there is confusion among Simenon's translators as to whether his actual rank is inspector, detective, or detective sergeant.

Maigret is considered unique in the annals of fictional detective for eschewing traditional methods of ratiocination in favor of intuition. His normal modus operandi is to go to the crime scene and establish a daily routine in the vicinity while his subordinates conduct a background investigation. The first Maigret novel was *The Death of Monsieur Gallet* (1931). Because of poor health, Simenon stopped writing in the early 1970s, having written over two hundred books, including almost eighty Maigret novels. This series has also inspired numerous big-screen and television adaptations.

SOURCES: William Amos, *The Originals*, 1985; Chris Steinbrunner and Otto Penzler, *EMD*, 1976.

MALET, WILLIAM. Malet was one of William the Conqueror's best-known sheriffs. Appointed to the position of sheriff* under Edward the Confessor, Malet served the victor of the Battle of Hastings (1066) as well. William entrusted Malet to find the body of the defeated Anglo-Saxon leader, King Harold, and have it buried in an unmarked grave in order to guard against it becoming a rallying point for patriotic Anglo-Saxons against the Norman conquerors. In 1068 King William appointed Malet sheriff of Yorkshire and sent him north to pursue insurrectionists. The following year he was taken captive in York by rebel forces and was not rescued until months later. He returned south from Scotland but was killed not long after while attempting to suppress another rebellion.

SOURCE: Irene Gladwin, *The Sheriff*, 1984.

MANGANO, ANGELO. (b. 1920) Born in the Sicilian village of San Giovanni de Giarre, Mangano knew he wanted to be a policeman from his youth. During World War II he served in the Italian Army on the African front, but he deserted to return home and fight with the Italian underground against the German allies of Italy. Following the war he joined the Italian National Police and soon was waging a one-man war against the Mafia in southern Italy.

Originally known as "Little Mangano," an ironic play on words for such a large man, he soon won enough respect to be considered a "Super Policeman" by his underworld adversaries. In one incident he narrowly escaped death after surviving three shotgun blasts. His greatest achievement was the arrest and subsequent conviction of Mafia leader Luciano Liggio, known as "The Godfather of Corleone."

SOURCE: Bruce Henderson and Sam Summerlin, *The Super Sleuths* 1976.

MAPLE, JACK. (b. 1952) Raised in the Richmond Hills section of Queens, New York City, Maple attended college briefly before earning a reputation as an eccentric police officer while working as a "cave cop," or "mole," for the New York City Transit Police beginning in 1970. A detective by the age of twenty-seven, he was reportedly the youngest detective on the force. Known for his trademark sartorial elegance and the omnipresent carnation in his lapel, he came to prominence after he was profiled in *New York* magazine by Michael Daly. Maple was the transit police lieutenant in charge of the Central Robbery Squad when William J. Bratton* took over as chief of the unit in 1990. Maple had already established his reputation for bravado as a member of decoy squads. After Bratton gave Maple a forum to discuss his ideas for improving the transit police, Bratton charged Maple with leading the transformation of the unit by changing the way in which it pursued criminals. Bratton and Maple's collaboration between 1990 and 1992 resulted in subway felonies dropping by 27 percent and robberies by one-third. In 1994 Bratton was appointed police commissioner for all of New York City, and he brought along Maple as his strategist and as deputy commissioner for crime control strategies and, later, deputy commissioner for operations. Due to Maple's almost photographic memory for crime statistics, some of his colleagues began referring to him as "Rain Man." Maple demanded that every precinct map out shootings, gun arrests, and narcotics violations in order to more accurately deploy police officers.

As chief strategist, Maple introduced a groundbreaking computerized map system that was given the moniker Comstat, short for "computer statistics." Comstat began a revolution in policing, and during twice-weekly meetings at One Police Plaza,* Maple demonstrated crime-fighting strategies to the police brass using the latest technology. Between 1993 and 1995, New York City homicides and robberies saw their most significant drop in decades. As crime continued to plunge, Maple's strategies were adopted by cities across the United States. In 1996 Mayor Rudolph Giuliani used the drop in crime as his platform for reelection and almost immediately replaced Bratton with the then-current fire commissioner, Howard Safir, a far less colorful personality. Out of respect to his patron, Matron resigned soon after.

Before the year was out, Maple was contacted by management consultant John Linder and queried about moving to New Orleans, Louisiana, to help clean up one of the most corrupt and dysfunctional police departments in the country. With the support of the New Orleans Police Foundation, Maple and Linder were offered a half-million dollars to try to duplicate the New York City miracle, a herculean undertaking that has not yet come to fruition.

Maple's strengths lay in ideas and concepts. While he could orally articulate them, they often seemed weak on paper. Bratton credited Maple with devising the crime control strategy that turned around crime in New York City. His strategy hinged on accurate and timely intelligence, rapid deployment, effective tactics, and relentless follow-up and assessment. Maple described his transition from transit lieutenant to the man in charge of NYPD crime strategies as "the biggest leap in the history of law enforcement" (Remnick).

SOURCES: William Bratton with Peter Knobler, *Turnaround*, 1998; David Remnick, "The Crime Buster," *New Yorker*, February 24, 1997; March 3, 1997; Jack Maple with Chris Mitchell, *The Crime Fighter: Putting the Bad Guys out of Business*, 1999.

MAPP V. OHIO. In this landmark 1961 Supreme Court Decision, the exclusionary rule was extended to the states. The decision overturned Dollree Mapp's conviction for illegal possession of obscene materials on the grounds of illegal search and seizure, since police claimed to be searching for a fugitive and illegal gambling activities.

In 1970 Dollree Mapp was arrested by the New York Police Department for suspicion of receiving stolen property. New York police detectives searched her home without a search warrant and found stolen property and heroin worth more than one hundred thousand dollars. The following year, Mapp was convicted of the felonious possession of drugs even though the search was for stolen property.

She was subsequently sentenced to from twenty years to life in prison. In 1980 the New York governor commuted her sentence, and she was paroled the following day.

SOURCE: William G. Bailey, ed., *The Encyclopedia of Police Science*, 1995.

MARÉCHAUSÉE. The precursor to the Gendarmerie Nationale,* the *maréchausée* was a military police force who could trace their origins to the era of the Crusades, when they acted as the king's bodyguard during battles. Members of the Gendarmerie Nationale's Republican Guard still stand guard outside the front door of the president of France. The *maréchausée* is also required to police the royal armies. The very name is derived from *maréchaux*, or *marshals*, referring to commanders of the royal armies and the medieval military police. After a brief respite during the French Revolution, the force was reorganized; it was renamed the Gendarmerie Nationale in 1791.

SOURCE: Philip John Stead, *The Police of France*, 1983.

MASTERSON, EDWARD J. (1852–1878) Born in Henryville, Quebec, Canada, Edward left home with his younger brother (and future lawman and sportswriter), William Bartholomew "Bat" Masterson,* to hunt buffalo in 1872. He began his law enforcement career in 1877 when he was appointed assistant marshal of Dodge City, Kansas, under Wyatt Berry Stapp Earp.* Later that year he replaced Earp as the cowtown's marshal after he was wounded in the chest during a gunfight. After a quick recuperation, Masterson returned to duty, only to be killed while attempting to disarm a drunken cowboy the following year. A model of restraint when compared to most of his counterparts, Masterson is credited with introducing progressive reforms such as replacing jail time with community service.

SOURCES: Fred Huston, "Ed Masterson—He Was More Than Just Bat's Brother!" *Golden West*, January 1974; Nyle H. Miller and Joseph W. Snell, *Great Gunfighters of the Kansas Cowtowns, 1867–1886*, 1967.

MASTERSON, JAMES P. "JIM." (1855–1895) Born in Henryville, Quebec, Canada, James moved to Wichita, Kansas, with his family in 1871. The youngest brother of William Bartholomew "Bat" Masterson,* he hunted buffalo before entering law enforcement as a Dodge City policeman in 1878. He served as deputy sheriff (see SHERIFF) under Bat from 1878 to 1880 in Ford County before moving up to city marshal of Dodge City in 1879. Two years later he was forced to resign with the election of new municipal officials. He left Dodge City following a gunfight with a bartender but returned in 1889. Masterson soon relocated to the Oklahoma Territory and became the first settler of Guthrie and deputy sheriff of Logan County, Oklahoma. In 1893, U.S. marshal Evett Dumas Nix* appointed James as his deputy. Masterson came to prominence during an

1893 gun battle with the Doolins at Ingalls, Oklahoma. Tuberculosis and alcoholism led to his death two years later; he was still wearing the badge of deputy marshal.

SOURCES: Nyle H. Miller and Joseph W. Snell, *Great Gunfighters of the Kansas Cowtowns, 1867–1886*, 1967; Jay Robert Nash, *EWLO*, 1994.

MASTERSON, WILLIAM BARTHOLOMEW "BAT". (1853–1921) One of seven children, Masterson was born in Henryville, Quebec, Canada. He traded his given name for William Barclay, or the more familiar "Bat," in early adulthood. In 1861 his family emigrated to the United States, making stops in rural New York State, Illinois, and Missouri, before finally settling in Kansas. In 1871 Masterson left home with his brother (and future lawman) Edward J. Masterson,* to hunt buffalo on the West Kansas plains. Over the next six years he worked in railroad construction, hunted buffalo, worked as a scout for General Nelson Miles, and participated in the Battle of Adobe Walls in the Texas panhandle.

Masterson came to prominence as a gunman following a gunfight in which he killed an army corporal in a fight over a woman, who was also shot in the fracas. He first worked as a peace officer in 1876 when he served as a Dodge City policeman. An avid follower of the sporting life, Masterson found time to win election as the Ford County, Kansas, sheriff* in 1877. The following year his brother, Dodge City marshal Edward Masterson, was killed by cowboys on a drinking spree and reportedly died in Bat's arms.

After losing the next election in 1879, Masterson gambled in the Colorado mining camps and then served as a peace officer under Wyatt Earp in Tombstone, Arizona. Over the next two decades he occasionally returned to law enforcement, pursued gambling interests, and got married. Restlessly roaming the West for several years, he finally turned to sportswriting in 1884 and then settled in Denver, Colorado.

In 1902 Masterson moved to New York City and wrote for the *Morning Telegraph*. Three years later he was appointed deputy U.S. marshal (see U.S. MARSHALS SERVICE) of the southern district of New York by President Theodore Roosevelt.* Masterson collaborated with writer Alfred Henry Lewis in a series of six articles that ran in the monthly *Human Life* in 1907 and 1908. He died at his desk of a heart attack while writing his column, "Masterson's Views on Timely Topics," which appeared three times a week in the *Telegraph*.

SOURCES: Robert K. DeArment, *Bat Masterson: The Man and the Legend*, 1979; Richard O'Connor, *Bat Masterson*, 1957.

***MATAI* SYSTEM.** On the island of Samoa, a local form of law enforcement very similar to England's tithing system* is used. The *matai* system relies on the custom of family control to deter potential lawbreakers and is used mostly in the more isolated parts of Western Samoa. Today, most internal disputes outside the capital city of Apia are settled by the *matai*, which continues to enforce rules and provide security within individual villages. Judgments by the *matai* are enforced with fines and occasionally banishment from the village.

SOURCES: James Cramer, *The World's Police*, 1964; U.S. Department of State, Samoa Country Report on Human Rights Practices for 1998, February 26, 1999.

MATHER, DAVE "MYSTERIOUS DAVE." (b. 1845) Born in Connecticut, Mather claimed to be a lineal descendent of clergyman Cotton Mather. By the time he was eighteen, he was rustling cattle in Arkansas. In 1874 he took up buffalo hunting and then relocated to Dodge City, Kansas, where his life was saved in the town's first "major surgery" following a knife fight. Mather was a member of several lynch mobs and participated in a series of gunfights before becoming assistant marshal and then deputy sheriff (see SHERIFF) in Dodge City in 1883. The following year he was succeeded as assistant marshal by Thomas C. Nixon. Mather harbored resentment, which resulted in him killing his replacement in a gunfight several months later. Following his acquittal, Mather killed a man over a gambling argument and left Dodge City for Kansas, where he once again donned a star as marshal of New Kiowa. The rest of his life is shrouded in mystery. Some reports indicate he joined the Royal Canadian Mounted Police (RCMP)* and retired to Canada. To this day, the place and date of his death remain uncertain.

SOURCES: Colin Rickards, *Mysterious Dave Mather*, 1968; Joseph W. Snell, *Gunfighters of the Kansas Cowtowns, 1867–1886*, 1967.

MATRONS. *See* POLICE MATRONS.

MATSELL, GEORGE W. (1811–1877) The son of Irish immigrants, Matsell was born in New York City and worked in his father's bookstore as a young boy. Probably the only bookstore owner to become a police commissioner, Matsell got his start in law enforcement in 1840 when he was appointed a police magistrate. Keenly aware that the night watch* system was outdated, Matsell organized a group of citizens who regularly patrolled the city's more crime-ridden areas. An early proponent of preventive policing, Matsell's reform agenda began to come to fruition when the 1844 New York City Municipal Police Act was passed. Matsell was quickly appointed to lead the improved police force.

During his tenure as chief, Matsell implemented the provisions mandated by the act, such as better patrol methods and stricter discipline. His force faced one of its greatest challenges during the Astor Place Riot* and periodic Election Day rioting. Matsell lobbied for a special river police, but he became a victim of political infighting in 1857 when the Metropolitan Police Act superseded the Municipal Police Act, replacing local control with a police commission, and Matsell was forced to step down. Fourteen years later he was appointed to superintendent of police and then commissioner. In his last years Matsell left policing for his law practice.

SOURCES: James F. Richardson, *The New York Police*, 1970; Charles Phillips and Alan Axelrod, *CCC*, 1996.

MAU MAU INSURGENCY. The force formerly known as the Mombasa Police Force and then the British East Africa Police was, by the 1920s, renamed the Kenya Police. The years 1952 to 1956 were probably the most turbulent ones for the force. During this period the police force, along with British troops, engaged in a bloody conflict with the Mau Mau, a secret society of the Kikuyu tribe. Under the banner of nationalism, the Mau Mau conducted a campaign of murder and terrorism against both the African and the European inhabitants of Kenya. The Kenya Police were charged with rounding up suspected society members who had fled into the almost impenetrable forests. During the insurgency, the Mau Mau were credited with killing close to six hundred security personnel and almost two thousand civilians.

SOURCE: James Cramer, *The World's Police*, 1964.

MAYNE, SIR RICHARD. (1796–1868) Born in Dublin, Ireland, Mayne was educated at Trinity College, Dublin, and then Trinity College, Cambridge, before entering the legal profession in 1822. On September 29, 1829, he, along with Sir Charles Rowan,* was selected as commissioner of the new police force of Sir Robert Peel,* a position that Mayne would hold for almost four decades. The new commissioners instituted a program of preventive policing as they trained and organized the new police force.

When Rowan resigned in 1849, Mayne was appointed chief commissioner. Over the next two decades he had to contend with mounting riots and civil disturbances. During the 1866 Hyde Park labor riots, Mayne was charged with with condoning police brutality, which tarnished the twilight of his career. Mayne was roundly criticized as having grown too old and being out of touch with new social conditions. Despite suggestions by the Disraeli government that he should resign, he stayed on and died in office two years later.

SOURCES: *DNB*, 5, Vol. 13; Wilbur R. Miller, *Cops and Bobbies*, 1973; John Wilkes, *The London Police in the Nineteenth Century*, 1977.

MAYO, KATHERINE. (1867–1940) Mayo traveled around the world with her prospector father under the spell of gold fever. Although wealth was elusive, Mayo developed a compassion for the underprivileged and devoted her early life as a journalist to exposing social injustice. She is best remembered in law enforcement circles for her books in support of state policing, including *Justice to All: The Story of the Pennsylvania State Police* (1917).

SOURCES: Kerry Segrave: *Policewomen: A History*, 1995; Dorothy Moses Schulz, *From Social Worker to Crimefighter*, 1995.

MEADE, WILLIAM KIDDER. (1851–1918) Born in Virginia, Meade relocated to Arizona and worked as a miner before entering the local political arena. Although his political goals went unfulfilled, President Grover Cleveland appointed him U.S. marshal (see U.S. MARSHALS SERVICE) from 1885 to 1890 and 1893 to 1897 (coinciding with Cleveland's nonconsecutive terms in office). Meade affiliated himself with the Behan faction during the conflict with the Earps (see EARP, MORGAN; EARP, VIRGIL; EARP, WYATT BERRY STAPP) in Tombstone, Arizona.

Initially Meade pursued a reform agenda, which included hiring deputies favorably disposed to Mormon constituents (who had suffered at the hands of the previous administration). Ironically, his first term in office was marred by an incident involving the Mormon community. Following the robbery of an army paymaster, Meade pursued the robbers into a Mormon settlement and arrested seven church leaders. Suspicion of malfeasance was directed at Meade and his deputies when it came to light that a five-hundred-dollar reward was offered for each arrest. The Mormon leaders were subsequently exonerated.

Meade rose to prominence in 1888 when he led a posse into Mexico in pursuit of a gang train robbers. This controversial incident led Mexican police to detain Meade and his posse for two weeks. Although the incident had short-lived international repercussions, lawman Robert Havlin "Bob" Paul* clandestinely received permission to hunt down the band in Mexico. With a lifelong interest in the mining business, Meade had mining investments in Tombstone and, like Wyatt Earp, took part in the Alaskan gold rush. He died in Tombstone in 1918.

SOURCES: Larry D. Ball, *The United States Marshals of New Mexico and Arizona Territories, 1846–1912*, 1978; Larry D. Ball, "This High-Handed Outrage: Marshal William Kidder Meade in a Mexican Jail," *Journal of Arizona History* 17, Summer 1976, pp. 219–232.

MEAGHER, MICHAEL. (c. 1843–1881) Born in County Cavar, Ireland, Meagher fought in the Civil War and was a Kansas stagecoach driver prior to his appointment as marshal of Wichita, Kansas, in April 1871. Three years later he resigned and set out for the Indian Territory, where he worked as a carpenter and freighter. He returned to Wichita and served briefly as deputy U.S. marshal and in 1875 was once again elected city marshal. Although he eschewed gunplay for the most part, he shot and killed an inebriated stage driver on New Year's Day, 1877. Meagher moved to Caldwell, Kansas, and was elected mayor in 1880; the following year he served as city marshal. On December 17, 1881, he was shot and killed by a drunken Texas cowboy.

SOURCES: Nyle H. Miller and Joseph W. Snell, *Great Gunfighters of the Kansas Cowtowns, 1867–1886*, 1967; Dan L. Thrapp, ed., *EFB*, Vol. 2, 1988.

MEANS, GASTON BULLOCK. (1880–1938) Born in North Carolina, Means led a rather undistinguished life as a towel salesman and occasional lawyer before joining the William John Burns* Detective Agency in 1910. As a detective he found his true calling. Burns, a future chief of the Bureau of Investigation, described Means as "the greatest natural detective ever known." However, on leaving the agency in 1915, Means embarked on a world-class career as one of the century's greatest con men. Means was suspected of swindling heiresses while serving as bodyguard and financial manager. During World War I he worked as a spy for both the British and Germans before offering his services to U.S. Army Intelligence.

When Burns was selected during the Warren Harding presidential administration to lead the Bureau of Investigation (in 1921), he brought along his former agency detective, Means. Riddled with corruption at the start, Means elevated the graft system within the Bureau to the next level. Harding's wife reportedly hired Means to investigate her husband's extracurricular affairs. Not long afterward, Means was indicted for swindling bootleggers and then attempted to blackmail President Harding over his supposed illegitimate child with Nan Britton. Means would go to jail for his incessant bribery and swindling pursuits, but not before collaborating on a book with Britton titled *The President's Daughter*. In 1930 he published the best-selling *The Strange Death of President Harding*, which suggested that he had been poisoned by his wife. One of his last and most elaborate scams involved collecting ransom money from a wealthy heiress to solve the Lindbergh kidnapping. When his ruse was uncovered (but not the ransom), Means went to jail for fifteen years. On his deathbed in 1938, Federal Bureau of Investigation (FBI)* agents queried him as to where they might find the $100,000 he had collected to find the Lindbergh baby. Means reportedly smiled and then closed his eyes forever.

SOURCE: Carl Sifakis, *The Encyclopedia of American Crime*, 1982.

MEAT-EATERS. According to the 1972 Knapp Commission* report, corrupt police officers, known as meat-eaters, represent a smaller percentage of the force than the so-called grass-eaters.* Meat-eaters tend to spend a significant amount of their working time and energy looking for opportunities to exploit for financial gain, including gambling, drugs, and serious infractions, from which they can extort exorbitant payments.

SOURCE: Whitman Knapp, chairman, *The Knapp Commission Report on Police Corruption*, 1972.

MEHEGAN, ALBERT D. (1886–1983) Born in Lafayette, Indiana, and educated at Purdue University, Mehegan joined the Federal Bureau of Investigation (FBI)* as a special agent in 1922. He retiring in 1975 at the age of eighty-eight; his fifty-three-year tenure with the force was the longest in the agency's history.

Forty-three of these years were spent in the Chicago field office, from which he participated in numerous high-profile cases. He worked undercover in West Virginia during the Hatfield-McCoy feud and he investigated gangsters John Dillinger and Baby Face Nelson. However, prior to joining the Bureau he had worked in the railway industry and his acumen in this area was second to none. For most of his career Mehegan focused on crimes involving interstate transportation theft and, working from the Chicago office, he served as an intermediary between the FBI and the major railroads.

SOURCE: Athan G. Theoharis, ed., *The FBI*, 1999.

MELVILLE-LEE, W. L. (1865–1955) Melville-Lee had aspired to be a policeman in England but was forced to give up his goal when he suffered a debilitating polo injury. Instead he became an influential proponent of police professionalism and a barrister. During the Victorian era he championed a new breed of police officer, who was committed to public service and preventive policing. Melville-Lee distinguished himself as a counterintelligence officer during the World War I.

SOURCE: W. L. Melville-Lee, *A History of Police in England and Wales*, 1901.

MESILLA SCOUTS. Due to the Posse Comitatus Act (see *POSSE COMITATUS*, the regular U.S. Army was barred from assisting local law enforcement in the pursuit of outlaw bands. By the 1880s the New Mexico Territory was teeming with gangs of rustlers. Governor Lew Wallace authorized militia units to go after these criminal bands. One of the most prominent was the Mesilla Scouts out of Dona Ana County The unit was led by Major Albert J. Fountain, and many citizens despised it because it was predominantly composed of Hispanic members. Locals disparagingly referred to the unit as "The Greaser Militia."

SOURCE: Larry D. Ball, *The United States Marshals of New Mexico and Arizona Territories, 1846–1912*, 1978.

MET, THE. This is London police slang for the London Metropolitan Police,* distinguishing it from the other branches and divisions of the London police.

SOURCE: Peter Laurie, *Scotland Yard*, 1970.

METROPOLITAN POLICE ACT OF 1829. This act is credited with introducing the modern model of policing, in which the primary duty of the police officer is to prevent crime by regular patrolling rather than just arresting suspects following the commission of a criminal act. Introduced by British Home Secretary Sir Robert Peel,* the "Act for Improving the Police in and Near the Metropolis" was the result of seven years of failed attempts to create a professional police force. Opposition to the force came from both the Parliament and the public. The London Metropolitan Police* force served as a model for urban police departments in the United States and throughout the British Empire.

SOURCE: Wilbur R. Miller, *Cops and Bobbies*, 1973.

MEXICO CITY MASSACRE. On October 2, 1968, ten thousand people gathered on the square in Tlatelolco, Mexico, to listen to unarmed student leaders protest the country's traditional one-party rule, the detention of hundreds of political prisoners without trial, and the oppression of free speech on campus. Five thousand police officers and soldiers stood by, and suddenly a helicopter descended on the crowd and began strafing the unarmed protestors. Over the next half-hour, the police and soldiers fired their weapons at the helpless crowd. To this day the government has only admitted killing twenty people. However, most estimates suggest that over three hundred people were killed and thousands wounded. In Mexico this tragic event is remembered as "sad night of Tlatelolco."

SOURCE: Elena Poniatowska, *Massacre in Mexico*, 1971.

MILLER, RICHARD WILLIAM. (b. 1936) Born in Los Angeles and educated at Brigham Young University, Miller joined the Federal Bureau of Investigation (FBI)* in 1964. However, besides fluency in Spanish, he was mediocre in almost every other facet of the job. Roundly criticized for poor job performance and being overweight, Miller was typically employed in low-priority posts. In 1983 he was assigned to interview Russian emigrants when he came under the spell of Svetlana Ogorodnikova, a Soviet spy. During their involvement, Miller gave her classified FBI manuals.

On being arrested the following year, Miller weakly claimed he was conducting a one-man counterintelligence operation. He was convicted in 1990 after three trials. Sentenced to twenty years in prison, Miller has the dubious distinction of being the first FBI agent arrested for espionage. Miller was released from prison in 1994.

SOURCES: Athan G. Theoharis, ed., *The FBI*, 1999; Charles Phillips and Alan Axelrod, *CCC*, 1996.

MILLER, ZEKE. (d. 1909) Along with Bass Reeves* and Grant Johnson,* Miller was one of the most prominent African-American deputy U.S. marshals (see U.S. MARSHALS SERVICE) to serve in the Indian Territory. From 1894 to 1907 he was credited with hunting down many desperadoes without ever having to shoot a man. Born in Ohio, he was originally employed as a mine inspector and only moved to the Indian Territory after a friend offered him the job as deputy marshal. When Oklahoma became a state, Miller traded in his badge for a business career.

SOURCE: Art Burton, *Black, Red, and Deadly*, 1991.

MILLS, MAKE. (1871–1956) A Polish immigrant, Mills joined the Chicago Police Department (CPD)* in 1896 and led its anarchist Squad for almost fifty years. Mills was promoted from sergeant to lieutenant in 1924. In 1927 Mills was also placed in charge of the newly created Missing Persons Bureau, but he would eventually leave this post on being appointed to head the Bomb Squad and the Unit of Foreign Investigation. Although Chicago law required mandatory retirement at the age of sixty-three, Mills was allowed to work until he was seventy-six. During his lifelong war against subversive activity, he became a nationally recognized expert on bombs and explosive devices.

SOURCES: Thomas A. Reppetto, *The Blue Parade*, 1978; Raphael W. Marrow and Harriet I. Carter, *In Pursuit of Crime*, 1996.

MILTON, JEFF DAVIS. (1861–1947) Born in Marianna, Florida, Milton was the last of ten children born to the Civil War governor of Florida John Milton. At the age of sixteen he moved to Navasota, Texas, before working cattle near Fort Phantom Hill and supervising convicts on a Huntsville prison farm. Milton began a three-year stint with the Texas Rangers* in 1880. After a rather un-eventful term with the Rangers, he resigned at the rank of corporal and worked in a general store shortly before returning to law enforcement in 1884 as deputy sheriff in Socorro County, New Mexico. In one incident he and another cowboy killed three bandits who tried to ambush them.

Milton served as a mounted inspector along the Arizona-Mexico border in 1887 and in 1895 was police chief of El Paso, Texas. Over the next five years he was involved in several deadly gunfights, including one in 1890 while work-ing as an express messenger for the Wells Fargo Detective Bureau,* in which he fought five members of the Burt Alvord* gang. During his last years he worked as a railroad conductor and prospected for gold and oil in the Sierra Madres and Texas. While at the wheel of a Model T Ford in 1917, in Tomb-stone, Arizona, he captured and wounded a bank robber. Although he suffered several gunshot wounds, including a debilitating injury to his arm in the 1900 gunfight, he worked into his seventies and filled his last peacekeeping position as an Immigration Service inspector on the Arizona-California border, where he was assigned to stem the smuggling of illegal Chinese immigrants.

SOURCES: J. Evetts Haley, *Jeff Milton, a Good Man with a Gun*, 1948; Bill O'Neal, *Encyclopedia of Western Gunfighters* 1979.

MIMS, HENRY. (1816–1925) Mims was reportedly the longest living of the Texas Rangers* when he died in 1925, approaching 110 years old. Even more remarkable is the fact that he was one of the few men to survive a scalping, having accomplished this feat after being left for dead by Indians near Duncan Prairie in 1865.

SOURCE: *Texas Rangers Sesquicentennial Anniversary*, 1973.

MIRANDA V. ARIZONA. This landmark case stemmed from the arrest of Ernesto Miranda (1940–1976) for rape and kidnapping on March 13, 1963. Miranda claimed that police officers coerced him into confessing to the crime during a two-hour interrogation and that he was not allowed to consult an attorney. Miranda was convicted of the crime over the objections of his attorney, who protested that Miranda had not been informed of his rights or given legal counsel to apprise him of his protection against self-incrimination under the Fifth Amendment. When *Miranda v. Arizona* reached the Supreme Court in 1966, the conviction was overturned.

In the court decision, Chief Justice Earl Warren wrote that before being questioned, all individuals must be notified of their constitutional rights, including the right to have an attorney present during questioning. This landmark case substantially altered American police practices in the interviewing of suspects. Lauded by civil libertarians, the "Miranda decision" has been roundly criticized by law enforcement and was later modified under the more police-friendly Warren Burger court in the 1980s. Miranda was retried and reconvicted. Four years after his release from prison in 1972, he was stabbed to death in a bar fight.

SOURCE: William G. Bailey, ed., *The Encyclopedia of Police Science*, 1995.

MIRELES, EDMUNDO, JR. Born in Alice, Texas, and educated at the University of Maryland, Mireles joined the Federal Bureau of Investigation (FBI)* in 1979. While serving the Miami field office in 1986 Mireles became the first recipient of the FBI's Medal of Valor after participating in the killing of two bank robbers. He was one of seven FBI agents shot during a gunfight in April 1986, in which two FBI agents were killed. It was considered the bloodiest day in FBI history. The deaths of agents Jerry L. Dove* and Benjamin P. Grogan* and the wounding of five other agents led to better FBI firearms training.

SOURCE: Athan G. Theoharis, ed., *The FBI*, 1999.

MOLLEN COMMISSION. In September 1992 the Mollen Commission convened in New York City to investigate police corruption once more among New York's Finest.* Led by Milton Mollen, the commission would uncover evidence of cocaine-dealing cops, cops protecting drug dealers, and police participating in murders and holdups. The hearings were dominated by the testimony of rogue cop Michael Dowd, a contemporary Harry Gross.* Dowd was a drug user and admitted to running his own crew of about fifteen corrupt patrolmen. Former Police Commissioner Lee Patrick Brown* would have a hard time answering charges that the department should have taken notice of Dowd, who drove a $30,000 Corvette and owned four homes, including his $300,000 main residence, while bringing home only $400 a week in police pay.

SOURCE: James Lardner, *Crusader*, 1996.

MONRO, JAMES. (1838–1920) Educated at Edinburgh and Berlin Universities, Monro succeeded Sir Howard Vincent* as head of London's Criminal Investigation Department (CID)* in 1884. Formerly the chief of police in Bengal, India, as assistant commissioner of the CID, Monro was almost immediately confronted by the Fenian bombing campaign of the Irish Republican Brotherhood, which he finally brought under control.

Well respected as a police official, Monro, was credited with curtailing crime and championing pension reform for policemen. He left the CID in 1888 and served as the unofficial head of detective service until 1890. Subsequently, Monro founded a Christian Medical Mission and cut short his retirement in Darjeeling, India, to return to Great Britain for his last years.

SOURCES: Paul Begg, Martin Fido, and Keith Skinner, *The Jack the Ripper A to Z*, 1991; Sir Basil Thomson,* *The Story of Scotland Yard*, 1936.

MOORE, MERLYN D. (b. 1942) Moore is nationally recognized for his expertise in the analysis of police operations and has served as consultant to the Enforcement Division of the Law Enforcement Assistance Agency (LEAA) on the Atlanta child murders and the National Center for the Analysis of Violent Crime at the Federal Bureau of Investigation (FBI)* Behavior Science Unit at Quantico, Virginia.* Moore has also served as field manager for the National Missing/Abducted Children and Serial Murder Tracking and Prevention Program and as project director for the Multi-Agency Investigation Project on Serial Murders for the National Institute of Justice. He is currently a criminal justice professor at Sam Houston State University and a senior consultant at Moore, Bieck, Heck, and Associates, a consulting firm specializing in police- and security-related work.

SOURCE: Mitchel Roth, *Fulfilling a Mandate*, 1997.

MOORE, ROY K. (b. 1914) Born in Hood River, Oregon, Moore joined the Federal Bureau of Investigation (FBI)* in 1938 following service in the U.S. Marines. Promoted to agent status in 1940, Moore worked out of the Albany field office. During the 1950s he would serve as special agent in charge of the Milwaukee, Wisconsin; Chicago; and then the Denver field offices. While in Denver, Moore was instrumental in the conviction of Jack Gilbert Graham for an airplane bombing, concluding the first such investigation by the FBI in the United States.

In the 1960s, while a special agent in charge of the Little Rock, Arkansas, office, Moore was assigned to investigate the 1963 church bombing in Birmingham, Alabama, that resulted in the deaths of four African-American girls. FBI director John Edgar Hoover* selected Moore to head up the Jackson, Mississippi, field office in July 1964. During his tenure in Mississippi he investigated over two hundred cases of violence, most related to the civil rights struggle.

During the 1970s Moore investigated left-wing radicals in Pennsylvania, worked as a special agent in charge of the Chicago office, and spent stints in the Virgin Islands and then back at Jackson, Mississippi, before attempting to break the impasse during the Wounded Knee siege.* He retired from the FBI in 1974 and entered the banking business.

SOURCES: Athan G. Theoharis, ed., *The FBI*, 1999; William W. Turner, *Hoover's FBI*, 1970; reprint, 1993.

MORRISON, ALEXANDER L., SR. (b. 1832) Born in Ireland, Morrison arrived in America in time to fight in the Mexican-American War. After service in New Mexico he moved to Chicago, served a stint in the state legislature, and then returned to New Mexico, where he had developed an affinity for the downtrodden Hispanic population. In 1882 he was appointed U.S. Marshal (see U.S. MARSHALS SERVICE), succeeding a Democrat, John E. Sherman Jr. Morrison's tenure in office was tainted when two of his deputies, including Timothy Isaiah "Long-Haired Jim" Courtright,* were arrested in connection with the murder of several local settlers. Their initial escape to Texas led newspaper editors to warn the marshal to pick his deputies more carefully in the future. Morrison later appointed his son, Alexander, Jr., as chief deputy. During the 1880s Morrison took part in the "Rustler War" against local bandits and devoted considerable effort toward stemming the illicit whiskey trade near the Navajo Reservation. In 1885 a change in political administrations led to his resignation.

SOURCE: Larry D. Ball, *The United States Marshals of New Mexico and Arizona Territories, 1846–1912*, 1978.

MORSE, HENRY NICHOLSON "HARRY." (1835–1912) Born in New York City, Morse went to sea as a young boy, eventually appearing in San Francisco in 1849. After a disappointing spell in the gold fields he worked at a series of service-oriented jobs before finding his career in law enforcement, beginning with his appointment as deputy provost marshal* for Alameda County, California, in 1863. Later that year he was elected sheriff* of the same county. He quickly developed a reputation as a tenacious manhunter. Among his most infamous quarries was Tomas "Procopio" Bustamante, nephew of the legendary Joaquin Murrieta, in 1872. In 1874 he caught the Tiburcio Vasquez gang after pursuing them for two months in one of the West's longest manhunts.

During his career as a peace officer, Morse invested wisely. Wearying of the political infighting and bureaucracy so characteristic of early law enforcement, he retired in 1878. However, the lure of his profession was too strong, and soon after his "retirement," he created a private detective force composed of close to sixty agents. Morse was instrumental in the 1883 capture of Black Bart and helped defend Theodore Durrant in what were then termed the "crime of the century" murders. However, he was thwarted by the detective skills of Captain Isaiah Wrigley Lees,* and the defendant went to the gallows in 1898. As he approached death, he could nonetheless feel confident and proud that his grandson would lead the Morse detective agency into the next century.

SOURCES: John Boessenecker, *Lawman: The Life and Times of Harry Morse, 1835–1912*, 1998; William B. Secrest *Lawmen and Desperadoes*, 1994; Charles Howard Shinn, *Graphic Description of Pacific Coast Outlaws*, reprint, 1958.

MOSSMAN, BURTON C. (1867–1956) Born in Illinois and raised in Minnesota, Mossman moved to New Mexico at sixteen. Following a string of jobs as a surveyor, cowboy, and ranch manager, Mossman became an expert at outwitting rustlers and bandits, and in 1901 he became the first captain of the Arizona Rangers,* a force modeled after the Texas Rangers.* Mossman focused his attention on the lawless southeastern section of the territory. During his one year with the Rangers, he tracked down Augustino Chacon, the confessed killer of over fifty men. Mossman left the force, after one year, as he had promised, and led a successful career as a businessman and owner of the Diamond A ranch.

SOURCES: Jay J. Wagoner, *Arizona Territory, 1863–1912: A Political History*, 1970; Bill O'Neal, *The Arizona Rangers*, 1987.

MOUCHARDS. The French police used a system of informants known as the *mouchards*. Although its implementation has been credited to Lieutenant-General Gabriel Nicolas de La Reynie* in the seventeenth century, it was probably used prior to his administration.

SOURCE: Philip John Stead, *The Police of Paris*, 1957.

MULLANEY, PATRICK J. (b. 1935) Born in New York City and educated at Catholic University and Manhattan College, Mullaney joined the Federal Bureau of Investigation (FBI)* in 1966. After postings in the Jacksonville, Florida; Los Angeles; and New York City field offices, Mullaney was assigned to the instructional staff at the FBI Academy at Quantico, Virginia,* in 1972. He subsequently developed new hostage negotiation techniques and introduced counseling for posttraumatic shooting experiences.

Mullaney served in the terrorism section of the Criminal Investigation Division in 1977 and two years later headed up the Baltimore, Maryland, field office. Promoted to inspector, he served in a variety of capacities in the 1980s before retiring in 1986. He is best known for developing the FBI's criminal behavior–profiling techniques with Howard Teton.*

SOURCE: Athan G. Theoharis, ed., *The FBI*, 1999.

MURPHY, PATRICK VINCENT. (b. 1920) Murphy began his career as a New York City Police Department (NYPD)*patrolman following World War II. He would serve stints with police departments in Syracuse, New York; Detroit,

Michigan; and Washington, D.C. Murphy succeeded Howard R. Leary as New York City police commissioner in 1970 after he resigned over the corruption scandal investigated by the Knapp Commission.* Credited with restoring integrity to the force, placing more restrictions on the police use of deadly force, and implementing "neighborhood policing" in New York City, Murphy retired in 1973 to head the Police Foundation, a nonprofit police research organization headquartered in Washington, D.C.

SOURCES: Thomas J. Deakin, *Police Professionalism: The Renaissance of American Law Enforcement*, 1988; Robert Daley, *Target Blue*, 1973.

MURTAUGH, GEORGE JOHN, JR. As Detective Sergeant with the Chicago Police Department (CPD),* "Duke" Murtaugh played a prominent role in the manhunt for the killer of eight nurses in July 1966. Murtaugh had joined the force in 1945 and had investigated more than a thousand homicides prior to Richard Speck's murderous rampage. Murtaugh would eventually lead the investigative team after the intruder's description was revealed by the lone survivor. Sixty-seven hours after the mass murder, Murtaugh had arrested the perpetrator of the era's "crime of the century."

SOURCES: Dennis L. Breo and William J. Martin, *The Crime of the Century*, 1993; Bruce Henderson and Sam Summerlin, *The Super Sleuths*, 1976.

MUSGRAVE, THOMAS. Sheriff* of Yorkshire in the 1350s and 1360s, in 1366 Musgrave became the first sheriff in recorded history to be brought to court on charges by a private individual for wrongful arrest. The plaintiffs accused Musgrave of having them imprisoned "without process of law or indictment or any manner of appeal." Musgrave ultimately was removed as sheriff after the court ruled in favor of the defendants.

SOURCE: Irene Gladwin, *The Sheriff*, 1984.

MUTAWWIUN. The *mutawwiun* is Saudi Arabia's autonomous religious police. They serve on certain judicial committees dealing with public morality. A form of public security police, members ensure strict compliance with the Islamic legal system and are renowned for their vigorous enforcement of such Islamic requirements as proper attire for women and prohibitions against the use of liquor.

SOURCE: George Thomas Kurian, *World Encyclopedia of Police Forces and Penal Systems*, 1989.

MVD. The Soviet Union's Ministry for Internal Affairs, or MVD, was responsible for a major portion of the country's internal security and most routine national police functions prior to the fall of communism in the late 1980s. Established as one organization in 1953 following the death of Joseph Stalin, the

MVD then absorbed the functions of the former Ministry of State Security (MGB). Lavrenti Pavlovich Beria* took over its control during its first year, shortly before he was arrested. Following Beria's execution, the KGB* emerged as the main state security organ.

In 1960 the MVD was abolished and replaced by Public Order Detachments. Members of these units came from all walks of life, including farmers, teachers, students, and workers. They were required to wear badges and patrol the local neighborhoods; their existence was predicated on a system of preventive policing using over 2.5 million citizens.

SOURCES: James Cramer, *The World's Police*, 1964; Robert Conquest, ed., *The Soviet Police System*, 1968.

N

NAPIER, SIR CHARLES JAMES. (1782–1853) During his lifetime in the military, Napier distinguished himself in the Napoleonic Wars and was promoted to commander in 1841. Posted to India, Napier was charged with administering the crime-ridden province of Sind. In 1843 he was instrumental in establishing the Indian Police Service. This police service was strongly influenced by the Royal Irish Constabulary,* being structured along military lines, but separate from the army. While both forces remained separate, they occasionally collaborated to quell civil disorder.

Napier's police force was commanded by British officers and entirely separate from the army. Under Napier, the Indian police was so effective in reducing crime that in the following decade, Bombay and Madras introduced police forces based on his model. Napier wrote *Lights and Shadows of Military Life* (1851).

SOURCES: Philip John Stead, *The Police of Britain*, 1985; Charles Phillips and Alan Axelrod, *CCC*, 1996.

NAPOLEONIC POLICING. One of Napoleon Bonaparte's most enduring accomplishments was the Napoleonic Code, which left France and many countries in the French orbit with a unitary system of law that was equally applicable to all citizens. Another of Napoleon's greatest legacies was the French police system. Under the centralized Napoleonic system of policing, every community of 5,000 citizens was given a commissioner of police, who was appointed by the central government. In similar fashion, commissioners general were appointed for cities of 100,000. This system was reinforced by the Gendarmerie Nationale,* which numbered close to 30,000 by the end of his regime. The Gendarmerie Nationale influenced similar units around the world. By the early 1800s the force was being used increasingly for civil police work and espionage activity. Napoleon also reinstituted the position of police chief of Paris in 1800. Formerly the lieutenant-general of police,* it was resurrected under the title of prefect of police of Paris. Joseph Fouché* would serve as head of the Ministry of General Police for most of the Napoleonic era.

SOURCES: Philip John Stead, *The Police of France*, 1983; Clive Emsley, *Policing and Its Context, 1750–1870*, 1983.

NATAL MOUNTED POLICE. The Natal Mounted Police was organized in 1873 in response to a rebellion in South Africa by the Hlubi Chieftain Langalilbalele. Established by a retired veteran of the Crimean War and the Indian Mutiny, the new force was modeled after the Cape Mounted Rifles. Unlike that force, however, the Natal Mounted Police were responsible for an entire province rather than a limited frontier border. They were also charged with preventing intertribal conflict. The Natal unit was initially composed of fifty Europeans, who supplied their own mounts. Two native troopers were recruited for every European, a ratio that was later reversed.

SOURCE: Mitchel Roth, "Mounted Police Forces: A Comparative History," *Policing* 21(4) (Fall 1998).

NATIONAL MOTOR VEHICLE THEFT ACT. In 1919 Congress passed the National Motor Vehicle Theft Act, better known as the Dyer Act, which expanded the policing powers of the Bureau of Investigation (in 1935, it would become the Federal Bureau of Investigation [FBI]*). The act was passed in response to the theft of 29,399 automobiles the previous year. This act made it a federal crime to transport a stolen motor vehicle across a state line and inaugurated a long debate over states' rights. Congress uses the commerce and tax clauses of Article 1 of the United States Constitution to either create new federal agencies, such as the Border Patrol or the Alcohol, Tobacco, and Firearms* (ATF) Bureau or to expand the law enforcement powers of existing federal agencies, such as the FBI. The FBI was brought into the hunt for John Dillinger in 1934 when he crossed the Indiana-Illinois state line in a stolen automobile. Prior to this incident, the legendary bandit had only violated state and local laws, but this crime would seal his fate, leading to his death at the hands of FBI agents outside Chicago's Biograph Theater later that year. Although the Dyer Act did not solve the car theft problem, it had a major impact in expanding the role of the FBI in national law enforcement beyond its original mandate.

SOURCES: Don Whitehead, *The FBI Story*, 1956; Carl Sifakis, *The Encyclopedia of American Crime*, 1982.

NATIONAL ORDER OF BLACK LAW ENFORCEMENT EXECUTIVES (NOBLE). Founded in 1976, NOBLE was established by black police administrators and is regarded as one of the most progressive police organizations in the United States. Its annual meetings have become as valuable to its membership as those of the International Association of Chiefs of Police (IACP).* At its annual meetings constituents of NOBLE discuss new methods of crime prevention, community policing, and many topics that are addressed at IACP meetings. NOBLE's visibility has been enhanced by the fact that half the nation's largest cities had black police chiefs by the 1980s. Prominent members of the organization included Lee Patrick Brown* and Hubert Williams.*

SOURCE: W. Marvin Dulaney, *Black Police in America*, 1996.

NATIVE POLICE FORCES. *See* NEW SOUTH WALES MOUNTED DIVISION.

NATIVIST RIOTS OF 1844. Destructive and bloody nativist riots in Philadelphia, Pennsylvania, in 1844 mobilized support for a "London-style" police force whose mandate would include preventing civil disorder. These riots were the culmination of years of tension between Philadelphia's nativeborn and immigrant Irish Catholic communities. Similar conflicts would be played out in other East Coast American cities in the 1840s and served as a clarion call for police reform.

SOURCE: David R. Johnson, *Policing the Urban Underworld*, 1979.

NEAGLE, DAVID BUTLER. (1847–1925) Born in Boston, Massachusetts, Neagle moved to San Francisco, California, with his parents five years later. After stints as a miner in the gold fields of Idaho and then the silver mines of Virginia City, Nevada, Neagle married and was involved in several gunfights. In 1874 he opened a saloon near the gold camp of Panamint, California. Over the subsequent five years, Neagle either prospected for mineral riches or worked in service-oriented businesses adjacent to the camps.

In 1879 Neagle moved to Tombstone, Arizona, and two years later entered law enforcement as deputy sheriff of Cochise County. It was during this period that he began his friendship with noted lawman Wyatt Berry Stapp Earp.* The following year Neagle was defeated in his bid for sheriff.* Soon after he returned to mining, and eventually he moved to San Francisco, where he was appointed deputy sheriff and license collector by the Democratic Party city bosses. Physically unimposing at five feet, eight inches, and weighing less than 150 pounds, Neagle nevertheless acquired a reputation as a no-nonsense peace officer.

In 1889 Neagle killed ex–state supreme court justice David S. Terry in a controversial incident, but eyewitness testimony vindicated him. Neagle left local law enforcement to work as a bodyguard and gunman on the Southern Pacific railroad. He retired to Oakland, California, in 1920, where he died five years later.

SOURCES: William B. Secrest, *Lawmen and Desperadoes*, 1994; Stacey Osgood, "The Life and Times of David Neagle,' in *The Westerners' Brand Book*, Vol. 19, April 1962.

NEEDLES, THOMAS B. Prior to the opening of the Oklahoma Territory to settlers, on March 1, 1889, Congress approved an act establishing Muskogee as the first court for whites in the Indian Territory. The Oklahoma District became the responsibility of the Muskogee and Wichita courts. Operating out of Muskogee, Thomas B. Needles was the first marshal appointed for the Indian Territory. Shortly before the land rush, he appointed three hundred additional deputies to control the settlers and to suppress the "sooners," who attempted to claim land before the land rush began. In 1891 Needles sent deputy marshal Henry Andrew "Heck" Thomas* in pursuit of Bob Dalton after he killed a farmer. Needles was replaced as marshal after only four years.

SOURCES: Glenn Shirley, *West of Hell's Fringe*, 1978; Frank Richard Prassel, *The Western Peace Officer*, 1972.

NEIL, JOHN. (b. 1850) Born in County Cork, Ireland, Neil joined the London Metropolitan Police* in 1875. Posted to the J Division as a constable (see CONSTABLES) and assigned to patrol the Bethnal Green section of London, Neil discovered the body of Jack the Ripper victim Mary Ann Nichols and witnessed the subsequent inquest. Neil resigned from the force in 1897.

SOURCE: Paul Begg, Martin Fido, and Keith Skinner, *The Jack the Ripper A to Z*, 1991.

NEPOTE, JEAN. (b. 1915) Born in Normandy, France, Nepote received a law degree from the University of Lyons before entering the French civil service in 1935. After service in the military, he was appointed commissioner of the French police in 1941. He distinguished himself during World War II when he fought with the French resistance. Following the war he worked for the Police Judicial Headquarters and then was instrumental in professionalizing and creating the Paris-based International Criminal Police Organization (Interpol*). Nepote was appointed deputy secretary-general of Interpol in 1958, and in 1963 he was promoted to secretary-general. He retired in 1978 after forty years in law enforcement and is remembered as one of the founders of Interpol.

SOURCE: Charles Phillips and Alan Axelrod, *CCC*, 1996.

NESS, ELIOT. (1902–1957) Ness came to the public's attention as head of the Untouchables* unit in Chicago during the heyday of nemesis Al Capone. He attended the University of Chicago prior to being chosen to lead a special Prohibition unit in that city. Authorized to crush organized crime–controlled breweries and distilleries, Ness personally selected members for his so-called Untouchables unit. Despite the credit accorded the Ness legend, the Untouchables, as with most Prohibition-oriented law enforcement units, was rather ineffective in its war against Al Capone's bootleg empire. Capone would be eventually brought to justice by the U.S. Internal Revenue Service in 1931. With the crime lord out of the way, Ness turned to Capone subordinates such as Frank Nitti and, later, moonshine operations in the hills of Kentucky, Tennessee, and Ohio.

Ness and his Untouchables made great newspaper copy but were rather underwhelming in their war against booze. The efforts of Ness and his protégés would cause Capone's alcohol production to drop by 80 percent as he was forced to buy overpriced liquor from other locations. Ness would survive three assassination attempts by Capone henchmen, including a drive-by, a car bomb, and a runover.

Ness was more successful in his next position as public safety director of Cleveland, Ohio. Following the repeal of Prohibition, he moved to Cleveland in 1935 and made short work of a police department riddled with corruption, forcing several hundred policemen to resign and sending at least a dozen officers to state prison. Under Ness's leadership, the Cleveland police department forced mob leader Moe Dalitz to move his syndicate operations out of the city. Ness did not crack every case, however. Particularly frustrating was his inability to identify and capture the "Torso" serial killer. Ness went on to establish the Cleveland Boys' Town and a police academy and to reorganize the city traffic department.

By the 1940s Ness's squeaky-clean reputation was marred by a divorce and a drunk-driving case, and he left law enforcement in 1942. Falling on hard times, he was living in obscurity as a salesman in Pennsylvania when an old friend from his youth, journalist Oscar Fraley, collaborated with Ness on the book *The Untouchables*, which chronicled Ness's Prohibition days in Chicago. Ness succumbed to a heart attack shortly before the book went to print.

SOURCES: Oscar Fraley, *The Untouchables*, 1957; Oscar Fraley, *Four against the Mob*, 1976; Steve Nickel, *Torso*, 1989.

NEVILL, CHARLES L. (1855–1906) Born in Carthage, Alabama, Nevill moved with his family to Fayette County, Texas in his youth. In 1874 he joined the Frontier Battalion of the Texas Rangers.* Nevill rose to prominence in the late 1870s while attempting to contain the Horrell-Higgins Feud in Lampasas, Texas. In 1878 he tracked down noted outlaw Sam Bass near Round Rock, Texas. Severely wounded during a shoot-out, Bass died in the local jail shortly after surrendering to Nevill. Two years later, Nevill was instrumental in the pursuit of the Jesse Evans gang and then the Potter outfit. Nevill left the Rangers in 1882 and served as sheriff* of Presidio County from 1882 to 1888 before moving to San Antonio. He continued his career in the Alamo city as chief deputy sheriff.

SOURCES: Robert W. Stephens, *Texas Ranger Sketches*, 1972; James B. Gillett, *Six Years with the Texas Rangers*, 1963.

NEW JERSEY STATE POLICE. The emergence of the New Jersey State Police force in 1921 is considered a turning point in the history of American state policing. The impetus for its creation was the ineffectiveness of county law enforcement and a rash of violent industrial disorders that plagued the Garden State between 1910 and 1915. In addition, the state was bordered by several large metropolitan areas, which afforded protection to criminals, and the increasing popularity of motor vehicles gave these lawbreakers the opportunity and mobility to escape local law enforcement rather easily. Opposition to a state police force came from the ranks of city bosses, who worried that the state police apparatus would interfere with the corruption of city politics. The New Jersey State Police was commanded by a superintendent appointed for a five-year term and imbued with the power to select the members of the force. Over the protestations of the local political machine, twenty-five-year-old West Point graduate Captain Herbert Norman Schwarzkopf* was selected as the first superintendent of the force on July 1, 1921.

The new superintendent wasted no time in introducing the military model of policing. Initially, eighty-one troopers were selected after completing training and meeting the requirements of having had two years of commissioned military service and agreeing to enlist for two years. Those who attempted to resign early could be charged with a misdemeanor, and troopers could not marry during their initial tour of duty. Troopers lived in barracks and were provided with pistols and rifles. During patrol, those assigned to the northern part of the state were given motorcycles, while those in the more rural, southern parts were assigned horses. With the proliferation of the automobile, troopers would soon trade horses for cars, but the motorcycle would persist for three decades and proved more deadly, taking the lives of fifteen officers, as opposed to five killed in the line of duty. The state police force was not well received in the South Jersey Piney Woods and other rural enclaves, but because it eschewed strike-breaking activities, unlike the Pennsylvania State Police,* the New Jersey State Police retained amicable relations with organized labor. The force, however, was almost undone by its botched handling of the 1932 Lindbergh kidnapping case. Schwarzkopf subsequently lost his job following the execution of Bruno Hauptman in 1936.

SOURCES: Thomas A. Reppetto, *The Blue Parade*, 1978; H. Kenneth Bechtel, *State Police in the United States*, 1995.

NEWMAN, KENNETH. (b. 1926) Born in Sussex, England, Newman enlisted in the Royal Air Force (RAF) in 1944 and then left to join the Palestine Police Force in 1947. The following year he began a twenty-four year stint with the London Metropolitan Police* and in 1972 he transferred to Scotland Yard.* The next year he was named Deputy Chief Constable of the Royal Ulster Constabulary. In 1976 he was appointed chief constable (see CONSTABLES), and two years later he was knighted.

Nicknamed "Mighty Mouse" and "ET," Newman was appointed commissioner in 1982 and, over the next five years, directed the transformation of the Metropolitan Police. Despite attempts at rectifying the rising crime problem, accusations of racial discrimination, and violations of civil rights, most indices indicate that Newman failed to meet his objectives. Furthermore, he contributed to the racial tensions by referring to the black community as "colored." Newman was succeeded by Peter Impbert in August 1987.

SOURCE: Paul Begg and Keith Skinner, *The Scotland Yard Files*, 1992.

NEW MEXICO MOUNTED POLICE. In February 1905, the Legislative Assembly of the Territory of New Mexico created the New Mexico Mounted Police (see HORSE MOUNTED POLICE) "for the protection of the frontier" and "for the preservation of the peace and the capture of persons charged with crime." The governor was authorized to appoint the members of this force, officers included. While the Pennsylvania State Police* is usually credited with introducing the military model to state policing, it was recognized independently by other contemporary forces that this model would be the best one for this level of law enforcement. In Section 9 of the bill creating the New Mexico force, it stated "That the troops raised under and by the virtue of this act shall be governed by the rules and regulations of the army of the USA." The New Mexico Mounted Police ultimately was abolished because of a combination of factors, not the least of which was occasional friction with local law enforcement.

SOURCES: Frank Richard Prassel, *The Western Peace Officer*, 1972; Mitchel Roth, "Mounted Police Forces: A Comparative History," *Policing* 21(4), Fall 1998.

NEW ORLEANS CIVIL GUARD. By the 1780s, Charleston, South Carolina had established a paramilitary police force to control the local slave populace. Subsequently, leading southern cities, including Mobile, Alabama; Savannah, Georgia; and New Orleans had established similar police forces, called city guards. The members of the city guard units wore police uniforms,* predating their Northeastern counterparts by decades, and were outfitted with weapons such as muskets and swords. Although they mimicked the militia, they were an altogether distinct force, which patrolled at night.

In 1804, New Orleans Mayor Etienne Bore introduced a mounted patrol to apprehend runaway slaves. His proposal to form this unit was a precursor to establishing the city's first distinct police force the following year. In 1805 the city council approved the Gendarmerie (see GENDARMERIE NATIONALE) to continue its slave-catching services while performing police duties. In 1806 the Gendarmerie was disbanded and replaced, three years later, by a less militaristic version called the city guard. It was noteworthy for employing several African-American members at a time when the majority of similar units were devoid of black members. However, mounting tension led to no further recruitment of black members after 1830, and they would not appear in New Orleans policing again until Reconstruction.

This military-style force would be demilitarized in little more than two decades. Eschewing uniforms and formidable weaponry, a daytime force was established to complement the nighttime unit. Although there is much controversy as to whether these innovations accord New Orleans an important role in American police reform, there is little doubt that the city was a center of police experimentation in the years prior to the creation of the New York City Police Department (NYPD)* force in 1845.

SOURCES: Clive Emsley, *Policing and Its Context*, 1983; Dennis C. Rousey, *Policing the Southern City: New Orleans, 1805–1889*, 1996.

NEW POLICE ACT OF 1829. The New Police Act of 1829 formally established the guidelines for all police systems of the United Kingdom. Known for its emphasis on preventive policing, its standard of effectiveness remained the absence of crime. According to this revolutionary legislation, police constables* were responsible for the security of life and property of citizens on their beat, as well as the preservation of peace and order.

The police act explicitly defined crimes in terms of felonies and misdemeanors and stated that "the first duty of a constable is always to prevent the commission of a crime." Also identified were the police ranks of chief constable, superintendent, inspector, sergeant, and police constable. One sergeant was charged with the supervision of nine police constables. The remainder of the police act describes procedures for enforcing the law and acts related to the law.

SOURCES: T. A. Critchley, *A History of Police in England and Wales, 900–1966*, 1967; "An Act for Improving the Police in and near the Metropolis" in *Parliamentary Bills, Papers*, Vol. 2, June 19, 1829.

NEW SOUTH WALES MOUNTED DIVISION. The New South Wales Mounted Police Division claims to be the oldest continuous horse mounted police* unit in the world. Created in 1825 by the colony's governor to control the growing bush-ranging threat (bandit menace in more rural areas) and apprehend runaway convicts in rural districts, like most mounted forces, it followed a military model. Recruited from the army, officers and men were awarded army pay according to army rank, with extra allowances for police* duty. Most of the subsequent Australian colonies adopted the mounted police model because it was so well adapted to the terrain.

In 1838 this force grew to over 160 men and was divided into three branches. The force proved to be too small to check the growing depredations of the highwaymen and lawless indigenous peoples. Despite the best efforts of the mounted force, crime increased by 80 percent in 1840 over the previous year. The efficiency of the mounted force declined in the 1840s, in part because of recruiting problems and public criticism of its methods in despatching local outlaws. In 1849 opposition prevailed and the corps was reduced in number, before being done away with altogether the following year.

In addition to the traditional mounted forces culled from the military ranks, there was a native contingent beginning in the 1840s. By 1844 it comprised twenty-nine mounted police out of forty-four. During the Australian gold rush of the 1850s, they were responsible for most law enforcement in the gold fields. Because of tribal rivalries, each detachment had to be recruited from the same group. The native contingent was phased out just before the turn of the century, although its members stayed on as trackers.

Rioting in Sydney in 1850 led to the reorganization of the police and the creation of a horse patrol. Further reorganization was required in the 1860s in response to anti-Chinese rioting in the gold fields and the continuing bush-ranging menace. Frontier conditions clearly influenced the development of law enforcement in Australia. Conflict with the indigenous population required the creation of a specialized and highly mobile police force. The most specialized response to the "aboriginal problem" in Australia was the formation of the Native Police Forces, which was staffed by native troopers and European officers, a common arrangement in the British Empire. This innovation was initially proposed by penal reformer Alexander Maconochie in 1837 and combined advantages of European firepower and horses with aboriginal bush and tracking skills.

Mounted forces in Australia have been maintained to this day. The New South Wales mounted force currently assists the police on special operations such as traffic control at major celebrations and sporting events; searches for missing persons in wilderness areas; and searches for escapees, drug plantations, and stolen livestock.

SOURCES: M. Finane, ed., *Policing in Australia: Historical Perspectives*, 1987; H. Senoir, *Constabulary: The Rise of Police Institutions in Britain, the Commonwealth, and the USA*, 1997; G. M. O'Brien, *The Australian Police Forces*, 1960; Mitchel Roth, "Mounted Police Forces: A Comparative History," *Policing* 21(4), Fall 1998.

NEW YORK CITY DRAFT RIOTS. New York City endured three days of bloody rioting resulting in two thousand people dead and eight thousand injured, beginning on July 13, 1863. The riots stemmed from President Abraham Lincoln's conscription laws, which antagonized Irish immigrants and fueled racial hatreds. Finding themselves the lowest rungs of the social ladder, Irish immigrants resented the fact that they should fight a war to free the blacks and worried that freedom would bring black migration North to compete for jobs. Irish gangs, however, saw the opportunity to loot and pillage unimpeded.

The unrest began as a seething protest, and by the second day had degenerated into lynchings of any black the Irish mobs could find. Irish criminals targeted military armories, where they murdered and tortured Union soldiers who resisted. The rioters and the forces of order, like those during the 1840s, were often divided along religious lines. Hundreds of buildings, including Protestant churches, were burned to the ground by the largely Catholic mobs, while Catholic churches were left standing.

During the three days of mayhem, unspeakable acts were committed by the rioters. Policemen, soldiers, and blacks were murdered. The children picked the bodies clean of clothing and wore the garments as bloodstained badges of honor. Crowds were estimated at between fifty and seventy thousand persons, more than a match for the police force. Black bodies were left mutilated and hanging from lampposts; some were burned. Women played a prominent role in the savagery, lagging behind the men to pour oil into knife wounds and set corpses on fire.

The crowds descended on black neighborhoods and targeted police stations, all the while searching for weapons. One of many heroes, Officer George Rallings, spirited children from a black orphanage when he learned that the mobs were on their way. His actions saved the lives of all the inhabitants except for a little girl who was left behind. Even Police Superintendent John Alexander Kennedy* was severely beaten as the mobs burned police precinct houses with impunity. Drilled in military and some riot control tactics following the Astor Place Riot* of the 1840s, one Metropolitan contingent of two hundred policemen turned back a mob of over two thousand on lower Broadway and was credited with probably saving City Hall and other civic buildings from destruction.

The tide turned only when troops headed toward the epic battle at Gettysburg, Pennsylvania, were rerouted to New York City on July 15. The riot had formally ended the next day, and when the regiments tallied their losses from the pitched battles with the mobs, they counted at least 350 dead or wounded. However, the totals for the entire riot were more appalling. The 2,000 deaths exceeded the mortality at the Battles of Bull Run and Shiloh. In the end, not one rioter was convicted of murder and only twenty went to trial. By the following week, the draft resumed and victorious Union troops filled New York streets.

SOURCES: Irving Werstein, *July 1863: The Incredible Story of the New York City Draft Riots*, 1957; Joel T. Headley, *The Great Riots of New York, 1712–1873*, 1873; James F. Richardson, *The New York Police: Colonial Times to 1901*, 1970.

NEW YORK CITY POLICE DEPARTMENT (NYPD). The first police organization in New York City was the *schout fiscal*,* maintained by the original Dutch settlers of what was initially called New Amsterdam. Created in 1624, the schout fiscal, or sheriff attorney, was imbued with the powers of both policeman and prosecutor and was charged with enforcing civil and military laws as well as the ordinances of the Dutch monarchy. In 1632 a new administration added penal functions to the schout's duties. In 1643 the "burgher guard," an early incarnation of the municipal police, was introduced.

As the town grew into a city over the next decade, the *ratel wacht** (rattle-watch*) a night patrol that summoned aid with rattles,* was introduced in 1653.

Within five years the rattle-watch had become an organized force of eight paid watchman (see NIGHT WATCH; WATCH AND WARD SYSTEM). In 1664 the Dutch turned the colony over to the British. The English initially used a combination of both Dutch and British police methods, primitive as they were. In 1693 a "bellman," the first uniformed police officer, replaced the nocturnal rattle-watch, and four year later the streets received the first street light. By the turn of the century, New York City mayor Isaac De Reimer created a constable's watch consisting of one constable and twelve watchmen. As the population grew to five thousand, the first police station, or watch house, was built at the corner of Broad and Wall streets in 1731.

Until the 1840s New York City policing remained fundamentally an amateur business of volunteer or poorly paid watchmen and constables.* Marshals and other functionaries complemented the law enforcement apparatus, but the only true professionals in criminal justice remained the criminals themselves. However, between 1790 and 1845 the city saw phenomenal growth, as the population grew from thirty-three thousand to four hundred thousand.

The old system of constables and nightwatchmen was soon overwhelmed by the problems accompanying the new economic and social order. Rioting, the growth of slums, and rising crime led to a growing sentiment for a police force on the London model, which called for a disciplined uniformed force with a rank hierarchy. Although many citizens feared a standing army, there were few sensible alternatives, and in the early 1840s a police bill was passed, coming to fruition in 1845 with the creation of a nine-hundred-man municipal police force under New York City's first chief of police, George W. Matsell.*

SOURCES: Augustine Costello, *Our Police Protectors*, 1885; James F. Richardson, *The New York Police*, 1970; Wilbur R. Miller, *Cops and Bobbies*, 1973.

NEW YORK METROPOLITAN POLICE.

NEW YORK METROPOLITAN POLICE. The New York Metropolitan Police Law in 1857 transferred control of the New York Police Department (NYPD)* to state officials. Members of the state legislature supported this action because of reluctance by Mayor Fernando Wood to suppress the city's vice problems and unwillingness to enforce the 1855 Prohibition law. When Wood's opponents won the governor's office and became the majority of the state legislature in 1856, the legislature created a special police district composed of the cities of New York, Brooklyn, and several adjacent cities. All current members of the local police forces automatically became members of the newly organized force, which was commanded by a police board consisting of five appointees by the governor and the mayors of New York and Brooklyn.

Wood defied the state officials by having the New York City Council adopt an ordinance creating a municipal police force, using the London Metropolitan Police* as its model. For a short time New York residents were confounded by the presence of two police forces. Tension escalated between the rival forces, culminating in a riot between the two in 1857, in which the metropolitans were routed by the municipals. When the state court of appeals ruled in favor of the new police law, Wood disbanded the municipal police and took his seat as a member of the metropolitan board. The metropolitan police were disbanded in 1870, and New York City police control was returned to the city.

SOURCES: James F. Richardson, *The New York Police*, 1970; Wilbur R. Miller, *Cops and Bobbies*, 1973.

NEW YORK'S FINEST. This phrase, referring to the New York City police, originated in the mid-1870s. According to one authority, it was used "ambiguously" by New Yorkers, who saw the force as either corrupt and ineffective or were proud to have protectors who were allowed more latitude and freedom than their London counterparts.

SOURCE: Wilbur R. Miller, *Cops and Bobbies*, 1973.

NEW YORK STATE POLICE. After reading *Justice to All* by Katherine Mayo,* which is slavishly devoted to the heroic exploits of the Pennsylvania State Police,* Theodore Roosevelt* sent a copy of the book to each member of the New York State Legislature, which was then contemplating a force on the Pennsylvania model. In 1917 the New York State Police force was established, with George Chandler, M.D., as its superintendent. Based on the Pennsylvania military constabulary model, the force was mostly responsible for traffic and crime control in the rural areas and small towns.

The New York legislature had considered a state police force in the years prior to 1917, in part because of the success of the neighboring Pennsylvania unit, as well as the inadequacy of New York's rural police. America's entrance into World War I apparently provided the impetus for the force. A large force of 232 men and officers, like its neighbor, it was commanded by a superintendent appointed by the governor. Unlike its neighbor, however, it developed a rapport with organized labor because it was not imbued with the powers to suppress riots in cities without the approval of the governor and was not used for strike breaking. In addition it had the power to arrest, without warrant, anyone violating state or federal laws throughout the state.

SOURCES: New York Division of State Police, *The New York State Police: The First Fifty Years: 1917–1967*, 1967; Thomas A. Reppetto, *The Blue Parade*, 1978; H. Kenneth Bechtel, *State Police in the United States*, 1995.

NIEDERHOFFER, ARTHUR. (1917–1981) Neiderhoffer was born in New York City and educated at Brooklyn College and Brooklyn Law School. With a dearth of opportunities for lawyers during the Depression, following his admission to the state bar in 1940 he joined the New York City Police Department (NYPD).* He was promoted to sergeant in 1951 and five years later to lieutenant. During his tenure with the force he was the recipient of four departmental awards for meritorious service. In the latter part of his twenty-one-year career with the force, Niederhoffer was a popular instructor and supervisor at the city's police-training academy.

Niederhoffer returned to college in 1956 and received a graduate degree in sociology and two year later coauthored his first book, *The Gang: A Study of Adolescent Behavior*. Retiring from the force in 1961, he was granted a Ph.D. in sociology two years later and began a second career in academia. After a series of teaching jobs he began a fourteen-year affiliation with the sociology department at John Jay College of Criminal Justice. As a former practitioner, he understood the pressures and realities of policing as well as anyone. In 1967 he published *Behind the Shield: The Police in Urban Society*, a sociological study of policing.

In 1968 Niederhoffer helped Mayor John Lindsay organize local residents into a community police corps to patrol Harlem. In 1971 he directed a two-year study of three hundred proposals submitted to the National Institute of Law Enforcement and Criminal Justice Technical Assistance in Criminal Justice through auspices of the Law Enforcement Assistance Administration (LEAA).* He continued to publish, teach, and consult on police matters until he died of lymphoma in 1981, following an eight-year battle with the disease.

SOURCE: Elaine Niederhoffer, "Arthur Niederhoffer," in *The Encyclopedia of Police Science*, ed. William G. Bailey, 1995.

NIGHT WATCH. With the absence of an efficient police force during the eighteenth century, European and American cities relied on the night watch for nocturnal protection. A medieval institution, watchmen were notoriously inept. Their main duties included watching out for crime, making regular announcements of the time and weather conditions, and spotting fires. Night watch duties varied somewhat from city to city, with southern watchmen expected to observe slaves and indentured servants on the streets after dark.

Boston established one of the earliest and most chronicled night watches as early as 1631. Peter Stuyvesant established the Burgher Guard in New Amsterdam in the 1650s, another early American incarnation of the night watch. By 1658, with the increased threats of Indian attacks, a rattle-watch* was inaugurated, consisting of a captain and eight men. The seventeenth-century night watch performed similar duties in both America and Europe.

SOURCES: William J. Bopp and Donald O. Scultz, *A Short History of American Law Enforcement*, 1972; Douglas Greenberg, *Crime and Law Enforcement in the Colony of New York, 1691–1776*, 1976.

NIX, EVETT DUMAS. (1861–1946) Born near Coldwater, Kentucky, he arrived in Guthrie, Oklahoma in 1889. Following a short business career he was appointed U.S. marshal in 1893. Among his deputies were a number of legendary western lawmen, including William Matthew "Bill" Tilghman, Jr.,* Chris Madsen,* Henry Andrew "Heck" Thomas,* Frank M. Canton (Joe Horner),* and James P. "Jim" Masterson.* Their main jurisdiction was the Oklahoma region. Nix claimed his force was responsible for sixty thousand arrests. While Nix participated in few gunfights himself, he supervised the capture of the Doolin gang and many others. Following his career as a lawman he went into the wholesale grocery business in Missouri.

SOURCES: Evett Dumas Nix, as told to Gordon Hines, *Oklahombres, Particularly the Wilder Ones*, 1929; Glenn Shirley, *Guardian of the Law: The Life and Times of William Matthew Tilghman*, 1988.

NKVD. With the abolition of the Soviet Cheka* in 1921, the State Political Administration (GPU) was created under the direction of the People's Commissariat of Internal Affairs (NKVD). By the 1930s the NKVD controlled all Soviet police forces for the next seven years. According to historian Robert Conquest, "the Soviet police forces reached their full development" under the NKVD.

Primarily charged with protecting order, state security, and public property, the NKVD also controlled numerous other agencies that functioned as state security forces, fire guards, border and internal guards, corrective labor camps, and many others. In 1941 the agency was divided into two Commissariats responsible for Internal Affairs (NKVD) and State Security (NKGB). With the outbreak of the Russo-German War, the NKVD was once again given complete control of both Commissariats. Following World War II, the NKVD became the Ministry of Internal Affairs (MVD*) and the NKGB became the Ministry of State Security (MGB).

SOURCES: Robert Conquest, *The Soviet Police System*, 1968; James Cramer, *The World's Police*, 1964.

NOBLE, JAMES MERVYN. (b. 1924) Noble was born near Belfast, Ireland, but his family immigrated to Toronto, Canada, when he was four. Following high school he joined the Royal Canadian Air Force (in 1944), but he missed serving in the war in Europe. Leaving the air force, in 1946, he joined the Toronto police department and soon rose to prominence as a detective. In 1961 he was transferred to the homicide squad and in 1969 became its chief. In 1973 he was promoted to the rank of inspector, making his home at the Metropolitan Toronto Police Department headquarters. Credited with solving over one hundred cases, Noble was later elevated to staff superintendent in charge of a police district covering one-forth of Toronto.

SOURCE: Bruce Henderson and Sam Summerlin, *The Super Sleuths*, 1976.

NOBLE, JORDAN B. (1800–1870s) Born in Georgia, Noble served as a drummer boy at the Battle of New Orleans in 1815, fought in the 1830s Seminole wars in Florida, and then fought in the Mexican-American War. Born a free man, he earned the rank of captain in the Seventh Louisiana Colored Infantry during the Civil War. According to one authority, he was "the most distinguished of the black policemen with Civil War service" on the New Orleans police force.

SOURCE: Dennis C. Rousey, *Policing the Southern City*, 1996.

NOOTBAAR, MAX. Born in Germany and educated at Heidelberg University, Nootbaar served in the German Army and then the U.S. Cavalry before joining the Chicago Police Department (CPD)* in 1896. During his early years on the force, he was credited with attempting to clean up the Levee vice district. Nootbaar rose through the ranks, thanks in part to his relationship with superintendent Francis O'Neill.* In 1910 Nootbaar was placed in charge of the training division. While most police officers were criticized for their behavior during the 1919 Chicago race riots, Nootbaar was credited with attempting to quell the violence diplomatically. His career was cut short when injuries suffered in a car wreck forced him to retire in 1922.

SOURCES: Thomas A. Reppetto, *The Blue Parade*, 1978; Raphael W. Marrow and Harriet I. Carter, *In Pursuit of Crime*, 1996.

NORFLEET, J. FRANK (1864–c. 1961) Stopping at a Dallas hotel in 1919, Texas cattleman Frank Norfleet was swindled by confidence men. Norfleet had fallen for a classic scam in which he found a wallet that had been planted so he would find it, returned it to the owner, and then refused a $100 reward. Posing as a wealthy investor, the owner of the wallet said he would invest the money for him. The next day he gave Norfleet $3,000, telling him that the investment had paid off handsomely. Norfleet told him to keep it and give him an update the following day. The following day he was told the investment was worth $200,000, but in a variation of the "big store" racket, Norfleet would have to put up collateral as a security deposit to get his money. He ended up emptying his bank account of $45,000 as security. The "investors" then quickly disappeared with the money.

When Norfleet was unsatisfied with the response from the Dallas, Texas, Police Department and various professional detective services, he vowed to hunt down the men on his own. During a forty-thousand-mile, four-year, international search, he captured every one of the swindlers. Thrilled by the hunt, Norfleet gave up ranching to become one of the preeminent bounty hunters of his time.

SOURCE: Carl Sifakis, *Encyclopedia of American Crime*, 1982.

NORTON, JOHN. (d. 1950) Formerly a private detective for the Northwestern Railroad, Norton joined the Chicago Police Department (CPD)* in 1891. He was assigned to the detective bureau, and during the next forty-six years he never walked a beat. Among the most prominent homicide investigations in which he participated were the murders of "Big Jim" Colosimo, Eleanor Ellis, Maybelle Exley, and Rudolph Wolf. In 1928 he was appointed head of the homicide squad, and two years later "Old Sandy" was promoted to chief of detectives. In 1934 Norton was assigned to the Maxwell Street District, where he was charged with breaking up the Forty-Two gang. During his long career he survived five gunshot wounds before retiring in 1937.

SOURCE: Raphael W. Marrow and Harriet I. Carter, *In Pursuit of Crime*, 1996.

NOTT-BOWER, JOHN REGINALD HORNBY. (1892–1972) The son of the City of London Police* commissioner William Nott-Bower during the era of the Sidney Street Siege,* Nott-Bower served twenty years in India with the Indian Police Service and twenty with the London Metropolitan Police,* beginning in 1933. When he succeeded Harold Scott as Criminal Investigation Department (CID)* commissioner, he became what one critic described as one of the "least memorable" of the nineteen commissioners to hold office. In 1958 he was replaced by his deputy, Joseph Simpson.

SOURCE: Paul Begg and Keith Skinner, *The Scotland Yard Files*, 1992.

OBSERVATIONS ON THE OFFICE OF CONSTABLE. Published in 1754 and written by Saunders Welch,* the high constable of Holburn, this early pamphlet on law enforcement offers recommendations for the appropriate conduct of constables* as well as suggestions for performance of their duties. His instructions have been considered a harbinger and precursor of the police bill of Sir Robert Peel.*

SOURCE: Patrick Pringle, *Hue and Cry*, 1955.

OBSERVATIONS ON THE PRACTICE OF A JUSTICE OF THE PEACE. Written by Thomas De Veil,* the first Bow Street police magistrate in 1747, this early book discusses, rather superficially, the collection of fees and fines and the role of magistrates in the fledgling criminal justice system.

SOURCE: Patrick Pringle, *Hue and Cry*, 1955.

O'CONNOR'S GUNNERS. In 1927, at the height of the Chicago gang wars of the 1920s, chief of detectives William O'Connor publicly announced the creation of an armored car force of police armed with machine guns. More a publicity ploy than a genuine law enforcement strategy, O'Connor reportedly recruited men who had seen service in World War I and were familiar with the operation of automatic weapons. In the end O'Connor's gunners were as inefficient as the rest of the Chicago Police Department (CPD)* in stopping the Prohibition-related carnage.

SOURCE: Carl Sifakis, *The Encyclopedia of American Crime*, 1982.

O'FARRELL, VALERIAN. (1876–1934) Following college O'Farrell began a twelve-year stint with the New York City Police Department (NYPD)* in 1900. Subsequently he left the force and opened his own detective agency, primarily serving as a sleuth for wealthy clients ranging from Arnold Rothstein and Charles Becker* to the Vanderbilts and Broadway actors. In the 1930s, he was mentioned as a possible replacement for John Edgar Hoover* as head of the Bureau of Investigation. Part of the rationale for this consideration was that O'Farrell was an experienced policeman and Hoover as the nation's "top cop" had never made an arrest. In reality, however, O'Farrell was so mediocre at solving crimes that when employed by a newspaper to examine major New York City crimes, his deduction was so faulty that a ghost writer was hired to offer better insight into the investigations.

SOURCES: Thomas A. Reppetto, *The Blue Parade*, 1978; *New York Times*, October 8, 1934; " 'Profile' of the J. E. Hoover," *New Yorker*, November 2, 1937.

OLD, WILLIAM A. (c. 1874–1914) Old was born in Uvalde, Texas, soon after the death of his father at the battle of Adobe Walls in the Texas panhandle. According to some accounts, he served briefly in the Texas Rangers* before joining the Arizona Rangers* in 1904. In 1904 he participated in the arrest of noted rustler Antonio Nunez, who while taken alive, had previously vowed to die fighting. By 1905 Old had been promoted to sergeant.

While stationed in Wheeler in 1909, Lieutenant Old took command of the Rangers during the absence of Captain Harry C. Wheeler.* He served in the force rising to the rank of lieutenant, until it was disbanded in 1910. He was best remembered for his predilection for bringing his prey in alive. Old's last years are obscured in mystery. Some accounts have him going down to Mexico to track down the killers of his friend Jefferson P. "Jeff" Kidder,* and others suggest that his wife killed him during a domestic argument in 1914.

SOURCES: Joseph Miller, ed., *The Arizona Rangers*, 1972; Bill O'Neal, *The Arizona Rangers*, 1987.

OLD CHARLIES. This is a pejorative nickname for New York City watch men (see NIGHT WATCH; WATCH AND WARD SYSTEM) in the 1830s. See also LEATHERHEADS; CHARLEYS.

SOURCE: Augustine Costello, *Our Police Protectors*, 1885; reprint, 1972.

OLDFIELD, GEORGE. (1924–1985) Oldfield left the British Royal Navy for a law enforcement career in 1947. While assigned to the Criminal Investigative Division (CID)* he was instrumental in solving several highly publicized crimes and in 1976 was promoted to assistant chief constable (see CONSTABLES). During the late 1970s, his mishandling of the hunt for the Yorkshire Ripper serial killer tarnished his career. He was roundly criticized for his microman-agement of the investigation, and when it became public knowledge that the actual perpetrator had been interviewed and released six times, the media had a field day. Oldfield was transferred to another position for health reasons shortly before the capture of the perpetrator, Peter Sutcliffe, in 1981.

SOURCE: Charles Phillips and Alan Axelrod, *CCC*, 1996.

OLINGER, ROBERT AMERIDTH. (c. 1841–1881) Born in Ohio, Olinger moved to the Oklahoma territory in his youth. He entered law enforcement as marshal of Seven Rivers in Lincoln County, New Mexico, in 1876 but was dismissed soon after for suspected ties to local criminals. In 1878 he fought in the Lincoln County War and was suspected of several killings. Olinger returned to policing in 1881 when he was appointed deputy U.S. marshal (see U.S. MAR-SHALS SERVICE).

Olinger was not well liked in New Mexico, and although he apparently liked to be called "Pecos Bob," most people considered him a bully and a loudmouth. On April 28, 1881, Olinger, along with Lincoln County Deputy J. W. Bell,* was assigned by Sheriff* Patrick Floyd Jarvis "Pat" Garrett* to guard William "Billy the Kid" Bonney at the Lincoln jail while he awaited his date with the hangman. However, the Kid escaped from custody, killing both Olinger and Bell in the process. Olinger was reportedly felled with a shotgun blast from the second floor of the jail overlooking the street. He was apparently responding to gunfire when Billy appeared from above and snarled "Hello Bob," before killing him. Following his murder, Olinger's mother reportedly commented, "Bob was a murderer from the cradle and if there is a hell, I know he is in it" (Bullis).

SOURCES: William A. Keleher, *Violence in Lincoln County*, 1957; Don Bullis, *New Mexico's Finest: Peace Officers Killed in the Line of Duty, 1847–1996*, 1996.

O'MEARA, STEPHEN J. (1854–1918) Born in Charlottetown, Prince Edward Island, Canada, O'Meara immigrated to America with his family when he was ten. Eight years later he entered journalism with the *Boston Globe*, rising to editor in chief and then publisher, in 1896. In 1906 he was selected as the first commissioner of the Boston Police Department. An advocate for professional-ism, he worked hard to separate politics from policing and improve policing standards. He supported his patrolmen in their pursuit of better pay and would probably have been able to settle the labor dispute that led to the Boston Police strike of 1919* were it not for his death the previous year. He was succeeded by Edwin Upton Curtis,* who is blamed for much of the acrimony of 1919.

SOURCE: Leonard Vance Harrison, *Police and Administration in Boston*, 1934.

O'NEILL, FRANCIS. (1849–1936) Born in Ireland and educated at Bantry, Ireland, O'Neill went to sea as a cabin boy in 1865 and eventually debarked at the port of San Francisco. He arrived in Chicago in 1867 and joined the Chicago Police Department (CPD)* force in 1873. That same year he was shot in the chest while apprehending a burglar.

O'Neill eventually became the chief of police in 1901. His tenure as chief was marked by conflict with reformers who noted that Chicago had one of the worst arrest records of any large city. However, O'Neill was quick to respond that this was due to the numerical inadequacy of a 2,300-man force (with only 500 men on duty at any one time) expected to patrol a city of 2 million people. In 1904 the department adopted fingerprinting* to supplement the Bertillon system.* O'Neill resigned from the force in 1905, but not before appointing the first African-American officer to a supervisory position on the force. During his retirement he became an authority on Irish folk music and wrote several books on the topic.

SOURCES: John J. Flinn, *History of the Chicago Police*, 1887; revised, 1973; Raphael W. Marrow and Harriet I. Carter, *In Pursuit of Crime*, 1996.

O'NEILL, WILLIAM OWEN "BUCKEY." (1860–1898) O'Neill, the son of Irish immigrants, was probably born in St. Louis, Missouri, although some accounts cite his birthplace as Ireland. He worked as a printer's apprentice prior to relocating to Phoenix, Arizona Territory, in 1879 and first entered law enforcement as a part-time special deputy. An habitué of Phoenix's gambling halls and saloons, it was during this time that he received the sobriquet "Buckey," referring to his predilection for beating the odds at the faro tables, or "bucking the tiger."

O'Neill worked as a typesetter for the *Phoenix Herald* during his first year before leaving for various mining towns, including Tombstone. In 1883 he worked as editor for the *Arizona Miner* and served in the local militia. Five years later he was elected sheriff* of Yavapai County, where he came to prominence when he led a posse on a successful six-hundred-mile pursuit of four train robbers. He also won acclaim for his relief work following the Walnut Creek Dam disaster, which saw numerous mining camps wiped out.

During the last decade of his short life he ran unsuccessfully for Congress as a Populist, struck it rich mining, served as adjutant general of the Arizona Territory, and was elected sheriff of Yavapai County, Arizona. In 1898 he captained the Arizona contingent in the legendary Rough Riders of Theodore Roosevelt* during the Spanish-American War. He was killed instantly by sniper's fire near Kettle Hill and buried on the spot in Cuba. The following year he was reburied at Arlington Cemetery.

SOURCES: Dale L. Walker, *Death Was the Black Horse: The Story of Rough Rider Buckey O'Neill*, 1975; Dale L. Walker, "Buckey O'Neill," *ANB*, Vol. 16, 1999; Charles Herner, *The Arizona Rough Riders*, 1970.

ONE POLICE PLAZA. The headquarters since the 1970s of the New York City Police Department (NYPD),* One Police Plaza can best be described as a rather bland, red brick, high-rise structure. The ultramodern headquarters is located closer to city hall and other municipal offices than its predecessors, which were at 250 Centre Street and the Mulberry Street locations.

SOURCE: H. Paul Jeffers, *Commissioner Roosevelt*, 1994.

ONION FIELD, THE. On March 9, 1963, Los Angeles Police Department (LAPD) Hollywood Division officers Ian Campbell and Karl Hettinger were working in a plainclothes squad felony car when they stopped Jimmy Smith and Gregory Powell for a minor traffic violation. Subsequently, the two officers were captured and forced to surrender their weapons. Handcuffed and kidnapped, the two lawmen were driven ninety-five miles away to onion fields thirty miles south of Bakersfield, where Powell murdered Campbell and Hettinger managed to escape. Powell and Smith were sentenced to death twice but were saved by the 1972 Furman decision and sentenced to life in prison. Hettinger's life went into free fall following the case. He was arrested for shoplifting and subsequently resigned from the force. Hettinger later found employment as a greenhouse manager and in 1977 was selected as an aide to Kern County Supervisor Harvey. This notorious crime was chronicled in the best-selling book by Joseph Aloysious Wambaugh Jr., *The Onion Field*, and then in a popular motion picture of the same name starring Ted Danson, John Savage, and James Woods.

SOURCES: Arthur Sjoquist (historical text by), *Los Angeles Police Department Commemorative Book, 1869–1984*, 1984; John M. Reilly, ed., *Twentieth-Century Crime and Mystery Writers*, 1985.

OPRICHNINA. Established by Czar Ivan the Terrible in the 1560s, this political police force was used as a tool of terror by the Russian czars and is considered a precursor to Soviet police forces such as the Cheka.*

SOURCE: Richard J. Terrill, *World Criminal Justice Systems: A Survey*, 1992.

ORDO SYSTEM. Following the Roman invasion of Britain, a system of policing based on Roman antecedents was established in British towns. Primitive in design, it was composed of an ex-magistrate who was assisted by members of the local elite. Eventually the Ordo system was replaced by Roman soldiers who had completed their terms of duty.

SOURCE: James Cramer, *The World's Police*, 1964.

ORWELL, GEORGE [ERIC ARTHUR BLAIR]. (1903–1950) Born Eric Blair in Motihari, India, Orwell attended Eton College in England before joining the Indian Imperial Police in Burma in 1922. The future author of *Animal Farm* and *1984* chronicled the British colonial police system in his 1934 novel *Burmese Days*, a scathing indictment of the treatment of colonial subjects by British officials. His tenure on the police force no doubt inspired some of his characterizations of the Thought Police as well as the terrorist tactics of state political police in his influential novel *1984*, which was published in 1948.

SOURCE: *DNB*, 1941–1950 supplement.

OUR POLICE PROTECTORS. Written in 1885 by Augustine Costello,* *Our Police Protectors* is a detailed history of the New York City police from the Dutch era until 1885. Although this chronicle often leans toward the hagiographic, it does contain a splendid account of police practices and problems of this earlier era. The most glaring deficiency of the book is the inability of the author to place policing within any type of social or political context.

SOURCE: Augustine E. Costello, *Our Police Protectors*, 1885; reprint, with introduction by Theodore N. Ferdinand, 1972.

OUTLAW, BASS. (c. 1865–1894) After killing a man in his native Georgia, Outlaw relocated to Texas. He joined the Texas Rangers* in 1885, serving stints in both Company E and D. Cultivated and apparently educated, he demonstrated refined manners when sober; however, the enigmatic Outlaw became a menacing figure when drunk, a fact that would lead to his dismissal from the Rangers just two years later. He later won appointment as a U.S. deputy marshal, (see U.S. MARSHALS SERVICE) and was involved in numerous deadly skirmishes. In 1894 he was mortally wounded by constable John Henry Selman* during a brawl in an El Paso, Texas, brothel in which Outlaw shot and killed Texas ranger Joe McKidrict.

SOURCES: Leon Metz, *John Selman: Texas Gunfighter*, 1966; Dan L. Thrapp, ed., *EFB*, Vol. 3, 1988.

OWENS, COMMODORE PERRY. (1852–1919) Born in Tennessee, Owens was named after naval hero Commodore Oliver Perry. He farmed in Indiana before reaching Texas in the 1870s and working as a cowboy. Over the next decade he would earn a reputation as a gunman as he moved to New Mexico and then Arizona. He began his law enforcement career as deputy sheriff of Apache County in 1886.

Soon after being elected sheriff* he was involved in one of the West's classic gunfights. On September 4, 1887, Owens rode up to a home in Holbrook, Arizona, looking for a suspected killer. He found the recalcitrant gunman and three associates, and in the ensuing confrontation, Owens shot all four. Only one survived. The flamboyant Owens made a memorable first impression with his long hair, a pair of .45s on his hips, and a rifle in hand. In 1895 he became the first sheriff of Navajo County, Arizona, for one year, and during the remainder of his life he served as a detective for the Santa Fe Railroad and an express messenger for the Wells Fargo Detective Bureau.*

SOURCES: Bill O'Neal, *Encyclopedia of Western Gunfighters*, 1979; Glenn G. Boyer, "Commodore Perry Owens Revisited," *Real West*, October 1982.

OWENS, MARIE. The widow of a Chicago Police Department (CPD)* officer, in 1893 Marie Owens became the first woman hired directly as a police officer (see POLICEWOMEN). Over the next thirty years Owens, who is generally acknowledged as the "first woman with full arrest powers conferred by a municipal law enforcement agency" (Schulz), visited courts and aided detectives in cases involving women and children. Officially listed as a "patrolman" in the Chicago police record books, when Owens retired in 1923 she was awarded a pension. Although Anne Loucks received much fanfare when she became Chicago's first civil service policewoman in 1913, Owens preceded her by twenty years, even though she was not formally designated as a policewoman.

SOURCES: Dorothy Moses Schulz, *From Social Worker to Crimefighter*, 1995; Kerry Segrave, *Policewomen: A History*, 1995.

P

PALMER, WILLIAM. Palmer joined the London Metropolitan Police* in 1847 and twenty-one years later had reached the rank of inspector. Palmer played an instrumental role in the detective department between 1869 and 1876. In 1870 he was promoted to chief inspector, and for the next seven years he was considered one of the right hand men of Superintendent Adolphus Frederick Williamson.* Palmer's career was destroyed when, along with Inspectors John Meiklejohn, and Nathaniel Druscovitch,* he was found guilty of accepting bribes from a gang of criminals in 1876 and sentenced to prison and hard labor for two years. This incident is remembered as one of the darkest days of Scotland Yard* and is referred to by several names including the De Goncourt case, the Turf Fraud scandal, the Montgomery scandal, and the Great Scotland Yard scandal. Following his release from prison, Palmer opened a pub.

SOURCES: Paul Begg and Keith Skinner, *The Scotland Yard Files*, 1992; Belton Cobb, *Critical Years at the Yard*, 1956.

PALMER RAIDS. A product of anti-Bolshevik hysteria, the Palmer Raids were initiated by U.S. Attorney General A. Mitchell Palmer in 1920. An adversary of organized labor, Palmer was the target of an unsuccessful bombing attempt in 1919, following which he swore vengeance on Bolshevik supporters. With his eyes set on higher office and with popular support from American citizens, Palmer used the Sedition Act to authorize the arrest of more than four thousand people on January 1, 1920. Hundreds of government agents rounded up individuals and held them in jail for a week without even charging them, in a flagrant violation of constitutional protections.

Palmer's popularity was short-lived and his actions were soon challenged by litigation and some members of the Woodrow Wilson administration for the erratic nature of the arrests. Although the individuals who were arrested were subjected to the threat of deportation, most were released for lack of evidence. When Palmer's predictions of a Bolshevik Mayday uprising failed to manifest themselves, he lost support. In the end Palmer was instrumental in the deportation of hundreds of suspected Bolsheviks, including noted anarchists Emma Goldman and Alexander Berkman.

SOURCES: George C. Kohn, *Encyclopedia of American Scandal*, 1989; Carl Sifakis, *The Encyclopedia of American Crime*, 1982.

PAPICH, SAMUEL J. "SAM." (c. 1919) Born and raised in Montana, Papich received an engineering degree from Northwestern University in 1936 and then attended law school. He joined the Federal Bureau of Investigation (FBI)* in 1941 and was assigned to the Special Intelligence Service unit, which handled counterespionage during World War II, Papich collaborated with the German double-agent Dusko Popov, who was credited with informing the FBI about the Nazi microdot communication system. After the attack on Pearl Harbor, Papich worked as an undercover agent in South America and was later selected as the FBI's legal attaché in Rio de Janeiro. In 1947 he was reassigned by his request to the San Francisco, California, field office.

During the 1950s John Edgar Hoover* appointed Papich as the liaison between the FBI and the Central Intelligence Agency (CIA), a position he would hold until his retirement in 1970. Papich handled several controversial cases that embroiled both agencies during the Cold War era. One of the most notable involved the authenticity of two communist defectors. One of the defectors, named Yuri Nosenko, claimed that Kennedy assassin Lee Harvey Oswald had no links to the KGB.* The other defector, Anatoliy Golitsyn, claimed that Nosenko was offering disinformation-intelligence to cast doubts on KGB links to the presidential assassination. While the FBI believed Golitsyn to be the actual disinformation source, the CIA gave him validation and saw Nonsenko as the disinformation-carrying agent. In 1970 relations between the two intelligence agencies had deteriorated to such a point the liaison position was discarded and Papich retired.

SOURCE: Athan G. Theoharis, ed., *The FBI*, 1999.

PARKER, ANDREW D. Parker was appointed New York City police commissioner in 1895 along with Theodore Roosevelt* and Colonel Frederick Dent Grant, the eldest son of the former president. Prior to taking this position Parker had practiced law and served as assistant district attorney. A Democrat, Parker was considered loyal to Tammany Hall, and usually at odds with the Republican Roosevelt. He was credited with transferring the bellicose Max Schmittberger* to the Jewish ghetto, where he made the transition from bribe collector to honest cop. Despite Parker's prominence in the 1890s, no mention is found of him after

1897. According to Roosevelt biographer Edmund Morris, he disappeared "from history as he entered it, a handsome, smiling, enigma."

SOURCES: Edmund Morris, *The Rise of Theodore Roosevelt*, 1979; H. Paul Jeffers, *Commissioner Roosevelt*, 1994.

PARKER, ELLIS. (1873–1940) Parker won renown as the so-called cornfield Sherlock Holmes* during a forty-year career as a New Jersey detective. A Burlington County detective since 1893, Parker claimed to have successfully investigated twenty thousand crimes and was a strong opponent of state policing. Shortly before the execution of Bruno Hauptmann for the death of Lindbergh's child, Parker muddled the situation by introducing evidence that he claimed proved that a New York mental patient was the real killer. Parker's detectives seized the suspect in New York and forcibly took him to New Jersey. He was subsequently indicted for kidnapping and convicted under the federal Lindbergh Law in 1937, earning him a stint in a federal penitentiary, where he died in 1940. The Lindbergh kidnapping turned out to be Parker's last case.

SOURCES: Thomas A. Reppetto, *The Blue Parade*, 1978; Fletcher Pratt, *The Cunning Mulatto and Other Cases of Ellis Parker, American Detective*, 1930.

PARKER, ISAAC CHARLES. (1838–1896) Born and educated in Ohio, Parker opened a law practice in St. Joseph, Missouri, in 1859. In between stints as an attorney he served briefly in a Missouri regiment during the Civil War. Following a term in Congress from 1871 to 1875, he was appointed judge of the U.S. district court for western Arkansas beginning in 1875 and ending with his death twenty-one years later.

Parker was an austere Methodist and an advocate of Indian rights, and his jurisdiction included the Indian Territory (later Oklahoma) and nine counties in the Fort Smith area, comprising a region of 74,000 square miles. One of his first acts upon taking office was appointing two hundred deputy marshals, sixty-five of whom would be killed in the line of duty. Between May 10, 1875, and September 1, 1896, he tried 13,490 cases and won more than 8,500 convictions. More than 85 percent of the cases dealt with cases in the Indian Territory. Until 1889 there was no appeal from a Parker decision. However, that year the U.S. Supreme Court began allowing appeals from the Indian Territory, and in 1895 alone it overturned thirty out of forty-six cases it reviewed.

Although Parker was known as the "Hanging Judge," during his two decades in office, of the 172 individuals sentenced to death, only 88 met their fates on the gallows. Parker created a gallows that could accommodate six criminals at a time and introduced each death sentence with the words: "I do not desire to hang you men. It is the law" (Burton). After watching each execution, he put his head down and cried. Congress withdrew the Indian Territory from Parker's authority in 1895, but he died before the jurisdictional change was officially implemented. Notified of his death, the Fort Smith jail erupted in a cacophony of applause. The 1898 Harman biography, *Hell on the Border*, has contributed to Parker's undeserved reputation as a bloodthirsty executioner.

SOURCES: Art Burton, *Black, Red, and Deadly: Black and Indian Gunfighters of the Indian Territories*, 1991; S. W. Harman, *Hell on the Border*, 1898.

PARKER, WILLIAM HENRY. (1902–1966) Born in Lead, South Dakota, Parker came from a distinguished family that included his grandfather, who served as a frontier lawman, and his father, who was superintendent of the largest gold mine in America. Parker moved to California in the 1920s and joined the Los Angeles Police Department (LAPD)* in 1927. At night he studied law, earning his degree three years later. His rise through the ranks was rather meteoric before leaving to fight in World War II. Parker distinguished himself in the war, earning a Purple Heart during the Normandy invasion. Following the war, Parker helped organize new police systems in Munich and Frankfurt, Germany. Returning to Los Angeles he rejoined the LAPD and in 1950 was appointed police chief, a position he would hold for the next sixteen years.

As police chief, Parker implemented higher standards for police officers and encouraged his recruits to pursue additional academic training. An advocate of professionalism, Parker introduced the internal affairs division; coauthored the board of rights procedure, which guaranteed the separation of police discipline from municipal politics; and founded the bureau of administration.

The radio and, then, television show *Dragnet** promoted Parker and the LAPD, which became a nationally recognized police department by the 1950s. The 1952 Kefauver Crime Investigation commended Parker's department for its crime-fighting prowess. The 1957 release of *Parker on Police*, edited by Orlando Winfield "O. W." Wilson,* did much to enhance Parker's impact on the professionalization of American policing.

Parker's tenure as police chief was tarnished by racial conflict in Los Angeles. Viewed by many as a reactionary, Parker regarded the growing liberal shift in the 1960s with suspicion as well. In 1962 Parker was accused of racial bigotry and discrimination by a group of Los Angeles religious leaders and in 1965 the Watts Riots erupted. By the time the national guard had restored order, thirty-six people were dead, nine hundred injured, and four thousand arrested. The accusations of the religious leaders seemed to have been borne out following the riots, when Parker tried to explain the behavior of the mobs during the riots, commenting "One person threw a rock and then, like monkeys in a zoo, others started throwing rocks" (Domanick). Despite a public outcry for his resignation Parker refused to step down. However, soon after he took a leave of absence for health reasons and went for heart surgery at the Mayo Clinic. On July 16, 1996, he collapsed at a testimonial dinner in his honor and died of heart failure on the way to the hospital.

SOURCES: O. W. Wilson, ed., *Parker on Police*, 1957; Joe Domanick, *To Protect and Serve*, 1994.

PARKHURST, CHARLES. (1842–1933) Born in Massachusetts and educated at Amherst College, Parkhurst rose to prominence in the 1890s as an advocate for police reform in New York City. Parkhurst had led a congregation in New England for many years before opening a pastorate at the Madison Square Square Presbyterian Church in 1880. For his first twelve years he rarely mentioned vice or police corruption in his sermons, but in 1892 he informed a reporter for the New York *World* that he would be delivering a sermon worth remembering. Parkhurst proceeded to about vice and police corruption, citing details that could not be substantiated. Unwilling to give in, the ever-resolute Parkhurst then hired a private detective to accompany him on a survey of the city's vice-ridden neighborhoods. Having accumulated the evidence he needed to demonstrate what a den of iniquity the city had become, the minister delivered a blistering sermon, mentioning specific names and places where vice was currently flourishing.

Although many saw Parkhurst as a religious zealot and a publicity hound, his revelations spurred the municipal government to investigate the police and create the commission headed by Clarence Lexow.* Parkurst's crusade resulted in a wave of reform and the resignation, dismissal, and indictment of numerous police officers. Tammany Hall forces returned to power five years later, but the minister continued his campaign unabated and is credited with being instrumental in the removal of police chief William Devery* from office. Parkhurst retired from the pulpit in 1918 but was honored twelve years later during an assemblage of modern reformers. In 1933 the minister died when he sleepwalked out of his second-story window.

SOURCES: Thomas A. Reppetto, *The Blue Parade*, 1978; H. Paul Jeffers, *Commissioner Roosevelt*, 1994; Carl Sifakis *The Encyclopedia of American Crime*, 1982.

PATTERROLLERS. During the seventeenth century, most American colonies created laws regulating the conduct of slaves. Extreme penalties and punishments for misbehavior were enforced by slave patrols,* whose members were known as patterrollers. According to one authority these patrols should be considered America's first distinctive police system. Since most slaves lived on plantations, the patterrollers were mostly a rural phenomenon.

SOURCE: W. Marvin Dulaney, *Black Police in America*, 1996.

PAUL, ROBERT HAVLIN "BOB." (1830–1901) Born in Lowell, Massachusetts, Paul got his first taste of adventure before reaching his teens when he went to sea as a cabin boy on a whaling ship. Following a string of adventures in various foreign ports he landed in the gold rush port of San Francisco in 1849. Over the next few years he worked in the mine fields before entering law enforcement in 1854, winning election as constable (see CONSTABLES), and soon after was appointed deputy sheriff in Calaveras County.

Paul forged a reputation as a frontier peace officer beginning with his apprehension of the Rancheria killers in 1855 and the tracking down of the Tom Bell gang the following year. In 1857 he was appointed undersheriff of Calaveras County and two years later was elected sheriff,* a position he would hold until his defeat in 1863. After losing the sheriff's race once more in 1871, he joined the Wells Fargo Detective Bureau* as a shotgun messenger in 1874. In 1878 he relocated to Pima County, Arizona, continuing to serve Wells Fargo as guard and detective. In 1880 he won the first of several consecutive races for sheriff of Pima County. His last days in law enforcement were spent as a detective for the Southern Pacific railroad and as U.S. marshal (see U.S. MARSHALS SERVICE) for the Arizona Territory beginning in 1891.

SOURCES: William B. Secrest, *Lawmen and Desperadoes*, 1994; Jay Robert Nash, *EWLO*, 1994.

PEAK, JUNIUS "JUNE." (1845–1934) Born in Warsaw, Kentucky, Peak moved with his family to Dallas County, Texas, in 1855. Following service in the Civil War he served as a deputy sheriff in Dallas and then as city marshal from 1874 to 1878. In the late 1870s he was commissioned as a lieutenant in a special detachment of Company B of the Texas Rangers* during the manhunt for Sam Bass. He left the Rangers and law enforcement in 1880 and spent his remaining years working for the Mexican Central Railroad, cattle ranching, and as a Dallas merchant.

SOURCES: Robert Stephens, *Texas Ranger Sketches*, 1972; "Captain June Peak," *Frontier Times* 11, August 1927; 12, September 1927.

PEARCE, NICHOLAS. (b. 1800) Born in St. Anthony, Cornwall, England, Pearce joined the London Metropolitan Police,* serving in the Whitechapel area of London. He was promoted to inspector by 1840 and was charged with investigating serious murder cases out of the A Division of Scotland Yard.* Among his most high-profile cases was the murder of Lord John Russell in 1840. Pearce led the investigation that resulted in the apprehension and conviction of Russell's valet, François Courvoisier. The subsequent execution of the culprit was witnessed by Charles Dickens* and William Makepeace Thackeray. This murder case, along with several other prominent cases, eventually resulted in the formation of the Scotland Yard detective branch.

Pearce also played an instrumental role in the 1842 Daniel Good case, which some sources describe as the "single most influential incident leading to the formal creation of the Detective" force. On August 15, 1842, the Detective Branch was established. Forty years later it would become known as the Criminal Investigation Department (CID).* Pearce stayed with the "Detective" until 1844, when he was promoted to superintendent of F Division.

SOURCE: Paul Begg and Keith Skinner, *The Scotland Yard Files*, 1992.

PEEL, SIR ROBERT. (1788–1850) Born into a wealthy manufacturing family, Peel served in Parliament in 1809 and then as chief secretary for Ireland from 1812 to 1818. While serving as home secretary in the 1820s, Peel championed the reform of the English judicial system. However, Peel is best remembered in the criminal justice realm for the police reforms that culminated in Parliament's passage of the Metropolitan Police Act of 1829.* Although Peel has received most of the credit for developing modern policing, some scholars subscribe to the notion that he deserves credit mainly for introducing the bill that inaugurated the London police experiment and his selection of Sir Charles Rowan* and Sir Richard Mayne,* who actually organized and planned the new police force.

Having established the principles upon which most modern police forces operate in the Western world, Peel created a police force along military lines. The Metropolitan Police were better trained and disciplined than any previous police organization and were expected to maintain a good rapport with their constituents. Prior to Peel, peacekeeping was based on responding to crimes after they had been committed. The new force introduced preventive policing to the streets of London, as uniformed officers patrolled streets rather than lounging around the police station waiting for a crime to be committed. Each constable patrolled a "beat" and became familiar with his turf. Blue police uniforms* set them apart in contrast to the military scarlet warn by the more bellicose militiamen and soldiers.

Initially, the police force was headquartered at 4 Whitehall Place, with a back door facing Scotland Yard.* Due to the fact that most officers used this entranceway, the building shortly became known as Scotland Yard. The new police force was so identified with Peel that its members were often referred to as Bobbies or Peelers.* Although Peel's police force was often embroiled in controversy during its early years it was rapidly accepted in London as crime levels began to drop and relations improved between the public and peace keepers. Peel continued his career in public service and was elected prime minister three times. He died in a horseback-riding accident on July 2, 1850.

SOURCES: Charles Reith, *The Blind Eye of History*, 1952; Philip John Stead, *The Police of Britain*, 1985; Anthony Babington, *A House in Bow Street*, 1969.

PEELERS. The term "Peelers" was an early popular reference to the London Metropolitan Police* of Sir Robert Peel.* A more common designation for the London peace officers is "Bobbies."

SOURCE: Jay Robert Nash, *Dictionary of Crime*, 1989.

PEIST, WILLIAM. (b. 1948) Formerly a prize-winning chef and graduate of the Waldorf-Astoria cooking program, Peist joined the New York City Police Department (NYPD)* in 1974, but was soon laid off during the city's financial fiasco. He was welcomed back to the force five years later after apprehending two arsonists while out on the town. Upon his return he worked as an informant for the bureau of internal affairs. While off duty he was in a car accident that resulted in the loss of a leg. When his pension compensation claim was rejected by the department, he turned on the force and began passing information to organized crime figures.

Together with his cousin Peter Mavis, who owed gambling debts to the mob, from 1990 to 1992 he supplied Gambino crime boss John Gotti with inside information that allowed him to escape conviction so many times that he became known as the "Teflon Don." Federal Bureau of Investigation (FBI)* wiretaps on Gotti revealed the existence of a turncoat on the force. Peist was eventually arrested and convicted of racketeering and obstruction of justice.

SOURCE: Charles Phillips and Alan Axelrod, *CCC*, 1996.

PELLICANO, ANTHONY. (b 1944) Born in Chicago, Pellicano worked as a debt collector before finding his bailiwick as a private investigator. Specializing in acoustics analysis, Anthony Joseph Pellicano Investigative Consultants forged a reputation as experts in this forensics field while parrying criticism that the agency utilized intimidation and illegal practices. Pellicano's agency received widespread publicity while collaborating with the Warren Commission investigation into the John F. Kennedy assassination. Pellicano's analysis of recorded sounds from the motorcade concluded that additional gunshot noises were actually motor vehicle backfires.

Pellicano rose to prominence in 1983 when his testimony helped John De-Lorean gain an acquittal following a taped sting operation. Ten years later he was hired by pop star Michael Jackson, who claimed that he had been accused of sexual molestation as an extortion attempt. However, the detective withdrew from Jackson's case later that year.

SOURCE: Charles Phillips and Alan Axelrod, *CCC*, 1996.

PENNSYLVANIA STATE POLICE. The state of Pennsylvania had been beset by widespread rural crime, industrial disorder, and ethnic conflict since the 1850s, when Irish, English, and Welsh miners descended on the state's coal and mine fields. In one of the most publicized cases, the Irish secret society known as the Molly Maguires allegedly killed a number of mining officials until they were infiltrated by Pinkerton's National Detective Agency* agent James Mc-Parland* in the 1870s. McParland's testimony led to twenty hangings and, subsequently, the destruction of the Mollies.

By the late nineteenth century, immigrants from Eastern Europe and Italy were drawn to the mine fields and industrial disorder broke out at the Carnegie steel plant in Homestead, Pennsylvania, in 1892. Three hundred Pinkertons were hired to protect the plant during the Homestead Strike,* and soon a pitched battle raged between strikers and the Pinkertons. The Pinkertons surrendered and many were unceremoniously beaten, leading the Governor to call in the state militia to restore order.

By the following century little had changed as widespread strikes paralyzed Pennsylvania's economy. With the ascendance of Samuel Whitaker Pennypacker* to the governorship in 1902, steps were initiated toward creating a state police force based on the Philippines Constabulary* and the Royal Irish Constabulary* military models. In 1905 the Pennsylvania State Police was created, led by Spanish-American war veteran John C. Groome.* Initially his 220-man force was selected from the ranks of the armed forces and required to be unmarried and to live in barracks. While they were charged with policing the entire state, for the most part the force patrolled the immigrant-dominated mining districts. Mounted on horses and equipped with carbines, pistols, and riot batons they became known as the Cossacks* to the opposition and were revered as the Black Hussars* by their supporters.

Katherine Mayo,* the Pennsylvania State police hagiographer and its foremost advocate, saw the state police as 100 percent Americans protecting the country from foreigners, labor agitators, and people of color. It was not long before the new force was at loggerheads with local law enforcement during jurisdictional disputes. During the first decade of their existence the state troopers were involved in numerous bloody clashes, including a 1909 steelworkers' strike at McKee's Rocks, where three troopers were shot, two fatally. The following year the troopers successfully put down a violent streetcar strike in Philadelphia.

During the World War I era, the same United Mine Workers that had called for the disbandment of the force had to ask the state police for protection against the more violent and radical International Workers of the World (IWW) workers. As the labor strikes of the 1910s diminished, the state police became more involved in rural crime and traffic problems as well as enforcing Prohibition laws. Ironically, the force began to reflect the heterogeneous nature of the state's population as well.

SOURCES: Philip Conti, *The Pennsylvania State Police: A History of Service to the Commonwealth, 1905 to the Present,* 1977; H. Kenneth Bechtel, *State Police in the United States,* 1995.

PENNYPACKER, SAMUEL WHITAKER. (1843–1916) Pennypacker distinguished himself as a member of the Twenty-sixth Pennsylvania Emergency Volunteers during the battle of Gettysburg in 1863. Following his military service he graduated from law school and was appointed a state judge in 1889. Thirteen years later he won support of the state political machine in a campaign for Pennsylvania governor. Considered by many to be the father of America's state police, Pennypacker had already served as a respected judge, historian, and trustee of the University of Pennsylvania prior to winning the governorship of Pennsylvania in 1902.

Pennypacker was attracted to state policing during the fierce labor strikes in the western Pennsylvania coal fields. The National Guard proved inadequate at keeping order, and after the new governor saw the state lose millions of dollars in revenues and wages, he proposed creating a state police force that would be used during emergencies. In 1905 a law establishing the Pennsylvania State Police* force was passed, making it one of the first state police forces of the twentieth century. In time it became a model for similar state units that would follow.

SOURCES: Thomas A. Reppetto, *The Blue Parade*, 1978; Katherine Mayo, *Justice to All*, 1917.

PENTLOW, WILLIAM. William Pentlow was an early member of the Bow Street Runners.* In 1751 Sir Henry Fielding* helped Pentlow obtain the lucrative position of prison keeper at the New Prison, Clerkenwell, for demonstrating bravery while apprehending a gang of robbers. Pentlow's son would also work as a runner.

SOURCE: Patrick Pringle, *Hue and Cry*, 1955.

PEOPLES, CLINTON THOMAS. (1910–1992) Born in Bridgeport, Texas, during an almost six-decade career in Texas law enforcement, Peoples wore ten different badges and probably served in more law enforcement agencies on a variety of levels than any other peace officer in Western history. Peoples entered law enforcement as a deputy sheriff in Montgomery County in 1930. He joined the Texas Department of Public Safety* in 1941 and five years later joined the vaunted Texas Rangers.* In 1953 he was promoted to captain and then in 1969 to senior Ranger captain. Peoples was the first Texas Ranger since John Salmon "RIP" Ford* in 1858 to be awarded the latter title, and he retired in this position five years later.

Peoples came to prominence in the 1950s while working undercover in Duval County, Texas. His investigation led to the conviction of George "the Duke of Duval County" Parr. In 1960 he investigated the murder of a U.S. Department of Agriculture official who was an important witness in the Billy Sol Estes case. Peoples was credited with developing the Texas Ranger Museum in Waco, Texas, and was the recipient of many honors during his long career, including an appointment as executive marshal by President Ronald Reagan during White House ceremonies in 1988. Peoples died in an automobile accident in Waco on June 22, 1992.

SOURCES: James M. Day, *Captain Clint Peoples, Texas Ranger: Fifty Years a Lawman*, 1980; *Courtesy, Service, and Protection*, 1995.

PEOPLES COMMISSARIAT OF INTERNAL AFFAIRS. *See* NKVD.

PETROSINO, JOSEPH "JOE." (1860–1909) Born in Salerno, Sicily, Petrosino immigrated with his family to Manhattan's Little Sicily in 1866. He joined the New York City Police Department (NYPD)* in 1883, an era characterized by the growth of Italian organized crime. After several years as a beat cop, he was promoted to detective and devoted the rest of his life to investigating the Mafia and related criminal groups. Petrosino was directed to create a detective squad of nativeborn Italians to keep tabs on the Black Hand extortion groups, and by 1896, the "Italian Squad" numbered fifty officers.

As Petrosino continued to investigate the Black Hand and Mafia groups he traced the source of power to Sicily, and with approval from the top brass, went to Sicily to gather evidence. A month after arriving in Sicily he was assassinated in Palermo. Petrosino became the first New York City detective to be killed outside the United States. The detective's murder led to the dismissal of the police chiefs of New York and Palermo. His funeral in Manhattan drew nearly two hundred thousand people.

SOURCE: Arrigo Petacco, *Joe Petrosino*, 1974.

PHELPS, EDWARD. Born in California, Phelps served as surgeon-in-chief at Fort Whipple, Arizona, when he was selected to follow Milton B. Duffield* as marshal (see U.S. MARSHALS SERVICE) of New Mexico in 1866. Wholly unqualified for the job, Phelps was the target of criticism for much of his term. In 1869 jurors were griping about nonpayment for services and local newspaper editors criticized him for beginning the census months behind schedule. While he tended to his medical practice on the side, city fathers continued to complain about his failure to devote attention to his job. Chronically dissatisfied with law enforcement work and its meager wages, Phelps absconded for Mexico with twelve thousand dollars in federal money in 1871. Not long after, he was murdered and robbed of his booty by Mexican outlaws.

SOURCE: Larry D. Ball, *The United States Marshals of New Mexico and Arizona Territories, 1846–1912*, 1978.

PHILIPPINES CONSTABULARY. Following the Spanish-American War of 1898, American armed forces were confronted with a native insurrection on the Philippine Islands seized from Spain. More American soldiers would see action here than in Cuba. Unprepared for counterinsurgency warfare, a constabulary force composed of American officers and native enlisted men was organized in the Philippines to combat the guerrilla threat in 1901. Inspired by the Royal Irish Constabulary* model of policing, the Philippines Constabulary would eventually number 250 Anglo officers and 7,000 enlisted men, drawn primarily from the indigenous population. The methods employed by the force were often brutal and unorthodox, and despite press censorship, word of their bloody search-and-destroy missions began to appear in American newspapers. Despite the controversy surrounding the constabulary, it was considered instrumental in bringing an end to the counterinsurgency movement by 1913. The Pennsylvania State Police* was reportedly inspired by the Philippines Constabulary.

SOURCE: Thomas A. Reppetto, *The Blue Parade*, 1978.

PHILLIPS, WILLIAM. New York City Police Department (NYPD)* Officer William Phillips was a decorated police officer with fourteen years of service when he testified on behalf of the Knapp Commission* on police corruption in 1970. Phillips had served in a radio patrol car and as a beat officer and was credited with making arrests in every Manhattan precinct. Phillips admitted to being corrupt for most of his career, having spent significant portions of it as a patrolman in the Twenty-Fifth Precinct in East Harlem, which at that time was the headquarters for organized crime gambling operations. He admitted to being a "super thief" and participating in all manner of petty theft, ranging from bowling alleys and garages to construction sites and bars. He also participated in shakedowns of gamblers, loan sharks, and pimps.

Phillips's subsequent testimony was not the result of some moral reawakening but rather the result of being arrested for bribery by the commission. He agreed to testify about corruption and work as an undercover agent during the commission investigation. He went on to participate in sixty-nine operations in which tape-recorded conversations involving corruption were obtained. His work resulted in the indictment of seventeen police officers.

Attention was drawn to Phillips in this case when he admitted shaking down a brothel madam in 1965. A private detective hired by the Knapp Commission to conduct surveillance on the apartment of Xaviera Hollander, of *Happy Hooker* fame, caught Phillips on tape offering protection. Although Frank Serpico was the highest-profile witness to testify in front of the Knapp Commission, most authorities on the trial agree that Phillips's testimony was the most damaging to the department. Following his testimony, the NYPD helped moved Phillips to another city because of death threats. While drawing full pay, Phillips collaborated with Leonard Schechter on the book *On the Pad*, which chronicled his life as a corrupt cop. In 1972 Phillips was indicted for the double murder of a pimp and a prostitute in 1968, and although represented by F. Lee Bailey, he was convicted and sent to prison.

SOURCES: Whitman, Knapp, chairman, *The Knapp Commission Report on Police Corruption*, 1972; Brian McDonald, *My Father's Gun*, 1999.

PICKERING, JAMES. Pickering served three terms as sheriff* of Yorkshire between 1389 and 1397. According to contemporary law three years had to elapse between each year as sheriff. He subsequently went on to serve as a member of Parliament, and in 1378 and 1383 was elected speaker for the Commons.

SOURCE: Irene Gladwin, *The Sheriff*, 1984.

PICKERT, HEINRICH A. (1886–1949) After distinguished service during World War I, which included a Purple Heart and a personal citation from General John J. Pershing, Pickert returned to America and a career in the Michigan National Guard. In 1929 President Herbert Hoover appointed Pickert, now a brigadier general in the national guard, to the post of customs collector. Five years later he was selected as commissioner of the Detroit police force. Pickert is credited with modernizing the force by introducing radio-equipped police cars and quicker response times to police calls. During protests and strikes at General Motors plants in 1937 by United Auto Workers, Pickert was criticized for responding with brutal strike-breaking tactics; to others, he was a hero standing firm in the face of civil disorder. He resigned as police commissioner two years later.

SOURCE: Charles Phillips and A an Axelrod, *CCC*, 1996.

PICKETT, TOM. (1856–1934) Pickett was born in Camp Throckmorton, Texas. After a youthful interlude as a cattle rustler, he joined the Frontier Battalion of the Texas Rangers,* in 1876. He left the force the following year and in 1879 moved to New Mexico, where he joined the Las Vegas police force. Pickett worked at a series of jobs, including as a ranch hand for William "Billy the Kid" Bonney associate Charlie Bowdre, and he soon fell in with Billy the Kid and a group of horse rustlers. He narrowly escaped several ambushes in which some of his fellow rustlers were killed and in 1882 was hired as marshal in Golden, New Mexico. Soon after he was forced out of office, and after a foray into Mexico that resulted in the killing of four Mexicans, he next reappeared in Arizona, where he affiliated himself with the Hash Knife gang during the Graham-Tewksbury feud. Pickett survived a gunshot wound to his leg and returned to cattle ranching. His last stint in law enforcement was as deputy sheriff (see SHERIFF) in Arizona between 1912 and 1914. He died from nephritis after having one of his legs amputated.

SOURCES: Philip J. Rasch, "He Rode with the Kid: The Life of Tom Pickett," in *English Westerners' 10th Anniversary Publication*, 1964.

PIETRI, JOACHIM. Born in Corsica, Pietri served as prefect of police for Paris from 1852 to 1858. Under his leadership the police force grew in numbers and became more efficient. He later studied the organization of Scotland Yard* and is credited with adopting the London model of twenty-four-hour beat patrols as well as the utilization of both uniformed and plainclothes officers* in targeted areas so they could become more familiar with their environment.

SOURCES: Philip John Stead, *The Police of France*, 1983; Philip John Stead, *The Police of Paris*, 1957.

PILSBURY, AMOS. As an early chief executive officer of the New York City Police Department (NYPD)* antisabbatarians referred to Pilsbury as "pious Pilsbury" for his support of Sunday blue laws. However, recent scholarship suggests that he was no tougher than his superiors in the crusade against Sunday drinking. In 1860 Pilsbury was succeeded as superintendent, by John Alexander Kennedy,* less than a year after his appointment.

SOURCE: Wilbur R. Miller, *Cops and Bobbies*, 1973.

PINKERTON, ALLAN, II. (1876–1930) The son of Robert Allan Pinkerton,* Allan Pinkerton, II, joined Pinkerton's National Detective Agency* in 1896 following graduation from the Harvard Business School. He served an apprenticeship, as his father and uncle did under his grandfather, being mentored by such outstanding superintendents as James McParland* and George Henry Bangs.* With the death of his father in 1907, he tried to fill his father's shoes but often came into conflict with his uncle William over the direction of the agency. In 1913 he turned down an invitation to be the police commissioner of New York City.

Following America's entry into World War I, Allan enlisted in the army. During the war he served as chief of the criminal-investigating unit of the provost marshal,* under General John Joseph Pershing. However, he was soon sent back to the United States to recuperate after surviving a gas attack at the front. With the death of William in 1923, Allan II took over the agency. During his tenure he opened more branches both nationally and internationally and expanded detective functions to include racetrack, guard, and security duties. With Allan II's death in 1930, his son, Robert Allan II, left Wall Street to become the last link between the agency and its namesake. By the 1940s the Pinkertons had lost their cachet as a detective agency and had made the transition to becoming a private security firm. Two years before his death in 1967 Robert Allan changed the name of the agency to Pinkerton's Inc.

SOURCES: James Mackay, *Allan Pinkerton: The First Private Eye*, 1996; Frank Morn, *"The Eye That Never Sleeps,"* 1982; James D. Horan, *The Pinkertons*, 1968.

PINKERTON, ALLAN J. (1819–1884) Born in Glasgow, Scotland, the son of a police officer, Pinkerton migrated to America in 1842 and established a cooper's works in Dundee, Indiana. Soon after he found his life's calling after playing an instrumental role in the capture of a gang of counterfeiters. He entered law enforcement in 1846 as deputy sheriff (see SHERIFF) of Kane County and then Cook County. In 1850 Pinkerton gave up his cooperage to become the first detective hired by the Chicago Police Department (CPD).* Pinkerton was hired to battle counterfeiters by the U.S. Treasury Department* on several occasions in the 1850s and served as deputy sheriff for Cook County and then special agent in the Chicago postal system.

In 1855 Pinkerton opened his own firm, Pinkerton's National Detective

Agency.* His investigative innovations included the first rogues' gallery, which displayed characteristics and idiosyncracies of known criminals. During the railroad expansion of the 1850s, Pinkerton was hired to create a spying system to keep railroad conductors from stealing fares. Soon after Pinkerton created an all-seeing eye as the symbol for the company, hence its motto, "The Eye That Never Sleeps."

A rabid abolitionist, in 1859 he reportedly sheltered John Brown and eleven runaway slaves in his home. Pinkerton rose to national prominence when he uncovered a plot to kill President-elect Abraham Lincoln on his way to Washington, D.C. He was subsequently placed in charge of Civil War operations under General George B. McClellan until 1863, when McClellan was dismissed. Pinkerton then returned to his private practice and opened offices in several major cities. Having successfully countered the skimming of fares by railroad conductors, he made the transition to tracking down train robbers, such as the James, Younger, and Dalton gangs.

During his lifetime Pinkerton began to earn the animosity of organized labor, but it would become more pronounced after his death. The Pinkertons earned a reputation as the enemy of labor and the ally of big business after infiltrating and exposing the Molly Maguires in the 1860s and 1870s. In the two decades following the Civil War, the Pinkerton agency became the largest and most visible private detective force in America. Following Pinkerton's death in 1884, his sons Robert Allan Pinkerton* and William Allan Pinkerton led the agency into the twentieth century.

Allan Pinkerton attempted to enhance the agency's tarnished image in his last years by supervising the writing of books about the agency that dramatized past crime-fighting exploits. Between 1874 and 1884 Pinkerton published sixteen books, including *The Expressman and the Detective* (1874), *Claude Melnotte as a Detective and Other Stories* (1875), *The Model Town and the Detectives* (1876), *The Molly Maguires and the Detectives* (1877), *The Spiritualists and the Detectives* (1877), *Strikers, Communists, Tramps and Detectives* (1878), *Mississippi Outlaws and the Detectives* (1879), *The Gypsies and the Detectives* (1879), *Professional Thieves and the Detectives* (1880), *The Rail-Road Forger and the Detectives* (1881), *Bank Robbers and the Detectives* (1882), *Bucholz and the Detectives* (1880), *The Spy and the Rebellion* (1883), *A Double Life and the Detectives* (1884), and *Thirty Years a Detective* (1884).

SOURCES: James Mackay, *Allan Pinkerton: The First Private Eye*, 1996; Frank Morn, *"The Eye That Never Sleeps," A History of the Pinkerton National Detective Agency*, 1982; James D. Horan, *The Pinkertons: The Detective Dynasty That Made History*, 1968.

PINKERTON, ROBERT ALLAN. (1848–1907) Robert Pinkerton and a twin sister, Joan, were born in Chicago. In 1864 Robert was sworn into Pinkerton's National Detective Agency as a deputy by the lieutenant of the New Orleans Office of the Provost Marshal.* When his father's health went into decline in

1869, Robert, along with his brother William Allan Pinkerton,* took over day-to-day operations of the detective agency. His son Allan Pinkerton II,* born in 1876, would be the only Pinkerton to carry the family name into the next century. Robert and his brother William investigated the 1866 Adams Express Company robbery and the Molly Maguires, trailed noted criminal Adam Worth, and, in the late nineteenth century, organized racetrack security measures. Robert's son Allan II later joined the agency, and although overshadowed by his famous uncle William, he, too, implemented new innovations in the organization.

SOURCES: James D. Horan, *The Pinkertons: The Detective Dynasty That Made History*, 1968; Frank Morn, *"The Eye That Never Sleeps,"* 1982.

PINKERTON, WILLIAM ALLAN. (1846–1923) The oldest of the six children of Allan Pinkerton,* "Willie" joined his father at field headquarters during the 1862 Seven Days campaign. Working as his father's aide, he demonstrated courage while still a teenager by working as a dispatch rider and then as an observer in a balloon as the battle raged below. He is credited with participating in the first aerial reconnaissance in the history of warfare. By 1864, William was working as an operative for his father out of the Department of the Mississippi. Following the Civil War, he supervised Pinkerton business in the West and Midwest out of the Chicago office.

Following Allan's stroke, by 1869 William and his brother Robert supervised all Pinkerton operations. In 1875 William was accused of leading the raid on Jesse James's mother's house, which resulted in the death of Jesse's eight-year-old half-brother Archie and the serious wounding of his mother. Allan Pinkerton deflected the blame on other detectives, but he never revealed the names of the operatives that night. Following the death of his father in 1884, William ran the agency with his brother Robert Allan Pinkerton.*

During his career with the Pinkertons, William investigated the 1866 Adams Express robbery of seven hundred thousand dollars at Cos Cob, Massachusetts, the largest haul of this era; helped his father investigate the Molly Maguires; and chased the Reno gang. In the 1890s he investigated America's "Bluebeard," Herman Mudgett, who confessed to murdering twenty-seven women and children before he was hanged in 1896. William also directed the investigations of the David Peter Hennessy* murder, the murder of ex-governor Frank Steunenberg in Idaho, and sent agents to South America after members of the Wild Bunch. In 1911, at the request of British Home Secretary Winston Churchill, William provided protection for King George V's coronation in London. He received criticism for his handling of San Francisco's Tom Mooney bombing case and the botching of the Atlanta, Georgia, investigation into the murder of Mary Phagan, which resulted in the hanging of an innocent man, Leo Frank.

SOURCES: James D. Horan, *The Pinkertons: The Detective Dynasty That Made History*, 1968; Frank Morn, *"The Eye That Never Sleeps,"* 1982; James Mackay, *Allan Pinkerton: The First Private Eye*, 1996.

PINKERTON'S NATIONAL DETECTIVE AGENCY. Considered the premier detective organization, Pinkerton's National Detective Agency was founded by Allan J. Pinkerton* as the North West Police Agency in 1855. The agency originally handled far-flung cases in communities with limited law enforcement expertise. However, in the ensuing decades the Pinkertons became increasingly recognized for its handling of labor-management disputes. Pinkerton agents gained a reputation for subterfuge and deceit for their handling of the 1888 Texas and Pacific Railroad strike; the infiltration of the miner's union in Coeur d'Alene, Idaho; and the 1905 investigation of the murder of ex-governor Frank Steunenberg in Idaho. It was not until 1937 that the Pinkertons were forced to disengage themselves from labor issues following the passage of a congressional resolution.

The agency saw its greatest expansion in the years following the Civil War, and it became officially known as the National Detective Agency in the 1860s. Much of their efforts in the 1860s were spent pursuing railroad bandits such as the Reno, Younger, and Dalton gangs. In many areas of the Midwest, the Pinkertons were vilified and their adversaries elevated to hero status. The Pinkertons further added to their reputation as agent provocateurs during the infiltration of the Molly Maguire terrorist group in the Pennsylvania coal fields between 1867 and 1877. Subsequent testimony by Pinkerton undercover agent James McParland* led to the conviction and execution of numerous miners. Following Allan Pinkerton's death, the business continued to flourish under the direction of his sons William Allan Pinkerton* and Robert Allan Pinkerton.*

With the advent of the Federal Bureau of Investigation (FBI)* in the early twentieth century, much of the criminal work once handled by the Pinkertons passed to the FBI and other official police forces. Pinkerton's still deals with criminal investigation on behalf of business and industry and for over seventy-five years has been the official detective agency of the Jewellers' Security Alliance. Its criminal investigation department at its New York headquarters at one time had the nation's most extensive files on jewel thieves and fences. The Pinkertons continue to offer a uniformed guard service to protect against theft, vandalism, burglary, and fire, as well as investigative services.

SOURCES: James Mackay, *Allan Pinkerton: The First Private Eye*, 1996; James D. Horan, *The Pinkertons: The Detective Dynasty That Made History*, 1968; Frank Morn, *"The Eye That Never Sleeps": A History of the Pinkerton National Detective Agency*, 1982.

PIPER, ALEXANDER. *See* PIPERS.

PIPERIZER. *See* PIPERS.

PIPERS. Referring to the practice of employing spies inside a police department, the term *pipers* (more commonly known as shooflies*) originated in Chicago in 1903. That year Captain Alexander Piper from the New York City Police Department (NYPD)* was selected to make a secret investigation of the Chicago Police Department (CPD).* Published the following year, his study excoriated the department for inefficiency, citing poor discipline and physical conditioning, corruption, and instances of police brutality. Subsequently, Piper, a future deputy police commissioner in New York, was charged with creating a spy system within the department to identify incompetent officers. These undercover operatives became known as pipers. However, the pipers were not totally effective and in many instances were deceived by frame-ups of honest cops, who were unceremoniously discharged from the force. In this manner one more barrier to payoffs and corruption was eliminated.

SOURCES: Carl Sifakis, *The Encyclopedia of American Crime*, 1982; Thomas A. Reppetto, *The Blue Parade*, 1978.

PISTONE, JOSEPH D. (b. c. 1940) Born in Pennsylvania, Pistone taught middle school and worked as a civilian agent for the Office of Naval Intelligence before joining the Federal Bureau of Investigation (FBI)* in 1969. He worked in the Jacksonville, Florida, and Alexandria, Virginia, field offices and then took courses at the FBI Academy at Quantico, Virginia. At the Academy he studied gambling investigation and took undercover and Special Weapons and Tactics (SWAT)* training. Reassigned to the New York City office, in 1974 he was assigned to undercover work.

In 1976, under the name Donnie Brasco*, Pistone infiltrated the Mafia as a deep-cover agent for five years. Pistone's stint as Donnie Brasco was the most successful infiltration into a mob family by a government agent. He initially was working in a relatively unimportant FBI operation in Tampa, Florida, in 1975. Later, while posing as a jewel thief, Pistone as Brasco frequented mob hangouts before gradually being accepted into the milieu. Over the following months, he was mentored by Bonnano family member Benjamin "Lefty Guns" Ruggiero.

After testifying against the organization, a half-million-dollar contract was placed on Pistone's head. His story was chronicled in his autobiography, *Donnie Brasco: My Undercover Life in the Mafia* (1988) and a highly successful film of the same name starring Johnny Depp. In 1983 Pistone was awarded the Attorney General's Distinguished Service Award, and three years later he retired from the FBI. Pistone and his family decided against being placed in the Witness Protection Program and instead changed their names and moved far from New York City.

SOURCES: Joe D. Pistone with R. Woodley, *Donnie Brasco: My Undercover Life in the Mafia*, 1988; Athan G. Theoharis, ed., *The FBI*, 1999.

PLAINCLOTHES OFFICERS. Following the creation of Sir Robert Peel's*
police in 1829, plainclothes policemen were occasionally employed for clandestine duties. For a public that was initially reluctant to accept a professional
police force, it became incumbent for the new police force to assure the citizens
that these "plainclothesmen" were not spies or informers. According to the early
1830s *Police Orders* issued by Commissioner Rowan,* plainclothesmen were
to be used to catch pickpockets and thieves. However, these tactics seemed to
diverge from the preventive duties promised by the new force. Some citizens
suggested that using plainclothesmen to watch for thieves in crowd situations
was just a step away from spying on conversations in local taverns.

The 1845 *Police Orders* proclaimed that policemen could not disguise themselves for police work without orders from the superintendent. Still, due to
concerns with public suspicions of the police, it was not until 1869 that a formal
detective division was created during the tenure of Sir Edmund Henderson* as
commissioner. Henderson also relaxed the prohibition against plainclothes policing.

American plainclothes divisions can be traced back to the sordid wardmen.
Dressed down in civilian clothing to divert attention from their graft-collecting
activities, they were little more than bagmen for nineteenth-century precinct
captains. By the 1940s, plainclothes police officers in the New York City Police
Department (NYPD) were often caught up in the corruption of the very underworld they were charged with investigating. Today, cities such as New York
have done away with plainclothes divisions. Following the 1972 Knapp Commission* investigation, this division was disbanded and replaced with the Organized Crime Control Bureau, which was to investigate gambling, vice, and
narcotics violations.

SOURCES: Paul Begg and Keith Skinner, *The Scotland Yard Files*, 1992; Brian
McDonald, *My Father's Gun: One Family, Three Badges, One Hundred Years in the
NYPD*, 1999.

*PLAN FOR PREVENTING ROBBERIES WITHIN TWENTY MILES OF
LONDON.* Published by Sir John Fielding* in 1755, this pamphlet proposed
that people whose houses were located between five and twenty miles from
London should band together and each contribute two guineas per year to an
appointed treasurer. Thereafter, whenever a highway robbery was reported in
their jurisdiction, they would use their treasury to hire a horse and messenger
to relay the particulars of the incident to the Bow Street office. According to
Fielding's instructions, reports should include the name and address of the victim, and as the messenger made his way to London, he was supposed to stop
at every inn, tavern, and turnpike and give a description of the highwayman and
his horse. When the messenger finally reached his destination, the Bow Street
magistrates would decide whether to send police officers to the scene or to
simply put a notice of the particulars in the *Public Advertiser*. All expenses
would come from the local treasury.

SOURCES: Patrick Pringle, *Hue and Cry*, 1955; Anthony Babington, *A House in Bow Street*, 1969.

PLUMMER, WILLIAM HENRY HANDY. (1837–1864) Recent research casts doubt on many of the accepted facts of Plummer's life, including the spelling of his name, which is spelled "Plumer" in his only two extant signatures. Plummer won renown as the prototype of the corrupt Western peace officer. Born in Maine, Plummer apparently was fairly well educated for the times. He arrived in Nevada City, California in the waning days of the gold rush. After stints in a series of dead-end jobs Plummer entered the baker's trade and participated in numerous business dealings with local saloons and brothels, eventually creating a political base that included close associations with various unsavory characters.

After selling his interest in the bakery business, he was defeated in his run for city marshal but was appointed a deputy by the victor in 1855. The following year he made sure he won the next election by enlisting local roughnecks to threaten opponents at the ballot box. However, Plummer's career as marshal would be tarnished by several episodes that brought into question his judgment as peace officer. Perhaps his most flagrant mistake was killing the husband of a woman he had helped in a domestic assault after he caught Plummer and the woman flagrante delicto during a late-night interlude. Plummer was convicted of second-degree murder and sentenced to ten years at San Quentin State Prison beginning in 1859.

In just a few months Plummer concocted an elaborate ruse to get out of prison. After persuading prison physicians that he was stricken with tuberculosis, his friends began a letter-writing campaign on his behalf that succeeded in gaining him a pardon to enjoy his last days in a more convivial atmosphere. He returned to Nevada City, and after a "miraculous" recovery, was appointed city constable. Soon after, he lost his job after severely injuring an adversary in a brothel brawl. Unwilling to wait around to see whether the injured party would recover, the ex-con peace officer left for Carson City, Nevada.

In 1861 Plummer was once again involved in a violent fracas and arrested. Recovering in jail from a deep knife wound to the head, the ever-vigilant Plummer escaped from jail. Over the next several months, Plummer's life took a more criminal turn, including several robberies and murders. In 1862 he organized a gang of criminals in Idaho while working in a Lewiston casino. Later that year he won election as sheriff* in Bannack, Montana, where he crusaded under the guise of a vigilante from Idaho. However, his gang of criminals, which was known as the "Innocents," continued to flourish. When it came time to construct gallows to execute members of this organization, Plummer ensured their protection and instead hanged members of his own deputy force.

The Innocents grew into such a large organization that it became necessary to develop secret methods of identification employing secret handshakes and code words. However, Plummer's luck was about to run out. Plummer shot one of his former colleagues who was trying to blackmail him for some of the take; however, he survived to give testimony to Plummer's secret criminal side. While local vigilance committees rooted out numerous members of the Innocents, Plummer was left untouched, and to his detriment, did not attempt to flee. Some sources indicate he had made a deal with the vigilantes and thought he would be protected. However, Plummer mounted the gallows steps with two other members of the gang on January 10, 1864, and despite pleas for mercy, the reputed killer of fifteen men was finally executed.

SOURCES: Jay Robert Nash, *EWLO*, 1994; William B. Secrest, *Lawmen and Desperadoes*, 1994; R. E. Mather and F. E. Boswell, *Hanging the Sheriff*, 1987.

POE, JOHN WILLIAM. (1851–1923) Born in Maysville, Kentucky, Poe worked as a buffalo hunter on the southern Plains in 1875. He served a one-year stint as marshal (see U.S. MARSHALS SERVICE) of Fort Griffin, Texas, and then five years as a U.S. deputy marshal. Poe reached Lincoln County, New Mexico, in 1881, where he served as a deputy sheriff under Patrick Floyd Jarvis "Pat" Garrett.* He reportedly informed Garrett where he could find Billy the Kid and was present when Garrett killed him at Fort Sumner in 1881. In 1883 he succeeded Garrett as sheriff* of Lincoln County. He left law enforcement in 1885 for banking and ranching. Poe chronicled the killing of Billy the Kid in a pamphlet that was first published in 1919 and then released as the book *Billy the Kid, Notorious New Mexico Outlaw.*

SOURCE: William A. Keleher, *Violence in Lincoln County, 1869–1881*, 1957.

POLICE. This term can be traced back to the Greek *politeia*, which referred to all affairs that affected the survival and order of the state. By the 1700s, European states used *la police* (French) and *die Polizei* (German) to refer to the internal administration, safety, protection, and surveillance of a territory. While the English eschewed the word *police* because of its absolutist connotations, the term gained increasing currency in France. The word was probably imported into England from France at the beginning of the eighteenth century. The term initially referred to good government through the introduction of sanitation, street lighting, and the like. By the end of the eighteenth century, the term was used more in England, and as a preventive police force developed in the first decades of the nineteenth century, the term seemed to have lost much of its stigma.

SOURCES: John Fitzgerald Moylan, *Scotland Yard and the Metropolitan Police*, 1929; Clive Emsley, "The Origins of the Modern Police." *History Today*, April 1999.

POLICE ACT OF 1964. From 1960 to 1962, the fifth Royal Commission on the Police of England and Wales met to decide on how to reform the English police. Their recommendations resulted in the Police Act of 1964, which allowed the British home secretary to make regulations for police service. This act marked a decisive stage in British police development and strengthened the role of the central government in modern policing by repealing sixty-one Acts of Parliament dating back to 1801. Most of these statutes were considered obsolete. For the first time in the history of the English police, an attempt was made to define the respective functions and duties of the home secretary, police author- ities, and chief constables. The bill also gave statutory recognition to the many changes that had been effected without statutory authority over the preceding thirty years.

Statutory recognition was given to many agencies, including the Police Col- lege, district police training centers, forensic science laboratories, and wireless depots, as well as common service arrangements. In addition, a Police Advisory Board mandated to advise the home secretary replaced the Police Council that was created by the Police Act of 1919. Constables* were no longer restricted by jurisdictional barriers to their own locality but now had powers and privileges of a constable throughout England and Wales. The bill also cultivated better procedures for dealing with complaints against police by allowing a chief officer of police to call on an officer of another force to investigate complaints. The multifaceted bill came into force in stages after it received the Royal Assent in June 1964.

SOURCES: Philip John Stead, *The Police of Britain*, 1985; T. A. Critchley, *A History of Police in England and Wales, 900–1966*, 1967.

POLICE FILMS. Since the silent film era, police dramas as well as comedies have been a staple of Hollywood motion pictures. Like Shakespeare's bumbling Dogberry,* the first stock characters of police films were the buffoonish Key- stone Kops,* introduced during the early decades of the twentieth century. How- ever, not everyone was amused by their antics. In particular, in 1910 the International Association of Chiefs of Police (IACP)* criticized these films as undermining the credibility of modern police officers. Many scholars of urban America would probably argue that the Keystone Kops were indeed emblematic of the current state of affairs, when political patronage and corruption rendered big city policing ineffective and often laughable.

By the 1930s police professionalization had elevated many departments to a higher standing in the minds of the public and few films made in this era lam- pooned policing. Heralding the new age of policing were dozens of the films promoting the G-men* of John Edgar Hoover.* In 1935 alone, over sixty films were made chronicling the exploits of the Federal Bureau of Investigation (FBI).* Hoover himself played an important role in reshaping celluloid stereo- types of police. He was instrumental in the making of *G-Men* (1935), starring James Cagney, which utilized documentary techniques to publicize FBI training and investigative methods. In addition, the passage of the Hays Code in 1934 required that movies demonstrate that "crime must not pay," necessitating the apprehension or killing of the criminals by the end of the last movie reel.

The 1940s introduced film noir detectives and femmes fatales, and police procedurals were rare. However, the 1948 *Naked City* offered a proto-documentary portrait of policing in an unglamorized nuanced style. Shot on location in New York City, it eschewed the more glamorous aspects of policing, instead preferring to offer a more realistic rendering, which emphasized the tedious aspects of policing. It also introduced the voice-over narrative, which kept the viewer apprised of police minutiae, facts, and figures. Television programs such as *Dragnet,** *Highway Patrol,** and *Adam Twelve* were heavily influenced by this narrative style.

The rash of Supreme Court decisions that supported victims' rights and attempted to restrict police powers were not well reflected in the films of the 1960s. Television more often took the lead in introducing minorities and women to entertainment audiences, as the white male police bureaucracy came under fire for being out of touch.

The 1970s signaled a new wave of films that reflected a more conservative crime control mood in the country, with iconoclastic cops, such as Clint Eastwood in *Dirty Harry*, taking the law into their own hands like vigilantes. Critics credit these films with creating an image of policing that has little concern for the rights of citizens as witnesses and in which suspects are liberally smacked around and threatened in order to obtain information.

By the 1980s, television shows such as *Hill Street Blues* and *Miami Vice* were offering a grittier side of policing. Unlike the clone-like cops of *Dragnet* and *Adam 12*, the police officers in these series had emotional problems and were often in conflict within their personal lives and jobs. By the late 1980s, Hollywood police films had generally degenerated into ultra-violent entertainment catering to adolescent fantasies. Films such as the *Lethal Weapon* series and *RoboCop* introduced policemen who often had to resort to superhuman tactics to confront more violent criminals.

SOURCES: James Robert Parish, *The Great Cop Pictures*, 1990; Larry Langman and Daniel Finn, *A Guide to American Silent Crime Films*, 1994; Neal King, *Heroes in Hard Times: Cop Action Movies in the United States*, 1999.

POLICE GAZETTE. In 1773, Sir John Fielding* applied for, and was awarded, a grant to finance a bulletin that would offer details on wanted criminals and herald the exploits of the Bow Street Runners.* The previous year he had already established *The Weekly or Extraordinary Pursuit* at his own expense. This precursor to the *Gazette* was circulated gratis to magistrates throughout England. Initially, the new bulletin was called *The Public Hue and Cry*, and then simply *The Hue and Cry*. With the creation of the London Metropolitan Police* in 1829, it received its more familiar title of *Police Gazette*. It was published out of the Bow Street office until 1883, when it was relocated to Scotland Yard.*

SOURCES: Anthony Babington, *A House in Bow Street*, 1969; Patrick Pringle, *Hue and Cry*, 1955.

POLICE MATRONS. Policing was a male-dominated field well into the 1960s. However, in the nineteenth century, women were given some opportunities to participate in law enforcement as police matrons. As early as the 1830s, matrons supervised female inmates in some correctional facilities. In 1878 the first women were hired by police departments to take care of female prisoners. By 1890, as a result of a campaign led by the Women's Christian Temperance Union and the General Federation of Women's Clubs, thirty-six city police departments hired police matrons. In 1891, New York City hired its first police matron. During the first decade of the twentieth century, a policewomen's movement (see POLICEWOMEN) would build on the accomplishments of the police matrons.

SOURCES: Kerry Segrave, *Policewomen: A History*, 1995; Dorothy Moses Schulz, *From Social Worker to Crimefighter*, 1995.

POLICE MUNICIPALE. Also called the "Mayors' police forces," or *la garde des maires*, the French *police municipale* is made up of approximately twenty-five thousand officers nationwide, who are controlled on the local level. President François Mitterrand and his Socialist party were instrumental in creating this force in order to decentralize the police and increase local control over government services. The duties of these units vary from town to town. Some cities maintain these small forces to fight crime or maintain order during busy tourist seasons. With limited enforcement powers and no general investigative powers, the *police municipale* is considered mainly a supplementary force to the *police nationale*.* Most cities do not have municipal police units.

SOURCE: Richard R. E. Kania, "The French Municipal Police Experiment," *Police Studies* 12, 1989, pp. 125–131.

POLICE NATIONALE. Of France's two police forces, the *police nationale* is the largest with over 150,000 employees. Responsible for urban policing, this force operates in cities with over ten thousand inhabitants and is supervised by a director general under the Ministry of the Interior.

SOURCE: Richard R. E. Kania, "The Return of the Municipal Police," *Criminal Justice International* 6(20), 1990.

POLICE PHOTOGRAPHY. Soon after the advent of photography in the late 1830s, its application was discovered by law enforcement. In 1846 Mathew Brady photographed prisoners in New York City's Blackwell's Island prison. The resulting daguerreotype images were published in the phrenological reformist Maramaduke Sampson's *The Rationale of Crime* in 1846.

As early as 1860, Switzerland was reportedly the first country to mention crime-scene photography. By the 1850s, police departments such as San Francisco's were keeping daguerreotype rogues' gallery collections of criminals for identification. Other major police departments followed suit; the New York City Police Department (NYPD),* by 1858; Danzig, Germany, in 1864; Moscow, three years later; London, in 1870; and by 1874, Paris introduced a full police laboratory.

During the Paris Commune, following the 1871 Franco-Prussian War, revolutionary insurgents chronicled their revolt with photographs but lived to regret it. When the Paris Commune fell after only three months, French troops used the photos to track down and execute former Communards. Not long after, the French police adopted the system of identification developed by Alphonse Bertillon,* supplementing it with two photographs that are now referred to as mug shots. The Bertillon system* was widely heralded in the United States following its introduction at the Columbian Exposition in 1893. The next year the Chicago Police Department (CPD)* adopted the system, and within five years it had established the National Bureau of Criminal Identification. Bertillon's system lost its credibility in 1903 when two men named William West could not be distinguished from each other using Bertillon's measurements. Fingerprinting soon ruled the day as the identification method of choice; however, nothing would diminish the value of photography.

By the late 1880s, few respectable police forces or private police agencies such as Pinkerton's* National Detective Agency,* were without mug shot books. Ever the self-promotor, in 1886 New York City police inspector Thomas F. Byrnes* published *Professional Criminals of America*, replete with rogues' gallery photographs and captions describing their criminal professions. Byrnes's professed goal in publishing this work was to suppress criminal activity, on grounds that criminals would keep a lower profile if their visage were well known. However, many criminals ended up reveling in their own notoriety.

The growth of tabloid newspapers in the 1930s created new outlets for crime-related photographs. With little in the way of censorship, editors published graphic images of killings and robberies. The New York *Daily News* devoted a third of its space to crime coverage, helping to elevate it to the largest circulation tabloid by 1926. Sensational murder trials such as the Fatty Arbuckle trial, the Snyder-Gray trial, and the trial of Leopold and Loeb grabbed the public's attention, thanks in part to the voluminous photographs of the perpetrators and victims. The addition of the New York *Evening Graphic* to the tabloid scene in 1924 offered sensational photographs, which were often touched up to make the images even more explicitly violent.

Photographs of high-profile crime scenes such as the 1929 St. Valentine's Day massacre* and the killing of John Dillinger at the Biograph Theater generated tremendous publicity for law enforcement agencies, such as the Federal Bureau of Investigation (FBI)* in the case of Dillinger. As director of the FBI, John Edgar Hoover* introduced the Ten Most Wanted List* campaign. This publicity gimmick entered popular culture through media glorification and such artists as Andy Warhol, who depicted it in his 1964 series *Most Wanted Men*.

In the 160 years since the emergence of photography it has become a primary tool of the police, who use it to identify criminals, establish evidence, and construct or reconstruct crime scenes.

SOURCES: Sandra S. Phillips, Mark Haworth-Booth, and Carol Squiers, *Police Pictures: The Photograph as Evidence*, 1997; Weegee, *Naked City*, 1945; Luc Sante, *Evidence*, 1992; Thomas Byrnes, *Rogues' Gallery*, reprint, 1969.

POLICE RIOTS OF 1857. Conflict between New York City's two rival police departments deteriorated into violence in 1857. The rivalry stemmed from the New York State Legislature's decision in 1853 to abolish the Municipal Police and replace it with the New York Metropolitan Police.* The new police force, to be controlled by the governor, was created to stem the political patronage and corruption that were endemic in the municipal force. However, the mayor refused to disband the city police force. Superintendent George W. Matsell,* fifteen captains, and eight hundred patrolmen supported Mayor Fernando Wood.* Violence erupted when Captain George Washington Walling,* a supporter of the new force, came to arrest the recalcitrant mayor. Vastly outnumbered by three hundred municipal officers inside city hall, Walling was unceremoniously removed from the building. Decked in frock coats and plug hats, fifty metropolitan officers descended on city hall and a pitched battle erupted from the streets into the hall. Fifty-two policemen were injured during the rout of the outnumbered metropolitans. The conflict came to a head when the national guard was called in by the Metropolitan Police Board. Subsequently, Wood was arrested and released on bail.

Throughout the summer, both police forces attempted to carry out business as usual, but the feud between the forces led to an inexorable rise in crime as neither was willing to cooperate with the other, to the detriment of the city. A municipal officer would arrest a suspect, only to have a metropolitan officer release him. Naturally, the other force then reciprocated. Mayor Wood finally abolished the municipals following a Supreme Court decision that supported the initial action, together with rising public disatisfaction with local policing. Soon after the riot, the fifty-two injured police filed suit against Mayor Wood. They each eventually collected $250 in damages, which was paid by the city coffers.

SOURCES: Thomas A. Reppetto, *The Blue Parade*, 1978; Wilbur R. Miller, *Cops and Bobbies*, 1973.

POLICEWOMEN. By 1845 women entered law enforcement, albeit at an inferior status, as police matrons.* It would be almost fifty years before Marie Owens* became the first woman selected to execute police duties in Chicago. Moreover, it was not until 1910 that Alice Stebbins Wells* became the first full-time paid policewoman in America. Over the next five years, twenty-five cities appointed policewomen to the forces. Initially, policewomen were charged with suppressing dance hall vice, helping children, and returning runaway girls. In 1915 the International Association of Policewomen* was established in Baltimore, Maryland, leading the effort to include more women in the police profession. Three years later, Ellen O'Grady became the deputy police commissioner of New York City. The first African-American policewoman killed in the line of duty was Washington, D.C., officer Gail A. Cobb.*

SOURCE: Dorothy Moses Schulz, *From Social Worker to Crimefighter*, 1995.

POLIZIA DI STATO. The Polizia di Stato is the Italian state police. Each of Italy's ninety-two provinces is commanded by a local prefect. Special units within the organization are responsible for offenses in such jurisdictions as highways, railways, and the postal service.

SOURCE: Philip L. Reichel, *Comparative Criminal Justice Systems*, 1999.

POLLARD, BENJAMIN. (d. 1836) Following graduation from Harvard, Pollard was appointed clerk of the Massachusetts House, serving from 1811 to 1815. A failed poet with literary ambitions, Pollard was selected as Boston's first city marshal in June 1823. As marshal, Pollard was responsible for enforcing health ordinances as well as civil and criminal laws. His powers allowed him to enter any house between sunrise and sunset to alleviate any sanitary threat. In addition, he was charged with supervising constables on city duty, teamsters, and cartmen, as well as his own deputies.

SOURCE: Roger Lane, *Policing the City*, 1967.

POLYGRAPH. *See* LIE DETECTOR.

PORTEOUS, JOHN. (d. 1736) A captain of the Edinburgh City Guard (an early Scottish police force), Porteous was charged with leading a security force to ensure the execution of a notorious smuggler. The smuggler was hanged at the appointed hour, but as his body was being cut down, a mob gathered and unleashed a torrent of stones and abuse on the soldiers, who fired back in self-defense, killing and wounding numerous citizens. Porteous, a strict, by-the-book police officer, was an unpopular figure in Edinburgh, and the citizens identified much more with the recently deceased convict. As leader of the security force, Captain Porteous was arrested for the deaths of the onlookers and convicted of murder. He soon won a pardon, but before he could leave the jail, a mob descended on it and overpowered the guards. Despite efforts to escape, Porteous was seized by the mob and hanged over a dyer's pole.

SOURCE: Sir Harold Scott, *The Concise Encyclopedia of Crime and Criminals*, 1961.

POSSE COMITATUS. Under English common law, all male persons over the age of fifteen were required to assist in law enforcement when summoned by the sheriff* through the hue and cry.* This group was the *posse comitatus.*

SOURCE: George E. Rush, *The Dictionary of Criminal Justice*, 1994.

PRATT, JOHN. Born in Massachusetts, following a stint in the Second Kansas Cavalry during the Civil War, Pratt served as marshal (see U.S. MARSHALS SERVICE) of the New Mexico Territory beginning on March 3, 1866. Aligned with the Republican party, Pratt came under the influence of the Santa Fe Ring political machine led by District Attorney Stephen B. Elkins and Thomas B. Catron. Pratt assisted in the prosecution of his predecessor, former marshal Abraham Cutler, for embezzlement. During his ten years in office, Pratt was credited with breaking up a slavery ring that violated state peonage laws, improving relations with county deputies, and improving the administration of the marshal's office. His close association with the local political machine led to charges of cronyism and conflicts of interest. He received some of his strongest criticism for his handling of the Colfax County War, in which he refused to arrest killers associated with the Santa Fe Crime Ring. A victim of political factionalism, in 1876 Pratt was replaced by John H. Sherman, Jr.* Subsequently, President Ulysses S. Grant rewarded Pratt, a staunch Unionist and Republican, with the position of secretary of the New Mexico Territory.

SOURCE: Larry D. Ball, *The United States Marshals of New Mexico and Arizona Territories, 1846–1912*, 1978.

PREECE, THOMAS WILLIAM. (1856–1928) Born in Salt Lake City, Utah, "Billy" Preece worked as a freighter and on the local Uintah Ute Indian reservation before winning election as sheriff* for Uintah County in 1896. Preece came to prominence following skirmishes with the Wild Bunch and for his role in the capture of noted desperado Harry Tracy and associates after the killing of a rancher in 1898. Two years later he killed rustler George "Flat Nose" Curry. In 1906 he left Uintah County to become a deputy U.S. marshal at Whiterocks, Utah. His last position in law enforcement was as city marshal (see U.S. MARSHALS SERVICE) of Vernal, Utah. Preece died of dropsy in 1928.

SOURCE: Edward M. Kirby and Mary C. Preece, "Billy Preece: Frontier Lawman," *Real West*, July 1979.

PRIVATE EYE. The term *private eye* is derived from the logo of Pinkerton's National Detective Agency,* which featured an eye and the slogan, "We Never Sleep." As the agency became more prominent criminals distinguished the "private eye" or "Eye" of private policing from the prying eyes of the police.

SOURCE: Frank Morn, *"The Eye That Never Sleeps,"* 1982.

PROHIBITION AGENTS. Unpopular with both the public and organized crime, Prohibition agents were drawn from a relatively weak pool of applicants. The qualifications and pay were so lackluster that many agents lined their pockets with bribes and kickbacks. One agent was reportedly offered three hundred thousand dollars per week. In an era characterized by corruption, it should not be surprising that many agents were attracted by the lucrative prospects for graft. The U.S. Treasury Department* fired over seven hundred agents for larceny between 1920 and 1928. The following year, the U.S. Department of Justice* took over the enforcement of Prohibition. In Chicago, Elliot Ness* reportedly had to go outside the Windy City to find enough honest agents to fill the ranks of the Untouchables* in 1929. The two most famous Prohibition agents were New Yorkers Izzy Einstein and Moe Smith (Izzy and Moe*), referred to by the press as Tweedledum and Tweedledee and credited with making almost five thousand arrests between them.

SOURCES: Oliver Cyriax, *Crime: An Encyclopedia*, 1993; John Slate and R. U. Steinberg, *Lawmen, Crimebusters, and Champions of Justice*, 1991.

PROVOST MARSHAL. The precursor to the Royal Military Police, the law enforcement position of provost marshal emerged out of sixteenth-century England. During the era's many military campaigns, the provost marshal decided where merchants could sell their goods and who could fix the price of food; he was also imbued with arrest powers to enforce the articles of war. Other responsibilities included confining prisoners, informing the night watch* of the night's password, preventing gambling, and suppressing prostitution in military camps.

According to contemporary sources any common woman caught within an army campsite could be branded on the face. Demonstrating how zealously the army maintained discipline in the seventeenth century, provost marshals were often characterized as "hangmen" or "executioners for the army" because they were required to conduct the execution and torture of prisoners.

As the British Empire established colonies in the far-flung corners of the world in the eighteenth and nineteenth centuries, the provost marshal's position continued to evolve. In the Caribbean, some corrupt provost marshals manipulated local politics, and in the American colony of Virginia they were responsible for sending prisoners to the galleys. American spy Nathan Hale was executed by a provost marshal, and by the nineteenth century one marshal complained of overwork during executions in Delhi, India, that involved tying captives to canons and then lighting the fuse.

The provost marshals were recognized as military police officers by the end of the Boer War, but they did not gain full recognition as such until 1953. By the twentieth century, the "Redcaps" (the Royal Military Police) had become a respected military force. Originally used primarily to enforce discipline in the armed services, they made the transition to playing a crucial role in traffic control on the myriad battlefields of the twentieth century, including the Falklands and the Gulf Wars.

SOURCES: R.A.J. Tyler, *Bloody Provost*, 1980; G. D. Sheffield, *The Redcaps*, 1994.

PUBLIC ENEMIES. Although the concept of "public enemies" was credited to the Federal Bureau of Investigation (FBI),* it was actually the brainchild of the Chicago Crime Commission, a watchdog group formed in 1919 to investigate the prevalence of crime in Chicago. The commission issued its first public enemies list in 1930; it was headed by none other than "Public Enemy Number One" Al Capone. The FBI later capitalized on the "public enemies" idea and, through a shrewd marketing campaign, put out the idea Ten Most Wanted List.* Initially, John Edgar Hoover* was against ranking criminals by number, but he soon relented.

SOURCE: William Helmer with Rick Mattix, *Public Enemies: America's Criminal Past, 1919–1940*, 1998.

PURVIS, MELVIN. (1903–1960) Born in Timmonsville, South Carolina, and educated at the University of South Carolina, Purvis rose from obscurity to become one of the best known Federal Bureau of Investigation (FBI)* agents of his era following his successful pursuit of John Dillinger. A former South Carolina lawyer, Purvis joined the FBI in 1927 and was subsequently promoted to the Chicago field office. He led one of the two teams during the Little Bohemia debacle, in which agent W. Carter Baum* was slain and John Dillinger escaped.

After a string of daring bank robberies and prison escapes in the 1930s, John Dillinger was named Public Enemy Number One (see PUBLIC ENEMIES) by the FBI. Purvis was tabbed to bring the bandit hero to justice in 1934. A tip from one of Dillinger's lovers, Anna Sage (more romantically remembered as the "Lady in Red"), led the authorities to Chicago's Biograph Theater on June 22, 1934, where Dillinger was gunned down after he refused to surrender to Purvis. For a brief time Purvis was a national hero, but he was soon forced to resign from the FBI because of what was described as "inappropriate" behavior. In reality, his popularity had begun to eclipse that of director John Edgar Hoover,* and when he refused to lower his high-profile stance, Hoover embarked on a crusade to destroy his reputation. After Purvis resigned in 1935, Hoover downplayed his role in the Dillinger case and promoted Samuel P. Cowley* as the architect of Dillinger's demise.

The rest of Purvis's life was rather anticlimactic, if not sad. He worked in Hollywood as a technical advisor on crime films and then served as an announcer for a children's radio show called "Junior G-Man" (see G-MEN). In 1936 he penned his autobiography, *American Agent*, and during World War II, he worked in military intelligence. Over the years he became increasingly depressed as his former boss, Hoover, attempted to deflect credit from Purvis to another agent for killing Dillinger. Purvis committed suicide in 1960, apparently with the same gun that killed John Dillinger.

SOURCES: Melvin Purvis, *American Agent*, 1936; Curt Gentry, *J. Edgar Hoover: The Man and His Secrets*, 1991; Athan G. Theoharis, ed., *The FBI*, 1999.

PUSSER, BUFORD. (1938–1974) Born and raised in McNairy County, Tennessee, following service in the Marines, he returned to find his hometown riddled with organized crime activity. In 1964 he won election as county sheriff* and embarked on a one-man war against gambling, prostitution, and moonshining. The six-foot, six-inch, 250-pound sheriff rose to prominence in the South for personally destroying gambling equipment and contraband while brandishing a huge wooden club. He was seriously wounded numerous times yet survived seven assassination attempts. Responding to these attacks with his own ruthless brand of violence, Pusser was himself the target of criticism for his brutal tactics.

Pusser's closest brush with death came in 1967 when he was shot in the face and his wife was killed during an ambush along a country road near New Hope, Tennessee. Despite requiring fourteen operations to repair his face, he continued to serve as sheriff until his defeat in 1970. Pusser's life was the subject of several books by W. R. Morris, including *The Twelfth of August: The Story of Buford Pusser* (1971) and *Buford: Story of the "Walking Tall" Sheriff, Buford Pusser* (1983). The 1972 low-budget film *Walking Tall*, starring Joe Don Baker, was a huge financial success as it was released at a time when Americans were wearying of the growing crime problem. Ironically, Pusser was killed in a car accident only hours after signing a contract to play himself in the sequel to *Walking Tall*.

SOURCE: W. R. Morris, *The Twelfth of August: The Story of Buford Pusser*, 1971.

Q

QUAI DES ORFEVRES. The current headquarters of the French police *judiciaire*, or sûreté,* can be found at 36 quai des Orfevres. On the top floor of the building is the prefecture library and museum. This location plays a central role in Georges Simenon's Inspector Jules Maigret* series and many other French detective stories.

SOURCE: Philip John Stead, *The Police of Paris*, 1957.

QUANTICO, VIRGINIA. The training of Federal Bureau of Investigation (FBI)* agents was initially conducted through the Washington, D.C., field office beginning in 1928. In 1972 an updated training facility was established on the U.S. Marine Corps base in Quantico, Virginia. Initially named the National Police Academy, in 1945 it was rechristened the FBI National Academy. It plays a major role in professionalizing law enforcement throughout the United States and the world. Classes were first offered here in 1935, but at that time there was little demand from police departments as it was prior to the police professionalization movement. As the demand for law enforcement training increased, the FBI moved out of the Marine Corps base and onto its own campus in 1972.

In 1984, the National Center for the Analysis of Violent Crime was established at Quantico and received national attention following the release of Thomas Harris's book *The Silence of the Lambs* and the subsequent movie. This center is located within the Profiling and Behavioral Assessment Unit of the Forensic Science Research and Training Center, which grew out of the Behavioral Science Unit in the 1970s and 1980s.

SOURCE: Athan G. Theoharis, ed., *The FBI: A Comprehensive Reference Guide*, 1999.

QUEIROZ, EUSEBIO DE. (1812–1868) Born in Luanda, Angola, Queiroz's father was a member of the Portuguese colony's high court. He moved to Brazil with his family in 1816 and in 1827 graduated from law school. He served in various judicial positions before being appointed Rio de Janeiro's police chief in 1833. Except for a six-month respite, he served as police chief for eleven years, the longest such tenure during Brazil's empire period. A founding member of the Conservative party, he is probably best remembered for declaring the transatlantic slave trade illegal in 1850. His career in public service also included a stint, from 1848 to 1852, as minister of justice, a post that gave him control of both the civilian and military police forces. In 1854 he became a senator, and the following year he was appointed to the Council of State. In 1867 he ascended to a seat on the Supreme Tribunal of Justice.

During his long career as police chief, Queiroz left his imprint on the newly created force and built it into a centralized authoritarian institution. With the judicial reforms of 1841, Queiroz had more opportunities to mold the evolving police force as the position of police chief became increasingly powerful. Formerly constrained by the old system, with the 1841 reforms, police officials replaced the elected judges in local districts and were imbued with the authority to arrest, judge, and sentence petty offenders in the police station without the formality of the traditional judicial process.

SOURCE: Thomas H. Holloway *Policing Rio de Janeiro*, 1993.

QUESTORES PARICIDII. During Rome's early republic, the *questores paricidii*, or trackers of murder, were employed by the consuls to capture killers whenever their activities seemed to threaten the community. As the official policemen of early Rome, their numbers were few and they were required to make sure that suspected murderers appeared before the assembly following their apprehension. This was done merely by blowing a trumpet outside the residence of the accused.

SOURCE: Charles Reith, *The Blind Eye of History*, 1952.

QUINN, PATRICK. An Irishman from County Mayo, Quinn was the second commander of the Special Branch of the Metropolitan Police.* He had formerly been one of Queen Victoria's bodyguards. As head of the Special Branch between 1903 and 1918, he helped catch German spy Siegfried Helm in 1910 as he mapped fortifications at Portsmouth. Although Helm was released soon after his capture, Quinn would be instrumental in the apprehension of other spies during World War I, the conviction of Roger Casement, and the suppression of suffragists.

SOURCE: Rupert Allason, *The Branch*, 1983.

R

RAILROAD POLICE (UNITED STATES). American railroad policing began in Pennsylvania in 1865 and, over the following decades, followed the railroads west to other states and territories. Railroad police had their hands full between 1865 and the turn of the century chasing bandits such as Butch Cassidy and the Sundance Kid. By the 1980s, this obscure law enforcement unit was composed of twenty-five hundred officers divided among the major railroad companies. Although they don the traditional badges and guns, they are not employed by any city, state, county, or federal agency, but are more like a shadow unit that tracks railroad crime across the nation through several states. Their investigative duties run the gamut from protecting sensitive cargoes such as space shuttle rocket boosters, and presidents to solving burglaries, vandalism, robberies, and assaults.

SOURCE: Frank Richard Prassel, *The Western Peace Officer*, 1972; reprint, 1981.

RAILWAY POLICE (GREAT BRITAIN). Great Britain introduced the first railway police in the 1820s. They were charged with watching railroads and mining sites in order to suppress theft and minimize accidents. Up until 1831, railway companies hired their own police officers, but as the railway system expanded in the 1830s, Parliament stepped in with the Special Constables Act, which authorized railway companies to officially appoint "special constables" to patrol and protect railway lines. Under a statute that originated in the seventeenth century, these constables* were sworn in by local magistrates and financed by local authorities. This statute introduced what has become one of the longest-lasting problems in policing—jurisdictional conflicts. As one railroad line passed from one jurisdiction to another, disputes arose over apprehending fugitives because the special constables could not arrest suspects outside railway property, thus allowing criminals to easily escape the scene of their crime.

Some of these jurisdictional problems were resolved following the formation of the Great Western Railway police force in 1835. Within a few years it had grown to over 170 officers, who were given arrest powers equivalent to those of the regular constables. Attired in uniforms modeled on the early metropolitan force, officers were identified with the letters "GWR" as well as a number on a stand-up collar in scarlet cloth. Each constable was armed with an eighteen-inch-long truncheon.* In a day when the working classes rarely possessed a timepiece, each constable was issued a watch to ensure a timely delay between trains entering each section of track and thus avoid collisions. According to most sources, the aphorism "If you want to know the time, ask a policeman" originated with the railway police.

By the 1840s, these transport police were criticized for protecting companies against passengers but not protecting the passengers. In response, the government reduced lineside duties so that they could concentrate on criminal activity. The introduction of the telegraph freed policemen from time-consuming traffic regulation. Over the following decades, the railway police had their jurisdictions expanded to effectively pursue suspects. Parliament introduced a number of acts to better empower the police to deal with changing crime patterns.

In 1858 the first railway policeman was murdered, and six years later the force recorded the first murder to take place on railway property. There is little doubt that the most famous criminal case involving the British transport police was a 1963 railway theft better known as the Great Train Robbery. On August 8, 1963, fifteen train robbers waylaid the Glasgow-to-London Royal Mail train and escaped with more than 2.5 million British pounds. Subsequent bungling by the intrepid train robbers led to the arrest of twelve of them, although a thirteenth, Ronnie Biggs, managed to escape to South America and live a life of celebrity. The transportation police have had to deal with rail crashes and related disasters; the 1987 King's Cross fire, when thirty-one passengers were killed in the subway; and football hooliganism; and they must remain vigilant because of terroristic threats.

SOURCE: Pauline Appleby, *A Force on the Move: The Story of the British Transport Police, 1825–1995*, 1995.

RAMSAY, NATHANIEL. (b. 1741) Following graduation from the College of New Jersey in 1767, Ramsay enjoyed a lucrative career as a lawyer and wealthy landowner. Captured by British forces at the Battle of Monmouth Courthouse in 1778, he was paroled two years later. Between 1785 and 1787, he served as a Maryland representative in the Second Continental Congress. On September 26, 1789, President George Washington appointed Ramsay as the first marshal with the U.S. Marshals Service.*

SOURCE: Frederick S. Calhoun, *The Lawmen*, 1991.

RAPELJE, HIRAM LEE. (1851–1919) Born in Ontario, Canada, Rapelje moved to California with his family in 1867. Following stints as a stagecoach driver, he was appointed deputy sheriff in the early 1880s, beginning a thirty-year career as a Fresno County lawman. Rapelje apprehended several horse thieves and robbers before returning to stagecoach driving in 1887. In 1892 he returned to law enforcement as a deputy sheriff in Fresno County. He rose to prominence following the gun battle that resulted in the apprehension of train robbers Chris Evans and John Sontag.

Beginning in 1894, "Hi" Rapelje began working as a watchman in Chinatown. His salary was paid by the saloon owners and local merchants, leading to charges of conflicts of interest. Rapelje apparently reveled in his capacity as "mayor of West Fresno," a title bestowed on him by the Chinese community. In the late 1890s he became embroiled in the conflict between various Chinese Tong gang members from San Francisco who were trying to grab a piece of the Fresno action. Rapelje left his position of deputy sheriff at the time of the gang war over control of the Fresno Chinatown, and in one particularly notorious incident he was involved in a shoot-out that left three Chinese men dead. In his last years, Rapelje returned to law enforcement as a deputy sheriff in Kern County and as an officer for the Huntington Lake Power Company.

SOURCES: William B. Secrest, *Lawmen and Desperadoes*, 1994; Hu Maxwell, *Evans and Sontag*, reprint, 1981.

RATTLES. One of the earliest police alarm systems was the rattle. In the early seventeenth century, one early police force was known as the rattle-watch.* Rattles were used by early night watchmen (see NIGHT WATCH; WATCH AND WARD SYSTEM) as an alarm system to summon help when threatened by lawbreakers in the days before professional police training. Rattles came in a variety of incarnations; some were iron weighted and could be wielded like a baton, while others were single or double ratchet. Most were well constructed out of hardwood and would make a characteristic loud "rat-a-tat-tat" noise when the handle was swung around rapidly, causing a club-like part to hit a center board. Early police rattles were handmade and often were inscribed with the owner's initials. Later models were identifiable by the companies that manufactured them, such as Bagshaw & Falls; P. Gaylord; and Schuyler, Hartley & Graham.

SOURCE: George E. Virgines, *Police Relics*, 1982.

RATTLE-WATCH. On August 12, 1651, the Dutch colony of New Netherlands introduced the law enforcement position of *ratel wacht*, or rattle-watch, so named because of the rattles* used as signal mechanisms. By 1658 a paid rattle-watch composed of eight men functioned as night watchmen (see NIGHT WATCH: WATCH AND WARD SYSTEM) from 9 o'clock at night until sunrise. All male citizens were required to serve stints in this position and were paid the equivalent of fifty cents per night from a tax paid by each property owner. Guards caught sleeping on duty were subject to fines and were penalized for fighting, swearing, and inebriation.

SOURCE: Augustine Costello, *Our Police Protectors*, 1885; reprint, 1972.

REDDIN, THOMAS. (b. 1916) Born in New York City, Reddin joined the Los Angeles Police Department (LAPD)* in 1941 and ascended to chief of police in 1967. Prior to achieving the top post Reddin commanded the detective bureau and bureau of Corrections and was superintendent of training. Like William Henry Parker* and Edward M. Davis,* during his twenty-seven months as police chief, Reddin was known as an independent chief who would not be bullied by politicians. However, he often found himself in conflict with the hard-core, macho police officers. His willingness to meet with civil rights leaders and members of the Black Panther party was seen as a weakness, as was his attendance at most Los Angeles cultural events. When Reddin asked patrolmen to turn on their headlights in honor of the recently assassinated Martin Luther King, Jr., less than one-quarter complied.

Despite his predilection for diplomacy, Reddin helped develop the Special Weapons and Tactics Team (SWAT),* ordered the surveillance of the Black Panthers, and defended the bloody police riots against Century City antiwar demonstrators in 1967. Reddin resigned in April 1969 after a turbulent stint as police chief, which included involvement following Sirhan Sirhan's assassination of Bobby Kennedy, shoot-outs with Black Panthers, and civil disorder in the Watts and Century City areas. Reddin's retirement was rather anticlimactic; he made a failed run for mayor and proved a disaster as a television news broadcaster.

SOURCES: Joe Domanick, *To Protect and Serve*, 1994; Daryl F. Gates, *Chief: My Life in the LAPD*, 1992.

RED TOMAHAWK. (c. 1853–1931) Born in South Dakota, Red Tomahawk was a sergeant of the Indian police* at the Standing Rock Agency in South Dakota during the Ghost Dance troubles in the late 1880s. Red Tomahawk, Lieutenant Bull Head, and forty-three Indian police were ordered to arrest Sitting Bull on December 15, 1890. What started out as a peaceful arrest turned into carnage as a gunfight quickly broke out between the Indian police and Sitting Bull's followers. In the ensuing skirmish, Bull Head, Sitting Bull, and several Indian police* officers were killed. Red Tomahawk is generally considered to have fired the shot that killed the legendary Sioux Indian chief and survived the affair unscathed.

SOURCES: Robert M. Utley, *The Last Days of the Sioux Nation*, 1963; Frederick J. Dockstander, *Great American Indians*, 1977.

REEVES, BASS. (1838–1910) Born into a slave family in Paris, Texas, Reeves became the first African-American to be commissioned a U.S. deputy marshal (see U.S. MARSHALS SERVICE) west of the Mississippi River. He left Texas in the 1850s after fighting with his young master and fled into the Indian Territory. Over the next decade he lived with various Indian tribes before leaving Oklahoma in 1863, after the Emancipation Proclamation was issued. Moving to Van Buren, Arkansas, he married and began a family and occasionally served as a scout for deputy U.S. marshals working on the periphery of the Indian Territory.

Reeves began his thirty-two-year law enforcement career in 1874 when he was among two hundred deputy marshals hired in Fort Smith, Arkansas, to hunt down wanted criminals in the Indian Territory. During the territorial era, deputy marshals were the only peace officers authorized to perform this task. By 1907, Reeves had killed fourteen wanted men, including the notorious horse thief and killer Jim Webb. A dependable and efficient lawman, on one occasion Reeves was even required to arrest his own son for murder. Reeves was forced to retire as U.S. deputy marshal in 1907, when Oklahoma became a state and implemented Jim Crow laws. Federal marshals were replaced by the state and Reeves joined the Muskogee police, walking a segregated beat for two years.

SOURCE: Art Burton, *Black, Red, and Deadly: Black and Indian Gunfighters of the Indian Territory, 1870–1907*, 1991.

REGULATORS, THE. In 1767 a group of vigilantes known as the Regulators was formed in the South Carolina backcountry. Probably the first vigilante movement in American history, its initial goal was to wipe out the outlaw scourge that was plaguing the region. Prior to the establishment of effective law enforcement and a legitimate court system, leading citizens organized the Regulators after help from Charleston was not forthcoming. The Regulator campaign against the outlaw gangs finally received the attention of the governor, who authorized two groups of mounted rangers to rid the region of the lawlessness. With the end of the bandit scourge, the Regulators evolved into an instrument of oppression, this time targeting the lower classes. As the new arbiters of moral behavior the Regulators' "Plan of Regulation" included the use of flogging and other corporal punishments to help "reform" vagrants, ne'er-do-wells, and "loose" women.

SOURCE: Richard Maxwell Brown, *The South Carolina Regulators*, 1963.

REHM, JACOB. Jacob Rehm was appointed city marshal of Chicago in 1858, and in 1861 he was appointed deputy superintendent of the newly created Chicago Police Department (CPD) force. In 1863 he was appointed chief of police, and despite his unscrupulous tendencies toward corruption, he was appointed to this position five times. He served on the Board of Police in 1871 and four years later was indicted in federal court for conspiring to defraud the government of liquor revenues in the great Whiskey Fraud cases. That same year he was convicted in the federal court and sentenced to a six-month jail term and a ten-thousand-dollar fine.

SOURCES: Raphael W. Marrow and Harriet I. Carter, *In Pursuit of Crime*, 1996; John J. Flinn, *History of the Chicago Police*, 1887; revised, 1973.

REID, EDMUND JOHN JAMES. (b. 1846) Reid joined the London Metropolitan Police* in 1872 following a series of jobs including ship's steward and pastry cook. He entered the Criminal Investigation Department (CID)* in 1874 and four years later was promoted to sergeant. In 1884 he rose to Detective Inspector at Scotland Yard.* After organizing the J Division CID at Bethnal Green, he was selected to succeed Frederick George Abberline* as head of the Whitechapel CID in 1888. He rose to prominence in the late 1880s during the hunt for Jack the Ripper in Whitechapel.

A man of many talents, Reid acted and sang on stage, and he reached record heights as a balloonist in the 1880s. He reportedly made the first parachute jump in England from over one thousand feet. Reid's exploits inspired the Detective Dier character in a series of ten novels written by Charles Gibbon. He retired from CID in 1896 as the longest serving detective inspector of Whitechapel. In several interviews at the turn of the century, Reid suggested that Jack the Ripper was responsible for nine murders.

SOURCE: Paul Begg, Martin Fido, and Keith Skinner, *The Jack the Ripper A to Z*, 1991.

REIS, ALBERT JOHN, JR. (b. 1922) Born in Wisconsin and educated at Marquette University and the University of Chicago, Reis taught criminology at several universities before settling down at Yale. In 1971 he completed the first examination of police brutality in America. In preparation, he accompanied police officers on patrol in Chicago, Boston, and Washington, D.C. According to his findings, African-Americans were twice as likely to be the targets of police brutality as their white counterparts. His study motivated police departments to become more compassionate in the treatment of minorities.

SOURCE: Charles Phillips and Alan Axelrod, *CCC*, 1996.

REY, OCTAVE. (1837–1908) Born in New Orleans, Rey was originally a cooper before fighting for the Union army in the Sixth Louisiana Colored Infantry during the Civil War. He left the army in 1863 to recuperate from a leg wound due to racial conflict within the Union army. Soon after he joined the New Orleans Metropolitan Police and was appointed captain in the Fourth Precinct. He lost his position during the Redemption process of 1876 and 1877 that accompanied the post–Civil War Reconstruction. Rey was one of the highest-ranking African-American policemen on the New Orleans force in the nineteenth century. Following his police service, he remained a well-respected member of the community. In 1882 he served as chief of special election marshals for the First Congressional District during the November election, and four years later he was involved in a shooting fracas.

SOURCE: Dennis C. Rousey, *Policing the Southern City: New Orleans, 1805–1889*, 1996.

REYNOLDS, GLENN. (1853–1889) Born in Texas, Reynolds fought Comanches during the 1860s and worked as a trail hand on Kansas cattle drives before winning election as sheriff* of Throckmorton County, Texas. In 1885 he raised sheep and then started a ranch in the vicinity of Pleasant Valley, Arizona. He relocated his family to Globe following the outbreak of violence known as the Pleasant Valley War. In 1888 the town elected him sheriff. Over the next year he tracked various bandits, both Apaches and whites. In 1889 Reynolds was assigned to transport the Apache Kid and several convicts to meet a train for the territorial prison. The prisoners overpowered Reynolds and his two deputies, and during the escape attempt, they killed Reynolds.

SOURCES: Jess G. Hayes, *Apache Vengeance*, 1954; Dan L. Thrapp, ed., *EFB*, Vol. 3, 1988.

RICHARZ, HENRY JOSEPH. (1822–1910) Born near Cologne in what is now Germany, Richarz came to America following the Marxist upheavals of 1848. By the early 1850s he was living in Texas, where he worked as postmaster until the outbreak of the Civil War. Following service in the home guard during the conflict, he was commissioned captain of Company of the Texas Rangers* (Frontier Battalion) in 1870. During his tenure with the Rangers, Richarz was mostly charged with handling the Indian threat and even pursued Kickapoo raiders into Mexico. In late 1870 his son was killed by Comanches, and during the first half of the following year he led his company on the trail of hostile Indians. In June of 1871, his Ranger company was disbanded due to a dearth of state funds. Richarz later served in the Texas State Legislature in 1880.

SOURCE: Mike Cox, *Texas Ranger Tales II*, 1999.

RICHEY (RICCI), LARRY. Growing up in Philadelphia, Richey (originally Ricci) worked as a newsboy before beginning his stellar career with the U.S. Secret Service* in 1898. Teamed with veteran Secret Service agent William John Burns,* Richey began a long affiliation with the future Federal Bureau of Investigation (FBI)* director and investigated one of the largest counterfeiting operations in American history. In 1906, Richey, who was of Italian descent, worked undercover in New York's Little Italy investigating the Black Hand extortion groups. His unit would collaborate with the Black Hand Squad of Joseph "Joe" Petrosino.*

During his tenure with the U.S. Secret Service, Richey investigated land fraud scandals for the Interior Department in Colorado and in 1910 helped arrest several brothel managers who worked for Big Jim Colosimo in Chicago's Levee district. In the early 1920s, when Attorney General Harlan Fiske Stone was looking for a candidate to lead the FBI, Richey suggested his friend John Edgar Hoover.*

SOURCE: Thomas A. Reppetto, *The Blue Parade*, 1978.

RIFKIN, STAN. The son of Russian-Jewish immigrants, Rifkin was raised in a New York City orphanage. He later joined the U.S. Marines and then, beginning in the 1950s, worked as a bounty hunter for over forty years. His career inspired the Steve McQueen movie *The Hunter*, and actor Robert DeNiro rode with Rifkin to prepare for his role as a bounty hunter in the movie *Midnight Run*. He claimed in an interview to have at one time used a motor home that contained a cell and bore the special license plate "Bounty Hunter Rifkin."

SOURCE: Jacqueline Pope, *Bounty Hunters, Marshals, and Sheriffs*, 1998.

RIGGS, CLINTON E. (1911–1997) Police officer Riggs was credited with creating the "Yield" traffic sign in 1939, while attending the Northwestern Traffic Institute. Over the next ten years he experimented with various prototypes before the first "Yield Right-of-Way" sign was installed at a Tulsa intersection in 1950. Riggs was also instrumental in establishing the Tulsa Police Academy and the Tulsa police officer badge.

Riggs apparently first came up with the idea for the yield sign, which both controls traffic at intersections and assigns liability in the event of a collision, while working traffic control as a member of the Oklahoma State Highway Patrol. Riggs graduated from the University of Tulsa Law School in 1954 and wrote several law enforcement handbooks, including *Law of Arrest for Police Officers* and *The Police Officer Witness*.

SOURCE: "Ex-Officer Who Created 'Yield' Sign Dies," *Houston Chronicle*, May 25, 1997.

RIIS, JACOB. (1849–1914) Riis moved to New York City in 1877, seven years after arriving in America from his native Denmark. Having lived in poverty himself during his peregrinations since leaving his homeland, Riis had a natural empathy for the impoverished. He found his calling while working as a police reporter for the *New York Tribune*. As a social reformer, photographer, and journalist, he became famous for documenting the miserable conditions of New York City tenement life during the late nineteenth century. Riis, along with Lincoln Steffens,* accompanied police board president Theodore Roosevelt* on midnight excursions to the seedier police precincts with the hope of exposing police corruption and dereliction of duty. Riis chronicled the struggles of the poor and downtrodden in *The Children of the Poor* (1892), *How the Other Half*

Lives (1890), and *The Making of an American* (1901), and then wrote a biography of Roosevelt entitled *Theodore Roosevelt, the Citizen* (1904).

SOURCES: Jacob Riis, *The Making of an American*, 1901; H. Paul Jeffers, *Commissioner Roosevelt*, 1994; Thomas A. Reppetto, *The Blue Parade*, 1978.

RIOS, ARIEL. (1954–1982) Born in New Haven, Connecticut, Rios graduated from the John Jay College of Criminal Justice in 1976 before beginning his law enforcement career with various New York police agencies. In 1978 he joined the Alcohol, Tobacco and Firearms* (ATF) Bureau and began working undercover in Connecticut. Rios was killed while making an undercover drug purchase in South Florida on December 2, 1982. He became a media hero and a symbol for the federal government's "war on drugs" during the Reagan era.

SOURCE: Charles Phillips and Alan Axelrod, *CCC*, 1996.

RIZZO, FRANK L. (1920–1991) The son of a policeman, Rizzo was born in Philadelphia, Pennsylvania. A high school dropout, Rizzo joined the navy in 1938 but was discharged for medical reasons the following year. Joining his father on the Philadelphia police force in 1943, he quickly earned a reputation as an aggressive, no-nonsense street cop and was promoted to acting sergeant; at one point he was even his father's supervisor.

In 1952 he was assigned to the highway patrol* and officially promoted to sergeant; he rose to inspector seven years later. A staunchly conservative proponent of law and order, Rizzo became identified with the use of police brutality and poor relations with the African-American community. In 1962 he criticized the courts and the American Civil Liberties Union (ACLU) as being soft on crime while testifying before the McClellan Senate Subcommittee on Crime. Promoted the following year to deputy commissioner, during the 1960s Rizzo would lead his force in confrontations with Vietnam War and civil rights protestors, thus embellishing his strident law-and-order image.

Rizzo was promoted to police commissioner in 1967, and in 1972 he became the first incumbent police chief to be elected mayor of Philadelphia. Because of term limits, Rizzo was forced to step aside following two consecutive terms in office, and in 1980 he unsuccessfully attempted to revise the city charter to allow him to run again. Despite future attempts to regain the mayor's seat, his political career was effectively finished by the 1980s when the city elected its first black mayor. When Rizzo died in 1991, the city honored its last political boss with one of Philadelphia's largest funerals.

SOURCES: S. A. Paolantonio, *Frank Rizzo: The Last Big Man in Big City America*, 1993; Jonathan Rubinstein, *City Police*, 1973; Fred Hamilton, *Rizzo: From Cop to Mayor of Philadelphia*, 1993.

ROBERTS, DANIEL WEBSTER. (1841–1935) Born in Winston County, Mississippi, he moved with his family to Blanco County, Texas, in 1843. In

1874 he joined Company D unit of the Frontier Battalion of the Texas Rangers.* He rose to the rank of captain during his tenure with the Rangers in the 1870s and rose to prominence by 1880 during conflicts with the Mason County Mob and the Jesse Evans and Potter gangs. A popular Ranger captain, his men conferred on him the homage of "one of God's noblemen" (*Frontier Times*). He suffered a serious leg wound during an Indian fight sometime in 1877–1878, and in 1882 he resigned from the force to take care of his ailing wife. In 1914 he published his memoirs chronicling his Ranger exploits.

SOURCES: "Captain Dan W. Roberts," *Frontier Times* 4 (11) August 1927; Robert W. Stephens, *Texas Ranger Indian War Pensions*, 1975.

ROBERTS, JAMES F. (1858–1934) Born in Bevier, Missouri, Roberts moved West in 1876 and started a cattle ranch near Globe, Arizona. In 1887–1988 he sided with the Tewksbury faction during the Pleasant Valley War. A highly skilled gunman, he was involved in several gunfights during the feud and was exonerated of several murder charges.

In 1889 he turned to law enforcement as deputy under Sheriff* William Owen "Buckey" O'Neill* in Jerome, Arizona. Three years later he began an eleven-year stint as constable for Jerome. In 1904 he won election as the town marshal.* Subsequently he moved to Clarkdale, Arizona and served as a special officer (with a deputy sheriff's commission) for the United Verde Company during his remaining years. The seventy-year-old Roberts was prominent in 1928 for his apprehension of Earl Nelson and the killing of his accomplice during a bank robbery. When Roberts died of a heart attack in 1935, he was the last remaining survivor of the famous Pleasant Valley War.

SOURCES: Earl R. Forrest, *Arizona's Dark and Bloody Ground*, 1964; Clara T. Woody and Milton Schwartz, *Globe, Arizona*, 1977.

ROBERTS, PATRICK ELTON. (d. 1990) Deputy Sheriff Roberts was reportedly the first American peace officer to die from AIDS contracted in the line of duty. He was infected while investigating a crime scene.

SOURCE: Craig W. Floyd and Kelley Lang Helms, *To Protect and Serve*, 1995.

ROBINSON, GEORGIA. In 1919 Georgia Robinson was promoted from matron to the Los Angeles Police Department (LAPD),* making her the first African-American woman hired as a municipal police officer in America. However, it took a year-long campaign by black activists before she was hired as a policewoman (see POLICEWOMEN). Her appointment was an attempt by the LAPD to enforce the law without criminalizing suspects. To further the department's reform agenda, Robinson attempted to keep wayward black women off the streets and tried referring them to other social agencies in the black community.

SOURCE: Craig W. Floyd and Kelley Lang Helms, *To Protect and Serve*, 1995.

ROEMER, WILLIAM F., JR. (1926–1996) The son of a former Jesuit seminarian, Roemer attended the University of Notre Dame before embarking on a legal career. During his thirty-year career with the Federal Bureau of Investigation (FBI)* Roemer was selected by John Edgar Hoover* for the Bureau's elite Top Hoodlum Program, beginning at its inception in 1957. An indefatigable lawman, Roemer conducted surveillance and gathered evidence on top Chicago mob bosses Sam Giancana and Murray "The Camel" Humphreys. After leaving the FBI, Roemer worked as a private attorney and served as a consultant on the Chicago Crime Commission. In 1983 he testified as a witness before the U.S. Senate rackets committee in Chicago. He went on to write several books chronicling his efforts against organized crime, including *Roemer: Man Against the Mob* (1989), *Tony Accardo: The Genuine Godfather*, and *The Enforcer*. He also wrote the novels *War of the Godfathers* and *Mob Power Plays*, which were based on actual mob stories.

SOURCE: John J. Flood, "William F. Roemer, Jr. (1926–1996)," Spilotro's Vegas Website, July 28, 1999, available at www.ipsn.org/roemer.html, Internet.

ROGERS, MARY CECILIA. (1820–1841) The inept Mary Rogers murder investigation in 1841 is considered by many police scholars to be a clarion call for police reform in America. Reportedly a beautiful woman who clerked in a New York City tobacco shop, Rogers counted as customers leading literary figures such as James Fenimore Cooper, Washington Irving, and Edgar Alan Poe. She would later supply the inspiration for the victim in Poe's classic detective story *The Mystery of Marie Roget*, published in 1842.

The real Mary Rogers was found murdered in July 1841. Subsequently, numerous theories emerged concerning her last fateful evening. The coroner's autopsy and the inadequate police investigation demonstrated the limits of contemporary policing. Since the body was found near Hoboken, New Jersey, the New York City police were reluctant to investigate. Of course it should be taken into account that there was not a twenty-four-hour police force and that law enforcement was primarily conducted by poorly paid and untrained night watchmen (see NIGHT WATCH; WATCH AND WARD SYSTEM) and roundsmen.* Newspaper criticism of the roundsmen created the impetus for an investigation. Although the case was never solved, the murder led to a reform campaign for more effective policing, and within five years the New York City police would be entirely reorganized and steps would be made toward professionalism.

SOURCE: Raymond Paul, *Who Murdered Mary Rogers?* 1971.

ROHAN, ANDY. (d. 1912) Rohan joined the Chicago Police Department (CPD)* in 1874 and, after serving with distinction as a beat cop for eight years, was promoted to detective. He was initially teamed with Michael Schaack, who later became an inspector on the force. In earlier years he had reportedly palled around with Frank and Jesse James while they were on the lam in Nashville following the Northfield bank raid; Rohan was unaware of their true identities. In 1901 he was cocommander of the detective bureau of the CPD, and in 1910 he retired. Three of his sons would also serve on the CPD.

SOURCE: Raphael W. Marrow and Harriet I. Carter, *In Pursuit of Crime*, 1996.

ROOSEVELT, THEODORE. (1858–1919) After graduating from Harvard in 1880, Roosevelt embarked on a career of public service that would catapult him to the presidency in 1901. As a police commissioner (he was one of four) in New York City from 1895 to 1897, Roosevelt was instrumental in exposing departmental corruption and rooting out unscrupulous police officials such as Alexander S. "Clubber" Williams* and William Devery,* Roosevelt introduced a variety of reforms, including a promotion system based on merit rather than patronage. He was also credited with implementing telephone communications, better police training, and a twenty-nine-member bicycle squad known as the "Scorcher Squad," which was charged with apprehending speeding horse-drawn carriages.

Roosevelt was a supporter of the Pennsylvania State Constabulary and, as president in 1908, created the Bureau of Investigation. A friend and confidant of legendary lawmen Patrick Floyd Jarvis "Pat" Garrett* and William Bartholomew "Bat" Masterson,* as New York City police commissioner he reorganized the police in an attempt to take control of the force out of the hands of local political bosses. Under his tenure he instilled paramilitary discipline and administration while weeding out vestiges of the Tammany Hall machine. By 1897, New York State Republicans had apparently wearied of his reform campaign, and in order to get him out of New York City, reportedly arranged to have him appointed assistant secretary of the navy.

SOURCES: Edmund Morris, *The Rise of Theodore Roosevelt*, 1979; H. Paul Jeffers, *Commissioner Roosevelt*, 1994; Theodore Roosevelt, *An Autobiography*, 1913.

ROSS, PETER F. (1836–1909) Born in Missouri, he moved with his family to Texas at the age of two. He was appointed captain in the Texas Rangers* in 1858 and then served in the Sixth Texas Cavalry during the Civil War. Following the war he went into the cattle business, spent several years in California, and in 1875 was elected sheriff* of McClennan County, Texas.

SOURCES: J. W. Ellison, "Scouted on Pease River," *Frontier Times*, December. 1927; Walter Prescott Webb, H. Bailey Carroll, eds., *Handbook of Texas*, 1952.

ROUNDSMEN. An early incarnation of the American policeman, roundsmen were the daytime counterpart to the night watchman (see NIGHT WATCH; WATCH AND WARD SYSTEM). Unlike other watchmen, who wore leather helmets, (hence their sobriquet leatherheads*), roundsmen worked as plain-clothesmen and did not wear the customary helmet. Roundsmen were typically laborers who supplemented their wages as amateur detectives. It is doubtful that they solved many crimes, but since they were unpaid, renumeration was generated through rewards and the return of stolen property. Like the thief-takers (see THIEF-TAKER GENERAL) of eighteenth-century London, roundsmen often collaborated with the criminal element in order to collect rewards for returning merchandise stolen by local criminals. In 1845 New York City replaced the incompetent roundsmen with a professional police force.

SOURCE: Carl Sifakis, *The Encyclopedia of American Crime*, 1982.

ROUSE, CHARLES. (d. 1820) Rouse is remembered as the last of the London Charleys.* He worked as a watchman (see NIGHT WATCH; WATCH AND WARD SYSTEM) in Kennington, England, until his death in 1820. His box served as a both a place of confinement and a place for the watchmen to keep warm and rest. He is typically featured carrying a lantern in one hand and a stave in the other. He was also equipped with a sword and rattle (see RATTLES).

SOURCE: George Howard, *Guardians of the Queen's Peace*, 1953.

ROWAN, SIR CHARLES. (1783–1852) Rowan was a retired officer who had been wounded at the Battle of Waterloo when he was appointed, along with Sir Richard Mayne,* as commissioner of the new London Metropolitan Police* of Sir Robert Peel* in 1829. A bachelor with no public school or university education, he was working as a magistrate in Ireland following a distinguished military career when Peel convinced him to come to London. The two commissioners became innovators, introducing preventive law enforcement to the streets of London. Most scholarship suggests that Peel met privately with Mayne and Rowan in order to come up with the accoutrements and appearance of the new police. Rowan retired in 1850 after being diagnosed with colonic cancer.

SOURCES: Charles Reith, *A New Study of Police History*, 1956; John Wilkes, *The London Police in the Nineteenth Century*, 1977.

ROYAL CANADIAN MOUNTED POLICE (RCMP). One of the best-known horse mounted police* forces in the world and one of the most widely recognized symbols of Canada, the North West Mounted Police was established in 1873 by the Canadian government to police the vast areas of western Canada that today comprise Saskatchewan and Alberta. At first there were 150 recruits, but this was soon doubled. Strongly military in character, the force adopted the now familiar scarlet tunic of the British Army.

Reports reaching the government indicated that some form of control was needed as free raiders roamed at will exchanging alcohol for furs and horses. News that a gang of wolf hunters had massacred a camp of Assiniboine Indians precipitated the formation of the North West Mounted Police. During its first decades, it established friendly relations with the Indians, suppressed lawlessness, assisted the militia, and patrolled the gold fields during the Yukon gold rush in the 1890s.

In 1904 King Edward VII granted the force use of the prefix "Royal," and it became the Royal North-West Mounted Police. In 1920 it absorbed the Dominion Police and its title was changed to the Royal Canadian Mounted Police. Its mission was upgraded as well, and was now to enforce federal legislation throughout the entire country.

During World War II, the RCMP was responsible for maintaining Canada's internal security, and in the intervening years it has assumed many provincial-policing duties. Today the force consists of more than sixteen thousand peace officers and acts as the municipal police force in about two hundred Canadian towns and cities. It has contract agreements to provide provincial police services in eight out of ten provinces (Ontario and Quebec have their own police forces). The RCMP enforces 140 federal laws and statutes dealing with narcotics, commercial crime, immigration and passport control, customs, and counterfeiting.

SOURCE: Mitchel P. Roth, "Mounted Police Forces: A Comparative History," *Policing* 21 (4), Fall 1998; R. C. Fetherstonhaugh, *The Royal Canadian Mounted Police*, 1938.

ROYAL IRISH CONSTABULARY. Ireland was the only corner of the British Empire that never embraced the police organization propounded by Sir Robert Peel* 1829. However, the continued conflict between a Catholic majority, which favored the overthrow of British rule, and the Protestant bastion of Ulster led to the creation of the Irish Constabulary in 1836. This unit was not designated the Royal Irish Constabulary* (RIC) until after 1867. Earlier precursors to this police force included a military-style "peace preservation" force established by chief secretary for Ireland Sir Robert Peel in 1814. Four years later, four provincial police forces, organized by county and numbering over five thousand officers, were established. Since Peel was tied to the creation of both the RIC and the English police, to distinguish the two, the Irish force was referred to as Peelers* and the English force as bobbies, in deference to Sir Robert.

The force grew to thirteen thousand by the 1850s and was characterized by paramilitary features; used a beat system to patrol the countryside much like its counterpart in urban London. Although officers were usually English, the rank and file were typically Irish Catholics. The RIC had the mind-set of an army of occupation and was often faced with suppressing riots and revolutionary activities. The RIC became the dominant model for British colonial policing in the far-flung British Empire.

RIC officers were often assigned to lead police forces in the British colonies and were typically better educated than other police officers, many having graduated from Eton, Harrow, and the Royal Military College at Sandhurst. The RIC was criticized for allowing the Ulster Protestants and southern Catholics to build private armies prior to World War I. By 1919, the power of the RIC had diminished, and it would not be resurrected until 1922, with the establishment of the Royal Ulster Constabulary (RUC).

SOURCES: Seamus Breatnach, *The Irish Police*, 1974; Sir Charles Jeffries, *The Colonial Police*, 1952; Charles Reith, *The Blind Eye of History*, 1952.

RUDITSKY, BARNETT "BARNEY." (1898–1962) Born in London, England, Ruditsky's family immigrated to New York's East Side during the first decade of the twentieth century. Ruditsky joined the army and served along the Mexican border and in France during World War I. He joined the New York City Police* Department (NYPD)* in 1921 and three years later was promoted to detective. He was partnered with Detective John "Johnny" Broderick,* and the dramatic duo provided good copy for newspapers that reported their exploits against underworld figures such as Legs Diamond and Dutch Schultz. Among Ruditsky's best-known arrests were those of Bugsy Siegel and Abe "Kid Twist" Reles, and in 1950 he bravely testified at the Kefauver Hearings on Organized Crime.

Ruditsky retired from the force in 1941 and served in the army during World War II in the African campaign, where he was wounded by shrapnel. During his stint in the army he also finished his memories as a policeman, "Angel's Corner." Following the war he opened a liquor store in Los Angeles and operated a private detective firm. His collection of bad debts for Las Vegas casinos, including Bugsy Siegel's operation, would come back to haunt him when a syndicated columnist leaked the information in his column, and Ruditsky's good cop image lost some of its luster. However, this did not deter him from becoming embroiled in more shady dealings. Joe DiMaggio hired him to dig up dirt on Marilyn Monroe during their divorce proceedings in 1954.

In 1959 Ruditsky's unpublished memoir, "Angel's Corner," was picked up by the NBC network and became a summer television series called *The Lawless Years*, with the author as technical advisor. According to William Howard Moore, after the show was canceled in 1961, it inspired ABC's more successful *The Untouchables*.

SOURCES: *New York Times*, October 19, 1962, obituary page; William Howard Moore, "Barney Ruditsky," *ANB*, Vol. 19, 1999.

RURALES. In the tradition of the Texas Rangers* and other frontier horse mounted police,* Benito Juarez founded the Mexican Rural Police Force, the Rurales, in 1861. The main focus of the force was to suppress the bandit problem. Outfitted much like their bandit counterparts, what differentiated the Rurales was their sombrero, which bore the number of the corps to which they belonged.

Considered formidable agents of the government, by 1875 more than 1,000 Rurales patrolled rural Mexico, particularly the central valley. Five years later the force was expanded to 1,767 men. Initially, Rurales were recruited from the bandit element, but by the 1880s, enlistees were drawn from the ranks of *campesinos* and artisans. With little chance for advancement, it was obvious that many joined to earn a temporary wage until something better came along. It is estimated that of those who enlisted between 1880 and 1910, half were from the countryside and the rest from urban areas, Most were illiterate with an average age in the mid- to late twenties. During the first decade of the twentieth century more than one-third of the Rurales deserted. By comparison, the Canadian Northwest Mounted Police had a 6 percent desertion rate and the U.S. Army, a 6.7 percent desertion rate.

SOURCE: P. J. Vanderwood, *Disorder and Progress: Bandits, Police, and Mexican Development*, 1981.

RUSK, DAVID VANCEL. Rusk fought at the Battle of San Jacinto in 1836 and then worked as a ferry operator before being appointed the first sheriff* of Texas and the American West in 1837.

SOURCE: "Texas' First Sheriff," *Sheriff's Association of Texas Magazine*, Vol. 1 (11), April 1932.

RUSSELL, RICHARD ROBERTSON. (1858–1922) Born in Dawson County, Georgia, he moved to Texas with his family in 1870. In 1879 he joined the Texas Rangers* but left a year later to pursue his lifelong interest in cattle ranching. In 1886 he began a ten-year stint as sheriff* of Menard County. During this period his cattle business flourished, and he was instrumental in founding the local bank. He left law enforcement in 1896 and soon joined the ranks of the millionaires and moved to San Antonio.

SOURCES: Robert W. Stephens, *Texas Ranger Sketches*, 1972; "R. R. (Dick) Russell" *Frontier Times* 4 (11), August 1927.

RYNNING, THOMAS H. (1866–1941) Born in Beloit, Wisconsin, Rynning, who had lost his parents as a youth, traveled west to Texas in 1882 and three years later joined the Eighth U.S. Cavalry. He participated in the final actions of the Geronimo campaign in Arizona. Rynning would spend the next few years performing in Buffalo Bill's Wild West Show and served with the Rough Riders of Theodore Roosevelt* at San Juan Hill during the Spanish-American War.

In 1902 he inaugurated his law enforcement career when he was appointed captain of the Arizona Rangers.* During his five years with the Rangers he was involved in several gunfights with Mexican miners, gamblers, and other sordid characters. In 1907 he began a five-year stint as warden of Yuma Territorial

Prison. After serving as warden he once again wore a badge, as U.S. marshal (see U.S. MARSHALS SERVICE) and the undersheriff in San Diego in the 1930s.

SOURCES: Bill O'Neal, *The Arizona Rangers*, 1987; Jay Robert Nash, *EWLO*, 1994.

S

SAGAR, ROBERT. (1852–1924) Chief Constable Sagar played a leading role in the Jack the Ripper investigation. He left medical training to join the London police (see LONDON METROPOLITAN POLICE) in 1880. Between 1880 and 1890, he was promoted to detective constable, sergeant, detective sergeant, and detective inspector. He reported in his memoirs that he suspected an insane man who had worked on Butcher's Row prior to confinement to an asylum likely to have been the Ripper. Unfortunately, scholars of Jack the Ripper have been unable to track down Sagar's memoirs. He retired from the force in 1905.

SOURCE: Paul Begg, Martin Fido, and Keith Skinner, *The Jack the Ripper A to Z*, 1991.

ST. JOHN, JOHN. (b. 1912) Born in Los Angeles California, St. John spent over three decades in the Los Angeles Police Department (LAPD),* twenty-five of them as a murder investigator. He earned the moniker "Jigsaw John" and became one of the city's most celebrated police officers while working on such notorious murder cases as the 1947 "Black Dahlia" murder. His exploits as Detective Badge No. 1 inspired the 1975 book *Jigsaw John* and then a television series.

SOURCE: Al Martinez, *Jigsaw John*, 1975.

ST. LEON, ERNEST. (d. 1891) The son of French immigrants, St. Leon grew up in San Antonio, Texas. He gave up his law aspirations to join the U.S. Cavalry and participated in a number of Indian campaigns before joining Company D of the Texas Rangers* in the 1880s. He was given the moniker "Diamond Dick" for his predilection for large diamonds. Although he was initially cashiered out of the Rangers for drinking, he was reinstated after successfully conducting an undercover operation for John Reynolds Hughes.* His skills as a clandestine operator led to similar missions, including one in which he posed as an ore thief and led three cronies to an abandoned mine where Rangers were waiting. In the ensuing gunfight, all three thieves were killed. In 1891 St. Leon died from wounds suffered in a barroom gunfight with several cowboys.

SOURCE: Jay Robert Nash, *EWLO*, 1994.

ST. LOUIS, MISSOURI, POLICE DEPARTMENT. The origins of the St. Louis Police Department are rooted in a combination of police models, including an 1808 constabulary based on French traditions and the London Metropolitan Police* of Sir Robert Peel.* The constabulary relied on conscripted officers, who had to supply their own weapons. Any attempts by white males between the ages of eighteen and sixty to evade service was punishable by a one-dollar fine. Besides enforcing the requisite local ordinances, the untrained and unmotivated police were most concerned with controlling the local slave population. As the city grew throughout the early nineteenth century, the police force made attempts at reorganization and expansion in 1818 and 1826, and in 1839 the city guard was inaugurated to supplement the night watch.*

Great steps toward creating a more modern police force were taken in the 1840s when the old city guard and the day police were consolidated into a full-time force. In 1856 the St. Louis Police Department made the official transition to a twenty-four-hour police force under its first chief of police, Daniel A. Rawlings. Under the new ordinance, a separate detective squad was created to complement the paid, uniformed beat patrol officers.

In 1861 a new police bill created a board of police commissioners. The bill authorized the board to appoint police officers to four-year terms, which could be extended if the officers was considered meritorious. In addition, the bill established a relief fund for the families of officers killed or injured while on duty. By placing the force under the control of a board of commissioners appointed by the governor, the establishment of the Metropolitan Police System effectively removed the force from the clutches of the mayor's office.

The 1860s marked a turning point in St. Louis policing, beginning an era of modernization and innovation. In 1867 a horse mounted police* force was initiated, and in 1881 telephones were adopted. By the late 1890s the force was using the Bertillon system* of identification, which in 1927 was replaced by fingerprinting.* In 1903 the first patrol car took to the streets, and in 1907 it was joined by motorcycles. Although formal police training began in the 1880s, a police academy was not created until 1969. In 1991 Clarence Harmon became the department's first African-American chief of police.

SOURCES: Victor E. Kappeler, "St. Louis Police Department," *The Encyclopedia of Police Science*, ed. William G. Bailey, 1995; Allen Wagner, "Establishing a Metropolitan

Police Force: The Civil War and the First St. Louis Board of Police Commissioners," *Gateway Heritage*, Spring 1999.

ST. VALENTINE'S DAY MASSACRE. On February 14, 1929, gangsters masquerading as members of the Chicago Police Department (CPD)* brutally dispatched seven men connected with the Bugs Moran gang in a Chicago garage. Carried out in broad daylight in a neighborhood teeming with activity, the murders provided a clarion call for police reform in a city racked by gang war between the Capone mob and its adversaries. Soon after the massacre, a citizens' committee was convened to address the shortcomings of the police force. Noted police authority Bruce Smith* was hired to direct the survey.

SOURCE: Thomas A. Repetto, *The Blue Parade*, 1978.

SAN FRANCISCO COMMITTEE OF VIGILANCE. Without an adequate police force, San Francisco citizens created vigilance committee in 1851 to end the rampant lawlessness that had plagued the city following the discovery of gold. In June that year Sam Brannan,* a former Mormon elder, and eleven other civic leaders organized the San Francisco Committee of Vigilance. Unlike other forms of extralegal law enforcement, this committee afforded those it arrested a reasonably fair trial before sentencing them to hang. The committee outlined its powers and goals in a constitution that made it clear that it would take the law into its own hands when warranted.

Although the city police chief and his twelve-member department attempted to intervene prior to the first hanging, they were no match for the vigilantes who directed the execution in front of a huge throng of approving onlookers. Before disbanding several months later, three more criminals would meet their fates on the gallows.

Subsequently, following these hangings, crime declined. However, by 1855 crime was rising again, and in response, a new vigilance committee was organized in 1856. The punishment meted out by this second committee was widely supported as the city seemed to have come under the control of criminal syndicates. Unlike other examples of lynch law in the American West, this vigilante committee was hailed as restoring law and order, as well as honest government, to San Francisco.

SOURCES: Hubert H. Bancroft, *Popular Tribunals*, 1887; Robert M. Senkewicz, *Vigilantes in Gold Rush San Francisco*, 1985.

SAN FRANCISCO POLICE DEPARTMENT. With the influx of population precipitated by the 1849 discovery of gold, San Francisco's leading citizens established a volunteer police force of 230 policemen in the summer of 1849. The following year Malachi Fallon* became the city's first elected marshal (see U.S. MARSHALS SERVICE). By 1851 an official police force had been created, composed of twelve officers. However, they were overwhelmed by the burgeoning criminal element, and the San Francisco Vigilance Committee* took the law into their own hands. In response, the police department was reorganized and the number of officers was increased to fifty.

Following the lead of other urban American police forces, in 1853 the local board of aldermen passed an ordinance that reorganized the police force. Initially the force consisted of day and night forces composed of fifty-six officers each. However, in 1856 another, larger vigilante group took action when it became disatisfied with the crime control actions of the current police force. That same year a law was passed that replaced the city marshal with the office of chief of police. In addition, the police force was tripled in size, to 150 men. In the ensuing election for the city's first chief of police, James Curtis, the vigilante leader, was elected.

During the next two decades, the police had to contend with increased organized gang activities. These gangs earned a reputation for unparalleled violence, leading at least one authority to suggest that the term *hoodlum* originated in response to their activities. During this era the Barbary Coast area became one of the most truculent police beats, leading officers to supplement their arsenal of weapons with knives to use in hand-to-hand combat. According to an unsubstantiated story, on one occasion in the 1890s six policemen were beaten into submission and shanghaied out to sea. Considered an apocryphal story but recounted in the department's official history, when the officers returned from their enforced journey, they drew straws to determine who would kill the orchestrator of their abduction. The winner supposedly shot the victim six times, once for each officer.

Following the great earthquake of 1906, the police force introduced its first written civil service tests and the department was increased to seven hundred men. The force had, for the most part, reversed its course and image from one predicated by political patronage to that of a more reform-minded and independent administration.

One of the biggest mysteries in San Francisco police history revolved around the disappearance of police chief William Biggy in 1908. Appointed chief of police the previous year, he soon became embroiled in the Ruef scandals and was suspected of ordering the assassination of state witnesses in October 1908. Biggy denied all charges against him and reportedly considered resigning until he could clear his name. However, the police commissioner cajoled him into staying in office. On the evening of November 30, 1908, Biggy disappeared from a police patrol boat on its return trip across San Francisco Bay. The pilot of the boat, Officer William Murphy, reported that Biggy seemed in a cheerful mood and that there were no forebodings of suicide. Murphy was questioned about the disappearance and exonerated. The body of Biggy did not turn up until it was found floating in the bay on December 15. The coroner's report indicated no signs of a struggle, and the death was ruled accidental. Newspapers speculated on the death for months, but it remains a mystery to this day.

The early decades of the twentieth century saw the cleanup of the notorious vice districts of the Barbary Coast and Morton Street. San Francisco policing adopted numerous innovations, including patrol cars and wagons with hand-cranked sirens. Each police station was equiped with one of the latter, called "jitneys," but the majority of police tasks were still handled by foot patrols. During the 1920s the police had not contend to only with bootleggers and Prohibition-inspired violence, but with Tong wars in Chinatown as Chinese gangs resisted attempts to suppress their brothels, gambling parlors, and opium dens.

Between 1920 and 1940, the San Francisco police force saw incredible technological progress as it adopted radio communications and created a motorcycle corps known as the "Flying Squad." The force was beleaguered by labor unrest throughout the 1930s, leading to new crowd control strategies and techniques. Besides teargas, aerial reconnaisance was also used, a harbinger of the development of a helicopter squad almost four decades later.

During the 1940s the police department was most concerned with wartime espionage and fears of a Japanese invasion. Throughout the war years, the city had to contend with an onslaught of population drawn by wartime job opportunities. Rising crime rates accompanied the economic boom of the 1940s, and as the city became more commuter oriented in the decades following World War II, walking beat officers were gradually phased out and replaced by patrol cars with two-way radios. In the 1960s and 1970s the police force was plagued by recurring antiwar protests, radical political activities, and a growing counterculture. San Francisco remains a familiar setting for Hollywood police films and mystery novels. Consequently, "Dirty Harry Callihan," *The Streets of San Francisco*, and the Continental Op* of (Samuel) Dashiell Hammett* remain among the more recognizable symbols of San Francisco's rich police heritage.

SOURCES: Thomas S. Duke, *Celebrated Criminal Cases of America*, 1910; Wes Van Winkle, *San Francisco Police Department 1982*, 1982; Thomas Reppetto, *The Blue Parade*, 1978.

SARTINES, ANTOINE GABRIEL DE. (1729–1801) Born in Barcelona, Spain, Sartines was lieutenant-general of police* of Paris from 1759 to 1774. Considered an expert in secret police work and an expert interrogator, in the years before the innovations of Joseph Fouché,* Sartines had been consulted on secret police* matters by the Pope, Catherine the Great of Russia, and the Empress Maria Theresa. Sartines demonstrated a flair for the dramatic and a penchant for wearing wigs as he earned a reputation as one of Paris' finest police administrators. During his tenure he directed the improvement of the fire and river rescue services and enhanced the street-lighting program by making the transition from candled lanterns to oil lamps. When Sartines introduced the more effective oil lamps in 1769 it dramatically reduced the number of lamplighters required to light the city from 435 men to 150.

Sartines was credited with founding a free school of design for city artisans; he also began construction of the Corn Market and encouraged public sanitation through street- and drain-cleaning projects. During his tenure he maintained order in Paris, and when he resigned in 1774 he became secretary of state for the navy.

SOURCES: Alan Williams, *The Police of Paris, 1718–1789*, 1979; Philip John Stead, *The Police of France*, 1983; Philip John Stead, *The Police of Paris*, 1957.

SAVAGE, EDWARD HARTWELL. (1812–1893) Born in rural New England, Savage joined the Boston police department in 1851 in an attempt to pay off his debts. Three years later he was promoted to captain, and in 1861 was made deputy chief. During the 1860s Savage introduced a rogues' gallery, the first traffic squad, the civil service code, and the policeman's ball.

As Boston's popular police chief between 1870 and 1878, Savage proved a perspicacious idealist who championed preventive policing and rehabilitation before they were in vogue. He is chiefly remembered for writing *Police Records and Recollections; or Boston by Daylight and Gaslight for Two Hundred and Forty Years* (1866). This book is considered by many to be the first full-length history of a police department. In 1878 Savage left policing to become the city's first probation officer. Savage's emphasis on rehabilitation had a profound impact on the creation of the 1870 National Prison Association and the founding of the International Association of Chiefs of Police (IACP).*

SOURCES: Edward H. Savage, *Police Records and Recollections*, reprint, with introduction by Roger Lane, 1971; Roger Lane, *Policing the City*, 1967.

SAVAGE, PERCY. (b. 1878) Born in a room above the cells of the Acton, England, police station, Savage's father, Frederick, was a member of the London Metropolitan Police.* In 1900 Percy emulated his father and joined the force as well. Later in his career he became a superintendent of the Criminal Investigation Department (CID)* at Scotland Yard* and a member of the Big Four.

SOURCE: Paul Begg and Keith Skinner, *The Scotland Yard Files*, 1992.

SAVAK. The Sazeman Ettelaat va Amniyat Kashvar (or National Intelligence and Security Organization), better known by its acronym, SAVAK, was the secret police force that operated under the regime of the shah of Iran beginning in 1957. Early on it earned a reputation for brutality under its first director, a Kurd, Teimur Bakhtiar. SAVAK initially was organized to arrest members of the outlawed Tudeh party, but over time, its mission expanded to include the surveillance of opposition and press censorship.

In 1974 it was estimated that this force consisted of from thirty to sixty thousand agents. Its network of informants was so well entrenched in Iran that, according to one estimate, one out of every ten Iranians worked in some capacity for the SAVAK informant network. SAVAK was known for its use of torture during interrogations as it targeted suspected communists and other subversives.

It was abolished in 1979 with the inauguration of the Islamic regime. Today, under the Islamic regime it is known as the SAVAMA (with M standing for nation), and uses many of the same techniques of its predecessor.

SOURCES: Thomas Plate and Andrea Darvi, *Secret Police*, 1981; George Thomas Kurian, *World Encyclopedia of Police Forces and Penal Systems*, 1988.

SAYER, JOHN. An early member of the Bow Street Runners,* like his colleague John Townsend,* he found his position a lucrative one, and at his death left an estate of close to thirty thousand pounds. Sayer, along with Townsend, worked as a bodyguard for King George III after the king was attacked by a crazed woman in 1786.

SOURCE: Anthony Babington, *A House in Bow Street*, 1969.

SCARBOROUGH, GEORGE A. (1859–1900) Born in Louisiana, the son of a preacher, Scarborough moved to Texas and worked as a cowboy in his youth. He began his law enforcement career as the Jones County sheriff* in 1885. Several years later he was appointed deputy U.S. marshal (see U.S. MARSHALS SERVICE) for El Paso. In April 1896 Scarborough rose to prominence when he killed John Henry Selman,* the slayer of noted outlaw John Wesley Hardin. Although most evidence suggests that his killing of Selman was probably closer to murder, he was exonerated nonetheless. Following this incident Scarborough left Texas and became a detective for the Grant County Cattleman's Association. While tracking rustlers and former members of the Butch Cassidy gang, Scarborough was shot in the leg, had it amputated, and died, on April 6, 1900, exactly four years after he had killed Selman.

SOURCE: Robert K. DeArment, *George Scarborough: The Life and Death of a Lawman on the Closing Frontier*, 1992.

SCHENGEN AGREEMENT. In 1985, Belgium, France, Germany, Luxembourg, and the Netherlands signed an agreement in Schengen, Luxembourg. Six years later this group was augmented with the addition of Portugal and Spain. The goal of the agreement was to allow easier travel among the member states while at the same time maintaining strict identity controls at airports, seaports, and land borders for travelers from outside the European Union and to insure translational cooperation in the war against international crime. Among the most important issues addressed by this agreement were jurisdictional matters dealing with policing, particularly the sharing of information and how far police could pursue criminals across borders. Critics of this agreement maintain that there is an inherent "Big Brother" syndrome at work here that violates the privacy of travelers. Others argue that unless those countries that have decided not to participate or are prevented from joining are added to the agreement, it will not work. However, many criminal justice experts expect other European countries to sign the agreement by the end of the century.

SOURCE: John Benyon, "The Developing System of Police Cooperation in the European Union," in *Crime and Law Enforcement in the Global Village*, ed. W. F. McDonald, 1997.

SCHINDLER, RAYMOND CAMPBELL. (1882–1959) Born in Mexico, New York, and educated in Wisconsin, Schindler moved to California and survived the 1906 San Francisco earthquake. Subsequently he became an insurance investigator, catching the attention of William John Burns,* who hired him shortly after. In 1910 Schindler was managing the New York City office of the Burns Detective Agency. However, two years later he set out on his own to establish what became known as the Schindler Bureau of Investigation. Schindler's investigative skills were credited with solving numerous highly publicized cases, ranging from the 1911 murder of little Marie Smith in New Jersey to the acquittal of Sir Henry Oakes in the Marigny murder case in the Bahamas. During the world wars Schindler performed counterespionage services for the federal government.

SOURCES: Rupert Hughes, *Complete Detective: Being the Life and Strange and Exciting Cases of Raymond Schindler, Master Detective*, 1950; Frank Smyth and Myles Ludwig, *The Detectives*, 1978.

SCHMITTBERGER, MAX. (d. 1917) Born to German immigrant parents in Hoboken, New Jersey, in his youth Schmittberger worked as an apprentice to a pastry cook. After joining the New York City Police Department (NYPD), Schmittberger, who was initially reluctant to take part in the traditional bribe system that was employed in New York City, eventually got with the system and rose through the ranks of the department. Rising to captain he became the unofficial collector in the tenderloin* district, which was run by crooked inspector Alexander S. "Clubber" Williams.*

Schmittberger was called to testify in front of the committee chaired by Clarence Lexow,* and he impressed its members with his vivid testimony of the graft problem in the city police force. His testimony was instrumental in placing Theodore Roosevelt* in the office of police commissioner. Impressed by Schmittberger's sincere testimony, reformer Lincoln Steffens exclaimed, "Cannot an honest man do dishonest things and remain honest?" (Jeffers). Surprisingly, even the Reverend Charles H. Parkhurst* agreed with Steffens, and the two men set about rehabilitating the fallen cop.

SOURCES: Thomas A. Reppetto, *The Blue Parade*, 1978; H. Paul Jeffers, *Commissioner Roosevelt*, 1994.

SCHOBER, JOHANN. (1874–1932) Born in Austria, Schober devoted his life to his country's civil service. Following World War I Schober was appointed by the Hapsburg ruler, Kaiser Karl, to take charge of the central bureau of police. With the disintegration of much of Austria's infrastructure during the war and finding itself faced by marauding bands of unemployed soldiers, the police force was all that stood between chaos and government control. In 1921 Schober's administrative panache led to his elevation to chancellor. The following year he was pressured to resign, and he returned to law enforcement. In an attempt to renew attempts at creating an international law enforcement agency, which had been in the planning stage before the war, Schober convened the International Criminal Police Conference in Vienna in 1923. Little did Schober realize that this meeting would lead to the creation of the International Criminal Police Organization (Interpol)* following World War II.

SOURCE: Charles Phillips and Alan Axelrod, *CCC*, 1996.

SCHOEMAKER, WILLIAM. (d. 1936) Born and raised in Chicago, Schoemaker joined the Chicago Police Department (CPD),* in 1903 and was assigned to the West Lake station. During his subsequent career, Schoemaker would hold more important police posts than any other member in the history of the department. He served as chief of detectives from 1924 to 1927 and then from 1931 to 1934 and was cited for bravery twenty-three times. On three other occasions he received awards for meritorious duty.

Schoemaker headed the vice squads in 1917, earning the moniker "Shoes." Despite his active career he never shot another person. He was instrumental in investigating the murder of Harvey Church, the bombing of the federal building, the Dearborn Street and the Evergreen Park mail robberies, and the Vincent Altman murder. He retired in 1934 and died two years later.

SOURCE: Raphael W. Marrow and Harriet I. Carter, *In Pursuit of Crime: The Police of Chicago*, 1996.

SCHOUT FISCAL. One of the earliest peace officers in America was the *schout fiscal* in the Dutch colony of New Netherland in the 1620s. In New Amsterdam, the progenitor of New York City, the colonial council under Peter Minuet appointed these officers, who were given duties typically on par with those of a sheriff* and an attorney general. Among the charges was the enforcement of laws and the execution of court orders. Although the officers were not considered salaried officials, they were compensated with certain court fees. The *schout fiscal* had little autonomy and was unable to pursue any action without the direction of the colonial directors. In fact, they were only allowed to arrest perpetrators caught in the act. By the 1650s the *schout fiscal* was considered the most important police functionary in the colony. In most criminal cases the *schout fiscal* was responsible for the county prosecution.

SOURCE: Augustine Costello, *Our Police Protectors*, 1885; reprint, 1972.

SCHUETTLER, HERMAN. (1861–1918) Schuettler was appointed to the Chicago Police Department (CPD)* in 1883 and was rapidly promoted through the ranks to chief of the homicide squad and then, in 1891, to captain. He was initially assigned to a lawless area known as "Little Hell," where he earned a reputation for bravado. He survived numerous gunfights, and in one incident beat an ex-convict to death while enjoying some off-duty time in a local tavern. In 1886 he played a prominent role during the investigation of anarchists, and in a fight with the radical Louis Lingg, he bit the man's thumb off to prevent being shot, a story that entered the lore of the CPD. Schuettler also was instrumental in the investigation of the murder of Dr. Cronin by the Clan-na-Gael, the Luetgart murder, and many other high-profile murder cases.

Although six hundred people perished in the 1903 fire at the Iroquois Theater, Schuettler was credited with rushing into the burning building during the conflagration and helping to save hundreds of lives. The 300-pound Schuetller, who was also the tallest man on the force, would serve as Chicago's deputy police chief intermittently between 1901 and 1917. In 1917 he was appointed chief of police, a position he held until his death in 1918. Unfortunately, his tenure as chief was blemished by payoffs and corruption among the rank and file.

SOURCES: Thomas A. Reppetto, *The Blue Parade*, 1978; Raphael W. Marrow and Harriet I. Carter, *In Pursuit of Crime*, 1996.

SCHWARZKOPF, HERBERT NORMAN. (1895–1958) Born in Newark, New Jersey, the son of second-generation German-Americans, Schwarzkopf attended West Point, where he graduated 88th in a class of 139. Following graduation he dropped his first name and became known as H. Norman. Schwarzkopf saw service in France during World War I and then along the Mexican border as a military police officer. In 1920 he left the service and returned to New Jersey, and the following year he was selected to head the New Jersey State Police. Schwarzkopf immediately implemented military-style discipline and training. Among his most famous cases was the 1922 Hall-Mills murder case, involving the deaths of a choir singer and a socially prominent minister involved in an adulterous affair. In its time this was referred to as the "crime of the century." The case was never solved.

Schwarzkopf was initially appointed for a five-year term, but he was reappointed in 1926 and again in 1931. As head of the New Jersey State Police, Schwarzkopf rose to prominence during his investigation of the Lindbergh kidnapping in 1932. Since the Hopewell, New Jersey, police force consisted of only two men, Schwarzkopf directed the state police manhunt that eventually led to the arrest and execution of Bruno Hauptman after a two-year pursuit. Schwarzkopf testified at the trial, using this as a springboard for a more public career as a commentator on the radio program *Gang Busters* after being forced to resign from the state police in the wake of the controversy surrounding the Lindbergh case.

During World War Two II Schwarzkopf returned to his military career and organized Iran's 20,000-man military police force. In 1951 he was appointed administrative director of the New Jersey Department of Law and Public Safety. He was credited with making inroads against waterfront crime during the 1950s before retiring in 1956. His career has been overshadowed by the achievements of his son and namesake, H. Norman Schwarzkopf, Jr., who successfully guided coalition forces in the 1990–1991 Persian Gulf War against Iraq.

SOURCES: *New York Times*, November 27, 1958; Thomas A. Reppetto, *The Blue Parade*. 1978.

SCOTLAND YARD. The origins of Scotland Yard can be traced to early nineteenth century London, where the police force of Sir Robert Peel* was headquartered at Whitehall Palace in the Great Scotland Yard. Beginning in the sixteenth century, Scotland Yard was the site of a palatial residence used by medieval Scottish royalty when visiting the English Court. In 1890 it was replaced by a more modern structure on the Thames embankment, across from the Home Office. The storied edifice was supplanted by the New Scotland Yard erected near Victoria Station in 1967. Scotland Yard remains the central office for the administration and control of the London Metropolitan Police.*

SOURCE: Sir Basil Thomson, *The Story of Scotland Yard*, 1936.

SCUDERIE DETETIVE LE COCQ. Following the 1964 killing of Milton Le Cocq de Oliviera,* Brazil's most revered detective, the Scuderie Detetive Le Cocq was organized in his memory in 1965. Founded by thirteen of Le Cocq's colleagues and close friends, the organization was supported by policemen. However, it is open to nonpolicemen as well as long as an individual is proposed for membership by two members, has no police record, and is popular with neighbors and debtors alike. Growing to over two thousand members in its first decade, it was devoted to uniting all Brazilian police officers in pursuit of common goals of promoting a positive image of policing and enhancing police professionalism. In its first decade the Scuderie could boast branches in eight Brazilian states and had representatives in countries all over the world. In addition it maintained contacts with Scotland Yard,* the Federal Bureau of Investigation (FBI)* and the International Criminal Police Organization (Interpol).*

SOURCE: Bruce Henderson and Sam Summerlin, *The Super Sleuths*, 1976.

SCYTHIAN POLICE. Ancient Athens employed Scythian archers as its only institutional form of police. While evidence remains sketchy concerning most of their activities, according to the Greeks, the name Scythian referred to their origins as "Northern Barbarians" from northern Europe. As depicted on Greek vases, these police apparently wore trousers as opposed to the more traditional attire. Taken as slaves, they were eventually offered the opportunity to gain their freedom. The Scythian archers were sheltered in tents. They were employed as town guards and carried out conventional police duties on the highways.

SOURCES: Charles Reith, *The Blind Eye of History*, 1952; Robert J. Bonner and Gertrude Smith, *The Administration of Justice from Homer to Aristotle*, 1930.

SEABURY INVESTIGATION. The 1930 Seabury Investigation began as a probe of the New York Magistrates' Court after several judges were linked to Arnold Rothstein and other mobsters. Judge Samuel Seabury, a direct descendant of John and Priscilla Alden, concluded that not much had changed since the Lexow Committee (see LEXOW, CLARENCE) investigation of the 1890s and that the police department was riddled with corruption. His findings led to the dismissal of twenty members of the vice squad and the exposure of rampant political bribery and corruption among city leaders, including police commissioners and the mayor. It led to the resignation of Mayor Jimmy Walker and to the reform administration of Fiorello LaGuardia.

SOURCE: Thomas A. Reppetto, *The Blue Parade*, 1978.

SEALY, LLOYD GEORGE. (1917–1985) Born in Manhattan, following graduation from Brooklyn College in 1935, Sealy worked for the Government Accounting Office and then as a railway mail clerk before joining the New York City Police Department (NYPD)* in 1942. Sealy encountered discrimination because he was African-American, and he was usually assigned beats in the all-black neighborhoods. In 1947 he was promoted to sergeant with the caveat that he could only work in the youth division. During the late 1940s Sealy returned to school and earned a law degree from Brooklyn Law School. Over the following decades he would become the first African-American to hold a variety of high posts with the NYPD, rising to lieutenant in 1959 and four years later to captain. He is credited with quelling riots in Harlem in the 1960s and in 1966 was promoted to assistant chief inspector, the highest position held by an African-American in the department up to that time. Sealy left policing in 1969 for an academic post at the John Jay College of Criminal Justice.

SOURCE: Charles Phillips and Alan Axelrod, *CCC*, 1996.

SEAVEY, WEBBER S. (1841–1915) Born in Maine, Seavey relocated to Wisconsin in 1857 and two years later embarked for the Colorado gold rush. During the Civil War he served in the Fifth Iowa Cavalry. Following the war he worked as a clerk on a Mississippi River steamboat and then entered law enforcement as the city marshal of Santa Barbara, California, from 1874 to 1879. He left policing and for six years led a life of adventure as a trader in the South Seas Islands. In 1887 he was appointed the chief of police of Omaha, Nebraska. Five years later he joined Chicago police superintendent Robert McLaughrey in lobbying North American police chiefs to organize an association of chiefs of police for cities of more than ten thousand population. The National Police Chiefs Union was organized the following year, and Seavey was elected its first president. Nine years later it was renamed the (more familiar) International Association of Chiefs of Police (IACP).*

SOURCE: Charles Phillips and Alan Axelrod, *CCC*, 1996.

SEBASTIAN, CHARLES E. Born in Missouri, Sebastian moved to Los Angeles following service in the Spanish-American War. Sebastian joined the Los Angeles Police Department (LAPD)* in 1900 and rose to prominence in 1907 as head of the "Chinatown Squad," which controlled vice in the gambling district and attempted to suppress the periodic Chinese Tong wars. His promotion to police chief in 1911 brought stability to the office. As the Los Angelenos took to the automobile, Sebastian championed uniform speed laws, automobile registration practices, the prohibition of drinking when driving, driver's tests, and other traffic reforms. Sebastian built a solid reputation as police chief and used it as a stepping stone to the mayor's office after resigning as police chief in July 1915. He was the first police officer to be elected Los Angeles mayor.

SOURCES: Gerald Woods, *The Police in Los Angeles*, 1993; Arthur W. Sjoquist (historical text by), *Los Angeles Police Department Commemorative Book, 1869–1984*, 1984.

SECRET POLICE. By the time of the French Revolution, Napoleon had introduced the precursor to modern state secret police forces. Between 1804 and 1810, Joseph Fouché* served as Minister of Police under Napoleon. As the first secret police chief of the modern era, he created one of the most effective instruments conceived in the protracted struggle against human rights. Over the next two centuries the secret police concept would be refined by Herman Goering's Gestapo,* the NKVD* of Lavrentia Pavlovich Beria,* the shah of Iran's SAVAK,* and Arturo Bocchini's Opera Vigilanze Repressione (OVRA) in Italy.

SOURCE: Thomas Plate and Andrea Darvi, *Secret Police*, 1981.

SECRET POLICE SYSTEM OF SPARTA. More than twenty-five hundred years ago, Sparta developed a police force of young men to track down any slaves suspected of seditious activity. With a population of 12,000 free citizens, 80,000 noncitizen freemen, and perhaps 200,000 slaves, it was incumbent on the state to maintain constant vigilance lest an insurrection or uprising occur. The Spartan police were a mobile unit, which was shuttled about the country to root out discontent and subversion and could arbitrarily execute suspected insurrectionists. The police force acted under the direction of a council of elders plus five leading elders known as the *ephors*, who were elected annually.

SOURCE: Charles Reith, *The Blind Eye of History*, 1952.

SECRET SERVICE. *See* U.S. SECRET SERVICE.

SELMAN, JOHN HENRY. (1839–1896) Born in Madison County, Arkansas, Selman moved with his family to Grayson County, Texas, in his youth. Selman joined the Twenty-second Texas Cavalry in 1861 but deserted two years later and went to Fort Davis, Texas, where he enlisted in the state militia in 1864. After an arrest for desertion he either escaped or was acquitted. He soon started a family and by 1870 had moved to New Mexico. His first venture in law enforcement was probably with a vigilante group in the Clear Fork region of the Brazos River. In 1874 Selman joined with the nefarious John Larn and organized another vigilante group near Fort Griffin. During the 1870s Selman reportedly killed several Indians as well as several unsavory whites.

In 1878 Selman fled Texas and apparently became involved in the 1878 Lincoln County conflict in New Mexico. Later that year, together with his brother and several other desperate characters, Selman formed the Seven Rivers Gang and participated in more killings. As the band disintegrated, Selman survived an attack of smallpox and disappeared for awhile, only to reappear in El Paso in 1888. Three years later he narrowly escaped an assassination attempt. He was elected constable (see CONSTABLES) at El Paso in 1892 and two years later killed deputy U.S. marshal Bass Outlaw,* who, while inebriated earlier, had murdered one of the Texas Rangers* in a brothel. In 1895 he killed John Wesley Hardin under questionable circumstances. The next year Selman was killed by deputy U.S. marshal George A. Scarborough.*

SOURCE: Leon Metz, *John Selman, Gunfighter*, 1966.

SEMINOLE LIGHTHORSE. In the Indian Territory that would later become Oklahoma, laws were enforced by the Seminole Lighthorse, a unit that included a captain, lieutenant, and eight privates. Known for their swift administration of justice, members of the lighthorse were represented by members of the Indian nations. As soon as they captured a criminal, the individual was brought before the tribal court. Since there were no jails, justice was meted out summarily. Minor crimes were punished with twenty-five strokes with a six-foot hickory switch. Recidivists received double the punishment. Murder and other serious crimes were punished by a firing squad.

SOURCE: Art Burton, *Black, Red, and Deadly*, 1991.

SERPICO, FRANK. (b. 1936) Born Francisco Vincent Serpico in New York City, Serpico joined the New York City Police Department (NYPD)* in 1959. He came to national attention in the 1970s for reporting corrupt colleagues, first to his superiors, who ignored him, and then to the *New York Times*. With this act, Serpico had broken the unwritten police prohibition against whistleblowing. Early in his career he had discovered that numerous cops took protection money and illegal contributions from underworld characters. Shortly after testifying against one of his fellow officers, Serpico was shot in the face while making an arrest. Most beat cops considered him a "rat" and eschewed the timeworn tradition of visiting wounded officers in the hospital. Instead, someone sent Serpico a card that read, "With sincere sympathy . . . that you didn't get your brains blown out you rat bastard" (Slate and Steinberg).

After publication of a series of investigative pieces by the *New York Times* an investigation into police corruption was opened. The findings of the 1971 Knapp Commission* led to mass resignations from the department. Serpico retired in 1974. However, the Peter Maas best-seller *Serpico* and the subsequent highly successful movie version starring Al Pacino transformed him into a minor celebrity. He soon left the United States for an expatriate life in Europe.

SOURCES: Peter Maas, *Serpico*, 1971; John Slate and R. U. Steinberg, *Lawmen, Crimebusters, and Champions of Justice*, 1991.

SESSIONS, WILLIAM STEELE. (b. 1930) Born in Fort Smith, Arkansas, this clergyman's son was raised in Kansas City before joining the U.S. Air Force in 1951. He left the service in 1956 to pursue a law degree at Baylor University. Sessions practiced law in Waco, Texas, from 1959 to 1969, when he relocated to Washington, D.C., to serve as chief of the government operations section of the criminal division for the U.S. Department of Justice.*

In 1971 President Richard M. Nixon appointed Sessions U.S. attorney for the Western District of Texas. Three years later President Gerald Ford selected him as district judge in El Paso, and after six years he was appointed to a similar position in San Antonio. Sessions developed a reputation as a law-and-order conservative, leading President Ronald Reagan to appoint him to head the Federal Bureau of Investigation (FBI)* in 1987. Following on the heels of the resignation of William H. Webster,* Sessions was pressured to investigate discrimination against minorities in the FBI. When the report was released two years later, during the George Bush presidency, the conclusions of the investigation stated that there was no discrimination in the agency. In the midst of a ten-year term, Sessions was fired over policy disagreements and accusations of misconduct in 1993 and replaced by Louis J. Freeh.*

SOURCE: Athan G. Theoharis, ed , *The FBI*, 1999.

SEVENTEENTH WARD GERMAN RIOT. In July 1857 the New York Metropolitan Police* force shot and killed an unarmed bystander while attempting to suppress a riot in the Seventeenth Ward over the Sunday enforcement of liquor laws. Three days of rioting led to the injury of five policemen as a crowd of five thousand threatened to take their rampage further. This incident was one of the earliest reports chronicling the police use of firearms while upholding the law, and it led to public outrage against the new force. However, not long after this a patrolman was killed while trying to apprehend a burglar, and public sympathy over this incident soon blunted the public criticism over the German riot.

SOURCES: Wilbur R. Miller, *Cops and Bobbies*, 1973; James F. Richardson, *The New York Police*, 1970.

SHADLEY, LAFAYETTE "LAFE." (d. 1893) Shadley rose to prominence in the 1890s during skirmishes with the Doolin-Dalton gangs. In 1892 he wounded bank robber Dan "Dynamite Dick" Clifton in Osage County. Shadley was a peace officer near Ingalls, Oklahoma, when, along with James P. "Jim" Masterson* and eleven other officers, he encountered seven members of the Doolin Gang and a pitched gunfight ensued. Bill Dalton is credited with fatally wounding Shadley during this incident.

SOURCE: Glenn Shirley, *West of Hell's Fringe*, 1978.

SHADOWS. In the 1850s, detectives were called shadows.

SOURCE: Jay Robert Nash, *Dictionary of Crime*, 1989; reprint, 1992.

SHANAHAN, EDWIN C. (1898–1925) Born in Chicago, Illinois, Shanahan joined the Bureau of Investigation in 1920 following service in the U.S. Army during World War I. On October 11, 1925, he became the first Bureau agent to be killed in the line of duty when he was shot by car thief Martin James Durkin. Ironically, Durkin was subsequently arrested and served twenty-eight years in prison, while Shanahan's son went on to a twenty-eight-year career with the Federal Bureau of Investigation (FBI)* beginning in 1948.

SOURCE: Athan G. Theoharis, ed., *The FBI*, 1999.

SHANKLIN, JAMES GORDON. (1910–1988) Born in Kentucky, Shanklin graduated from Vanderbilt University Law School before joining the Federal Bureau of Investigation (FBI)* in 1943. After stints at various postings, he was assigned as a special agent in charge of the Dallas, Texas, office in 1963. Shanklin led the FBI investigation into the John F. Kennedy assassination in Dallas, but received his greatest notoriety for destroying a letter written by the assassin, Lee Harvey Oswald, which had been hidden away by his agents. Following the president's death, Shanklin was informed of the existence of the Oswald letter, and in order to avoid accusations of incompetence, he ordered it destroyed. In Shanklin's defense the letter did not imply any threats on the president's life, but the mere destruction of a piece of evidence in the conspiracy-laden climate of the 1960s cast doubt on many of the conclusions of the Warren Commission.

SOURCE: Charles Phillips and Alan Axelrod, *CCC*, 1996.

SHARPEVILLE MASSACRE. On March 16, 1960, the leader of the Pan-African Congress (PAC) notified the commissioner of the South African Police (SAP)* that his organization was going to hold a peaceful protest against apartheid pass laws (required black individuals to carry ID cards to go from township to township) throughout South Africa on March 21. However, protestors failed to materialize except in locations such as Sharpeville and Langa. Demonstration leaders had little control over the unemployed and angry young protestors. The Sharpeville police station was manned by three white officers and thirty-five black officers. When the police found themselves confronted by some twenty thousand protestors, police reinforcements entered the fray. Vastly outnumbered, the police used aircraft to strafe the crowd before ground officers opened fire. Most reports indicate that the crowd did not fire weapons, nor was an order to fire on the protestors given. However, 69 demonstrators were killed and 180 were wounded. The police were subsequently exonerated of the killings, whereupon bloody riots broke out around South Africa. On March 30, 1960, the government declared a state of emergency and banned opposition parties such as the PAC.

SOURCE: John D. Brewer, *Black and Blue: Policing in South Africa*, 1994.

SHEA, JOHN. (188–1903) Born in rural Illinois, Shea moved to Chicago shortly after the Great Fire of 1871 and joined the Chicago Police Department (CPD).* He rapidly rose to detective and worked on some of the most famous cases of the 1870s. He was teamed with fellow detective Joseph Kipley,* and in a short time they became one of the best recognized police teams in the history of the Chicago police force.

SOURCE: Raphael W. Marrow and Harriet I. Carter, *In Pursuit of Crime*, 1996.

SHEEHAN, TIMOTHY J. Wounded four times during service in the Civil War and the Sioux conflict of 1862, Sheehan left the army a lieutenant colonel in 1865 and headed back to his home state of Minnesota. During the next twelve years he was sheriff* of Freeborn County, Minnesota, and then worked as an Indian agent at the White Earth agency. Sheehan was appointed deputy U.S. marshal in 1890. In 1898 Sheehan accompanied a small force of soldiers to the Leech Lake Reservation to suppress the sale of liquor on the reservation. The subsequent pursuit of the Indians led to a skirmish after a soldier accidentally fired his weapon leading to an exchange of gunfire, in which Sheehan and ten soldiers received gunshot wounds and six died. Another skirmish followed and reinforcements were sent to the scene leading the Indians to accept a negotiated settlement. The Leech Lake disturbance of 1898 was the last violent encounter between Indians and the U.S. Marshals Service* for seventy years.

SOURCE: Frederick S. Calhoun, *The Lawmen*, 1991.

SHERIDAN, WILLIAM PATRICK HENRY. (1861–1934) Born in New York City, Sheridan was educated briefly at the College of the City of New York but left school for a position with Western Union. In 1886 he joined the

New York City Police Department (NYPD); and during his first year he was elevated to detective. During his twenty years on the force, Sheridan was remembered for his photographic memory. In 1909, in an attempt to grab some business from Pinkerton's National Detective Agency,* the retired Sheridan joined with William John Burns* to create the Burns and Sheridan Detective Agency. Sheridan sold his share of the agency to Burns in 1911 because of differences over the pace of expansion. Sheridan then established his own detective business in New York City.

SOURCE: Gene Caesar, *Incredible Detective: The Biography of William J. Burns*, 1968.

SHERIFF. The ancient law enforcement position of sheriff was established in Anglo-Saxon England prior to the Norman Conquest of 1066. The word is derived from *shire reeve*, with *shire* meaning "county" and *reeve* meaning "agent of the king." Originally responsible for collecting taxes, by the time of Edward the Confessor the sheriff had acquired increased prestige and had acquired additional powers. Imbued with financial, judicial, policing, and military authority, the position became a lucrative one during the Norman period. However, the sheriff's powers peaked during the reign of King John in the early thirteenth century. With the enactment of the Statute of Westminster* in 1285, sheriffs were given the responsibility of chasing lawbreakers, raising the hue and cry,* and bringing culprits to justice.

During the colonial era in America, the first sheriffs appeared and the office soon became an elected one. Colonial sheriffs served process papers, maintained law and order, collected taxes, and maintained jails. Following the American Revolution, the sheriff remained an essential ingredient of the developing criminal justice system. Terms were generally limited, sometimes to as short as one year. With the power to collect taxes and conduct elections, the sheriff remained a dominant influence as America moved west.

The American sheriff became prominent during the settlement of the nineteenth-century West, an especially active era when communities were often poorly protected and the population was sparse. Sheriffs were given the power of *posse comitatus,** which allowed them to deputize common citizens to pursue fugitives from justice. Although posses are rarely used today, the sheriff continues to be a dominant figure in rural policing. Tenure in office is typically limited to two or three terms, and while there are literally thousands of counties in the United States, not all appoint or elect sheriffs. Sheriffs are popularly elected in all states except Rhode Island. Duties vary from state to state, as does the pattern of renumeration.

SOURCES: Frank Richard Prassel, *The Western Peace Officer*, 1972; Sir Harold Scott, ed., *The Concise Encyclopedia of Crime and Criminals*, 1961.

SHERIFF'S BALL. Prior to the Civil War, sheriffs and other officials sent out invitations to hangings, which they called "sheriff's balls." This was considered a lucrative opportunity, since tickets were then sold to scalpers for the best seats, which they sold for prices ranging from five to twenty-five dollars. Front-row seats were often purchased by criminal associates, who bought them out of respect or to be privy to any gallows confession that might implicate them. At one notorious New York City execution in 1860, ten thousand spectators paid their respects. However, because the hanging took place on a small island thirty feet from the shore, good seats were at a premium. According to one report, Captain Isaiah Rynders supervised the event and cleared a thousand dollars after expenses.

SOURCE: Carl Sifakis, *The Encyclopedia of America Crime*, 1982.

SHERMAN, JOHN E., JR. (1846–1912) The nephew of General William Tecumseh Sherman, John E. Sherman left Ohio for the West, where he was appointed New Mexico marshal in 1876, succeeding John Pratt.* Sherman was unpopular and viewed as a tool of the local Santa Fe Crime ring. Crime flourished under his watch, and range wars continued unimpeded in Lincoln and Colfax Counties. Sherman obtained federal murder warrants for the apprehension of Billy the Kid and ordered Deputy Marshal Patrick Floyd Jarvis "Pat" Garrett* to lead a posse in pursuit of William Bonney and his associates. With the arrest of Billy the Kid, on December 23, 1881, Sherman reveled in the subsequent media attention for his instrumental role in bringing in America's most famous desperado. When the Kid escaped from jail prior to his hanging, he reportedly intended to kill Sherman as soon as the opportunity presented itself, but instead Garrett killed the Kid before he could make good on his threat.

In 1882 Sherman was forced out of office. Unlike his predecessors, during his six years as marshal Sherman demonstrated a surprising political independence from the Santa Fe Ring; however, this did not overcome his failures in office, where he was accused of public intoxication, failure to compensate jurors, and inability to assuage the liquor traffic to Indian reservations.

SOURCE: Larry D. Ball, *The United States Marshals of New Mexico and Arizona Territories, 1846–1912*, 1978.

SHIELD CLUB. The Shield Club was formed following the 1946 Euclid Beach Incident in Cleveland, Ohio, in which African-American policeman Lynn Coleman was suspended from the force for attempting to protect members of the Congress of Racial Equality (CORE) during a meeting to discuss the integration of a public dance hall. Coleman and his partner were severely beaten by private guards hired by the dance hall. Subsequently, Coleman was suspended without pay for "conduct unbecoming an officer." African-American policemen rallied in Coleman's support and organized the Shield Club as a vehicle to voice their grievances against the Cleveland Police Department.

Police associations were prohibited by the department, and members of the nascent organization faced harassment from their supervisors. Nonetheless, the

Shield Club soon became active in community activities, sponsoring food drives and trips for needy youths. It also led in efforts to recruit more minority officers.

SOURCE: W. Marvin Dulaney, *Black Police in America*, 1996.

SHIPPY, GEORGE M. Shippy joined the Chicago Police Department (CPD)* in 1887 and over the next twelve years served in a variety of capacities before becoming a captain in 1898 and an inspector in 1904. During his tenure as police chief beginning in 1907, he earned the sobriquet "Iron Chief." In 1908 Shippy survived an assassination attempt by an anarchist in Shippy's own home. In the subsequent gunfight, Shippy's son was shot in the chest and a patrolman was shot in the hand. The assailant, however, was fatally wounded. Shippy resigned from the force in August 1909.

SOURCE: Raphael W. Marrow and Harriet I. Carter, *In Pursuit of Crime*, 1996.

SHOOFLY. A term originally used by the underworld in the 1890s, it referred to gang members who kept watch on police movements. It later alluded to internal affairs officers, such as Pipers,* who worked in state, federal, or local police agencies and were responsible for rooting out internal corruption.

SOURCE: Jay Robert Nash, *Dictionary of Crime*, 1989.

SHORE, JOHN. One of the older and more experienced members of the force, Shore played a major role in detective department investigations for Scotland Yard* between 1869 and 1876. He had formerly served two years on the Bristol City police before joining the London Metropolitan Police* at the age of twenty-four. Two years later he made detective sergeant and earned the sobriquet "John Blunt" for "his bluff and breezy manner" (Lock). During an epidemic of pick-pocketing and racecourse thefts, he won renown for his ability to catch them in the act. In 1878 he was promoted to chief inspector. Although not well educated, Shore succeeded Adolphus Frederick Williamson* as superintendent in 1889.

SOURCES: Joan Lock, *Dreadful Deeds and Awful Murders*, 1990; Belton Cobb, *Critical Years at the Yard*, 1956.

SIDNEY STREET SIEGE. The East End of London was a hotbed of revolutionary activity during the first decade of the twentieth century. Numerous political exiles from czarist Russia found sanctuary in London, where they clandestinely planned many of the bombings and assassinations in Russia before the revolution. One of the more notorious groups of anarchist expatriates was the "Flame." Led by "Peter the Painter," the Flame resorted to criminal activity in order to raise money to further their political aspirations. In December 1910 members of the Flame killed three policemen and permanently disabled two others while fleeing a bungled jewelry robbery. The Houndstitch murders, also called the "Tottenham Outrage," led to a police manhunt that culminated in the tracking down of two perpetrators to a tenement at 100 Sidney Street just one month later.

Police quickly surrounded the block of tenement buildings and made preparations for an assault. Over the next seven hours police reinforcements were called up to battle the two anarchists while large crowds gathered to watch the action. Several were hit by ricocheting bullets. Police forces were intent on avenging the deaths of their comrades the previous month and wanted to storm the building. Before an assault could be mounted, the tenement mysteriously was set ablaze. Both men died in the fire.

Controversy followed, with newspapers questioning the need for such a disproportionate number of police and militiamen against two individuals. In addition British immigration policy and the control of aliens in the country became a source of debate. Peter the Painter, the actual killer of the three policemen, was never caught. He was later identified as Jacob Peters, who later became the head of the Soviet Cheka.*

SOURCES: Donald Rumbelow, *The Siege of Sidney Street: The True Story of Winston Churchill and the Anarchist Rebellion of 1911*, 1973; Sir Harold Scott, ed., *The Concise Encyclopedia of Crime and Criminals*, 1961.

SIEGE OF SIDNEY STREET. *See* SIDNEY STREET SIEGE.

SIEKER, EDWARD ARMON, JR. (1853–1901) Born in Baltimore, Maryland, Sieker, along with his three brothers, joined the Texas Rangers* in the 1870s. In 1874 he enlisted in Captain Cicero Perry's Company D of the Frontier Battalion. He eventually rose to the rank of sergeant and gained prominence during the pursuit of the Jesse Evans gang in the Big Bend region. Sieker left the Rangers in 1881 and relocated to Menard, Texas, where he flourished as a justice of the peace,* cattle rancher, and state oil inspector.

SOURCES: "Serg't Ed. A. Sieker," *Frontier Times* 4 (11), August 1927; Robert W. Stephens, *Texas Ranger Sketches*, 1972.

SIEKER, LAMARTINE PEMBERTON. (1848–1914) Born in Baltimore, Maryland, Sieker was one of four brothers who saw service in the Texas Rangers.* Prior to moving to Texas in 1873, at age fifteen, he distinguished himself as a Confederate soldier under General James Longstreet during the Civil War. Like his brother Edward Armon Sieker, Jr.,* Lamartine Sieker joined Texas Ranger Company D in 1874, and over the next eight years earned the captain's rank during meritorious service against Indians and border outlaws. In 1885 he was appointed quartermaster for the Austin, Texas, force, and in 1889 he was elevated to assistant adjutant general. After leaving the Rangers in 1905, Sieker ran a hotel.

SOURCES: Robert W. Stephens, *Texas Ranger Sketches*, 1972; "Colonel Lamartine P. Sieker, Texas Ranger," *Frontier Times* 5 (2), November 1927.

SIMON, CARLETON. (1871–1951) Following European training in the fields of psychiatry and criminology, Simon rose to prominence as chief pathologist during the investigation of President William McKinley's assassin. Appointed deputy police commissioner of New York City in 1920 and head of the narcotics force, Simon is credited with temporarily clamping down on the drug trade. In 1926 he left his position to pursue new methods of criminal investigation, including the study of eyeprints. Considered a pioneer in this field, Simon examined patterns of blood vessels in the human retina and found that each individual's eyeprint was unique. Simon was given impetus to study alternatives to fingerprinting* after John Dillinger had his fingerprints surgically altered. Simon is recognized for developing the first identification procedures for this investigative technique in the United States. He also worked as a criminologist for the International Association of Chiefs of Police (IACP).*

SOURCE: Charles Phillips and Alan Axelrod, *CCC*, 1996.

SIMPSON, CEDRIC KEITH. (1907–1985) Born in Brighton, England, and educated at Guy's Hospital Medical School, Simpson became an authority in forensic detection and lectured on the subject at London University from 1937 to 1962. Simpson rose to prominence with the publication of his textbook *Forensic Medicine* in 1947. A later edition of this work won the 1958 Royal Society of Arts Swiney prize for the best medicolegal work published in the previous decade.

Among Simpson's most famous murder investigations were the 1949 acid bath murders by John George Haigh and the 1942 Dobkin case. In the latter case he uncovered evidence in a bombed-out London church that sent Harry Dobkin to the gallows for the murder of his wife. A pioneer in forensic dentistry, he is credited with being the first investigator to identify a suspect from teeth marks left on a victim's body. An advocate for the return of hanging, in 1965 Simpson secured the first successful conviction of an individual for battered baby syndrome. During his long career, he published over two hundred articles, coauthored and edited several books, and in 1978 penned his best-selling autobiography, *Forty Years of Murder*. He died from a brain tumor.

SOURCES: Cedric Keith Simpson, *Forty Years of Murder*, 1978; Frank Smyth, *Cause of Death*, 1980; Richard Whittington-Egan and Molly Whittington-Egan, *The Bedside Book of Murder*, 1988.

SIMPSON, JOSEPH. (1909–1967) A graduate of the Hendon Police College in Great Britain, Simpson was the first Scotland Yard* commissioner to ascend through the police ranks to the top job. His meteoric rise began in 1931 when he joined the London Metropolitan Police.* Six years later he was promoted to assistant chief constable of Lincolnshire; he then held the same position in Northumberland and Surrey. In 1956 Simpson returned to the Met* as assistant commissioner of traffic and two years later became deputy commissioner. In 1958 he succeeded John Nott-Bower* in the top post.

SOURCE: Paul Begg and Keith Skinner, *The Scotland Yard Files*, 1992.

SIPPY, BENJAMIN "BEN." (prominent 1880s) Sippy fled a theft indictment in Parker County, Texas, for Arizona and in 1880 was elected city marshal (see U.S. MARSHALS SERVICE) of Tombstone, Arizona. Sippy subsequently won acclaim for saving Johnny-Behind-the-Deuce O'Rourke from a lynch mob and arresting Luke Short for the killing of Charlie Storms. Aligned with the Earp faction (see EARP, MORGAN; EARP, VIRGIL, EARP, WYATT BERRY STAPP), Sippy's name came up in connection with Doc Holliday's stagecoach robbery problems when Holliday was accused of robbing a stagecoach himself. Sippy mysteriously disappeared from Tombstone, and the historical record, in January 1881. He was replaced as marshal by Virgil Earp.

SOURCE: Ed Bartholomew, *Wyatt Earp: The Man and the Myth*, 1964.

SIRINGO, CHARLES ANGELO. (1855–1928) The son of Italian and Irish immigrants, Siringo was born on the Matagorda Peninsula in Texas. He became a cowboy at the age of eleven and worked at a series of odd jobs before finding employment in 1871 as a cowboy for Abel H. "Shanghai" Pierce in Wharton County, Texas. Over the next fourteen years, he trailed cattle on the Chisholm Trail, met Billy the Kid, and cofounded the LX Ranch. In 1885 he published *A Texas Cowboy*, the first autobiography written by a cowboy. The following year he entered law enforcement, first as a detective for Pinkerton's National Detective Agency* in Chicago, and then as a "cowboy detective" in Denver.

Over the next two decades, Siringo participated in many high-profile cases, including the investigation of the Haymarket anarchists and the infiltration of the miners' labor union in Coeur d'Alene, Idaho. He also served bodyguard duty during the "Big Bill" Haywood trial in 1906–1907. Siringo was reportedly inspired to turn to detective work in 1886. Through serendipity he happened to be in the city when radicals threw a bomb into a crowd during the Haymarket Riot,* killing several police officers; this provided the impetus for Siringo to enter law enforcement and begin a lifelong crusade against anarchism. During his career he also investigated countless other crimes involving train robbers, rustlers, murders, and kidnappings. In 1907 he resigned from the Pinkertons and became a free-lance detective; he then pursued rustlers and horse thieves while working as a ranger for the Cattle Sanitary Board of New Mexico from 1916 to 1918.

Siringo eventually published seven books, including *A Cowboy Detective: A True Story of Twenty-Two Years with a World Famous Detective Agency* (1912). Barred by litigation from mentioning the name of the detective agency, he referred to it instead as the Dickensen Detective Agency. In 1915 he published *Two Evil Isms: Pinkertonism and Anarchism. By a Cowboy Detective Who*

Knows, as He Spent Twenty-Two Years in the Inner Circle of Pinkerton's National Detective Agency. Clearly, Siringo had an axe to grind: Pinkerton's had filed an injunction to prevent him from revealing any company secrets in his earlier book. Siringo moved to California for health reasons in 1922 and became a familiar fixture around the nascent movie industry. After meeting Western actor William S. Hart, he was hired as a consultant for what became one of Hart's best films, *Tumbleweeds* (1925). Siringo published his last book, *Riata and Spurs*, in 1927; He died in Hollywood the following year.

SOURCES: Ben E. Pingenot, *Siringo*, 1989; Orlan Sawey, *Charles A. Siringo*, 1981; Frank Morn, *"The Eye That Never Sleeps,"* 1982.

SIXKILLER, SAMUEL "SAM." (1842–1886) Born in the Going Snake District of the Cherokee Nation, Sixkiller initially fought for the Confederacy during the Civil War, but he soon deserted and then joined Union troops under his father, First Lieutenant Redbird Sixkiller. Returning to the Cherokee Nation, he worked at a series of jobs before winning appointment as high sheriff of the Cherokee Nation in 1875. He also held an appointment as co-warden of the National Penitentiary at Tahlequah.

In 1879 Sixkiller was tried and acquitted of shooting a young Cherokee marauder who had fired at him first. Following this episode, which caused bad blood in the community, he relocated his family to the town of Muskogee in the Creek Nation. Here he was appointed captain of the Indian police* at the Union Agency in 1880 and soon after was again performing dual duties when he was commissioned as a deputy U.S. marshal (see U.S. MARSHALS SERVICE) by Judge Isaac Charles Parker* of Fort Smith, Arkansas. Over the next four years Sixkiller earned the respect of lawmen and lawbreakers alike as he pursued bootleggers, cattle thieves, rapists, train robbers, and other criminals laying low in the Indian Territory.

Sixkiller is credited with killing only two men during his six years with the Indian police, despite involvement in a plethora of gunfights. In 1886 Sixkiller had several confrontations with a mixed-blood Cherokee named Dick Vann who, following one arrest, had threatened revenge. On Christmas Eve 1886, an unarmed Sixkiller was ambushed and killed by Vann as he walked the streets of Muskogee.

SOURCES: Art Burton, *Black, Red, and Deadly*, 1991; William T. Hagan, *Indian Police and Judges*, 1966.

SLAUGHTER, JOHN HORTON. (1841–1922) Born in Louisiana, Slaughter relocated to Texas with his family when he was an infant. Raised in Lockhart, he worked as a cowboy, fought Comanche Indians, fought for the Confederacy during the Civil War, and served a brief stint with the Texas Rangers.* Slaughter worked in the cattle business in the 1870s and killed a man in a gunfight over a gambling argument. Arrested and released, he found he had contracted tuberculosis and for health reasons relocated to Arizona for the remainder of his life.

In the 1880s he ranched and then was elected sheriff* of Cochise County in 1886. In 1890 he retired from law enforcement and returned to the cattle business. The new sheriff, in a gesture of respect, appointed Slaughter deputy sheriff for life. Slaughter would serve one term in the Arizona Legislature, beginning in 1907, but his peace officer career was long behind him.

SOURCE: Allen A. Erwin, *The Southwest of John Erwin Slaughter*, 1965.

SLAVE PATROLS. As the slave population of the Southern states increased in the early eighteenth century, the colonies responded by organizing slave patrols to suppress insurrections and combat crime. Initially part of colonial militias, the first slave patrol was established in South Carolina in 1704. All ambulatory men between the ages of eighteen and fifty were required to volunteer for duty. All female heads of household were also required to serve on the patrols, but they were also allowed to hire a substitute instead. Typical duties required slave patrol members to inspect highways and inns every two weeks, being always on the alert for slaves absent without passes. Those who were caught without permission to be away from their plantation were taken into custody, tried at court, and then, usually, flogged. Patrols were imbued with police powers that many historians suggest made them precursors to modern policing.

SOURCES: Philip L. Reichel, "Southern Slave Patrols as a Transitional Police Type," *American Journal of Police* 7 (2), 1988; Michael S. Hindus, *Prison and Plantation: Crime, Justice and Authority in Massachusetts and South Carolina, 1767–1878*, 1980.

SLEEMAN, SIR WILLIAM HENRY. (1778–1856) Born at Stratton, Cornwall, England, Sleeman served in the British army in his twenties before rising to prominence for suppressing the Thuggee (Thugi) cult in India during the 1830s. The Thuggee were a secret society who believed they had been entrusted by the goddess Kali with the duty of murdering travelers. In 1835 Sleeman was appointed superintendent of operations against the Thuggee and was commissioner during their ultimate destruction in 1839. In the course of his campaign, four thousand Thuggee were brought to trial. Sleeman, who was conversant in several languages including Hindustani and Arabic, was able to infiltrate the secret organization by means of informers and, in the process, learned their secret language, recorded their confessions, and reported in detail their horrific rituals. Forty-seven years after debarking at Calcutta, Sleeman died of a heart attack near Ceylon while returning to his native England.

SOURCES: George Bruce, *The Stranglers*, 1969; Philip Mason, *The Men Who Ruled India*, 1985; A. J. Wightman, *No Friend for Travellers*, 1959.

SLICKERS. Overwhelmed by gangs of criminal predators, the citizens of Lincoln County, Missouri, took the law into their own hands in 1845. They formed a vigilante group called the "Slickers," in reference to the punishment of "slicking," or whipping with hickory sprouts. After they slicked a suspected criminal, he was given a short time to leave the county. Despite some opposition, the Slicker campaign of 1845–1846 was considered a successful endeavor.

SOURCE: Carl Sifakis, *The Encyclopedia of American Crime*, 1982.

SLIPPER, JACK. (b. 1924) Born in Ealing, Middlesex, England, Slipper worked as an electrician and served in the Royal Air Force during World War II. Following the war he returned to his trade before joining the London Metropolitan Police* in 1951. After five years as a uniformed constable he was transferred to the Criminal Investigation Department (CID),* and in 1962 he was transferred to the Flying Squad,* rising to sergeant several months later. Following several more promotions and transfers, he was made detective chief superintendent and transferred to lead the stolen car squad at Chalk Farm in 1971. Two years later he returned to the Flying Squad as operational chief superintendent, and in 1977 he was promoted to Detective Chief Superintendent at Wembley. He retired from policing at the end of 1979. During his legendary career, "Slipper of the Yard" investigated some of the most spectacular crimes of his era, including the twelve-million-pound Bank of America robbery, the Shepherd's Bush multiple police murders, and the Great Train Robbery. While operations chief of the Flying Squad, Slipper rose to prominence as the man who flew to Rio de Janeiro to find train robber Ronald Biggs. He chronicled his career in his 1981 autobiography, *Slipper of the Yard*.

SOURCE: Jack Slipper, *Slipper of the Yard*, 1981.

SLIWA, CURTIS. Curtis Sliwa founded the Guardian Angels* in 1979. His former wife, Lisa Sliwa, eventually became the organization's national director. Although this citizens' group styled itself as an auxiliary police unit, it sometimes came under fire for its vigilante activities and has been characterized as "a cross between a Special Forces military squad and a street gang" by its critics.

SOURCE: Martin Alan Greenberg, *Auxiliary Police*, 1984.

SMITH, BRUCE. (1892–1955) Born in Brooklyn, New York, the son of a banker and real estate broker, Smith attended Wesleyan and Columbia Universities. In 1916 he began his career as a police consultant and criminologist when he was hired by the New York Bureau of Municipal Research and studied the Harrisburg, Pennsylvania, police department. The following year he began a two-year stint in the air force during World War I. He returned to the bureau following the war, and as he rose through the ranks, he expanded his knowledge of policing by collaborating with the National Crime Commission, the Illinois

Association of Criminal Justice, and the Missouri Association for Criminal Justice.

Over the remainder of his life Smith continued to survey police departments, and after an extensive comparative study of European police procedures, he was instrumental in creating the *Uniform Crime Reports** in 1930. Cities that consulted Smith on how to improve their police forces included Chicago, Illinois; Baltimore, Maryland; San Francisco, California; Pittsburgh and Philadelphia, Penssylvania, and many others. Smith was not always successful. He had made numerous recommendations for reforming the New Orleans, Louisiana, Police Department, but when he returned over twenty years later, the same problems remained. As America's foremost expert on police operations, Smith was in constant demand at top universities and served as a visiting faculty member at the Federal Bureau of Investigation (FBI)* National Police Training Academy from its inception in 1935 until his death (from a lung ailment while sailing on his yacht, the *Lucifer*) in 1955. His most influential books included *Rural Crime Control* (1933), *Mobilizing Police for Emergency Duties* (1940), and *Police Systems in the United States* (1940).

SOURCE: William G. Bailey, "Bruce Smith," in *The Encyclopedia of Police Science*, ed. William G. Bailey, 1995.

SMITH, HENRY. (1835–1921) Born and educated in Scotland, Smith worked as a bookkeeper and then was commissioned in the Suffolk Artillery Militia in 1969. He attempted to gain a senior appointment in the City of London Police* for six years before being appointed chief superintendent in 1875. From 1890 to 1901 he served as commissioner. During the Jack the Ripper murders he took charge of the investigation when Commissioner James Fraser was on leave. Smith was credited with maintaining a good rapport with the press during his tenure. In his 1910 memoirs, *From Constable to Commissioner*, Smith claimed to know more about the Ripper case than any man alive. However, many of his claims have been called into question by Ripper scholars.

SOURCE: Paul Begg, Martin Fido, and Keith Skinner, *The Jack the Ripper A to Z*, 1991.

SMITH, MOE. *See* IZZY AND MOE.

SMITH, SYDNEY ALFRED. (1883–1969) Born in Roxburgh, New Zealand, and educated at Victoria College and then Edinburgh University, Smith became a forensic authority following an apprenticeship to Professor Harvey Littlejohn. Between 1917 and 1928, Smith served as the principal medicolegal expert to the Ministry of Justice in Egypt and professor of forensic medicine at the University of Egypt. He rose to international prominence following his investigation into the assassination of the Sirdar Sir Lee Stack Pasha in 1924.

Following Littlejohn's death in 1927, Smith replaced his mentor (in 1928) as professor of forensic medicine at Edinburgh University for the next twenty-five years. Smith was widely considered an authority in ballistics, toxicology, and microscopy. Often called on internationally as an expert witness and forensic investigator, he played instrumental roles in the Annie Hearn, Jeannie Donald, Sidney Fox, and Dr. Buck Ruxton murder cases. In the 1930s he received the Swiney Prize for his 1925 textbook *Forensic Medicine*. His autobiography, *Mostly Murder*, was published in 1959.

SOURCES: Frank Smyth, *Cause of Death*, 1980; Sir Sydney Smith, *Mostly Murder*, 1959; Richard Whittington-Egan and Molly Whittington-Egan, *The Bedside Book of Murder*, 1988.

SMITH, THOMAS JAMES "BEAR RIVER." (1840–1870) Smith was born in New York City. Following a stint as a professional boxer, he joined the New York City Police Department (NYPD).* After his acquittal in an accidental shooting, he left the force and moved West, where he served in the army and then worked as a teamster in Bear River City Wyoming. His proficiency with his fists landed him the job of town peace officer, and he was assigned to keeping order in the short-lived boom camp. Although he reportedly carried a brace of pistols, by 1869 he had apparently stopped using guns to enforce the law. In 1870 he was appointed peace officer in Greeley, Colorado, and soon after he was appointed marshal (see U.S. MARSHALS SERVICE) of Abilene, Kansas.

Smith came to prominence in Abilene for eschewing gunplay and making it an offense to carry firearms in the city limits. During his year in Abilene he survived at least one assassination attempt, killed no one, and typically relied on his fists to enforce the laws. Later he served as deputy and undersheriff of the county as well as town marshal.* He was killed on November 2, 1870, while arresting a murder suspect. Ironically, Smith was almost decapitated by an axe rather than falling a victim of gunplay, which he had always tried to avoid.

SOURCES: Carl W. Breihan, *Great Lawmen of the West*, 1963; Joseph G. Rosa, *The Gunfighter: Man or Myth?*, 1969.

SMITH, TOM. (d. 1892) Born in Texas, Smith came to prominence during the Jaybird-Woodpecker War in Fort Bend County, Texas, between 1888 and 1890. During the feud, Smith served as deputy in the Woodpecker faction and killed the leader of the Jaybirds. Smith played a role in another of the West's most notorious conflicts in 1892 when he became embroiled in the Johnson County War in Wyoming. He entered the fray when he was approached while working as a Wyoming stock detective and asked by cattlemen to recruit Texas gunmen for an invasion of Johnson County in an attempt to drive out small ranchers.

Returning to Texas, Smith had no problem recruiting experienced gunmen, favoring men who had served behind a badge against organized outlaw bands in the Brazos, Pecos, and Panhandle counties. Smith was instrumental in the killing of Nick Ray and Nate Champion during the noted siege at the KC Ranch House. When word got out about this outrage, fellow ranchers besieged the Texas gunmen, who were rescued by U.S. cavalry troops and taken into custody. The Texans were allowed to return home without a trial. Smith met an ignominious end when he was killed by an African-American desperado on a train in Indian Territory.

SOURCES: Helena Huntington Smith, *The War on the Powder River*, 1966; Ed Bartholomew, *Western Hard-Cases*, 1960.

SMITH, WILLIAM. (1848–1908) Born in Leicestershire, England, "Bill" Smith immigrated with his family to Utica, New York, in 1853. The following year the family moved to Lawrence, Kansas. After serving in the Civil War, he moved to Wichita, Kansas, and established a sawmill. He served as deputy sheriff and sheriff* in 1873 and then was appointed deputy U.S. marshal. In 1874 he was appointed marshal of Wichita, Kansas, and also served as constable (see CONSTABLES). He moved on to Galena, Kansas, in 1877 and served as one of its earliest mayors in 1895.

SOURCES: Ed Bartholomew, *Wyatt Earp: The Untold Story*, 1963; Dan L. Thrapp, ed., *EFB*, Vol. 3, 1988.

SODERMAN, HARRY. (1903–1956) The son of a police administrator and sheriff, Soderman was born in Stockholm, Sweden. Shortly after graduating from college in 1925, he began studying police departments around the world. During his two-year research trip, he supported his work by writing articles for the *Swedish Police Journal*. He studied police science under Edmond Locard at the French Police Laboratory and graduated with a doctorate from the University of Lyons. He taught police science in his native Sweden and in 1939 founded the National Institute of Technical Police, Sweden's incarnation of the Federal Bureau of Investigation (FBI).* He served as its first director from 1939 to 1953. Following World War II he was instrumental in founding the International Criminal Police Organization (Interpol).* Soderman published numerous books and articles, but he is best known for *Modern Criminal Investigation* (1935), which he coauthored with John J. O'Connell.

SOURCES: Harry Soderman, *Policeman's Lot*, 1956; Charles Phillips and Alan Axelrod, *CCC*, 1996.

SOURYAL, SAM S. Born in Cairo, Egypt, and educated at a variety of institutions, including the Higher Institute of Police Sciences in Cairo, Souryal entered policing as a cadet at the National Police Academy in Cairo at the age of sixteen. After four years of police studies, he was assigned to the Zeiton Police Station for two years and then served stints with several other departments before being promoted to lieutenant in the nation's "Flying Squad." He ascended to captain in the Cairo police in 1960, and was a founding member of the Cairo

Special Weapons and Tactics (SWAT)* team, a unit that preceded the famous Los Angeles unit. Over the next five years, Souryal rose to prominence in several high-profile crime cases. In 1965 he turned to academia, and over the last thirty-five years he published widely in police sciences, criminal investigation, police operations and ethics. In 1999, Souryal was selected by the United Nations to be its representative for the high commissioner on human rights in Indonesia.

SOURCE: Sam S. Souryal, interview with author, November 1999.

SOUTH AFRICAN POLICE (SAP). Modeled on military discipline and command structure, the South African Police force was divorced from the local population and staffed by British officers. Since these rural-based forces were paramilitary in nature, they were easily transformed into military units in time of war, which occurred often during nineteenth-century colonial expansion. The policeman-soldier can be readily discerned in both the British and Afrikaner models of policing.

Formed in 1822, the Cape Mounted Police were the earliest incarnation of the horse mounted police* tradition in South Africa. At their zenith they numbered eight hundred. Over the next fifty years the police force was reorganized several times, and in 1878 it was divided into two branches, each commanded by a separate lieutenant commander and both supervised by a general officer. Besides fighting in various colonial wars, the Cape Mounted Police was required to perform police duties ranging from stock theft and the collection of dog taxes to the apprehension of those without appropriate gun licenses.

Other South African police forces engaged in colonial police matters included the Natal Mounted Police* and the Zululand Mounted police, all inspired by the early Royal Irish Constabulary* model. In 1873 the Natal Mounted police was organized in response to a tribal rebellion, and for over a generation they would be supported by the Zululand Mounted. During the Boer War the Zululand force was incorporated into the Natal Mounted, and by 1904 it was disbanded altogether.

Following the British victory in the Boer War, the South African Constabulary (SAC) was organized into three divisions, two of which were controlled by British officers and one by Colonel Samuel Benfield "Sam" Steele* of the Canadian Royal North-West Mounted Police. With the end of hostilities, the force stood at 10,500 men, making it the largest mounted police force in the world. There was apparently never a lack of friction between the SAC and local police. According to Steele, "I may say that we seldom had the support of local law enforcement." With the creation of the Union of South Africa in 1910, all of the South African police units were united under a single banner. In 1913 the South African Constabulary, Cape Mounted Rifles, Natal Mounted Police, and others formally became the nucleus of the South African Police.

SOURCES: Mitchel Roth, "Mounted Police Forces: A Comparative History," *Policing* 21 (4), Fall 1998; J. Brewer, *Black and Blue: Policing in South Africa*, 1994; Sam Steele, *Forty Years in Canada*, 1972; H. Senior, *Constabulary*, 1997.

SPECIAL BRANCH OF THE METROPOLITAN POLICE. The creation of the Special Branch of the Metropolitan Police was precipitated by the bombing campaign orchestrated by the American-based Fenian movement. Beginning in the late 1860s Fenians inaugurated a bombing campaign in England in order to win Home Rule for Ireland. In 1883 Fenian terrorists bombed several public buildings and Scotland Yard* established the Special Irish Branch (later changed to Special Branch) on March 17, 1883, the first specialist section of the Criminal Investigation Department (CID). The first members of this branch were predominately Irish. Chosen to lead the nascent unit were James Monro, John Sweeney, and Adolphus Frederick Williamson.* Within two years they had smashed the terror campaign.

The success of the Special Branch led to its utilization as bodyguards for protecting Queen Victoria and foreign dignitaries during the 1897 Jubilee festivities. The Special Branch would later be involved in the 1911 Sidney Street Siege,* investigate German espionage networks during World War I, communist trials in the 1920s, and, more recently, Irish Republican Army (IRA) terrorists and Soviet spy rings. It remains a unique secret service and political police organization that bridges the divide between British Intelligence and Scotland Yard.

SOURCE: Rupert Allason, *The Branch: A History of the Metropolitan Police Special Branch, 1883–1983*, 1983.

SPECIAL WEAPONS AND TACTICS (SWAT). The Philadelphia Police Department established the precursor to the Special Weapons and Tactics (SWAT) teams in 1964, when it established its one-hundred-member Special Weapons and Tactics Squad. Designed to respond quickly and decisively to bank robberies in progress, it was soon also used to resolve other types of incidents involving heavily armed criminals. Its media popularity and successful field implementation led other police forces to develop similar units, most notably the Los Angeles Police Department (LAFD).*

Although then-Los Angeles Police chief Daryl F. Gates* claimed credit for introducing the name of the Special Weapons and Tactics teams (SWAT)* in the late 1960s when he was deputy chief, he initially wanted to call the units Special Weapons Attack Teams. However, deputy chief Edward M. Davis* objected to the bellicosity projected in the word *attack*, and it was changed to the more familiar rendering. The creation of SWAT teams was a response to new trends in criminal violence which included skyjackings, shoot-outs, and hostage taking. However, the 1974 shoot-out with Symbionese Liberation Army (SLA) members catapulted the units to national prominence.

American SWAT teams have distinctive qualities that differentiate them from other police units. Most teams average twelve members and are organized into two types. The assault units are used to enter and clear structures, while cover groups provide cover protection and protect the periphery of the incident in progress. All teams are on-call twenty-four hours a day. Teams are mainly used in predicaments that are hostage related, sniper situations that pose a threat to civilians, barricade incidents in neighborhoods or commercial sectors, and for antisniper protection for visiting luminaries.

SOURCES: Joe Domanick, *To Protect and Serve*, 1994; John A. Kolman, *A Guide to the Development of Special Weapons and Tactics Teams*, 1982.

SPILSBURY, SIR BERNARD HENRY. (1877–1947) Born at Leamington Spa, Warwickshire, England, and educated at Magdalen College, Oxford, Spilsbury came under the influence of several forensics pioneers while pursuing his medical education at St. Mary's Hospital. Following graduation, he was hired by St. Mary's as the resident assistant pathologist. In 1910 Spilsbury rose to prominence as a leading exponent of forensic science during the murder trial of Dr. Hawley Harvey Crippen. Over the next decade he was viewed as the greatest medicolegal expert of his era. A vision of sartorial splendor in a Savile Row suit and top hat, Spilsbury testified in most high-profile murder cases of his time, including the Brighton Trunk Murders, Herbert Armstrong, Patrick Mahon, Donald Merret, George Joseph Smith, and many others.

Toward the end of his career, Spilsbury's skills became somewhat diminished, and the accuracy of his findings was frequently brought into question. Hampered by arthritis, Spilsbury retired from full-time work in 1934. The man whose name became synonymous with forensic pathology conducted more than twenty-five thousand autopsies during a remarkable career, but his last years were marked by a series of personal tragedies and he became more reclusive. At the age of seventy he committed suicide, gassing himself in his university laboratory.

SOURCES: Richard Whittington-Egan and Molly Whittington-Egan, *The Bedside Book of Murder*, 1988; Frank Smyth, *Cause of Death*, 1980.

SPRADLEY, A. JOHN. (1853–1940) Born in Simpson County, Mississippi, Spradley killed two brothers in a gunfight in 1871 and fled to Nagocdoches, Texas, where he worked in a relative's mill for several years. In 1880 he was appointed deputy sheriff of Nagocdoches County. The following year he started a thirty-year tenure as county sheriff.* While on duty he reportedly wore, under his clothes, a steel shirt, an early prototype of the bullet-proof vest. In 1884 Spradley narrowly survived a serious gunshot wound while making an arrest. He participated in several other gunfights and made the transition from tavern owner to rabid prohibitionist after one too many encounters with drunken hoodlums. After retiring from law enforcement, Spradley farmed and stayed active in local politics.

SOURCE: Jay Robert Nash, *EWLO*, 1992.

STALKER, JOHN. (b. 1939) Born in Manchester, England, Stalker graduated from the Police Staff College in 1969 and later the Royal College of Defence Studies in 1983. He entered law enforcement as a detective on the Greater Manchester Police force in 1958. In 1977 he was promoted to chief detective of the Warwickshire County Police. Three years later he began a seven-year stint as head of the detective division of the Greater Manchester Police force. However, he resigned in 1987 when he was denied permission to finish an investigation into the police shootings of six unarmed civilians in Northern Ireland. He had been withdrawn from the investigation soon after he accused British police of purposely killing the civilians. Stalker inflamed the matter by suggesting that authorities were participating in a cover-up. After leaving the force, he chronicled this incident in *The Stalker Affair*, which was published in 1988.

SOURCE: John Stalker, *The Stalker Affair*, 1988.

STANDEFER, WILEY W. (prominent 1870s) Born in Georgia, prior to entering law enforcement in Arizona, Standefer was a rancher in California. Taking advantage of political connections, he was appointed Arizona marshal in August 1876, replacing Francis Goodwin. During his two-year stint, Standefer pursued a myriad of outlaw gangs in the territory and supervised the first federally mandated hanging in Arizona history. The only blemish on his short-lived tenure as marshal was the death of popular Arizona bandit Jack Swilling in the Yuma Jail due to appalling conditions. Swilling's death was blamed by local constituents on the highhanded actions of federal law enforcement, and it elevated the bandit to martyr status. Standefer soon resigned and was replaced by Crawley P. Dake* in June 1878.

SOURCE: Larry D. Ball, *The United States Marshals of New Mexico and Arizona Territories, 1846–1912*, 1978.

STANDLEY, JEREMIAH. (1845–1908) Born in Andrew County, Missouri, Standley moved to California with his family in 1853. He received his sobriquet "Doc" in his youth when he helped save the life of a sick cow. In 1864 he was named deputy sheriff of Mendocino County. He rose to prominence as a manhunter after solving a series of high-profile local cases and apprehending several killers. In 1882 he began a ten-year tenure as sheriff,* during which he was credited with solving thirteen out of the fourteen stagecoach robberies he investigated. After retiring, he moved to Alaska, where he prospected for gold and served as Nome deputy sheriff.

SOURCE: Charles Phillips and Alan Axelrod, *CCC*, 1996.

STAR POLICE. Prior to the introduction of police uniforms* in 1853, the New York City police were only identifiable by the eight-pointed shield introduced by police chief George W. Matsell.*

SOURCE: James F. Richardson, *The New York Police*, 1970.

STATUTE OF WINCHESTER. This statute was the only general public measure of any consequence enacted in England to regulate policing between the Norman Conquest (1066) and the Metropolitan Police Act of a 1829.* Introduced in 1285, the Statute of Winchester is considered an early milestone in the development of law enforcement strategy. A blending of Saxon and Norman ideas, it proposed a watch and ward system,* which introduced the town watchman to supplement the duties performed by traditional constables.* Here for the first time a distinction is made between urban and rural law enforcement.

According to the statute, towns were required to station watchmen at every gate of walled towns from sunset to sunrise. Imbued with arrest powers, watchmen were to confine transients during the hours of darkness. The statute was also notable for its requirement that the hue and cry* be raised in the event a perpetrator is on the loose. In order to put some teeth into the law, the Assize of Arms* was maintained, requiring all males between fifteen and sixty to possess a weapon that could be used in the pursuit of a suspect.

SOURCE: T. A. Critchley, *A History of Police in England and Wales, 900–1966,* 1967.

STEELE, SAMUEL BENFIELD "SAM." (1849–1919) Born in Ontario province, Canada, Steele served in the militia while still in his teens and participated in the Red River Campaign of 1870–1871. After distinguishing himself in the Royal Canadian Artillery, Steele was appointed sergeant major of the recently established North West Mounted Police, the forerunner of the Royal Canadian Mounted Police* (RCMP)* in 1873. He was instrumental in establishing a string of outposts and mediating disputes between settlers, trappers, and Indians. He was promoted to superintendent in 1885 and led troops in that year's Northwest Rebellion. During the late 1890s he was credited with preventing the sort of lawlessness that typically accompanied mineral rushes by using the mounted police to perform municipal jobs such as tax collectors and postal workers while at the same time solving crimes. He later saw service in the Boer War in South Africa and was knighted in 1918.

SOURCE: Robert Stewart, *Sam Steele: Lion of the Frontier,* 1979.

STEFFENS, LINCOLN. (d. 1936) A prominent "muckraking" journalist of the Progressive era and an unrelenting critic of police corruption, Steffens championed the underclasses and was a confidante of New York City police commissioner Theodore Roosevelt.* in the 1890s. His autobiography, unimaginatively entitled *Autobiography* (1931), is loaded with valuable anecdotes about policing in New York City from the 1890s into the early twentieth century. He became increasingly infatuated with communism in the 1920s and 1930s and won a following among American communists and "fellow travelers."

SOURCE: H. Paul Jeffers, *Commissioner Roosevelt,* 1994.

STERLING, ALBERT D. (c. 1853–1882) Born in Ohio, Sterling exhibited a lifelong fascination with Native American culture. He worked as chief of scouts at Fort Cummings, New Mexico, before accepting the position of chief of the Indian police* at the San Carlos Reservation in August 1880. Except for a one-year respite, he served in this position until his death. On April 19, 1882, Sterling and an Indian policeman were killed while attempting to abort an attack by Sierra Madre Apache raiders on the San Carlos reservation. The raiders reportedly cut off Sterling's head and played with it like a football.

SOURCES: Dan L. Thrapp, *Conquest of Apacheria, General Crook and the Sierra Madre Adventure*, 1967; Dan L. Thrapp, ed., *EFB*, Vol. 3, 1988.

STERLING, WILLIAM WARREN. (1891–1960) Born in Bell County, Texas, Sterling grew up on a ranch near Cotulla. He attended Texas A&M College before joining the Texas Rangers* in 1915. Known to his friends as "General Bill," Sterling was the only Ranger to hold every rank from private to adjutant general during the 1930s. Sterling chronicled his career in *Trails and Trials of a Texas Ranger* (1959).

SOURCES: William Warren Sterling, *Trails and Trials of a Texas Ranger*, reprint, 1968; *Texas Rangers Sesquicentennial Anniversary*, 1973.

STOCKLEY, JAMES. (1863–1954) Stockley was reportedly the last living policeman from the Jack the Ripper case when he died in 1954. He joined the London Metropolitan Police* in 1885 and played a rather insignificant role in the hunt for the Ripper, but he did work wearing various disguises while policing in the Whitechapel area during the investigation. He retired from the force in 1911 and worked as a private detective. One of his clients was the Singer sewing machine heiress, Miss Florence Pratt. Following her death in 1934 she left Stockley her fortune of one million pounds. Although it was later contested, he lived comfortably in retirement on the interest from his inheritance.

SOURCE: Paul Begg, Martin Fido, and Keith Skinner, *The Jack the Ripper A to Z*, 1991.

STOUDENMIRE, DALLAS. (1945–1882) Stoudenmire was born in Macon County, Alabama. Following service in the Confederacy during the Civil War, he moved West. He earned a reputation as a gunman in Columbus, Texas, before winning appointment as city marshal of El Paso, Texas, in 1881. He added to his reputation early on by killing three men in a gunfight. During his first year on the job he killed the previous town marshal,* who was trying to ambush him.

Before long he entered a simmering feud with the well-connected Manning Brothers, who later killed his brother-in-law, Doc Cummings. Stoudenmire had developed a fondness for alcohol and repeatedly threatened the Mannings (who had been acquitted of killing Cummings), citing self-defense. In 1882 Stoudenmire was forced to resign by the local vigilance committee. On September 18, 1882, the former marshal accosted one of the Manning brothers in a saloon. While they were fighting one of his brothers interceded, killing Stoudenmire with a gunshot to the head; once again, the brothers were exonerated.

SOURCES: Leon Metz, *Dallas Stoudenmire: El Paso Marshal*, 1969; Leon Metz, *The Shooters*, 1976.

STRANGLERS, THE. The "Stranglers" was a small vigilante organization composed of only fourteen members. Led by Granville Stuart, a Montana cattle rancher, these regulators were primarily leading ranchers in the area that banded together to end the rustling scourge between 1884 and 1886. Although lynch law justice had fallen out of favor, the Stranglers were credited with hanging seventy rustlers. Stuart went on to a stellar political career.

SOURCE: Carl Sifakis, *The Encyclopedia of American Crime*, 1982.

STRECHER, VICTOR G. (b. 1931) Born in Milwaukee, Wisconsin, Strecher was educated at the University of Wisconsin, Michigan State University, and Washington University, where he received a Ph.D. in Sociology in 1968. Strecher entered law enforcement with the Michigan State University Police Department in 1953. In 1956 he began a three-year stint teaching criminal justice at Michigan State University before serving as a police and security advisor to the Government of South Vietnam from 1959 to 1961. Over the next thirty years Strecher was Director of the St. Louis Metropolitan Police Department Academy (1961–1966) and then of the Law Enforcement Policy Study Center at Washington University (1966–1968). In 1969 U.S. Attorney General John Mitchell appointed Strecher to the Commission on Minority Employment in Law Enforcement. He continued to focus on criminal justice administration as professor and Director of the Arizona State University Criminal Justice Center (1976–1978) and then as Dean and Director of the Criminal Justice Center and College of Criminal Justice at Sam Houston State University, Huntsville, Texas. Strecher published several books and numerous articles including *The Environment of Law Enforcement* (1971) and *Planning Community Policing* (1997).

SOURCES: Interview with author, November 1999; Mitchel Roth, *Fulfilling a Mandate*, 1997.

STRIKEBREAKERS, POLICE AS. During the 1890s most local police forces in the United States were still generally ineffective in suppressing crime and civil disorder. With the labor unrest that accompanied the rise of big business and the labor unions, Pinkerton's National Detective Agency* found a niche supplying guards and strikebreakers to America's industrial giants. However, the Pinkertons tarnished their reputation almost beyond repair with their participation in the 1892 Homestead Strike* at the Carnegie steel plant in Pennsylvania.

Pennsylvania persisted as a hotspot for labor unrest into the early twentieth century. In 1902, strikes in the anthracite coal fields required the militia to quell the disturbance. Many historians credit disputes between labor and management for providing the impetus for the establishment of the Pennsylvania State Police* in 1905. The presence of recent immigrants from eastern and southern Europe predicated the creation of state police agencies in some cases and obviated against the inauguration of such forces in others.

SOURCE: H. Kenneth Bechtel, *State Police in the United States*, 1995.

SUGHRUE, MICHAEL. (1844–1901) Born in County Kerry, Ireland, like his twin brother Patrick F. Sughrue,* he served as a peace officer in Kansas. Following service in the Seventh Kansas Cavalry during the Civil War, he was appointed deputy by his brother in Ford County, Kansas. In 1884 he was appointed town marshal* of Ashland, Kansas, after tracking down a wanted killer. The next year he became the first sheriff of Clark County, Kansas, serving until 1890 and then again from 1899 to 1900.

SOURCE: Wayne T. Walker, "The Twin Sheriffs of Western Kansas," *The West*, April 1969.

SUGHRUE, PATRICK F. (1844–1906) Born in County Kerry, Ireland, Sughrue was the twin brother of fellow Kansas lawman Michael Sughrue.* While living in Leavenworth, he worked as a blacksmith before he found his bailiwick as a policeman in Dodge City in March 1877. The following year he was elected constable* (see CONSTABLES), and in 1879 he was credited with apprehending horse thief Charles Trask.

In 1883 Sughrue was elected sheriff* of Ford County, Kansas. During his four-year tenure, he arrested Dave "Mysterious Dave" Mather* for the killing of assistant marshal Tom Nixon. Sughrue saw the transition of Dodge City from a wide-open destination for cowboys to the era of state Prohibition and the end of the cattle drives in the 1880s.

SOURCES: Wayne T. Walker, "The Twin Sheriffs of Western Kansas," *The West*, April 1969; Nyle H. Miller and Joseph W. Snell, "Some Notes on Kansas Cowtown Police Officers and Gunfighters," *Kansas Historical Quarterly*, Summer 1962.

SULLIVAN, JOSEPH. Federal Bureau of Investigation (FBI)* director John Edgar Hoover* used Sullivan as an FBI troubleshooter in the 1960s. In 1964 he was charged with investigating the murder of three civil rights workers in Mississippi. Sullivan was reportedly the model for actor Efrem Zimbalist's Inspector Erskine in the *FBI* television series in the 1960s.

SOURCE: Athan G. Theoharis, ed. *The FBI*, 1999.

SULLIVAN, WILLIAM CORNELIUS. (1912–1977) Born and raised in Boston, Massachusetts, Sullivan earned a bachelor's degree in history from American University and served in the Internal Revenue Service before joining the Federal Bureau of Investigation (FBI)* in 1941. During World War II, he got his first taste of counterintelligence work while investigating the local German community out of the Milwaukee, Wisconsin, field office. During the 1940s he continued his counterintelligence work out of a variety of field offices before being assigned to the domestic intelligence division, where he oversaw intelligence operations in Mexico and South America.

Following the war, Sullivan made an easy transition to focusing on communist activities. During the 1950s and 1960s he continued his intelligence work and was reportedly the main ghostwriter for the John Edgar Hoover* work *A Study in Communism* (1962). Sullivan supervised the FBI's investigation of the John F. Kennedy assassination and the wiretapping of Martin Luther King, Jr. Suspected as a communist sympathizer, Sullivan is credited with directing the scurrilous campaign against King, which included attempts at gathering compromising evidence on the civil rights leader by bugging his hotel rooms.

During the Richard Nixon years, Sullivan was ordered to maintain FBI wiretap records on White House staff members accused of leaking sensitive materials to the press and of bugging the Paris residence of columnist Joseph Kraft. In 1970, Sullivan rose to the number three position in the FBI, and many officials considered him a natural successor to Hoover. Not long after his promotion, Sullivan began to criticize Hoover's policies, which restricted FBI surveillance of radical extremists and antiwar activists. By publicly criticizing his chief, Sullivan hoped to diminish Hoover's power and lead to his removal. However, his attempts backfired, and Hoover fired Sullivan on October 1, 1971, for insubordination.

Sullivan remains one of the Bureau's most controversial figures. Following his sacking he unleashed accusations against Hoover and the Bureau that tarnished the image of the once-elite unit. However, Sullivan's legacy remains equally tarnished, as he has been credited with the development of the FBI's counterintelligence program (COINTELPRO*) during the antiwar era. According to former FBI director Clarence Marion Kelly,* some of Sullivan's critics called him "Crazy Billy." Sullivan chronicled his FBI experiences in the book *The Bureau*, published posthumously in 1979. Following his dismissal from the FBI, he was appointed director of the Department of Justice's Office of National Narcotics Intelligence. Sullivan died in a hunting accident in 1977.

SOURCES: William C. Sullivan, with Bill Brown, *The Bureau: My Thirty Years in Hoover's FBI*, 1979; Curt Gentry, *J. Edgar Hoover: The Man and His Secrets*, 1991.

SUPERGRASS. The derivation of this expression, which is used in Great Britain to describe police informants, is somewhat obscure. Among the derivations suggested are "grasshopper" for copper* and "in the grass," referring to being on the lam from the police or prison. Synonymous with *supergrass* are the expressions *squealer, snitch, squawker,* and *stool pigeon.* While the 1970s are considered the era of the supergrasses, the tradition of police informants can be traced back as far back as the ancient world and to the thief-takers (see THIEF-TAKER GENERAL) such as Jonathan Wild.*

SOURCE: James Morton, *Supergrasses and Informers: An Informal History of Undercover Police Work,* 1995

SÛRETÉ. The development of the Sûreté in France can be traced to the innovations of Eugene François Vidocq* in the nineteenth century. Vidocq's handpicked security brigade (Brigade de Sûreté) of twenty ex-convicts was the precursor of the modern Sûreté. Vidocq was considered a pioneer in the utilization of detection techniques, including graphology and paper-and-ink analysis.

Drawing on his own recruitment by the police from the criminal underworld, Vidocq made extensive use of his former colleagues in crime. Petty bickering and professional jealousy over his success as a detective chief led to his resignation and to a brief stint as a private detective. However, this was short-lived and in 1832 he was appointed chief of the Sûreté for a term of several months. His successor, Louis Canler, saw the detectives of the Sûreté incorporated as official affiliates of the police in 1833.

The late nineteenth century witnessed the transformation of the Sûreté into a highly professional detective police force as it was institutionalized into a separate unit. It won international renown for its meticulous information gathering and is generally considered the inspiration for the International Criminal Police Organization (Interpol)* and the Scotland Yard* Criminal Investigation Department (CID)*. In 1966 the Sûreté was merged with the police of Paris to form the National Police.

SOURCES: Philip John Stead, *The Police of Paris,* 1957; Clive Emsley, *Policing and Its Context, 1750–1870,* 1983.

SWANSON, DONALD SUTHERLAND. (1848–1924) Born in Thurso, Scotland, Swanson joined the London Metropolitan Police* in 1868, and over the next twenty years would ascend to the rank of chief inspector of the Criminal Investigation Department (CID).* In 1896 he was promoted to superintendent. He retired in 1903. During the Jack the Ripper killings, he was in charge of the investigation from September to October 1888. His most celebrated cases included the recovery of the Countess of Dysart's jewels and, then, of a stolen Gainsborough painting and his suppression of a gang that blackmailed homosexual prostitutes. Other highly publicized cases followed, including the apprehension of railway murderer Percy LeFroy Mapleton and the subduing of Fenian terrorists.

SOURCE: Paul Begg, Martin Fido, and Keith Skinner, *The Jack the Ripper A to Z,* 1991.

SWEATBOX. Some early police stations maintained a small, cramped room adjacent to a hot furnace for interrogation purposes. Prior to the creation of the American Civil Liberties Union and other civil libertarian groups suspects were subjected to the third degree* in these sweatboxes in order to coerce confessions. Washington, D.C., police superintendent Richard Sylvester* delivered a presentation to the annual meeting of the International Association of Chiefs of Police (IACP)* condemning the use of the sweatbox in 1910.

SOURCES: Thomas J. Deakin, *Police Professionalism*, 1988; Richard Sylvester, "Sweat Box," International Association of Chiefs of Police: Seventeenth Annual Session, May 10–13, 1910, in *Proceedings of the Annual Conventions of the International Association of Chiefs of Police: 1906–1912*, Vol. 2; reprint, 1971.

SWISS GUARD. Assigned to protect the Pope, the papal palace, and Vatican City, the Swiss Guard was founded in 1506 by Pope Julius II, making it one of the oldest police forces still in existence. Pope Paul VI abolished three other guard forces in 1970, which included the Papal Gendarmie, the Palatine Guard, and the Noble Guard.

SOURCES: George Thomas Kurian, *World Encyclopedia of Police Forces and Penal Systems*, 1989; James Cramer, *The World's Police*, 1964.

SYLVESTER, RICHARD. (flourished 1898–1915) Prior to entering law enforcement, Sylvester studied law, worked as a journalist and as a disbursement officer for the Ute Indian Commission, and then joined the Washington, D.C., police as chief clerk. In 1894 he finished writing the history of this police force, and in 1898 he began a seventeen-year career as superintendent of the Washington, D.C., police.

Sylvester was elected president of the National Police Chief's Union in 1901 (renamed the International Association of Chiefs of Police [IACP]* in 1902), succeeding Webber S. Seavey.* During his fifteen-year tenure, Sylvester led the transition of this organization into a powerful voice for police reform and professionalization. During the annual meetings of the IACP, Sylvester delivered presentations ranging from "A History of the Sweat Box" (1910) to "The Third Degree" (1910) and emphasized the need for preventive policing and vice control and the importance of probation. His efforts paid off, and the IACP unanimously voted to ban third degree methods of interrogation. Sylvester led probably the earliest campaign against the movie industry, criticizing the nascent film industry for its degrading portrayal of police officers as Keystone Kops.*

SOURCES: Thomas J. Deakin, *Police Professionalism: The Renaissance of American Law Enforcement*, 1988; Richard Sylvester, "A History of the Sweat Box," and Richard Sylvester, "Third Degree," in *International Association of Chiefs of Police: Seventeenth Annual Session*, 1910; Charles Phillips and Alan Axelrod, *CCC*, 1996.

T

TAFOLLA, CARLOS. (d. 1901) An original member of the Arizona Rangers,*
Tafolla was killed in the second month of the company's existence and was the
only Arizona Ranger killed in the line of duty. Tafolla had prior experience in
law enforcement when he joined the force in 1901. He was with a posse of
Rangers searching for the Bill Smith gang of horse rustlers when they were
ambushed and Tafolla received two mortal gunshot wounds. He succumbed to
his injuries by midnight.

SOURCE: Bill O'Neal, *The Arizona Rangers*, 1987.

TAMM, QUINN. (1910–1986) Born in Seattle, Washington, and educated at
the University of Virginia, Tamm joined the Federal Bureau of Investigation
(FBI)* in 1934. He parlayed his initial appointment as a messenger into the
position of assistant chief technician of the crime laboratory. In 1938 he was
promoted to chief of the identification division. Over the next two decades
Tamm supervised the identification division and then the training and inspection
division. After resigning from the FBI in 1961, he accepted the directorship of
the International Association of Chiefs of Police (IACP) field service division
the following year. Later that year he became the executive director after his
predecessor stepped down for health reasons. Under Tamm's tenure, the IACP
more than doubled its membership while fending off criticism by civil libertarians who were concerned about relations between the police and an increasingly
heterogeneous American culture. Tamm retired from the IACP in 1975.

SOURCES: Charles Phillips and Alan Axelrod, *CCC*, 1996; Athan G. Theoharis, ed.,
The FBI, 1999.

TAMRUAT. The term *tamruat* ("police") can be found in the court chronicles of sixteenth-century Thailand. The Tamruat Luang, or Royal Police, was apparently a clandestine police force used by ancient monarchs to watch for subversive activity and was responsible for maintaining order in the rural hinterlands. Thailand adopted more modern police methods in 1861.

SOURCE: James Cramer, *The World's Police*, 1964.

TANNER, RICHARD. (c. 1832–1873) Sergeant Richard Tanner was one of the original members of the Detective Branch, having begun his service in Scotland Yard* in the early 1850s. Promoted to inspector in 1864, he was forced to retire five years later because of rheumatism. During his career he was instrumental in solving the James Mullins murder case as well as the first murder committed on the railway. His work on the latter case resulted in the conviction and hanging of Franz Muller after his extradition from America.

SOURCES: Paul Begg and Keith Skinner, *The Scotland Yard Files*, 1992; Joan Lock, *Dreadful Deeds and Awful Murders*, 1990.

TASER. Introduced to law enforcement in 1975, TASER is the acronym for Tom Swift's Electric Rifle. More than one hundred law enforcement agencies use this nonlethal weapon, which shoots small barbed contacts connected to wires at a target in order to shock the assailant into submission. It is not necessary for the dart to penetrate the skin since the electrical charge will reach the body even if only imbedded in the clothing.

SOURCE: George E. Rush, *The Dictionary of Criminal Justice*, 1994.

TEARE, ROBERT DONALD. (1911–1979) Educated at King William's College, Isle of Mann, Teare then studied medicine at Gonvile and Caius College at Cambridge and then London's St. George's Hospital. During his career he became one of England's leading forensic pathologists. His high-profile cases included the Jones and Hulton, Camb, Raven, Timothy Evans, Hume, Straffen, Chesney, and Podola murders. Teare, together with pathologists Sydney Alfred Smith* and Francis Edward camps*, were collectively referred to as the "Three Musketeers." Of the three, Teare was the least publicity conscious, and over time, frequent clashes between Camps and Smith precipitated a break in the once-vaunted clique. Teare taught forensic medicine at St. Bartholomew's Hospital Medical College and then at Charing Cross Hospital Medical School before retiring in 1975.

SOURCE: Richard Whittington-Egan and Molly Whittington-Egan, *The Bedside Book of Murder*, 1988.

TECHNOLOGY AND POLICING. Until the nineteenth century, except for the introduction of firearms (the Colt .45*), police technology had changed but little from its medieval antecedents. One of the first areas to be impacted by the technological advances of the nineteenth century was communications equipment with the introduction of telegraph police callboxes in 1867. This device was improved by the Gamewell Company, which invented the Gamewell Police Signal System,* a callbox with more than a single signal, allowing routine police reporting, emergency assistance calls, and better coordination between headquarters and beat cops.

Two years after the invention of the telephone, Washington, D.C., led the way by installing its first telephone in a police station in 1878. Chicago installed them in boxes on policemen's beats two years later. The Cincinnati, Ohio, police force is credited as the first force to replace the telegraph with the telephone. In the 1920s the teletypewriter became a familiar fixture in police departments, and by the early 1900s police photography* was an accepted investigative tool. Improvements in telephotography led to the capture of a criminal in Pittsburgh in 1911 after his mug shot was transmitted by facsimile from New York City.

Many accepted modes of police technology were first popularized by the Berkeley, California, Police Department,* including the first police owned and operated radio system. Police forces in New York City and Detroit added scorcher squads of bicycle police in the 1890s, and in 1913 the Fitchburg, Massachusetts, police implemented a motorcycle unit. In 1910 Akron, Ohio, was credited with introducing the world's first police car (a Model T Ford), and two years later, the first motorized patrol wagon was cruising the streets of Cincinnati.

Although radio broadcasting of news and entertainment had become common in American homes by the 1920s, the widespread adoption of the technology by police departments was hindered by the reluctance of the Federal Radio Commission to recognize the importance of radios to police work. While August Vollmer* and introduced the first two-way radio police car with the Berkeley Police Department in 1921, and William P. Rutledge implemented it with the Detroit Police Department, the systems did not perform satisfactorily initially, mainly because the police department was not given its own wavelength and broadcasts went out over public airwaves. By the late 1920s radio use increased among police departments, which reported improved response times to crime scenes. Police administrators also realized how much better they could supervise patrol officers.

Beginning in the 1920s, telephone wiretaps were used by police to prosecute gangsters for major Prohibition violations. However, court cases such as *Olmstead v. United States* (1928) soon placed certain limits on this investigative procedure. Electronic surveillance has played an important but controversial role in law enforcement's arsenal of technology in the war against crime.

Technological advances in weaponry are also about to take policing into the twenty-first century. Law enforcement has recently emerged as one of the fastest growing markets for high-tech gadgets, particularly in the realm of less-than-lethal weapons and tools. These weapons include sticky foam, a substance that can be effectively fired at a suspect from thirty feet, quickly immobilizing the fugitive. However, there is some reticence about this product among police officers who are worried that a suspect could suffocate if shot in the face. Other weapons and tools that are either ready or on the drawing board include the snare net, the smart gun, strobe goggles, rear-seat air bags to control arrestees, millimeter wave cameras to detect concealed weapons, and backscatter X-ray scanners for detecting drug shipments.

SOURCES: Robert M. Regoli and John D. Hewitt, *Criminal Justice*, 1996; George W. Bailey, ed., *The Encyclopedia of Police Science*, 1995; Mike Grudowski, "Not-So-Lethal Weapons," *New York Times Magazine*, August 13, 1995.

TENDERLOIN. The use of this term to denote an area of town that offered opportunities for police corruption because of the presence of vice can be reportedly traced back to 1870s New York City Police Department (NYPD)* Captain Alexander S. "Clubber" Williams,* who, when he heard that he was to be assigned to an area of New York heavily concentrated with vice resorts, reportedly exclaimed, "All my life I've never had anything but chuck steak, now I'm going to get me some tenderloin" (Reppetto).

SOURCES: Thomas A. Reppetto, *The Blue Parade*, 1978; H. Paul Jeffers, *Commissioner Roosevelt*, 1994.

TEN MOST WANTED LIST. The Federal Bureau of Investigation (FBI)* introduced the Ten Most Wanted Program on March 14, 1950. The first number one on the list was a convicted train robber and murderer named Thomas J. Holden. John Edgar Hoover* loved publicity, and here he found a perfect tool for trumpeting the FBI's war against the underworld. What is less known was he borrowed the idea from a newspaper reporter who wrote a popular story based on names and descriptions of the ten fugitives the FBI would most like to apprehend. According to the FBI, the list was created to publicize certain fugitives. As testimony to its success rate, more than one-quarter of those captured were located through the assistance of citizens familiar with the well-publicized list.

When suspected serial killer Rafael Resendez-Ramirez was placed on the list in June 1999, he became the 457th person to appear on it. Fugitives are only removed from the list when they are captured, charges are dropped, or when they no longer meet the criteria for "Most Wanted" status. The FBI boasts a 94 percent success rate, having captured 428 fugitives.

The names of fugitives placed on the list are submitted by the fifty-six FBI field offices and then reviewed by the agency's Criminal Investigative Division (CID) and the Office of Public and Congressional Affairs. Criminals who are selected for the list must either have lengthy records or pose a serious threat to the public. If a criminal is already notorious, it is doubtful he or she will make the list. The changing nature of America's crime problem is reflected by each decade's Most Wanted lists. In the 1950s it was dominated by bank robbers, car thieves, and burglars, whereas the 1960s lists contained radicals wanted for the destruction of government property and kidnapping. In subsequent decades terrorists and organized crime figures predominated, as well as serial killers and drug kingpins.

SOURCES: Mark Sabljak and Martin H. Greenberg, *Most Wanted: A History of the FBI's Ten Most Wanted List*, 1990. S. K. Bardwell, "Serial Killing Suspect Joins Most Wanted," *Houston Chronicle*, June 22, 1999.

TERRY V. OHIO. This was a 1968 Supreme Court decision that expanded the right of police officers to search for weapons when interrogating a suspect. In this case, John Terry and another man had been convicted of carrying a concealed weapon. A Cleveland, Ohio, police detective discovered the weapon when he searched them after suspecting them of casing a burglary target. Although no crime had been committed, the men were arrested, charged, and convicted of carrying concealed weapons. Terry appealed the case to the Supreme Court on the grounds that it violated his Fourth Amendment right against unreasonable search and seizure, and therefore the gun should not have been entered as evidence in court. This ruling validated an officer's right to stop, question, and even search a person who acted suspiciously as long as the officer had reasonable grounds for doing so. During a decade that was notable for placing restrictions on police powers, *Terry v. Ohio* clearly augured a new climate that was more favorable for enhancing them.

SOURCE: Kenneth J. Peak, *Policing America*, 1993.

TETON, HOWARD. Teton joined the Federal Bureau of Investigation (FBI)* in 1962, following service in the U.S. Marine Corps; the Orange County, California Sheriff's Department; and the San Leandro, California, Police Department. He is credited, along with Patrick J. Mullaney,* with introducing the FBI to criminal behavior profiling. While teaching criminology at the FBI Academy in 1969, he began consulting Dr. James Arnold Brussel* whose profile of the "mad bomber" in 1957 gave this investigatory tool its first real credibility. Teton stayed with the Behavioral Science Unit in Quantico, Virginia,* until his retirement in 1986.

SOURCE: Athan G. Theoharis, ed., *The FBI*, 1999.

TEXAS DEPARTMENT OF PUBLIC SAFETY. In January 1935, Texas Governor James V. Allred called for the reorganization of the Texas Rangers* and Texas state law enforcement in general. Allred's crusade was in part a response to a rising crime control problem. Under the previous administration of Governor "Ma" Ferguson, the Texas Rangers had deteriorated as a law enforcement organization. After winning the governor's race in 1932, in which the

Rangers supported her opponent, Ferguson discharged the experienced Rangers and began handing out appointments to her supporters. Having cut funding to the once esteemed organization and staffed inexperienced supporters, Texas was ill prepared to handle the rising crime wave of the 1930s.

Ferguson's political appointments became a liability as state committees investigated them for involvement in vice operations, embezzlement, and murder, and in 1934 the governor decided not to seek reelection. Among the most hotly debated issues of the following gubernatorial campaign were stronger law enforcement and the resurrection of the Texas Rangers. Attorney-general and gubernatorial candidate Allred argued most emphatically for the overhauling of the once elite organization. He was in favor of combining the Rangers and the Highway Patrol, as well as creating an identification bureau and a central broadcasting network, and on August 10, 1935, Allred brought the Rangers and the Texas Highway Patrol under one banner. Together with the Headquarters Division, these three divisions formed the nucleus of the department as it exists today. Under the bill creating the Texas Department of Public Safety (DPS), the State Highway Patrol was transferred from the Highway Department to the DPS and redesignated as the Texas Highway Patrol. Similarly, the Rangers were transferred from the Adjutant's General Department to the new department, retaining full police authority in regard to the enforcement of Texas criminal laws.

The main responsibilities of the DPS fell under three categories: general crime suppression and control; motor vehicle transportation management; and disaster and emergency activities. Directors of the DPS from its inception include: Louis G. Phares (September 1, 1935–May 8, 1936); H. H. Carmichael (May 8, 1936–September 24, 1938); Homer Garrison, Jr.* (September 26, 1938–May 7, 1968); Wilson E. Speir (May 7, 1968–December 31, 1979); James B. Adams (January 1, 1980–May 31, 1987); Leo E. Gossett (June 1, 1987–July 31, 1988); Joe Milner (August 1, 1988–August 31, 1991); and James R. Wilson (September 1, 1991–August 30, 1999); Dudley M. Thomas (September 1, 1996–March 30, 2000); Thomas A. Davis (April 1, 2000–present). During the 1990s, the DPS was often at the center of internationally publicized law enforcement crises, which included the 1991 Luby's Cafeteria massacre in Killeen, the 1993 Branch Davidian Siege in Waco, and the Republic of Texas stand-off in West Texas.

SOURCES: Mitchel Roth (historical text by), *Courtesy, Service, and Protection*, 1995; James W. Robinson, *The DPS Story*, 1975.

TEXAS RANGERS. The Texas Rangers were created by Stephen Austin in 1823, although they did not appear in official legislation as the "Texas Rangers" until 1874. Their reputation is such that it is often hard to separate reality from fiction. During the nineteenth century they would have an on-and-off existence. A formally organized force of Texas Rangers did not appear until the outbreak of the Texas Revolution in 1835, when they were formed as an auxiliary military body. Formal historical records of the Rangers prior to 1860 are scarce due to fires that periodically ravaged the records at the state capitol as well as the fact that this force often operated as an irregular militia, loosely organized without a headquarters, written records or reports.

The Rangers originally consisted of ten volunteers whose duties were to "range" over the seemingly endless Texas landscape and reconnoiter the movements of the local Indian groups, most notably the Comanches. It is from this "ranging" activity that the Rangers derived their name. With wages of fifteen dollars a month, payable in land, these men were in a constant state of preparedness. During the fifty years between the creation of Stephen Austin's colony in Texas and the establishment of a permanent force, the functions of the Texas Rangers continued to evolve.

On October 17, 1835, a Corps of Rangers was created by a council of local government representatives. With the main goal of eliminating the Indian threat, Rangers were paid $1.25 a day and were responsible for electing their own officers. Rangers had to furnish their own mounts and equipment. Originally known as superintendents rather than captains, they each commanded twenty-five Rangers. The following month, the provisional government created "a corps of rangers under the command of a major to consist of 150 men" (Webb). Some of the early Ranger legends entered Ranger lore during the 1830s, including John Coffee "Jack" Hays* and Erasmus "Deaf" Smith.

The popular conception of the Texas Rangers began in 1840 when the Texas government decided to form standing companies of Rangers to patrol the frontiers. Emergencies in the early 1840s included raids by Comanches and Cherokees as well as the constant threat of invasion from Mexico. On December 29, 1845, Texas became the twenty-eighth state. Following annexation, federal troops took over border patrols and the Rangers were disbanded. Faced with border raiders and Comanche depredations, it was only a short time before Texas reorganized the force.

In 1850, the Rangers came back into existence for a brief period. While they were often referred to as mounted volunteers, they were essentially following in the ranging tradition of law enforcement, responsible for protecting the wide-ranging Texas frontier from Indian attacks.

Following the Civil War, a separate state police was created to rid Texas of the lawless conditions accompanying Reconstruction. During the 1870s the state police, like the Rangers, remained highly mobile and came into conflict with local law enforcement. In 1874 the Texas Rangers assumed the role relinquished by the state police as the legislature created two forces to enforce the laws of Texas and protect the frontier. This era revealed a new emphasis in law enforcement for the Rangers as their duties shifted from border and Indian fighting to straight police work against the growing outlaw scourge.

The Rangers were once again reorganized in 1900 with the disbanding of the Frontier Battalion. The years between 1910 and 1919 presented many challenges to Rangers assigned to the region of the Rio Grande as they often became embroiled in problems growing out of the Mexican Revolution and World War I. Between 1919 and 1935, the Rangers were faced with new social problems as Texas made the transition from the frontier era, including labor strikes, border raids, Prohibition violations, boomtown violence, and surging Ku Klux Klan activities.

By the 1930s the Texas Ranger tradition was in dire need of updating. Traditionally undermanned, their numbers were cut back and were in danger of obsolescence because of urbanization and modern science. With the introduction of the automobile and the train, the Rangers' days as an effective mounted police force became a nostalgic memory, and in 1935 they were consolidated into the Texas Department of Public Safety.*

SOURCES: Mitchel Roth, "Mounted Police Forces: A Comparative History," *Policing* 21(4) Fall 1998; Mitchel Roth (historical text by), *Courtesy, Service, and Protection*, 1995; Walter P. Webb, *The Texas Rangers*, 1935; John L. Davis, *The Texas Rangers: Their First 150 Years*, 1975.

THACKER, JOHN NELSON. (1837–1913) Born in rural Missouri, Thacker moved west to Nevada sometime in the early 1860s. He entered law enforcement, serving one term as sheriff, of Humboldt County in 1868. Subsequently he served stints as a ranch foreman and as a shotgun messenger for the Wells Fargo Detective Bureau.* He would later return to the stage company and become one of the most prominent Wells Fargo employees during his long career, mostly as lieutenant to the company's chief special officer and detective, the legendary James Bunyan Hume.*

During his tenure with the stage company Thacker helped Hume accumulate their renowned "Robbers Record" report published in 1885. A noted achievement for its time, the record enumerated all Wells Fargo robberies between 1870 and 1884, listing all pertinent information about each incident. Thacker was prominent in the capture of stage robber Charles E. Boles, better known as "Black Bart," and was also credited with planning the strategy that resulted in the capture and wounding of train robbers Evans and Sontag in 1893. With the death of James B. Hume in 1903, Thacker was appointed as his replacement. Thacker, too, was moving into his twilight years; he would join his mentor in death four years later.

SOURCES: William B. Secrest, *Lawmen and Desperadoes*, 1994; Richard Dillon, *Wells Fargo Detective*, 1969.

THAMES RIVER POLICE. Formerly known as the Marine River Establishment and now as the Thames Division, this police unit established in 1798 is generally considered to be the world's first uniformed police force (see POLICE UNIFORMS). For over two centuries this force has guarded the Thames River of London from river pirates, thieves, and corrupt officials. It was at the behest of magistrates and police reformers Patrick Colquhoun* and John Harriott that a strategy for policing the Thames River was formulated. According to Colquhoun's research, in the 1790s there were 37,000 river workers, 11,000 known criminals, and more than 1,000 pirates operating along the river. The entreaties of these reformers, with the assistance of Jeremy Bentham, convinced Parliament to authorize the creation of this force on July 2, 1798.

SOURCE: T. A. Critchley, *A History of Police in England and Wales, 900–1966*, 1967.

THICK (E), WILLIAM. (1845–1930) William Thick was one of the prominent H Division detectives during the London search for Jack the Ripper. He joined the London Metropolitan Police* in 1868, where he won the sobriquet "Johnny Upright," which, according to Walter Dew,* was awarded on the basis of his upright walk and police methods. Writer Jack London, however, demurs, suggesting the moniker was given to him by a convicted criminal. Thick spent almost his entire twenty-five-year career in the same police division and retired in 1893.

SOURCE: Paul Begg, Martin Fido and Keith Skinner, *The Jack the Ripper A to Z*, 1991.

THIEF-TAKER GENERAL. In 1692 the profession of thief-taking was inaugurated by an Act for Encouraging the Apprehending of Highwaymen. Without a public police force and suffering a tremendous outlaw problem, the English government began offering a forty-pound reward for the arrest and successful prosecution of any highwayman. In addition thief-takers were entitled to the highwayman's horse, harness, arms, and goods, unless they proved to be stolen. Initially thief-takers were typically bandits who turned in accomplices for the promised blood money. However, despite the best intentions of the Highwayman Act, highway robbery continued unabated.

   In 1715 underworld boss Jonathan Wild* elevated thief-taking to a science, and over the next ten years he was credited with sending over one hundred criminals to the London gallows. Wild's exploits earned him the title of thief-taker general, even though he followed his colleagues to the gallows himself in 1725. Thief taking was considered a precursor to the 1740s Bow Street Runners* of Sir Henry Fielding.*

SOURCE: Gerald Howson, *Thief-Taker General: The Rise and Fall of Jonathan Wild*, 1970.

THIRD DEGREE, THE. The term *third degree* refers to police sanctioned brutality, which was more prevalent during the pre–*Miranda* rights era. In the 1930s, parlance ranging from "shellacking" and "massaging" to "breaking the news" and "giving him the works" was synonymous with giving a crime suspect the third degree. Many police departments condoned the beating of suspects to extract confessions. Methods of third-degree questioning included the water cure, which involved forcing water down the nostrils of a supine victim, beatings with a rubber hose, and drilling into the nerves of the teeth. The *Eleventh Report of the National Commission on Law and Observance and Enforcement* reported 106 appellate court cases in which the third degree was the basis for reversal of the previous conviction.

Although recent cases suggest that the third degree is still practiced in certain jurisdictions, the 1966 *Miranda* decision is credited with diminishing the amount of brutality complaints stemming from this traditional police tactic.

SOURCES: Ernest Jerome Hopkins, *Our Lawless Police*, 1931; Emanuel H. Lavine, *The Third Degree*, 1930.

THOMAS, HENRY ANDREW "HECK." (1850–1912) Born in Oxford, Georgia, a twelve-year-old Thomas reportedly served under Confederate General Thomas "Stonewall" Jackson during the Civil War. He entered law enforcement in 1868 as a policeman in Atlanta, Georgia, and was wounded there during a race riot. Relocating to Texas, Thomas found employment as an express messenger and then opened his own detective agency in Fort Worth. While in Texas, he was credited with destroying the Lee outlaw gang and saw action against the Sam Bass gang. Thomas reportedly turned down an offer by the governor, following his destruction of the Lees, to join the Texas Rangers* and instead left the state.

In 1886 he was appointed deputy U.S. marshal by Judge Charles Isaac Parker* of Fort Smith, Arkansas, who was responsible for policing the Indian Territory. Over the next six years he was linked with fellow lawmen Chris Madsen* and William Matthew "Bill" Tilghman* as one of the "Three Guardsmen." Thomas was credited with tracking down and killing Bill Doolin. However, recent scholarship suggests this is myth making and that Doolin was probably dead by the time Thomas arrived on the scene. According to another version of the story, Thomas found Doolin dead of tuberculosis, shot the corpse with his shotgun, and brought the body in for the $5,000 reward, which he then gave to the victim's impoverished widow. From 1893 to 1900, Thomas served as a deputy marshal in the Indian Territory and then as chief of police for Lawton, Oklahoma. He retired in 1909 and died from Bright's disease three years later.

SOURCES: Glenn Shirley, *Heck Thomas: Frontier Marshal*, 1962; Bill O'Neal, *Encyclopedia of Western Gunfighters*, 1979.

THOMPSON, BEN. (1842–1884) Born in Knottingly, England, Ben immigrated with his family to Austin, Texas, while still a young boy. He fought for the Confederacy during the Civil War and, like many veterans, had a hard time adjusting to civilian life in the defeated South. Arrested for murder in Austin, Texas, Thompson escaped to Mexico, joining Emperor Maximilian's forces in their ill-fated imperialist venture south of the border. Returning to the United

States in 1867, Thompson opened up a gambling hall in Austin, but after another brush with the law, he was sentenced to two years in the Huntsville Penitentiary.

Following his release from prison Thompson ran for Austin city marshal, winning in his second attempt. His tenure as a peace officer was relatively effective. However, Thompson would prove his own worst enemy. After a night of gambling, drinking and womanizing in San Antonio's Vaudeville Variety Theater, he shot the owner, Jack Harris, to death after a dispute over a gambling debt. After resigning as city marshal, Thompson was tried and acquitted of the murder. Returning to the gambling den with friend and noted gunman John King Fisher,* the two were confronted by friends of Harris who unleashed a withering fusillade on the two visitors, killing them both instantly.

SOURCES: Floyd B. Streeter, *Ben Thompson: Man With a Gun*, 1957; W. M. Walton, *Life and Adventures of Ben Thompson, the Famous Texan*, 1884.

THOMPSON, JOHN HENRY. (1861–1934) Born in Bell County, Texas, Thompson moved to the Arizona Territory in 1880. Ten years later he was appointed sheriff* of Gila County. He was initially ordered by the board of supervisors to confiscate guns and pistols, and after furnishing the courthouse with one for each office, he was to sell the rest at auction. That same year Thompson apprehended members of the notorious Apache Kid gang. He was reelected sheriff in 1893 and continued his responsibilities for a five-thousand-square-mile territory, which included several Apache reservations, mining camps, and cattle ranches.

In 1894 Thompson distinguished himself while fighting a fire that destroyed a large section of Globe, Arizona. In the late 1890s he sought his fortune in the Yukon wilderness during the gold rush. He then returned to Globe in 1900 and again won election as sheriff; in 1908 he was elected to his sixth term in office. In 1910 he investigated the death of the Apache leader Captain Jack on the San Carlos reservation. He was elected to a seventh stint as sheriff in 1910. After retiring from law enforcement, Thompson worked for the Arizona State Highway Department and pursued mining and ranching businesses, with moderate success.

SOURCE: Jess G. Hayes, *Sheriff Thompson's Day*, 1968.

THOMSON, BASIL HOME. (1861–1939) Born in York, England, and educated at Eton and Oxford, Thomson served with the Colonial Office. He was also prime minister of Tonga; governor of Dartmoor, Cardiff, and Wormwood Scrubs Prisons; inspector of prisons; and secretary to the prison commissioners. In 1896 he was called to the bar.

Thomson won the favor of Winston Churchill in 1909 following his assistance in organizing the Central Association for the Aid of Discharged Convicts, a project initiated by Churchill. In 1913 Thomson succeeded Sir Melville Macnaghten as Head of the Criminal Investigation Department (CID)* of Scotland

Yard.* Six years later he conferred on himself the title of director of intelligence as he led the battle against the incipient communist threat. He retired in 1921 and established a career as a writer of books and plays. His books included *Queer People* (1922), *The Criminal* (1925), *The Story of Scotland Yard* (1935), and *The Scene Changes* (1939).

SOURCES: Paul Begg, Martin Fido, and Keith Skinner, *The Jack the Ripper A to Z*, 1991; Rupert Allason, *The Branch*, 1983.

THOMSON, JAMES JACOB. (prominent 1860s) The son of a merchant, Thomson was born in the Middle East and moved with his family to London in 1844. Fluent in several languages, Thomson joined the Detective Branch of Scotland Yard* in 1866. That same year his investigation into the "Great Stamp Office Robbery" in Manchester led to the arrest of the perpetrators the following year. He was eventually promoted to divisional superintendent.

SOURCE: Joan Lock, *Dreadful Deeds and Awful Murders*, 1990.

THORN, BENJAMIN KENT. (1829–1905) Born in Plattsburg, New York, Thorn and his family moved to Chicago when he was a child. After stints as a farm worker, clerk, and teacher, he sought his fortunes in California following the discovery of gold in 1849. In 1855 he was appointed deputy sheriff and then was elected constable (see CONSTABLES), beginning a long, distinguished career as a Calaveras County peace officer. Thorn earned respect rather early in his career by capturing the killer Sam Brown in his first year as a lawman.

Over the next forty years, Thorn brought numerous desperadoes to justice, including, in 1859, multiple murderer Santiago Molino, who was killed during a gunfight with Thorn and a deputy. That same year he was appointed under-sheriff by Robert Havlin "Bob" Paul.* After serving in different capacities as a peace officer, in 1867 Thorn himself became sheriff,* a position he would hold for the next three decades. One of his greatest pieces of detective work resulted in the capture of stagecoach robber "Black Bart." In 1883 Thorn uncovered several of Bart's possessions, including a handkerchief with a mark from a particular San Francisco laundry, which ultimately led lawmen to their quarry. Thorn won his last election in 1898 and died six years later.

SOURCES: William B. Secrest, *Lawmen and Desperadoes*, 1994; Richard Dillon, *Wells Fargo Detective*, 1969.

THORNTON, STEPHEN. (1803–1861) Born in Epsom, England, Thornton joined the London Metropolitan Police* in 1832. In 1839 he investigated Chartists in northern England, and in 1842 he was selected as one of the original members of the Detective Branch. Thornton rose to prominence in connection with the search for the Manning brothers following their 1845 murder of Patrick O'Connor. In 1849, the Mannings were hanged together. This execution was witnessed by Charles Dickens,* who wrote an anti–capital punishment piece on the event for the *Times*. Dickens described Thornton as "middle aged and ruddy-faced" (Lock) when he met him in the 1840s.

SOURCES: Joan Lock, *Dreadful Deeds and Awful Murders*, 1992; Paul Begg and Keith Skinner, *The Scotland Yard Files*, 1992.

THREE GUARDSMEN. Deputy marshals Henry Andrew "Heck" Thomas,* Chris Madsen,* and William Matthew "Bill" Tilghman,* were often referred to collectively as Oklahoma's "Three Guardsmen." Working the Indian Territory for Fort Smith's Judge Isaac Charles Parker,* they were credited with tracking down criminal luminaries such as the Doolins and Daltons and many others. Their accomplishments and parallels to Dumas's Three Musketeers served as inspiration for many Hollywood westerns in the 1930s and 1940s.

SOURCE: Glenn Shirley, *West of Hell's Fringe*, 1978.

TILGHMAN, WILLIAM MATTHEW "BILL," JR. (1854–1924) Born in Fort Dodge, Iowa, and raised in Atchison, Kansas, Tilghman first entered law enforcement in 1877 as a deputy sheriff under Charles E. Bassett* in Dodge City, Kansas. Seven years later Tilghman became the marshal of Dodge City, where he introduced the no-guns policy, which has often been credited to Wyatt Berry Stapp Earp.*

Tilghman moved to the Oklahoma Territory shortly after the "Land Rush," and by 1892 had been appointed deputy U.S. Marshal by Marshal Evett Dumas Nix.* Along with fellow Oklahoma lawmen Chris Madsen* and Henry Andrew "Heck" Thomas,* Tilghman earned his place in Western history as one of the Three Guardsmen.* Over the next decade Tilghman carved out a reputation as one of the toughest manhunters in the territory, tracking down numerous outlaws, including "Arkansas Tom" Jones, "Bitter Creek" Newcomb, as well as the notorious Bill Doolin gang. Tilghman was appointed sheriff* of Lincoln County, Oklahoma, in 1900 and in 1911 became police chief of Oklahoma City.

In his last year Tilghman became infatuated with the fledgling motion picture industry and was featured in several silent pictures. He formed the Eagle Film Company, with E. D. Nix and Chris Madsen, to make a realistic Western film, *The Passing of the Oklahoma Outlaws*, in response to the fictionalized films of the day that romanticized desperadoes. A peace officer to the end, in 1924 Tilghman was lured out of retirement to bring order to the Oklahoma boom town of Cromwell. It was a fatal decision, for later that year he was killed while trying to arrest an inebriated law breaker. The twice-married lawman had sired seven children, but ironically, three of his sons would serve time behind bars, including one convicted for manslaughter.

SOURCES: Glenn Shirley, *West of Hell's Fringe: Crime, Criminals, and the Federal Peace Officer in Oklahoma Territory, 1889–1907*, 1978; Glenn Shirley, *Guardian of the Law: The Life and Times of William Matthew Tilghman*, 1988.

TIPPIT, J. D. (1924–1963) Often forgotten in the rush to judgment following the assassination of John F. Kennedy was assassin Lee Harvey Oswald's killing of Dallas Police officer J. D. Tippit as he attempted to make his escape. Tippit was eating lunch when he received a radio call that Kennedy had been shot. At about 1:00 P.M., Tippit spotted a suspect who matched the description of the assassin. As he left his squad car to question Oswald, he was shot four times with a .38 caliber revolver and expired on the way to the hospital. Oswald was subsequently arrested while watching the movie *War Is Hell* and booked for the murder of Tippit. Initially police were not aware of any links between Oswald and the killing of the president. Tippit had joined the Dallas force in 1952 and three years later had been awarded a citation for bravery. He left a wife and three children.

SOURCE: Craig W. Floyd and Kelley Lang Helms, eds. *To Serve and Protect*, 1995.

TITHING SYSTEM. The tithing (tything) system was an early example of community law enforcement in Anglo-Saxon England. From the era of King Alfred, the main responsibility for keeping the peace fell upon each community through a well-understood principle of social obligation. Every freeman was to belong to a group called a tithing, organized for police purposes. Each tithing was a collection of ten families. Each member of the group was bound by a pledge to be answerable to the lawful behavior of the other members of the group. The leader of each group was called the tithingman. If any member of the group committed a crime, the others had to bring him or her to trial. If they failed, they had to pay compensation to the victim's family. Tithings were organized into unions of ten comprising approximately one hundred families, hence the designation hundred; these were each headed by a hundredman. Following the Norman conquest in 1066, these simple arrangements were adopted and modified.

SOURCES: T. A. Critchley, *A History of Police in England and Wales: 900–1966*, 1967; Charles Reith, *The Blind Eye of History*, 1952.

TOLSON, CLYDE ANDERSON. (1900–1975) Born near Laredo, Missouri, Tolson was raised and educated in Cedar Rapids, Iowa, before relocating to Washington, D.C. After a meteoric rise through various positions in the War Department during World War I, he was appointed confidential secretary to the secretary of war. After receiving his law degree from George Washington University, he left the War Department to join the Bureau of Investigation as an agent. After four months in the Boston office, John Edgar Hoover* had him return to Washington, D.C., where he placed him in charge of the clerical staff and gave him the title of chief clerk.

Tolson soon became the protégé and lifelong friend of director J. Edgar Hoover. Following Tolson's two short stints in the field, Hoover promoted him several times; to assistant director in 1930; assistant to the director (1938); and associate director (1947), a rank he held until he retired in 1972. Possessing a near-photographic memory, Tolson proved invaluable to the FBI's labyrinthine bureaucracy. He served as Hoover's chief of staff, and in the 1960s, after his thirty-seventh year with the bureau, he was awarded the President's Distinguished Federal Civilian Service Medal.

An unremarkable agent, Tolson shunned publicity, but his relationship with fellow lifelong-bachelor Hoover seemed unwholesome to many. Their association came under scrutiny since they went to work, ate lunch, and took vacations together, but suggestions that they had a homosexual relationship have never been substantiated. Poor health forced Tolson to resign from the FBI in 1972, shortly after the death of Hoover. Tolson inherited most of his colleague's estate, including Hoover's home.

SOURCES: *New York Times*, obituary page, April 15, 1975; Kenneth O'Reilly, "Clyde Anderson Tolson," *ANB*, Vol. 21, 1999.

TOMA, DAVID. (b. 1933) Born in Newark, New Jersey, Toma gave up college for minor league baseball before serving a stint in the Marine Corps. He joined the Newark Police Department after his honorable discharge and was promoted to detective after three years. A master undercover cop, Toma used deep cover tactics to infiltrate narcotics, gambling, and prostitution rackets. He also possessed a benevolent streak that allowed him to try to help rehabilitate some of his collars.

Toma rose to prominence and became a media sensation with the help of television and his amazing arrest record, which included ten thousand over a seventeen-year career. Eschewing gun and badge while on assignment, his undercover work resulted in a 98 percent conviction rate. The 1973 television show *Toma*, starring Tony Musante, was based on the real-life detective, as was the popular Robert Blake vehicle, *Baretta*. Toma emphasized the nondramatic aspects of policing in several books, including *Toma, the Compassionate Cop* (1974), *Toma Tells It Straight—With Love* (1981), and *Turning Your Life Around: David Toma's Guide for Teenagers* (1992). Following retirement he worked as a radio talk show host and toured the lecture circuit.

SOURCES: David Toma and Michael Brett, *Toma, the Compassionate Cop*, 1974; Charles Phillips and Alan Axelrod, *CCC*, 1996.

TONTON MACOUTES. This Haitian secret police organization evolved from an unofficial gang of thugs in the 1950s known as *cagoulards** into a force of five thousand uniformed armed state security enforcers. In order to decentralize the force, "Papa Doc" Duvalier forbid Macoute chiefs to communicate with each other and were expected to take their cues directly from the dictator. Under this system each region of Haiti had a Tonton Macoute commander; next in charge was a joint commander and then a first sergeant. At the bottom of this chain of command were the Macoutes themselves.

They were initially given cachet for their activities by "Papa Doc" Duvalier, who called them the Service Detectives (SD). Best known by their nickname "Tonton Macoutes" or "Bogeymen," the Tonton Macoutes earned an enduring reputation for brutality during the dictatorship of the Duvaliers beginning in the late 1950s. Although they were still referred to as the Macoutes, in an attempt to change the regime's image, in 1971 the government officially changed the name of its chief security force to Volunteers for National Security. That same year Jean Claude Duvalier took over control of Haiti following the death of his father. "Baby Doc" moved the Macoutes out of the urban areas and into the rural countryside and transferred most of their authority to his secret force known as the Leopards. With democratization in the 1980s and the exile of "Baby Doc," the Macoutes were targeted for revenge by many of their former victims.

SOURCES: Thomas Plate and Andrea Darvi, *Secret Police: The Inside Story of a Network of Terror*, 1981; James Cramer, *The World's Police*, 1964.

TOWN MARSHAL. The main law enforcement officer west of the Mississippi River, the town marshal functioned the same as a chief of police, even if he was a one-man force. Most nineteenth-century Western towns did not appoint a local marshal until the population was pushing a thousand. As territories made the transition to statehood federal marshals were replaced by local peace officers. Unlike the peace officer of popular culture, town marshals were more often involved in maintaining town jails, collecting taxes, serving civil papers, protecting property, and arresting the drunk and disorderly rather than pursuing wily desperadoes. Over time towns created police departments to handle local law enforcement, although the Western town marshal persists into the twenty-first century.

SOURCE: Frank Richard Prassel, *The Western Peace Officer*, 1972.

TOWNSEND, JOHN. (c. 1759–1832) Townsend was one of the most famous Bow Street Runners.* He was one of two assigned to protect the Royal Court following an attack on King George III by a crazed assailant. Originally a costermonger (produce seller), he attended Old Bailey trials, cavorted and mixed with notorious denizens of the London underworld, and was revered for his encyclopedic knowledge of crime and criminals. Townsend found his profession a lucrative one and went on to live a comfortable retirement.

SOURCES: George Howard, *Guardians of the Queen's Peace*, 1953; J. J. Tobias, *Nineteenth-Century Crime in England: Prevention and Punishment*, 1972; Anthony Babington, *A House in Bow Street*, 1969.

TRACY, DICK. The fictional creation of Chester Gould (b. 1900), Tracy is generally considered the first comic strip detective. Introduced as Plainclothes Tracy in 1931 as a civilian detective in Prohibition-era Chicago, he later appeared as an official detective. Next to Sherlock Holmes,* Tracy is probably the best recognized fictional sleuth in the world. In the 1930s Tracy was portrayed as an Federal Bureau of Investigation (FBI)* agent in four motion picture serials. These were followed in the 1940s with four feature films that follow the original source material more closely.

SOURCE: Chris Steinbrunner and Otto Penzler, *EMD*, 1976.

TRAFFIC POLICING. On June 27, 1652, New Amsterdam, the future New York City, passed the first traffic law in the New World. Designed to prevent accidents, all drivers and conductors were ordered to walk with wagons, carts, and sleighs within the city limits, under threat of fines and damages.

After the Dutch colony passed to the English, one of the earliest traffic regulations was implemented in 1791, requesting "Ladies and Gentlemen" to order their coachmen to conduct their carriages in the direction of the East River following a performance at the John Street Theater. By 1860 the New York City Police Department had inaugurated its first unit specifically designed to enforce traffic regulations.

Although it is generally accepted that traffic signals came into use following the introduction of the automobile in the twentieth century, mechanical devices were used to control traffic outside the British Parliament as early as 1868. The signal used two semaphore arms similar to those at today's railroad crossings in order to prevent the movement of oncoming traffic. Although Salt Lake City, Utah, and St. Paul, Minnesota, claim to have introduced the first automobile traffic control signal, Cleveland, Ohio, has been credited with introducing the now familiar green-red signal in 1914.

SOURCES: George E. Rush, *The Dictionary of Criminal Justice*, 1994; James F. Richardson, *Urban Police in the United States*, 1974.

TREASURY DEPARTMENT. *See* U.S. TREASURY DEPARTMENT.

TRENCHARD, VISCOUNT HUGH MONTAGUE. (1873–1956) Best known as the father of the Royal Air Force (RAF), Trenchard could trace his ancestry in England back to the Norman conquest. He served in the British armed forces in India and then in the South African Boer War, where he barely survived a chest wound. After a near miraculous recovery Trenchard joined the recently established Royal Flying Corps in 1912, and during World War I was instrumental in the development of strategic-bombing theory.

Following the war Trenchard was selected by the prime minister to reform the London Metropolitan Police.* Although his charges were initially reluctant, over the next decade he attempted to implement military-style regimentation. In the end his reform agenda was left unfulfilled, but he did eliminate much of the corruption that plagued the force. His most controversial proposal was to eliminate reporting unwitnessed robberies as crimes. By making this change, the crime rate seemed to be lower than it actually was. When he was forced to revert back to the old policy, crime rates, naturally, increased, and he took the brunt of criticism. He resigned in 1935 and focused his attention on the development of the modern RAF.

SOURCES: Andrew Boyle, *Trenchard*, 1962; H. R. Allen, *The Legacy of Lord Trenchard*, 1972.

TREVI. The terrorist campaigns in Europe during the 1970s led the police forces of the nine European Economic Community countries to form the anti-terrorist network known as TREVI, for Terrorism, Radicalism, and International Violence, in 1977.

SOURCE: Thomas Plate and Andrea Darvi, *Secret Police*, 1981.

TROJANOWICZ, ROBERT CHESTER. (1941–1994) The son of a police officer, Trojanowicz was born in Bay City, Michigan, and educated at Michigan State University. During his academic career at Michigan State University he championed the cause of community policing. In 1975 he coauthored *Community Based Crime Prevention* and followed it up seven years later with *An Evaluation of the Neighborhood Foot Patrol in Flint, Michigan*. He was a strident advocate of taking police out of their cars and placing them on community streets, where they could be instrumental in crime prevention. In 1983 he founded and was selected to head up the National Center for Community Policing. Until his death from a heart attack, he continued to publish research on police training and juvenile delinquency issues.

SOURCE: Charles Phillips and Alan Axelrod, *CCC*, 1996.

TRUNCHEON. A precursor to the modern police baton, early London constables* were armed with fifteen-inch-long wooden truncheons made of cocus wood and attached to a leather strap. Wooden truncheons or staffs were traditional weapons of the English country constables prior to the creation of the force of Sir Robert Peel.* While policemen were encouraged to exercise discipline when using these batons, by the late nineteenth century, American police officers such as Alexander S. "Clubber" Williams* were wielding these brutal instruments with remarkable dexterity.

SOURCE: J. F. Moylan, *Scotland Yard and the Metropolitan Police*, 1929.

TUKEY, MARSHAL FRANCIS. (b. 1814) Tukey moved to Boston from Maine to work as a mechanic, but he ended up answering another calling when he completed law school in two years. He accepted the position of marshal in

1846 and over the next six years led the Boston day and night watch.* With his appointment in 1846 the Boston watch was increased from twelve to thirty men. Other detectives and night officers were shortly added to the force.

A dynamic man with a flair for the dramatic, Tukey was fond of the limelight and delighted in staging secret raids and making sensational discoveries. An 1848 excavation on Boston Commons attracted an appreciative crowd which was delighted when a stash of stolen money was discovered. Tukey would probably have been more comfortable in the media driven world of today than staid Boston of the nineteenth century. Although he styled himself as Boston's own Eugene François Vidocq,* in reality his detectives were usually incompetent, particularly in the famous 1849 Parkman-Webster murder case.

In 1851 Tukey directed a series of raids against vice establishments, which culminated in the "Celebrated Ann Street" raid targeting gamblers and prostitutes, and resulted in 150 arrests. That same year he inaugurated a local spectacle, when he forced local representatives from the underworld to parade in front of the public and police so that they would be familiar faces in the event they were suspects in a criminal case.

Without any powerful political patrons to bolster his hold on the office, Tukey was vulnerable to negative public opinion. He incurred the opprobrium of the public on more than one occasion when he used the technique of mass arrests against the public for neglecting icy sidewalks or for dog law violations. Other complaints focused on Tukey's unenlightened attitudes toward juvenile delinquency. With a growing number of neglected children wandering Boston streets, Tukey felt compelled, if given the opportunity, to bound out such children as apprentices or domestics until they reached adulthood, rather than concede their predicament to other social factors. He was forced to resign in 1852 and later relocated to California.

SOURCE: Roger Lane, *Policing the City: Boston 1822–1885*, 1967.

TURROU, LEON G. (prominent 1930s) Turrou rose to prominence in several high-profile Federal Bureau of Investigation (FBI)* cases during the 1930s. During the investigation of the Lindbergh kidnapping he interrogated suspect Bruno Hauptmann and obtained handwriting samples that led to his conviction after they matched up with the original ransom notes. In the late 1930s Turrou worked undercover while investigating the pro-Nazi German-American Bund. His exploits in this case inspired the Edward G. Robinson film vehicle *Confessions of a Nazi Spy.*

Turrou resigned from the FBI in 1938 and attempted to cash in on his FBI exploits. He sold his account of his undercover activities to the press before the case went to trial and would write some of the first exposes of the FBI. He penned his own account of his anti-Nazi investigation, *The Nazi Spy in America*, and during World War II he worked for the Office of Strategic Services (OSS), the precursor to the Central Intelligence Agency (CIA). Although Turrou resigned on his own accord, John Edgar Hoover* attempted to change his file to suggest he was fired. Turrou later wrote a scathing critique of the FBI investigation of the Lindbergh case in *Where My Shadow Falls: Two Decades of Crime Detection.*

SOURCES: Athan G. Theoharis, ed., *The FBI*, 1999; Curt Gentry, *J. Edgar Hoover: The Man and His Secrets*, 1991.

TWEED, WILLIAM MARCY "BOSS." (1823–1878) This New York political boss became synonymous with the rampant corruption of nineteenth-century urban America. In 1870 New York City officials began examining the corrupt influence of Boss Tweed on the New York City Police Department (NYPD),* when it became public knowledge that this notorious dispenser of political patronage had a substantial number of police officers and their supervisors on his payroll, while others in the criminal justice system were reluctant to prosecute the powerful "Boss" of Tammany Hall. Subsequently, Republican and Democratic representatives attempted a variety of strategies to eliminate politics and corruption from police management.

SOURCES: James F. Richardson, *The New York Police*, 1970; George W. Walling, *Recollections of a New York Chief of Police*, 1887; reprint, 1972.

TYRELL, SIR JOHN. (d. 1437) Tyrell served as Sheriff* of Essex and of Hertfordshire in 1414 and 1423, respectively, and in 1428 he retained the same position in Suffolk. Tyrell fought in the battle of Agincourt and then was employed by the Duke of Gloucester as steward and chief financial agent until his death. Tyrell only spent three years as sheriff while retaining his affiliation to a great lord, a common arrangement in medieval times.

SOURCE: Irene Gladwin, *The Sheriff*, 1984.

U

UHNAK, DOROTHY. (b. 1933) Born in the Bronx, she attended the College of the City of New York before joining the New York City Transit Police Department. During her fourteen years on the force Uhnak rose to detective second grade and received an award for heroism. She left the force to write full time and earn a degree at the John Jay College of Criminal Justice. Her first book was the autobiographical *Policewoman* (1964), followed by several novels featuring a policewoman assigned to the Manhattan district attorney's staff. The first in the series, *The Bait* (1968), was the cowinner of the Mystery Writers of America Edgar award for best first novel for 1968.

SOURCE: Chris Steinbrunner and Otto Penzler, *EMD*, 1976.

UNIFORM CRIME REPORTS (UCR). The annual meetings of the International Chiefs of Police (IACP)* were credited with providing the impetus for the creation of a national system for the collection of uniform crime data. Implementation of the *UCR* began in 1930 when Congress passed legislation that directed the Justice Department to assume responsibility for collecting *UCR* data. In September of that year the Federal Bureau of Investigation (FBI)* was directed to serve as the clearinghouse for the information. Annual *Uniform Crime Reports* categorize "crimes known to the police" and arrest statistics. The reports gauge American crime trends using seven felonies as indicators: murder, forcible rape, robbery, burglary, larceny, aggravated assault, and auto theft. Incidentally, these are supposedly crimes most likely to be reported to the police.

Since the data is based on only reported crimes from American police departments the *UCR* has been criticized for delivering underreported crime statistics to the public. Among the most potent criticisms of the reports is the fact that if an individual is arrested for multiple offenses, only the highest order of offense is counted. Therefore, many cases of physical violence and property damage go unreported. However, it is generally acknowledged that the *UCR* has led to improved law enforcement and that the crime reporting has improved. The *UCR* was the most authoritative source for crime statistics until the introduction of the National Crime Victimization Survey (NCVS) in the 1970s.

SOURCES: Marvin E. Wolfgang, "Uniform Crime Reporting: A Critical Appraisal," *University of Pennsylvania Law Review*, no. 3 (1963); Samuel Walker, *Popular Justice*, 1998.

UNIFORMED POLICE. Uniformed police forces were introduced to the streets of Paris by Prefect of Police Louis-Marie Debelleyme* in 1829, several months before the London Metropolitan Police* of Sir Robert Peel* appeared in the streets of London and sixteen years before the New York City police followed suit. Debelleyme's contingent of one hundred policemen was dressed in blue uniforms with cocked hats.

SOURCES: Philip John Stead, *The Police of Paris*, 1957; Wilbur R. Miller, *Cops and Bobbies*, 1973.

UNION STATION MASSACRE. *See* KANSAS CITY MASSACRE.

UNTOUCHABLES, THE. On September 28, 1929, Chicago Prohibition agent Elliot Ness* was ordered by District Attorney George Q. Johnson to establish a special squad to eradicate gangster Al Capone's criminal empire. Ness picked nine men, almost half of whom came from outside the city to guarantee a modicum of integrity. Although they busted almost twenty distilleries and six breweries worth close to a million dollars during their first year in operation, the Untouchables had only a limited impact on the Capone empire.

The Untouchables received their moniker in 1930 following an incident when mobsters tossed a bomb into a vehicle bearing two members of the Ness team. Tossing the bundle back into the gangster's car, the Prohibition agents rushed back to Ness and reported the incident. Ness wasted no time in beating a path to local newspapers, who tabbed the crime-fighting unit with its famous nickname. Ness and his Untouchables were rarely off the front pages during the waning days of Prohibition as reporters often cadged rides with the squad as they went out after bootleggers.

SOURCES: Thomas A. Reppetto, *The Blue Parade*, 1978; Oliver Cyriax, *Crime: An Encyclopedia*, 1993.

U.S. BORDER PATROL. An agency within the Immigration and Naturalization Service (INS), the Border Patrol was established in 1924 with a contingent of 450 officers. It was initially organized to police American borders with Canada and Mexico. Probably the best-known agency of the INS, today it is most prominent in its nightly attempts to stop the flow of illegal immigrants across the borders of California, Texas, and Florida. Charged with policing eight thousand miles of border, agents are equipped, not only with weapons, but with full powers of arrest and of search and seizure.

SOURCE: Kenneth J. Peak, *Policing America*, 1993.

U.S. CAPITOL POLICE. Founded in 1801, the Capitol Police provide police and investigative service on the Capitol grounds, in annex buildings, and the Capitol Power Plant. With close to 1,250 uniformed officers, they are also charged with protecting members of Congress anywhere in the United States.

SOURCES: Donald A. Torres, *Handbook of Federal Police and Investigative Agencies*, 1985; Donald A. Torres, "Federal Police and Investigative Agencies," in *The Encyclopedia of Police Science*, ed. William G. Bailey, 1995.

U.S. CUSTOMS SERVICE. Concerned with a multimillion-dollar national debt following the American Revolution, Congress passed the Tariff Act of July 4, 1789, which established a tariff and a system for collecting duties. At the end of July, President George Washington nominated the first fifty-nine collectors of customs and other personnel, effectively founding the United States Customs Service. Initially charged with collecting tariffs and duties, the Customs Service grew into the federal government's largest agency by the 1790s with over 500 employees. Its role as a law enforcement agency did not begin until the early 1800s, when it became involved with patrolling the eastern seaboard.

SOURCE: Kenneth J. Peak, *Policing America*, 1993.

U.S. DEPARTMENT OF JUSTICE. Federal law enforcement in the United States remains the principal domain of the U.S. Treasury Department* and the U.S. Department of Justice.* The Department of Justice contains the oldest federal law enforcement, the U.S. Marshals Service* (1789), as well as the Federal Bureau of Investigation (FBI)* (1908), the best-known law enforcement agency in America if not the world. Also in this department are the Drug Enforcement Administration (DEA) and the Immigration and Naturalization Service (INS), which contains the U.S. Border Patrol.*

SOURCE: David R. Johnson, *American Law Enforcement: A History*, 1981.

U.S. MARSHALS SERVICE. The word *marshal* is a derivation of the Old High German words *marah*, for horse, and *calc*, which means servant. These words combine to mean *horsekeeper*. Formerly servants, marshals rose to the rank of knight and commanded cavalry units under the Frankish kings. Over many generations the marshals were given more duties, including the maintenance of law and order, and were permitted to hire deputies. This important law enforcement position survived in the British military tradition as provost marshal* and field marshal.

The marshal was transplanted to the English colonies in the sixteenth century, and was readily identifiable in most colonies. Occasionally the sheriff's office replaced the marshalcy. The Judiciary Act of September 24, 1789, established the federal judiciary and the United States marshal, America's first federal law enforcement officer. Since the American Revolution, U.S. marshals have played instrumental roles in the 1794 Whiskey Rebellion, enforcing Western law and order, Prohibition, and desegregation in the 1960s.

Initially, marshals were appointed by the president, with the consent of the Senate. The marshals, along with their subordinate deputies, were authorized to assist federal courts, hold federal prisoners, serve subpoenas, summonses, warrants, and court orders on behalf of the federal courts. Initially, marshals were not paid salaries but were paid fees for certain tasks.

The Judiciary Act empowered the marshals to employ deputy marshals to summon *posse comitatus*,* serve process papers, and to deputize temporary deputies. The sheriffs eventually found themselves under the control of judges and U.S. district attorneys. According to most reports, U.S. marshal Robert Forsyth was the first law enforcement officer killed in the line of duty following the American Revolution.

During the westward expansion of the nineteenth century, U.S. marshals played an important role in Western law enforcement as settlers moved onto federally controlled lands. Marshals and their deputies were initially concerned with only federal crimes, which included mail and train robbery. With much of the West part of the public domain, marshals were soon called on to solve murders committed on Western lands. As western territories made the transition to statehood, local peace officers such as town marshals and sheriffs took over most policing duties.

Today, U.S. Marshals continue to enforce federal criminal laws, transport federal prisoners, carry out federal court orders, handle the Witness Protection Program, and maintain order in the federal courts. Many of their duties correspond to those of the sheriff.* In 1988 Congress passed the U.S. Marshals Service Act, and the following year saw the two hundredth anniversary of the U.S. Marshals service.

SOURCES: Larry D. Ball, *The United States Marshals of New Mexico and Arizona Territories, 1846–1912*, 1978; Frank Richard Prassel, *The Western Peace Officer: A Legacy of Law and Order*, 1981; Frederick S. Calhoun, *The Lawmen*, 1991.

U.S. PARK POLICE. Founded in 1919, the six hundred members of the U.S. Park Police are controlled by the National Park Service. They are both a uniformed and an investigative force.

SOURCES: Donald A. Torres, *Handbook of Federal Police and Investigative Agencies*, 1985; Donald A. Torres, "Federal Police and Investigative Agencies," in *The Encyclopedia of Police Science*, ed. William G. Bailey, 1995.

U.S. SECRET SERVICE. The first general law enforcement agency of the federal government, the U.S. Secret Service was created in 1865 under the U.S. Treasury Department* for the purpose of combating counterfeiting. At that time it was estimated that one-third of all American paper currency in circulation was counterfeit. The agency was credited with suppressing the problem within the next decade.

Today the Secret Service is composed of two uniformed forces, the U.S. Secret Service Uniformed Division and the Treasury Police Force. The Treasury Police Force was established in 1789 and became part of the Secret Service in 1937. Initially, officers were expected to protect money shipments from the Bureau of Engraving and Printing, guard currency in the treasury vault, and ensure the security of the Treasury Building's cash room.

Over time the Secret Service has seen its charge expanded to include cases as diverse as the Teapot Oil Scandal, the Ku Klux Klan activities, wartime counterespionage, and Western land fraud cases. Although the Secret Service is usually associated with presidential protection, this mission came late to the service. Following the assassination of President William McKinley in 1901, Congress and public opinion demanded better protection for the chief executive, since this was the third presidential assassination in thirty-six years. While Congress authorized the Secret Service to protect the president, the legislation did not go into effect until 1906.

Secret Service protection has been expanded to include the president and vice president and their families, as well former presidents and families, major candidates for president and vice president, visiting foreign dignitaries, and other individuals selected by the chief executive. Agents are typically plainclothes officers* and carry a five-pointed silver star bearing the words "U.S. Secret Service." With more than 1,900 special agents as of 1995, the Secret Service currently has offices throughout the United States, Puerto Rico, and in Paris, France.

SOURCES: Walter S. Bowen and Harry E. Neal, *The United States Secret Service*, 1960; Dennis V. McCarthy and Philip W. Smith, *Presenting the President: The Inside Story of a Secret Service Agent*, 1985.

U.S. SUPREME COURT POLICE. Founded in 1939, the U.S. Supreme Court Police are responsible for the Supreme Court building and its contiguous grounds.

SOURCE: Donald A. Torres, *A Handbook of Federal Police and Investigative Agencies*, 1985.

U.S. TREASURY DEPARTMENT. Created in 1789, the Treasury Department of the United States Government today controls the Alcohol, Tobacco, and Firearms* Bureau, the U.S. Customs Service,* the Internal Revenue Service, and the U.S. Secret Service.* With a widespread mandate and myriad responsibilities, the U.S. Treasury Department also controls law enforcement personnel in the Office of Inspector General and the Bureau of Printing and Engraving.

During the 1920s Treasury agents enforcing the Prohibition laws were often referred to as "T-men." As the Federal Bureau of Investigation (FBI)* continued to increase its jurisdiction in the 1930s G-men* and T-men often found themselves in competition with one another over federal cases. However, the Treasury agents have yet to surpass their FBI counterparts in prestige.

SOURCES: Donald A. Torres, *A Handbook of Federal Police and Investigative Agencies*, 1985; Bela Rektor, *Federal Law Enforcement Agencies*, 1975.

V

VALENTINE, LEWIS JOSEPH. (1882–1946) Born in Brooklyn, Valentine initially wanted to enter the priesthood but family financial problems forced him to drop out of school and work in a department store. Valentine joined the New York City Police Department (NYPD),* force in 1903 and over the next decade led an undistinguished career as a beat cop in Brooklyn. In 1913 he was finally promoted to sergeant and three years later lieutenant of the "confidential squad" that investigated corruption in the department.

Under George V. McLaughlin. Valentine was appointed to captain in 1926 and then deputy inspector assigned to crack down on the city's gambling syndicates. When the zealous Valentine arrested politically connected Tammany Hall officials he was demoted to captain by the new police commissioner. In the 1931 Seabury Investigation Valentine testified against Tammany Hall corruption at the behest of Judge Samuel Seabury, leading to the slow death of the Tammany machine.

When reform mayor Fiorello LaGuardia was elected in 1934, he appointed Valentine as police commissioner. During his tenure as commissioner Valentine provided protection to voters at the ballot box, improved city street signs leading to a drop in pedestrian deaths, and interacted with community groups. In his first years he fired three hundred officers and reprimanded or fined eleven thousand others.

A tough law-and-order type, Valentine received perhaps his greatest criticism for his "mark 'em and muss 'em up" policy, which civil libertarians viewed with great alarm. Always tough on hoodlums, he even demanded that gangsters "tip their hats" to police officers. Thin-skinned at times, Valentine even stopped speaking to the press after unfavorable articles were printed. The incorruptible commissioner proved a favorite to the majority of New Yorkers, and when he helped bring in Murder Incorporated's Louis "Lepke" Buchalter, he was elevated to hero status.

In 1945 Valentine retired from policing to host *Gang Busters*, a reality-based radio program. Following the end of World War II, Valentine was selected by General Douglas MacArthur to oversee the reform of the Japanese police and penal systems. Later in 1945 he returned to the airwaves in the States, served on the editorial board of *True Police Cases*, and lectured on crime prevention. He chronicled his life in the autobiography *Night Stick*, published posthumously in 1947. On December 16, 1946, he succumbed to liver disease.

SOURCES: Lowell M. Limpus, *Honest Cop: Lewis J. Valentine*, 1939; Thomas A. Reppetto, *The Blue Parade*, 1978.

VAN WINKLE, MINA. (d. 1932) Well educated and a product of a religious upbringing, Van Winkle became a pioneer policewoman with the Washington, D.C., police. Van Winkle succeeded Alice Stebbins Wells* as head of the International Association of Policewomen (IAP)* in 1919 and is credited with establishing the Women's Bureau of the Washington, D.C., Metropolitan Police Department. Lieutenant Van Winkle was appointed the director of the new bureau in 1918. Her policewomen conformed to the similar units of that era in that they did not wear uniforms and devoted their attentions to women and children. Although she faced resistance in her efforts on behalf of female policing in the 1920s, she overcame many barriers to become a nationally prominent figure and head of the IAP. She was not only the organization's president, she was its main financial contributor, and when she died in 1932 the organization was disbanded as well.

SOURCES: Dorothy Moses Schulz, *From Social Worker to Crimefighter*, 1995; Kerry Segrave, *Policewomen: A History*, 1995.

VENARD, STEPHEN. (1824–1891) Born in Lebanon, Ohio, Venard traveled west to California during the gold rush in 1850. After working at several dead end jobs he entered law enforcement as deputy sheriff, and after a failed first attempt, was elected to terms as city marshal of Nevada City, California, in the 1860s. After an unsuccessful run for sheriff* in 1866, he came to the public's attention after joining a posse and then singlehandedly shooting three stage robbers. This incident elevated him to local deputy sheriff and won him a commission in the state militia as lieutenant colonel. The Wells Fargo Detective Bureau* awarded him a gold-mounted Henry rifle similar to the one used in the pursuit of the Wells Fargo robbers. Venard joined Wells Fargo as a shotgun guard and detective and in the early 1870s captured several stagecoach robbers. However, by 1883 he was working as a constable (see CONSTABLES) in Nevada City. He survived a near fatal stabbing and left law enforcement for ranching in the 1880s, succumbing to kidney problems in 1891, the penniless ex-peace officer was buried in Nevada City after funds were raised by old colleagues.

SOURCES: William B. Secrest, *Lawmen and Desperadoes*, 1994; Dan L. Thrapp, ed., *EFB*, Vol. 3, 1988.

VETTERLI, REED. (1904–1949) Federal Bureau of Investigation (FBI)* agent Reed Vetterli survived the so-called Kansas City massacre* in 1933 but soon lost favor with director John Edgar Hoover* following the debacle. A Mormon, Vetterli resigned in 1938 and returned to Utah where he lost elections for Congress and then governor. He served as police chief of Salt Lake City from 1940 to 1945. When he died in 1949, he had apparently fallen on bad times and was pedaling radio appliances.

SOURCE: Robert Unger, *The Union Station Massacre*, 1997.

VIANA, PAULO FERNANDES. (d. 1821) A native of Rio de Janeiro, Viana was the city's first intendant of police (see INTENDANCE OF POLICE). His thirteen-year tenure began in 1808 and ended with his removal by King Joao VI, following demands by civilian and military authorities that the government adopt a more liberal constitution after the royal family was transferred from Portugal back to Brazil. As intendant, Viana was credited as a savvy administrator whose public works projects, including street paving, installation of street-lamps, and better water supply, vastly improved the city's living conditions.

Viana's Guarda Real de Policia used torture devices such as thumbscrews to obtain confessions during interrogations. Established in 1809, the Guarda Real was modeled after a similar institution in Lisbon, Portugal. During Viana's term as intendant, members of the Guarda such as Miguel Nunes Vidigal* were seen as ruthless administrators of justice, who targeted transients, idlers, and vagrants. The Guarda is regarded as an early precursor to Rio de Janeiro's contemporary death squads. Viana apparently died from apoplexy after the prince regent spitefully ordered cavalry troops to ride over Viana's beloved formal garden, which was located directly across the street from his residence.

SOURCE: Thomas H. Holloway, *Policing Rio de Janeiro: Repression and Resistance in a Nineteenth-Century City*, 1993.

VIDIGAL, MIGUEL NUNES. One of the most notorious members of Rio de Janeiro's Guarda Real de Policia, Vidigal served in Brazil's colonial militia from 1770 until joining the Guarda in 1809. Vidigal first served as adjutant before moving to second in command under Paulo Fernandes Viana.* Regarded as a terror by vagrants, Vidigal and his policemen, whom he handpicked for their size and brute strength, would appear at late-night reveries held by common people and slaves outside the city limits. At these *batuques*, Vidigal and his force would select celebrators at random and then summarily beat them. According to local folklore, these brutal attacks became better-known as "shrimp dinners" because of the parallels between the beatings and the peeling of skin on shrimp to get to the edible pink flesh.

Vidigal led raids on encampments of escaped slaves and the brutality of their methodology has drawn comparisons with their modern-day counterparts. Following Viana's dismissal in 1821, Vidigal was promoted to general of the militia and then of the regular army, before being placed at the head of the Guarda Real de Policia. A recipient of many honors, he retired at the rank of field marshal in 1824. Despite the awards and commendations, Vidigal left a legacy of administering kangaroo court justice and corporal punishment, using race as the main criteria. An analysis of his tenure with the police indicates that most of those who were arrested or punished were of African origin.

SOURCE: Thomas H. Holloway, *Policing Rio de Janeiro: Repression and Resistance in a Nineteenth-Century City*, 1993.

VIDOCQ, EUGENE FRANÇOIS. (1775–1857) The son of a baker, Vidocq was born in Arras, France, and left home at an early age for a life of adventure. After a stint in the military he fell in with some unsavory characters before winding up behind bars. An escape artist, Vidocq won acclaim for breaking out of prison three times. Incarcerated in La Force prison in 1809 he offered to work as a spy and informant for the police. Vidocq was released and placed in command of a group of ex-convicts which became the nucleus of the Sûreté* (now the Police Judiciare). His thief-catching force soon expanded from four to twenty-four as Paris streets became markedly safer. Subsequently, Vidocq accumulated a personal fortune due to a clause in his agreement with authorities that allowed him to keep the spoils left behind by criminals he sent to jail.

Considered the world's first private detective, Vidocq employed numerous police detection techniques considered standard procedures today, including disguises, decoys, informants, autopsies, blood tests, ballistics, criminal files, and handwriting analysis. He directed the Sûreté from 1811 until he resigned in 1827. Except for a brief return to the Sûreté in 1832, Vidocq worked as a private detective the remainder of his law enforcement career.

Vidocq published several books, including a four volume, 350,000 word autobiography, *Memoirs* (there is some debate as to whether he was the actual author). In 1845, at the age of seventy the famous detective toured London with an exhibition of pictures and ephemera representing his life. A friend of both the celebrated and the damned, Vidocq returned to sleuthing as a counterespionage agent for Louis-Napoleon. Vidocq's exploits reportedly served as the inspiration for several fictional sleuths, including Edgar Allan Poe's Auguste C. Dupin,* Emile Gaboriau's Monsieur Lecoq,* and Honoré de Balzac's Jacques Collin.

SOURCES: Samuel Edwards, *The Vidocq Dossier: The Story of the World's First Detective*, 1977; Philip John Stead, *Vidocq: A Biography*, 1953; William Amos, *The Originals*, 1985.

VINCENT, SIR HOWARD. (1849–1908) Formerly a barrister and fluent in French, Vincent went to France and immersed himself in the French detective system. After submitting a report of his findings on the Paris police to a committee on the London Metropolitan Police,* it was recommended that the police should have a united and separate detective force and in March 1878 the Criminal Investigation Department (CID)* was created. Vincent was selected as its first director. Almost immediately Vincent set to reorganizing Scotland Yard* by reassigning 250 detectives and promoting Adolphus Frederick Williamson* to the new rank of chief superintendent. In the new scheme, Williamson would be charged with supervising 3 chief inspectors, 20 inspectors, and 159 sergeants arrayed over sixty London Divisions. Before retiring in 1884 Vincent had expanded to a force of roughly 600 officers. Following a rash of Irish nationalist bombings in London Vincent was credited with establishing the "Special Irish Branch," the world's first antiterrorist squad.

SOURCES: David Scoli, *The Queen's Peace*, 1979; John Fitzgerald Moylan, *Scotland Yard and the Metropolitan Police*, 1929; Rupert Allason, *The Branch*, 1983.

VIZZINI, SALVATORE. Vizzini joined the U.S. Marines at seventeen and saw action in the Japanese theater of World War II. During his training he became an expert in martial arts and fluent in six languages. In 1953 he began a thirteen-year stint with the Bureau of Narcotics. Working undercover for over a decade, Vizzini infiltrated a heroin factory in Palermo and exposed a heroin network that ran from Istanbul to Beirut to Marseilles. His cover was blown while working as a croupier in San Juan while investigating cocaine smuggling allegedly financed by Fidel Castro's regime. In 1967 he was selected by the governor of Florida to infiltrate the Mafia and expose its Florida connections. He subsequently served as chief of police for the city of South Miami, Florida.

SOURCE: Sal Vizzini, with Oscar Fraley and Marshall Smith, *Vizzini: The Secret Lives of America's Most Successful Undercover Agent*, 1972

VOICEPRINTING. In 1962 Lawrence G. Kersta described the new technique of voiceprint identification at the annual meeting of the Acoustical Society of America. Kersta had analyzed literally thousands of voiceprints while working as a researcher for Bell Telephone. Through his research he determined that no two human voices were exactly alike. By using a tape recorder and a spectrograph, an instrument that transforms speech sounds into perceptible diagrams, a trained technician can reportedly identify speakers with an accuracy of at least 99.65 percent. Police investigators have used this technique to solve telephone extortion schemes and apprehend obscene phone callers. Voiceprinting is still considered a controversial identification technique with a minority of states allowing the procedure as evidence in trial courts.

Voiceprinting has played an instrumental role in several criminal investigations, but the most famous use of voiceprinting was in the case of Clifford Irving's Howard Hughes hoax. Refusing to appear in public to attack the forged biography, the reclusive millionaire conducted a telephone interview with several reporters who knew him. Irving challenged the veracity of the interview, but prosecutors were prepared for Irving's claims that they did not speak to the real Hughes and hired Kersta and another voiceprint expert to compare the spectrographs of the Hughes telephone interview with earlier recordings. Science ultimately triumphed, and Irving went to jail for fraud. There continues to be much apprehension about voiceprinting among civil libertarians and "police state" critics, especially after the Federal Bureau of Investigation (FBI)* asked a radio station to record phone calls critical of President Richard Nixon in 1973 so they could be used for future voice analysis by the FBI and the Central Intelligence Agency (CIA).

SOURCES: Eugene Block, *Voiceprinting: How the Law Can Read the Voice of Crime*, 1975; Carl Sifakis, *The Encyclopedia of American Crime*, 1982.

VOLLMER, AUGUST. (1876–1955) Considered the father of the modern police organization, Vollmer was born in New Orleans, Louisiana, and educated abroad after being orphaned in his youth. Vollmer eventually settled in Berkeley, California, and distinguished himself in combat during the Philippines campaign of the Spanish-American War. In 1905 he was elected city marshal of Berkeley and four years later began a twenty-four-year career as Berkeley, California, Police Department* chief. In 1907 he was elected president of the California Chiefs of Police and in 1922 accepted the presidency of the International Association of Chiefs of Police (IACP).*

Vollmer rose to prominence for requiring prospective members of his police force to be college graduates in a time when high school educations were not required. His innovations included rigorous in-service training and probation for first-time offenders. He was the first police executive to champion the lie detector* as an investigative tool and in 1922 implemented a single fingerprint classification system. During the 1920s and 30s his police laboratory became a model for technicians in police departments throughout the country. Consistently at the forefront at adapting new technology to police work, prior to the two-way wireless radio Vollmer set up a system of blinking lights throughout Berkeley to alert patrolmen to contact headquarters for instructions.

In between teaching at the University of California and running his police department Vollmer was called on to reorganize the San Diego, California, Police Department (1915); the Los Angeles Police Department (LAPD)* (1923–1925); the Detroit Police Department (1925); the Havana, Cuba, Police Department (1926); the Chicago Police Department (CPD),* the Kansas City Police Department (1929), and the Minneapolis, Minnesota, Police Department (1930). After stepping down form the Berkeley Police Department he helped reorganize the Santa Barbara, California, Police Department (1936), and then agencies in Syracuse, New York (1943), Dallas, Texas (1944), and Portland, Oregon, (1945). Vollmer was also instrumental in the repeal of Prohibition with his contributions to the commission headed by George Woodward Wickersham* in 1931. Vollmer committed suicide in 1955. Vollmer was the author and coauthor of numerous books and articles, including *The Police and Modern Society* (1936), *The Criminal* (1949), and, with Alfred E. Parker, *Crime and the State Police* (1935) and *Crime, Crooks, and Cops* (1937).

SOURCES: Gene E. Carte and Elaine H. Carte, *Police Reform in the United States: The Era of August Vollmer*, 1975; Alfred E. Parker, *Crime Fighter: August Vollmer*, 1961; Alfred E. Parker, *The Berkeley Police Story*, 1972; and Donal E. J. MacNamara, "August Vollmer: The Vision of Police Professionalism," *Pioneers in Policing*, 1977.

VUCETICH, JUAN. (1858–1925) Born on an island off the Dalmatian coast, Vucetich moved to Argentina in his twenties. He made his first steps toward becoming a criminologist by joining La Plata Central Police Department as head of its statistical bureau. Unhappy with the prevailing system based on anthropometry,* after familiarizing himself with Galton's work on fingerprinting* Vucetich convinced the police force to adopt this new identification technique. It took the solution of a dramatic murder case with fingerprints for Vucetich to gain the critical support to make the transition from Bertillon system*–based methods to dactyloscopy (fingerprinting). In 1896 the Argentina police agency became the first in the world to use fingerprinting as its foremost criminal identification system. Vucetich self-published two books on the subject.

SOURCES: Frank Smyth, *Cause of Death*, 1980; Charles Phillips and Alan Axelrod, *CCC*, 1996.

W

WALDO, RHINELANDER. (1877–1927) Waldo graduated from West Point and served in the Philippines following the Spanish-American War. As New York City Police Department (NYPD)* commissioner under Mayor William J. Gaynor from 1911 to 1913, Waldo, who was formerly city fire commissioner, was credited with introducing a number of innovations, including the first automobile in the police department, new uniforms with heavy coats and large pockets to protect officers through the harsh winter months, and a three-shift platoon system. He abolished the position of roundsman (see ROUNDSMEN) and replaced it with the rank of sergeant. Waldo's tenure was short-lived since he was forced to resign in the wake of the Charles Becker* scandal. The subsequent Curran Committee investigation into Becker's murder of a small-time gambler found Waldo incompetent, and he resigned in 1913.

SOURCE: Thomas A. Reppetto, *The Blue Parade*, 1978.

WALKER REPORT ON THE 1968 CHICAGO DEMOCRATIC NATIONAL CONVENTION. Chicago police responded to demonstrations at the 1968 Chicago Democratic National Convention in a "club-swinging melee" that was televised live throughout the world. Most clashes between the police and demonstrators took place in the Grant Park–Michigan Avenue and Lincoln Park Areas. The subsequent investigation following the violent confrontation between police and demonstrators released its findings in the Walker Report, entitled *Rights in Conflict* and published in November 1968. Although this incident has been characterized as a police riot, further investigation noted that only a minority of the police officers were involved in the overzealous attacks on demonstrators and well-dressed middle-aged by-standers. This almost week-long series of confrontations became nightly fodder for national newscasts which broadcasted ample proof of police misconduct as it focused on out-of-control police on foot and horseback clubbing news photographers, rubber-neckers, and demonstrators. During these skirmishes fifty-nine police officers and 101 demonstrators were hospitalized for injuries and 668 people were arrested. What made the Walker Report so indelible to its readers was the use of a pictorial chronology of the police overreaction to the demonstrators. This 1968 episode resounded for years and continued to receive wide attention when eight people, including Abby Hoffman, Jerry Rubin, Bobby Seale, and Tom Hayden, were arrested on federal charges of conspiring to cross state lines to cause riots. The ensuing Chicago Conspiracy Trial drew attention to the convention riots for years.

SOURCE: Davis Faber, *Chicago '68*, 1988; John Schultz, *Chicago Conspiracy Trial*, 1993.

WALLACE, BENJAMIN "BEN." (d. 1946) At six feet, five inches, and tipping the scales at 280, "Big Ben" Wallace developed a reputation for killing black criminals in Harlem as a member of the New York City Police Department (NYPD)* between 1928 and 1946. By 1946 the African-American policeman had killed five men and wounded several others. His predilection to gun violence led to his own demise, when he was killed in a gunfight with several criminals. Before he died he killed his assailant.

SOURCE: W. Marvin Dulaney, *Black Police in America*, 1996.

WALLACE, WILLIAM ALEXANDER ANDERSON "BIG FOOT." (1817–1899) Born in Lexington, Virginia, Wallace moved to Texas in 1836 after finding out that his brother and cousin had been shot by Mexican troops during the Goliad massacre. Physically imposing at six feet, two inches, and weighing 240 pounds, "Big Foot" Wallace tried his hand at a variety of frontier occupations, including farming and buffalo hunting before joining the ill-fated Mier Expedition during its invasion of Mexico in 1842. Taken prisoner by Mexican troops, the Texans were held captive at Perote Prison, where Wallace reportedly earned his sobriquet "Big Foot," when he was unable to find size twelve shoes. Released from prison in 1844, Wallace promptly joined the Texas Rangers,* serving under Captain John Coffee "Jack" Hays* on the frontier and in the War with Mexico.

Wallace commanded his own Texas Ranger company in 1858, participating in numerous violent confrontations with border bandits and Comanches. During the years leading up to the Civil War, Wallace earned a reputation for his ability to track down escaped slaves in west Texas. To supplement his income, Wallace occasionally rode as a shotgun guard for the San Antonio–El Paso stagecoach lines. Following his Ranger career, he retired to a ranch in Frio County.

SOURCES: John C. Duval, *The Adventures of Big-Foot Wallace*, 1966; Walter P. Webb, *The Texas Rangers*, 1935.

WALLING, GEORGE WASHINGTON. (1823–1891) Born in Keyport, New Jersey, Walling left school at an early age. After a childhood of hard work he joined the New York City Municipal Police and was stationed in the Third Precinct in December 1847. Within six years he would be appointed to captain of the Eighteenth Ward. In 1866 he made inspector, and in 1874 he was appointed superintendent of the New York Metropolitan Police.*

Walling was a central participant in a series of police riots that racked New York in the 1850s. In 1857 Walling was appointed captain of the new Metropolitan police force formed under state control to replace the corrupt Municipal police force. Mayor Fernando Wood* refused to dismiss the Municipal force and accept the new state authorized one. Captain Walling was sent to arrest the mayor and riots soon broke out between the two police forces. The Metropolitan force would triumph following a year of conflict and by the 1860s Walling's force had won a reputation as a notoriously brutal agency. After the carnage of the New York Draft Riots* in 1863, his force garnered increasing support from his constituents. Walling distinguished himself during the epic rioting that resulted in hundreds of deaths. Walling was appointed superintendent of the rejuvenated Municipal Police in 1870 but was forced to retire in 1885 because of a mandatory retirement age.

SOURCE: George Walling, *Recollections of a New York Chief of Police*, 1888; Thomas A. Reppetto, *The Blue Parade*, 1978.

WAMBAUGH, JOSEPH ALOYSIUS, JR. (b. 1937) Born in East Pittsburgh, Pennsylvania, and educated at Chafey College and California State College, Wambaugh joined the Los Angeles Police Department (LAPD)* in 1960. He rose through the ranks to detective sergeant before leaving the force in 1974 to write full-time. Wambaugh rose to prominence with the publication of *The New Centurions* in 1971. Other books followed, including *The Blue Knight* (1972), *The Onion Field* (1973), *The Choirboys* (1975), *The Black Marble* (1978), *Finnegan's Week* (1993), *Fugitive Nights* (1992), *Secrets of Harry Bright* (1985), *The Delta Star* (1983), *The Glitter Dome* (1981), *Lines and Shadows* (1984), *Golden Orange* (1990), *The Blooding* (1989), and *Echoes in Darkness* (1987). Wambaugh's work inspired several movies and the television series *Police Story* and *The Blue Knight*.

SOURCE: John M. Reilly, ed., *Twentieth-Century Crime and Mystery Writers*, 1985.

WARD, BENJAMIN. (b. 1926) Following a career in law enforcement that included stints as New York City Department of Corrections Services commissioner (1975–1988), Housing Authority chief (1979), and commissioner of the Department of Corrections (1979–1983), Ward was appointed New York City

Police Department (NYPD)* commissioner by mayor Ed Koch in 1984. During his six-year tenure as commissioner, Ward was lauded for recruiting more minority police officers and reimplementing foot patrols on New York City streets. Ward is credited with introducing a community-based policing strategy known as the Community Patrol Officers Program. When Ward retired in 1989, crime was still a major problem but he was instrumental in making the force a more professional and ethnically diversified organization.

SOURCE: Charles Phillips and Alan Axelrod, *CCC*, 1996

WARD, JEROME L. (1833–1913) Born in Vernon, New York, Ward moved with his family to Wisconsin when he was ten and later was wounded in the Civil War while serving as a wagoner with the 1st Wisconsin Cavalry. In 1882 he won the election for sheriff* in Cochise County, Arizona, succeeding John Harris Behan.* The following year Ward won prominence for apprehending and supervising the execution of the five outlaws who perpetrated the "Bisbee Massacre" in which his deputy had been a victim. Ward was killed by a motor vehicle in 1913 while attending a parade in San Diego.

SOURCES: Dan L. Thrapp, ed., *EFB*, Vol. 3, 1988; Ed Bartholomew, *Wyatt Earp: The Man and the Myth*, 1964.

WARD, RICHARD H. (b. 1939) Born in New York City and educated at the University of California, Berkeley, and the John Jay College of Criminal Justice, Ward entered law enforcement as a patrol officer with the New York City Police Department (NYPD)* in 1962 after leaving the U.S. Marines. He would rise to detective before leaving the force for an academic career in 1970. Over the next three decades, Ward became internationally known for his acumen in police training, counterterrorism, and transnational crime. He is currently the dean and director of the Criminal Justice Center at Sam Houston State University, the largest criminal justice educational facility in the United States.

SOURCE: Kay Billingsley, "Dr. Souryal Returns from Indonedia Assignment," *The Mandate* 8 (1), Fall 1999.

WARNE, KATE. (1833–1868) In 1856 Warne became America's first female detective when she was hired by Pinkerton's National Detective Agency.* Within four years other women would join what Pinkerton described as his "Female Detective Bureau." Warne became the superintendent of the Female Detective Bureau and assisted Allan Pinkerton in foiling the Baltimore plot to kill Lincoln in 1861. Pinkerton frequently had to deflect criticism from his family members for hiring women. Because he had a penchant for flirtation many suspected his intention to hire female operatives as less than noble and following Allan's death in 1884 women were noticeably absent from the Agency payroll. In his will, Pinkerton ordered that the graves of Warne, Timothy "Tim" Webster,* and other employees buried in Chicago's Graceland Cemetery should "never be sold, graveled or aliened in any manner whatsoever" (Horan). In his 1875 book *The Expressman and Detective*, he called her "the greatest female detective who ever brought a case to a successful conclusion" (Horan).

SOURCES: James D. Horan, *The Pinkertons*, 1968; Frank Morn, *"The Eye That Never Sleeps,"* 1982; James Mackay, *Allan Pinkerton*, 1996.

WARREN, SIR CHARLES. (1840–1927) Educated at Cheltenham, Sandhurst, and Woolwich, Warren served in the British army with distinction during the 1877–1878 Kaffir War, where he was severely wounded. Returning to England as a Lieutenant-Colonel in 1880 he taught military engineering for a short spell before being asked to lead the search for a missing scientific expedition in Egypt in 1882. Warren's investigation uncovered the murders of the expedition members and led to the subsequent arrest and conviction of the perpetrators. After military service in Africa in the 1880s Queen Victoria appointed him to succeed London Metropolitan Police commissioner Sir Edmund Henderson* in 1886.

During his short tenure as police commissioner Warren was criticized for the inability of the police to track down serial killer Jack the Ripper. Ripperologists and police strategists alike have denounced Warren's ridiculous attempts at solving the great murder case. Warren's exploits made great fodder for newspaper writers who ridiculed his use of bloodhounds, which eventually became lost in the London fog and his suggestion that police use rubber soled shoes instead of police issue hobnailed boots in order to sneak up on the infamous killer. Warren is also blamed for destroying crucial evidence that implicated a Jewish perpetrator in order to avoid anti-Semitic rioting. Warren resigned from the police on November 9, 1888, the same day that Mary Jane Kelly's mutilated body was found. After two years as police commissioner Warren returned to the army, later fighting in the Boer War and playing an instrumental role in the Boy Scout movement.

SOURCE: Paul Begg, Martin Fido, and Keith Skinner, *The Jack the Ripper A to Z*, 1991.

WASHINGTON, SYLVESTER. One of the best-known African-American police officers in Chicago history, Washington served on the city's South side from 1934 and 1960 where he earned the moniker "Two-Gun Pete" for wielding two .375 magnum handguns, with which he shot and killed more than a dozen men. He claimed in one interview to have arrested more than twenty-thousand suspects in a sixteen-year period. His nickname was given to him by a *Chicago Defender* newspaper reporter in 1936.

SOURCE: W. Marvin Dulaney, *Black Police in America*, 1996.

WATCH AND WARD SYSTEM. In 1285 the Statute of Winchester* codified a variety of time-tested notions about early law enforcement. Many of these had been developing for decades but had not been formally introduced by statute. Among the most noteworthy in terms of policing was the system of watch and ward, which introduced the town watchman, a fixture in city life until the birth of modern policing some six hundred years later. The watchman augmented the existing institutions of law enforcement by supplementing the duties performed by the constables.* The Statute of Winchester required most towns to maintain a watch of up to sixteen men. Watchmen were to be stationed at the walled gates of town between the hours of sunset and sunrise and all strangers within city limits were to be confined during the hours of darkness. An unpaid, unprofessional position, all men were required to volunteer for regular service. Failure to comply usually resulted in a stint in the stocks.

SOURCE: T. A. Critchley, *A History of Police in England and Wales, 900–1966*, 1967.

WATCHMEN. *See* NIGHT WATCH; WATCH AND WARD SYSTEM.

WEBB, JOHN JOSHUA. (1847–1882) Born in Keokuk, Iowa, Webb worked as a hunter, teamster, and surveyor prior to entering law enforcement as an occasional deputy under sheriffs Charles E. Bassett* and William Bartolomew "Bat" Masterson* in Dodge City in 1877. When not working as a hired gun he worked as a special officer in Las Vegas, New Mexico, and then as that city's marshal in 1880. In March 1880 he was sentenced to hang for robbery and murder, but his sentence was commuted by Governor Lew Wallace. On September 19, 1881, he participated in a successful escape from the San Miguel County jail and reportedly disappeared in Mexico. Some sources claim that Webb died of smallpox in Winslow, Arizona, in 1882.

SOURCES: Peter Hertzog, *A Directory of New Mexico Desperadoes*, 1965; William A. Keleher, *Violence in Lincoln County, 1869–1881*, 1957; Nyle H. Miller and Joseph W. Snell, *Great Gunfighters of the Kansas Cowtowns, 1867–1886*, 1967.

WEBSTER, TIMOTHY "TIM." (1821–1861) Born in Newhaven, Sussex, England, Webster immigrated to the United States with his parents in 1832. Growing up in Princeton, New Jersey, he dreamed of joining the New York City Police Department (NYPD),* but without the right connections it seemed his goal would elude him. However, with the help of an acquaintance on the force, he won appointment in 1853. That same year Webster accepted an offer to join the Pinkerton's National Detective Agency.* In 1861 Webster narrowly escaped the gallows after he was arrested and suspected of being a Confederate spy, but was saved by the arrival of Alan Pinkerton. During the Civil War, Webster worked undercover in Tennessee and sent back some of the agencies' most meticulous reports. Webster is credited with uncovering the duplicity of Confederate spy Rose Greenhow, as well as an organization of southern sympathizers and supporters in Baltimore. The intrepid Webster at times played a double agent, reporting directly to Confederate War Secretary Judah P. Benjamin. He continued his dangerous game of cat and mouse until his identity was uncovered while behind enemy lines. Despite requests that his life be spared, he was executed by hanging on April 28, 1862, the first American executed for espionage since Nathan Hale in 1776.

SOURCES: James Mackay, *Allan Pinkerton: The First Private Eye*, 1996; Frank Morn, *"The Eye That Never Sleeps,"* 1982.

WEBSTER, WILLIAM H. (b. 1924) Raised in St. Louis, Missouri, and educated at Amherst College, Webster earned his law degree at Washington University following service in World War II. He later served in the navy during the Korean War before entering politics in 1960 as a Dwight Eisenhower appointee and then as a district court judge in 1972 under President Richard Nixon. Six years later, President Jimmy Carter selected Webster to lead the Federal Bureau of Investigation (FBI),* the first permanent head since the death of director John Edgar Hoover* in 1972. Webster is credited with launching the first successful federal offensive against organized crime, leading to the arrest of the bosses of New York City's "Five Families." During Webster's reign, the FBI was instrumental in solving several espionage cases, most notably the arrest of the John Walker ring. In 1987 President Ronald Reagan appointed Webster to head the Central Intelligence Agency after William Casey stepped down for health reasons. He retired from public office in May 1991.

SOURCES: Charles Phillips and Alan Axelrod, *CCC*, 1996; Athan G. Theoharis, ed., *The FBI*, 1999.

WELCH, SAUNDERS. (1711–1784) Born in Aylesbury, England, the child of paupers, young Welch grew up in a workhouse. Following an apprenticeship as a trunkmaker, he opened a grocery shop. Elected the High Constable of Holborn in 1747, Welch assisted Sir Henry Fielding* as an early member of the Bow Street Runners.* As co-commander of the Runners, Welch published the pamphlet "A Letter upon the Subject of Robbers" (1753) and *Observations on the Office of Constable** (1754). This set of guidelines suggested appropriate conduct for the Bow Street Runners. In 1755 he was appointed magistrate for Middlesex and then Westminster. Welch often worked cases on his own, like the Fielding brothers, and was apparently popular with the working classes for his diplomacy skills in the face of social disorder accompanying the industrial revolution. Prior to his retirement in 1776, Welch opened a Magistrate's Office on Litchfield Street, supervised the Runners, and supplemented Fielding's judicial responsibilities for six years until they became estranged over petty differences. He subsequently moved to Italy to try to recover his health, but would return to England, where he died just weeks before his friend Dr. Samuel Johnson.

SOURCES: Paul Begg and Keith Skinner, *The Scotland Yard Files*, 1992; Patrick Pringle, *Hue and Cry*, 1955; Anthony Babington, *A House in Bow Street*, 1969.

WELLS, ALICE STEBBINS. (prominent 1910–1920s) Born in Kansas, Wells moved to the New York City area as a young woman and found employment as an assistant to a Congregational minister. Subsequently, she studied theology for two years at a Hartford, Connecticut, seminary and then traveled the lecture circuit spreading the gospel of Christianity. She is credited with being the first woman to be a pastor of her own congregation in Maine and Oklahoma.

A strong advocate for women in modern police work, she lobbied Los Angeles social and political leaders for her cause, leading to her appointment on September 12, 1910, as the first sworn female police officer in America (see POLICEWOMEN). That year she was hired by the Los Angeles Police Department (LAPD)* According to her job requirements, she was expected to "enforce laws concerning dance halls, skating rinks, penny arcades, picture shows, and other similar places of recreation; the suppression of unwholesome billboard displays; and maintenance of a general information bureau for women seeking advice on matters within the scope of the Police Department" (Sjoquist).

A charismatic speaker, Wells toured over one hundred cities in support of female police officers. Wells was at the forefront of the first national policewomen's organization and in 1915 was elected as the first president of the International Association of Policewomen (IAP).* Wells is also credited with creating the first class dealing specifically with women police, offered through the UCLA Criminology Department in 1928.

SOURCES: B. R. Price and S. Gavin, "A Century of Women in Policing," in *The Criminal Justice System and Women*, ed. B. R. Price and N. J. Skoloff, 1982; P. Horne, *Women in Law Enforcement*, 1980; Arthur W. Sjoquist (historical text by), *Los Angeles Police Department Commemorative Book, 1869–1984*, 1984.

WELLS FARGO DETECTIVE BUREAU. In 1850 Henry Wells, an Albany, New York, express agent, joined with William G. Fargo of Onondaga, New York, to form the American Express Company. Two years later, as the business expanded farther west, they decided to carve out two express jurisdictions. The original company had hegemony in the East, while all business west of the Mississippi and Missouri Rivers would be handled by the newly inaugurated Wells Fargo and Company.

On July 1, 1852, Wells Fargo started business, based out of San Francisco. Within five years it established express agencies in 87 locations, and by 1859 it had expanded to 126 agencies between Canada and Mexico. In 1861 it took over the financially desperate Pony Express. Besides shipping food, tools, and liquor on its "fast freights" the express conveyed shipments of nineteenth-century treasure such as gold and silver bullion across the West, guarded by Wells Fargo employees. Transportation was accomplished via Concord stages, railroad cars, steamboats, and ocean-going vessels.

The most valuable commodities including gold dust and nuggets, gold and silver bullion, and currency were transported in Wells Fargo's trademark green-painted wooden box, secured with strap iron and sealed with a hasp and lock. Only company agents at each end of the line possessed keys for the locks. Not even drivers or Wells Fargo express guards were provided with keys. This in part explains the cliché of the highwayman shooting or chiseling off the locks to get to the contents. Advertising that no customer would ever have to face a loss, the company created an elaborate security system. Although coaches were typically protected by armed guards, successful robberies were followed by the relentless pursuit of the perpetrators by specially trained agents.

In order to protect the precious cargo, each strongbox concealed a waybill and a duplicate of the invoice was sent to the intended destination. In the event of a robbery, Wells Fargo detectives could copy the invoice to further their investigation. As outlaws became more accustomed to this system, the express company responded by replacing wooden boxes with iron ones which were then bolted to the coach, requiring highwaymen to use dynamite to separate the precious cargo from the stage.

The company continued to flourish into 1880s and 1890s. Much of its success was due to its policy of instantly replacing all losses and employing its detective force to hunt down the perpetrators. In the 1870s noted California lawman James Bunyan Hume* was hired to lead its detective bureau. As its chief special officer until his retirement in 1904, Hume was instrumental in apprehending numerous criminals, most notably "Black Bart."

In an era when Western peace officers were usually imbued with unlimited powers, Hume, although only a private detective, was allowed to investigate, search, interrogate, arrest, detain, and transport suspected criminals as he saw fit. However, today's Wells Fargo agents are only allowed to make arrests outside San Francisco County where they are deputized and only in cases dealing with Wells Fargo bank matters and with the approval of that jurisdiction's law enforcement agency.

SOURCE: Richard Dillon, *Wells Fargo Detective: A Biography of James B. Hume*, 1969.

WENSLEY, FREDERICK PORTER "THE WEASEL." (1865–1949) Wensley joined the London Metropolitan Police* in 1888 and rose to prominence in 1896 when he arrested William Seaman for the Turner Street murders that same year. After many years in the H Division of the Criminal Investigation Division (CID),* he was promoted to Chief Constable in charge of CID. Wensley retired in 1929 and two years later published his memoirs, *Detective Days*. Wensley patrolled the Whitechapel area during the hunt for Jack the Ripper and was one of the few police officers to rise from the ranks to acceptance among the "gentlemen" at the top of the London police hierarchy. Among the most notable cases Wensley was instrumental in solving were the murder of Emi-

unheeded. Its main achievement, however, was in informing the public that the American criminal justice system needed to be reevaluated and improved. Among the harshest critics of the committee's findings were police executives who found that many of the conclusions were hastily drawn. Wickersham died of a heart attack in 1936.

SOURCES: George E. Mowry, "George Woodward Wickersham," *DAB*, Vol. 11, 1958; Robert C. McManus, "Unhappy Warrior: A Portrait of George W. Wickersham," *Outlook and Independent*, September 17, 1930.

WICKERSHAM COMMISSION. *See* WICKERSHAM, GEORGE WOOD-WARD.

WIDENMANN, ROBERT. (1852–1930) Born in Ann Arbor, Michigan, Widenmann arrived in Lincoln County, New Mexico, in 1877 and became affiliated with the John Tunstall faction during the Lincoln County War. He worked in Tunstall's general store until he was appointed a deputy marshal thanks to his father's acquaintance with Interior Secretary Carl Schurz, a fellow Bavarian. Widenmann was with the Tunstall party the day John Tunstall was murdered in February 1878. Widenmann was later instructed to arrest the suspected killers. Siding with the Chisum faction, he selected a posse from the cattleman's ranch hands. Among them was the teenaged William Bonney, later better known as Billy the Kid. Over the next several months the posse hunted the suspected killers of Tunstall, leading to a number of deadly shoot-outs with the Dolan cattle faction, including the death of Deputy Marshal William Brady.* On April 1, 1878, Widenmann and Bonney were arrested for the murder of Brady and Sheriff* George Hindman. Widenmann was released and soon after forced to turn in his badge. He left New Mexico and law enforcement forever.

SOURCES: Jay Robert Nash, *EWLO*, 1994; Dan L. Thrapp, ed., *EFB*, Vol. 3, 1988; Frederick S. Calhoun, *The Lawmen*, 1989.

WILD, JONATHAN. (1682–1725) As the leading criminal of London in the first half of the eighteenth century, Wild dominated the underworld of London from 1715 until his death in 1725. During the 1720s London suffered one of its worst crime waves. Since most powerful criminals were protected from prosecution through bribes and graft, the only response the government could come up with was to pay rewards for the capture of robbers and prescribe the death penalty for most offenses.

A master at self-promotion, he called himself thief-taker general.* Wild exploited the law to the fullest and his posse of thief-catchers is considered by many to be a precursor to police departments. For ten years he was considered the most efficient gang breaker and thief catcher in England. Wild improved an ingenious system for receiving stolen goods developed by Moll Cutpurse in the previous century. The system involved getting higher prices for stolen goods by selling them back to the original owners who were willing to pay more. Wild improved on this system by first posing as a private thief taker who went after offenders to subsequently collect a reward once the objects were returned. He then organized bands of thieves whom he directed in his various schemes. Any thieves that attempted to compete with him he would be set up for arrest and execution. Therefore, by aiding the law in his capacity as thief-taker, Wild used the law to fatten his own coffers.

Wild's days were numbered when an act was passed in 1717 that made this activity a capital crime. At his trial Wild claimed that he had provided evidence that sent seventy-six men to their deaths. Despite supporters who argued that he helped control the crime problem Wild was hanged in 1725.

SOURCE: Gerald Howson, *Thief-Taker General: The Rise and Fall of Jonathan Wild*, 1970.

WILKIE, JOHN ELBERT. (1860–1934) Born in Chicago, Wilkie worked as a journalist for several local newspapers before moving to London in 1893 to pursue other business opportunities. Three years later he returned to the States and became a private investigator. The seeming inability of the U.S. Secret Service* in the 1890s to control the counterfeiting problem led to the dismissal of its director and the appointment of Wilkie as his replacement in 1898. Under Wilkie's direction the Secret Service busted a notorious ring of counterfeiters during the Monroe Note investigation. In another high profile case Secret Service agents infiltrated Coxey's army during the organized march on Washington, resulting in many arrests. During the 1890s the Secret Service was increasingly involved in the growing internal upheavals in American society.

During the Spanish-American War, Wilkie set up a counterespionage network to trap Spanish spies and sympathizers. Wilkie met great resistance in his attempt to dispense with informants, the most valuable source for getting to counterfeiters, but he was instrumental in improving investigative methods and abolishing the appointment of agents through the patronage system. During Wilkie's tenure, the Secret Service was not yet formally responsible for the protection of presidents. However, although agents were present when President McKinley was assassinated in 1901, they could not prevent the tragedy when an official asked to trade places with an agent so he could stand next to the president. In 1903 agents were permanently assigned to protect the president. Wilkie left the service in 1913 for more lucrative opportunities in the railroad business.

SOURCES: Charles Phillips and Alan Axelrod, *CCC*, 1996; Thomas A. Reppetto, *The Blue Parade*, 1978.

WILLEMSE, CORNELIUS W. (c. 1872–1942) A Dutch immigrant, Willemse worked as a bouncer in the Bowery and a counterman at the Eagle Hotel before beginning a distinguished career with the New York City Police Department (NYPD) in 1899. Willemse was fond of recounting how police commissioner

Theodore Roosevelt* had once turned him down for a job with the force because he worked in a vice area. In 1931 he published his autobiography, *Behind the Green Lights*, in which he recounted using rubber hoses and blackjacks when employing the third degree.* Willemse also wrote *A Cop Remembers* (1933).

SOURCES: H. Paul Jeffers, *Commissioner Roosevelt*, 1994; James F. Richardson, *The New York Police*, 1970.

WILLIAMS, ALEXANDER S. "CLUBBER." (1839–1910) In an era of corrupt cops, none was more unscrupulous than Williams. Born in Nova Scotia, Canada, Williams worked as a ship's carpenter in Key West, Florida, and Japan before arriving in New York City in 1866. Joining the New York Metropolitan Police,* for two years he patrolled the most violent sectors of the city. Physically imposing, Williams earned the nickname "Clubber" for his dexterity with a nightstick. On one occasion Williams reportedly bragged, "There is more law at the end of a policeman's nightstick than in any ruling of the Supreme Court" (Repetto). Journalist and reformer Jacob Riis* reported how on one occasion Williams clobbered a bearded citizen who would not disperse when given the order to by "Clubber." Riis recognized the victim and reportedly informed Williams he had just clubbed former president Ulysses S. Grant.

In 1871 he was promoted to captain of the Gashouse district and five years later was rewarded with a transfer to the tenderloin,* leading the colorful cop to exclaim "I've had nothing but chuck steak for a long time, and now I'm going to get a little of the tenderloin" (Reppetto). Williams reportedly beat journalist Augustine Costello* senseless with his club for publishing the tenderloin comment in his hagiographic history of the police department, *Our Police Protectors*. Except for a two-year interlude as superintendent of street cleaning, Williams served as captain of the lucrative tenderloin area until 1887. During his eleven years in the tenderloin district, the influential Williams was accused and exonerated of eighteen brutality complaints.

When the Lexow Committee (see LEXOW, CLARENCE) investigated Williams in 1894 it found that on an annual salary of $3,500, Williams had amassed more than $1 million in assets, including a Connecticut vacation home and a $30,000 dock for his spacious yacht. His explanation for such wealth was that he had made savvy real estate investments in Japan. The following year Williams was forced to resign from the force.

SOURCES: H. Paul Jeffers, *Commissioner Roosevelt*, 1994; Thomas A. Reppetto, *The Blue Parade*, 1978.

WILLIAMS, HUBERT. Williams's tenure as Newark, New Jersey, police director, from 1974 to 1985, was the longest up to that time. An African-American, Williams was credited with restoring confidence in the police department after years of unresponsiveness. Among the innovations implemented by Williams were a 911 system, the use of police decoys to deter muggers, police sweeps of high crime areas, roadblocks to deter drunk drivers, a task force to attack the truancy problem and suppress juvenile crime, and "color-conscious" policies, which assigned African-American police officers to areas that were overwhelmingly black. His accomplishments led to his appointment as the first African-American president of the Police Foundation.

SOURCE: W. Marvin Dulaney, *Black Police in America*, 1996.

WILLIAMS, WILLIAM L. "WILLIE." (b. 1943) Born in Philadelphia, Williams left his father's meat-packing plant for his first stint in law enforcement, with the Philadelphia Park Guards. In 1972 this unarmed force that protected city parks was incorporated into the city police department, bringing Williams into the orbit of professional policing. Williams distinguished himself on the civil service exams and rose rapidly through the department to captain.

In 1982, with a recent associate's college degree in hand, Williams was the top candidate for the position of commissioner. In 1988 he was promoted by the new mayor Wilson Goode. Williams led the healing process that had racially cleaved the force during the Frank L. Rizzo* years. He was instrumental in opening substations in the most impoverished neighborhoods. Following the Rodney King* beating in 1991, the subsequent release of racially insensitive comments by Los Angeles Police Department (LAPD)* officers, and then the Los Angeles riots, Los Angeles Mayor Tom Bradley* convinced Daryl F. Gates* to step down, and in 1992 Willie L. Williams became the first African-American police chief of Los Angeles. However, the transition was fraught with complications, since it was complicated by the fact that Wilson was the first chief hired from outside the department since 1949.

SOURCES: W. Marvin Dulaney, *Black Police in America*, 1996; Charles Phillips and Alan Axelrod, *CCC*, 1996.

WILLIAMSON, ADOLPHUS FREDERICK. (1831–1889) Considered one of the greatest investigators of all time, Williamson joined Scotland Yard* in 1850. Two years later he was promoted from constable to sergeant and transferred to the Detective Branch. Over the following decades he was promoted to inspector, chief inspector, superintendent, and chief constable. Variously known as "Dolly," short for Adolphus, or the "philosopher," Williamson was fluent in French and is credited by many to have led Scotland Yard into an internationally recognized law enforcement agency. Williams rose to prominence early in his career in 1855 following his investigation of the "Great Bullion Robbery."

Mentored by Jonathan Whicher,* Sergeant Williamson was one of the original members of the Detective Branch. By 1863 Williamson and Richard Tanner* were charged with supervising the Detective Branch. In the following decade Williamson rose to the rank of detective superintendent, directing three chief inspectors, three inspectors, and nineteen sergeants.

Following the creation of the Special Branch of the Metropolitan Police* in

1883, Williamson was placed in charge of the Irish Bureau, devoting his attention to the Irish Fenian threat, which typically employed bombing campaigns like the IRA of today. Williamson resigned from the Yard in 1886 following a forty-year career after three of his detectives were arrested in a bribery investigation. During his brilliant career Williamson participated in the Constance Kent case, the Jack the Ripper case, and investigated Fenian bombings, but unfortunately he left no memoirs to document his thoughts and exploits.

SOURCES: Leonard Gribble, *Great Manhunters of the Yard*, 1966; Paul Begg and Keith Skinner, *The Scotland Yard Files*, 1992; Joan Lock, *Dreadful Deeds and Awful Murders*, 1990.

WILSON, FRANK J. (1887–1970) Best remembered as the federal agent who nabbed Al Capone, Wilson joined the U.S. Treasury Department* Intelligence Unit in 1920. In 1930 Elmer Lincoln Irey,* chief of the Internal Revenue's Enforcement Branch assigned Wilson with the task of prosecuting the crime boss using a 1927 Supreme Court decision that made illegal income subject to income tax.

Wilson was faced with an onerous assignment since Capone had not filed income tax returns for several years, nor did he hold property or bank accounts in his own name and had endorsed no checks. Without a paper trail, Wilson had to base his analysis on his estimation of net worth and net expenditures. Capone got wind of the investigation and hired a hit team to kill Wilson. Capone was eventually pressured by associates to pull off the killers and soon after Wilson's persistence and evidence sent Capone to prison.

Wilson also played a prominent role in the Lindbergh kidnapping investigation by insisting that the serial numbers of the ransom be recorded. Beginning in 1936, Wilson headed the U.S. Secret Service* for eleven years and is credited with reducing the counterfeiting problem to an all-time low. He also implemented what are today's standard presidential security measures. He retired from public service in 1947.

SOURCES: Frank Spiering, *The Man Who Got Capone*, 1976; Andrew Tully, *Treasury Agent*, 1958.

WILSON, ORLANDO WINFIELD "O.W." (1900–1972) Born in Veblen, South Dakota, Wilson was educated at the University of California, Berkeley. The son of a lawyer, it was only natural he should gravitate to the criminal justice discipline. During his tenure at the University of California from 1921 to 1925, he worked as a patrolman with the Berkeley, California, Police Department* under police chief August Vollmer.* The influential police reformer Vollmer is credited with directing Wilson toward a career in criminology.

Shortly after graduation, Wilson was appointed police chief of Fullerton, California, but he left several months later after clashing with city fathers over his reform agenda. Before returning to policing, he worked for two years as an investigator for the Pacific Finance Corporation. In 1928, thanks to a recommendation from his mentor Vollmer, he accepted the police chief job for Wichita, Kansas. Within five years Wilson had revamped the corruption-plagued force. He was instrumental in introducing unmarked police cars, mobile crime laboratories, lie detectors, and hiring part-time students as police officers.

Wilson left the force due to pressures from political patrons of the Wichita racketeers, which he had pursued zealously. Resigning in May 1939, he quickly found employment with Chicago's Public Administration Service, which hired him to survey and write reports on various city police forces. He found many forces were merely pawns of political bosses. Later that year Wilson was invited to teach police administration as a tenured professor at Berkeley. During World War II Wilson distinguished himself in the U.S. Army as lieutenant colonel of military police. Following the war he remained in Germany as the chief public safety officer.

Wilson returned to Berkeley in 1950 as dean of the School of Criminology, and despite attempts to diminish the academic standing of the criminology program, over the next decade he elevated the program to one of the best in the country. Sensitive to criticism that he lacked a Ph.D. and was a poor lecturer, Wilson was most at home visiting police departments around the nation, where his real acumen was appreciated.

In 1960 Wilson resigned his deanship to become commissioner of the Chicago Police Department (CPD).* Promised by Mayor Daley to be free of political meddling, Wilson reorganized the number of police districts to eradicate remnants of the patronage system and established the Internal Investigation Division to root out police corruption. By hiring hundreds of new employees, a thousand police officers could be released from clerical duties to pursue criminals on the streets.

Wilson watchers had learned to expect the unexpected. In 1966 he invited police critic and civil rights leader Martin Luther King, Jr. to police headquarters to discuss interactions between the police and African-Americans. King was quick to draw comparisons between his treatment at the hands of southern police with Wilson's department. That same year Wilson's force solved the murder of eight student nurses by Richard Speck in just one day. Wilson retired from the force in 1967. Of his books and articles, his most influential book was *Police Administration* (1963). He also edited the book by LAPD chief William Parker,* *Parker on Police* (1956). He died from a stroke in Poway, California.

SOURCES: William J. Bopp, *"O.W.": O.W. Wilson and the Search for a Police Profession*, 1977; O.W. Wilson, *Police Planning*, 1952.

WILSON, VERNON COKE. (1857–1892) Born in Petersburg, Virginia, Wilson joined Company A of the Texas Rangers* in 1875. The following year he killed noted cattle rustler "Seeley" Harris, despite suffering several gunshot wounds himself. In 1878 he was credited with making the legendary mad dash from Austin to San Saba County to notify Rangers that Sam Bass was in his hideout at Round Rock. In 1885 he was appointed to a four-year term as chief of the Mounted Inspectors in Arizona and New Mexico by President Grover Cleveland. Working as a special detective for the Southern Pacific Railroad in 1892, he was charged with investigating the Evans-Sontag train robbers in California. Credited with killing twenty-seven desperadoes himself, Wilson was killed on September 13, 1892 while attempting to capture Evans and Sontag in Fresno County, California. Chris Evans reportedly fired the fatal shot.

SOURCE: Dan L. Thrapp, ed., *EFB*, Vol. 3, 1988.

WINSTEAD, CHARLES B. (1891–1973) Born in Sherman, Texas, Winstead worked as deputy sheriff in Brownsville, an Army field clerk, and then chief clerk in the U.S. attorney's office in El Paso before joining the Federal Bureau of Investigation (FBI)* in 1926. In the 1930s he was posted to the "Flying Squad" operating out of Oklahoma City in pursuit of John Dillinger. Winstead is credited with killing the noted desperado as he exited the Biograph Theater. Winstead waited in the lobby and trailed him outside the theater where he shot Dillinger three times as he drew his gun.

Winstead took part in the Lester "Baby Face Nelson" Gillis and Barker-Karpis gang investigations and claimed to have killed "Ma" Barker in Florida during a 1935 gunfight. He went on to serve in a variety of field offices before joining the army as assistant director of intelligence during World War II. Winstead reportedly left the FBI after John Edgar Hoover* ordered him to apologize to a reporter for telling her that her opinions about Russia were "not worth doodleyshit" (Gentry). When he refused to apologize Hoover relegated him to Oklahoma City, one of the least desirous field offices. Winstead told Hoover to go to hell and resigned to join the army. He was rebuffed in his attempts to return to the FBI after the war.

SOURCES: Curt Gentry, *J. Edgar Hoover: The Man and His Secrets*, 1991; William C. Sullivan with Bill Brown, *The Bureau*, 1979; Athan G. Theoharis, ed., *The FBI*, 1999.

WISE, CONSTABLE. One of the early-eighteenth-century English constables,* Wise testified against under-city-marshal Charles Hitchen,* who was accused of consorting with thieves and thief-takers (see THIEF-TAKER GENERAL) as well as being a thief himself. Wise reported that Hitchen frequented taverns and could often be seen in the company of well-known criminals. Constable Wise once apprehended six pickpockets, but Hitchen accused him of overstepping his jurisdiction and took custody of the men and probably set them free.

SOURCE: Gerald Howson, *Thief-Taker General*, 1970.

WOLFF, ALBERT. (1903–1998) Born and raised in Chicago, Wolf became interested in law enforcement in his youth after reading stories of Western lawmen and frontier justice. Educated at Northwestern University, he became a bailiff's assistant following graduation and earned the nickname "Wallpaper Wolff" for seizing everything but the wallpaper from bankrupt companies to pay for court-ordered judgments. In 1928 he joined the Department of Justice's Bureau of Prohibition. Initially he was assigned to raid stills in rural Kentucky, but in 1929 he became part of the Secret Six, a clandestine Chicago agency formed by local businessmen, under the command of the U.S. Department of Justice* to counter Prohibition gangs.

When Eliot Ness* created the Untouchables* in 1929, Wolff was assigned to the unit. His undercover work took him into many dangerous situations, prompting him to maintain a large insurance policy. Wolff began accompanying Ness on large-scale operations after it was learned that one of the Untouchables was consorting with gangsters. He left federal law enforcement after World War II and pursued various business endeavors in the Chicago area. Wolff worked as actor Kevin Costner's technical advisor during the filming of *The Untouchables*. The incorruptible Wolff admitted that, despite numerous raids on Capone bootlegging operations, the only time he met the mobster was when he was at a health spa in Hot Springs, Arkansas, and Capone introduced himself, saying, "So you are Wallpaper Wolff." When Albert Wolff died in 1998, he was believed to be the last surviving member of the Untouchables.

SOURCE: Richard Goldstein, "Albert Wolff, 95, Capone Nemesis as Member of Untouchables," *New York Times*, March 25, 1998.

WOOD, FERNANDO. (1812–1881) Born in Philadelphia, Wood moved to New York City with his family as a child. After an unsuccessful stint in the cigar business he found success operating a waterfront tavern and grocery store. During the gold rush era of the late 1840s he was able to capitalize on the California trade and together with his lucrative real estate investments was able to retire in 1849 and shifted his concentration to city politics. Following a term in Congress and an unsuccessful bid for New York City mayor in 1850, Wood won the mayoral election in 1854. Regarded as a tool of Tammany Hall, Wood organized corruption on a grand scale as the Municipal Police controlled elections and collected graft payments.

Wood drew inspiration from military traditions for his conception of the Municipal police. He wanted police officers to wear uniforms even when off duty and prescribed merit badges for the officers, which he doled out in May 1855 at a full-dress review and parade. During his tenure as mayor he served as a member of the three-man Board of Police Commissioners, but unlike his predecessors, Wood hoped the mayoralty would lead him to higher political offices and he attempted to use his position to enhance his personal power through the control of the police department. In order to block his goals, opponents in the state legislature responded by authorizing the 1857 Metropolitan Police Act, which effectively transferred responsibility for police control from the mayor's office to state officials. Wood resisted and refused to abolish the Municipal police force, leading to the Police Riots of 1857,* which pitted Wood's police against the New York Metropolitan Police.*

Following a spate of citizen complaints against the Municipal police, the Republicans, who were in control of the state government, took over the police department and amended the city charter by creating a larger police district and the new Metropolitan police department which controlled Manhattan, Brooklyn, Staten Island, and the Bronx. During its existence between 1857 and 1870, it was controlled by a board of commissioners appointed by the governor. When Wood refused to disband the Municipal force state authorities ordered police commissioner Daniel D. Concver to arrest Wood on charges of inciting to riot and violence. Attempts to arrest the mayor led to what became known as the police riots of 1857, the largest gang fight in New York City history prior to the 1863 New York City Draft Riots.*

SOURCES: James F. Richardson, *The New York Police: Colonial Times to 1901*, 1970; Thomas A. Reppetto, *The Blue Parade*, 1978.

WOOD, WILLIAM P. (1824–1903) A veteran of the Mexican War, Wood parlayed his friendship with Lincoln's secretary of war Edwin Stanton into an appointment in 1865 as the first chief of the U.S. Secret Service.* Their friendship was solidified when Wood gave perjured testimony for Stanton's firm in order to win a patent suit related to the McCormick Reaper. During the Civil War Stanton made him warden of the Old Capitol Prison, which housed Confederate spies and the like. Soon, the ever-resourceful, and some would say unscrupulous, Wood had used his position as warden to create a network of informers.

As Secret Service chief, Wood initially supervised thirty agents who had been experienced detectives. Its main charge was to maintain the public's confidence in the nation's currency. The country faced an incredible counterfeiting problem following the end of the Civil War, and according to the secretary of the treasury, the only way to control it was to establish a full-time agency. Wood was considered an obvious choice for the job because of his contacts in the black market and his success at investigating war-related fraud. He often resorted to unethical and illegal investigative methods, but nonetheless, in the first year of operation, Wood could cite over two hundred arrests as well as a decrease in counterfeit money. Wood left the Secret Service in 1869.

SOURCES: James Mackay, *Allan Pinkerton: The First Private Eye*, 1996; James D. Horan, *The Pinkertons*, 1968; Charles Phillips and Alan Axelrod, *CCC*, 1996.

WOODCOCK, SIR JOHN. (b. 1932) Born in Preston, Lancashire, Woodcock joined the local constabulary in the late 1940s. Following two years in the Army Special Investigation Branch, he returned to his old police job in 1952 and was promoted to chief inspector thirteen years later. He was awarded several high appointments over the next fifteen years, culminating in his promotion to Her Majesty's Inspector of Constabulary for Wales and Midlands in 1983. Seven years later he was put in charge of all forty-three British police forces, a position he held for three years. A popular career police officer, Woodcock emphasized the new realities of policing by recruiting minorities and championing police sensitivity to the public.

SOURCE: Charles Phillips and Alan Axelrod, *CCC*, 1996.

WOODRIFFE, EDWIN R. (1941–1969) Born and raised in Brooklyn, New York, Woodriffe joined the U.S. Department of the Treasury* following graduation from Fordham University. In 1967 he joined the Federal Bureau of Investigation (FBI)* and worked out of the Cleveland, Ohio, and Washington, D.C., field offices. On January 8, 1969, he became the first African-American FBI special agent to be killed in the line of duty when he and his partner were shot from ambush in Washington, D.C., while pursuing a bank robbery suspect.

SOURCE: Athan G. Theoharis, ed., *The FBI*, 1999.

WOODS, ARTHUR. (1870–1942) Harvard-educated and a former English teacher at Groton, Woods was appointed to head the New York City detective bureau in 1907. Woods, who had pursued postgraduate work in Europe, returned to the Continent to study European detective bureaus and brought back to New York the specialized squad strategy. Woods had become a protégé of Theodore Roosevelt,* having taught his children at Groton. His connections led to his advancement to deputy commissioner and then police commissioner of the ten-thousand-man force in 1914.

During his tenure Woods vigorously attacked the vice problem, but he made his greatest contributions in the realm of police training and professionalism. Influenced by Scotland Yard* and other European police organizations, he introduced a homicide clinic and psychopathic laboratory to train homicide and sex crime investigators and established the first school for patrolmen, a precursor to the New York City police academy.

In 1916 Woods was called on the carpet for illegal wiretapping, but the matter was later dropped. A progressive reformer, Woods resigned in 1917, when a Tammany Hall mayoral candidate defeated the reform mayor and Woods's patron John Purroy Mitchel. Woods continued to lecture on behalf of police reform, and in 1918, his platform was explained in his book, *Policeman and Public*. He later entered national politics in 1919 by joining the Herbert Hoover administration.

SOURCES: Thomas A. Reppetto, *The Blue Parade*, 1978; Charles Phillips and Alan Axelrod, *CCC*, 1996.

WOOLRIDGE, CLIFTON. (1850–1915) While his early life is shrouded in mystery, Woolridge joined the Chicago Police Department * (CPD) in 1888 and rapidly achieved the rank of detective. Over the next twenty-two years he was credited with making 3 arrests a day, or 19,500 during his career. Referred to as "that damned little flycop' by his criminal adversaries, Woolridge concentrated much of his attention on the vice lords and was responsible for shutting down over one hundred brothels. He claimed to have been the target of at least forty-four gunshots, suffering twenty-three wounds in the line of duty. Unlike most of his contemporaries Woolridge, a crack shot, reportedly claimed that he never shot to kill a man. A colorful man and an extrovert, he claimed to be a latter-day Sherlock Holmes* and "the World's Greatest Detective" in his autobiographical *Hands Up! In the World of Crime* (1901). Fearless as well as incorruptible, he refused thousands of dollars in bribes. He retired from policing in 1910.

SOURCES: Carl Sifakis, *The Encyclopedia of American Crime*, 1982; Clifton Woolridge, *Hands Up! In the World of Crime*, 1901.

WOUNDED KNEE SIEGE. During the late 1960s and early 1970s the American Indian Movement (AIM) became increasingly militant. In 1970 AIM members took over Alcatraz Island in an attempt to draw attention to the plight of American Indians. The following year AIM occupied the Twin City Naval Air Station near Minneapolis and disrupted the operation of the facility. The U.S. marshals responded by sending in the recently created Special Operations Group (SOG), resulting in a violent clash with the Indians who were armed with clubs and knives. Up until this time the federal government had allowed the occupation of Alcatraz as AIM continued to publicize its demands. In June 1971, SOG deputies moved in and the occupation ended without incident.

AIM continued to agitate for Indian rights as U.S. Marshals monitored their activities. In late 1972 and early 1973 word reached the U.S. Marshals Service* that AIM had targeted the Bureau of Indian Affairs (BIA) at the Pine Ridge Reservation in South Dakota. SOG deputies were sent in to train BIA police and to fortify the BIA building. AIM led numerous demonstrations, and following several incidents in which Indians were arrested for carrying weapons, AIM members took over the historic site of Wounded Knee, scene of the 1890 Indian massacre, rather than the BIA building. As the residents of Wounded Knee were held captive by the activists, the Federal Bureau of Investigation (FBI)* and BIA police set up roadblocks. U.S. Marshals Service chief Wayne B. Colburn* dispatched more than one hundred deputies to Wounded Knee.

By the beginning of March, marshals and FBI agents had set up a perimeter around the historic village. AIM leaders Russell Means and Dennis Banks released demands for Senate investigations into the treatment of Indians and the operation of the BIA. Several gunfights erupted during the siege, and although they were conducted from great distances two Indians were killed and U.S.

Marshal Lloyd Grimm was paralyzed by a gunshot wound to the spine. The developing Watergate scandal immobilized the government in Washington, D.C., and without the approval to move in with armored personnel carriers negotiations dragged on until spring. On May 7, 1973, after seventy-one days, the marshals moved in after an agreement was reached between both sides. For most of the members of the U.S. Marshals Service who weathered Wounded Knee, it was a high point in their careers and the first time they had served under fire. The success of the operation also demonstrated to Colburn that the paramilitary SOG unit was worth the training and highlighted the agency's discipline and professionalism.

SOURCES: Frederick S. Calhoun, *The Lawmen*, 1991; Robin Langley Sommer, *The History of the U.S. Marshals*, 1993.

Y

YEHUDAI, YOSEF. (1947–1989) Born in Romania, he immigrated to Israel in 1961 and three years later joined the Israeli military. Following his service with the border guards he entered law enforcement as a police officer, rising to Jerusalem police chief in 1986. Following the outbreak of Palestine Liberation Organization–inspired rioting, Yehudai was forced to enforce emergency security measures which included curfews in the Arab section of town. His command, while controversial, was instrumental in saving many lives.

SOURCE: Charles Phillips and Alan Axelrod, *CCC*, 1996.

YULCH, ADAM. (1885–1950) While working for New York's Nassau County Police Department in the 1930s Yulch established a Laundry-Mark Identification Bureau. Although laundry mark identification had been used by investigators for years, Yulch made the system more efficient and earned an international reputation as the "laundry-mark hawkshaw." Yulch collaborated with many other law enforcement agencies, including the Royal Canadian Mounted Police (RCMP).* He is generally credited with setting up the most complete laundry identification bureau in America.

SOURCE: Carl Sifakis, *The Encyclopedia of American Crime*, 1982.

Z

ZANETH, FRANK [FRANCI ZANETTI]. (1890–1971) Born Franci Zanetti, southwest of Milan, Italy, Zaneth immigrated to Canada from Springfield, Massachusetts, in 1911. He joined the Royal North-West Mounted Police following a stab at homesteading near Moose Jaw on the Canadian frontier. Zaneth became the most secret operative of the Royal Canadian Mounted Police (RCMP)* between 1917 and the 1940s. He proved an ideal choice for clandestine investigation. Fluent in several languages and a natural actor, his diminutive appearance ran counter to the image of the tall, rugged Mountie.

Within two years of his enlistment, he was promoted to detective corporal. In 1920 he became detective sergeant and in 1932 was elevated to detective staff sergeant. Two years later he became the first member of the RCMP to hold the rank of detective inspector. Over the following decade he worked on numerous difficult cases before moving into administration. In 1945 he was promoted to superintendent and four years later to assistant commissioner. He retired in 1951.

In the 1920s he successfully worked undercover against bootleggers, Mafioso, and drug runners. He also helped suppress alien smuggling operations and handled the Quebec conscription riots in 1918, post–World War I labor conflict, moneylaundering operations, and Cold War espionage, often in disguise.

SOURCE: James Durbo and Robin Rowland, *Undercover: Cases of the RCMP's Most Secret Operative*, 1992.

ZULULAND MOUNTED. *See* SOUTH AFRICAN POLICE (SAP).

Appendices

Appendix 1: Leaders of the Bureau of Investigation and FBI

Stanley Wellington Finch*	July 26, 1908
A. Bruce Bielaski	April 30, 1912
William E. Allen	February 10, 1919
William J. Flynn	July 1, 1919
William John Burns*	August 22, 1921
John Edgar Hoover*	May 10, 1924
Clyde Anderson Tolson*	May 2, 1972
Louis Patrick Gray III*	May 3, 1972
William D. Ruckelshaus	April 27, 1973
Clarence Marion Kelley*	July 9, 1973
William H. Webster*	February 23, 1978
John Otto	May 26, 1987
William Steele Sessions*	November 2, 1987
Floyd Clarke	July 19, 1993
Louis J. Freeh*	September 1, 1993

Source: Athan G. Theoharis, ed., *The FBI: A Comprehensive Reference Guide*, 1999.

Appendix 2: Commissioners of the London Metropolitan Police

July 7, 1829: Joint Commissioners, Colonel Sir Charles Rowan* and Sir Richard Mayne*

January 5, 1850: Rowan retired

January 6, 1850: Captain William Hay jointly appointed with Mayne

August 29, 1855: Hay died

December 26, 1868: Mayne died in office

December 27, 1868: Col. D.W.P. Labolmondiere, acting commissioner

February 13, 1869: Col. Sir Edmund Henderson* appointed

March 26, 1886: Henderson resigned

March 29, 1886: Gen. Sir Charles Warren* appointed

December 1, 1888: Warren resigned

December 3, 1888: James Monro appointed

June 21, 1890: Monro resigned

June 23, 1890: Col. Sir Edward Bradford appointed

March 4, 1903: Bradford retired

May 31, 1903: Sir Edward Richard Henry* appointed

August 31, 1918: Henry resigned

August 31, 1918: Gen. Sir Nevil Macready appointed

April 1920: Macready resigned

April 1920: Brig. Gen. Sir William Horwood appointed

November 7, 1928: Horwood retired

November 8, 1928: Gen. Lord Byng of Vimy appointed

September 30, 1931: Byng retired

November 2, 1931: Viscount Hugh Montague Trenchard* appointed

November 11, 1935: Trenchard retired

November 29, 1935: Sir Philip W. Game appointed

May 31, 1945: Game retired

June 1, 1945: Sir Harold Scott appointed

August 13, 1953: Scott retired

August 14, 1953: Sir John R. H. Nott Bower appointed

August 31, 1958: Nott Bower retired

September 1, 1958: Sir Joseph Simpson appointed

March 20, 1968: Simpson died in office

March 21, 1968: Sir John Waldron appointed

April 16, 1972: Waldron retired

April 17, 1972: Sir Robert Mark appointed

March 12, 1977: Mark retired

March 13, 1977: Sir Davis McNee appointed

October 1, 1982: McNee retired

October 2, 1982: Sir Kenneth Newman appointed

August 1, 1987: Newman retired

August 2, 1987: Sir Peter Imbert appointed

February 1, 1993: Imbert retired

February 1, 1993: Paul Condon appointed

Sources: Bill Waddell, *The Black Museum: New Scotland Yard*, 1993; Rupert Allason, *The Branch: A History of the Metropolitan Police Special Branch, 1883–1983*, 1983.

Appendix 3: Heads of the Special Branch of the Metropolitan Police*

John Littlechild	1883–1903
Patrick Quinn*	1903–1918
James McBrien	1918–1929
Edward Parker	1929–1936
Albert Canning	1936–1946
Leonard Burt*	1946–1958
Evan Jones	1958–1966
Ferguson Smith	1966–1972
Victor Gilbert	1972–1977
Robert Bryan	1977–1981
Colin Hewett	1981–1983

Source: Rupert Allason, *The Branch: A History of the Metropolitan Police Special Branch, 1883–1983*, 1983.

Appendix 4: New York City Police Department Commissioners, 1901–1996

Michael C. Murphy	2/22/1901–1/1/02
John N. Partridge	1/1/02–1/1/03
Francis V. Greene	1/1/03–1/1/04
William McAdoo	1/1/04–1/1/06
Theodore A. Bingham	1/1/06–7/1/09
William F. Baker	1/1/09–10/20/10
James C. Cropsey	10/20/10–5/23/11
Rhinelander Waldo*	5/23/11–12/31/13
Douglas I. Mckay	12/31/13–4/8/14
Arthur Woods*	4/8/14–1/1/18
Frederick H. Bugher	1/1/18–1/23/18
Richard Edward Enright*	1/23/18–12/30/25
George V. McLaughlin	1/1/26–4/12/27
Joseph A. Warren	4/12/27–12/18/28
Grover A. Whalen	12/18/28–5/21/30
Edward P. Mulrooney	5/21/30–4/12/33
James S. Bolan	4/15/33–12/31/33
John F. O'Ryan	1/1/34–9/24/34
Lewis Joseph Valentine*	9/25/34–9/14/45
Arthur W. Wallander	9/23/45–2/28/45
William P. O'Brien	3/1/49–9/25/50
Thomas E. Murphy	9/26/50–7/5/51

George P. Monaghan	7/9/51–12/31/53
Francis W. H. Adams	1/1/54–8/1/55
Stephen Patrick Kennedy*	8/2/55–2/22/61
Michael J. Murphy	2/23/61–6/6/65
Vincent I. Broderick	6/7/65–2/21/66
Howard R. Leary	2/22/66–10/8/70
Patrick V. Murphy	10/9/70–5/12/73
Donald E. Cawley	5/13/73–1/11/74
Michael Codd	1/12/74–12/31/77
Robert J. McGuire	1/1/78–12/29/83
William Devine	12/30/83–12/31/83 (interim position only)
Benjamin Ward	1/1/84–10/22/89
Richard J. Condon	10/23/89–1/21/90
Lee Patrick Brown*	1/22/90–9/1/92
Raymond W. Kelly	9/1/92–1/9/94
William J. Bratton*	1/10/94–4/15/96
Howard Safir	4/15/96–

The New York City Police Department has been under the direction of a single police commissioner since February 22, 1901. Prior to that time, the department was jointly run by a board made up of four to six police commissioners, one of whom would act as the president of the board. The most famous president of the board was Roosevelt,* who served from May 6, 1895, to April 19, 1897.

Source: NYPD homepage, July 12, 1999, available at: www.ci.nyc.ny.us/html/3100/commish.html, Internet.

Appendix 5: Los Angeles Police Chiefs, 1876–2000

Jacob T. Gerkins	12/18/1876–12/26/77
Emil Harris*	12/27/77–12/5/78
Henry King	12/5/78–12/11/80
George E. Guard	12/12/80–12/10/81
Henry King	12/11/81–6/30/83
Thomas J. Cuddy	7/_/83–1/1/85
Edward McCarthy	1/2/85–5/12/85
James W. Davis	12/22/85–12/8/86
John K. Skinner	12/13/86–8/29/87
P. M. Darcy	9/5/87–1/22/88
Thomas J. Cuddy	1/23/88–9/4/88
L. G. Loomis	9/5/88–9/30/88
Hubert H. Benedict	10/1/88–1/1/89
Terrence Cooney	1/1/89–4/1/89
James E. Burns	4/1/89–7/17/89
John M. Glass	7/17/89–1/1/1900
Charles Elton	1/1/1900–4/5/04
William A. Hammell	4/6/04–10/31/05
Walter H. Auble	11/1/05–11/20/06
Edward Kern	11/20/06–1/5/09
Thomas Broadhead	1/5/09–4/12/09
Edward F. Dishman	4/13/09–1/25/10

Alexander Galloway	2/14/10–12/27/10
Charles E. Sebastian	1/3/11–7/16/15
Clarence E. Snively	07/17/15–10/15/16
John L. Butler	10/16/16–07/16/19
George K. Home	7/17/19–9/30/20
Alexander W. Murray	10/01/20–10/31/20
Lyle Pendegast	11/1/20–7/4/21
Charles A. Jones	7/5/21–1/3/22
James W. Everington	1/4/22–4/21/22
Louis D. Oaks	4/22/22–8/1/23
August Vollmer*	8/1/23–8/1/24
R. Lee Heath	8/1/24–3/31/26
James Edgar Davis*	4/1/26–12/29/29
Roy E. Steckel	12/30/29–8/9/33
James E. Davis	8/10/33–11/18/38
D. A. Davidson	11/19/38–6/23/39
Arthur C. Hohmann	6/24/39–6/5/41
Clarence B. Horrall	6/16/41–6/28/49
William A. Worton	6/30/49–8/9/50
William Henry Parker*	8/9/50–7/16/66
Thad F. Brown	7/18/66–2/17/67
Thomas Reddin*	2/18/67–5/5/69
Roger E. Murdock	5/6/69–8/28/69
Edward M. Davis*	8/29/69–1/15/78
Robert F. Rock	1/16/78–03/27/78
Daryl F. Gates*	3/28/78–5/31/92
William L. "Willie" Williams*	6/1/92–8/21/97
Bayan Lewis	1997
Bernard Parks	8/22/97–present

Source: Arthur W. Sjoquist (historical text by), *Los Angeles Police Department Commemorative Book, 1869–1984*, 1984.

Appendix 6: Past Superintendents and Commissioners of the Pennsylvania State Police*

SUPERINTENDENTS OF THE PENNSYLVANIA STATE POLICE

John C. Groome*	Appointed July 1, 1905
George F. Lumb	Appointed June 3, 1919
Lynn G. Adams	Appointed March 1, 1920

SUPERINTENDENTS OF THE PENNSYLVANIA STATE HIGHWAY PATROL

Wilson C. Price	Appointed May 18, 1923
Deputy Supt. Philip J. Dorr	(Acting) February 29, 1936
Lt. Earl J. Henry	(Acting) March 16, 1936
Charles H. Quarles	Appointed April 13, 1936
Lt. Earl J. Henry	(Acting) February 28, 1937

COMMISSIONERS OF THE PENNSYLVANIA MOTOR POLICE

Col. Percy W. Foote	Appointed June 29, 1937
Lt. Col. C. M. Wilhelm	Appointed January 25, 1939
Col. Lynn G. Adams	Appointed May 31, 1939
Col. C. M. Wilhelm	Appointed January 20, 1943

COMMISSIONERS OF THE PENNSYLVANIA STATE POLICE

Col. C. M. Wilhelm	Appointed June 1, 1943
Col. E. J. Henry	Appointed March 28, 1955
Col. Frank G. McCartney	Appointed February 26, 1959
Col. E. Wilson Purdy	Appointed January 29, 1963
Lt. Col. Paul A. Rittelman	(Acting) April 8, 1966
Col. Frank McKetta	Appointed January 17, 1967
Col. Rocco P. Urella	Appointed January 25, 1971
Col. James D. Barger	Appointed January 2, 1973
Col. Paul J. Chylak	Appointed February 15, 1977
Col. Daniel F. Dunn	Appointed March 1, 1979 (died in office)
Lt. Col. Cyril J. Laffey	(Acting) May 16, 1984
Lt. Col. Nicholas Dellarciprete	(Acting) December 1, 1984
Col. Jay Cochran, Jr.	Appointed March 6, 1985
Col. John K. Schafer	Appointed January 30, 1987 (died in office)
Col. Ronald M. Sharpe	Appointed August 3, 1987
Col. Glenn A. Walp	Appointed April 23, 1991
Maj. James B. Hazen	(Acting) January 17, 1995
Col. Paul J. Evanko	Appointed February 15, 1995

Source: Pennsylvania State Police homepage, November 1999, available at: www.psp.state.pa.us/PA_Exec/State_Police/info/commish, Internet.

Appendix 7: The Position of Lieutenant-General of Police,* Paris

La Reynie, Gabriel Nicolas de,* 1667–1697

Argenson, Marc René de Voyer, 1697–1718

Arnouville, Louis-Charles de Marchault d', 1718–1720

Argenson, Pierre-Marc Levoyer de Faulmy, 1720

Baudry, Gabriel Taschereau de, 1720–1722

Argenson, Pierre-Marc Levoyer de Paulmy, 1722–1724

Ombreval, Nicolas-Jean-Baptiste Ravot d', 1724–1725

Herault, René, 1725–1739

Marville, Claude-Henri Feydeau de, 1739–1747

Berryer, Nicolas-René, 1747–1757

Bertin, Henri-Leonard-Jean-Baptiste, 1757–1759

Sartines, Antoine Gabriel de,* 1759–1774

Albert, Joseph-François-Ildefonse-Remond, 1775–1776

Lenoir, Jean Charles,* 1776–1785

Crosne, Louis Thiroux de,* 1785–1789

Sources: Philip John Stead, *The Police of Paris* 1957; Alan Williams, *The Police of Paris, 1718–1789*, 1979.

Appendix 8: Prefects of the Paris Police Through 1956

Dubois, Louis	March 1800–October 1810
Pasquier, Etienne	October 1810–May 1814
Beugnot, Jacques	May 1814–December 1814
André, Antoine	December 1814–March 1815
Bourrienne, Louis	March 1815
Real, Pierre	March 1815–July 1815
Courtin, Eustache	July 1815
Decazes, Elie	July 1815–September 1815
Angles, Julien	September 1815–December 1821
Delavau, Guy	December 1821–January 1828
Debelleyme, Louis-Marie*	January 1828–August 1829
Mangin, Jean	August 1829–July 1830
Bavoux, Jacques	July 1830
Girod, Louis	August 1830–November 1830
Treilhard, Achille	November 1830–December 1830
Baude, Jean	December 1830–February 1831
Vivien, Alexandre	February 1831–September 1831
Saulnier, Sebastien	September 1831–October 1831
Gisquet, Henri	October 1831–September 1836
Delessert, Gabriel	September 1836–February 1848
Sobrier, Marie	February 1848
Caussidiere, Marc	February 1848–March 1848

Trouve-Chauvel, Arist	May 1848–July 1848
Ducoux, François	July 1848–October 1848
Gervais, François	October 1848–December 1848
Rebillot, Charles	December 1848–November 1849
Carlier, Pierre	November 1849–October 1851
Maupas, Charlemagne	October 1851–January 1852
Blot, Sylvain	January 1852
Pietri, Joachim	January 1852–March 1858
Boitelle, Edouard	March 1858–February 1866
Pietri, Joseph	February 1866–September 1870
Keratry, Emile	September 1870–October 1870
Adam, Edmond	October 1870–November 1870
Cresson, Ernest	November 1870–February 1871
Choppin, Albert	February 1871–March 1871
Valentin, Louis	March 1871–November 1871
Renault, Leon	November 1871–February 1876
Voisin, Felix	February 1876–December 1877
Gigot, Albert	December 1877–March 1879
Andrieux, Louis	March 1879–July 1881
Camescasse, Jean	July 1881–April 1885
Gragnon, Arthur	April 1885–November 1887
Bourgeois, Leon	November 1887–March 1888
Loze, Henry	March 1888–July 1893
Lepine, Louis	July 1893–October 1897
Blanc, Charles	October 1897–June 1899
Lepine, Louis	June 1899–March 1913
Hennion, Celestin	March 1913–September 1914
Laurent, Emile	September 1914–June 1917
Hudelo, Louis	June 1917–November 1917
Raux, Fernand	November 1917–May 1921
Leullier, Robert	May 1921–July 1922
Naudin, Armand	July 1922–August 1924
Morain, Alfred	August 1924–April 1927
Chiappe, Jean	April 1927–February 1934
Bonnefoy-Sibour, Adrien	February 1934–March 1934
Langeron, Roger	March 1934–February 1941
Marchand, Camille	February 1941–May 1941

Bard, François	June 1941–May 1942
Bussière, Amedée	May 1942–August 1944
Luizet, Charles	August 1944–March 1947
Ziwes, Armand	March 1947–May 1947
Leonard, Roger	April 1951–July 1954
Baylot, Jean	April 1951–July 1954
Dubois, André	July 1954–November 1955
Genebrier, Roger	November 1955–

Source: Philip John Stead, *The Police of Paris*, 1957.

Appendix 9: Attorneys General of the United States, 1908–1998

Charles Joseph Bonaparte*	December 17, 1906–March 4, 1909
George W. Wickersham*	March 5, 1909–March 5, 1913
James C. McReynolds	March 5, 1913–August 29, 1914
Thomas Watt Gregory	August 20, 1914–March 5, 1919
A. Mitchell Palmer	March 5, 1919–March 5, 1921
Harry M. Daughtery	March 4, 1921–March 28, 1924
Harlan Fiske Stone	April 7, 1924–March 2, 1925
John T. Sargent	March 17, 1925–March 5, 1929
William D. Mitchell	March 5, 1929–March 3, 1933
Homer S. Cummings	March 4, 1933–January 2, 1939
Frank Murphy	January 2, 1939–January 18, 1940
Robert H. Jackson	January 18, 1940–July 10, 1941
Francis Biddle	September 5, 1941–June 30, 1945
Tom C. Clark	July 1, 1945–August 24, 1949
J. Howard McGrath	August 24, 1949–April 7, 1952
James P. McGranery	May 27, 1952–January 20, 1953
Herbert Brownell, Jr.	January 21, 1953–November 8, 1957
William P. Rogers	November 8, 1957–January 20, 1961
Robert F. Kennedy	January 21, 1961–September 3, 1964
Nicholas D. Katzenbach (Acting)	September 4, 1964–February 11, 1965
Nicholas D. Katzenbach	February 11, 1965–October 2, 1966

Ramsey Clark (Acting)   October 3, 1966–March 2, 1967

Ramsey Clark   March 2, 1967–January 20, 1969

John N. Mitchell   January 21, 1969–March 1, 1972

Richard G. Kleindienst   March 2, 1972–June 12, 1972
    (Acting)

Richard G. Kleindienst   June 12, 1972–May 24, 1973

Eliot L. Richardson   March 25, 1973–October 20, 1973

William B. Saxbe   January 4, 1974–February 3, 1975

Edward H. Levi   February 5, 1975–January 20, 1977

Griffin Bell   January 26, 1977–August 16, 1979

Benjamin Civiletti   August 16, 1979–January 19, 1981

William French Smith   January 23, 1981–February 1985

Edwin Meese III   March 25, 1985–August 12, 1988

Richard Thornburgh   August 12, 1988–August 15, 1991

William Barr   November 20, 1991–August 15, 1991

Janet Reno   March 12, 1993–

Source: Athan G. Theoharis, ed., *The FBI: A Comprehensive Reference Guide*, 1999.

Appendix 10: Chronology of American Policing

1631	First night watch* established in Boston
1704	First of the slave patrols* established in the South
1710	Publication of *The Constables Pocket-Book*
1767	Emergence of the Regulators,* a South Carolina vigilante group
1789	U.S. Marshals Service* established
1823	Texas Rangers* established
1829	The first modern police force established, in London
1845	The first twenty-four-hour unified police force in America established, in New York City
1853	New York City police become first American police to adopt the wearing of uniforms
1867	Publication of Allan J. Pinkerton's* *General Principles of Pinkerton's National Police Agency*
1871	First National Police Convention is held in St. Louis, Missouri
1874	John Philip Clum* establishes the first Indian police* force
1878	First police matrons* hired
1887	George Washington Walling* publishes *Recollections of a New York City Chief of Police*
1890	Publication of George M. Roe's *Our Police: A History of the Cincinnati Police Force from the Earliest Period until the Present Day*
1893	Marie Owens* is hired by the Chicago Police Department*
1894	Lexow Committee on police corruption (headed by Clarence Lexow*) convenes in New York City

1895	Theodore Roosevelt* hired as New York City police commissioner
1905	Lola Baldwin* hired by Portland, Oregon, Police Department
1908	Police cars introduced in Louisville, Kentucky
1909	Publication of *Police Administration* by Leonhard Felix Fuld*
1910	Washington, D.C., police superintendent Richard Sylvester* addresses the International Association of Chief of Police* concerning the use of the third degree*
1911	Berkeley, California, Police Department* chief August Vollmer* puts entire police force on bicycles
1912	August Vollmer introduces motorcycle patrols
1919	Publication of *Policeman and Public* by Arthur Woods*; Boston Police Strike of 1919*
1920	Publication of *American Police Systems* by Raymond Blaine Fosdick*
1921	August Vollmer adopts the first lie detector* in a police laboratory
1921	Vollmer introduces police car radios in patrolling
1924	John Edgar Hoover* appointed director of the Bureau of Investigation (see Federal Bureau of Investigation [FBI], origins of*)
1930	Bureau of Investigation placed in charge of *Uniform Crime Reports**
1931	Wickersham Commission releases *Report on Police* (see Wickersham, George Woodward*)
1935	Bureau of Investigation renamed Federal Bureau of Investigation (FBI); FBI establishes National Police Academy
1950	Publication of *Police Administration* by Orlando Winfield "O. W." Wilson*; William Henry Parker* appointed Los Angeles Police Department (LAPD)* chief
1961	*Mapp v. Ohio**
1966	*Miranda v. Arizona**
1968	Publication of James Q. Wilson's *Varieties of Police Behavior*; Indianapolis, Indiana, Police Department becomes the first American police department to assign women on routine patrol duty
1972	Knapp Commission* convenes
1982	Publication of "Broken Windows"* by James Q. Wilson and George Kelling
1991	Rodney King* beating
1992	Christopher Commission* delivers report on LAPD
1994	Publication of David H. Bayley's *Police for the Future*

Sources: Bryan Vila and Cynthia Morris, eds., *The Role of Police in American Society*, 1999; William G. Bailey, ed., *The Encyclopedia of Police Science*, 1995.

Appendix 11: Chronology of British Policing

1798	River Police founded
1829	Metropolitan Police founded by the Metropolitan Police Act of 1929* with headquarters at 4 Whitehall Place
1837	Mounted Police combined into Metropolitan Police force
1839	River Police taken into Metropolitan Police; Bow Street Runners* disbanded; City of London Police* established
1840	Divisional detectives first utilized
1842	Scotland Yard* detectives posted at police headquarters (HQ)
1850	Sir Charles Rowan* retires
1856	First assistant commissioners appointed
1862	Police strength at 7,800 men
1868	Sir Richard Mayne* dies in office
1878	Detective Branch reorganized as Criminal Investigation Department (CID)
1882	Police strength at 11,700 men
1883	Special Irish Branch set up
1888	Police strength at 14,200 men; the Whitechapel Murders occur
1889	Photography used to identify criminals
1890	Move to new Scotland Yard
1900	Police strength at 16,000 men
1901	Adoption of bicycle patrols; Sir Edward Richard Henry* develops fingerprinting system at Scotland Yard
1910–1911	Sidney Street Siege*

Source: John Wilkes, *The London Police in the Nineteenth Century*, 1977; reprint, 1984.

Appendix 12: American State Departments—Date and Name of First State Agency

Alabama	1919	Special Force
Alaska	1941	Highway Patrol
Arizona	1901	Arizona Rangers*
Arkansas	1929	State Road Patrol
California	1929	Highway Patrol
Colorado	1917	Department of Safety
Connecticut	1903	State Police
Delaware	1898	State Detectives
Florida	1939	Department of Public Safety
Georgia	1917	Home Guard
Hawaii		Each island has its own police force
Idaho	1919	State Constabulary
Illinois	1921	Highway Patrol Officers
Indiana	1921	Deputies
Iowa	1915	Special Agents
Kansas	1933	Traffic Inspectors
Kentucky	1932	Highway Police
Louisiana	1928	Highway Police
Maine	1917	Special Constables
Maryland	1916	Motorcycle Deputies
Massachusetts	1865	State Police
Michigan	1917	State Troops

Minnesota	1929	Highway Patrol
Mississippi	1938	Highway Patrol
Missouri	1931	Highway Patrol
Montana	1935	Highway Patrol
Nebraska	1919	Special Assistants
Nevada	1908	State Police
New Hampshire	1937	State Police
New Jersey	1921	State Police
New Mexico	1905	Mounted Police*
New York	1917	State Police
North Carolina	1929	Highway Patrol
North Dakota	1935	Highway Patrol
Ohio	1933	Highway Patrol
Oklahoma	1937	Highway Patrol
Oregon	1921	Field Deputies
Pennsylvania	1905	State Police
Rhode Island	1917	Constabulary
South Carolina	1868	State Police
South Dakota	1917	State Constabulary
Tennessee	1915	State Constabulary
Texas	1835	Texas Rangers*
Utah	1923	Traffic Patrols
Vermont	1925	Traffic Enforcement Officers
Virginia	1924	Motor Vehicle Inspectors
Washington	1921	Highway Patrol
West Virginia	1919	Department of Public Safety
Wisconsin	1939	Traffic Inspectors
Wyoming	1935	Department of Law Enforcement

Source: H. Kenneth Bechtel, *State Police in the United States: A Sociohistorical Analysis*, 1995.

Appendix 13: Original Members of Scotland Yard's Detective Branch

Inspector Nicholas Pearce*
Inspector John Haynes
Sergeant Stephen Thornton*
Sergeant William Gerrett
Sergeant Frederick Shaw
Sergeant Braddick
Sergeant Charles Burgess Goff
Sergeant Jonathan Whicher*

Source: Paul Begg and Keith Skinner, *The Scotland Yard Files: 150 Years of the C.I.D., 1842–1992*, 1992.

Appendix 14: FBI Agents Killed in the Line of Duty

Edwin C. Shanahan*	October 11, 1925
Paul E. Reynolds	August 9, 1929
Albert L. Ingle	November 24, 1931
Raymond J. Caffey*	June 17, 1933
W. Carter Baum*	April 22, 1934
Herman E. Hollis	November 27, 1934
Samuel P. Cowley*	November 28, 1934
Nelson B. Klein	August 16, 1935
Wimberly W. Baker	April 17, 1937
Truett E. Rowe	June 1, 1937
William R. Ramsey	May 3, 1938
Hubert J. Treacy	March 13, 1942
Percy E. Foxworth	January 15, 1943
Harold Dennis Haberfeld	January 15, 1943
Richard Blackstone Brown	July 14, 1943
Joseph J. Brock	July 26, 1952
John Brady Murphy	September 26, 1953
Richard Purcell Horan	April 13, 1957
Terry R. Anderson	May 17, 1966
Douglas M. Price	April 25, 1968
Anthony Palmisano	January 8, 1969
Edwin R. Woodriffe*	January 8, 1969

Gregory W. Spinelli	March 15, 1973
Jack R. Coler	June 26, 1975
Ronald A. Williams	June 26, 1975
Trenwith S. Basford	August 25, 1977
Mark A. Kirkland	August 25, 1977
Johnnie L. Oliver	August 9, 1979
Charles W. Elmore	August 9, 1979
Jared Robert Porter	August 9, 1979
Terry Burnett Hereford	December 16, 1982
Robert W. Conners	December 16, 1982
Charles L. Ellington	December 16, 1982
Michael James Lynch	December 16, 1982
Robin L. Ahrens*	October 5, 1985
Jerry L. Dove*	April 11, 1986
Benjamin P. Grogan*	April 11, 1986
James K. McAllister	April 18, 1986
Scott K. Carey	May 10, 1988
L. Douglas Abram	January 19, 1990
John L. Bailey	June 25, 1990
Stanley Ronquest	March 11, 1992
Martha Dixon Martinez	November 22, 1994
Michael John Miller	November 22, 1994
William Christian Jr.	May 29, 1995
Charles Leo Reed	March 22, 1996

Source: Federal Bureau of Investigation, in Athan G. Theoharis, ed., *The FBI: A Comprehensive Reference Guide*, 1999.

Appendix 15: Chicago Police Department (CPD) Firsts, 1833-1933

Accident Prevention Squad	1924
African-American Policeman	1872
African-American Police Official	1905
Automobile Made for CPD	1905
Automobile Patrol	1908
Call Box	1880
Canine Corps	1961
Chief of Detectives	1874
Chief of Police	1855
Constable	1835
High Constable	1837
Scientific Crime Lab	1938
Detective Division	1861
Eight-hour Day	1910
Electric Traffic Signals	1925
Female Detective	1878
Fingerprint System	1904
Street Gaslights	1850
Homicide Squad	1905
Mounted Horse Patrol	1906
Bureau of Identification	1884

Marine Police Division	1878
City Marshal	1842
Police Matron*	1881
Missing Persons Bureau	1927
Motorcycles	1910
Park Police	1913
Horsedrawn Patrolwagons	1880
Official Police Department	1855
Policeman Killed in Line of Duty	1855
Police Pension	1874
Policewoman	1913
Precinct Station	1855
Radio Division	1930
Radio-equipped Squad Cars	1922
Sex Homicide Bureau	1938
Uniforms	1858

Sources: Raphael W. Marrow and Harriet I. Carter, *In Pursuit of Crime: The Police of Chicago, Chronicle of a Hundred Years, 1833–1933*, 1996; John J. Flinn, *History of the Chicago Police*, 1887; rev. ed., 1973.

Appendix 16: Chicago Police Chiefs, 1855–1933

Cyrus P. Bradley	1855–1863
Jacob Rehm	1863
Cyrus P. Bradley	1864
William Turtle	1864–1865
Jacob Rehm	1866–1871
W. W. Kennedy	1871–1872
Elmer Washburn	1873–1874
Jacob Rehm	1874–1875
Michael Hickey	1875–1878
V. A. Seavey	1878–1879
Simon O'Donnell	1880
William McGarigle	1880–1882
Austin Doyle	1882–1885
Fred Ebersold	1885–1888
George W. Hubbard	1888–1889
Fred Marsh	1890–1891
Bob McCullough	1891
Robert W. McClaughry	1892–1893
Michael Brennan	1893–1895
John J. Badenoch	1895–1897
Joseph Kipley*	1897–1901
Francis O'Neill	1901–1905

John M. Collins	1905–1907
George M. Shippy*	1907–1909
LeRoy T. Steward	1909–1911
John McWeeny*	1911–1913
James J. Gleason	1913–1915
Charles Healey	1915–1916
Herman Schuettler*	1917–1918
John J. Garrity	1918–1920
Charles C. Fitzmorris	1920–1923
Morgan Collins	1924–1927
Michael Hughes*	1927–1928
William F. Russell	1928–1930
John H. Alcock	1931
James Allman	1931–1933

Sources: Raphael W. Marrow and Harriet I. Carter, *In Pursuit of Crime: The Police of Chicago*, 1996; John J. Flinn, *History of the Chicago Police*, 1887; rev. ed., 1973.

Appendix 17: Year of First African-American Police Appointments in Selected Cities

Chicago	1872
Pittsburgh	1875
Indianapolis	1876
Boston	1873
Cleveland	1881
Philadelphia	1881
Columbus, Ohio	1885
Los Angeles	1886
Cincinnati	1886
Detroit	1890
Brooklyn, N.Y.	1891
St. Louis	1901
New York City	1911

Source: W. Marvin Dulaney, *Black Police in America*, 1996.

Appendix 18: U.S. Marshals

John Arnold

R. P. Baker

Henry D. Barrows

Doug Beaman

Charles Bingham

John Brooks

J. H. Burdick

William A. Carroll

Robert I. Chester

Wayne B. Colburn*

Chapman Coleman

Mott L. Crawford

Crawley P. Dake*

Charles Denvens

Isaac Q. Dickason

Edward Dodd

Frederick Douglass

Faith Evans

James F. Fagan

Jabez Fitch

Creighton M. Foraker*

Robert Forsyth

George P. Foster

Watson Freeman

Nathaniel Garrow

Tom Green

W. M. Griffith

Lloyd H. Grimm

Frank Hadsell

Edward L. Hall

William E. Hall

William C. Hecht

Ward Hill Lamon

David Lenox

William Morel

Stanley E. Morris

Kenneth Muir

Evett Dumas Nix*

Richard T. O'Connor

Lewis S. Partridge

Tony Perez

J. H. Pierce

Fred Pinder

John Pratt*

James Prince

Nathaniel Ramsay*

Daniel A. Robertson

Logan H. Roots

John E. Sherman, Jr.*

John Smith

William H. Smythe

Benjamin Spooner

Wiley W. Standefer*

Daniel H. Stewart

Paul Strobach

Henry Talmadge

Thomas G. Thornton

Zan L. Tidball

Carl C. Turner

George Turner

John J. Twomey

George Tyng

R. M. Wallace

Morton A. Waring

Edward S. Wheat

Doug Wiggs

Ralph Zurita

Sources: Larry D. Ball, *The United States Marshals of New Mexico and Arizona Territories, 1846–1912*, 1978; Frederick S. Calhoun, *The Lawmen: United States Marshals and Their Deputies, 1789–1989*, 1991; Robin Langley Sommer, *The History of the U.S. Marshals*, 1993.

Appendix 19: U.S. Deputy Marshals

Willis H. Blayney

Samuel Bradford

William Brady*

Al Butler

Ada Carnutt

Robert Cheshire

Benjamin J. Churchill

James Davis

Ellis Duley

R. T. Dunn

Virgil Earp*

Wyatt Berry Stapp Earp*

John C. Elliot

Don Forsht

Patrick Floyd Jarvis "Pat" Garrett*

D. K. Goodin

Jesse Grider

Bob Haslip

William O. Hildreth

John Hixon

Ham Hueston

Jacob K. Lowe

Chris Madsen*

James P. "Jim" Masterson*

Alexander Mattison

Cecil Miller

Jeff Davis Milton*

David Butler Neagle*

Jacob Owens

Ransome Payne

Joseph Peavy

J. Herbert Ray

Gene Same

George A. Scarborough*

Lafayette "Lafe" Shadley*

Timothy J. Sheehan

Dick Speed

Henry Andrew "Heck" Thomas*

William Matthew "Bill" Tilghman, Jr.*

Frank Vandegrift

Robert Widenmann*

H. A. Wilson

C. H. Wisler

Sources: Frederick S. Calhoun, *The Lawmen: United States Marshals and Their Deputie*, 1991; Larry D. Ball, *The United States Marshals of New Mexico and Arizona Territories, 1846–1912*, 1978; Robin Langley Sommer, *The History of the U.S. Marshals*, 1993.

Appendix 20: Police Origins Worldwide

Afghanistan	1880s
Algeria	1962
Andorra	Andorran Police, 1931
Angola	People's Police Corps of Angola, 1978
Anguilla	Anguillan Police, 1972
Antigua and Barbuda	Antigua and Barbuda Police, 1886
Argentina	federal police, 1880
Australia	1788
Austria	City Guard, 1569
Bahamas	Royal Bahamas Police Force, 1840
Bahrain	Bahrain Police, 1926
Bangladesh	provincial police, 1861
Barbados	Barbados Police Force, 1835
Belgium	gendarmerie, 1795
Belize	British Honduras Police Force, 1885
Bermuda	1879
Bolivia	1886
Botswana	Bechuanaland Mounted Police, 1884
Brunei	Straits Settlement Police, 1905
Burundi	judicial police, 1967
Cameroon	Cameroon National Gendarmerie, 1960
Canada	Quebec, 1651

Chad	Sûreté, 1961
Chile	Queen's Dragoons, 1758
China	"runners," Confucian China; public security, 1949
Colombia	1853
Congo	National Gendarmerie, 1961
Cyprus	1960
Denmark	Copenhagen, 1590
Dominican Republic	National Police, 1936
Ecuador	municipal police, 1830
El Salvador	National Guard, 1912
Ethiopia	1935
Finland	"servants of the town," 1700s
France	commissaire-enquêteurs, 615; maréchausée,* 1544
Gambia	River Police, 1855
Germany	1732
Ghana	Gold Coast Militia and Police, 1844
Gibraltar	Gibraltar Police, 1830
Greece	Gendarmerie (Khorofylaki), 1833
Grenada	Grenada Militia, 1783
Guyana	Guyana Police Force, 1891
Honduras	Special Security Corps, 1963
Hong Kong	Royal Hong Kong Police Force, 1841
India	Sind constabulary model, 1843
Indonesia	Dutch Alegmeene Politie, pre-1947
Iran	Gendarmerie, 1911
Iraq	Iraqi Police Force, 1919
Ireland	provincial police, 1822
Israel	Palestine police force, 1926
Italy	Carabinieri, 1814
Ivory Coast	Gendarmerie, 1854
Jamaica	Jamaica Constabulary Force, 1867
Japan	1871
Jordan	1956
Kampuchea	1970
Kenya	1886
Korea, South	paramilitary constabulary, 1945
Laos	1945

Lesotho	Lesotho Mounted Police, 1872
Liberia	Liberian National Police Force, 1924
Liechtenstein	Princely Liechtenstein Corps, 1933
Luxembourg	*maréchausée*, seventeenth century
Malawi	Malawi Police Force, 1921
Malaysia	British police force, 1806
Malta	Malta Police Force, 1814
Mauritius	Mauritius Police Force, 1859
Monaco	1867
Mozambique	Public Security Force, 1975
Nepal	Raksha Dal, c. 1952
Netherlands	1795
New Zealand	armed constabulary, 1846
Nigeria	Lagos Police Force, c. 1890s
Norway	local police, twelfth century; first chief constable appointed, 1686
Oman	askars tribal police, no date; Muscat Police Force, 1931
Panama	Corps of National Police, 1904
Paraguay	Paraguayan Police, 1951
Peru	Civil Guard, early twentieth century
Philippines	Philippines Constabulary,* 1901
Poland	National Police, 1918
Portugal	sixteenth century
Puerto Rico	Civil Guard, 1868
Qatar	Qatar Police, 1948
Russian Federation	The Cheka,* 1917
St. Helena	constabulary, 1865
St. Lucia	St. Lucia Police, 1834
Senegal	National Gendarmerie, 1843
Seychelles	1775
Sierra Leone	Sierra Leone Police Force, 1829
Singapore	Singapore Police Force, 1827
Somalia	armed constabulary, 1884
South Africa	Cape Constabulary and similar forces, nineteenth century
Spain	Carabineros, 1829
Sri Lanka	Vidanes, 1806
Sudan	Sudan Police Force, 1898
Suriname	Armed Police Corps, 1865

Tanzania	British East Africa Police, 1919
Thailand	*tararuat*,* sixteenth century
Trinidad and Tobago	Trinidad Constabulary Force, early 1900s
Turkey	Jandarma, 1845
Tuvalu	Gilbert and Ellice Islands Armed Constabulary, 1892
Uganda	Armed Constabulary, 1900
United Arab Emirates	1974
United Kingdom	tithings,* A.D. 800; New Police, 1829
United States	*schout fiscal*,* 1640s
Uruguay	National Police of Uruguay, 1829
Vatican City	Swiss Guard,* 1506
Western Samoa	Western Samoan Police, 1900
Yemen	Aden Police Force, 1937

Sources: George Thomas Kurian, *World Encyclopedia of Police Forces and Penal Systems*, 1989; James Cramer, *The World's Police*, 1964.

Appendix 21: Soviet State Security Leadership

1917–26	Felix Edmundovich Dzerzhinsky*
1926–34	Vyacheslav Menzhinsky
1934–36	Genrikh Yagoda
1936–38	Nikolay Yezhov
1938–41 (February)	Lavrenti Pavlovich Beria* (NKVD* [People's Commissariat of Internal Affairs])
1941–41 (July)	Vsevolod Merkulov (NKGB [People's Commissariat of State Security])
1941–43 (April)	Lavrenti Pavlovich Beria (NKVD)
1943–46 (March)	Vsevolod Merkulov (NKGB)
1943–46 (October)	Viktor Abakumov (SMERSH ["Death to Spies": popular title of Armed Forces Counterintelligence Directorate, 1943–1946])
1946–46 (October)	Vsevolod Merkulov (MGB)
1946–51 (August)	Viktor Abakumov (MGB)
1951 (December)	Sergey Ogoltsov (MGB [Ministry of State Security])
1951–53 (March)	Semyon Ignatyev (MGB)
1953 (June)	Lavrenti Pavlovich Beria (MVD [Ministry of Internal Affairs])
1953–54	Sergey Kruglov (MVD)
1954–58	Ivan Serov (KGB* [Committee for State Security])
1958–61	Alexander Shelepin

1961–67	Vladimir Semichastnyy
1967–82	Yuri Andropov
1982 (December)	Vitaliy Fedorchuk
1982–1988	Viktor Chebrikov

Sources: John J. Dziak, *Chekisty: A History of the KGB*, 1988; George Thomas Kurian, *World Encyclopedia of Police Forces and Penal Systems*, 1989.

Appendix 22: Members of Interpol*

Albania

Algeria

Andorra

Angola

Antigua and Barbuda

Argentina

Armenia

Aruba

Australia

Austria

Azerbaijan

Bahamas

Bahrain

Bangladesh

Barbados

Belarus

Belgium

Belize

Benin

Bolivia

Bosnia-Herzegovina

Botswana

Brazil

Brunei

Bulgaria

Burkina Faso

Burundi

Cambodia

Cameroon

Canada

Cape Verde

Central African Republic

Chad

Chile

China

Colombia

Congo

Congo (Democratic Republic)

Costa Rica

Croatia

Cuba

Cyprus

Czech Republic

Denmark

Djibouti	Japan
Dominican Republic	Jordan
Dutch Antilles	Kazakhstan
Egypt	Kenya
El Salvador	Kirghizistan
Equador	Laos
Estonia	Lesotho
Ethiopia	Liberia
Fiji	Libya
Finland	Liechtenstein
France	Lithuania
Gabon	Luxembourg
Gambia	Madagascar
Georgia	Malaysia
Germany	Malawi
Ghana	Maldives
Great Britain	Mali
Greece	Malta
Grenada	Marshall Islands
Guatamala	Mauritania
Guinea	Mexico
Guinea Bissau	Moldova
Guinea Equatorial	Monaco
Guyana	Morocco
Haiti	Mongolia
Honduras	Mozambique
Hungary	Myanmar
Iceland	Namibia
India	Nauru
Indonesia	Nepal
Iraq	New Zealand
Iran	Nicaragua
Ireland	Niger
Israel	Nigeria
Italy	Norway
Ivory Coast	Oman
Jamaica	Pakistan

Panama

Papua New Guinea

Paraguay

Peru

Philippines

Portugal

Qatar

Rumania

Russia

Rwanda

St. Kitts and Nevis

St. Lucia

St. Vincent and Grenadines

Saudi Arabia

Senegal

Seychelles

Sierra Leone

Singapore

Slovak Republic

Slovenia

Somalia

South Africa

South Korea

Spain

Sri Lanka

Sudan

Sweden

Switzerland

Suriname

Swaziland

Syria

Tanzania

Thailand

Togo

Tonga

Trinidad and Tobago

Tunisia

Turkey

Uganda

Ukraine

United Arab Emirates

United States

Uruguay

Uzbekistan

Venezuela

Vietnam

Yemen

Zambia

Zimbabwe

Source: Appendix 1: List of ICPO-Interpol Member States (177), Interpol homepage, October 30, 1997, available at: 193.123.144.14/interpol.com/index2.htm, Internet.

Appendix 23: Chief Inspectors for the U.S. Postal Inspection Service through 1958

David B. Parker   July 1, 1878–October 15, 1883

A. G. Sharp   October 16, 1883–October 1, 1885

W. A. West   October 2, 1885–April 19, 1889

E. G. Rathbone   April 20, 1889–July 17, 1891

Moses D. Wheeler   July 18, 1891–August 1, 1897

G. B. Hamlet   August 3, 1897–November 24, 1898

W. E. Cochran   November 25, 1898–June 30, 1904

W. J. Vickery   July 1, 1904–January 1, 1908

F. E. McMillan   January 2, 1908–July 31, 1909

Theodore Ingalls   August 1, 1909–May 3, 1910

Robert S. Sharp   May 4, 1910–February 16, 1913

C. B. Keene   February 17, 1913–June 30, 1913

Joe P. Johnston   July 1, 1913–March 31, 1913

J. C. Koons   April 1, 1915–September 2, 1916

J. W. Johnston   September 3, 1916–March 31, 1917

G. M. Sutton   April 1, 1917–April 6, 1921

Rush D. Simmons   April 7, 1921–December 31, 1926

G. B. Miller   January 1, 1927–November 31, 1929

W. R. Spilman   January 1, 1930–August 25, 1930

Thomas M. Milligan   November 6, 1930–April 11, 1933

K. P. Aldrich   April 12, 1933–February 28, 1943

Jesse M. Donaldson   March 1, 1943–July 15, 1945
J. J. Doran   August 15, 1945–July 17, 1949
C. C. Garner   July 18, 1949–February 5, 1953
David H. Stephens   February 6, 1953–

Source: John N. Makris, *The Silent Investigators: The Great Untold Story of the U.S. Postal Inspection Service*, 1959.

Appendix 24: Directors of the Texas Department of Public Safety*

Louis G. Phares	September 1, 1935–May 8, 1936
H. H. Carmichael	May 8, 1936–September 24, 1938
Homer Garrison, Jr.*	September 26, 1938–May 7, 1968
Wilson E. Speir	May 7, 1968–December 31, 1979
James B. Adams*	January 1, 1980–May 31, 1987
Leo E. Gossett	June 1, 1987–July 31, 1988
Joe Milner	August 1, 1988–August 31, 1991
James R. Wilson	September 1, 1991–

Source: Mike Cox et al., eds., *Courtesy, Service, and Protection: The Texas Department of Public Safety's Sixtieth Anniversary*, 1995.

Appendix 25: High Points in French Police History

615	Clotare appoints commissaire-enquêteurs to maintain police
1544	The *maréchausée* established as military police force
1667	Louis XIV reorganizes Paris Police and introduces the *lieutenant-general* as commander
1789	French Revolution abolishes Prefecture of Police; Thiroux de Crosne* becomes last lieutenant-general
1790	Decree creates forty-eight *commissaires of police* for Paris
1799	Joseph Fouché* appointed minister of police
1800	Prefecture of Police of Paris created
1802	Napoleon abolishes the Ministry of Police
1804	Ministry of Police is restored, headed by Fouché
1810	Fouché is dismissed
1811–27	Eugene François Vidocq* creates the Sûreté* branch at Prefecture of Police
1829	*Sergeants de ville* appointed as street patrol in Paris
1832	The Sûreté is reorganized
1851	Lyons is given a state police force
1854	Paris adopts the London system of beat policing
1856	Inauguration of political police squads
1883	Prefecture's training school for police officers established
1883–1914	Alphonse Bertillon* at Prefecture of Police
1893	Adoption of fingerprinting*
1894	Police general intelligence unit established

1923   Interpol* inaugurated in Vienna (moves to Paris in 1946)

1941   State police assigned to towns with over 10,000 inhabitants

Sources: Philip John Stead, *The Police of France*, 1983; George Thomas Kurian, *World Encyclopedia of Police Forces and Penal Systems*, 1989; Harold K. Becker, *Police Systems of Europe: A Survey of Selected Police Organizations*, 1973.

Appendix 26: Arizona Rangers* Roster, with Tenure

Allison, William D., 1903–1904

Anderson, Robert M., 1902–1908

Baggerly, Roy, 1906

Bailey, James D., 1903–1905

Barefoot, Fred S., 1901–1903

Bassett, James H., 1902–1905

Bates, W. F., 1902–1905

Beaty, Clarence L.,* 1903–1907

Black, Samuel C., 1908

Brooks, John J., 1903–1905

Burnett, Reuben E., 1905–1906

Byrne, Cy, 1907–1909

Campbell, John E., 1901–1903

Carpenter, William L., 1908–1909

Chase, Arthur F., 1908

Clarke, John R., 1906–1908

Coffee, Garland, 1905

Davis, Wayne, 1906–1908

Devilbiss, George W., 1904

Doak, Boyd M., 1905

Ehle, A. E., 1907–1908

Ensor, William, 1903–1905

Eperson, Charles A., 1903–1906

Farnsworth, Clark H., 1905

Felton, Oscar, 1902–1905

Ferguson, William F., 1903–1904

Ford, Frank A., 1907

Foster, John, 1902–1907

Foster, William K., 1903

Fraser, J. A., 1907–1908

Gadberry, M. Tom, 1909

Graham, Dayton, 1902

Gray, Henry S., 1901–1905

Greenwood, John F., 1905–1906

Grover, Herbert E., 1901–1902

Gunner, Rudolph, 1907–1909

Hamblin, Duane, 1901–1902

Hayhurst, Samuel J., 1903–1909

Heflin, C. W., 1908

Henshaw, Samuel, 1903

Hickey, Marion M., 1905–1906

Hicks, O. F., 1909

Hilburn, J. R., 1904

Holland, Thomas J., 1901–1902

Holmes, James T., 1902–1909

Hopkins, Arthur A., 1903–1906

Horne, R. D., 1907–1908

Humm, George, 1908

Johnson, Don, 1901–1902

Jorgenson, Louis, 1903

Kidder, Jefferson P.,* 1903–1908

King, Orrie, 1908–1909

Larn, William A., 1907

Lenz, Emil R., 1908–1909

MacDonald, Alex R., 1903–1904

McAda, Oscar, 1907–1909

McDonald, James Porter, 1905–1907

McGarr, Charles E., 1905–1907

McGee, E. S., 1907–1909

McGee, James E., 1904–1906

McKinney, Joseph T., 1905–1906

McPhaul, Henry H.,* 1905–1906

Mayer, George L., 1907

Mickey, Lew H., 1905–1909

Miles, J. T., 1907–1908

Moran, James, 1904–1905

Mossman, Burton C.,* 1901–1902

Mullen, John Oscar, 1903

Neill, Reuben L., 1904–1906

Old, William A.,* 1904–1909

Olney, Benjamin W., 1906–1909

Page, Leonard S., 1901–1902

Parmer, William C., 1908–1909

Pearce, Joseph H., 1903–1905

Pearson, Pollard, 1902–1903

Peterson, William S., 1902–1905

Poole, Travis B., 1907

Redmond, John M., 1908–1909

Rhodes, John, 1906–1908

Richardson, Frank, 1901–1902

Rie, Charles, 1903–1904

Robinson, McDonald, 1901–1902

Rollins, Jesse W., 1906–1907

Rountree, Oscar J., 1903–1906

Rynning, Thomas H.,* 1902–1907

Scarborough, George E., 1901–1902

Short, Luke, 1908

Shute, Eugene H., 1905–1906

Smith, James, 1907

Sparks, William, 1903–1909

Speed, William S., 1906–1909

Splawn, C. T., 1905

Stanford, Tip, 1903–1909

Stanton, Richard H., 1901

Stiles, William L. 1902

Tafolla, Carlos,* 1901

Thompson, Ray, 1905–1907
Warford, David E., 1903
Warren, James, 1901–1902
Webb, William W., 1902–1903
Wheeler, Frank S., 1902–1909
Wheeler, Harry C.,* 1903–1909
Wilson, Owen C., 1903
Wilson, W. N., 1906–1909
Woods, Herbert E., 1908–1909
Woods, Leslie K., 1906

Source: Bill O'Neal, *The Arizona Rangers*, 1987.

Appendix 27: How to Join the North-West Mounted Police Force, 1906

MEMORANDUM FOR THE INFORMATION OF APPLICANTS FOR ENGAGEMENT IN THE ROYAL NORTH-WEST MOUNTED POLICE

1. Applicants must be between the ages of twenty-two and forty, active able-bodied men of thoroughly sound constitution, and must produce *certificate of exemplary character*.

2. They must be able to read and write either the English or French language, must understand the care and management of horses, and be able to ride well.

3. The term of engagement is five years.

4. The rates of pay are as follows:

4 Staff-Sergeants	$2.00 per day
Other Staff-Sergeants	$1.50 to $1.75 per day
Other Non-Commissioned Officers	$1.10 to $1.25 per day
Constable—1st year's service	60c. per day
Constable—9th year's service	$1.00 per day

Extra pay is allowed to a limited number of blacksmiths, carpenters, and other artisans.

5. Members of the Force are supplied with free rations, a free kit on joining and periodical issues during the term of service. Kit to be kept in serviceable condition at the expense of the N.-C. Officer or Constable.

6. Married men will not be engaged.

7. The minimum height is 5 feet and 8 inches, the minimum chest measurement 35 inches, and the maximum weight 175 lb.

8. Application to join the Force must be made to the Commissioner, Regina, Sask., or to the Comptroller, Ottawa.

9. No expenses, travelling or otherwise, of applicants can be paid from public funds.

10. Section 38, chapter 91, of the Revised Statutes, 1906, provides as follows:—

Every person who, by concealing the fact of his having been dismissed from the Force or by false or forged certificates or false representations, obtains admission into the Force, or obtains any pay, gratuity or pension, shall, on summary conviction, be liable to a fine not exceeding eighty dollars, or to imprisonment, with or without hard labour, for any term not exceeding six months, or to both fine and imprisonment.

Source: A. L. Haydon, *Riders of the Plains: A Record of the Royal North-West Mounted Police of Canada, 1873–1910*, 1910; reprint, 1973, pp. 371–372.

Selected Bibliography

GENERAL

Amos, William. *The Originals: An A-Z of Fiction's Real-Life Characters.* 1985.
Bailey, William G. ed. *The Encyclopedia of Police Science.* 1995.
Becker, Howard K. *Police Systems of Europe: A Survey of Selected Police Organizations.* 1973.
Brewer, John D. *Black and Blue: Policing in South Africa.* 1994.
Conquest, Robert, ed. *The Soviet Police System.* 1968.
Cramer, James. *The World's Police.* 1964.
Cyriax, Oliver. *Crime: An Encyclopedia.* 1993.
Denny, Cecil E. *The Law Marches West.* 1939.
Durbo, James, and Robin Rowland. *Undercover: Cases of the RCMP's Most Secret Operative.* 1992.
Dziak, John. *Chekisty: A History of the KGB.* 1988.
Fetherstonhaugh, R. C. *The Royal Canadian Mounted Police.* 1938.
Hall, Augus, ed. *The Crime Busters: The FBI, Scotland Yard, Interpol—The Story of Criminal Detection.* 1976.
Hattersley, Alan F. *The First South African Detectives.* 1960.
Haydon, A. L. *The Riders of the Plains: A Record of the Royal North-West Mounted Police of Canada, 1873–1910.* 1910; reprint, 1973.
Holloway, Thomas H. *Policing Rio de Janeiro: Repression and Resistance in a Nineteenth-Century City.* 1993.
Ingleton, Roy D. *Police of the World.* 1979.
Knight, Amy. *Beria: Stalin's First Lieutenant.* 1993.
Kurian, George Thomas. *World Encyclopedia of Police Forces and Penal Systems.* 1989.
McArdle, Phil, and Karen McArdle. *Fatal Fascination: Where Fact Meets Fiction in Police Work.* 1988.
Morton, James. *Supergrasses and Informers: An Informal History of Undercover Police Work.* 1995.

Mosse, George L., ed. *Police Forces in History*. 1975.

O'Brien, G. M. *The Australian Police Forces*. 1960.

Ousby, Ian. *Guilty Parties: A Mystery Lover's Companion*. 1997.

Penzler, Otto. *The Private Lives of Private Eyes*. 1977.

Phillips, Charles, and Alan Axelrod. *Cops, Crooks, and Criminologists: An International Biographical Dictionary of Law Enforcement*. 1996.

Plate, Thomas, and Andrea Darvi. *Secret Police: The Inside Story of a Network of Terror*. 1981.

Pope, Jacqueline. *Bounty Hunters, Marshals, and Sheriffs: Forward to the Past*. 1998.

Rhodes, Henry T. F. *Alphonse Bertillon: Father of Scientific Detection*. 1956.

Roth, Mitchel. "Mounted Police Forces: A Comparative History." *Policing* 21 (4): 1998.

Scott, Harold, ed. *The Concise Encyclopedia of Crime and Criminals*. 1961.

Siegel, Jeff. *The American Detective: An Illustrated History*. 1993.

Slate, John, and R. U. Steinberg. *Lawmen, Crimebusters, and Champions of Justice*. 1991.

Smyth, Frank, and Myles Ludwig. *The Detectives: Crime and Detection in Fact and Fiction*. 1978.

Stead, Philip John. *The Police of France*. 1983.

———. *The Police of Paris*. 1957.

Steinbrunner, Chris, and Otto Penzler. *Encyclopedia of Mystery and Detection*. 1976.

Symons, Julian. *Crime and Detection: An Illustrated History*. 1966.

Williams, Alan. *The Police of Paris, 1718–1789*. 1979.

Woeller, Waltraud, and Bruce Cassiday. *The Literature of Crime and Detection*. 1988.

AMERICAN POLICING

Ball, Larry D. *Desert Lawmen: The High Sheriffs of New Mexico and Arizona, 1846–1912*. 1992.

———. *The United States Marshals of New Mexico and Arizona Territories, 1846–1912*. 1978.

Bechtel, H. Kenneth. *State Police in the United States: A Socio-Historical Analysis*. 1995.

Bopp, William J. *O.W.: O.W. Wilson and the Search for a Police Profession*. 1977.

Bullis, Don. *New Mexico's Finest: Peace Officers Killed in the Line of Duty, 1847–1996*. 1996.

Burton, Art. *Black, Red, and Deadly: Black and Indian Gunfighters of the Indian Territory, 1870–1907*. 1991.

Calhoun, Frederick S. *The Lawmen: United States Marshals and Their Deputies, 1789–1989*. 1991.

Costello, Augustine E. *Our Police Protectors: A History of the New York Police*. 1885; reprint, with introduction by Theodore N. Ferdinand, 1972.

Cresswell, Stephen. *Mormons, Moonshiners and Cowboys, Klansmen: Federal Law Enforcement in the South and West, 1870–1893*. 1991.

Daley, Robert. *Prince of the City*. 1978.

———. *Target Blue: An Insider's View of the N.Y.P.D.* 1973.

Dillon, Richard. *Wells Fargo Detective: A Biography of James Hume*. 1969.

Domanick, Joe. *To Protect and Serve: The LAPD's Century of War in the City of Dreams*. 1994.

Dulaney, W. Marvin. *Black Police in America*. 1996.

Flinn, John J. *History of the Chicago Police.* 1887; revised, 1973.

Floyd, Craig W. and Kelley Lang Helms, eds., *To Serve and Protect: A Tribute to American Law Enforcement Officers.* 1995.

Gates, Daryl F., with Diane K. Shah. *Chief: My Life in the LAPD.* 1992.

Greenberg, Martin Alan. *Auxiliary Police.* 1984.

Hagan, William T. *Indian Police and Judges: Experiments in Acculturation and Control.* 1966.

Horan, James D. *The Pinkertons: The Detective Dynasty That Made History.* 1968.

Jeffers, H. Paul. *Commissioner Roosevelt: The Story of Theodore Roosevelt and the New York City Police, 1895–1897.* 1994.

Johnson, David R. *American Law Enforcement: A History.* 1981.

———. *Policing the Urban Underworld: The Impact of Crime on the Development of the American Police, 1800–1887.* 1979.

Kenney, John P. *The California Police.* 1964.

Knapp, Whitman, Chairman of Committee. *Knapp Commission Report on Police Corruption.* 1972.

Lane, Roger. *Policing the City: Boston 1822–1885.* 1967.

Lardner, James. *Crusader: The Hell-Raising Police Career of Detective David Durk.* 1996.

McDonald, Brian. *My Father's Gun: One Family, Three Badges, One Hundred Years in the NYPD.* 1999.

Mackay, James. *Allan Pinkerton: The First Private Eye.* 1996.

Makris, John N. *The Silent Investigators: The Great Untold Story of the U.S. Postal Inspection Service.* 1959.

Marrow, Raphael W., and Harriet I. Carter. *In Pursuit of Crime: The Police of Chicago, Chronicle of a Hundred Years, 1833–1933.* 1996.

Mayo, Katherine. *Justice to All: The Story of the Pennsylvania State Police.* 1917.

Miller, Joseph. *The Arizona Rangers.* 1972.

Morn, Frank. *"The Eye That Never Sleeps": A History of the Pinkerton National Detective Agency.* 1982.

Nash, Jay Robert. *Encyclopedia of Western Lawmen and Outlaws.* 1994.

Nunnelley, William A. *Bull Connor.* 1991.

O'Neal, Bill. *The Arizona Rangers.* 1987.

Parker, Alfred E. *The Berkeley Police Story.* 1972.

Peak, Kenneth J. *Policing America: Methods, Issues, Challenges.* 1993.

Prassel, Frank Richard. *The Western Peace Officer: A Legacy of Law and Order.* 1972; reprint, 1981.

Reppetto, Thomas A. *The Blue Parade* 1978.

Richardson, James F. *The New York Police: Colonial Times to 1901.* 1970.

———. *Urban Police in the United States.* 1974.

Rousey, Dennis C. *Policing the Southern City: New Orleans, 1805–1889.* 1996.

Rubinstein, Jonathan. *City Police.* 1973

Russell, Francis. *A City in Terror: 1919, the Boston Police Strike.* 1975.

Savage, Edward H. *Police Records and Recollections; or Boston by Daylight and Gaslight for Two Hundred and Forty Years.* Reprint, 1973.

Schulz, Dorothy Moses. *From Social Worker to Crimefighter: Women in United States Municipal Policing.* 1995.

Secrest, William B. *Lawmen and Desperadoes: A Compendium of Noted, Early California Peace Officers, Badmen and Outlaws, 1850–1900.* 1994.

Segrave, Kerry. *Policewomen: A History.* 1995.

Shirley, Glenn. *West of Hell's Fringe: Crime, Criminals, and the Federal Peace Officer in Oklahoma Territory, 1889–1907.* 1978.

Sifakis, Carl. *The Encyclopedia of American Crime.* 1982.

Sjoquist, Arthur W. (historical text by). *Los Angles Police Department Commemorative Book, 1869–1984.* 1984.

Sommer, Robin Langley. *The History of the U.S. Marshals.* 1993.

Thrapp, Dan L., ed. *Encyclopedia of Frontier Biography.* 3 volumes. 1988.

U.S. Department of Justice. Law Enforcement Assistance Administration. *Two Hundred Years of American Criminal Justice.* 1976.

Viano, Emilio C., and Jeffrey H. Reiman, eds. *The Police in Society.* 1999.

Vila, Bryan, and Cynthia Morris, eds. *The Role of Police in American Society.* 1999.

Walker, Samuel. *Popular Justice: A History of American Criminal Justice.* 1998.

Walling, George W. *Recollections of a New York City Police Chief.* 1887; reprint, 1972.

Whitehead, Don. *Border Guard: The Story of the United States Customs Service.* 1963.

BRITISH POLICING

Allason, Rupert. *The Branch: A History of the Metropolitan Police Special Branch, 1883–1983.* 1983.

Appleby, Pauline. *A Force on the Move: The Story of the British Transport Police, 1825–1995.* 1995.

Babington, Anthony. *A House in Bow Street: Crime and the Magistracy, 1740–1881.* 1969.

Begg, Paul, Martin Fido, and Keith Skinner. *The Jack the Ripper A to Z.* 1991.

Begg, Paul, and Keith Skinner. *The Scotland Yard Files: 150 Years of the C.I.D., 1842–1992.* 1992.

Briggs, John et al. *Crime and Punishment in England: An Introductory History.* 1996.

Camps, Francis E. *The Investigation of Murder.* 1966.

Cobb, Belton. *Critical Years at the Yard, 1860–1889.* 1956.

———. *The First Detectives and the Early Career of Richard Mayne, Commissioner of Police.* 1957.

———. *Murdered on Duty: A Chronicle of the Killing of Policemen.* 1961.

Collins, Philip. *Dickens and Crime.* 1968.

Critchley, T. A. *A History of Police in England and Wales, 900–1966.* 1967.

Emsley, Clive. *The English Police: A Political and Social History.* 1991.

———. *Policing and Its Context, 1750–1870.* 1983.

Fido, Martin and Keith Skinner. *The Official Encyclopedia of Scotland Yard.* 1999.

Gladwin, Irene. *The Sheriff: The Man and His Office.* 1984.

Howard, George. *Guardians of the Queen's Peace: The Development and Work of Britain's Police.* 1953.

Howson, Gerald. *Thief-Taker General: The Rise and Fall of Jonathan Wild.* 1970.

Ingleton, Roy. *The Gentlemen at War: Policing Britain, 1939–1945.* 1994.

Jackson, Richard. *Occupied with Crime.* 1967.

Laurie, Peter. *Scotland Yard: A Study of the Metropolitan Police.* 1970.

Lock, Joan. *Dreadful Deeds and Awful Murders: Scotland Yard's First Detectives, 1829–1878*. 1990.

Miller, Wilbur R. *Cops and Bobbies: Police Authority in New York and London, 1830–1870*. 1973.

Moylan, John Fitzgerald. *Scotland Yard and the Metropolitan Police*. 1929.

Potter, John Deane. *Scotland Yard*. 1972.

Pringle, Patrick. *Hue and Cry: The Story of Henry and John Fielding and Their Bow Street Runners*, 1955.

Reith, Charles. *The Blind Eye of History: A Study of the Origins of the Present Police Era*. 1952.

———. *A New Study of Police History*. 1956.

Reynolds, Elaine A. *Before the Bobbies: The Night Watch and Police Reform in Metropolitan London, 1720–1830*. 1998.

Rumbelow, Donald. *I Spy Blue: The Police and Crime in the City of London from Elizabeth I to Victoria*. 1971.

Sheffield, G. D. *The Redcaps: A History of the Royal Military Police and Its Antecedents from the Middle Ages to the Gulf War*. 1994.

Speed, P. F. *Police and Prisons*. 1977.

Stead, Philip John. *The Police of Britain*. 1985.

Thomson, Sir Basil. *The Story of Scotland Yard*. 1936.

Tobias, J. J. *Crime and Police in England, 1700–1900*. 1979.

———. *Nineteenth-Century Crime in England: Prevention and Punishment*. 1972.

Tyler, R.A.J. *Bloody Provost*. 1980.

Waddell, Bill. *The Black Museum: New Scotland Yard*. 1993.

Whittington-Egan, Richard, and Molly Whittington-Egan. *The Bedside Book of Murder*. 1988.

Wilkes, John. *The London Police in the Nineteenth Century*. 1977; reprint, 1984.

FEDERAL BUREAU OF INVESTIGATION

Cook, Fred. *The FBI Nobody Knows*. 1964.

DeLoach, Cartha. *Hoover's FBI: The Inside Story by Hoover's Trusted Lieutenant*. 1995.

Gentry, Curt. *J. Edgar Hoover: The Man and the Secrets*. 1991.

Greenberg, Martin, and Mark Sabljak. *Most Wanted: A History of the FBI's Most Wanted List*. 1990.

Helmer, William, with Rick Mattix. *Public Enemies: America's Criminal Past, 1919–1940*. 1998.

Pistone, Joseph. *Donnie Brasco: My Undercover Life in the Mafia*. 1987.

Powers, Richard Gid. *G-Men: Hoover's FBI in American Popular Culture*. 1983.

———. *Secrecy and Power: The Life of J. Edgar Hoover*. 1987.

Purvis, Melvin. *American Agent*. 1936.

Roemer, William. *Roemer: Man against the Mob*. 1989.

Schott, Joseph. *No Left Turns: The FBI in Peace and War*. 1975.

Sullivan, William. *The Bureau: My Thirty Years in Hoover's FBI*. 1979.

Theoharis, Athan. *J. Edgar Hoover, Sex and Crime: An Historical Antidote*. 1955.

———. ed. *The FBI: A Comprehensive Reference Guide*. 1999.

Tully, Andrew. *The FBI's Most Famous Cases*. 1965.

Turner, William. *Hoover's FBI: The Man and the Myth*. 1970; reprint, 1993.
Ungar, Sanford. *F.B.I.* 1976.
Unger, Robert. *The Union Station Massacre: The Original Sin of J. Edgar Hoover's FBI*. 1997.
Whitehead, Don. *The FBI Story: A Report to the People*. 1956.

TEXAS RANGERS

Baenzigger, Ann Patton. "The Texas State Police Force during Reconstruction: A Re-examination." *Southwest Historical Quarterly*, April 1969.
Cox, Mike. *Texas Ranger Tales: Stories That Need Telling*. 1997.
———. *Texas Ranger Tales II*. 1999.
Davis, John L. *The Texas Rangers: Their First 150 Years*, 1975.
Day, James M. *Captain Clint Peoples, Texas Ranger: Fifty Years a Lawman*. 1980.
Douglas, C. L. *The Gentlemen in the White Hats: Dramatic Episodes in the History of the Texas Rangers*. 1934.
Ford, John Salmon. *Rip Ford's Texas*. Edited by Stephen Oates. 1963.
Frost, H. Gordon, and John H. Jenkins, *"I'm Frank Hamer,"* 1968.
Greer, James K. *Colonel Jack Hays: Texas Frontier Leader and California Builder*. 1952.
Keating, Bern. *An Illustrated History of the Texas Rangers*. 1975.
Kilgore, D. E. *A Ranger Legacy: 150 Years' Service to Texas*. 1973.
Knowles, Thomas W. *They Rode for the Lone Star: The Saga of the Texas Rangers*. 1999.
Malsch, Brownson. *Captain M. T. "Lone Wolf" Gonzaullas: The Only Texas Ranger Captain of Spanish Descent*. 1980.
Paine, Albert Bigelow. *Captain Bill McDonald, Texas Ranger: A Story of Frontier Reform*. 1909.
Proctor, Ben. *Just One Riot: Episodes of Texas Rangers in the Twentieth Century*, 1991.
Rangers of Texas. 1969.
Robinson, James W. *The DPS Story*. 1975.
Roth, Mitchel (historical text by). *Courtesy, Service, and Protection: The Texas Department of Public Safety*, edited by Mike Cox et al. 1995.
Sterling, William Warren. *Trails and Trials of a Texas Ranger*. 1959.
Texas Rangers: Sesquicentennial Anniversary. 1973.
Ward, James Randolph. "The Texas Rangers, 1915–1935: A Study in Law Enforcement." Ph.D. dissertation, Texas Christian University, 1972.
Webb, Walter Prescott. *The Texas Rangers*. 1935.

Index

Boldface page numbers indicate location of main entries.

About the Author

MITCHEL P. ROTH is Associate Professor of History and Criminal Justice at Sam Houston State University. His earlier books include *Historical Dictionary of War Journalism* (Greenwood, 1997).